Conducting Choral Music

ROBERT L. GARRETSON

PRENTICE HALL, Upper Saddle River, New Jersey 07458

Library of Congress Cataloging-in-Publication Data

Garretson, Robert L.
    Conducting choral music / Robert L. Garretson. — 8th ed.
        p.   cm.
    Includes bibliographical references and index.
    ISBN 0-13-775735-2 (pbk. : alk. paper)
    1. Choral conducting   I. Title.
MT85.G175C6   1998
782.5'145--DC21   97-36067

Acquisitions editor: Bud Therien
Editorial/Production Supervision: Edie Riker
Cover designer: Kiwi Design
Manufacturing buyer: Robert Anderson
Editorial assistant: Gianna Caradona
Marketing manager: Sheryl Adams

This book was set in 10.5/12 Goudy Old Style by Preparé/Emilcomp
and was printed and bound by Courier Companies, Inc.
The cover was printed by Phoenix Color Comp.

Printed in the United States of America

10   9   8   7   6   5   4   3   2

ISBN 0-13-775735-2

Prentice-Hall International (UK) Limited,London
Prentice-Hall of Australia Pty. Limited, Sydney
Prentice-Hall Canada Inc., Toronto
Prentice-Hall Hispanoamericana, S.A., Mexico
Prentice-Hall of India Private Limited, New Delhi
Prentice-Hall of Japan, Inc., Tokyo
Pearson Education Asia Pte. Ltd., Singapore
Editora Prentice-Hall do Brasil, Ltda., Rio de Janeiro

Conducting
Choral Music

To
Katie and **Chris**

I am sincerely grateful to **Lee Egbert** who,
on the death of my husband, Robert,
gave of himself without hesitation by completing
responses to editor's notes and by reading
the page proofs for the entire book.

—*Aretha Garretson*

Contents

3   MAINTAINING VOCAL HEALTH   123

Preface

This eighth edition of Conducting Choral Music begins with the aspiring conductor's most immediate concerns dealing with conducting techniques, progresses through specific and practical matters dealing with tone and diction, maintaining vocal health, children's voices and the boy's changing voice, style and interpretation, the rehearsal of choirs and choruses, programs and concerts, and ends with a discussion of planning and managerial procedures.

As the choral conducting profession grows, our responsibilities increase and we need greater knowledge. This eighth edition includes new sections on: Uses and Application of Supermetric Conducting Patterns, Ethnic and Multicultural Perspectives — and Lists of Selected Choral Music, The Choir/Chorus Retreat, Responsibilities of the Choir Member — A Self-Assessment, Suggestions for Adjudicators of Choral Music Festivals, and firms dealing with Choir Travel/Tour Services.

Several topics have been enlarged or expanded, including Styles of Diction (with some humorous errors in enunciation), Conducting Choral/Orchestral Works, and Considering the Audience (in program planning). The list of references at the end of each chapter has been updated; however, a number of older publications that are out of print, but available in libraries, have been retained if you wish to make some comparative analysis of the ideas presented in choral music texts over the decades. If these books are not available in a nearby library, inquire about obtaining them through interlibrary loan. In recent years publishers have produced instructional videotapes on conducting techniques, vocal tone production and techniques, rehearsal techniques, show choir choreography, and publicity and public relations. Available videotapes and their producers are listed at the end of each respective chapter pertaining to these topics. The source information in the Appendix has also been revised and updated, with special attention given to the chronological list of choral composers, the inclusion of new choral octavo publications and extended choral works, current addresses of music publishers/distributors, and sources for obtaining choir apparel and various types of musical equipment.

This book is addressed to conductors of school choirs and choruses, to church choir directors, to leaders of community choral groups, and to students who wish to improve their understanding of the art of choral singing. It may also be of interest and help to administrators and other individuals seeking a knowledge of the aims and objectives of the choral conductor. Its design and content are intended to deal with the principles and techniques studied in college and university courses in choral conducting, choral methods and materials, and secondary school music.

Results of a study by the author focus attention upon the fact that many choral conductors regard their professional training as inadequate. It was the consensus of a large group of conductors, whose views were sought, that their training should have been more practical. With this guiding thought in mind, an approach to the solution of particular problems that conductors are likely to meet, especially during their first few years of conducting experience, is presented. Specific practices and techniques have been presented to give you the utmost assistance. Since few teaching situations are identical, the inclusion of basic principles will be helpful in increasing your insight and in providing a general approach for meeting and solving problems as they arise.

Areas of particular concern to choral conductors and necessary in their professional training are conducting techniques, tone and diction, maintaining vocal health, children's voices and the boy's changing voice, style and interpretation, rehearsal techniques, program and concerts, and planning and management. A chapter, therefore, is devoted to each of these areas. It is hoped that this book, based on the teaching needs of numerous choral conductors, will contribute to the betterment of choral singing.

Many persons have contributed to my concepts as presented in this book. Some of the ideas have been formulated through observation and discussion with choral conductors throughout the country. The techniques suggested have crystallized during my application of them while working with various groups: with school choirs and choruses, church choirs, and choral groups on the university level. To all concerned—conductors and singers—I express my gratitude.

For permission to use excerpts from their choral publications, I am indebted to the following music publishers: Art Masters Studios, Inc.; Augsburg Fortress Publishing House; Boosey & Hawkes, Inc.; Broude Brothers, Ltd.; Curtis Music Press; Oliver Ditson Company; European American Music Corp.; Galaxy Music Corp.; Hinshaw Music, Inc.; Neil A. Kjos Music Co.; Hal Leonard

Publishing Corp.; Edward B. Marks Music Corp.; MCA Music, Inc.; Otto Heinrich Noetzel Verlag (Wilhelm-shaven BRD); Plymouth Music Co.; Theodore Presser Co.; G. Ricordi & Co.; E. C. Schirmer Music Co.; G. Schirmer, Inc.; Shawnee Press, Inc.; Walton Music Corp.; Warner Bros. Publications and World Library Publications.

For permission to quote from their publications, I express appreciation to Oxford University Press; W. W. Norton & Co., Inc.; *The NATS Bulletin*; Harcourt Brace Jovanovich, Inc.; and Macmillan (London and Basingstoke.)

To my many friends and colleagues who over the years have made helpful comments and suggestions regarding the various editions of this book I am very grateful. I would particularly like to express my appreciation to two colleagues at Colorado State University who provided helpful comments for this eighth edition. To Lee Egbert, Director of Choral Activities, for his ideas on and use of the term "Supermetric Conducting Patterns," and to Wilfred Schwartz, string specialist and founder, music director/conductor of the Fort Collins Symphony Orchestra, for his critique of the section on Conducting Choral/Orchestral works, I am most grateful.

To the many music publishers who submitted choral music for review and consideration for the new listing in this edition of Ethnic/Multicultural Music, I wish to give my sincere thanks. To Laurence Kaptein, Director of Choral activities at the University of Colorado in Boulder, for his assistance in helping to identify these publishers, I wish to express my sincere appreciation. And finally, to my wife Aretha, who has offered continual encouragement, I am particularly grateful.

Introduction

During the twentieth century, particularly since World War I, choral singing has assumed a position of increasing importance and popularity in our society. School and college choirs and choruses, church choirs, community choruses, and choruses sponsored by industrial and commercial firms have increased in size and in quality. Individuals are quite naturally drawn to activities that they enjoy. Let us examine some of the underlying reasons for this increase and development of choral singing.

Considerable credit should be given schools and colleges for this phenomenal growth. Choral music has progressed from a largely extracurricular activity to an integral part of the school curriculum. This would not have occurred without at least some degree of recognition of the values of music participation. Without attempting an exhaustive consideration of these values, for our purpose they may be summarized as follows.

Although the benefits of choral singing are many, the *aesthetic* and *expressive* values of music are considered to be the most important. All persons need to develop a sensitivity to beauty in music and other art forms, because understanding and appreciation of them may serve to refine and humanize their entire existence. Because music is a significant and integral part of our culture, it is the school's responsibility to help students become more intelligent consumers of music. Participation in musical activities can serve as a means through which individual musical taste may be improved. Through a study of the vast wealth of music literature, students may learn to discriminate between the musically trite

1

and the rich musical heritage that is the right and the privilege of every individual. All people have a need for individual self-expression in as many varied ways as possible. Although many concepts and ideas may be expressed through language, other aspects of our experience can be best expressed through various other art forms. The aesthetic and expressive values of music are, therefore, the principal justifications for its inclusion in the school curriculum.

The *personal-social* values of choral singing also deserve consideration. All individuals need the opportunity to engage in activities that promote physical development and that feeling of well-being which is characteristic of good mental health. Music participation can contribute to these ends. Correct posture and proper breathing techniques are emphasized as an adjunct of choral singing and are a necessary attainment of the well-trained choral group. Music also serves as a wholesome outlet for and expression of individual emotions. Through music, individuals not only can express themselves, but also can release pent-up feelings of frustration so common in our present-day society.

By contributing time and talent to various social organizations, and through being accepted by other members of such groups, people fulfill their need "to belong": their social beings find expression. A characteristic of the adolescent, as he or she strives to become a social being, is the strong desire to belong, inasmuch as membership in various groups usually results in satisfaction and acceptance by members of the peer group. Through cooperative group endeavor, the chorus or choir provides additional opportunity for the development of democratic attitudes and a wholesome channeling of interests toward members of the opposite sex. Students in music activities develop pride in being identified with a fine musical organization and make many social adjustments through the close association with their peers. Certain critics of present-day society say that it has become too individually oriented and that what we need are activities necessitating more group effort. Choral singing certainly fulfills this need.

Finally, and not to be overlooked, are the *avocational* and *vocational* values that accrue from music participation. Changes in the attitudes of our society, coupled with many modern living improvements, have resulted in a greater amount of leisure time for some individuals. These changes are highly desirable and offer increased opportunity for individuals to explore many possible areas. As a result of improved educational programs, many people have discovered music to be an area from which they may derive great personal enjoyment and satisfaction. If continuing programs of music instruction are to be maintained in our society, vocational needs must also be met. In addition to a teaching career, opportunities exist in the area of professional music. To be eminently successful in these areas of endeavor, knowledge and skills must be developed at a reasonably early age.

Many institutions other than schools have contributed to influencing the status of choral music. Increasing awareness of the importance of music as a force in religious worship has resulted in a resurgence of emphasis on church music programs. An increasing number of churches employ full-time people to assume responsibility for the development of the music program. Often these individuals carry the title of minister of music, and in effect their duties reflect this title. Choirs for children of elementary school age, for junior and senior high school youth, and for adults are maintained to meet the musical and social needs of all age groups.

Industry's increasing awareness of the importance of rapport in a cohesive, closely knit organization has prompted the establishment of numerous company choruses and other related music activities. Under capable leadership, these organizations have improved employees' morale, developed a feeling of belonging, improved labor and management relationships, and through periodic concerts have strengthened community ties.

The media of radio, television, motion pictures, and recordings have considerably influenced the tastes of the listening public in recent years. Radio has promoted greater understanding and has brought various sections of the country closer together. Remote and isolated areas have reaped a particular benefit. Music of many types has been made available to interested listeners at a minimum cost. Many FM stations, in particular, continue to present music of a high quality.

The impact of television has been overwhelming, but its cumulative effects have not been fully evaluated. Although an increase in the quality and the quantity of musical programs seems desirable, a limited number of excellent programs are being presented. Forward-looking teachers have brought these programs to their students' attention and have used them as a valuable educational tool.

Some choirs and choruses have been fortunate enough to make periodic appearances on television. Such experiences, by motivating a choral organization toward maximum group effort, can contribute substantially to the attainment of higher musical standards. The increased use of videotape for such programs also provides a choral group with opportunities to observe and to evaluate the visual as well as the musical aspects of their performance. Educational television especially has utilized the talents of amateur choral groups, and has presented a number of other programs designed to promote musical understanding and appreciation. Since choral music programs may be televised with a minimum of staging and production costs, further possibilities will undoubtedly be explored in the future.

Music serves effectively to heighten the intensity of dramatic situations in motion pictures; and the public is currently experiencing a barrage of tonal sounds and effects associated with theatrical and television productions and the modern dance. Although choral music per se has been too infrequently featured, this background music has perhaps to some extent developed a general awareness of a variety of vocal tone qualities and instrumental tone colors.

Recorded music, especially since the advent of the long-playing record, has made available to the listening public more music of a high quality than ever before. Numerous recordings of college and university choirs, church choirs, and professional choruses from the United States and Europe are presently available. Previously produced recordings of choral organizations number in the hundreds, and new recordings are being released periodically. Especially strong interest has developed with the advent of high-fidelity, stereophonic, and digital recordings. Although some of this interest may stem from mechanical or engineering factors, rather than musical aspects, this development has been generally beneficial to the improvement of musical tastes. Inherent in choral recordings are tremendous educational possibilities that, if effectively utilized in educational programs, may further improve the quality of choral singing in America.

Choral music has grown considerably and is still growing in America. However, the previously discussed influences are bound to reap a desirable cumulative harvest. Capable and inspired leadership—emphasizing wide participation and high musical standards—will ultimately place choral music in its proper sphere as a social and an aesthetic art.

1

Conducting
Techniques

When conducting a choir, the director should by means of poise, gestures, facial expressions, and eye contact not only energize the singers but also elicit the proper interpretation of the music from the choir. Through these varied means a conductor may instill life and vitality into the music—the result of which can be a truly thrilling and genuinely aesthetic experience for both the participants and the listening audience.

The conductor must be more than a mere time beater. Your musical knowledge and interpretative wishes should be conveyed through your conducting technique. Of course, demonstrations and verbal explanations are important, but during rehearsals, keep them to a minimum. It is through *technique*[1] that the experienced conductor can more quickly help the group achieve the desired interpretation.

---

[1] *Technique* in this context refers to the multitude of devices used by a conductor to convey the intent of the music and to achieve musical and artistic results. Fundamental conducting patterns, important as they are, are really subservient to the bodily and facial expressions that reflect the mood of the music. Nevertheless, they provide a necessary basis from which to start.

FUNDAMENTAL CONDUCTING PATTERNS

Each conductor is likely to have his or her own methods, but the fundamental patterns are the same. The student conductor should practice the basic movements until they become automatic. For the purpose of clarification, each of the basic meter patterns, as illustrated in Figures 1 through 5, is presented in at least two ways. The first diagram in each figure indicates the basic direction of the beats within the pattern. The subsequent patterns illustrate the manner in which you may apply them in the interpretation of music. The dotted lines in these conducting diagrams are called *rebounds* or *afterstrokes*. Although they should be considered subordinate to the basic movements within the pattern, they serve as connecting motions between the various beats and as preparatory motions to each subsequent beat. A degree of tension should occur toward the end, or point, of each beat, which is followed by a degree of relaxation during the rebound. Combined, these factors serve to give your conducting movements definition, clarity, and smoothness or flow—all of which are essential to artistic conducting.

In conducting fast tempi in triple meter (Figure 2c), negate or omit the second and third beats and utilize only the first or primary beat. In such instances, a slight pause generally occurs at the bottom of this beat; however, the faster the tempo, the less opportunity for pause.

The pattern for conducting quadruple meter is illustrated in Figure 3. Diagram *a* illustrates only the general directions of the beats (down, left, right, up); *b* illustrates how the pattern may be utilized with music of a moderate tempo in a legato style. Note that, following the downbeat and the initial rebound, beats two, three, and four are conducted on a horizontal plane, with the rebound of the fourth beat returning to one. A pitfall into which the young conductor often falls is using a beat that is too rounded in style, with the third beat sometimes rebounding too high, so as to appear as an additional downbeat in the measure.

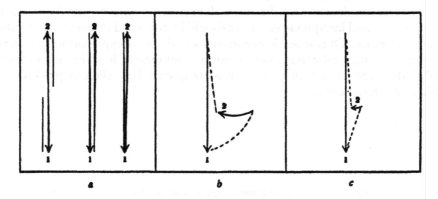

FIGURE 1 Duple meter (2/4, 2/2, 2/8): (*a*) the general direction of the pattern (i.e., down, up), (*b*) the pattern for slower tempi, and (*c*) the pattern for faster tempi.

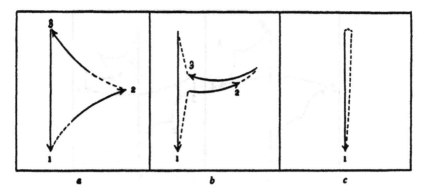

FIGURE 2   Triple meter (3/4, 3/8, 3/2): (*a*) the basic directions of the pattern, (*b*) application of the pattern for moderately slow and medium tempi, and (*c*) pattern for fast 3/4 or 3/8 tempi.

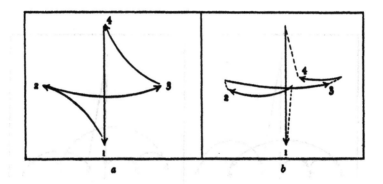

FIGURE 3   Quadruple meter (4/4, 4/2): (*a*) the basic directions of the pattern, and (*b*) application of the pattern to music of a moderate tempo.

Thus the conducting pattern is often unclear and confusing to the singers. In summary, keep beats two, three, and four on a horizontal plane.

Three different patterns for conducting sextuple meter are presented in Figures 4 through 6. In Figure 4, diagram *a* illustrates the general directions of the pattern, and diagram *b* illustrates how the pattern may be applied in the conducting of actual music. Many conductors prefer such a pattern because the fourth beat is clearly defined with a movement in a direction opposite from the first three beats and from the gradual stepwise return to the next downbeat.

Figure 5, however, illustrates an alternative pattern, with one clear downbeat and the other beats indicated on a somewhat horizontal plane. Pattern *a* illustrates the general directions of the beats, whereas pattern *b* illustrates how the movements might be applied in the conducting of actual music. The advantage of this pattern is simply that there can be no doubt there is only one downbeat in the measure.

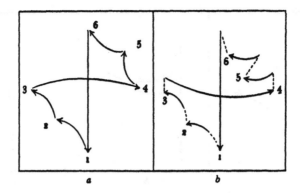

FIGURE 4   Sextuple meter (6/8, 6/4): (*a*) the basic directions of the pattern, and (*b*) application of the pattern to music of a moderate tempo.

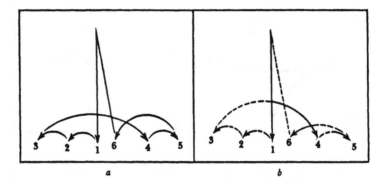

FIGURE 5   Sextuple meter (6/8, 6/4): (*a*) the basic directions of the pattern, and (*b*) application of the pattern to music of a moderate tempo. Note that all beats, with the exception of the downbeat, are on about the same plane, and the pattern may be used as an alternative to Figure 4.

Still another alternative is illustrated in Figure 6. The advantage of this pattern is the similarity in the direction of the fourth beat. In pattern *a*, six beats are indicated; in pattern *b*, the secondary beats—that is, two, three, five, and six—are negated or omitted so that the pattern may be adapted for use with faster tempi. Because of the similar direction of the primary beats (one and four), you may more easily alternate between one pattern and the other. This flexibility allows the movements in Figure 6 to be used with music involving irregular or changing tempi.

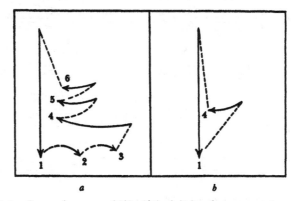

FIGURE 6   Sextuple meter (6/8, 6/4): (a) for slower tempi, and (b) for faster tempi.

IRREGULAR METER

Music in irregular meter—that is, 5/4, 7/4, and so on—may be analyzed in combinations of two and three or three and two, and three and four, or four and three, depending on the strong and weak syllables of the text structure. Irregular meter occurs rather infrequently in choral music; when it is encountered, however, it is generally more effective to utilize combinations of the duple, triple, and quadruple meters previously presented. For example, "Nächtens" ("Nightly"), by Johannes Brahms (G. Schirmer, No. 10133), written in 5/4 meter, should be conducted throughout by combining duple- and triple-meter patterns (Figure 7). Conduct the second downbeat, however, on a slightly lower plane so as not to elicit any undue stress on the third beat of the measure. (Actually, the movement should not even be considered as a downbeat, since the gesture for this beat is very small and implies or evokes no particular stress. In contrast, a real downbeat begins from a higher plane, the movement has greater length, and through supporting facial expressions and body gestures elicits a particular degree of stress and intensity.)

In "To Agni" (from the *Rig Veda*), by Gustav Holst, also written in 5/4 meter, conduct every other measure with a triple- and duple-meter pattern, and alternate measures with a duple and a triple pattern.[2]

You may encounter occasional exceptions, however, to the use of such patterns. For example, in measure 19 of "Walking on the Green Grass," by Michael Hennagin (Boosey & Hawkes, No. 5443), the rhythmic notation is 5/4 ♪♪♩.♪ and should be analyzed not as 2 + 3, or 3 + 2, but as 1 + 4. This becomes apparent in

[2] To develop alertness and the flexibility to move from one meter pattern to another, practice conducting the following sequence of changing meters:

2/4, 3/4, 4/4, 5/4, 6/4, 7/4

Devise various other combinations of patterns to conduct, and write them on the chalkboard. Another alternative is for one person, through various hand signals, to indicate a changing and varying sequence of patterns.

FIGURE 7 Excerpt from "Nächtens," by Johannes Brahms (Op. 112, No. 2) in 5/4 meter, which may be conducted by combining double- and triple-meter patterns, Copyright G. Schirmer, Inc., 1953. Used by permission.

examining the score, and you should be guided by the dictates of the music. Thus you should employ a downbeat, followed by another downbeat on a lower plane and a regular 4/4 pattern.

MUSIC IN FREE RHYTHM

Occasionally you will encounter music without a time signature and measure bars, and seemingly without any regular or systematic rhythmic accent or pulsation. In such instances it is desirable to conduct all the beats downward, with the exception of the last beat in the phrase, which generally should be upward. The beginning of the phrase should receive a regular precise downbeat; the subsequent words should be treated with a slight downward movement, varying in length according to the relative importance of the words. To determine the frequency and the appropriate size of the downward movements, analyze the text of the music carefully. The final measures of "Our Father," by Alexander Gretchaninov (Presser, No. 332-13000), necessitate this type of conducting treatment (Figure 8).[3] The downward movements are indicated under the music.

SUBDIVIDED BEATS

In conducting music of a moderate tempo, the patterns previously illustrated are effective. However, as these patterns are applied to slower tempi, there comes a point where the precision of the beat may become lost and the pattern becomes relatively ineffective. The solution to this problem, therefore, is not simply to slow the beat down further, but to subdivide the beats within the pattern so that in effect they *consume more time by moving through more space*. Through this means, the rhythmic pulsations of your conducting patterns become more marked and are distinguished by greater clarity; as a result, you are able to obtain a higher degree of precision from the group. When the music is of an exceptionally slow tempo, often indicated by the musical markings *largo* and *grave*, use the divided beat to clarify your musical intentions.

Two well-known examples of choral music that require a subdivided beat, as illustrated in Figure 9, are "Crucifixus" (from the B Minor Mass), by Johann S. Bach (E. C. Schirmer, No. 1174), and "Surely He Hath Borne Our Griefs" (from *Messiah*), by George F. Handel (G. Schirmer, No. 6598). Excerpts from these selections are shown in Figures 10 and 11.

A subdivision of the conducting beat may also be desirable when the rhythmic movement of a particular passage needs to be emphasized or brought

[3] Other examples of music in free rhythm are "Glory Be to God," by Rachmaninoff (Kjos; H. W. Gray), "Gladsome Radiance," by Gretchaninov (H. W. Gray), and "To Thee We Sing," Russian liturgy, arr. Tkach (Kjos).

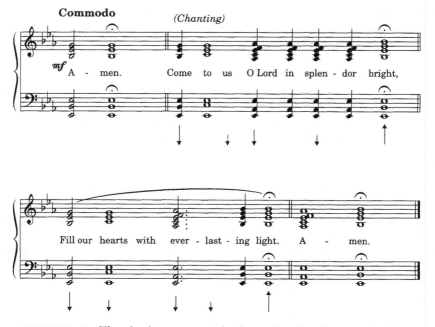

FIGURE 8 The final measures of Alexander Gretchaninov's "Our Father," with all but the last beat in the phrase conducted downward. Copyright 1916, Oliver Ditson Company. Used by permission.

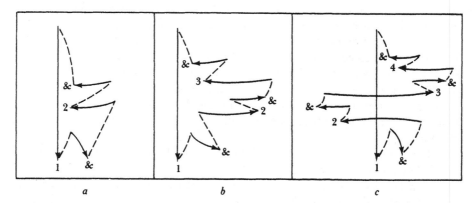

FIGURE 9   (a) Subdivided duple meter, (b) subdivided triple meter, and (c) subdivided quadruple meter.

out, and during a ritardando, when the rhythmic precision of the group needs to be stabilized. Such instances are likely to occur at the ends of phrases and in the final few measures of a composition. However, any of the beats within a given measure may be subdivided if the tempo of the selection allows sufficient time for the additional movements. The subdivided beat should not be utilized unless there is adequate time for the rebound of the subdivided or second half of the

FIGURE 10   Excerpt from "Crucifixus" (from the B Minor Mass), by J. S. Bach, which should be conducted with a subdivided triple-meter pattern.

beat, as well as for the rebound for the principal beat strokes. Figure 12 offers a case in point, and the correct treatment depends on the tempo being utilized. Thus, if the tempo was approximately M.M. ♩ = 54, the use of the subdivided beat as illustrated in Figure 12*a* would be most appropriate. On the other hand,

FIGURE 11   From the introduction to "Surely He Hath Borne Our Griefs" (from *Messiah*), by G. F. Handel, in which the subdivided quadruple-meter pattern should be used.

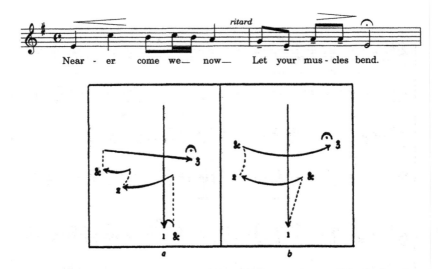

FIGURE 12   "Volga Boatmen" (folk song). In conducting the final measure, shown here, pattern *a* is utilized with very slow tempi, pattern *b* with moderate tempi.

if the music was conducted at approximately M. M. ♩ = 70, the added motion of the divided beat would undoubtedly detract from the clarity of your movements. In this and similar cases involving moderate tempi, avoid the subdivided beat pattern and simply accentuate the rebound of beats one and two, as illustrated in Figure 12*b*. In this treatment a slight pause should occur at the end of each rebound prior to the stroke of the subsequent beat. This serves to accentuate the rhythmic movement of the divided beat.

Where you have a choice of the preceding alternatives, consider thoughtfully the tempo of the music and the conducting pattern appropriate to the music's most effective interpretation.[4]

SUPERMETRIC PATTERNS

The meter signature of music normally indicates a conducting pattern to be used for each measure. However, there are exceptions where, to conduct more accurately the shape and contour of the phrase over several measures, it is desirable to use a conducting pattern which may compound repetitive meters. These are called supermetric patterns. Such patterns are not uncommon and usually necessitated where music occurs at a tempo so fast that conducting its stated meter (say, 3/8 in repetitive 1-beats) does not serve its broader phrasing. Thus, each *measure*, or group of measures, in regular meter usually would correspond to its supermetric *beat*. Beethoven indicates a section to be played in 3-beat units, but that each measure should be conducted in one, in particular, his "ritmo di tre [or quattro] battuta" (Scherzo, *Ninth Symphony*) means that three (or four) measures in fast tempo are to be grouped together (as one supermetric measure). For example, conducting in supermetric patterns in the French Carol, *Bring a Torch, Jeanette, Isabella* (Figure 13) better serves the work's harmonic structure and prosody. In reality, four of these repetitive 3/8 measures become the metrical equivalent of a 12/8 measure, and is best served by supermetric 4-beat patterns.

FIGURE 13   *Bring A Torch, Jeannette, Isabella* (French Carol). Use of a supermetric pattern (four recurring measures of 3/8 meter compounding to one 12/8 measure, and conducted in a 4-beat pattern).

[4] For further discussion of tempo, see "Determining the Tempo" later in this chapter.

Further, measures 17 and 18 of this piece ("Ah! Ah!") illustrates that an irregular phrasing may occur and has necessitated the interjection of a singular 2-beat pattern (or two 1-beats) before resumption of a regular supermetric 4-beat pattern.

In the motet *Ave Verum Corpus*, by W. A. Mozart, K. 618 (Figure 14), the meter is ¢, or Alla Breve (half note = the beat), and the tempo Adagio ($\lesssim$ = 48). Although a 4/4 conducting pattern is sometimes employed, the Alla breve here initially suggests a repetitive 2/2 (2-beat) conducting pattern. Closer examination suggests that a 4/2 supermetric pattern would better shape the contour of phrases, and also eliminate an extra and unmusical downbeat of measure 3.

The use of supermetric patterns may be found particularly useful in conducting certain passages of various other choral works from the Renaissance to the present. For example, in this section of the last movement of Beethoven's *Ninth Symphony* (Figure 15), the music appears in 6/8 meter, suggesting 2 conducting beats per measure. Because of its textual phrasing and fast tempo, however, a supermetric 4-beat pattern is suggested; that is, with one beat for each measure of the 6/8 meter. Here a four-beat pattern compounds four 6/8 measures.

Still another example where a 4-beat pattern may be effectively used occurs in the "Polovetsian Dance and Chorus" (from *Prince Igor*), by Alexander P. Borodin (Figure 16), beginning at letter F. From this point to letter G, the music, set in ¾ meter, divides itself into four measure phrases where a 4-beat pattern may be effectively used. Set in such a quick tempo, the meter would suggest repetitive 1-beat patterns for every ¾ measure; however, both music and text ultimately group these ¾ measures into groups of fours. (Last, supermetric patterns may also be employed in music of irregular meters, such as 5/8, 7/4, 11/8 and others.)

THE PREPARATORY BEAT AND ATTACKS AND RELEASES

To be effective, attacks and releases must be executed by the entire ensemble at precisely the same time. To achieve this precision, the group must be alert, it must respond to the rhythmic pulsation of the music, and the conductor must give a clear and precise preparatory beat or movement for each attack or release.

Always give the preparatory beat at the same rate of speed you want in the subsequent measures. Prior to beginning a selection, consider your desired tempo and the appropriate preparatory movement. This is especially important to the beginning conductor; later, as you gain experience, this process becomes automatic. In general, the preparatory beat should approximate the direction of the movement preceding the beat on which the music begins. For example, if the music begins on the first beat of a measure in quadruple meter, the preparatory movement should occur on the fourth beat preceding and should be made in the same general direction of the beat utilized for the standard conducting pattern for quadruple meter. Of course, when the music begins on the first beat of a measure in triple meter, the preparatory movement will occur on the third beat preceding the downbeat or actual attack (Figure 17).

FIGURE 14 "Ave Verus Corpus," by W. A. Mozart, K. 618. The use of a 4/4 pattern is suggested for every four measures as indicated.

FIGURE 15 *Ninth Symphony* (last movement) of Ludwig van Beethoven. In acknowledgment of a four measure phrasing, and rather than use the suggested repetitive 2-beat pattern in 6/8, note the use of a supermetric 4-beat pattern for every four measures beginning at letter M.

Effective and precise attacks depend not only on adequate preparatory movements executed by the hand and arm, but also on an alert physical stance of the body and appropriate facial expressions. The attack is facilitated if you are alert to the readiness of the singers, breathe with the group during the preparatory movement, and mouth the words in the first measure or so of the text.

You must also prepare adequately for releases to achieve any degree of precision. A slight upward movement is usually sufficient as a preparatory motion to the actual release, which is generally a precise downward or sideways movement. The size of these movements (the preparation and the actual release) should coincide with the mood of the music and the general size of the conducting pattern being utilized. That is, the preparation and the release of music of a soft, subdued nature demands a shorter upward preparation and downstroke, whereas

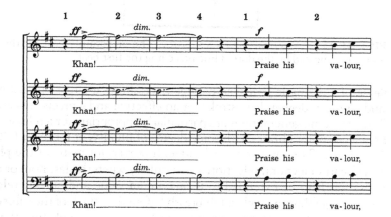

FIGURE 16 Excerpt from "Polovetsian Dance and Chorus" (from *Prince Igor*) by Alexander P. Borodin, where the use of supermetric 4-beat phrasing will clarify dynamics, show textual phrasing, and eliminate the unnecessary repetitive downbeat at the beginning of each 3/4 measure.

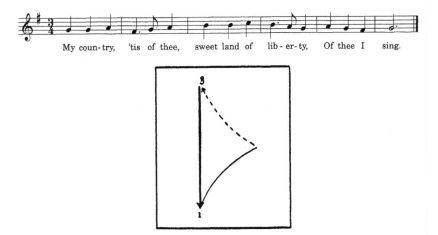

My coun-try,   'tis of thee,   sweet land of   lib-er-ty,   Of thee I   sing.

FIGURE 17   "America," by Henry Carey. The preparatory beat for the attack is indicated by the dotted line preceding the first beat.

the release of a dramatic *fortissimo* passage necessitates a larger upward movement and a longer, deeper downstroke for an effective and a precise release.

The preceding general rules are particularly appropriate for a release at the end of a selection, for phrases with some degree of finality, or for those followed by a slight pause. Try a modified technique, however, for many of the phrases within the heart of a choral selection—particularly when the last note or chord in a phrase needs to be extended to its maximum value and quickly released, with the group grabbing a quick catch breath before the attack of the subsequent phrase. A suggested movement to utilize in such cases is to simply turn the palm of the hand over and close it. This movement has been likened to turning off a water faucet. In certain musical selections one or more of the parts may need to be cut off while the others are sustained. When these voice parts are to your right, this subtle release may be done with the right hand; when they are to your left, the left hand may be used for the release while the basic conducting pattern is continued with the right hand. At the end of a piece, the final note does not always need to be beat out as long as there are no other moving parts in the measure and the rhythm (or pulsation) has basically ceased.

There is far more to the function of preparatory movements than starting and stopping the music. The achievement of any degree of rhythmic control by the conductor is dependent on the clarity of the preparatory beat. Leonard Bernstein comments: "The chief element in the conductor's technique of communication is the preparation. Everything must be shown ... before it happens."[5] Likewise, Wilhelm Furtwängler states that "it is not the moment of the downbeat itself, nor the accuracy and sharpness with which this downbeat is given,

[5] Leonard Bernstein, "The Art of Conducting," in *The Conductor's Art*, ed. Carl Bamberger (New York: McGraw-Hill, 1965), p. 272.

which determines the precision achieved by the orchestra, but the preparation which the conductor gives to this downbeat."[6]

George Szell, when conductor of the Cleveland Orchestra, once met with a group of the orchestra's players for a beer following a rehearsal. As he was leaving one of the players called out, "See you on the downbeat!" Szell quickly replied, "No! On the preparation!"[7]

Attacks on Incomplete Measures

Problems in achieving precise, accurate attacks most frequently occur when dealing with *incomplete measures*. Following are several variants and suggested techniques for dealing with each.

1. When a composition begins on a full or complete beat, prepare the group by conducting the preceding beat as a preparatory movement. For example, when in quadruple meter the music begins on the fourth beat, utilize the third beat as the preparatory movement (Figure 18).
2. When a composition begins on the second half of the beat, give the first half of the beat as the preparation (Figure 19).
3. When a composition begins after the second half of the beat and is closer to the following than to the preceding beat, use a full or complete beat as the preparatory movement according to rule 1 (Figure 20).

Note that no special treatment is utilized in Figure 20 for the sixteenth note preceding the fourth beat. Since this note falls more closely to the following

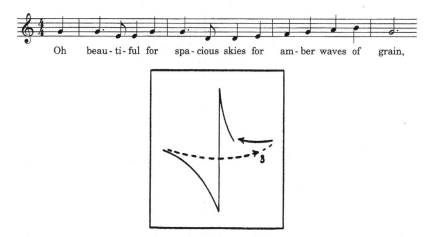

FIGURE 18   "America, the Beautiful," by Samuel A. Ward. The preparatory beat is indicated by the dotted line preceding the fourth beat.

[6] Wilhelm Furtwängler, "About the Handicraft of the Conductor," in *The Conductor's Art*, ed. Carl Bamberger (New York: McGraw-Hill, 1965), p. 211.

[7] Don V. Moses, et al., *Face to Face with an Orchestra* (Princeton, N.J.: Prestige, 1987), p. 27.

I— wish I was— in de land ob cot - ton.

FIGURE 19 "Dixie," by Daniel Emmett. The preparatory beat is indicated by the dotted line.

Ye sons of France, a - wake to glo - ry!

FIGURE 20 "La Marsellaise" (French national anthem), by Rouget de Lisle. The preparatory beat is indicated by the dotted line preceding the fourth beat.

(fourth) beat than to the preceding (third) beat, the same preparatory movement is utilized as that for any music beginning on a full or complete beat (compare the diagram in Figure 20 with that suggested for use with "America, the Beautiful" [Figure 18]).

An exception to the treatment of a sixteenth note occurs with the note following the fermata in Figure 21.

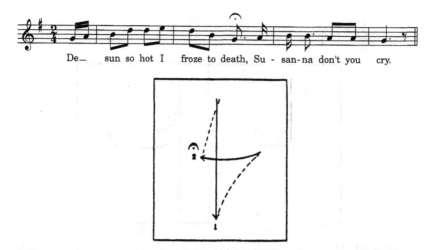

De— sun so hot I froze to death, Su - san-na don't you cry.

FIGURE 21 Excerpt from "Oh! Susanna," by Stephen Foster. The preparatory movement (following the fermata) is the upward motion that precedes the first of the following measure.

FERMATAS

You must prepare for all *fermatas*, or holds, if you expect precision in performance; that is, the movements preceding the fermata should be especially clear, concise, and definite. When a slight ritardando precedes the fermata, as is often the case, enlarge the pattern of your beat slightly as a means of gaining attention and preparing the group for the fermata. Raising the plane or height of the beat on which the fermata occurs is often helpful when the group is sustaining a *forte* passage. This is not always necessary, however, when the group is singing *piano*. [8]

During the hold, continue a slow, steady movement of the beat and avoid a stationary position in midair. Musical tone is continuing—not static—and this suggested slight movement will assist the singers in maintaining an even, steady flow of breath necessary for adequate tonal support.

The release of the fermata, or hold, is as important as the preparation, and either of two procedures may be utilized, depending on the interpretative effect desired. One procedure is to cut off completely the tone following the hold; the alternative is to carry over the tone to the succeeding phrase without a break in the flow of the breath. The conducting patterns for these two procedures are illustrated in Figure 22.

[8] When singing softly there is a tendency for singers to lessen the breath support, thus causing intonation problems. To avoid this difficulty, singers should have the illusion of using more and not less energy when singing softly.

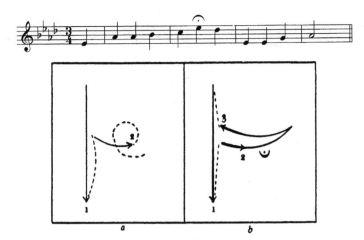

FIGURE 22   "Flow Gently, Sweet Afton." Two procedures for releasing the fermata: (*a*) complete release, and (*b*) carryover.

UNIFYING THE TECHNIQUE

As soon as you have a knowledge of the basic patterns, begin to apply them in ways that are meaningfully related to the music and at the same time try to integrate them into your total conducting technique. Various factors need to be carefully considered at this point, including correct posture, surety of beat patterns, facial expressions that reflect the mood of the music, coordination of the movements of the wrist, elbow, and hand, and even whether or not to use a baton.

Body Attitudes

The correct posture of a choral conductor can be described as "a body position that enables the conductor to most effectively achieve his or her task." In this sense, the posture resembles somewhat the correct posture of the singer (see Figure 48 in Chapter 2): Place one foot several inches ahead of the other and spread your feet apart to provide a solid foundation; this position allows you to remain alert and responsive to the musical situation.[9] Conducting gestures or movements should occur only in the upper body. From the waistline down, the body should generally be stationary. This does not preclude occasionally moving closer to the group during rehearsals or moving from one side of the room to the other to assist various sections. But for the most part, and certainly during a concert, *stand still.* On the podium you must assert a necessary degree of forcefulness, based on a knowledge and surety of the music. Your job is to communicate the composer's intentions to the singers. Shyness, coyness, and the like must be masked. Strive for clarity and definition.

[9] When your feet are in this position, be careful not to rock back and forth or to bend the upper body too far forward. Should either of these situations occur, it may be helpful to place your feet in a more parallel position.

One pitfall to which beginning conductors often succumb is the tendency to merely draw the patterns in the air in a somewhat mechanical way. To minimize this tendency, study the music carefully, identifying the various tensions created through rhythmic and harmonic movement and letting them be reflected in your conducting. Conducting thus becomes a real means of communicating musical ideas to a group of singers and not merely a mechanical exercise.

Your facial expressions should reflect the mood or character of the music. In short, the best advice is to try to "look like the music." Regular practice before a full-length mirror helps improve this aspect of conducting technique.

Self Analysis

It is essential that you eliminate undesirable traits in the beginning stages and not allow them to become reinforced and habitual. Following are some specific tips for young conductors:

1. Hold the wrist firmly, but never rigidly![10] Any looseness or floppiness of the wrist is distracting and lessens the clarity of the point of each beat.
2. Keep the elbows flexible and not held too closely to the body, since freedom of movement is inhibited. They should at least be high enough to allow the palms of the hands to face the floor. Conversely, do not extend the elbows too far outward because that also is distracting and possibly disabling to the shoulder.
3. Hold the fingers close together. With young conductors there may be a tendency to spread them somewhat apart, and this is not only distracting but sometimes even humorous to the singers. Spread fingers have been referred to as "Dracula" hands, and an extended little finger has been described as the "teacup hand position."
4. Most of the time, conduct primarily in front of the body so that the singers can perceive your beat patterns or gestures as related to your facial expressions and thus integrate them into a whole. Extended movements to one side of the body may be utilized for a special purpose only, but they should be the exception rather than the rule.
5. Maintain eye contact with the singers to the greatest extent possible and never bury your nose in the music. It is essential to maintain eye contact at the beginning and ending of phrases, at fermatas, and during any change of tempo. Be familiar enough with the score so you only need to use it as an occasional reference point.

If you could view yourself as others see you, many problems would be eliminated or at least minimized. This is possible, of course, on a videotape: The various points just mentioned become not only more meaningful but sometimes also shockingly real. It is essential for the young conductor striving for proficiency to practice on specific aspects of technique on a daily basis. Practicing in front of a mirror is helpful, but it is of even greater benefit for two persons to pair off, to practice conducting each other alternately, and then to provide immediate feedback to the other's conducting.

---

[10] Like a firm mattress, the wrist is flexible, but not rigid.

Use of a Baton

The use of a baton has a distinct advantage in that it helps to delineate the point of each beat to a greater extent, thus providing a degree of necessary and desirable discipline. The baton serves as an extension of the hand and arm and is helpful in working with larger groups, particularly with a large chorus or orchestra, or both.

The advantage of using the hands only—rather than a baton—is that the conductor is able to achieve a somewhat more fluid and flexible beat. This is particularly advantageous in legato sections of a piece. Some conductors, however, have been known to use both techniques with a particular choral work—a baton when conducting the larger choral and orchestral forces and the hands only during a more subdued, legato choral section of a work. A choral conductor who anticipates working with combined choral and instrumental organizations would be well advised to develop an adequate baton technique.

The conductor who has skill in both use of a baton and conducting with hands only will enjoy a much fuller range of possibilities in musical style and performance than the conductor who solely uses one or the other technique. The basic question of whether or not to use a baton should be, "How will the music best be served?"—not a conductor saying, "I just simply don't like using a baton," or "I don't feel comfortable using a baton, so I don't use one!" Conductors should discipline themselves with/without a baton, so that they get beyond inhibitions and make decisions based on musical needs.

Some considerations—hands or baton?

1. *Size of performing forces*: As the distance between the conductor and the performers (instrumental and/or choral) becomes greater, the clarity of the beat becomes increasingly difficult to see, thus making the decision to use a baton more reasonable and attractive.
2. *Character of the music*: More rhythmically intricate pieces are better served by a baton, whereas long sustained lines might find better expression with the use of the hands only.
3. *Limited rehearsal time*: A baton is helpful when assembling several musical forces together in a very short period of time. Often, a choir has only two or three final rehearsals with an orchestra, thus making clarity of gesture all the more critical.

As to the differences in technique, the patterns utilized in conducting instrumental groups are often more sharp and angular, with the objective in mind of achieving precision from the instrumentalists; but they should not be too extreme, or overdone. Ehmann states that "when applied to singing, [overly sharp gestures] result in tight and throaty voice production and the consequent loss of pitch.[11] Ehmann advocates that the beat patterns used for instrumental groups be "rounded off" and swing more to the outside. In place of primarily vertical movements, conductors should strive for more horizontal movement. "The

---

[11] Wilhelm Ehmann, *Choral Directing* (Minneapolis: Augsburg, 1968), p. 115.

director and singers should think of an imaginary horizontal plane at the level of the solar plexis, and imagine that the music moves back and forth on this plane."[12]

Some conductors feel strongly that using a baton does not and should not interfere with the ability to conduct choral groups in a very legato passage. The success of many orchestral conductors is advanced as evidence. And so the debate continues! In summary, the proof lies in the results each conductor personally achieves, and his or her final choice will be made after experience and careful evaluation of the musical results achieved with each approach.

Determining the Tempo

Performing a musical work in the proper tempo is an important aspect of artistic interpretation. In the process of determining a tempo, you should consider a number of factors.

Style and Historical Period

Any consideration of tempo should begin with an analysis of the musical style and the characteristics of the historical period from which the music was an outgrowth. Artistic forms of expression are shaped by various social, economic, and political forces that influence a composer. Tempo, therefore, as well as other interpretative considerations, should reflect the basic spirit of the times. (For a discussion of tempo during the various historical periods, see Chapter 5.)

Changes between historical periods were not abrupt, but evolved slowly. Within a given period, we may find unique differences among the styles of individual composers. With a concept of the general characteristics of particular periods as a starting point, you should carefully analyze the style of the composer whose music you are preparing to perform. Although such a procedure may seem like a neverending task, all efforts in this direction will contribute to a clearer understanding of the essential factors influencing interpretation.

Metronome Markings

Some music contains metronome markings indicating the desired tempo of the composer or the arranger. The metronome marking indicates the number of beats occurring within the duration of a minute and the type of note that receives the basic pulse. For example, the abbreviation M.M. $\quarternote$ = 60 indicates that 60 quarter notes may be sounded in the duration of one minute, or 1 quarter note each second.[13] If the metronome marking was M.M. $\quarternote$ = 120, the tempo

[12] Ibid., pp. 115–116.

[13] The metronome, a mechanical device used to indicate a particular desired tempo, was invented in 1816 by Johannes Maelzel; hence the name Maelzel Metronome, or the abbreviation M.M.

would be double, and 120 quarter notes would be sounded in the duration of one minute, or 2 quarter notes each second. Prior to introducing a new selection to the group, check your own tempo concept with the metronome marking. Although such markings need not be slavishly followed, they can provide a basis for determining your ultimate tempo.

Tempo Markings

Although not all composers include metronome markings on their music, many indicate the approximate desired tempo through the use of appropriate words, sometimes in English, but usually in Italian. Following is a basic group of Italian tempo markings:

Very slow:	*Largo*—large, broad, stately
	Grave—heavy, slow, ponderous
Slow:	*Larghetto*—slow (the diminutive of largo)
	Lento—slow
	Adagio—slow, leisurely
Moderate:	*Andante*—moderately slow, at a walking pace
	Moderato—moderate (tempo)
Moderately fast:	*Allegretto*—quite lively, moderately fast
Fast:	*Allegro*—lively, brisk, fast
	Vivace—brisk, spirited
Very fast:	*Presto*—very fast, rapid
	Prestissimo—as fast as possible

Although these Italian terms are only relative indications of tempo, they do provide a general way to determine the approximate tempo suggested by the composer or the editor. Equally important, however, are those terms indicating a change in the basic tempo. Here are some of the more common terms:

Accelerando—gradually increasing in tempo
Ritardando—gradually decreasing in tempo
Rallentando—gradually decreasing in tempo
Allargando—gradual broadening of tempo, with slight increase in volume
Calando—gradual decrease in tempo and volume
Stingendo—gradually increasing in tempo and excitement
A poco a poco—little by little, gradually
Poco meno mosso—a little slower
Poco più mosso—a little faster
A tempo—return to the original tempo

In addition to the preceding terms, you will encounter many others, particularly those pertaining to musical expression. Until you become thoroughly acquainted with all such markings, consult a standard dictionary of musical terms.

FIGURE 23 "Go Tell It on the Mountain" (Christmas spiritual). Copyright © 1945, 1973 by Galaxy Music Corporation. Used by permission.

Mood of the Text

A thorough study of the mood of the text provides additional insight in determining the most desirable tempo. An excerpt from the Christmas spiritual "Go Tell It on the Mountain" (Galaxy, No. 1532) is included for illustrative purposes (Figure 23).

We have heard this spiritual performed at various tempi, ranging from approximately M.M. ♩ = 60 to M.M. ♩ = 130. With such a wide variance in tempi, just what should be the conductor's guiding criterion? Although the mood of some spirituals is somber and serious, the text of this particular one describes the joyous, happy news that "Jesus Christ is born!" With this prevailing thought in mind, we are inclined to select a beginning tempo of approximately M.M. ♩ = 100. The tempo of contrasting sections within the music, however, should be considered separately in light of the prevailing mood of the text.

Ability of the Singers

The complexity of various vocal lines and the harmonic aspects of the music are highly important factors in determining the correct tempo. Certainly the skill with which the singers can execute a difficult florid passage must be considered. For singers with limited technique, it is a far better practice to perform a selection at a slightly slower tempo and to sing it *well*, rather than quickly in a slovenly, unmusical manner. Straightforward folk song arrangements can often be sung at a more rapid tempo without sacrificing tonal stability than music with an unusual harmonic treatment.

Acoustics of the Performance Room

The acoustical properties of the rehearsal room or the auditorium have a telling influence on the total musical effectiveness of a selection. In comparison with instruments, the human voice—especially that of an inexperienced singer—has less sustaining quality. In rooms with little reverberation, a lifeless tonal quality, with an insufficient connection between various tones within the musical phrase, will often result. In such instances music may sound best at a slightly faster tempo than you would normally use in an auditorium or a room with reasonably good acoustics. Conversely, the conductor will find it desirable to employ restraint when rehearsing or performing in rooms with exceptionally live acoustical properties.

ACHIEVING EXPRESSIVE CONDUCTING

In developing conducting technique, the fundamental patterns merely provide a necessary basis from which to begin. The conductor must also consider the conducting plane or height of the beat, the size of the beat in relationship to tempo and dynamics, negating the beat, clarifying the beat, the style of the beat in relationship to the manner of articulation, preparing for changes in tempo and dynamics, the length of the musical phrase, the use of the left hand, and the cueing of entrances.

The Conducting Plane

The level of the conducting beat is determined by the size of the musical organization and the eye level of the singers. If the size of the organization is reasonably small and if the group is seated on risers, the plane of the conductor's beat, for the most part, should be from the shoulder level down to the waist. If the musical organization is exceptionally large, raise the conducting plane slightly so that all singers may clearly see the beat.

The conducting plane may be raised or lowered to effectively indicate the shape of a phrase or an increase and decrease of phrasewise tension within the musical phrase. The choral selection "A Thought Like Music," by Brahms (Plymouth, No. A.S. 103), is an excellent example of music requiring this treatment (Figure 24). The phrase should be begun with a beat about chest high and gradually raised to the peak of the phrase in the second measure. After the peak of the phrase is reached, the conducting plane is gradually lowered. Another example of this treatment occurs in "How Lovely Is Thy Dwelling Place," by Brahms (Carl Fischer, No. 632).

Size of the Beat

The size of the conductor's beat is determined by the dynamic level, the tempo and rhythm of the music, and the style of articulation (discussed in a following section), as well as by the general mood or character of the music. Determine the appropriate dynamics of the music and adapt the size of the beat accordingly. Music of a high dynamic level generally necessitates a larger, broader beat, whereas music of a low dynamic level requires a relatively smaller movement. Particularly with music of a subdued nature, some conductors are inclined to use movements that are too large and often, therefore, imprecise and

FIGURE 24   Excerpt from "A Thought Like Music," by Johannes Brahms, in which the conducting plane may be raised and lowered to indicate the rise and fall or increase and decrease of tension within the phrase. Copyright © 1958 by Plymouth Music Company, Inc. Used by permission.

unclear.[14] For example, in the choral selection "Since All Is Passing," by Paul Hindemith (Schott, No. AP37), the size of the conducting pattern that is appropriate to the first phrase—marked *piano* (*p*)—need not be more than six inches in height; for the second phrase marked *pianissimo* (*pp*)—the pattern should necessarily be reduced slightly in height; the third phrase—marked *forte* (*f*)—should be prepared for vigorously and should be approximately fourteen to sixteen inches in height. The dynamic level of the final phrase is identical to the

---

[14] The conducting movements for music of a low dynamic level should, for the most part be immediately in front of the body; thus a more coordinated effort between the hand and arm movements and the facial expressions may be achieved.

FIGURE 25 Excerpt from "Since All Is Passing" (Puisque tout passe) (No. 3, of *Six Chansons*), by Paul Hindemith. The size of the conducting pattern for this phrase, which is marked *p*, need not be more than six inches in height. Copyright © 1943 by B. Schott's Sönne, Mainz. Copyright renewed 1970. Used by permission of European American Music Distributors Corporation.

second and should be conducted accordingly (see Figure 25). ["Since All Is Passing" is the third of a group of *Six Chansons* for Four-Part Chorus of Mixed Voices, Unaccompanied, and based on original French poems by Rainer Maria Rilke. The chansons are often performed as a set and are: "The Doe" (La Biche), "A Swan" (Un Cygne), "Since All Is Passing" (Puisque tout passe), "Springtime" (Printemps), "In Winter" (En Hiver), and "Orchard" (Verger)].

In the motet "Create in Me, O God, a Pure Heart," by Brahms (G. Schirmer, No. 7504), an extremely quiet beginning is necessary and the conductor must strive for an appropriate dynamic level (Figure 26). To help achieve the desired effect, your initial preparatory movement should be extremely small—only a precise movement of several inches is necessary, since a larger movement may elicit too loud a response.[15]

[15] The size of the beat should also be minimized before important entrances, so that the strong beat on the entrance will be more obvious and clearer.

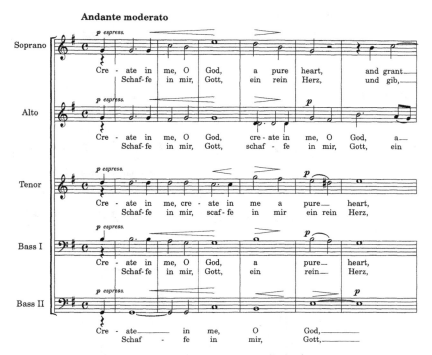

FIGURE 26 Excerpt from "Create in Me, O God, a Pure Heart," by Johannes Brahms, in which the conductor must use an exceptionally small beat in the beginning to achieve the desired dynamic level. Copyright G. Schirmer, Inc., 1931. Used by permission.

Dynamic contrast is a problem of considerable concern to many directors, some of whom have often stated—somewhat in jest—that their choral groups seem to know only two dynamic levels—loud and louder. In view of this seeming dilemma, give careful consideration to the appropriate size of your conducting movements as they relate to the dynamic level of the music. This is essential if your groups are ever to sing in an expressive manner.

The tempo of the music is also an important factor influencing the size of the beat. Because of physical limitations, you must limit the scope of the beat with music of a relatively fast tempo to achieve any degree of precision. For example, in the well-known Ukrainian carol, "Carol of the Bells," by Leontovich (Carl Fischer, No. CM 4604), the tempo necessitates a relatively small beat. Although some parts of the music may be conducted one beat to a measure, the introductory section in particular requires a small, crisp three-beat pattern. Thus if the pattern is to be clear and precise, it must be relatively small.

In conducting certain figures or patterns containing notes of unequal duration, it is often desirable, particularly in legato music, to reduce the size or scope

Adagio non tanto

FIGURE 27 Excerpt from "My Lord, What a Mornin'" (spiritual), arr. H. T. Burleigh (© 1924 by G. Ricordi & Co., New York; used by permission of Franco Colombo Publications, a division of Belwin Mills Publishing Corp.), in which the conducting patterns are modified (*a*) for the rhythmic pattern $\frac{4}{4}$♩♩♫, and (*b*) for the rhythmic pattern $\frac{4}{4}$♩♩.♩.. Note the rebound of the first beat and the relatively short strokes of the following beats. Compare these patterns with Figure 3.

of the beat on unaccented pulses (Figure 27). For example, in conducting the spiritual "My Lord, What a Mornin'" (Ricordi, No. 412), minimize the movements for the second and third beats in measures 1, 3, and 4 (Figure 27*a*) and the movements for all beats except the first in measure 2 (Figure 27*b*). This modification is more expressive of the music, it serves to lessen the singers' physical response on unaccented pulses, and it facilitates a more legato effect. Although this is but one example, the principle is basic and may be applied in numerous rhythmic patterns as a means of eliciting a more musical response.[16]

Negating the Conducting Beats

Negation involves minimizing the size of the conducting pattern and, in some cases, omitting the pattern of the beat entirely. Negation is often used (1) during rests, (2) to clarify the rhythm, and (3) before important choral entrances. The word *negation* implies the act of or an instance of denying. As indicated, in its application to choral conducting, it means omitting certain beats in a conducting pattern when the music is not moving rhythmically, as in the instance of rests. Even very small movements, such as those advocated for "My Lord, What a Mornin' " (Figure 27), may be considered negation. You will encounter many other situations, however, where hardly any or no movement is required. For example, in measure 4 of "Glory to God," by J. S. Bach (see Figure 28), no movement needs to occur on the third and fourth beats of the measure, except for a preparatory movement to the succeeding measure. In "Jesus, Priceless Treasure," by J. S. Bach, where the fermatas occur in both the second and

FIGURE 28 Excerpt from "Glory to God" by J. S. Bach. The conductor should negate the third and fourth beats of measure 4, followed by a preparatory beat to the next measure.

---

[16] Practice conducting various rhythm patterns with the objective of negating or reducing the size of beats where there are rests or little rhythmic movement. For example:

$$\frac{3}{4} \text{ } \text{♩♩♩|♩♩♩♩|♩♩|♩♩♩♩| } etc.$$

Devise various other rhythmic patterns to conduct.

1. Je - sus, price - less   Treas - ure, Source of pur - est pleas - ure,
2. Hence, all fear and   sad - ness! For the Lord of glad - ness,

FIGURE 29 Excerpt from "Jesus, Priceless Treasure," by J. S. Bach. Only the third beat is conducted in the measures with fematas, followed, of course, by the preparatory beat to the next measure.

fourth measures (see Figure 29), a relatively firm beat will be given on the third beats of each of these measures, after which there need not be any conducting gestures except for the preparatory movement to the following measure.

Also, in "Kyrie Eleison," by W. A. Mozart (see Figure 30), a firm beat will be given on the first beat of the measure, followed by a very slight movement on the second beat (just lightly touching the beat). On the half-note rests following "Kyrie" in measures 1, 2, and 3, the third and fourth beats in each of these measures may be negated or only lightly touched—just enough to give a cue to the orchestra or the piano accompanist for the third beat of the measure. In either case, the fourth beat will be completely negated. The only movement following this will be the preparation (an upward gesture) for the next measure. The preceding are given only as examples where the concept of negation should be applied. In choral literature, however, you will find numerous examples where there is no rhythmical movement, and where the conducting pattern should reflect the music. Following are some other examples of music necessitating this treatment. Examine them carefully and determine how best to conduct them.

There are exceptions to all rules, and in this instance, the exception occurs when the choir is singing a long sustained note, for example, [musical notation], which involves a gradual *crescendo*, or building of intensity. Here the conductor's initial gestures should be relatively small, but gradually increase in size to reflect the changing dynamics of the music.

An overlooked and underused negation is the one used immediately before important entrances where you want a very precise attack. Excessive or unnecessary baton or arm movements prior to an entrance can sometimes be misleading or confusing to singers, thus lessening the unanimity and force of the attack.

Clarifying the Beat

With fast tempi there may not be adequate time to conduct each beat in the pattern in a clear, distinct manner. Although decreasing the size of the beat pattern will help (so that the hand does not have to move through so much space), sometimes the only solution is to eliminate or leave out certain beats in

FIGURE 30 Excerpt from "Kyrie Eleison," by W. A. Mozart, edited by Rod Walker, Hal Leonard Publishing Corporation, 1982. Used by permission. The fourth beat of measures 1, 2, and 3 should be negated and the third beat either negated, or slightly touched—just enough to give a cue to the orchestra or the accompanist.

FIGURE 31 Excerpt from "Neighbors' Chorus" from *La Jolie Parfumeuse*, by Jacques Offenbach, in which beats two and three are either negated or reduced in size to clarify the conductor's gestures. Copyright Broude Brothers, 1954. Used by permission.

a measure. As was discussed, this is often referred to as *negation*. For example, in the "Neighbors' Chorus," by Jacques Offenbach (Broude Brothers, No. 130), the meter is 3/8 and the tempo marking is ♩. = 69 (Figure 31). Therefore, the most effective gesture is simply to conduct the music with one strong beat to a measure, thus negating, or at least minimizing the size of, beats two and three in each measure. Occasionally, however, three small beats per measure may be conducted to indicate the restraint necessary at the end of a phrase, such as in measures 11 and 12. Measure 13, of course, returns to the original tempo.

The reverse of this situation occurs in "All Breathing Life, Sing and Praise Ye the Lord," by J. S. Bach (G. Schirmer, No. 7470) (Figure 32). In contrast, utilize a small three-beat pattern to set the tempo and to indicate the rhythmic movement of the sixteenth-note figure. Then, two or three measures of this pattern may be followed by a "one-to-a-measure" pattern (with beats two and three being negated) for the remainder of the phrase. At the beginning of most phrases, however, the conductor will generally revert to the small three-beat pattern.

Style of the Beat

It is highly important that your beat reflect the manner or style of articulation of the music—that is, legato, staccato, or marcato.[17] In conducting music in a legato style, you should maintain a continuous movement to the beat, for when it stops, the natural tendency is for the singers to stop also, or at least to lessen the flow of the breath. One of the difficulties involved, especially in slow, sustained passages, is maintaining control of the arm movement. When the arm moves too quickly and the end of the beat is reached too soon, the conducting appears jerky and the smooth legato effect is lost. To eliminate this fault, imagine a definite resistance to your movements. Pretending to move your hand through a pool of water will often produce the desired feeling.

Music in a staccato style must be conducted in a crisp, detached manner to indicate the desired articulation of the music. To do so effectively, however, use a relatively small beat. Because singing in a marcato style necessitates a sharp inward movement of the abdominal muscles on each note marked >, this action should be reflected in your motions. Thus music in a marcato style demands a vigorous movement, with a precise and definite point to each beat. Although there are many compositions that are in either legato or staccato styles throughout, few if any compositions are in marcato style throughout.[18] Phrases indicating marcato are so marked for special effect, and to be effective, should be in contrast to other sections. Figure 33 includes an excerpt from "The Last Words of David," by Randall Thompson (E. C. Schirmer, No. 2294), that illustrates a considerable use of marcato. Note the relationship of the marcato markings to the text of the music. "Glory to God," by J. S. Bach (Ricordi, No. NY 1397), is an excellent example for analysis and performance that alternates between marcato and legato styles. An example combining all three styles—legato, staccato, and marcato—is "When Love Is Kind" (English folk song), arr. Salli Terri (Lawson-Gould, No. 843).[19]

---

[17] For a discussion of the relationship of diction to these basic styles of articulation, see "Styles of Diction" in Chapter 2.

[18] For examples of music in legato, staccato, and marcato styles, see "Styles of Diction" in Chapter 2.

[19] Another style of articulation is *portato*—a style or manner of performance halfway between legato and staccato. The music notation is marked ♩ or ♩.

FIGURE 32 Excerpt from "All Breathing Life, Sing and Praise Ye the Lord," from the motet *Sing Ye to the Lord*, by J. S. Bach, in which a small, precise three-beat pattern is used to set the tempo and indicate the rhythmic movement of the sixteenth-note pattern.

FIGURE 33 Excerpt from "The Last Words of David," by Randall Thompson, illustrating a marcato style, which necessitates vigorous and marked conducting gestures. Copyright E. C. Schirmer Music Co., 1950. Used by permission.

Controlling Tempo and Dynamics

A conductor must retain absolute control of the tempo of a choral group. Under certain circumstances singers may be inclined either to rush or to drag the tempo—neither of which helps to achieve a musical performance. At the very least they may not be as responsive to the conductor as is necessary. When you are in control, you have the feeling that the singers will respond to the most subtle nuances in your gestures (almost like being in command of a mighty organ). First of all, the group must be trained to watch the conductor carefully, and you should not always necessarily conduct a piece at the same exact tempo (sometimes due to the varying acoustics of the performance halls). Also, the treatment of phrase endings may be handled slightly differently. So in this respect you should not always be predictable; if you are and the group feels they can second-guess you, so to speak, they are not likely to be as attentive as necessary.

Additionally, to control the tempo of an ensemble, two conditions are essential: the precision of the initial beat and the clarity of the afterstroke, or rebound. There should be a definite point to each beat followed by a clear rebound to the next beat. It is the preciseness of the point of each beat that enables a choir to maintain a steadiness of the pulse, and it is the nature of the rebound that enables you to change the tempo—either faster or slower.[20] Effective changes in tempo are not achieved by merely slowing down or speeding up the conducting pattern. Rather, the pattern must be modified in a way that will both attract the attention of the singers and signal your intentions.

To express your desire for accelerando, the overall conducting pattern should be lessened in size, but give particular attention to a gradual quickening of the rebound of each beat. For a ritardando, the first half of each beat should be gradually lengthened, but the rebound in particular should consume slightly more time by moving through more space; that is, the point of each subsequent beat is not reached quite so soon.

If the choir determines their own ritardandos (which they are sometimes inclined to do), there will be too many versions of tempi, inaccuracy, and overexaggeration of the ritard. To alleviate this problem, insist that the group maintain a steady tempo—like a team of horses pulling a heavy load (or use any other apt analogy), and "pull on the reins" ever so slightly when you feel it is necessary. Such an approach helps to maintain the intensity and the drive of the pulse and places you more in command of the choir.

As to dynamic changes, the size of the beat is paramount. An almost ludicrous situation arises when a conductor asks for a *pianissimo* verbally and

---

[20] To test the clarity of your conducting gestures, ask the choir or the members of your conducting class to respond by clapping their hands together on each beat. Try different tempi, moving from slow to fast and utilizing various pauses between beats (in a somewhat erratic manner). Can the group follow you? The test of your clarity as a conductor is whether all the clapping sounds occur precisely together, with *no* sounds occurring before or after the intended beat.

through facial expressions but continues to flail away with a relatively large conducting pattern. Soft passages necessitate a small, precise conducting pattern, which may be increased in size according to the relative level of dynamics. To become more sensitive to what is being asked of the choir, some periodic practice in front of a mirror can be most helpful. Ask yourself, "Do I like what I see, and how would I as a singer respond to the conducting gestures observed?"

Extending the Musical Phrase

Some singers are inclined to take unnecessary breaths between short phrases or in the middle of phrases. The conductor can eliminate some of this difficulty by making a circular movement toward the group—indicating that a breath is not to be taken and the musical phrase is to be extended. This circular movement should commence at least one beat, and in faster tempi, two beats, prior to the end of the phrase that is to be carried over.

The Left Hand

Conductors, as a general rule, are inclined to overuse the left hand. Some fall into the habit of allowing the left hand to follow the pattern of the right. Since overuse of the left hand renders it relatively ineffective for special situations, it should, for the most part, be held near the waistline. You may then more effectively use the left hand for special emphasis, such as sudden accents, abrupt changes in tempo, cueing entrances of certain sections, crescendo and decrescendo, and to assist in effecting clear, precise attacks and releases.

In actual practice many conductors do use both hands simultaneously in conducting the basic patterns. There is nothing terribly wrong with this practice, particularly when it is used, for example, to convey a certain dramatic intensity in the music or to rhythmically solidify a chorus of considerable size. It does become unnecessary, however, when conducting music of a restrained nature and a low dynamic level. In this instance, too much arm movement is inimical to the best artistic performance of the music and might best be described as overkill.

Cueing

Effective cueing should provide a sense of security to the singers and facilitate the precision of attacks and an improved musical interpretation. It also allows the singers to become more aware (if they watch) of important entering solo voices or sections that are generally of musical importance to the listeners. This concept should be communicated to the singers so they understand the necessity for some voices to occasionally predominate and others to be subservient to the melodic line.

Cueing has been referred to as "effective phrasing with a timely look in the proper direction." Several methods of cueing are currently utilized. Use any of the following approaches, depending on the tempo of the music, the style of the music, and the frequency of the entering parts:

1. Use of the *hands*, providing there is adequate time to execute the movements
2. Use of the *head*, when a multiplicity of entrances occur in the music
3. Use of *facial expressions*, appropriate in dealing with more subtle and delicate entrances
4. A *combination* of two or more of the preceding methods

Some subtle cues may be indicated by a very slight hand movement combined with appropriate facial expressions, such as a nod of the head, or perhaps by mouthing the vowels in the first word or so. Other entrances may necessitate a more vigorous motion, sometimes with both hands being used. The appropriate gesture depends, of course, on the dynamic level of the music, the tempo, and the number of entrances required.

A good many cues that involve the entrance of only one part may be best accomplished by simply pointing the beat or hand and arm in the direction of the group or section whose entrance needs to be assisted. When several sections or the entire choir is cued, it is generally best to reinforce the gesture by using both hands.

Cueing entrances of various parts is essential to rhythmic security. Give them the same careful treatment and preparation as you give the entire ensemble at the beginning of a choral selection.

CONDUCTING ACCENT AND CHANGING METER

Basic conducting patterns often need to be modified in a variety of ways to reflect the character of the music and to elicit the proper musical response from the group. Rhythm, meter, and accent account for many of these modifications; therefore, the following procedures are suggested for conducting syncopated figures, offbeat accents, displaced rhythmic accents, and changing meter and shifting accents.

Syncopated Figures

The conducting of certain syncopated figures may be made more effective by utilizing a vigorous rebound from the beat preceding each accented or syncopated note in the figure, and shortening or reducing the size of the following beat. See, for example, the excerpt from "Ching-A-Ring Chaw," adapted by Aaron Copland (Figure 34), and the illustration of the modified conducting pattern for the figure $\frac{2}{4}$ ♩ ♪ ♩ ♩ ♪.

For a similar example involving the same conducting principle—yet somewhat more complex—see the final three measures of "Now Is the Hour of Darkness Past," by Daniel Pinkham (Figure 35). Note that the accents fall on the second beat, the second half of the third beat, and the second beat of the fol-

FIGURE 34 Excerpt from "Ching-A-Ring Chaw" (minstrel song), from *Old American Songs*. Adapted by Aaron Copland; arranged for SATB by Irving Fine. A modified conducting pattern is used for the syncopated figure ${}^2_4$ ♩ ♪♫♩ ♩ —(*a*) for faster tempi, as in the example, and (*b*) for music with slower tempi. A slight pause occurs at the top of the rebound, especially in conducting faster tempi © 1954, 1955 by Aaron Copland. Reprinted by permission of Aaron Copland, Copyright Owner, and Boosey & Hawkes, Inc., Sole Publisher and Licensees.

lowing measure, and that the music is marked *senza rall.* While a conductor might initially be inclined to simply conduct the rhythm of the words, this creates difficulties in terms of rhythmic accuracy. Instead, conduct a strict three-beat pattern with an accentuated rebound on the second half of the third beat in measure 3. The size of the first beat in the following measure should be negated or minimized to allow for a clearer emphasis on the accented second beat.[21]

---

[21] In addition to your gestures, it is helpful, in this instance, to ask the chorus to count aloud together—one, *two*, three *and*, one, *two*, three, *one*, and so on. In counting, emphasize the accents and repeat as many times as necessary.

FIGURE 35 Excerpt from "Now Is the Hour of Darkness Past," by Daniel Pinkman, in which the conductor combines an accentuated rebound and negation to achieve clarity. Copyright 1975 by Ione Press, Inc. Sole selling agent: E. C. Schirmer Music Co., Boston. Used by permission.

Offbeat Accents

A group of offbeat accents—that is, those occurring on the second half of each beat or pulse—may be conducted effectively by utilizing a slight downward movement of the hands and arm on the first half of the beat followed by a definite and precise upward movement on the second half of the beat. The pattern should be entirely up and down, with the rebound retracing the path of the downbeat (see the excerpt from "Ezekiel Saw the Wheel" and the illustration of the suggested conducting pattern in Figure 36.

Displaced Rhythmic Accents

The accenting of beats other than those expected—that is, the strong beats of a measure—is a rhythmic device used by various contemporary composers. One means is the use of traditional rhythmic patterns in nonsymmetrical forms. For example, in the composition "It Is Good to Be Merry," by Jean Berger (Kjos, No. 5293), the traditional 9/8 pattern of 3 + 3 + 3 is altered to 2 + 2 + 2 + 3 (see Figure 37). In Leonard Bernstein's "America" (from *West Side Story*), the 6/8 pattern of 3 + 3 is altered to 3 + 3 + 2 + 2 + 2 (see Figure 34). In "Ballad of Green Broom" by Benjamin Britten (Boosey & Hawkes, No. 1875), the 6/8 pattern of 3 + 3 is altered to 3 + $1\frac{1}{2}$ + $1\frac{1}{2}$ and $1\frac{1}{2}$ + $1\frac{1}{2}$ + 3 (see Figure 39).

In conducting such patterns, first analyze the music for the shift of accents and then determine the most appropriate movements to convey clarity and evoke rhythmic precision from the group. The conducting pattern should not be too large if precision is to be achieved. Following the downbeat, make the subsequent movements (beats) from right to left in a crisp, short, decisive manner (see Figures 33–35).

FIGURE 36 Excerpt from "Ezekiel Saw the Wheel" (spititual), arr. Sime-one, in which the modified pattern shown is used for conducting the offbeat accents $\frac{2}{4}$ ♩♪♪♩♪. . From the Fred Waring choral arrangement. © Copyright MCML, Shawnee Press, Inc., Delaware Water Gap, PA 18327. Used by permission.

Conducting Asymmetrical Patterns

In preparing to conduct asymmetrical patterns in music with changing meter and shifting accents, the conductor should carefully analyze the music, identify the significant aspects of the rhythm that need to be clarified or conveyed to the singers, and then determine the most appropriate gestures or patterns to convey musical meaning and the intentions of the composer. Additionally, try to use gestures or patterns that are physically adaptable and not unnecessarily complicated. For example, in Figure 37 "It Is Good to Be Merry," by Jean Berger, the 9/8 figure could be conducted with a simple 4-beat pattern, with a hesitation on the fourth beat and the rebound delayed for the ninth beat in the measure (2 + 2 + 2 + 3). A suggested altrenative, however, to

FIGURE 37 Excerpt from "It Is Good to Be Merry," by Jean Berger, together with a conducting pattern for the nonsymmetrical figure $\frac{9}{8}$ ♩♪♪♩♪ (2 + 2 + 2 + 3). Used by permission of Neil A. Kjos Music Co., San Diego, Calif. Copyright 1961.

this simple straightforward approach is illustred in the conducting pattern in Figure 34. Note how the plane of the pattern gradually rises higher—to reflect the rising pitch level, as well as the crescendo in the music. Practice using both approaches and adopt the one you feel most comfortable with and is the most musically effective.

In Figure 38, an excerpt from "America" from *West Side Story*, by Leonard Bemstein, conduct the first and third measures with a simple 2/4 pattern that is used for 6/8 meter of a moderate tempo. For the second and fourth measures, however, use your regular 3-beat pattern that accomodates the displaced accents.

Lightly

1. I like to be in A - me - ri - ca, O - kay by me in A - me - ri - ca.
2. Au-to - mo-bile in A - me - ri - ca, Chro-mi - um steel in A - me - ri - ca.

1. Oh,_____ A - me - ri - ca, Oh,_____ A - me - ri - ca.
2. Oh,_____ A - me - ri - ca, Oh,_____ A - me - ri - ca.

1. Oh,_____ A - me - ri - ca, Oh,_____ A - me - ri - ca.
2. Oh,_____ A - me - ri - ca, Oh,_____ A - me - ri - ca.

1. Oh,_____ A - me - ri - ca, Oh,_____ A - me - ri - ca.
2. Oh,_____ A - me - ri - ca, Oh,_____ A - me - ri - ca.

a   *b*

FIGURE 38 Excerpt from "America" from *West Side Story*, by Leonard Bernstein, arr. William Strickles, and patterns for conducting the nonsymmetrical figure ⁶⁄₈ ♪♪♪♪♪♪|♩♩♩ (3 + 3 + 2 + 2 + 2): (*a*) for measures 1 and 3, and (*b*) for measures 2 and 4. © 1957, 1959, by Leonard Bernestein and Stephen Sondheim. Used by Permission.

In Figure 39, "Ballad of Green Broom," by Benjamin Britten, you might be tempted to conduct with a simple 2/4 pattern allowing each individual line to do its own rhythms. While this approach might be utilized after the singers thoroughly know their music, it is not a good idea for the beginning stages of learning where they need help in handling the various offbeat rhythms. The conducting patterns illustrated in Figure 39 should help singers with these rhythmic patterns.

In Randall Thompson's "Glory to God in the Highest" (E. C. Schirmer, No. 2470) (see Figure 40), for example, the first six measures change alternately

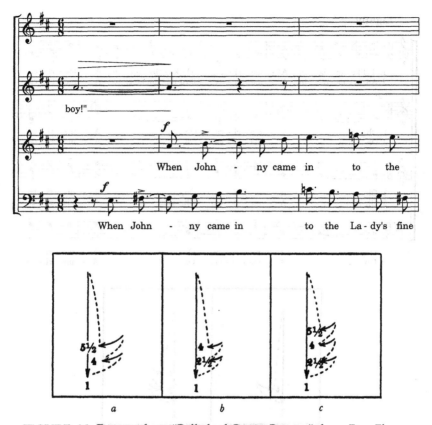

FIGURE 39 Excerpt from "Ballad of Green Broom," from *Five Flower Songs*, Op. 47, No. 5. Words anonymous; music by Benjamin Britten. Conducting pattern (*a*) for measure 1: ⁶₈♩♪.♪|, pattern (*b*) for measure 2: ⁶₈♪.♪♪♪♪| , and pattern (*c*) for measure 3: ⁶₈♪.♪.♪.♪|. © 1951 by Boosey & Co., Ltd. Renewed 1979. Reprinted by permission of Boosey & Hawkes, Inc.

from 2/4 to 3/8 to 2/4 (two measures) to 5/8 to 2/4.[22] A suggested approach to conducting this section of changing meter, as illustrated in Figure 40 is as follows: In measure 1 (in 2/4), use a two-beat pattern with a strong full downbeat and a short precise secondary beat. In measure 2 (in 3/8), because the eighth note maintains the same value as in the previous measure ($\downarrow$ = 120) and since it would be awkward, and not really necessary, to conduct three distinct movements, negate beats two and three and conduct only one strong beat in the measure. (Actually, there is a pause on the second beat, and the rebound from the downbeat occurs on the third beat.) Measures 3 and 4 should be conducted in two, as in measure 1. In measure 5 (in 5/8), conduct the first eighth note with a

[22] Other suggested selections for study with changing meter are "It Is Good to Be Merry," by Jean Berger (Kjos, No. 5293) and "Festival Te Deum," by Benjamin Britten (Boosey & Hawkes).

FIGURE 40 Excerpt from "Glory to God in the Highest," by Randall Thompson. Suggested conducting patterns for (*a*) measures 1 and 4, (*b*) measures 2 and 11, (*c*) measure 5, and (*d*) measure 12. Copyright E. C. Schirmer Music Co., 1958, Used by permission.

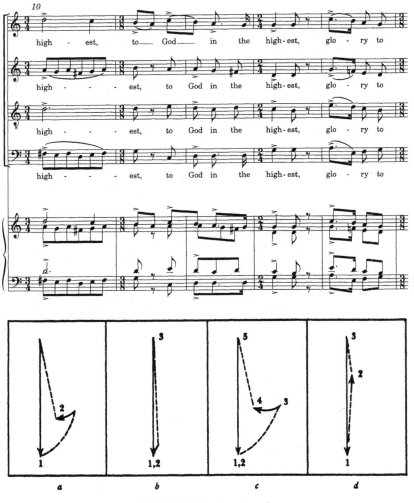

FIGURE 40 *(continued)*

downbeat, negate the beat on the second eighth note, and indicate the third eighth note by the rebound, which is restricted with the hand and arm returning only part way. You will thus be in a position for the secondary beat of a two-beat pattern, with the last two eighth notes in the measure conducted as in measure 1. The principal reasons for using this pattern, and particularly for negating the second beat in the measure, are the moderately rapid tempo ($\quad$ = 120) and the need for clarity in the conducting pattern. Each of the five eighth notes should be equal in duration, and if you execute the pattern as described, no problem of unevenness should occur. Conduct measure 6 (in 2/4) with a strong downbeat, but with a short movement on the secondary beat to indicate the duration of an eighth note followed by the eighth note rest.

In measures 11 through 13, the accents shift from the third beat to the second to the first. In measure 11 (in 3/8), conduct the first beat with a vigorous downbeat—but short and precise; negate the second beat (with a slight pause); and indicate the third-beat accent by a precise, directly upward movement or rebound. In measure 12, the downbeat on beat one should be followed by a precise upward rebound on beat two and negate the third beat. In measure 13, accent the first beat with a precise downbeat.

Another interesting example involving changing meter (see Figure 41) may be found in "Walking on the Green Grass," by Michael Hennagin (Boosey & Hawkes, No. 5443). Measure 12 (in 2/4) and measure 13 (in 6/8) are both

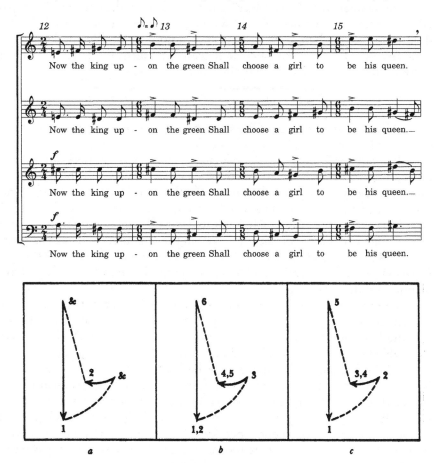

FIGURE 41 Excerpt from "Walking on the Green Grass," by Michael Hennagin, with suggested conducting patterns for measures 12-15: (*a*) for measure 12, (*b*) for measures 13 and 15, and (*c*) for measure 14. Note that the conducting pattern for measure 14 (in 5/8) uses the first half of the pattern for measure 12 (in 2/4) and the last half of the pattern for measure 13 (in 6/8). © 1962 by Boosey & Hawkes, Inc. Reprinted by permission.

conducted with a two-beat pattern; however, the tempo of the eighth note remains constant ($\flat = \flat$), with the rebound to the downbeat occurring on the second eighth note in the 2/4 meter and on the third and sixth eighth notes in the 6/8 meter. Measure 14 (in 5/8 meter) may be considered a composite of the two previous measures: The conducting pattern for the first two eighth notes is the same as that used for measure 12, and the pattern for the remaining quarter note and eighth note is the same as that used in the last half of measure 13. In other words, the rebound of the beat pattern used for 2/4 meter occurs on the second half of the beat, whereas the rebound for the 6/8 meter occurs on the third and sixth eighth notes in each measure.

Remember that the conducting pattern you use depends on the rhythm. For example, in measure 14 of "Walking on the Green Grass" the basic rhythm is 2 + 3, whereas in measure 5 of "Glory to God in the Highest" the basic rhythm is 3 + 2. Compare the suggested patterns for conducting each of these rhythms and practice each alternately as follows:

Alternate the practice of 5/8 patterns with 2/4 and 6/8 patterns until you can move from one to another with security.

Conducting 7/8 meter at a moderate-to-fast tempo also necessitates the use of a pattern different from that used for slow tempi. although the precise technique you use will vary according to the rhythm within each measure, a practical approach is to conduct a basic 4/4 pattern with an accentuated rebound on each beat except the last, which is negated with the rebound returning, on the seventh pulse (if felt or conducted in 8/8) in the measure, to the next downbeat (Figure 42). Benjamin Britten's "Festival Te Deum," Opus 32. (Boosey & Hawkes), contains several examples of 7/8 meter that may be conducted in the manner just described.

Another alternative is to conduct the 7/8 measures with the first two movements or beats of a triple-meter pattern (with the rebounds accentuated) and the last half of a 6/8 pattern, as illustrated in Figure 43. (This pattern is preferable for conducting the first three measures of the excerpt.)

The principle in the selection of beat patterns, then, is to analyze and break down the rhythmic patterns into their basic components, usually units of two or three (duple- or triple-meter patterns), and identify patterns or movements that are the simplest to coordinate, particularly during moderate-to-fast tempi. Economy of movement is necessary if rhythmic clarity and precision are to be achieved. Gestures that are too large and too numerous can impede rhythmic drive and lessen the intensity and effectiveness of the interpretation. In measures with irregular meter, look not only to the rhythm but also to the text to determine the most appropriate conducting patterns.[23]

---

[23] For further suggestions on conducting music in multimeter and nonsymmetrical patterns, see page 182.

FIGURE 42 Excerpt from "Festival Te Deum," Op. 32, words liturgical; music by Benjamin Britten, in which the measures in 7/8 may be conducted with the pattern indicated. © 1945 by Boosey & Co., Ltd.; renewed, 1972. Reprinted by permission of Boosey & Hawkes, Inc.

In conducting septuple meter at quick or fast tempi (allegro), use gestures that are very deft, precise, and economical—that is, limited in size or movement. The faster the tempo, the shorter the downbeat, the less space the gestures will take up, and the closer together they will be. Movements will become more vertical and less horizontal. In fact, they consume less time by moving through less space. [24] Figure 44 illustrates conducting patterns appropriate for use in the 7/8 portions of "Hosanna," by Knut Nystedt (Hinshaw Music, No. HMC-518),

[24] Compare this principle with that of conducting subdivided beats.

ma - jes - ty   of Thy   Glo - ry.

ma - jes - ty   of Thy   Glo - ry.

ma - jes - ty   of Thy   Glo - ry.

ma - jes - ty   of Thy   Glo - ry.

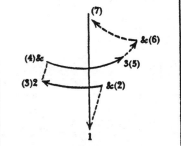

FIGURE 42   (*continued*)

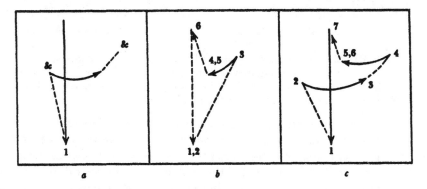

FIGURE 43   (*a*) First two movements of a triple-meter pattern (with accentuated rebounds), (*b*) last half of a 6/8 pattern, and (*c*) combination of *a* and *b* into a 7/8 pattern for conducting selected measures in Benjamin Britten's "Festival Te Deum."

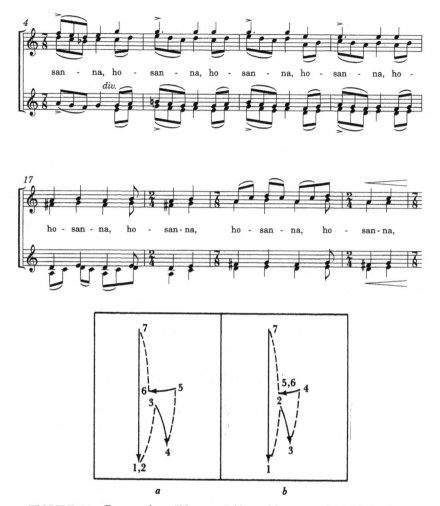

FIGURE 44 Excerpt from "Hosanna" (for treble voices; SSAA), by Knut Nystedt, with suggested patterns for conducting 7/8 meters at fast tempi (♩ = 120): (a) for 3 + 2 + 2, and (b) for 2 + 2 + 3. Copyright Hinshaw Music, Inc., 1981. Used by permission.

with a tempo marking of ♩ = 120. The music necessitates the use of patterns appropriate for both 3 + 2 + 2 and 2 + 2 + 3 rhythms. Figure 44a and b (2 + 2 + 3) is also appropriate for use in conducting the 7/4 portion of *Chichester Psalms* (Part 1), by Leonard Bernstein (G. Schirmer, No. ED 2656), marked *Allegro Molto*, ♪ = ♩ = 120 (c + 3/4).

Following is a list of other examples of choral music containing changing meters, in many but not all instances, from measure to measure. These are all

excellent study as well as performance pieces. Each should be thoroughly analyzed to determine the most appropriate and effective conducting patterns. Practice until your technique becomes stable and secure. The sequence of meter
changes is indicated following each selection.

Hindsight—Brent Pierce. Walton Music Corp. No. 2964. (6/8, 5/8, 6/8, 5/8, etc.)

A Fancy—Emma Lou Diemer. Carl Fischer No. CM8011. (2/2, 3/2, 2/2, 3/2, etc.)

Who Hath a Right to Sing?—Lloyd Pfautsch. Lawson-Gould No. 52048. (6/8, 5/8, 6/8, 5/8, etc.)

Shout the Glad Tidings—Larry Willcoxen. Harold Flammer No. A-5583. (3/8, 5/8, 9/8, 5/8, etc.)

The Ninth of January—Dmitri Shostakovitch. G. Schimer No. 12123. (6/8, 5/8, 3/8, 3/4, 4/4, 7/8,
    5/8, 3/8, 2/4, etc.)

Praise Ye the Lord—John Rutter. Oxford University Press No. 42.357. (3/4, 4/4, 3/8, 5/8, 3/8, 4/4,
    7/8, 4/4, 6/8, 4/4, etc.)

Mary Hynes (from Reincarnations)—Samuel Barber. G. Schirmer No. 8908. (4/4, 3/2, 3/8, 4/4, 3/8,
    5/8, 3/4, etc.)

Festival Te Deum—Benjamin Britten. Boosey & Hawkes. (3/4, 5/8, 7/8, 4/4, 3/4, 3/8, 5/8, 2/4 ...;
    2/4, 7/8, 3/4, 11/8, 7/8, 5/8, 2/4, ...; 6/8, 18/8, 4/8, 5/4, 4/4, 7/8, 3/4, 5/8, 3/4, etc.)

Symphony of Psalms—Igor Stravinsky. Boosey & Hawkes. (Part I: 2/4, 4/4, 1/4, 3/2, 4/4, 3/2, etc.; Part
    II: 4/8, 3/8, 2/8, 4/8, etc.; Part III: 4/4, 3/2, 4/4, 3/2, 2/2, 3/2, etc.)

Chichester Psalms-Leonard Bernstein. G. Schirmer, Inc. (Part I: 6/4, 3/4, 3/8, 5/4, 2/4, 5/8, 6/4, 2/4,
    5/4, 7/4, etc.; Part II: 3/4, 2/4, 3/4, ¢, 3/2, 3/4, C, ¢; Part III: 9/4, 10/4, 5/2, 9/2, 12/2.)

STUDYING THE SCORE

In preparing for a rehearsal, first study the score thoroughly (singers generally
resent the conductor who learns the music along with the choir). There are five
basic steps involved in score study:

1. Perusing the text to determine the overall mood and message of the music.
2. Analyzing the music to determine its form, tonality (major, minor, or atonal), texture
   (monophonic, homophonic, polyphonic, or a combination), dynamics, and tempo.
3. Identifying troublesome spots in the music.
4. Determining the appropriate conducting gestures for the music.
5. Thinking about what you should relate to the choir about the overall style and
   interpretation of the music.

A perusal of the text reveals the basic mood of the music and provides a
basis for understanding a composer's use of various musical devices to highlight
the text. A good text begets good music! (A poor text may be one criterion for
opting to discontinue study of the music.) Regarding the close relationship
between words and music, the eminent composer Ned Rorem states, "In the finest
lyrics the music comes from the words and so enriches, reinforces, illuminates
them. We will recapture this art of illuminating only when we have musicians
capable of literary discrimination, capable of selecting *cantabile* words, and of feel-

ing the fine shades of their timbre, of their minor hurries and delays."[25] After perusing the text, play the entire piece through on the piano to get an overview.

Regarding the form of the music, is it stropic, that is, using the same music for all stanzas, as in a hymn or chorale, or is it binary (AB), ternary (ABA), with a B section for contrast, or a repeated A section to establish unity? Or is it a rondo form (ABACA), theme and variations, or a free compositional form? Is there an identifiable reason for the form used by the composer? If it can be identified it would be helpful to explain this to the singers.

Is the tonality modal, major, minor, or atonal? Is its use seemingly related at all to the text of the music and what the composer is endeavoring to communicate? Does the music have a key center, and if so, does it modulate from one key to another? Note any suspensions in the music that may have to be leaned on to maximize their effectiveness. Is the texture monophonic (a single melodic line), homophonic (chordal, or hymnlike, with all voices moving together), polyphonic (several independent vocal lines), or possibly a combination of two or more of these styles?

How are the dynamics related to the text of the music, and how do they achieve either the quiet or dramatic qualities the composer is striving for? To determine the proper tempo of the music, you may refer to the metronome markings, but remember that the metronome was invented in the nineteenth century. Thus no metronome markings appear on music of the Renaissance, Baroque, or Classic periods, unless some editor has placed them there. Whatever the metronome markings, they should only be used as a beginning point. You must study the notation and the text of the music carefully to determine the appropriate tempo. For music of the romantic and contemporary periods, the notation, if carefully studied, can give clues as to the appropriate tempo so that all notes receive their proper treatment.

To save rehearsal time it is important to identify any particular troublesome or difficult spots in the music beforehand. Difficulties for singers may occur with intricate rhythms or unusual intervals. For challenging rhythms, a helpful procedure is to clap the rhythms with the singers responding, and then have the entire group recite the words of the music in their proper rhythm. Unusual or difficult intervals can be played on the piano, with the singers responding. A better way, however, is to relate the intervals to the beginning pitches in a familiar song. For example, for the interval of an ascending augmented fourth, , ask the singers to recall the beginning pitches of "Maria" from Leonard Bernstein's *West Side Story*. Just the mere mention of this, however, will be of minimal help. Ask the singers to repeat the interval several times, and as a follow-up, ask them again at the next rehearsal to sing this interval. Use the same procedure for all troublesome intervals. (For a list of songs with various intervals to be used for this purpose, see pp. 214–16.)

[25] Ned Rorem, *Settling the Score* (New York: Harcourt Brace Jovanovich, 1988), p. 84.

After careful study, mark your score by either underlining, encircling, or drawing over portions of the music. For example, underline or encircle tempo and dynamic indications; circle accents, phrasing lines, changing meter signs, and moving parts that need to be emphasized or brought out. (Some conductors prefer to highlight their markings by using a red or blue pencil.) These markings may effectively serve as a reminder for the use of appropriate conducting gestures during either subsequent study or actual rehearsals.

In studying the score, read through the music and try to conceptualize your interpretation. Give specific consideration to each measure and leave nothing to guesswork. To illustrate this point, guidelines for preparing the first twelve measures of "Create in Me, O God, a Pure Heart," by Brahms (G. Schirmer, No. 7504) are given in Figure 45.

After you have carefully studied and prepared the score, try using mental imagery. Without actually conducting, follow the score and mentally imagine the gestures that would be most appropriate and would best convey to the singers the intent of the music. Freedom from unnecessary muscular tension and more refined conducting skills may result. While such an approach should obviously be interspersed between the actual practice of conducting gestures, its importance should not be overlooked! Your ultimate goal should be to make the

MEASURE	SUGGESTED CONDUCTING GESTURES
Incomplete	Use extremely small movement, because a large gesture will elicit too loud a response.
1	Use small beat pattern; negate beats two and three.
2	Raise plane of beat slightly; place slight stress on third beat.
3	Negate beats two and three; support tone with left hand.
4	Lower plane of beat; indicate decrescendo with left hand.
5	Negate beats two and four; make precise sideways movement (from left to right) to indicate the release of the second and the beginning of the third beat in measure.
6	Negate first beat; cue soprano line on second beat.
7	Conduct quarter-note movement in baritone line.
8	Restrain volume with left hand; raise plane of beat gradually.
9	Continue to restrain volume on first beat; gradual crescendo beginning with second beat may be indicated by raising slightly the conducting plane.
10	Lower conducting plane gradually; indicate decrescendo by lowering the left hand.
11	Negate second beat; cue and stress entrance of bass line on third beat.
12	Indicate decrescendo of tenor line by lowering left hand and conducting plane.

FIGURE 45   Guidelines for conducting the first twelve measures of "Create in Me, O God, a Pure Heart," by Johannes Brahms.

technique automatic, so that it will flow naturally, emanate from, and express the intent of the music. [26]

The final step in score study involves what you are going to say to the singers about the composer and the overall style and interpretation of the music. While specific points need not be made at the initial reading, you should at least express a general idea of the composer's as well as your own objectives. Offer a brief explanation of who the composer was, when and where he or she lived, and any other pertinent facts relating to the composition. This is important so the singers can relate the period in which the composer lived to information previously gained from humanities and/or history classes. As to the music itself—the form, tonality, texture, dynamics, and the tempo—decide what you will say at the initial and the subsequent rehearsals.

In summary, conducting should never be simply a matter of establishing the tempo, conducting a meter pattern, and then "watching the notes go by." Young conductors, in particular, should know their scores, develop some specific musical expectancies, and then express them to the choir both verbally and through their conducting. Try preparing a number of selections in detail, as previously indicated, and then note the development of your conducting technique!

SUMMARY: DEVELOPING CONDUCTING SKILLS

Choral conducting involves the development of skills and specific techniques not entirely dissimilar to the development of techniques in voice or on an instrument. For example, the playing of long tones and the practice of scales and arpeggios in all keys are essential to developing technique on woodwind instruments. Similarly, all instrumentalists have felt compelled to drill on certain passages in music with which they were having difficulty. Likewise, conducting involves certain basic skills and techniques that need to be isolated, practiced, and refined to the extent that they become automatic, so the conductor can concentrate on the interpretation of the music rather than on the technique per se.

Practice these specific techniques daily in front of a mirror or with a conducting partner who can provide helpful suggestions, but preferably before a video camera so you may evaluate your own conducting gestures. Following is a summary of the techniques, presented previously in this chapter, that you as a conductor must master. Once each technique has been perfected, or improved upon, apply it to the conducting of specific choral selections. Below each particular technique is a listing of selected octavo music (most of which is available in college and university libraries) that is particularly suitable for practice of that technique. Gradually expand this list by seeking other appropriate music to

---

[26] Studies have shown that the use of mental imagery is conducive to the development of various skills both in and outside of music. See, for example, Maxwell Maltz, *Psycho-Cybernetics* (New York Pocket Books, 1969), pp. 35–36. See also the section on Sports Psychology and Peak Performance on pp. 236–38 and the references on p. 250.

which the techniques may be applied. If you or others are critical of your conducting at any point, return periodically to practicing the specific techniques in isolation without the music.

1. Duple, triple, and quadruple meters   Practice conducting patterns in 2/4, 3/4, and 4/4, concentrating on the cleanness of the downbeat and the horizontal movement of the other beats in the pattern, particularly in 3/4 and 4/4 meters.

2/4: "Oh! Susanna"—Stephen Foster, arr. Mark Hayes. Shawnee Press, No. A-1745.
3/4: "Kyrie" (from Mass in G)—Franz Schubert. Kjos, No. 5989.
4/4: "Gloria in Excelsis"—Franz Joseph Haydn. Hal Leonard, No. 08679600.

2. Timing and flow   Practice moving your conducting hand back and forth in a tubful of water (or in a swimming pool). The natural resistance of the water will help you develop a feel for the proper timing and the flow of the beat.

"Sure on This Shining Night"—Samuel Barber. G. Schirmer, No. 10864.

3. Sextuple meter   Practice the three patterns for sextuple meter (pp. 8–9), and consider the advantages of each as applied to specific pieces.

"She's like the Swallow" (Newfoundland folk song)—arr. E. Chapman. Oxford, No. X64.
"Zamba for You"—Ariel Ramirez, arr. Eduardo Gomez. Lawson-Gould, No. 52242.
"Silent Night"—Franz Gruber, arr. Malcolm Sargent. Oxford, No. OCS 876.

4. Irregular meter   Practice conducting patterns in 5/4 and 7/4 in combinations of 2's and 3's and 3's and 4's, and vice versa. Minimize the size of the second downbeat in each pattern.

"Nächtens" ("Nightly")—Johannes Brahms. G. Schirmer, No. 10123.

5. Subdivided beats   Practice the suggested patterns (p. 12) in both 3/4 and 4/4 meter, making certain that your beat is precise and clear and that you "consume more time by moving through more space."

3/4: "Crucifixus" (from B Minor Mass)—J. S. Bach. E. C. Schirmer, No. 1174.
4/4: "Surely He Hath Borne Our Griefs" (from Messiah)—G. F. Handel. G. Schirmer, No. 6598.
4/4: "Crucifixus"—W. A. Mozart. National Music Publishers, No. WHC-141.

6. Supermetric Patterns   Review the application of supermetric conducting patterns to the musical examples provided:

"Bring a Torch, Jeanette, Isabella"—French Carol
"Ave Verum Corpus"—W. A. Mozart
Ninth Symphony (last movement)—Ludwig van Beethoven
"Polovetsian Dance and Chorus" (from Prince Igor)—Alexander Borodin

Keeping in mind the basic purpose of using a supermetric conducting pattern, see how many other musical selections you can identify that would benefit from this treatment.

7. Attacks   Practice the three types of preparatory movements for beginning music on incomplete measures (pp. 18–19).

4/4 ♩♩ "A Sigh Goes Stirring through the Wood"—Johannes Brahms. Associated, No. A-379.

2/4 ♪♪♪|♫♩ "The Girl I Left Behind Me" (Irish folk song; in *Five Traditional Songs*)—arr. John Rutter. Oxford University Press.

4/4 ♪♫♩|♩ "La Marseillaise" (French national anthem)—Rouget de Lisle; in 357 *Songs We Love to Sing*. Schmitt, Hall & McCreary, No. 9015.

8. Releases   Practice releases with both the right hand and the left hand and at various tempi ranging from slow to fast (releases should be in the tempo of the music being performed).

Practice releases on all selections listed.

9. Fermatas   Practice the two types of fermatas—the complete release and the carryover technique.

"Chorales from The *Passion According to St. John*"—J. S. Bach. Lawson-Gould, No. 51145.

10. The conducting plane   Practice a pattern appropriate for a particular size of choral ensemble; for example, a chamber choir of 20 voices and a large choir of 120 voices. Following this, practice a pattern to reflect the line of various musical phrases.

"A Thought Like Music"—Johannes Brahms. Plymouth, No. AS 103.

11. Dynamics   Practice conducting patterns appropriate for *p*, *mf*, and *f* passages by varying the size of your beat.

"Since All Is Passing"—Paul Hindemith. Schott, No. AP 37.
"Locus iste a Deo factus est"—Anton Bruckner. C. F. Peters, No. 6314.
"Create in Me, O God, a Pure Heart"—Johannes Brahms. G. Schirmer, No. 7504.

12. Crescendo and decrescendo   Practice conducting a four-measure phrase (in 4/4 meter), starting from *pianissimo* with a gradual crescendo to *forte*, and after two measures followed by a gradual decrescendo to *pianissimo*.

"Ave Maria"—Sergei Rachmaninoff. Lawson-Gould, No. 52344.

13. Negation   Practice conducting various rhythmic patterns in which the size of the beats in different measures is minimized to reflect the notation of the music. For example:

4/4 ♩.♩♩.♩♪♩♩♩♩♩𝅝|

"My Lord, What a Mornin'" (spiritual)—arr. H. T. Burleigh. Ricordi, No. 412.
"Gloria in Excelsis"—W. A. Mozart. Frederick Harris Music Co., No. HC 4034.

14. *Clarifying the beat*   Practice moving from three beats (3/4 or 3/8) to one beat per measure, and then back, to maximize your assistance to the choral group and to assist them in singing in a precise and an articulate manner.

"Neighbors' Chorus" (from *La Jolie Parfumeuse*)—Jacques Offenbach. Broude Bros., No. 130.
"All Breathing Life, Sing and Praise Ye the Lord"—J. S. Bach. G. Schirmer, No. 7470.

15. *Style of the beat*   Conduct a pattern in 4/4 meter to coincide with different styles: *legato* (smooth and connected), *staccato* (short and detached), *portato* (a style halfway between legato and staccato), and *marcato* (accented beats or notes). Then, try combining two styles—for example, two beats legato, followed by two beats in marcato style: ⌐♩♩♩ and so on. Devise and practice all possible combinations.

"When Love Is Kind" (English folk song)—arr. Salli Terri. Lawson-Gould, No. 843.
"Glory to God"—J. S. Bach. Ricordi, No. NY1397.
"The Last Words of David"—Randall Thompson. E. C. Schirmer, No. 2294.

16. *Changing and controlling tempo*   The clarity of the *rebound* of each beat is the cue to control of the tempo. Practice this procedure (in 4/4 meter) with friends and ask them to clap their hands on each beat of your changes to see how clear your gestures are. If possible, try this procedure with your entire class.

17. *Cueing*   Practice cueing imaginary sections of the choir with the right hand by directing your beat toward that section. Know where your sections are located and devise exercises with entrances on various beats of a measure, to help develop maximum flexibility. Also utilize head movements and facial expressions as either alternatives or reinforcements to the primary cueing gestures. Watch yourself in a mirror and evaluate the clarity of your gestures. Can you follow yourself ?

"Sing a New Song"—Michael Haydn. Flammer, No. A-5970.
"Dona Nobis Pacem"—Ludwig van Beethoven. National Music Publishers, No. WHC-143.
"Hallelujah"—G. F. Handel. Music 70 Publishers, No. M70-330.
"Zigeunerleben" ("Gypsy Life")—Robert Schumann. Walton, No. 2706.

18. *Syncopation and offbeat accents*   Modify your conducting pattern by accentuating the rebound of your beat(s) to emphasize the rhythmic stress in the music. For example: $\frac{2}{4}$ ♩♪♩♩ | ♩♪♩♩ | (see pp. 42–44).

"Ching-a-Ring Chaw" (minstrel song)—adapted by Aaron Copland and arr. Irving Fine. Boosey & Hawkes, No. 5024.
"Ezekiel Saw the Wheel" (spiritual)—arr. H. Simeone. Shawnee Press, No. A-0130.

19. *Displaced rhythmic accents*   Analyze the following choral selections to determine the alteration of rhythmic stress, mark your score accordingly, and practice appropriate conducting patterns (see pp. 46–47).

"It Is Good to Be Merry"—Jean Berger. Kjos, No. 5293.

"America" (from *West Side Story*—choral selections)—Leonard Bernstein. G. Schirmer, No. 10703.
"Ballad of Green Broom"—Benjamin Britten. Boosey & Hawkes, No. 1875.

20. 5/8 (quintuple) meter   Is the rhythm 2 + 3 or 3 + 2? Conduct the first half of a 2/4 pattern and the last half of a 6/8 pattern, then vice versa. Practice both of these patterns in alternating measures so that moving from one to the other becomes automatic: ♪ ♩ ♪ ♪ ♩ | ♩ ♪ ♪ ♩ ♪ | and so on.

21. 7/8 (septuple) meter   Is the rhythm 2 + 2 + 3 or 3 + 2 + 2? Practice conducting the first two beats of a 3/4 meter pattern (with accentuated rebounds) and the last half of a 6/8 pattern (for 2 + 2 + 3). Then, conduct the first half of a 6/8 pattern followed by the second and third beats of a 3/4 pattern (with accentuated rebounds; for 3 + 2 + 2). Apply these patterns to the appropriate measures in the following music.

"Festival Te Deum"—Benjamin Britten. Boosey & Hawkes, No. H.15656.
"Hosanna"—Knut Nystedt. Hinshaw Music, Inc., No. HMC-518.

22. Conducting asymmetrical patterns   Practice conducting the patterns suggested on pages 45 through 58 for the changing meters of 2/4, 3/8, 2/4, 5/8, 2/4, 3/4, 3/8, and 2/4. Adjust your rebounds to fit the music!

"Glory to God in the Highest"—Randall Thompson. E. C. Schirmer, No. 2470.
"Walking on the Green Grass"—Michael Hennagin. Boosey & Hawkes, No. 5443.

(See also the listing of music with changing meters on page 58.)

23. Studying the score   Review the five basic steps involved in score study and apply them to the analysis of a number of choral works.

In addition to the choral octavo music previously suggested, you may find collections of choral music of various types and styles to be particularly helpful in furthering the aims of the conducting class. The following publications are recommended.

The Conductor's Manual of Choral Music Literature, by Lee Kjelson and James McCray. Belwin Mills Publishing Corp.
Choral Perspective, compiled by Don Malin. Edward B. Marks Music Corp.
Five Centuries of Choral Music, compiled by a committee of teachers in the Los Angeles Public Schools, William C. Hartshorn, Supervisor. G. Schirmer.

For additional choral collections, see the listing in the appendix. For a source of easy song material for beginning conductors, see the list of "Community Song Books."

TOPICS FOR DISCUSSION

1. Identify the personality attributes of successful conductors you have known. With this information as a basis, discuss the factors that you believe are important to conducting success.

2. Identify the facets of effective conducting technique that you have observed in various conductors.
3. Why do some choruses, when performing with an orchestra, sing behind the conductor's beat? How can such problems be corrected or at least minimized?
4. Discuss the differences in interpretation of a choral composition as illustrated in two or more recordings. Which interpretation do you believe is most effective, and why?
5. What effect do tempo, dynamics, accent, rhythm, phrasing, style, and mood of the music have on the basic conducting patterns?

SELECTED READINGS

BUSCH, BRIAN R. *The Complete Choral Conductor.* New York: Schirmer Books, 1984.

CAIN, NOBLE. *Choral Music and Its Practice,* Chap. 14. New York: M. Witmark & Sons, 1942.

CHRISTY, VAN A. *Glee Club and Chorus,* Chap. 1. New York: G. Schirmer, 1940.

DAVISON, ARCHIBALD T. *Choral Conducting.* Chaps. 1, 2. Cambridge, Mass.: Harvard University Press, 1945.

DECKER, HAROLD A. AND JULIUS HERFORD, *Choral Conducting Symposium* (2nd ed.). Chap. 5. Englewood Cliffs, N.J.: Prentice Hall, 1988.

FINN, WILLIAM J. *The Conductor Raises His Baton.* New York: Harper & Row, 1944.

GREEN, ELIZABETH A. H. *The Modern Conductor* (5th ed.). Englewood Cliffs, N.J.: Prentice Hall, 1992.

GREEN, ELIZABETH A. H., AND NICOLAI MALKO. *The Conductor and His Score.* Englewood Cliffs, N.J.: Prentice-Hall, 1975.

HUNSBERGER, DONALD, and ROY ERNST. *The Art of Conducting* (2d ed) McGraw Hill, 1992.

JONES, ARCHIE N. *Techniques in Choral Conducting.* New York: Carl Fischer, Inc., 1948.

KAPLAN, ABRAHAM. *Choral Conducting.* New York: W. W. Norton & Co., Inc., 1985.

KJELSON, LEE, AND JAMES MCCRAY. *The Conductor's Manual of Choral Music Literature.* Miami: Warner Bro. Pub., 1973.

KRONE, MAX T. *Expressive Conducting.* San Diego: Neil A. Kjos Music Co., 1949.

LABUTA, JOSEPH. *Basic Conducting Techniques.* Englewood Cliffs, N.J.: Prentice-Hall, 1973.

MCELHERAN, BROCK. *Conducting Techniques: For Beginners and Professionals.* New York: Oxford University Press, Inc., 1966.

MOE, DANIEL. *Problems in Conducting.* Minneapolis: Augsburg Publishing House, 1968.

POOLER, FRANK, AND BRENT PIERCE. *New Choral Notation.* New York: Walton Music Corp., 1971.

ROE, PAUL. *Choral Music Education* (2d ed.), chap. 8. Englewood Cliffs, N.J.: Prentice-Hall, 1983.

RUDOLF, MAX. *The Grammar of Conducting* (2d ed.). New York: Schirmer Books, 1980.

SATEREN, LELAND B. *Mixed Meter Music and Line in Choral Music.* Minneapolis: Augsburg Fortress Publishing House, 1968.

SIMONS, HARRIET. *Choral Conducting: A Leadership Teaching Approach.* Champaign, Ill.: Mark Foster Music Co., 1983.

STANTON, ROYAL. *The Dynamic Choral Conductor.* Chaps. 2, 3. Delaware Water Gap, Pa.: Shawnee Press, Inc., 1971.

VIDEOTAPES

Coming alive: Choral Directing, by Lloyd Pfautsch. Augsburg Fortress Publishing House.

Excellence in Conducting. "The Natural Approach," by Eph Ehly. Volume 1, *Basic Technique.* Hal Leonard Publishing Corporation, No. 08414140.

Tone and Diction

Tone quality is the very substance of choral singing. Without properly produced tones, coupled with correct diction, effective choral singing is impossible to attain. Dynamic contrasts, proper blend and balance, accurate pitch and intonation, and effective phrasing are all dependent on correct vocal production. Furthermore, projection of the mood or spirit of the music is dependent on correct diction, as well as on proper tone quality. Since good tone quality and correct diction are fundamental considerations in the training of choral groups, the conductor should develop a well-defined concept of all factors influencing tone and diction. Because choral groups react in varying ways, you should also develop a wide variety of techniques for achieving your objectives.

THE VOCAL INSTRUMENT

The human vocal instrument possesses the three components that are essential to the functioning of all musical instruments: an *actuator*, a *vibrator*, and a *resonator*. In addition, it has a component unique to the human voice: an *articulator*. Generally, the components of the vocal instrument (see Figure 46) may be identified as follows:

1. The respiratory, or breathing, muscles serve as the actuator.
2. The vocal cords (sometimes referred to as vocal folds) serve as the vibrator and are the source of the sound.

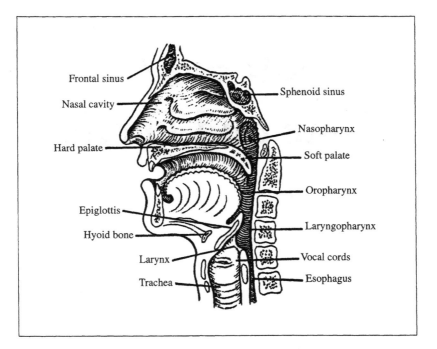

FIGURE 46 Relative locations of the larynx, the resonating cavities (pharynx, mouth, and nasal cavity), and the articulating organs (tongue, lips, teeth, palate, and lower jaw). Note the divisions of the palate (hard palate and velum, or soft palate), and the pharynx (laryngopharynx, oropharynx, and nasopharynx).

3. The pharynx, mouth, and nasal cavity serve as the resonator, which amplifies the sound.[1]
4. The tongue, lips, teeth, palate, and lower jaw serve as the articulator.

The principal muscles used in normal breathing are the diaphragm, the abdominal muscles, and the intercostal muscles. Although there is still some difference of opinion concerning the action of these muscles, the following is generally accepted. During inspiration, the diaphragm contracts and pushes

---

[1] Some authorities also consider the paranasal sinuses, the trachea, the bronchi, and the chest cavity to be part of the resonating system. The concept of the nasal and sinus cavities as resonating chambers appears to be rather widely accepted among voice teachers. There is a contrary opinion, however, that rejects the concept of both the nasal and the sinus cavities as resonating chambers, and scientific evidence is cited against the latter. For statements of these opinions, see Richard Luchsinger and Godfrey Arnold, *Voice-Speech Language* (Belmont, Calif.: Wadsworth, 1965), p. 458, and John Carroll Burgin, *Teaching Singing* (Metuchen, N.J.: Scarecrow, 1973), pp. 84–87. Whatever the opinion held by various persons, perhaps greater agreement might exist on at least the "sensation" of head resonance. This is not to say that it occurs physiologically, but that it is at the very least a pedagogical device for achieving voice placement.

downward while the contraction of the intercostal muscles lifts or raises the ribs. The combined action of these muscles enlarges the thorax, which allows the lungs to fill with air. During normal expiration, there is supposedly no muscle contraction necessary; the chest is decreased in size by the elastic recoil of the thoracic wall. In prolonged expiration, such as in singing a sustained note, the abdominal muscles gradually contract while the diaphragm slowly relaxes, and the intercostal muscles maintain enough tension to prevent bulging of the inter-costal spaces. During the act of singing, breath control is of the essence; therefore, a delicate interplay or balance must exist between these opposing sets of muscles. When one set contracts, the other set should relax—but not completely—since their mutual activity provides for the best utilization of the air in the lungs.

The larynx functions somewhat like a valve—when open, it allows the singer to inhale and exhale air to and from the lungs. The vocal cords or folds are the vibrating edge of the thyroarytenoid muscles, the posterior ends of which are attached to the arytenoid cartilages. The anterior, or front, ends of the vocal cords are attached to the thyroid cartilage, commonly known as the Adam's apple. The vocal cords are tensed by the contraction of the cricothyroid muscles. The tension of the vocal cords is decreased by the contraction of the thyroary-tenoid muscles, of which they are a part. The vocal cords are approximated or brought together by muscles controlling the position of the arytenoid cartilages, and are set into vibration by the flow or the pressure of the breath during exha-lation. The fissure or opening between the vocal cords is referred to as the glot-tis. During deep inspiration, the glottis assumes a somewhat round shape, but during quiet or normal breathing, it assumes a V-shaped position. When you sing a high pitch, the vocal cords come very close together and the glottis becomes a thin narrow slit or opening (see Figure 47).

The pitch of the tone is determined by the tension of the vocal cords and the pressure of the breath against the vocal cords. If this pressure or breath sup-port is inadequate, the laryngeal muscles often function incorrectly in their effort to obtain the correct pitch. This induces fatigue and undue strain on the voice.

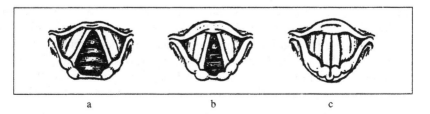

a   b   c

FIGURE 47   The larynx as observed through a laryngoscope, illustrating differences in the size of the glottis (*a*) while taking a deep breath, (*b*) dur-ing quiet or normal breathing, and (*c*) during phonation.

In general, the resonating cavities may be divided into two types—fixed and adjustable. The nasal cavity is fixed, whereas the pharynx and the mouth are capable of special utilization. On each side of and above the vocal cords are cavities that amplify the vibrations produced by the vocal cords and increase their intensity as they are projected from the larynx. These cavities are fully utilized as resonance chambers only when the throat is relaxed and kept open. Similarly, the mouth is best used as a resonance chamber when all the muscles, including the tongue, are relaxed and the cavity of the mouth is enlarged, thus allowing for an increased resonance chamber. The nasopharynx and the nasal cavity are most effectively utilized as resonance chambers when a slight opening between the oropharynx is maintained, thus allowing for an extension of the vibrating column of air emanating from the larynx.

Flexibility of the articulating organs—the tongue, the lips, the velum (soft palate), and the lower jaw—is highly important if the vocal mechanism is to function at optimum efficiency. Procedures for coordinating the various components of the vocal instrument are discussed in the following sections.

DEVELOPING CHORAL TONE

In the process of developing the tonal quality of a choral group, you must consider a number of factors: correct singing posture, proper breath control, prevocalizing warm-ups, the function and the value of particular vocalises, and the development of deep-set vowels and high-forward resonance. Development of the high range, particularly in male voices, and the achievement of vocal flexibility are also areas of special importance and concern.

Achieving Correct Posture

Correct posture is necessary to the development of good tone production. Since vocal tone is affected by all the muscles of the body, the singer must maintain an alert body position while singing, whether standing or sitting (Figure 48).

When in a standing position, place the feet approximately ten inches apart, with one foot several inches in front of the other. This stance affords the singer better balance and lays the foundation for the proper use of the breathing muscles. The weight of your body should rest to a great extent on the balls of the feet—not on the heels. The knees should be slightly flexed; they should never be in a locked position, because this contributes to unnecessary body rigidity and tension, as well as dizziness and possibly fainting. A check against locked knees is to raise each heel alternately off the floor, without raising the shoulders: if the knees are locked, you cannot raise the heel.[2]

---

[2] Excessive tension in the body, such as occurs when locking the knees, can constrict venous return of the blood from the legs, thus contributing to dizziness and fainting. Other relevant factors include overly warm room temperatures, decreased circulation, and singers being packed together too tightly and unable to move. Attention to proper posture, room temperature,

FIGURE 48   Correct posture for standing and sitting.

The abdomen should be drawn in, and the spine should be kept as straight as possible. The upper back should feel as wide as possible and the chest should be held relatively high, but without strain or excess tension. Since the throat functions as an organ pipe, the head must be kept perpendicular to the shoulders in order that this pipe be kept clear and open. The singers must hold their music in such a position that they may easily see the director without lowering or raising their heads, since any deviation in the position of the head is likely to affect the tone quality.

When seated, the correct posture from the waist up will be almost identical with the standing posture. The only basic difference is that the legs assume a bent position. While in a sitting position, the singer must keep both feet on the floor and lean slightly forward, away from the back of the chair, in order to maintain adequate breath support. Some of the body weight must be distributed to the lower limbs and the feet. The proper coordination between the breathing

and adequate ventilation, using an adequate number of choir risers to accommodate the choir, and moving singers into different standing arrangements between sets of music can help to minimize problems. For further information, see the section "The Singer's Posture and the Circulatory System," pages 129–34.

muscles and the vocal apparatus will result only if this correct posture is maintained while singing.[3]

Improving Breath Control

The next consideration in developing good choral tone is the establishment
of correct breathing habits. This is necessary to ensure the steady flow of the breath
to the vocal cords and is fundamental to both tone quality and tone control.

Clavicular, or collarbone, breathing does not fill the lungs to capacity and
the resultant tension in the upper chest and shoulder muscles affects the muscles
around the larynx and inhibits the proper action of the vocal cords.[4] Improper
breathing habits that have developed over a period of years are not always easily
corrected. First, singers must thoroughly understand the effect of poor breathing
habits on their own tone production and on the tone quality and blend of the
choir. They must achieve a conception of the correct method of breathing.

In singing, it is necessary to use the muscles around the entire midsection
of the body, not just the diaphragm. The muscles of the upper chest and shoulders should be relaxed, with the greater amount of work being done by the intercostal muscles, the diaphragm, and the abdominal muscles. These are the
muscles used in correct breathing technique (see "The Vocal Instrument" earlier
in this chapter).

As the director, you should continually emphasize the formula *Breathe
deeply, expand around the entire midsection—in the back and around the sides, as well
as in front.* Have the choir members bend over, from a standing position, until
the upper part of the body is parallel to the floor. In this posture clavicular
breathing is difficult and somewhat unnatural. By pressing the hands against the
waist, with thumbs to the back, singers can get the feel of correct breathing. Try
it! Another procedure, which is more easily managed in a crowded rehearsal
room, is to have the group lean forward in their chairs, placing one elbow on
the knee. Proper breath action may then be checked by pressing the other hand
against the waist.

---

[3] To augment the ideas presented on posture, you may wish to explore and study the
Alexander Technique, which is a process or procedure for increasing individual awareness of movement and posture habits that create tension and inefficient use of the body mechanism. It is used by
musicians (both vocal and instrumental), by actors, and by dancers, as well as by others, to help
reduce unnecessary effort and tension and to achieve greater efficiency in body movements, thus
contributing to their improved performance.

The Alexander Technique is best learned through individual instruction by a compe-
tent person trained in this technique. Information about qualified teachers in the United States is
available via the American Center for the Alexander Technique, 252 W. 102nd St. #1, New York,
NY 10025 and/or The North American Society of Teachers of the Alexander Technique (NAS-
TAT), P.O. Box 3992, Champaign, IL 61826-3992. For references on this subject, see the listing at
the end of this chapter.

[4] This type of incorrect breathing is exemplified in the inspiration movements used by a
child in preparation for blowing out a candle.

Abdominal breathing and control is essential particularly with music necessitating a *marcato* attack. To help singers get a feel for the use of the proper muscles, some conductors ask their singers to place their hands on their abdomens and then to "Bark like a dog" ("woof, woof"), "Grunt like a pig" ("oink, oink"), or "Laugh from your belly like Santa Claus" ("Ho, ho, ho"). Laughter, of course, is a good means of releasing muscular tension, as well as activating the proper action of the abdominal muscles. Following the Santa Claus laughs, have the group sing the three-part "Laughing Canon," by Luigi Cherubini.

After the singers learn how the muscles are utilized in correct breathing, they must strive toward the attainment of proper breath control until it becomes automatic. Proper breath support and control will improve only through continual emphasis.

Stretching Exercises (Prevocalizing Warm-ups)

The current popularity of physical fitness programs, including jogging, walking, swimming, and dance aerobics classes, has had an influence on choral music programs. Each of these activities emphasizes the importance of preparing for aerobic exercise through appropriate stretching and warm-up exercises to avoid any unnecessary muscle strain.

Choral directors have utilized some of these exercises, not necessarily to avoid muscle strain, but to increase blood circulation and to help singers to get in tune with their own bodies. The exercises may be done as a group at the beginning of rehearsal or undertaken on an individual basis prior to rehearsals. A suggested sequence to focus on is as follows: face, neck, shoulders, arms, and torso.

1. Facial muscle relaxation   Rubbing the facial muscles with both hands to release any excess or unnecessary tension is a good place to begin. Concentrate first on the forehead, then on the cheeks, and last on the lips and jaw.

The following exercises should be done from the *pelvic tilt* position. That is, stand with the feet approximately shoulder-width apart and the knees slightly bent. Tuck in the pelvis by tightening the lower abdominal muscles and contracting the muscles of the buttocks. This position helps prevent back strain and avoids swayback and undesirable shortening of the muscles of the lower back.

2. Neck stretches   Slowly lower the head frontward and then backward. Then dip the left ear to the left shoulder and the right ear to the right shoulder. Repeat several times. Following this, drop the head and slowly roll it to the left and then to the right (180 degrees). Do these movements slowly and avoid doing them too vigorously. Do not try to rotate the head in a 360-degree movement, because this may injure the spinal column.

Another variation of the side-to-side neck stretch is to reach behind and hold the left arm with the right hand before dipping the right ear to the shoulder. Then, before dipping the left ear to the shoulder, reach behind and hold the right arm with the left hand. Such use of the arms helps to keep the shoulders more level. Hold each stretch at least five or six seconds.

3. Shoulder shrugs   Raise the shoulders upward toward the neck and ears, and then depress the shoulders by stretching downward; push hands toward the floor.

4. Shoulder stretch   Place the left forearm above the head (with bent elbow). Place right hand on left elbow and pull easily but steadily to the right. Bend to the right from the waist. Repeat procedure by pulling right elbow with the left hand and bending from the waist to the left.

5. Arm and shoulder stretch   Place left arm in front of body. Place right hand on left elbow and pull easily but steadily to the right. Repeat procedure by pulling the right arm with the left hand.

6. Arm circles   Extend the arms to both sides of the body and slowly move them in circles—first frontward and then backward. Start with small movements and gradually increase their size. To provide adequate room for arm movements, turn 90 degrees to the left (or right). As an alternative, stretch the arms in front of the body before moving them in circles.

7. *Upward arm and torso stretches* Raise the arms over the head and attempt to reach toward the ceiling with first the right arm and then the left arm. Alternate reaching slowly right and then left—four or more times each side.

8. *Torso stretch* Reach left across the body with the right arm, and then reach to the right with the left arm. Repeat four or more times each side.

9. *Lower back stretch* Standing on the left leg, with the left knee slightly bent, bring the right knee toward the chest, feeling a gentle stretch in the lower back and posterior hip. Then repeat the stretch with the left knee. The buddy system (with persons next to each other in a back-to-back position) is useful in maintaining balance. Hold each stretch for ten to fifteen seconds.

Directors will likely find it best not to follow a rigid sequence of exercises, but to vary the selection, the order, and the time devoted to specific exercises, just as they would with vocalises. To achieve effective results, singers must totally understand and appreciate the purpose of the stretching exercises and must approach them with seriousness and in silence. Any single student or small group of students who makes light of a situation will lessen the benefit to the whole group. To minimize any problems, lead the group through the exercises in order to control not only the selection but also the pace of the routine.

After singers have focused on getting in tune with their bodies, then proceed to a series of vocalises from which they may now receive greater benefit than they would have without doing the stretching exercises. Stretching exercises should segue naturally into the vocalization period.[5]

Use of Vocalises

Choral conductors generally employ vocalises as a part of the vocal training of their choir members. They are used specifically for the improvement of choral tone and blend. Some conductors use vocal exercises only as a part of the warm-up period, as athletes use mild exercise to prepare themselves for the more strenuous rigors of competition. Other conductors feel that exercises employed for such purposes are largely a waste of time, since they are not directly connected with the immediate problem of improving the performance of the choral music. This latter group will often take a troublesome portion of the music out of context and use it as a vocal exercise.

---

[5] Exercise enthusiasts in the choir may mention other exercises, such as leg stretches, sit-ups, push-ups, and jumping jacks, which, although beneficial, are obviously inappropriate for class use. Suggest that they do them individually prior to rehearsals. Jogging in place for ten to fifteen seconds is one activity, however, that can be done in the rehearsal room.

Although some conductors may feel that only one of the previously mentioned procedures should be followed, it seems reasonable to assume that both practices have considerable merit and that each approach should be employed to some extent. To be effective, vocal exercises must be varied periodically. Continued concentration on particular devices or exercises will eventually lead to boredom, lack of concentration, and less than maximum physical effort. As a result, more harm than good may occur. Therefore, *variety* is the watchword—variety in vowel sounds, in the types of exercises, and in the time of the rehearsal period during which they are utilized.

Vocal exercises should be employed discriminately, since each exercise, if performed correctly, will produce a different type of color or tone quality. It is important to realize, then, that the overuse of one exercise to the neglect of another will not always produce the best or the desired results. For example, if the choir sings with an overly dark tone, the conductor should avoid too much vocalization on the darker vowels, such as **aw** and **oh**. It might be well for the choir director or the voice teacher to think of various vocal exercises as a physician might think of a prescription or a form of therapy—that is, as a remedy or a treatment for a specific individual or group need. For choral blend, a uniformity of vowel production must be achieved. Although you are definitely concerned with individual voices and needs, the problem in practice is, for the most part, one of dealing with the tone problems of a large group.

Let us first of all examine the type of tone quality desired for high school, college, and community choral groups. There are several schools of thought concerning the ideal quality, and in addition, certain choral selections require subtle changes in voice quality. Nevertheless, it is essential that you develop your concept of tone through private voice study and by listening to numerous choruses and choral recordings, and then strive toward that goal. A word of caution, however! Sometimes inexperienced high school conductors are overzealous in their attempts to achieve the mature quality found only in adult choirs, and in their eagerness develop a tenseness and a rigidity in the youthful voices. High school choirs have characteristic qualities common to that age level. Those qualities should be carefully nurtured and allowed to develop slowly. Only in this way will the ultimate in high school choral singing be achieved.[6]

Individuals participating for the first time in a choir generally display an abundance of technical faults. Some may sing with a throaty tone, others with white, nasal, or colorless tones. Without uniformity in tone production, blend is practically unattainable.

Just what type of voices are we endeavoring to develop? There are two characteristics that you should strive to develop in voices at the outset: (1) a deep-set vowel and (2) a high-forward resonance. When these two characteris-

---

[6] See also "Schools of Choral Singing," pages 106–13.

tics are present, the tone quality is rich and beautiful and capable of lending itself to the wide gamut of emotions found in choral literature. Various exercises contribute to the development of these qualities and are presented on the following pages.

Achieving Deep-Set Vowels

The deep-set vowel is usually associated with maturity and roundness of tone and with naturalness of production. It is achieved through minimizing unnecessary tension in the vocal apparatus and by correctly utilizing the resonance cavities of the mouth and throat. As discussed previously, correct posture and breath control are essential conditions. Clavicular breathing should be avoided, since the resultant tension in the shoulder muscles and the upper regions of the chest is often reflected in the muscles surrounding the larynx, thus inhibiting the proper functioning of the vocal mechanism. [7]

The writer has observed high school and adult choral groups in various sections of the country. One of the most objectionable faults is that many teenagers, as well as adults, sing with a tight, rigid jaw. Some individuals believe that this condition is a reflection of environmental tensions. More likely, the condition results from lack of proper vocal training and individual awareness of the problem. Whatever the exact cause, the effect is disastrous on choral singing. Tenseness in the jaw and facial muscles results in strident, pinched, and colorless tones. Depth of tone and subsequent choral blend are impossible to attain until the condition is alleviated. The following are suggested devices, techniques, and exercises to help eliminate this problem.

1. Singers should be instructed to concentrate on relaxing their facial muscles. Gently stroking the face with the fingertips is one means of eliminating excessive tension during rehearsals. To develop further the singers' understanding of the importance of this relaxation, choir members should be asked to observe the facial expressions of a recognized concert singer on television. In addition, they should compare their mental conception of this singer with their own facial expressions by checking in a mirror. (Enlargements of close-up group photographs taken during rehearsals provide a further objective means for the singers to analyze their difficulties.)

2. In addition to relaxing the lips and facial muscles, singers must relax their jaws and open their mouths wide if they are to achieve deep-set vowels. The darker vowels, such as **oh, aw,** and **ah,** should have a great deal of depth and should be formed low in the throat. In order to make them round and full, singers should think of singing the vowels up and down rather than across. The jaw should be free

---

[7] This is a particularly troublesome problem with high school boys, since large chest expansion seems to be associated with manliness. The problem here can be lessened somewhat by means of a frank and open discussion about the way athletes employ deep abdominal breathing in order to increase their own breath control.

from any rigidity. Exercise 1 is an excellent device for loosening the jaw and rounding out the tone.

EXERCISE 1

Yah, yah, yah, yah,   yah,   Yah, yah, yah, yah,   yah,   *etc.*

1. Vocalize from low Bb (below the staff) to Eb (fourth space, treble clef). Much of the value of the exercise is lost if it is sung in the extreme high range of the voice.

2. In this exercise use lots of jaw action. A helpful physical device is for the singer to place the tips of each index finger on the approximate hinge position of the jaw. This procedure serves to increase awareness of the jaw movement.

3. In singing this exercise, there is an unconscious tendency for some singers to pull the upper lip downward over the upper front teeth. This practice should be discouraged, since it is likely to darken the tone quality too much. Singers should be instructed to hold the upper lip stationary, with just a portion of the upper teeth remaining visible. A useful device is to have the singers check this position with a hand mirror. It should prove enlightening to them.

4. It has been found profitable for the singers to check one another's jaw movements on this exercise. This procedure seems to provide the proper motivation for people who have difficulty with the exercise.

When the vowel **ah** is used, Exercise 2 is also helpful in developing the deep-set vowel. It has an added ear-training value, in that it provides an opportunity for the singers to hear their parts more clearly in relationship to the other tones in the chord.

EXERCISE 2

1. Director should cue each entrance.

2. Singers should hold back the breath, explode the attack, and drop the jaw.

3. Crescendo, then decrescendo, on final chord.

4. Proceed upward or downward by half steps.

5. For the purpose of developing uniformity of vowel production, the exercise should also be sung on the various other vowels. Each vowel should be preceded by the consonant **m**.

Developing High-Forward Resonance

The preceding exercises, if used consistently, develop depth in the voices and transform the thin, shallow voices of inexperienced singers into rounder and deeper voices. If used to the total exclusion of other exercises, however, they will make the voices dark and throaty; as a result flatting sometimes occurs. To be most effective, these devices and exercises must be coupled with exercises designed to develop focus or high-forward resonance in the voices.

When sound is produced by vibration of the vocal cords, it moves in many directions and is resonated and amplified in the various cavities of the body— that is, the chest, the pharynx, the mouth, and the nasal cavity. A sound, unrestricted by muscular tension, will seek and utilize *all* these resonating areas. Muscular tension and interference, however, often limit the maximum use of these resonating chambers. Tension in the throat muscles prevents the most effective use of the pharynx as a resonator, and, as previously mentioned, a tight, rigid jaw and an unruly tongue reduce the size of the oral cavity and lessen its effectiveness as a resonator.

Of particular concern to the choral conductor is the development of focus or high-forward resonance in the voice. By this we simply mean the maximum utilization of the resonating cavities or chambers above the oropharynx and the mouth, specifically the nasopharynx and the nasal cavity. The key to the most effective use of these resonating areas is to maintain a sensation of an opening between the oropharynx and the nasopharynx. The organ that regulates the size of the opening is the velum, or soft palate (see Figure 49). When food is swallowed the velum moves posterosuperiorly and maintains contact with the posterior wall of the pharynx. This muscular adjustment also occurs in the articulation of certain consonants. If this adjustment did not occur, air would escape through the nose, and the precise articulation of these consonants could not be achieved. As the nasal consonants **m, n,** and **ng** are produced, the velum is in its relaxed, or lowered, position, the nasal port is widely open, and the nasopharynx and the nasal cavity serve as a more predominant center of tonal resonance. The velar opening, or nasal port, may be maintained, however, by a means other than relaxing or lowering the soft palate. It also may be opened by an upward and forward tension of the velum—as experienced in a deep yawn.[8] This suggested movement of the velum is contrary to the velopharyngeal contact utilized in articulating certain consonants.[9]

---

[8] Cf. G. Oscar Russell, *Speech and Voice* (New York: Macmillan, 1931), p. 18.

[9] Cf. Robert F. Hagerty and others, "Soft Palate Movement in Normals," *Journal of Speech and Hearing Research* 1, no. 4 (December 1958), 325–30.

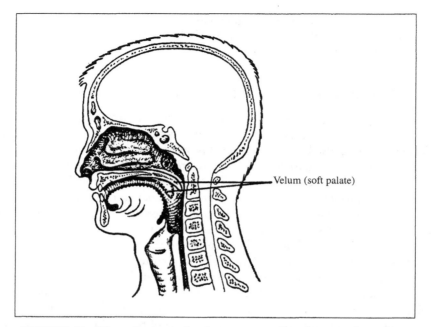

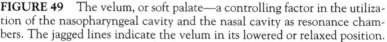
Velum (soft palate)

FIGURE 49   The velum, or soft palate—a controlling factor in the utilization of the nasopharyngeal cavity and the nasal cavity as resonance chambers. The jagged lines indicate the velum in its lowered or relaxed position.

According to a survey by Burgin, voice teachers generally accept the concept of a raised soft palate in singing. Yawning serves the purpose of raising the
soft palate, as well as opening the throat. Also, according to Burgin, "this device
[the yawn] appears to be among the most popularly accepted in the broad scope
of training the singing voice."[10]

Singers should strive to develop a high-forward arch to the velum, or soft
palate, so that the nasal port may remain slightly open, thus allowing for an
extension of the vibrating column of air emanating from the larynx and a more
effective use of the upper resonating cavities.[11]

Thus singers should think of the nasopharynx as an extension of the
oropharynx and should concentrate on drawing the breath "inward and
upward." Many choral conductors recommend yawning as a means of developing a sensation of the high-forward arch of the velum. Other directors simply
suggest singing with a sensation of a high arch in the back of the mouth. Both
devices, however, achieve the same desired purpose and can be utilized to facilitate this necessary physical adjustment.

[10] John Carroll Burgin, *Teaching Singing* (Metuchen, N.J.: Scarecrow, 1973), p. 77.

[11] There is not complete agreement on the extent of the opening between the oropharynx
and the nasopharynx. X-ray studies during phonation indicate a changing size, depending on the
vowel produced, and variations on the same vowel among different singers. However, regardless of
the size of the opening, the imagery of directing the tone through this space is helpful in achieving
high-forward resonance.

Muscles work in pairs throughout the body. When one set is in tension to effect a specific movement or action, the opposing set of muscles should be relaxed. When the opposing set of muscles is not relaxed, unnecessary tension occurs, resulting in wasted energy. The singer, therefore, must try to relax the opposing muscles, so that the others may function at optimum efficiency. This is the singer's goal. However, until the correct vocal adjustment becomes automatic in nature, the singer must apply a degree of conscious effort toward arching the velum and opening the passage between the oropharynx and the nasopharynx.

Sagging facial muscles are also detrimental to the development of high forward resonance. The feeling of a short upper lip and a lifting of the facial muscles directly above the upper lip will aid in the development of this resonance. When the correct singing sensation is achieved and the process becomes automatic, then the singer will be able to produce fully resonated tones with a minimum of effort. Exercises 3 through 5, and the specific suggestions pertaining to their use, will be helpful in developing high-forward resonance in the voice.

EXERCISE 3

Hah,   hah,   hah,   hah,   hah,   hah,   hah,   hah.

1. Vocalize on the descending major scales C, D♭ (C♯), D, and E♭. Sing each scale slowly, taking a catch breath between each scale step.
2. Sing with the tips of two fingers between the teeth. This ensures an open mouth and a freer emission of the tone.
3. The feeling of the high arched roof of the mouth, as in yawning, is necessary for the proper adjustment of the velum, or soft palate, and the correct focus of the tone or voice. Strive to develop this sensation.
4. When yawning, notice the position of the lips. In their most relaxed position they are extended away from the teeth; the upper lip is raised slightly and a portion of the upper teeth is visible.
5. Concentrate on the sensation of drawing the breath inward in a relatively narrow stream and focusing the tone in the resonating cavities behind the bridge of the nose. (Using various physical devices will assist the singer in achieving the correct tonal focus. Drawing the hand inward toward the body facilitates the singer's concept of the correct direction of the flow of the breath.[12] Placing the fingertips on the bridge of the nose is also a reminder of the correct point of tonal focus.)
6. Vocalize all voices to their lowest tones. Avoid forcing the voices in the lower register.
7. Avoid distorting and altering the vowel sound. A common pitfall is to change the vowel **ah** to **uh** when vocalizing in the lower register of the voice.

After a sufficient degree of progress has been made toward achieving correct resonance, Exercises 4 and 5 may be alternated with Exercise 3.

[12] The flow of the breath is actually from the lungs, through the larynx, and into the resonating chambers or cavities. The sensation of drawing the breath inward simply assists in directing the tone into the cavities above the pharynx and the oral cavity.

EXERCISE 4

Hah,————— hah,—————

hah,————— hah.—————

1. Sing each scale (C, D♭, D, E♭) slowly, taking a full breath between each descending scale.
2. Sing with the tips of two fingers between the teeth.
3. Vocalize all voices to their lowest tones. Avoid forcing the voices and distorting the vowel sounds in the lower register.
4. Concentrate on achieving correct tonal focus (see suggestions 3, 4, and 5 in Exercise 3).

EXERCISE 5

Hah,————— hah,————— *etc.*

1. Start on middle C and vocalize upward by half steps an octave or more.
2. Vocalize with the tips of two fingers between the teeth. A freer emission of the tone is thus assured.
3. Raise the upper lip and extend away from the teeth.
4. The feeling of the high arched roof of the mouth, as in yawning, is necessary for the proper adjustment of the velum. Strive to attain the sensation.

When practicing Exercise 5, male singers quite often become easily discouraged when their voices crack or break in the upper range. Considerable benefit can accrue to the singers if they are encouraged to continue the exercise upward in a light head voice or falsetto quality.

One of the obstacles to achieving the proper placement of voices relates to many singers' misconception that the darker vowels, such as **ah** and **oh**, are to be placed far back in the mouth or throat. In baritones and basses, in particular, this idea often results in an overly dark sound that is difficult to blend and too heavy to be properly supported by the breath, thus resulting in pitch and intonation problems for the choir. Exercises 6, 7, and 8, therefore, have the same basic objectives as Exercises 3, 4, and 5, but they may be used as alternatives and will be particularly helpful for lightening and focusing the tone.

EXERCISE 6

Ee— ah,——————— ee— ah————————— *etc.*

1. Vocalize upward by half steps, but stay primarily in the middle range of the voices.
2. Drop the relaxed jaw on the **ah** vowel, trying to keep the placement forward. Strive for a bright **ah** vowel, and avoid the darker sound that occurs if it is placed farther back in the mouth.

EXERCISE 7

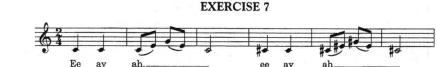

Ee   ay   ah,——————   ee   ay   ah—————

1. Vocalize upward by half steps, but stay primarily in the middle range of the voices.
2. Maintain a frontal placement on all vowels; that is, strive for a bright sound.

EXERCISE 8

Ee - ah,————————   ee - ah,——————   *etc.*

1. Vocalize upward by half steps, but stay primarily in the middle voice range.
2. Drop the relaxed jaw on the **ah** vowel and keep the placement or focus forward.

To afford further variety, Exercises 9, 10, and 11 also may be utilized periodically as warm-up exercises.

Exercise 9 may be notated on the chalkboard or introduced by means of syllables (all voices sing the interval of the octave—*do* to *do*; sopranos sustain *do*, altos descend to *mi*, tenors descend to *sol*, and basses descend to *do*).

EXERCISE 9

Ee - ah.—————

1. Singers should try to maintain the forward placement of the **ee** vowel throughout the exercise; however, as the sound changes to **ah** the jaw should drop and be kept relaxed.

2. Singers should maintain adequate breath support and should crescendo toward the end of the exercise.

3. The exercise may be repeated upward by half steps (not to exceed four or five half steps, depending on the maturity of the voices).

To afford variety, Exercises 10 and 11 may be alternated on subsequent days with Exercise 9.

EXERCISE 10

1. Sing the exercise in unison.
2. Combine two parts—**SA, TB, ST, AB.**
3. Sing in four parts.
4. Repeat upward or downward by half steps.

EXERCISE 11

The use of the nasal consonants (**m, n,** and **ng**) as a means of establishing a sensation for and a feeling of correct resonance is a somewhat controversial subject. One position states that "humming is not singing" and that the two acts require a different adjustment of the velum. In the broadest sense, this statement is true; that is, in humming, the velum is in its relaxed, or lowered, position, whereas in singing, this is seldom, if ever, the case.

The use of humming prior to singing, the use of the consonants **m, n,** and **ng** as a prefix to the vocalization of various vowels, and the vocalization of such words as *sing* and *hung* (immediately moving to and sustaining the **ng** sound) have become common practices. Proponents of the value of humming maintain that it provides the best muscular setting for the attainment of resonance. In this respect, the use of the nasal consonants has value, because during this act the vocal mechanism is well coordinated. Excessive tension in any aspect of the vocal mechanism will prevent the attainment of a fully resonated tone. Therefore, humming and the use of the other nasal consonants have value in that they facilitate the beginning of phonation without excessive muscular tension. Because of this relaxing effect, choir members should endeavor to retain the humming sensation while singing.

EXERCISE 12

Hm

The humming exercise shown in Exercise 12 may be used for the purpose just described. In addition, it has a certain ear-training value if the group is instructed to listen carefully and to hold the chord until it is perfectly in tune. Instruct the singers to avoid gasping for breath; when a breath is needed they should drop out of the ensemble, take a full breath, and then reenter as unobtrusively as possible. Some persons may hum incorrectly. To check, ask the group to open their mouths, while humming, at a given signal. If the tone changes into the vowel **ah,** the group is humming incorrectly. When the mouth is opened, the correctly produced tone should change from **hm** to **ng.** It is wise to use this checking device frequently. The **ng** sound has greater intensity than the **hm** sound, and may be preferable for use with certain selections calling for a humming background. Some high school directors have even found this exercise to be a profitable time saver—when the students in the chorus enter the rehearsal room, they immediately take their seats and commence humming their respective tones. After all the choir members have arrived, the director may immediately begin the rehearsal, since the group is in a more receptive frame of mind and less inclined toward verbal outbursts.

In striving for the development of deep-set vowels and a high-forward resonance, do not get the idea that one vocal characteristic should purposely be developed prior to the other. In practice, the two should be developed simultaneously.

If the utmost is to be gained from the previously mentioned exercises, they should be sung with a free, open throat. Excess tension in the muscles around the larynx should be eliminated insofar as possible. Vocalization on the vowel **oo** has been found to be helpful in opening the throat. When vocalizing on this vowel, place the tips of two fingers between the front teeth. This procedure assists in opening the throat and aids in a freer emission of the tone, substantially assisting in the development of the higher range of the voice.

Developing the Vocal Range

Limited vocal range prevents the performance of a considerable amount of choral literature. If music with an extreme tessitura is used, the voices are likely to sound harsh, strained, and unmusical. Under such circumstances, blend, balance, and good intonation are impossible to attain. Therefore, developing the singers' vocal range is an important and essential task of the choral conductor.

The singing of correctly produced high tones is dependent on an open throat (achieved through vocalization of the **oo** vowel) and a high-forward resonance (see Exercises 3 and 4). The heavy chest quality of the middle range is not easily produced in the upper limits of the voice, and any attempt to do so will often result in unmusical sounds and breaks in the flow of the tone; therefore, the singers should try to lighten their voice quality in vocalizing Exercise 13, which helps develop the upper range.

EXERCISE 13

1. Vocalize, in the beginning, on the vowel **oo**. This vowel opens the throat and facilitates a freer production of tone. As progress is made, however, it is desirable periodically to alternate the **oo** with the **ah** vowel. The latter vowel will give greater brilliance and "ring" to the voice.
2. Vocalize with the tips of two fingers between the teeth. This device facilitates the dropping of the jaw, which is an absolutely essential condition in singing the high tones.
3. When singing *high*, think *low*, and vice versa. This thought facilitates the necessary muscular adjustment.
4. Vocalize all voices up to the extreme limits of their range. Sopranos and tenors should vocalize up to high C, and altos and basses at least up to high A♭.

Female voices find Exercise 13 comparatively easy—that is, much easier than will the male voices. Female voices are able to sing the higher pitches without the unique muscular adjustment problem that occurs with male voices. With female voices, the range simply needs strengthening and developing. The problem is not quite the same with the male voice. In vocalizing Exercise 13, male voices will quite naturally and normally change into a falsetto quality at a certain point. At first there may be some embarrassment on the part of the younger singers, but this should be expected. They should be told of the many fine singers who have extended their ranges by first learning how to use their falsetto voice correctly. Indeed, there may even be places in the literature where such a quality will be desired by the tenor voices.

Exercise 14 is provided as an alternative to Exercise 13; however, it should be used sparingly and not until vocalization on the $\overline{oo}$ vowel has reasonably achieved its objective.

EXERCISE 14

Ah ——— *etc.*

1. Ascend by half steps.
2. Use procedures enumerated in 2, 3, and 4 for Exercise 13.

There will exist, however, many other instances where it will be necessary and desirable for the male singers to sing with a full resonant quality in their high range. In order to do so, it will be necessary to develop the so-called "covered" tone, in which the vowel sound is slightly altered or modified toward one that is more easily produced in the upper register. It is full and resonant and is devoid of any falsetto characteristics. In singing the covered tone, a certain firming of the vocal mechanism occurs and the vowels are slightly modified—generally toward the **uh** sound. [13] Exercise 15 is suggested as a means of obtaining the desired tone quality and placement.

EXERCISE 15

Beginning on the first line E (treble clef), slur up an octave, keeping the resonance high and forward. The sounds **ing** and **ay** are generally the best to begin with; however, eventually the other vowels should be used as well. Remember that the jaw must be dropped on all high tones. On the open vowels, sing with the tips of two fingers between the teeth. In singing the closed vowels **ee** and **ĭ**, the back sides of the tongue should be held against the upper back teeth. This device facilitates an easier and freer production of tone. Basses should eventually vocalize up to high A♭ and the tenors to high C.

In developing the lower range of the voice, have the singers vocalize, using the vowel **ah**, on the descending five-tone scale (see Exercise 28 in Chapter 8). The exercise should be begun on about first space F (treble clef) and should be sung slowly downward. The voices should not be forced, but should be produced with a naturally resonant quality. The greatest deterrent to developing the lower range in both male and female voices is that the singers often fail to drop the

---

[13] The covered tone versus the open tone has been a controversial subject for many years. For a historical background, as well as an experimental analysis, see Luchsinger and Arnold, *Voice-Speech Language*, pp. 103-106.

jaw. As a result, a considerable portion of the lower range of the voice frequently remains undeveloped. In addition, when the jaw is not dropped, the vowel sound will often change from **ah** to **uh**. Singing the exercise with the tips of two fingers between the teeth will help to alleviate this problem.

Developing Flexibility

A flexible voice is usually a freely produced voice—one that is devoid of excessive strain and tension. A marked degree of flexibility is essential if desired interpretative effects are to be achieved in choral music. Exercise 16 (a–f) should prove profitable in developing flexibility in voices.

EXERCISE 16

1. Vocalize only in the middle range of the voice. Proceed upward by half steps.
2. Insert the tips of two fingers between the teeth. This assists in a free emission of the tone.
3. Avoid singing too loudly. Excessive tension is sometimes created in this way, thus making the exercise more difficult and thereby decreasing the benefit from it.

4. At first, sing the exercise quite slowly—until the singer becomes acquainted with it; then gradually increase the tempo.
5. Practice exercises in both a legato style and a half-staccato style.

Developing the Unique, Characteristic Qualities of Voices

While the preceding vocalises can be of benefit to all singers, specific mention should be made concerning the voices in each section of the choir.[14]

Sopranos   Because this section is often called on to sing pitches in a quite high register, it is important that it be done with an appropriate tonal quality. The soprano voice generally has a light, flutelike, lyrical quality. One fault of sopranos is their tendency to carry the quality of the chest voice into the upper range. This is strenuous to the voice and often distorts the sound of the choir. Sopranos should endeavor to lighten the quality in the upper range. Practice singing the **oo** vowel on an arpeggio, as illustrated in Exercise 13, will help to lighten the voice quality in the upper range and help singers to find the important needed quality and placement or focus in the upper range of their voices. Vocalization can extend to the E above high C with the understanding that those singers who have difficulty may drop out when they feel any vocal strain. The sound model of the upper soprano voice, however, will have been established. As progress is made, the singers may alternate singing the o̅o̅ vowel with the **ah** vowel, which will give greater brilliance and ring to the voices. In developing the lower tones of the voice, sopranos should try to carry the resonance of their upper range into the lower registration to avoid the development of too heavy a quality. The second soprano voice is similar in range to the first soprano, but has a somewhat fuller, more dramatic quality.

Altos   The alto voice has a heavier, deeper quality, particularly in the middle and lower range, in comparison to the soprano voice. These singers should avoid carrying the quality of their lower voices into too high a range, as it can sound raucous. In vocalizing it is best to vocalize downward, carrying the quality of the middle voice into the lower range. The descending five-tone scale, as illustrated in Exercise 17, is suggested.

EXERCISE 17

Mah,_____   Mah,_____   *etc.*

Some authorities feel that there are relatively few true alto voices, and often singers assigned to this part are those who have a limited upper range and are bet-

---

[14] For the voice ranges of singers, see "Testing and Classifying Voices," pages 282–85.

ter music readers. In consideration of this it is suggested that altos never be forced into producing a quality they are physically incapable of achieving. Directors should focus on achieving flexibillity and purity of sound rather than weighty volume. Assignment of a singer to the soprano or alto section should be based on their tone quality and range—never just on their music reading ability.

Tenors   Tenor voices should possess a light, lyrical quality, particularly in the upper register. When too heavy a quality is used, there can be a tendency toward flatting. When singing in the high range, tenors should be encouraged to utilize their falsetto or light head voices whenever necessary, rather than employing a heavier, weightier tone quality. For tenors in particular, it is important to sing with a raised soft palate or with a sensation of a high-forward arch to the velum. An exercise particularly useful in helping tenors properly focus their higher pitches is slurring up an octave, first on **ing** and then on **ay**.[15] (See Exercise 18.)

EXERCISE 18

| ing, | ing, | ing, | | ing, | ing, | ing, | *etc.* |
| ay, | ay, | ay, | | ay, | ay, | ay, | |

1. Ascend by half steps. Tenors to B♭ and baritones to F or G.

Basses   Baritones and basses possess a heavier, darker quality than tenors and have a more fully developed middle and lower range. Vocalizes should focus on the **ah** vowel to promote roundness and fullness of tone, but they also must have a high-forward resonance. Otherwise they will be inclined to flat, and bring the rest of the choir down with them. Exercise 16 is also helpful in achieving the necessary tonal focus, along with Exercises 6, 7, 8, 9, and 10.

ACHIEVING CORRECT DICTION

Correct diction, necessary to the effective communication of the central thought of the text, is the overall manner of vocal utterance as it pertains to the conveying of meanings and ideas. Pronunciation, enunciation, and articulation are all integral aspects of diction; these terms are often used rather loosely, and frequently their precise meanings are misunderstood

Pronunciation is the manner of uttering the words, in particular the use of appropriate vowel and consonant sounds and the proper accent of words and phrases. "Sing as you speak" is a statement often heard. This advice would be worthwhile, providing everyone spoke correctly and there was a reasonable degree of uniformity in the speech mannerisms and habits of individuals. Care-

---

[15] See also Exercise 15, which describes the exercise in greater detail.

ful analysis of words spoken or sung by individuals will reveal a wide variety of similar, yet distinctly different, pronunciations of each vocal sound.

Vocal mannerisms characteristic of particular regional areas should be avoided, and a standardized general American approach to pronunciation, as utilized by most radio and television announcers, should be adopted. In an attempt to become educated, singers should avoid extreme alterations in pronunciation, or they will sound unnatural, affected, and ridiculous to local audiences. An exception to the use of a standardized general American approach to pronunciation in choral singing is readily evident in the performance of certain folk songs requiring a dialectal treatment. Pronunciation problems inherent in these choral selections should be carefully analyzed in regard to vowel and consonant sounds and accent or stress, and then diligently rehearsed. Careful attention must be given to all pronunciation problems if effective communication of the text is to be achieved.

Enunciation pertains to the manner of vocal utterance as regards distinctness and clarity of the various vowel and consonant sounds. Individuals who mumble their words and who slur or omit consonants have fallen into slovenly habits that are not conducive to good communication. Use every possible means to develop the singers' awareness of this problem. Demonstrating the singers' faults through imitation and playing back audio recordings of rehearsals and performances are suggested procedures for improving enunciation.[16] Only when effective enunciation is achieved will the central thought of the music be communicated to the listening audience.

Articulation pertains to the physical action of the articulating organs (tongue, lips, teeth, palate, and lower jaw) in forming and altering the channels and in projecting the various vocal sounds necessary to achieve intelligible communication. A further differentiation may be made between articulation and enunciation. When an individual is unable to speak distinctly because of lack of physical control, such as occurs with young children, he or she may be said to have poor articulation. When an individual's vocal utterance is indistinct because of slovenly diction and lack of concentrated effort, it may be said that his or her speech or singing is poorly enunciated.

Difference between Vowels and Consonants

The vowels are used for sustaining the singing tone, and the breath flow is continuous. In the sounding or the articulation of the consonants, the flow of breath is momentarily interrupted. This is the basic difference between the vowels and the consonants.

Vowels are the chief vehicle for sustaining the vocal tone, whereas consonants have shorter sustaining qualities and in some instances may detract from

---

[16] Imitation of singers' faults always should be done in a spirit of joviality—never in a ridiculing manner. Imitation should be followed immediately by the conductor's demonstration of correct procedures and the chorus's renewed efforts toward improvement.

the legato flow of the music. The vowels are all voiced sounds—that is, the vocal cords are set into vibration. However, approximately one third of the consonants are voiceless. Intelligibility of the consonants is dependent on the precise movements of the articulating organs; the vowels are dependent more on duration and resonance for their identity.[17] Singing a choral selection on the vowels only is a useful device for achieving uniformity of vowel production and improving tonal blend. Moreover, it demonstrates the fact that vowels have little meaning by themselves, and that intelligibility of the text is dependent primarily on the precise articulation of the consonants.

Vowels

If uniform tone production and tonal blend are to be achieved, you must be cognizant of the precise differences of vowel sounds used in speaking and singing, and you must develop a similar awareness on the part of your choristers. Singers as a group are usually familiar with the primary vowels (**ee, ay, ah, oh, oo**), since these are used extensively as a beginning point in vocalization. However, they are less familiar with the precise differences among the other vowel sounds. The vowel chart in Figure 50 illustrates the variety of vowel sounds that occur in the texts of choral literature. The International Phonetic Alphabet, with a specific symbol for each sound, was devised by phoneticians to provide an accurate means of identifying and differentiating among the various vowel and consonant sounds. In the first column of the chart, the phonetic symbols for the different vowel sounds are listed. The diacritical markings for these vowels, as used in English dictionaries, are listed in the second column. Both the phonetic symbols and the diacritical markings are presented primarily as a reference for the choral conductor. Because their precise meanings would not always be readily evident to a group of amateur singers, various illustrative symbols for each vowel are included in the third column, and are suggested for use with the choir members. When pronunciation difficulties occur in rehearsals, the conductor should identify and isolate particularly troublesome vowel sounds. These illustrative symbols may be written on the chalkboard, discussed, pronounced, and sung as a means of clarifying in the singers' minds the desired vowel sounds. Numerous examples of specific vowels as they occur in various words are also listed and may be used for illustrative or comparative purposes.

The formation of each vowel in Figure 51 requires distinctly different adjustments of the articulating organs, with the exception of the following: The vowel ɝ (**ûr**) is the counterpart of ɚ (**ẽr**) and the adjustment of the articulating organs is quite similar. The vowel ɝ (**ûr**) occurs only on stressed syllables and the sound ɚ (**ẽr**) occurs on unstressed syllables. Also, the vowel ʌ (**ŭ**) is the counterpart of ə and the position of the articulating organs is almost identical.

---

[17] The formation of intelligible vowel sounds is, of course, dependent on the adjustment of the articulating organs; however, the vowels are not so dependent on such a rapid and precise adjustment as the consonants.

PHONETIC SYMBOLS	DIACRITICAL MARKINGS	ILLUSTRATIVE SYMBOLS	EXAMPLES
i (long e)	ē	ee	see, each, tree, Easter, free, glee, feet, sleep, deep, sheep, wheel
ɪ (short i)	ĭ	ĭ	sing, is, will, him, thing, ship, wish, April, similar, crib, been, king
e (long a)	ā	ay	say, faith, age, angel, rain, same, maiden, away, day, way, great
ɛ (short e)	ĕ	eh	yet, end, enter, help, never, every, let, men, said, then
æ (short a)	ă	ă	at, rang, mantle, ashes, agony, began, can, cat, that, than
a	ȧ	ȧ	ask, grass, laugh, bath, calf, craft, raft, chance, chaff
ɑ	ä	ah	father, Amen, aims, army, far, heart, calm, palm, psalm
ɒ (short o)	ŏ	ŏ	stop, hot, sorry, olive, God, watch, wander, John, yon
ɔ	ô	aw	law, all, awe, autumn, always, walk, warm, dawn
o (long o)	ō	oh	flow, old, road, hope, low, soul, snow, open, so, boat, home, cold
ʊ	o͝o	o͝o	look, bosom, took, foot, stood, should, would, book, full, brook
u	o͞o	oo	who, too, moon, whose, blue, true, through, flew, soon, tomb
ɝ	ûr	ur	birth, early, earth, world, worth, perfect, burden, were
ɚ	ēr	er	ever, never, another, pleasure, mother, weather, measure
ə	ə, ȧ	uh	about, around, firmament, America, awhile, away, above
ʌ (short u)	ŭ	uh	but, sun, done, creation, other, until, wonder, thunder

FIGURE 50   The single vowels frequently occurring in choral literature, with symbols and examples that the conductor may use to illustrate and correct pronunciation difficulties.

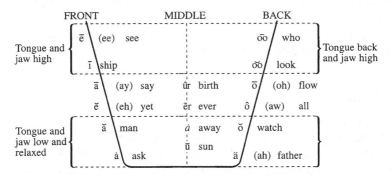

FIGURE 51   Front-to-back vowel formation.

The vowel ʌ (ŭ) occurs only on stressed syllables, whereas the vowel ə occurs only on unstressed syllables.

The various vowels are determined by the relative size and shape of the mouth and throat cavities. Specific determinants are the position of the tongue, the jaw, and the lips. As indicated in Figure 6, the vowels ee and ĭ are formed high and forward; the vowel oo is formed lower in the throat. In singing the ee and ĭ vowels, the tongue is relatively high, whereas in the oo vowel the tongue is back. In both cases the position of the jaw is high and the mouth is somewhat closed. Because of this condition, these sounds are often referred to as *closed vowels*. All other vowels are referred to as *open vowels*, even though the position of the tongue, lips, and jaw will vary to some extent. The tongue is most relaxed and the jaw at its lowest position while singing the vowel ah, as in the word *father*. Because of the lesser degree of tension, this vowel is the most freely produced and is therefore frequently used as a beginning point in vocalization. (See also Figure 52.)

In their exuberance, novice choristers may tense the tongue too much and restrict the proper functioning of the vocal mechanism; a thin, shallow tone quality is likely to result. Suggest to the singers that when singing the open vowels, the tongue remain in the relaxed position of the ah vowel. There is a limit, of course, to the practicality of this suggestion as it affects pronunciation; however, the idea does facilitate somewhat the reduction of excessive tension in the tongue muscle.

When singing the closed vowels ee and ĭ, suggest that the singers place the back sides of the tongue against the upper back teeth. When the position of the tongue is too high, this device serves to enlarge the oral cavity somewhat and allows for a freer emission of tone. It also prevents singers from forming these vowels too low in the throat, which may cause throatiness and flatting, especially in the upper range of the voice.

If a choral group sings with a nasal, white, or colorless tone, then vowels with extreme forward placement, such as ee and ĭ, should be used sparingly in vocalization, and the vowels formed lower in the throat, such as **aw, oh,** and **oo,** should be used. Conversely, if the group sings with an overly dark tone quality, then greater attention should be given the vowels formed high and forward. All the primary vowels (**ee, ay, ah, oh, oo**), however, should be utilized to some extent in vocalization, and concentration on any one group of vowels to the total exclusion of the others should be avoided.

Diphthongs

The diphthong may be defined as a compound vowel, or a syllable in which the sound changes from one vowel to another. In a simple or single vowel the articulating organs are held in a somewhat fixed position, whereas in a diphthong the articulating organs change position, thus altering the vowel sound. Figure 53 shows the diphthongs as they occur in English.

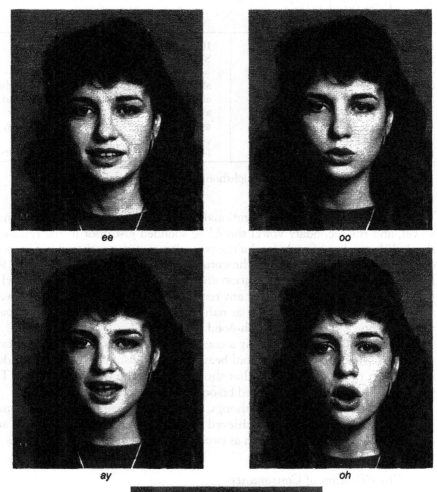

FIGURE 52 Relative positions of the lips and jaw in forming the primary vowels (*ee, ay, ah, oh, oo*). Compare with Figure 51.

PHONETIC SYMBOLS	DIACRITICAL MARKINGS	ILLUSTRATIVE SYMBOLS	EXAMPLES
aɪ or ɑɪ	ī (long i)	ah—ĭ	night, high, light
aʊ or ɑʊ	ou	ah—o͝o	our, now, round
ɔɪ	oi	aw—ĭ	oil, rejoice, joy
eɪ	ā	ay—ĭ	day, faith, they,
oʊ	ō	oh—o͝o	old, hope, low
ju or ɪʊ	ū	ĭ-o͞o—	beauty, few, view

FIGURE 53   The diphthongs as they occur in English.

Except for **ju** or **Iu,** the durational stress should be given to the primary vowel, and the secondary vowel should be sounded just prior to the release of the diphthong. It is often helpful if the secondary vowels are thought of in terms of the same durational stress as the consonants. This procedure should be followed whenever the musical notation and the tempo permit the *initial* vowel in the diphthong to be sustained for any reasonable length of time. Thus the word *night,* if sustained, would be sung as **nah—ĭt,** not **nah-eet,** and the word *round* would be sung **rah—ŏond,** not **rah-ŏond.**

The diphthong **ju** is actually a consonant-vowel combination. An example of this sound occurs in the word **beauty.** In this instance it is the secondary rather than the primary vowel that should receive the durational stress. The word should always be pronounced **bŭ‾oo—ty,** rather than **bee-oo-ty.**

In the treatment of all diphthongs, a smoother transition from the primary to the secondary vowel will be achieved if the diphthong is thought of as a single, connected sound, rather than as two separate and distinct vowel sounds.

Classification of Consonants

Generally the consonants may be classified into two types—the voiced and the voiceless (nonvoiced). The voiceless consonants include **k, p, t, f, h, s,** and **sh,** whereas the voiced consonants include **b, d, v, z, zh, l, g, j, w, r, y, m, n,** and **ng.** The consonant **th** is voiced in some words and voiceless in others. In producing the voiced consonants, the vocal cords are drawn together and set into vibration and the consonant is voiced as a result, whereas in the voiceless consonants there is no perceptible movement of the vocal cords. The voiced consonants are softer in character and less explosive than the voiceless (nonvoiced) consonants. Since the voiced consonants have a longer sustaining quality, they may be used effectively to bridge the gap between various vowel sounds, especially in legato singing. Developing the singers' awareness of the essential differences between these consonant sounds will result in improved enunciation.

For a number of consonants, the adjustment of the articulating organs is similar. Only one adjustment is necessary for the following paired consonants: **t-d, p-b, f-v, k-g, s-z,** and **sh-zh.** The first consonant in the pair is voiceless,

VOICELESS	VOICED
t—time, turtle, part	d—day, garden, afraid
p—pretty, happy, harp	b—bright, above, crib
f—faith, before, life	v—voices, ever, above
k—kind, because, music	g—garden, finger, flag
s—sing, asleep, peace	z—zenith, music, eyes
sh—sheep, ocean, wish	zh—Jacques, pleasure, rouge

FIGURE 54   Paired consonants, with similar articulator adjustments.

whereas the second consonant is voiced.[18] The words in Figure 54 illustrate further the similarities between the adjustment of the articulators and the differences in sound duration. Words are listed that include the use of an initial, a medial, and a final consonant.

Another means of classifying the consonants is by the manner in which the flow of the breath is released. The *explosive* consonants are **p, b, t, d, ch, j (dzh), k,** and **g.** The *continuants* are **w, wh, f, v, th, s, z, sh, zh, r, j (y), h, l, m, n,** and **ng.** In articulating the *explosive* consonants, the flow of the breath is momentarily interrupted by the contact between the articulating organs. An explosive sound is emitted as the articulating organs are separated precisely and the pressure of the breath is released. In producing the *continuants*, the articulating organs assume a relatively fixed position as the sound is emitted.

Still another means of classifying the consonants is by the position or placement of the articulating organs involved in producing the sounds. They are as follows:

Bilabial **(p, b, m, w)**   Bilabial consonants are formed by the lower and upper lips. In forming the consonants **p** and **b,** the flow of the breath is interrupted momentarily as the lips are drawn together, and the breath is released in an explosive manner as the lips are suddenly opened; **p** is voiceless, and **b** is a voiced consonant. The consonant **m** is voiced and is formed by closing the lips, thus causing the flow of the breath to be emitted through the nasal passages. The consonant **w** is voiced and is referred to as a *bilabial glide.* It is produced by the lips forming a position similar to the **u** vowel and then moving or gliding quickly to the subsequent vowel sound.

Labiodental **(f, v)**   Labiodental consonants are formed by the lower lips and the upper teeth. The lower lip and the upper teeth are brought together and the breath is forced audibly between the two articulating organs; **f** is a voiceless consonant and **v** is voiced.

Lingua-dental **(th)**   Lingua-dental consonants are formed by the tip of the tongue touching the back side of the upper front teeth. The breath is forced

---

[18] Exceptions to the pairing of voiced and voiceless consonants are **h, r, y, w, l, m, n,** and **ng.** All these consonants are voiced except the **h,** which is voiceless.

between these two articulators; **th,** as in the word *thousand,* is voiceless and the sound **th,** as in the word *there,* is voiced.

Lingua-alveolar (t, d, n, l, s, z)   Lingua-alveolar consonants are formed by the tip of the tongue and the upper teeth or gum ridge. In forming the consonants **t** and **d,** the flow of the breath is interrupted momentarily by the contact between these two articulating organs. The consonants are sounded and the breath is released in a slightly explosive manner as the contact between these organs is released; **t** is voiceless and **d** is voiced. The **n** is voiced and is formed by placing the tip of the tongue against the gum ridge and directing the sound through the nasal passages. In the consonant **l,** which is also voiced, the tongue is placed against the gum ridge and the sound is emitted over the sides of the tongue. In forming the consonants **s** and **z,** the sides of the tongue are kept in contact with the upper back teeth, and the tip of the tongue rests just behind the upper front teeth, although not touching directly. The flow of the breath is directed over the tongue where it strikes the back edge of the upper front teeth, thus causing the hissing sound descriptive of these two consonants. The **s** is voiceless and the **z** is voiced.

Lingua-palatal (sh, zh, ch, dzh, j, r)   Lingua-palatal consonants are formed by the contact between the tongue and the hard palate. In producing the consonants **sh** and **zh,** the sides of the tongue are placed against the upper back teeth, as in the position for the consonant **s,** except that the tongue is drawn slightly back; **sh** is voiceless and **zh** is voiced.

In sounding the consonant combinations **ch** and **dzh,** the tongue contacts the hard palate at a point slightly farther back than for the consonant **t.** The tongue comes in contact with the upper back teeth and the flow of the breath is interrupted momentarily. As the tongue is released, the breath is emitted in an explosive manner. The consonant **ch** is voiceless, but the **dzh** is voiced.

The consonant **j,** as it occurs in certain words, is pronounced **dzh,** as in *judge* and *joy.* In other words, such as *hallelujah,* it assumes a softer, nonexplosive quality as in the consonant **y** in such words as *yet, year,* and *beyond.* The **y** is considered by many authorities to be a voiced consonant; however, some writers classify it as a semivowel.

In pronouncing the consonant **r,** the sides of the tongue contact the upper back teeth. The tip of the tongue is curled or drawn back toward the hard palate and, as the sound is emitted, it glides smoothly to the adjustment necessary for the following vowel sound. This adjustment is common in such words as *run, around,* and *read.* In some words, however, the tongue assumes a much lower position in the mouth, and the glide occurs in reverse order. This action occurs in such words as *heard, her,* and *creator,* where the preceding vowel sound is stressed. In this case, the consonant is articulated as the syllable is released. The consonant **r** is a voiced consonant.

Velar (**k, g, ng**)   Velar consonants are formed by arching the back part of the tongue and pressing it lightly against the soft palate. In the **k** and **g** sounds, the flow of the breath is interrupted momentarily. As the contact is released and the tongue is lowered, the breath is exploded. The consonant **k** is voiceless, but the **g** is voiced. In forming the consonant **ng,** the position of the tongue is similar to that of the **k** and **g** sounds, except that the soft palate, or velum, is lowered slightly and the tongue is more relaxed, thus allowing the sound to be emitted through the nasal passages. The consonant **ng** is voiced.

Glottal (**h**)   Glottal sounds are formed in the glottis, or the opening between the vocal cords. The vocal cords come together in a position that restricts the flow of the breath slightly, but not enough to set the cords into vibration. The consonant **h** is voiceless and is produced by forcing the breath between the nonvibrating vocal cords. This sound is often referred to as the *aspirate h.*

Styles of Diction

There are three basic styles of choral diction, namely, *legato, staccato,* and *marcato.* Each of these styles is distinctly different and must be treated in a specific manner to achieve effective interpretation.

Legato diction is smooth and connected. A minimum of emphasis should be given to the rhythmic stress or pulsation of the music in legato style. Legato phrases should be thought of as long, soaring and descending musical lines. In addition, the explosive qualities of the consonants should be minimized if they are to be smoothly blended with the vowel sounds.[19] In achieving this effect, the singers should carry over the final consonants of one syllable or word to the following syllable or word. The following examples serve to illustrate this concept: *My Lord, what a mornin'* is sung **mah-ee law—rd hwah-tuh maw—rn-nĭn.** *Lost in the night* is sung **law—stĭ-n-thuh nah—ĭt.** *My love dwelt in a northern land* is sung **mah-ee luhv dweh-l-tĭn nuh naw-r-thern lă—nd.**

Any exception to this rule occurs when the diction becomes unintelligible or creates a somewhat ludicrous effect. In the following examples, it is desirable to separate the sounds, as indicated by the diagonal lines, with a slight break in the flow of the breath.

"She's / like the Swallow" (from "She's Like the Swallow," Newfoundland folk song, Oxford, No. X64).
"Slumbers / not nor sleeps" (from "He Watching over Israel"—Felix Mendelssohn, G. Schirmer, No. 2498).
"We Three Kings of Orient / Are" (John H. Hopkins).

[19] To achieve a smooth blending between the consonants and the vowels in legato diction ask the singers to sustain the consonants as well as the vowels. This device, although seemingly quite unorthodox, lessens the explosive qualities of the consonants and contributes substantially to the desired legato effect.

When the second syllable occurs on a stressed beat, you may further clarify the sound through careful articulation. That is, in the first example, articulate and emphasize the word *like* with a "capital L."

Imprecise diction can lead to some other highly humorous misunderstandings of various phrases, as follows:

"Gladly, the Cross I'd Bear" has been understood as "Gladly, the Cross-Eyed Bear."

"Scuse Me While I Kiss This Guy" has been heard as "Scuse me while I kiss the sky'"

"Ride on the Peace Train" has been heard as "Right on the pea strain"

"Every picture tells a story, don't it?" has been heard as "Every picture tells a story doughnut." [20]

To properly handle these and other similar aspects of diction it is important that final consonants be carefully articulated, and when necessary, an ever so brief seperation between specific words is essential.

EXERCISE 19

Bah, bah, bah, bah,   *etc.*

(repeat one half step higher, etc.)

1. Use various consonants on this exercise (**b, p, t, f, d,** and so on).
2. Vocalize only in the middle register.
3. Work for clearness and precision of consonants and for flexibility. Flexibility will aid in developing freedom of voice production.

Examples of choral octavo publications requiring a staccato treatment of diction are included in the following list.

"Cicirinella" (Italian folk song)—arr. Max Krone. Witmark, No. 5-W2952.

"Hasten Swiftly, Hasten Softly"—Richard Kountz. Galaxy, No. 1750.

"I Saw Three Ships" (traditional English)—arr. Alice Parker and Robert Shaw. G. Schirmer, No. 10188.

"Rock-a My Soul" (spiritual)—arr. Joseph De Vaux. Bourne, No. B-211128.

"Sleigh, The"—Richard Kountz. G. Schirmer, No. 7459.

"We Wish You a Merry Christmas" (English folk song)—arr. the Krones. Kjos, No. 4006.

"Younger Generation"—Aaron Copland. Boosey & Hawkes, No. 1723.

In **marcato diction,** each note is sung with an accent, and the rhythm is quite pronounced. Effective marcato diction necessitates correct muscular action, which is precisely a sharp inward movement of the abdominal muscles. [21] Perhaps the most effective means of teaching this concept is to ask the singers to grunt each note in the correct musical rhythm. By placing the hand on the abdomen, singers are more likely to feel the movement, thus facilitating the

[20] Gavin Edwards, "Scuse Me While I Kiss This Guy and Other Misheard Lyrics," *People Weekly* 43, no. 20 (May 22, 1995), 25.

[21] For a discussion of the function of the abdominal muscles in the respiratory process, see "The Vocal Instrument" earlier in this chapter.

achievement of this concept. With attention focused on this muscular move-ment, have the group recite the text in correct musical rhythm before attempt-ing further to apply the concept to actual singing. Exercise 20 is also helpful in achieving the correct muscular movement.

EXERCISE 20

Ho, ho, ho,   Hah, hah, hah,   Hee, hee, hee, hee,   hee   *(repeat upward by half steps)*

A marcato treatment of diction is required in sections of the following choral octavo publications, which are included for study and analysis.

Examples of octavo choral selections requiring a legato treatment of dic-tion are included in the following list. [22]

"Alleluia"—Randall Thompson. E. C. Schirmer, No. 1786.
"Ave Verum Corpus"—Wolfgang A. Mozart. G. Schirmer, No. 5471.
"God So Loved the World" (from *The Crucifixion*)—John Stainer. G. Schirmer, No. 3798.
"How Lovely Is Thy Dwelling Place"—Johannes Brahms. G. Schirmer, No. 5124.
"I Wonder as I Wander" (Appalachian carol)—arr. John Jacob Niles and Lewis Henry Horton. G. Schirmer, No. 8708.
"Lost in the Night" (Finnish folk song)—arr. F. Melius Christiansen. Augsburg, No. 119.
"Mary Had a Baby"—William L. Dawson. Kjos, No. T118.
"My Love Dwelt in a Northern Land"—Edward Elgar. G. Schirmer, No. 2366.
"O Divine Redeemer"—Charles Goouod. Schmitt, Hall & McCreary, No. 1602.

In **staccato diction**, the words should be sung in a detached style as if there were a slight rest between each note. Good staccato diction depends on distinct and precise articulation of the consonants. The lips should be flexible and devoid of excessive tension, and the lip movements should be exaggerated. The singers should refrain from singing too loudly, since excessive volume is likely to inhibit the precise articulation of the words. (Excessive volume tends to shift the focus from careful articulation to weighty tonal effects.) The vowels should be modified slightly and formed closer to the front of the mouth; words should be thought of as being formed on the lips, since sounds formed too far in the back of the mouth tend to become weighty, cumbersome, and difficult to artic-ulate in a short, detached style. Exercise 19 will be helpful in developing precise lip movements and in improving staccato diction.

"Hallelujah" (from *Mount of Olives*)—Ludwig van Beethoven. G. Schirmer, No. 2215.
"Hallelujah, Amen" (from *Judas Maccabaeus*)—George F. Handel. G. Schirmer, No. 9835.
"Hospodi Pomilui"—Alexis von Lvov, ed. Wilhousky. Carl Fischer, No. CM 6580.
"Let Their Celestial Concerts All Unite" (from *Samson*)—George F. Handel. E. C. Schirmer, No. 312.
"Psalm 150"—Louis Lewandowski, ed. H. R. Wilson. Schmitt, Hall & McCreary, No. 1640.

---

[22] For complete names and addresses of the publishers referred to in this and subsequent lists, see Appendix.

Although many choral compositions require only one specific style of diction, others contain contrasting sections and phrases, each requiring a different treatment. Prior to introducing a selection to the chorus, analyze the text and the music carefully, giving particular attention to the diction requirements. If in doubt about the style of diction, always look to the text of the music. The mood and emotional content of the text will reveal many things to you, including various shadings and nuances necessary for the most effective interpretation of the music.

The Sibilant S

Of the sibilants, or hissing sounds, in English (**s, z, sh, zh, ch,** and **j**), the most troublesome, especially in legato singing, is the consonant **s.** Unless handled correctly, the singing of this consonant may remind us of sounds emanating from a snake pit. An example of this may be found in the words "God so loved the world" from the chorus in John Stainer's *The Crucifixion.* Unless careful attention is given to the sibilant **s** in the word **so,** considerable difficulty may occur with amateur choral groups. Amateurs are often likely to sing the phrase as **Gaw—dsssssssoh—luh—vd thuh wuh—rld.** The difficulty here lies primarily in the lack of the singers' accurate response to the rhythmic duration of the first measure. The **s** is anticipated with a resultant hissing sound. Tight, rigid jaws also contribute to the problem. If the jaw is not relaxed and the mouth kept open, the consonants **d** and **s** will inevitably follow the preceding vowel sound too quickly.

A solution to this specific problem, which also will apply to other problems of a similar nature, is first to concentrate on the development of rhythmic accuracy in the chorus. The fact that the first measure has three beats must be understood and felt by all the singers. Having the group clap or tap the basic pulsation, or even conducting the traditional pattern for triple meter, will be helpful. Next, have the group sing the phrase on a neutral syllable, such as **loo.** After rhythmic accuracy has been achieved, the group should prefix the vowel sound **oh** in the second measure with the consonants **ds.** The final result should sound as shown in Figure 55.

Some directors have found it particularly helpful, in dealing with the hissing **s**'s, to assign the singing of them to only a particular portion of the chorus, with the remainder of the group singing only the vowel sound. The use of this approach certainly depends on the requirements of the musical situation, and

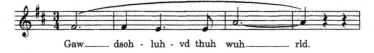

Gaw———— dsoh - luh - vd thuh wuh————— rld.

FIGURE 55 Excerpt from "God So Loved the World" (from John Stainer's *The Crucifixion*).

its success depends on a clear understanding on the part of the singers of their particular assignments.

In certain choral selections it will be helpful to minimize the s sound by changing it to the shorter z sound. Certainly the obvious advantage of this procedure becomes apparent in singing the words "slumbers not" from Mendelssohn's "He Watching over Israel."

The Troublesome R

The consonant **r** is often the source of unmusical sounds in amateur choral groups. The difficulty usually encountered is the overanticipation of the consonant, often caused through the singer's inaccurate response to the rhythmic duration of the music. Words such as *ever* and *world* are particular examples. How often have we heard the sound **eh-vuhrr** or the equally unpleasant sound of **wuhrrrr-ld?** To alleviate the problem, singers must not only be made more conscious of rhythmic duration, but must also be instructed to sustain the vowel preceding the consonant **r** sound, and to add the **r** only briefly upon the release of the syllable. Thus *ever* should be sung as **eh-vuh—r,** and *world* as **wuh—rld.**

The Consonants M, N, *und* L

Although most of the consonants have a comparatively short duration, the consonants **m, n,** and **l** are particular exceptions and have a certain degree of sustaining power. As such they may be effectively used, especially in legato singing, to bridge more smoothly the gap between the various vowel sounds. For example, when the group sings the word *amen*, the pronunciation **ah—mehn** contributes little to the smoothness of the legato phrase. A more effective procedure is to sing the word as **ah—m—mehn.** In this manner the consonant **m** serves to bridge the gap between the vowels **ah** and **eh,** thus creating an improved legato effect (Figure 56). To accomplish this successfully, the mouth must be closed momentarily on the release of the first vowel and opened on the attack of the second vowel sound. (Obviously, this treatment is appropriate only when dealing with legato diction. Utilizing this approach with a vigorous Handelian chorus would be out of character and highly inappropriate. In most cases the approach used will be dictated by the demands of the musical situation.)

A similar treatment is suggested in dealing with the consonant **n.** In the words *mine eyes*, the tongue should touch the back side of the upper front teeth

FIGURE 56 An example of bridging the gap between two vowels sounds. Note (*a*) how the word is written, and (*b*) how it is effectively sung.

as the **n** is sounded. The tongue should drop immediately before the first syllable of the word *eyes*. The phrase should be sung as **mah-een-nah-eez.**

In most cases, when dealing with the double consonants, the first of the two should be eliminated. Usually this procedure is dictated by common sense. For example, the word *better* is pronounced **beh—tuhr** and not **beht—tuhr;** the word *torrents* is pronounced **tŏ-rĕnts** and not **tŏr-rĕnts.** An exception to the rule, however, is the treatment of the double consonant **ll.** In the word *allelujah*, for example, both **l**'s should be sounded if legato diction is to be clear and connected. The word *allelujah* should be sung **ahl—lay—loo—jah,** rather than **ah—lay—loo—jah.** The initial **l** should be added upon the release of the first vowel, and the second **l** should prefix the second vowel. Examples of this suggested treatment may be found in the following compositions.

"Alleluia"—Wolfgang A. Mozart. Carl Fischer, No. 541.
"Alleluia"—Randall Thompson. E. C. Schirmer, No. 1786.

The Aspirate H

The aspirate **h** is effected by means of a rapid flow of the breath, and when this condition does not prevail, the sound is often strident and ineffective. For example, in the word *hallelujah* in the chorus "Hallelujah, Amen" from the oratorio *Judas Maccabaeus* by Handel, the initial consonant is often slighted, resulting in a poor attack and a tightening of the vocal mechanism. To avoid this pitfall, singers should be instructed to anticipate the attack and precede the initial vowel with a rapid push or flow of the breath. When singing in marcato style, a sharp inward movement of the abdominal muscles will help to activate the flow of the breath. Adequate preparation on the part of both the conductor and the chorus is essential. Singers should be poised, alert, and ready for the attack, and the conductor should provide a clear, precise preparatory beat.

The aspirate **h** will often cause difficulty when combined with another consonant. For example, the word *when* often is pronounced as **wehn** rather than **hwehn.** In addition to activating the flow of the breath, singers must strive for careful, precise lip action to ensure the correct articulation of this consonant combination.

Vowel–Consonant Balance

The concept of "singing on the vowel," important as it is, should not be stressed at the expense of the consonants. Overemphasis on the vowel sounds to the neglect of the consonants may result in beautiful choral tone, but the singing will generally lack luster and the desirable expressive characteristics.

To achieve correct, understandable diction, a balance must be maintained between the vowels and the consonants. When given only equal stress, the vowel sounds usually predominate over the consonants because of their sustaining characteristics. Therefore, to achieve a desirable balance the consonants should be overexaggerated—not in duration, but in the degree of intensity.[23] Emphasis should be placed on careful and precise articulation rather than on excessive duration of the consonants. It should be understood, however, that clear diction will not guarantee good voice production and that any attempt toward precise articulation should not cause unnecessary tension in the vocal mechanism. Articulation should occur away from the throat!

More effective results will be achieved by graphically illustrating on the chalkboard the relative degree of emphasis required in balancing the vowels and the consonants, as in Figure 57.

Final Consonants

Amateur singing groups often do not finish their words, especially at the ends of phrases. The poetic qualities of the text are thereby lost, and projection of the mood or spirit of the song becomes relatively ineffective. Be careful to provide a clear, precise release to the phrase so that the group may use this movement as a signal to add the final consonants. In addition, try to develop in your singers an increased consciousness of the problem. One effective approach is to sing a series of words from which the final consonants are omitted; then ask the singers to identify the words. The variety of guesses will serve to illustrate the importance of including the final consonants of all words.

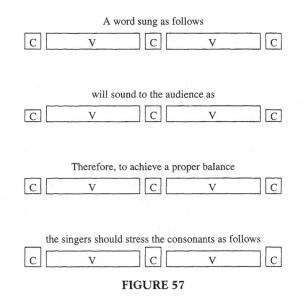

FIGURE 57

[23] A word of caution! An exception to this treatment occurs in dealing with music in a legato style, as discussed earlier in this chapter. Too much emphasis on the intensity of the consonants is likely to disturb the legato flow of the music. In this style, emphasis should be placed on the smooth connection of vowels and consonants.

Tone and diction are the chief means of transmitting the poetic qualities of the music to the audience. Without properly produced and appropriate tone quality, the effectiveness of the music is lessened considerably, and without correct diction, choral tone becomes meaningless and little more than instrumental in character. Good tone quality and correct diction are essential to effective interpretation and, to be achieved, must receive your detailed, exacting attention.

Commonly Mispronounced Words

A brief list of some common errors in pronunciation is shown in Figure 58.[24] This list, though incomplete, may serve as a starting point if you want to develop your own list of mispronounced words—or words that are troublesome in your particular locality.

SCHOOLS OF CHORAL SINGING

The principles of choral tone and diction presented earlier in this chapter are basic, like those any thoughtful voice teacher might prescribe, and allow the voice maximum flexibility in projecting human emotion as delineated in any musical style. Over the years, however, there have developed a number of schools of thought on the modification of these ideas to achieve specific musical objectives. This occurs because the ideas of particularly successful choral conductors have developed a considerable following from admiring students. The eminent choral conductor Howard Swan has identified six different schools of choral singing, which can be summarized as follows.[25]

School A   This school may be described as physical. For example, the movements used to develop correct posture include clasping the hands behind the head with the elbows almost touching in front. Singers are then urged to pull their arms up and away from the waist without lifting the shoulders. Overweight singers are asked to vocalize with the hands held high above the head while walking or standing on the toes.[26]

The basic vocalises are sung in a *staccato* manner. Emphasis is on an attack that is produced with the maximum degree of intensity. Women generally sing comparatively softly; men are asked to produce a big tone. The result in performance is one of a pyramid effect with the lower men's voices carrying the greater volume in contrast with the women's voices. "The men sing with a tone that is big and dark and the women with a sound that at times could be characterized as

---

[24] This list, of course, does not pertain to songs necessitating a dialectal treatment.

[25] For an elaboration of these ideas, see Howard Swan's chapter, "The Development of a Choral Instrument," in *Choral Conducting: A Symposium*, 2d ed., eds. Harold Decker and Julius Herford (Englewood Cliffs, N.J.: Prentice Hall, 1988).

[26] This school of thought was advocated by John Finley Williamson, the founder and first conductor of the Westminster Choir.

WORD	PRONUNCIATION
angel	ayn-j*eh*l, not ayn-juhl
beautiful	bĭo͞o-tĭ-fōōl), (bū-tĭ-fōōl) not be-oͦoͦ-tee-fuhl
Bethlehem	Bĕth-lē-hĕm, not Bĕth-lē-ham
can	kăn, not kĭn
Christmas	Chrĭs-más, not Chrĭs-muhs
creation	kree-ay-sh*uh*n (kre-ā-shŭn), not kree-ay-shĭn
dew	dĭ-*oo* (dū), not dōͦo. (Other words necessitating a similar pronunciation of the diphthong ĭ-oͦoͦ are: new, beauty, few, view, pure, and human.)
for	fŏr, not fûr
forget	fŏr-g*eh*t, not fŏr-gĭt
forgiveness	fŏr-gĭv-n*eh*s, not fŏr-gĭv-nuhs
Galilee	Gă-lĭ-lē, not Gă-luh-lē
get	g*eh*t, not git
glory	gl*oh*-ree, not glaw-ree
government	guh-*vern*-mehnt (gŭ-vĕrn-mĕnt), not guh-ver-mehnt
heaven	heh-*veh*n, not heh-vuhn
judgment	jŭj-mĕnt, not jŭj-muhnt
kindness	kah-ĭnd-n*eh*s (kīnd-nĕs), not kah-ĭnd-nuhs
listen	lĭs-*eh*n, not lĭs-uhn
Lord	La*w*rd (Lôrd), not Lahrd, or Lowrd
love	l*uh*v (lŭv), not lahv
manger	mayn-j*er* (mān-jēr), not mayn-jĭr
Mary	M*eh*-ree (Mâ-rē), not May-ree
mountain	moun-t*eh*n, not moun-uhn
night	n*ah*-ĭt (nīt), not naht, or nah-eet. (Other words containing the long ĭ [a diphthong] include high, sigh, fly, etc.)
open	oh-p*eh*n, not oh-puhn
poor	pŏor, not pohr
pretty	prĭ-*tē*, not prĭ-dē
roof	roͦoͦf, not ruhf
silent	sah-ĭ-l*eh*nt (sī-lĕnt), *not sah-ee-luhnt*
spirit	spĭ-rĭt, not spĭ-ruht
the	th*ee* before words beginning with a vowel, or the silent *h* (th*ee* everlasting, th*ee* hour); th*uh* before words beginning with a consonant (th*uh* night, th*uh* heavens).
triumphant	trī-ŭm fănt, not trī-ŭm-funt
virgin	vûr-jĭn, not vûr-juhn
wheel	*h*weel, not weel
when	*h*wĕn, not wĕn (wehn)
worship	wûr-shĭp, not wûr-shup
your	yŏor, not yuhr

FIGURE 58 Common errors in pronunciation.

shrill by some listeners."[27] In summary, choral balance is not achieved, and softer dynamics will not be heard.

You may question how this style of singing applies to our contemporary choral scene in terms of the performance of major choral works. The answer is

[27] Swan, p. 15.

that it can be most effective with such works as the last movement of Beethoven's *Ninth Symphony*, where volume and force are required. Here it can be effective especially in balancing the choral forces with the orchestra. Its application to other choral styles, however, may be highly questionable.

School B   The second school purports that vocalization with different vowels and consonants will result in sound colors related to orchestral instruments. No other individual school advocates such an exceptional amount of vocalization. All vowels are to be preceded by consonants, as it presumably focuses the tone and relieves a squeeze in the larynx.

According to this school of thought, vocalizing on the ee vowel will result in a string tone, the vowel o̅o̅ develops a sound like a flute, the vowel **ah** simulates a reed tone, and the vowel **aw** results in the sound of a French horn. Advocates of this school are interested in the performance of polyphonic music and do not consider good diction to be of primary importance. Vocalization is considered as the disciplining of singing and it is suggested that whenever possible vocalises be accompanied by the orchestral instrument whose timbre is being sought, and sung at a dynamic level of *pp*. This school strives to make all dramatic voices more lyrical and works toward excellence in the performance of polyphonic music.[28]

School C   The principle objective of School C is the development of a choral blend, which is achieved with a minimum amount of vocal vibrato. Singers are asked to submerge their own sound with that of the choir. Some persons categorize this style as straight tone singing, which they believe is inimical to the best interests of the solo singer.

Where it is most important for the choir to achieve an impersonal interpretation, choirs representing this school often sing with dynamic levels ranging from *pp* to *mf*, which is appropriate for the Renaissance style, but not for music from later periods. Desirable tone quality is the primary objective of the chorus, and other aspects of interpretation, such as style and performance practice, are considered subservient.

Singers are placed where they will achieve the best blend. The scrambled arrangement is not acceptable, however, presumably because of the polyphonic entering of voices from different sections of a choir. In achieving the ideal tone quality from voices, certain model singers in each section of the choir are considered important and helpful.

Advocates of this vocal approach refer to it as an *a cappella* tone and most suitable for the singing of *a cappella* music, particularly the sacred music of the fifteenth and sixteenth centuries. Vocalization is generally done at lower

---

[28] For further information on this point of view, see the writings of its principal advocate William J. Finn, *The Art of the Choral Conductor* (Evanston, Ill.: Summy Birchard Company, 1960).

dynamic levels, and matching sounds occur both within and between sections. [29] The initial advocate of this school of thought was F. Melius Christiansen, the first conductor of the St. Olaf Choir, who is said to have founded the *a cappella* school of singing in the 1930s.

School D   This approach is based on the importance of good diction and the application of tone syllables toward the achievement of this end. The use of tone syllables is credited to Fred Waring, whose fame arose from his ensemble, Fred Waring and His Pennsylvanians. The group presented weekly radio shows during the 1940s and television programs beginning in the 1950s. [30]

In using tone syllables, conductors should consider the following important procedures:

1. Ask singers to be aware of all vowel sounds and sing them with clarity.
2. Be aware of the consonants that have pitch: **m, n, ng, l,** and **y,** and exaggerate both their intensity and duration.
3. Try to achieve a continuity of tone from word to word and from syllable to syllable. Consonants at the end of a phrase should be articulated and never carried over to the next phrase.
4. In singing diphthongs give the secondary vowel a lesser amount of the time value of the notes. For example, in the word *home* where the word has a whole note value in 4/4 meter, sustain the oh vowel for three and a half beats, with the $\overline{oo}$ vowel receiving about one half a beat depending on the tempo of the music.

In a number of its earlier choral publications, Shawnee Press included the tone syllables underneath the regular text. (See the excerpt from "Awake My Soul" in Figure 59.) Note how the tone syllables guide the singer in pronunciation, duration of vowels and diphthongs, treatment of consonants, and phrasing. Specifically note the following:

1. In the word *awake* the consonant **k** is enunciated immediately before the word *my*.
2. The treatment of the diphthongs in the words *my* and *joy*.
3. The placement of the final consonant **l** in the word *joyful*.
4. The symbol *** indicates no breath is to be taken at this point and the musical phrase is to be continued.
5. The treatment of the words with double consonants (the first two **l**'s in hallelujah). Both **l**'s are clearly articulated.

Since tone syllables are not used in any publishers' music except Shawnee Press, and then only on limited publications, conductors who utilize these principles may identify troublesome problems of diction in the text and then write

---

[29] For further information, see Leland Sateran, *Those Straight Tone Choirs* (Minneapolis: Augsburg Publishing House, 1963). See also the articles by Olaf C. Christiansen in *Choral News* 1, no. 2; 2, no. 1; and 4, no. 2, published by Neil Kjos Music Company.

[30] Fred Waring is also known as founder of Shawnee Press and the author of *Tone Syllables* (Delaware Water Gap, Pa.: Shawnee Press, 1945, 1948, and 1951).

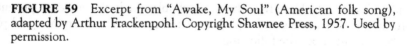

FIGURE 59 Excerpt from "Awake, My Soul" (American folk song), adapted by Arthur Frackenpohl. Copyright Shawnee Press, 1957. Used by permission.

on the chalkboard their suggested pronunciation/enunciation. The use of tone syllables is limited with polyphonic music. They are more applicable to homophonic music, and in particular, folk and popular music.

School E   Called the scientific approach to teaching, this school was started by a group of private voice teachers including Joseph J. Klein, Arnold Rose, Douglas Stanley, and John C. Wilcox.[31] Most of their ideas are considered revolutionary, or contrary to prevailing wisdom, and some even dangerous to a singer's vocal health. For example, most singers are taught to focus their tones. School E disagrees with this concept and states that good tone results from the correct conditions of all the processes involved in singing. Another conflicting

[31] For a detailed presentation of their methodology to the teaching of voice, see the following publications: Joseph J. Klein, *Singing Technique* (Princeton, N.J.: D. Van Nostrand, 1967); Arnold Rose, *The Singer and the Voice* (London: Faber and Faber, 1971); Douglas Stanley, *Your Voice* (Aulander, N.C.: Pitman, 1957); John C. Wilcox, *The Living Voice* (New York: Carl Fischer, 1935).

position is that most teachers ask their students to project their tone forward and upward. This group, however, advocates the sensation of focusing tones backward and downward. School E believes that good singing is throaty singing. Traditional teachers advocate that the tongue lie flat in the mouth with the tip touching the lower front teeth. School E, on the other hand, suggests that the tongue maintain a high position in the mouth so the throat can remain open.

Again, traditionalists believe that all vocalization for beginning singers should start in the middle voice range. School E, on the other hand, purports that it should begin in the lower register of a singer's voice. It also stresses the importance of a loose jaw, which is facilitated by the teacher gently stretching the jaw downward to help the student sing without unnecessary body tension. School E is basically designed for developing solo singers, not necessarily for singers in a choir. Also, School E advocates a tone that is big, full, and dark, so directors need to consider carefully the effects this would have on their singers' voices. Intensity of tone can create a situation of tension in a choir that is not properly guided in this technique.

Some directors may be attracted to this maturity of sound, feeling that their solo singers will be motivated to continue their vocal studies. In summary, choral directors should carefully consider the effects of this approach to choral singing before ever applying any aspect of it to their choirs.

School F   This school is based on the beliefs and practices of the eminent choral conductor Robert Shaw, who lists the techniques the choral conductor deals with as pitch, tone, dynamics, speech, and rhythm. Shaw emphasizes the importance of singers continually thinking about pitch by suggesting individuals check themselves with a tuning fork. Also, a chorus should be asked to (1) sing a chord in a given key without the use of a piano to obtain the pitch, and (2) sing a two-part chord with the interval as unfamiliar and dissonant as the director wishes.

To practice tone and dynamics, have your chorus sing phrases from music they are studying on various vowel sounds (in place of the text). In practicing *crescendo* and *diminuendo* have the chorus break down each beat into smaller units, such as

and practice as follows:

In the early stages of rehearsing a musical selection, do so at the dynamic levels of *mp* and *mf*, but no louder.

According to Shaw, the essential element of speech in song is drama. Strive to pronounce all the sounds of the word, including dipthongs and all consonants, and make certain that the sounds of all syllables coincide with the rhythmic pulse of the music; that is, sing them in tempo and in rhythm. Fine composers create a musical fabric that illuminates the text; however, if a choice is to be made the music is supreme.

For rhythm, some considerations for rehearsals are as follows:

1. Separate each dotted note from its following note.
2. Conduct the basic rhythm of the music rather than only the metrical rhythm.
3. Consider the proportion of each sound in a syllable and practice singing vowels, diphthongs, and consonants rhythmically.

Effective communication between the conductor and singers was of paramount importance to Robert Shaw. Through this means he strove to motivate singers to excel. Shaw was an inveterate writer of letters to his singers.[32] "Most of his letters dealt with fundamentals—rhythm and tempo, form, phrasing, score editing, enunciation, as well as with works in preparation, such as the requiems of Britten, Berlioz, Hindemith, and Verdi."[33] While working hard on musical disciplines is important, Shaw feels it is not enough. "But all that we have accomplished is worth nothing at all unless it releases the spirit to sing and shout, to laugh and cry, or pray the primitive prayer. I earnestly believe, too, that the spirit—and only the spirit—can guide us to the sound."[34]

Shaw feels that "good enunciation comes with the desire to communicate—and that is not a technique, but an attitude—a spirit ... unless each of us really loves each little sound, the 'disappearing' vowel in a diphthong, the hummed consonants, the exploded 't,' the final 'd'—unless each detail is precious to us—no set of rules can ever be effective."[35]

Shaw is noted for his superb musicianship and ability to instill in singers his own sense of joy and humility at having the opportunity to perform great music. He is also noted for his sense of humor and pointed one-liners, which serve to motivate singers toward a higher level of achievement and a desire to do their best to please their conductor.[36]

It must be understood that the techniques mentioned have worked well for Robert Shaw. While these basic ideas may be emulated, phrases should not be simply imitated, but only adapted to your personal style if and when a situation warrants it.

---

[32] For examples of these letters, see Joseph Mussulman, *Dear People . . . Robert Shaw, A Biography* (Bloomington: Indiana University Press, 1979).

[33] Ibid., p. 241.

[34] Ibid., p. 108.

[35] Ibid., p. 62.

[36] For examples of these one-liners, see Musselman, op. cit., p. 143.

Choral conductors attend music conventions and competition-festivals as well as programs in the concert hall, and hear and see things they both like and dislike. They are often inclined to adopt those ideas that appeal to them and thus slowly develop their own eclectic approach to choral conducting. The information here is meant to prepare directors for what they may hear or even read about. Thus they will be in a position to make better judgments. For example, some years ago the author heard a high school choir at a competition-festival using the choral tone advocated by School A. The initial impact of the sound was stunning; however, very shortly the choir began to have severe pitch and intonation problems. It became obvious that these young voices could not handle such a weighty type of tone. Their difficulty was akin to the exhaustion that comes about from carrying a heavy load up a mountain trail. In conclusion, before adopting any new ideas advocated by these six different schools of thought, study the writings of their advocates carefully.

TONE QUALITY AND HISTORICAL AUTHENTICITY

In the earlier part of this chapter the basic tenets of a desirable and appropriate type of vocal tone quality were presented along with suggested procedures for their achievement. This is the type of tone quality advocated by the majority of voice teachers in the Western world. As a matter of fact, when their students deviate from it at all, many teachers become upset, and some even try to influence their private voice students to pay little heed to any vocal techniques that differ from theirs. This is the basis for the disagreements between some college and university voice teachers and choral directors. With advice from two directions, the poor voice student can become very confused.

If the truth were told, the fundamentals of voice production presented here can be deviated from to a limited extent without any detrimental effect on singers. Certainly some deviation is necessary to achieve historical authenticity in performing choral music from different periods. The tone qualities advocated by some schools of singing are appropriate for the performance of particular styles of music, but not for others, as is pointed out in the following discussion of tone quality.

Renaissance Period

The masses and motets of the Renaissance are restrained in nature and should be performed as a prayer unto God. The tone quality should be kept light and clear, with a minimum of vibrato. A heavy dramatic voice quality and excessive vibrato are totally inappropriate for music of the period. The relatively straight tone initially formulated by F. Melius Christiansen (School C) is most appropriate for this style of music.

Baroque Period

In contrast to Renaissance performance practices, Baroque composers gave freer vent to their emotions. Even though the music was somewhat impersonal, the emotion came from the tumultuous and dramatic forces of that historical period. Tone quality then may be full and dramatic, yet under careful control, with a minimum of vibrato, and somewhat instrumental in nature. Excessive vibrato may adversely affect the intonation and blur the clarity of the polyphonic structure. School B, advocated by William J. Finn, is considered appropriate in many aspects for Baroque music because of its interest in the performance of polyphony and its focus on the clarity of vocal lines as would be achieved by other musical instruments. Also highly appropriate for Baroque music is School F, advocated by the eminent choral conductor Robert Shaw, as the tone is shaped and influenced by the musical forces of pitch, speech, and rhythm, and not by any abstract ideas unrelated to the music. Listening to Shaw's recording of J. S. Bach's *The Passion According to St. John* illustrates the musical integrity of this school of singing.

Classic Period

Composers of the Classic period strove for greater elegance and more delicate proportions than those of the Baroque period. Music of the Classic period was usually somewhat abstract in nature and discreet in taste and an integral part of a very sophisticated mode of living by the nobility, who were the prime supporters of the composers of the era. Thus, vocal tone was controlled and possessed a degree of restraint and clarity reflecting society's tastes. To the extent that it is impersonal in nature, the application of the tenets of School C is appropriate for music of the Classic period; however, all the approaches to School F are equally desirable. Adaptation of a combination of the two schools of thought should be considered.

Romantic Period

Composers of the Romantic period were not restricted as in previous periods, and sought to express emotion freely through tone color and other means. Composers sought to express sensuous beauty and tonal enchantment. In view of the composers' concerns with expression and textual aspects of the music, School F is the only avenue of thought that stresses the importance of these matters. The concepts of diction as set forth in School D are often applicable to music in a homophonic style. The principles of School A, however, with its emphasis on full, weighty, and vibrant tone, are applicable for use with such monumental works as the final movement of Beethoven's *Ninth Symphony*, where strength of voices is needed to balance the forces of the full orchestral sound. The tone of School A is appropriate for a number of other large choral/orchestral works as long as it is not overdone. For all such works, however, the premises of tone quality of School F should be carefully considered and applied.

Modern Period

The Modern period, beginning toward the end of the nineteenth century and continuing to the present time, includes a considerable variety of aesthetic movements and musical styles, which each necessitate a different type of tonal quality and treatment.

Impressionism With its minimal tension and rhythmic drive, Impressionism gives a feeling of vagueness, while being quite precise. It requires a comparatively small but light, clear, and flexible tone. For this music, consider the concepts of schools B and C as well as F.

Expressionism Expressionistic music is characterized by its intensity, dissonance, angular melody, complex rhythms, and fluctuating tempi. Voices performing this music obviously must be flexible and under careful control. Consider the premises advocated by schools E and F.

Neoclassicism Through Neoclassicism, composers endeavored to recapture the ideals of the eighteenth century, where the focus was on craftsmanship rather than on the emotional expression of the nineteenth century. For music of this period, consider the tenets of both schools C and F.

Neo-romanticism World War II created an atmosphere more conducive to romantic ideals and to a more personal means of communication by composers. Consider the tenets of schools D and F.

Avant-garde music During the decade of the late 1960s and the 1970s a variety of types of choral music were composed: choral music with electronic tape, choric speech, aleatoric (chance) music, and multimedia presentations. These musical expressions are so diverse that no one school of choral singing can be advocated for them. Simply apply the basic principles of singing as advocated in the first part of this chapter to all these types of musical expression.

Folk and popular music Effective communication is the essence of folk and popular music; therefore, only the premises of School D, which exemplifies the beliefs and techniques of Fred Waring, are appropriate. Clear and precise diction leading toward effective communication is the prime objective of this school, and the techniques advanced for effective communication of textual ideas are paramount.

A GLOSSARY OF TERMS ON CHORAL TONE AND DICTION

Actuator: Part of the vocal mechanism that actuates, or begins, the flow of the breath, i.e., the lungs, the diaphragm, the intercostal muscles, and the abdominal muscles.

Alveoli: The ridge of the gums above and behind the upper front teeth. In phonics, the consonants t and d are formed by touching the upper alveoli with the tip of the tongue.

Articulation: The action of physical adjustment of the articulating organs in the formation of intelligible sounds.

Articulators: Part of the vocal mechanism that forms or shapes the various language sounds and determines their particular distinguishable characteristics. Specific determiners are the tongue, lips, teeth, and lower jaw, the hard palate, and the velum, or soft palate.

Aspirate h: Vocal sound characterized by a slight constriction of the vocal cords; the cords are approximated, but not close enough to be set into vibration.

Bilabial: Consonants formed by the upper and lower lips (p, b, m, w).

Breath support: Flow or pressure of the breath against the vocal cords in an amount suffficient to effect the vibration necessary for a given pitch; considered to be adequate when phonation occurs without unnecessary constriction or tension in the laryngeal muscles.

Closed vowels: Vowels ee, ĭ, and oo, classified as such because of the relatively small oral cavity caused by the high position of the tongue in the mouth.

Consonants: Vocal sounds formed by precise, articulate movements of the lips, tongue, and jaw and characterized by an interruption or restriction of the flow of the breath. Consonants give intelligibility to vocal expression.

Covered tone: Slightly modified or altered vowel sound utilized by male singers in the production of tones in the upper register. The covered tone is full and resonant and lacking in any falsetto characteristics. A firming of the vocal mechanism occurs, and the vowel being sung is modified toward the uh vowel.

Deep set vowels: Vowels characterized by a roundness and a fullness of tone quality, and a naturalness of tone production, creating a sensation of being formed low in the throat. Essential physical conditions are a relaxed tongue and an open throat.

Diaphragm: Broad muscular partition located between the chest cavity and the abdomen. The diaphragm is one of the principal muscles used in inhalation. It is arched and dome-shaped in its relaxed state. As the diaphragm is tensed, it contracts and flattens out, thus pushing downward against the organs in the abdominal region. Coupled with the action of the rib muscles, the diaphragm contributes to the enlargement of the chest cavity, and as a result the air pressure is lowered. The lower air pressure is equalized by air entering the lungs. When the diaphragm relaxes, it returns to its normal state and pressure is exerted on the small air sacs in the lungs, thus causing exhalation, and completing the cycle of breathing.

Diphthong: Compound or double vowel, in which the vowel sounds change smoothly from one to the other. For example, the word *round* contains the diphthong ou (ah and oo) and is pronounced rah-oond.

Enunciation: Manner of vocal utterance as regards distinctness and clarity of vowels and consonants.

Falsetto: Light head voice, lying above the natural or normal range of the male voice. In a falsetto tone, only the inner edges of the vocal cords vibrate.

Final consonant: Last consonant in a word.

Glottal: Relating to or produced in the glottis; the aspirate consonant h, formed in the glottis.

Glottis: Fissure or opening between the vocal cords or bands.

Hard palate: Portion of the roof of the mouth between the alveoli and the velum, or soft palate. The hard palate is a structure of bone with a layer or cover of tissue.

High-forward resonance: Focusing of the tone in the "mask," or more specifically in the frontal cavities of the head. Essential physical conditions are an open throat and an arched velum.

Hooty tone: Muffled tone quality lacking in correct tonal focus.

Initial consonant: Consonant situated at the beginning of a word.

Intercostal muscles: Muscles that lie between the ribs and that partially control the process of respiration .

Labiodental: Consonants formed by the lower lip and the upper front teeth (**f, v**).

Laryngeal muscles: Muscles that regulate the size of the glottis, control the degree of tension of the vocal cords, and close off the larynx during swallowing.

Larynx: Sometimes referred to as the voice box; a cartilage that houses the vocal cords, situated at the upper part of the trachea, or windpipe.

Legato diction: Style of diction in which the vowels and the consonants are smoothly connected. The explosive qualities of the consonants are minimized, and the final consonants of most syllables or words are carried over to the prefix of the following syllable. For example, the words *night time* are sung **nah-ĭ taheem.**

Lingua-alveolar: Consonants **t, d, n, l, s,** and **z,** formed by the tip of the tongue touching the alveoli (teeth or gum ridge; portion of the jaw where the sockets for the upper teeth are situated; area between the teeth and the hard palate).

Lingua-dental: Consonants formed by the tip of the tongue touching the upper front teeth (**th** as in *thousand,* and **th** as in *there*).

Lingua-palatal: Consonants formed by the contact between the tongue and the hard palate (**sh, zh, ch, dzh, j,** and **r**).

Marcato diction: Style of diction in which each note in the music receives an accent and the explosive qualities of the consonants are exaggerated.

Medial consonant: Consonant situated within a word.

Nasality: Undesirable, exaggerated nasal quality often arising from some obstruction in the nasal cavity. When the nasal cavity becomes infected and swollen, as with a head cold, this quality usually occurs.

Open throat: Expression used to describe the feeling of a relaxed throat; an essential condition to correct voice production.

Open vowels: All the vowels with the exception of **ee, ĭ,** and **oo**. They are classified as open vowels because of the relaxed tongue position and the relatively low position of the jaw. The basic open vowel is **ah,** as in the word *father.* This vowel is the most naturally produced and is widely used as a beginning point in vocalization.

Palate: Roof of the mouth. (*See also* Hard palate; Velum.)

Pharynx: Cavity extending from the base of the skull to the esophagus.

Phonation: Act of uttering or producing vocal sounds in singing or speaking.

Pronunciation: Manner of pronouncing words as regards the selection of appropriate vowels and consonants, and the proper accent of words.

Registers: Compass or range of the voice in which the singer is able to sing without readjustment of the vocal cords. Principal classifications are the chest and head registers; however, some authorities consider the middle range of the voice as a third register. Certain other authorities emphatically deny the existence of vocal registers.

Resonance: Amplification and enrichment of a fundamental tone emanating from the larynx—by means of supplementary vibrations in the bodily resonance cavities.

Resonator: The part of the vocal mechanism that amplifies or resonates the tone and provides its characteristic timbre—specifically, the pharynx, the mouth, the nasal cavity, and the sinuses. (Some authorities believe that the trachea, the bronchi, and the chest cavity also contribute to vocal resonance.)

Respiration: Process of breathing, involving the alternate inhaling and expelling of the breath; inspiration followed by expiration.

Sibilants: Hissing sounds caused by the raised tongue position and the flow of the breath being directed at the back side of the upper teeth. The sibilants in English are **s, z, sh, zh, ch,** and **j.**

Soft palate: See Velum.

Sonorous: Full, richly resonant tone quality.

Staccato diction: Style of diction in which the notes and the words are distinctly separated or detached.

Strident quality: Harsh, grating, unpleasant tonal quality.

Sustained consonants: Consonants with a longer degree of sustaining power, such as **l, m,** and **n.**

Syllable: Single sound or a part of a word, which may be pronounced separately without interruption.

Tessitura: Average range of the melodic line or a voice part.

Throaty quality: Excessively dark tone quality sounded or resonated deep in the throat.

Tonal focus: Direction of the vocal tone to a particular localized area of the frontal resonators.

Tremolo: Excessively wide and slow vibrato that detracts from the expressive qualities of the voice.

Velar: Consonants formed by arching the back part of the tongue and pressing it against the velum, or soft palate (**k, g, ng**).

Velum, or Soft palate: Muscular membrane continuous with and attached to the bone of the hard palate. It serves an important function in phonation in that it may be raised to prevent the breath from entering the nasal passages during the articulation of certain consonants.

Vibrato: Rapid fluctuation of vocal tone alternately above and below a given pitch level—for the purpose of adding beauty and warmth to the tone.

Vibrator: Part of the vocal mechanism in which the sound originates; the vocal cords or membranes that are attached to the inner portion of the larynx and are set into motion or vibration by the flow of the breath.

Voiced consonant: Consonant phonated with a distinguishable movement of the vocal cords.

Voiceless consonant: Consonant phonated without movement of the vocal cords.

Vowels: Vocal sounds utilized for sustaining the tone and in which the flow of the breath is continuous. The primary vowels are **ee, ay, ah, oh,** and **oo.**

TOPICS FOR DISCUSSION

1. What environmental factors cause a singer to use clavicular or high-chest breathing, when, as a child, one quite naturally employs abdominal breathing?
2. Discuss the tone quality of various choirs and choruses you have heard either in concert or in recordings. What tonal characteristics do you feel are desirable? What characteristics are undesirable?
3. What is the relationship between flexibility and good tonal quality?
4. Differentiate between the terms *pronunciation, enunciation,* and *articulation.*
5. What truths and what fallacies exist in the statement "Sing as you speak"?
6. How may the choral conductor employ the concept of *front-to-back vowel placement* as a device for the improvement of tone quality?
7. Which consonants are likely to cause a choral group the most difficulties? Why? What procedures may be utilized to overcome these difficulties?
8. Why does each varying musical style require a distinct type of treatment in terms of diction? In terms of tone quality?
9. Why is it desirable for the choral conductor to have a *variety* of techniques for achieving good tonal quality and correct diction?

SELECTED READINGS

ADLER, KURT. *Phonetics and Diction in Singing: Italian, French, German, Spanish.* Minneapolis: University of Minnesota Press, 1967.

BURGIN, JOHN CARROL. *Teaching Singing.* Metuchen, N.J.: Scarecrow, 1973.

CAIN, NOBLE. *Choral Music and Its Practice.* Chap. 10. New York: M. Witmark & Sons, 1942.

CARUSO, ENRICO, AND LUISA TETRAZZINI. *Caruso and Tetrazzini on the Art of Singing.* New York: Dover Publications, 1975 (originally published by The Metropolitan Company, Publishers, New York, 1909).

CHRISTY, VAN A. *Glee Club and Chorus.* Chap. 4. New York: G. Schirmer, 1940.

COPP, AL, ET AL. *Sound for Ensemble Singing*. Kenosha, Wis.: Society for the Preservation and Encouragemnent of Barber Shop Quartet Singing in America, 1989.

DARROW, GERALD F. *Four Decades of Choral Training*. Metuchen, N.J.: Scarecrow, 1975.

DEWEY, PHILIP. *Bel Canto in Its Golden Age*. New York: King's Crown Press, Columbia University, 1950.

DYKEMA, PETER W., AND KARL W. GEHRKENS. *The Teaching and Administration of High School Music*, Chap. 8, pp. 90–94. Boston: C. C. Birchard, 1941.

FIELDS, VICTOR A. *Training the Singing Voice*. New York: King's Crown Press, Columbia University, 1947.

FINN, WILLIAM J. *The Art of the Choral Conductor*. Chaps. 2, 3, 4, 13, 14. Boston: C. C. Birchard, 1939.

FRISELL, ANTHONY. *The Tenor Voice*. Boston: Bruce Humphries, 1964.

HAASEMANN, FRAUKE, AND JAMES M. JORDAN. *Group Vocal Technique*. Chapel Hill, N.C.: Hinshaw Music, 1990.

——. *Group Vocal Technique: The Vocalise Cards*. Chapel Hill, N.C.: Hinshaw Music, 1990.

HAMMER, RUSSEL. *Singing—An Extension of Speech*. Metuchen, N.J.: Scarecrow, 1978.

HOWERTON, GEORGE. *Technique and Style in Choral Singing*. Chaps. 1–4. New York: Carl Fischer, 1958.

HULS, HELEN STEEN. *The Adolescent Voice: A Study*. New York: Vantage Press, 1957.

JONES, ARCHIE N. *Techniques in Choral Conducting*. Chaps. 2, 3. New York: Carl Fischer, 1948.

KAGEN, SERGIUS. *On Studying Singing*. New York: Holt, Rinehart & Winston, 1950. (Also Dover edition).

KNIGHT, MEL, ED. *Improving Vocal Techniques Through the Warm Up*. Kenosha, Wis.: Society for the Preservation and Encouragement of Barber Shop Quartet Singing in America, 1990.

KRONE, MAX T. *The Chorus and Its Conductor*. Chaps. 4, 5. San Diego: Neil A. Kjos Music Co., 1945.

MARSHALL, MADELINE. *The Singer's Manual of English Diction*. New York: G. Schirmer, 1953.

MAY, WILLIAM V., AND CRAIG TOLIN. *Pronunciation Guide for Choral Literature*. Reston, VA.: Music Educators National Conference, 1987.

MORIARTY, JOHN. *Diction*. Boston: E. C. Schirmer Music Co., 1975.

REID, CORNELIUS L. *The Free Voice*. New York Colman-Ross Co., Inc., 1965.

ROE, PAUL F. *Choral Music Education* (2d ed.). Chaps. 4, 5. Englewood Cliffs, N.J.: Prentice-Hall, 1983.

SHEWAN, ROBERT. *Voice Training for the High School Chorus*. West Nyack, N.Y.: Parker Publishing Company, 1973.

STANLEY, DOUGLAS. *Your Voice*. New York: Pitman Publishing Corporation, 1945.

STANTON, ROYAL. *The Dynamic Choral Conductor*. Chaps. 4, 5. Delaware Water Gap, Pa.: Shawnee Press, 1971.

SUNDERMAN, LLOYD F. *Some Techniques for Choral Success*. Chaps. 2, 3. Rockville Centre N.Y.: CPP/Belwin, 1952.

THURMAN, LEON. "Voice Health and Choral Singing: When Voice Classifications Limit Singing Ability," *The Choral Journal* 28, no. 10 (May 1988), 25–33.

VENNARD, WILLLIAM. *Developing Voices*. New York: Carl Fischer, Inc., 1973.

WESTERMAN, KENNETH N. *Emergent Voice* (2d ed.). Ann Arbor, Mich.: Privately published, 1955.

WILSON, HARRY R. *Artistic Choral Singing*. Chaps. 6, 7. New York: G. Schirmer, 1959.

The Performing Arts Health Information Services, Inc., has available a number of health information booklets written for specific groups, such as music instrumentalists, vocalists and dancers. They also publish a monthly (ten issues) magazine—Performing Arts Health News. Booklets of particular interest to singers and choral directors are as follows:

A Guide to the Prevention of Vocal Fold Problems in Singers and Actors (S300).
A Guide to Exercise and Fitness for Performers (B101).
A Guide to Nutrition and Diet for Performers (B102).
Complete Set of General Health Guides for Performers (S150/B101-103).
A Guide to Preventing Physical Injuries in Conductors (B206).
What Are Vocal Nodules and How Can You Prevent Them? (B302).
A Guide to the Treatment of Laryngitis in Singers and Actors (B303).

The Use of Strobovideolaryngoscopy in the Evaluation of the Voice (B303).
Complete Set of Vocalists' Health Guides (S350/B301-303).

For further information, write Performing Arts Health Network, Radio City Station, P.O. Box 566, New York. N.Y. 10101-0566.

References on the Anatomy and Physiology of the Human Vocal Mechanism

ALDERSON, RICHARD. *Complete Handbook of Voice Training*. Englewood Cliffs, N.J.: Parker Publishing, 1979.

APPELMAN, D. RALPH. *The Science of Vocal Pedagogy*. Bloomington: Indiana University Press, 1967.

BERG, JANWILLEM VAN DEN. "Calculations on a Model of the Vocal Tract for Vowel/i/ and on the Larynx." *Journal Acoustical Society of America*, 21 (1955), 332–38.

————."Myoelstic Aerodynamic Theory of Voice Production." *Journal of Speech and Hearing Research* 1, no. 3 (September 1958), 224–27.

————."Transmission of the Vocal Cavities." *Journal Acoustical Society of America* 27 (1955), 161–68.

————. And A. SPORR. "Microphonic Effect of the Larynx." *Nature* 179 (1957), 525-626.

————. J. T. ZANTEMA, and P. DOORNENBAL, JR. "On the Air Resistance and the Bernoulli Effect of the Human Larynx." *Journal Acoustical Society of America* 27 (1957), 626–31.

BOONE, DANIEL R. *The Voice and Voice Therapy* (3d ed.). Englewood Cliffs, N.J.: Prentice-Hall, 1983.

BORCHERS, ORVILLE I. "Practical Implications of Scientific Research for the Teaching of Voice." *Music Teachers National Association, Volume of Proceedings*, 1941, PP. 209–215.

————. "Vocal Timbre in Its Immediate and Successive Aspects." *Music Teachers National Association, Volume of Proceedings*, 1941, pp. 346–58.

BRODY, VIOLA. *An Experimental Study of the Emergence of the Process Involved in the Production of Song*. Unpublished Ph. D. thesis, University of Michigan, 1941.

DENES, PETER B. and ELLIOTT N. PINSON. *The Speech Chain: The Physics and Biology of Spoken Language*. Baltimore: Bell Telephone Laboratories, 1963.

FARNSWORTH, D.W. "High Speed Motion Pictures of the Human Vocal Cords" *Music Teachers National Association, Volume of Proceedings*, 1939, pp. 305–9.

HAGERTY, ROBERT F., et al. "Soft Palate Movement in Normals." *Journal of Speech and Hearing Research* 1, no. 4 (December 1958), 325–30.

HENDERSON, LARRA BROWNING. *How to Train Singers*, 2d Edition. West Nyack, New York: Parker Publishing Co., 1991.

HIXON E. *An X-Ray Study Comparing Oral and Pharyngeal Structures of Individuals with Nasal Voices and Individuals with Superior Voices*. Unpublished M.S. thesis, State University of Iowa, 1949.

HUSLER, FREDERICK, and YVONNE RODD-MARLING. *Singing: The Physical Nature of the Vocal Organ; A Guide to the Unlocking of the Singing Voice*. London: Faber & Faber Ltd., 1965.

JONES, DAVID S., RICHARD J. BEARGIE, and JOHN E. PAULY. "An Electromyographic Study of Some Muscles of Costal Respiration in Man." *The Anatomical Record* 117, no. 1 (December 1953), 17–24.

LEWIS, DON. "Vocal Resonance," *Journal Acoustical Society of America* 8 (1936), 91–99.

LUCHSINGER, RICHARD, and GODFREY ARNOLD. *Voice-Speech Language*. Belmont, Calif.: Wadsworth, 1965.

NEGUS, V.E. *The Mechanism of the Larynx*. London: William Heinemann Ltd., 1929.

NORRIS, M.A. *X-Ray Studies of Vowel Production as It Is Related to Voice*. Unpublished M.A. thesis, State University of Iowa, 1934.

RUSSELL, R. OSCAR. "First Preliminary X-Ray Consonant Study." *Journal Acoustical Society of America* 5 (1934), 247–51.

————. *Speech and Voice*. New York: Macmillan, 1931.

————. *The Vowel*. Columbus: Ohio State University Press, 1928.

————. "X-Ray Photographs of the Tongue and Vocal Organ Positions of Madame Bori." *Music Teachers National Association, Volume of Proceedings*, 27 (1932), 137.

SECORD, ARTHUR E. *An X-Ray Study of the Hyoid Bone, Thyroid Cartilage and Cricoid Cartilage in Relation to Pitch Change in the Human Larynx*. Unpublished Ph.D. thesis, University of Michigan, 1941.

STRONG, LEON H. "The Mechanism of Laryngeal Pitch." *Anatomical Record* 63, no. 1 (August 1935), 13-28.

VENNARD, WILLIAM. *Singing: The Mechanism and the Technic* (rev. ed.). New York: Carl Fischer, Inc., 1967.
WESTERMAN, KENNETH N. "Resonation." *Music Teachers National Association, Volume of Proceedings.* 1949, pp. 295–300.
WESTLAKE, HAROLD. *The Mechanics of Phonation, An X-Ray Study of the Larynx.* Unpublished Ph.D. thesis, University of Michigan, 1938.
WILLIAMS, R.L. "A Serial Radiographic Study of Velopharyngeal Closure and Tongue Positions in Certain Vowel Sounds." *Northwestern University Bulletin* 52, no. 17, 9–12.
WOLFE, W.G. *X-Ray Study of Certain Structures and Movements Involved in Naso-Pharyngeal Closure.* Unpublished M.A. thesis, State University of Iowa, 1942.

References on the Alexander Technique [37]

ALEXANDER, F. MATTHIAS. *Constructive Conscious Control of the Individual.* Long Beach, Calif.: Centerline Press, 1985.
————. *The Use of the Self.* Long Beach, Calif.: Centerline Press, 1984.
BARLOW, WILFRED. *The Alexander Technique.* Rochester, Vt.: Healing Arts Press, 1990.
BEN-OR, NELLY. "The Alexander Technique," in *Tensions in the Performance of Music,* ed. Carola Grindea. London: Kahn & Averill, 1978, pp. 84-95.
CAPLAN, DEBORAH. *Back Trouble.* Gainesville, Fla.: Triad Publishing Co., 1987.
GELB, MICHAEL. *Body Learning: An Introduction to the Alexander Technique.* New York: Delilah Books, 1981; London: Aurum Press, Ltd., 1981.
JONES, FRANK PIERCE. *Body Awareness in Action: A Study of the Alexander Technique.* New York: Schocken Press, 1976.
LEIBOWITZ, DEBORAH, and BILL CONNINGTON. *The Alexander Technique.* New York: Harper & Row, 1990.
WESTFELDT, LULIE, F. *Matthias Alexander: The Man and His Work.* Long Beach, Calif.: Centerline Press, 1986.

References on the Schools of Singing

FINN, WILLIAM J. *The Art of the Choral Conductor.* Evanston, Ill.: Summy Birchard Company, 1960.
KLEIN, JOSEPH J. *Singing Technique.* Princeton, N.J.: D. Van Nostrand, 1967.
MUSSULMAN, JOSEPH. *Dear People—Robert Shaw . . . A Biography.* Bloomington: Indiana University Press, 1979.
ROSE, ARNOLD. *The Singer and the Voice.* London: Faber and Faber, Ltd., 1971.
SATERAN, LELAND. *Those Straight Tone Choirs.* Minneapolis: Augsburg Publishing House, 1963.
STANLEY, DOUGLAS. *Your Voice.* Aulander, N.C.: Pitman Publishing Co., 1957.
SWAN, HOWARD. "The Development of the Choral Instrument," in *Choral Conducting: A Symposium* (2d ed.), eds. Harold A. Decker and Julius Herford. Englewood Cliffs, N.J.: Prentice Hall, 1988.
WARING, FRED. *Tone Syllables.* Delaware Water Gap, Pa.: Shawnee Press, 1945, 1948, and 1951.
WILCOX, JOHN C. *The Living Voice.* New York: Carl Fischer, 1935.

VIDEOTAPES [38]

A Practical Guide to Choral Improvement, by Roger Emerson. Hal Leonard Publishing Corporation, no. 40303431.

[37] The references in this section are generally available from Centerline Press, 2005 Palo Verde, Suite 325, Long Beach, CA 90815. A catalog listing these publications, as well as various others, is available upon request.

[38] For further information, as well as prices, contact the producers.

A *Voice Building Program for the Warm-Up Period*, by Bob Mucha. SPEBSQSA, Inc., no. 4022 (Society for the Preservation and Encouragement of Barber Shop Quartet Singing in America, Inc., 6315 Third Ave., Kenosha, WI 53143-5199).

Daily Workout for a Beautiful Voice, by Charlotte Adams. Santa Barbara Music Publishing, SBMP 21, Video no. 1.

Group Vocal Technique, by Frauke Haasemann. Hinshaw Music.

Vocal Master Class with Robert Merrill. Music Educators National Conference, no. 3061.

Vocal Production, by Fritz Mountford. Hal Leonard Publishing Corporation, no. 08417940.

Vowel Targets with Bill Myers. Society for the Preservation and Encouragement of Barber Shop Quartet Singing in America, Inc., no. 40480.

3

Maintaining
Vocal Health

Choral directors have become increasingly aware of the importance of maintaining vocal health. This chapter focuses on three broad topics. The first is whole body health, or factors that involve the singer's body and the singing voice, such as rest and exercise, diet, body hydration, the speaking voice, the common cold, and the singer's environment. The second section includes information on the singer and the laryngologist and "tips" from professional singers. The final topic examines the singer's posture and the circulatory system relative to maintaining alertness and avoiding dizziness and fainting spells.

WHOLE BODY HEALTH

Singers need to know how to take care of their voices adequately; it is important to them as individuals, as well as to the sound of the choir. It is generally understood that a singer's body is his or her instrument, and both physical condition and mental attitude have an effect on the singing voice. Therefore, directors should provide appropriate information on maintaining vocal health and continually stress its importance. Following are some important considerations.

Rest and Exercise

Bodily fatigue and mental stress can have a detrimental effect on the voice; therefore, adequate rest is important in the prevention of vocal problems. Exercise improves sleeping patterns, can reduce blood pressure, and is necessary to keep the body in tune. Exercise may also help maintain desired body weight. Singers should exercise at least every other day for a minimum of twenty minutes. Exercise should be moderate in nature and not overly strenuous. Swimming, walking, and cycling are all recommended; however, the activity must be one that a person enjoys, looks forward to, and achieves satisfaction from doing. While moderate exercise may reduce muscular tension and help a person sleep better, extremely vigorous exercise may be too fatiguing and detrimental to a singer's voice.

Diet

It is important for singers to maintain a balanced diet with at least one daily serving from each of the basic food groups.[1] Good nutrition cannot be overemphasized, since it contributes to overall good health. The old axiom "You are what you eat" might serve as a reminder to watch one's diet. Fatty foods should be avoided or eaten in moderation because they tend to be high in calories and low in nutrients.

The density of the laryngeal mucus is critical to singers because if it becomes too thick, congestion will occur, and coughing and clearing of the throat will usually result. Some mucus-causing foods that singers should avoid, particularly before a concert, are milk, ice cream, chocolate, coffee, condiments (such as pepper, mustard, and meat sauces), and highly spiced foods. Conversely, drinking water or hot herbal tea with honey and lemon and throat lozenges will usually increase the flow of laryngeal mucus secretions. While the use of antihistamines to control a postnasal drip has a drying effect, it also results in decreased vocal cord lubrication. Of course, the consumption of alcohol and the use of drugs can be disastrous to the human body and the singing voice. In some people, the chlorine in drinking water may have a drying effect on the mucus secretions around the vocal cords. If such should be the case, then singers may either drink only bottled water or boil their water before drinking it (keep well refrigerated until consumed). In such cases, singers should consult a larnygologist (a physician who specializes in vocal afflictions or difficulties) or an otolaryngologist (an ear, nose, and throat specialist). The physician can best advise them on their options.

Professional singers often refrain from eating before a singing engagement, and usually wait until after their performance. The reason is that a full stomach may often prevent effective use of the abdominal muscles in breathing, and gases

---

[1] It might prove beneficial to distribute information on this subject for the chorus to review individually, or have one or more chorus members provide a brief review for the group.

may be emitted that adversely affect the laryngeal mucus. With amateur singers this advice may not always be practical; however, they should at least be advised to eat lightly.

Body Hydration

Individuals should drink an adequate amount of liquid, preferably water, each day to avoid dehydration and subsequent dryness of the vocal mechanism. The vocal cords are covered with a watery, thin mucus, which serves to lubricate the mechanism. During phonation, the vocal cords vibrate and rub against each other approximately 256 times per second on middle C. To avoid irritation and minimize friction, a thin lubricant is necessary. The lubricant required is almost 99.9 percent water. As an analogy, recall washing your hands with soap and water and then, after drying them, repeating the procedure without soap. Without the lubrication of the soap there is considerably more friction. The amount of water a person drinks each day should be sufficient to keep the urine clear, that is, the color of tap water. [2]

Fainting can occur in individuals who contract any infectious disease, such as measles, mumps, chicken pox, scarlet fever, influenza, or even the common cold, because in battling such afflictions the body becomes dehydrated. Thus physicians always advise patients to "Get lots of rest and drink lots of liquids!" However, many persons when feeling poorly refrain from both eating and drinking liquids. To function properly, the body needs water and when it hasn't been ingested, water will be taken from the blood. As much as one liter, or 20 percent of the blood in the body, can be lost in this manner. As a result, there is an insufficient amount of blood in the circulatory system to be pumped to critical places, such as the brain, and fainting can occur. Drinking a reasonable amount of liquid can rectify this imbalance in a relatively short period of time. Fainting can also occur in persons who do not maintain correct singing posture. See the following section, "The Singer's Posture and the Circulatory System."

Misuse of the Voice

Singers, if they are to protect their delicate vocal mechanisms, should avoid unnecessary loud speaking, and particularly the yelling and screaming that often occur at school athletic events. While it may sometimes be difficult to control the enthusiasm of high school students, they should understand that such use of the voice is highly detrimental. Ask the singers, "How can you abuse your voice in this manner and expect to contribute to the choir as a singer?"

When a singer auditions for a choir, the director should note the general pitch levels of both the speaking voice and the singing voice. They should be approximately the same. When a teacher notices a wide difference between the

[2] Van Lawrence, "Sermon on Hydration (The Evils of Dry)," *The NATS Journal* 42, no. 4 (March/April 1986), 22–23.

two, then more careful voice testing is in order. Many students are inclined to speak too low, and that is detrimental to the singing voice. It may be noted that people in England often speak in more of a head voice. Suggest to singers that they try mixing the registers as they would in singing, since this can be beneficial to the singing voice.[3] Singers are taught to sing in the mask—that is, focus the tone in the frontal resonance chambers. Likewise, they should learn to speak in the mask, which is contrary to the practice of speaking too low and focusing the sound in the opposite direction.

If some persons appear to be misusing their voices, the director may wish to refer them to a speech pathologist—a specialist who diagnoses and treats misuse of the voice. Speech pathologists work closely with physicians and will not begin treatment until a physician examines the person and determines that the problem is of a nonorganic nature.

For teachers who deal with cheerleaders, here are two bits of advice for them: (1) Make sure all your yells have adequate breath support from the muscles of the abdominal region of the body with absolutely no tension on the muscles of the throat, and (2) alternate yells with a cheerleader partner. Use all appropriate body motions, but mouth the words. No one will ever know the difference! Also, save the voice in whatever ways you can, such as minimizing loud and usually unnecessary talking before and after yells, as well as during the course of the day.

If you use your voice in consecutive classes to demonstrate or correct troublesome passages you will have little voice left at the day's end. Such misuse can be injurious to the voice. Ask student volunteers to sing or demonstrate particular parts in the music. They generally are better vocal models anyway!

The Common Cold

The common head cold and sore throat seem to plague singers periodically, particularly when they least expect it. The cold virus is ever-present in the body, and when a person's resistance is lowered through fatigue, stress, poor diet, or exposure to the cold, the thin layer of protective mucus is disturbed and the virus is able to penetrate the nasal and throat cells and reproduce. The body, in turn, begins to fight the infection by stimulating increased blood flow into the areas involved. The blood contains antibodies that attack the virus. Part of the fluid from the additional blood drains out of the capillaries and into the nasopharynx. This fluid mixed with mucus results in the runny nose that is so troublesome.[4]

What to do? The best procedure is to get ample rest, keep warm, and drink lots of liquids, preferably warm. Also, don't sing with a sore throat. Warmth and

[3] See Morton Cooper, "Vocal Suicide in Singers," The NATS Bulletin 26, no. 3 (February/March 1970), 7–10.
[4] Tom Ferguson, "Grandmother Knew Best," The Mother Earth News 65 (September/October 1980), 140.

relaxation promote increased blood flow to the surface of the skin, and more antibodies are produced to fight the infection. Drinking warm liquids helps to replace the fluids lost through one's increased temperature (the body's attempt to fight the virus). Acidic liquids, such as orange, lemon, or grapefruit juice, help by acidifying the throat. Cold viruses cannot survive in an acidic environment.[5]

The Singer's Environment

The environment can have an important effect on the voice. Is the room dust free, or does it have drapes that serve as collectors of dust? Are there curtains surrounding the stage where some rehearsals or the final rehearsals are held? Is there adequate ventilation to clear dust particles and stale air from the room? Consider the consequences of such an environment for your singers.

People do, however, react differently to substances in their food and environment, and some may be allergic to certain substances that can have a detrimental effect on the delicate balance of laryngeal mucus, causing it to thicken and resulting in coughing and hoarseness. Some of these substances are tobacco smoke, dust, mold, and the pollen from weeds, grasses, and trees. These are among the many substances that can be tested for at an allergy clinic.

Most singers are particularly sensitive to an air-conditioned environment, because in the cooling process moisture is removed from the air. An extended period of time in an air-conditioned room requires singers to drink considerably more water. An extended trip in an airplane, which is air conditioned, will also have a drying effect on the laryngeal mucus. Also, when heating systems dry out the air, the use of a humidifier to replace the moisture is desirable, particularly in those parts of the country that have a dry climate and where there is relatively little humidity.

Professional singers' vocal health depends on where they live and how they live—that is, on their lifestyles and how they take care of themselves. They get ample rest and exercise, they watch what they eat and drink, and they are highly sensitive to their environment. Good singers won't compromise their health!

The Emotions and Hyperventilation

Hyperventilation is "an increased or forced respiration which results in carbon dioxide depletion with accompanied symptoms of lowered blood pressure, vasoconstriction, and faintness."[6]

To remain alert and physically adaptable persons must maintain a balance of oxygen and carbon dioxide in the blood. During hyperventilation the carbon dioxide level is decreased considerably and thus the balance is altered. When there is a lack of carbon dioxide in the blood the arteries, particularly

---

[5] Ibid.

[6] Alyce Bolander and Donald O. Bolander, *The Medical Dictionary*. New York: Lexicon Publications, Inc. 1986.

the large ones going to the brain, tend to constrict, thus decreasing the blood supply to the brain and other vital organs in the body. Constriction of the vessels results in "a reduced blood flow and a shortage of oxygen regardless of how much is going into the lungs."[7] This, of course, can cause dizziness and in some cases fainting. Hyperventilation occurs through very rapid breathing and can be avoided through slow, controlled abdominal breathing, like that advocated and taught by choral directors. To further control breathing patterns, slow breathing through one nostril at a time is advised (close the other nostril with the forefinger).

In group situations where considerable emotion can be involved, such as large group religious youth meetings and some rock concerts, a condition referred to by researchers as "epidemic hysteria" can occur. Due to the emotional climate within the group, when one persons faints others may follow suit. The question arises, "Can this happen with singers during a concert?" As singing involves the controlled expiration of the breath, rapid breathing is not likely to occur; however it could conceivably occur before a concert or between musical selections.

Singers should be advised of the consequences of quick, shallow breathing and directors should instruct their singers in proper breathing habits to be followed throughout their waking hours. That is, always breathe deeply utilizing the abdominal muscles to steady the rate and acquire the maximum amount of breath. Practicing some deep breathing exercises fully using the abdominal muscles ("belly breathing") and the muscles around the entire midsection of the body during rehearsals and prior to concerts can have only a beneficial effect.[8]

HEEDING THE ADVICE OF EXPERTS

The Singer and the Laryngologist

Become acquainted with physician-voice specialists in your community. To help identify the physician interested in working with singers, contact a university voice department, medical society, or local hospital for recommendations. Meet personally with the physician to discuss your objectives. Schedule a time after the physician's last appointment for the day so there can be ample time to talk. Try to find a laryngologist who has a special interest in helping singers and who enjoys this relationship. Invite the doctor to speak to your choir about maintaining vocal health. Such a physician is generally more than willing to accept such an invitation because he or she knows that prevention is the best approach to maintaining optimal vocal health. His or her comments can augment and reinforce the information you have already provided. After a general

[7] Flippin, Royce, "Slow Down, You Breathe Too Fast," *American Health* 11, no. 5 (June 1992), 72.

[8] For further suggestions on breathing and breath support see pp. 70–71.

presentation, a question-and-answer period is desirable. Such meetings can be highly beneficial to the members of a choir, since singers seem to place more credence in what a physician tells them than in what others tell them. After this meeting, the choir members will know whom to consult when they experience vocal difficulties. When problems occur, singers should arrange for the *last* appointment in the day so the physician will also have time to talk. Singers should introduce themselves and clearly state, "I am a singer and I need your help!" The conscientious physician will take the necessary time to provide guidance and to reassure the patient.

Some Advice from Professional Singers

Professional opera singers are careful to avoid roles that are inappropriate for their individual voices, which could involve either a tessitura that is too high (the range of notes where most of the part lies) or assuming too heavy a dramatic role, both of which can be injurious to the voice.[9] Luciano Pavarotti counsels, "Go easy. One new role a year is plenty." He also says, "Vocalize, vocalize … ten minutes, seven or eight times a day."[10]

Singing opera is a most athletic endeavor, and a strong body and good posture are essential. The bass Nicolai Ghiaurov emphasizes psychic well-being and "loving what you're doing." Too much emotion has a negative effect on vocal endurance if the emotion translates into physical tension and stress. Mirella Freni avoids singing the role of Butterfly because the character demands "raw passion, rage, and despair." Maintaining too busy a schedule is detrimental to the voice. Alfredo Kraus warns that if you sing in two cities on successive days, "your subconscious is working in both places, and it's too busy." Luciano Pavarotti says, "Remember the first lesson you ever took and believe it!" And finally, Birgit Nilsson comments, "There almost has to be another you, standing at your side, in full control."[11]

THE SINGER'S POSTURE AND THE CIRCULATORY SYSTEM[12]

All voice teachers and choir directors understand the importance of correct singing posture and most likely have spoken to their singers about the role of posture in achieving proper breath support and in the vitalization of tone. Nonetheless, even conscientious singers often need reminding. Have any of your

---

[9] Martha Duffy, "Why Golden Voices Fade," *Time*, May 6, 1991, p. 75.

[10] Ibid., p. 74.

[11] Ibid., p.75.

[12] An edited version of this section of the book was published in *The Choral Journal* 30, no. 9 (April 1990), 19–22.

singers ever experienced dizziness or fainting during a recital/concert? While it may occur only infrequently, steps should be taken to see that it *never* happens.

Some contributing causes of fainting can be an overheated performance hall and overcrowding on choir risers. Overheating can lead to increased skin blood flow to dissipate heat, thus "stealing" blood that would have gone to the brain. However, the primary cause of fainting is venous pooling, or a lack of blood being returned through the veins to the heart where it can be pumped to the brain and other parts of the body. This fact is apparently not well known or understood; there is little or nothing in the literature for musicians on the subject. Some directors believe the problem is psychological, and that one incident will provoke others to follow. It is possible that some subsequent fainting incidents may be psychological, but only in very emotional situations; most choirs, however, perform in a reasonably controlled situation. Whatever the cause, it is a rather common practice to ask a singer who exhibits dizziness to sit down on the choir risers, with the head between the legs (to allow for blood to flow to the head). It is essential that directors and their singers understand just how the circulatory system functions.

The heart pumps blood through the arteries in the body and returns it through the veins. The "used" blood is returned to the right ventricle and then through the pulmonary artery to the lungs where it is cleansed (it picks up oxygen and discards carbon dioxide), and then moves on to the left ventricle of the heart where the circulatory process continues. However, maintaining an upright position without any bodily movement may cause venous pooling of the blood in the lower extremities of the body, which can result in dizziness or fainting.

Venous return of the blood to the heart is normally aided by the rhythmic action of muscle contraction. If we stand still, the veins in our legs are filled with blood. As we begin to walk or move about, the muscles begin to pump the veins, and because the veins contain one-way valves, the blood is forced to flow back to the heart. When we stand still, the blood again begins to pool in the lower extremities of the body.[13] In addition, changes in thoracic pressure during normal breathing, as well as during singing, also affect venous return.[14] During inspiration more blood returns to the heart because of the negative pressure inside the chest, which expands the large veins near the heart. In contrast, during protracted expiration, as occurs while singing, the pressure within the chest is positive, which tends to compress the large veins and reduce blood return to the heart. Thus, with any activity that lessens the normal or natural rhythm of the thoracic pump, the effective functioning of the skeletal muscle pump (below the level of the diaphragm) becomes even more important.[15]

[13] T. C. Fung, *Biodynamics Circulation* (New York: Springer-Verlag, 1984), p. 201.

[14] James J. Smith and John P. Kampine, *Circulatory Physiology*, 2d ed. (Baltimore/London: Williams and Wilkins 1984), p. 102. See also Robert C. Little and William C. Little, *Physiology of the Heart and Circulation*, 4th ed. (Chicago: Yearbook Medical Publishers, 1989), p. 307.

[15] Discussion with Alan Tucker, Professor of Physiology, Colorado State University, Fort Collins.

The classic tilt table experiment further illustrates the effect of blood pooling in the lower extremities:

> The subject is strapped to a table that can pivot to different positions. The heart rate and blood pressure are stable as long as the subject remains horizontal. Once the table is tilted vertically, an uninterrupted column of blood exists from the subjects heart to toes. This . . . causes blood to pool in the lower extremities and results in a backup of fluid in the capillary bed that seeps into the surrounding tissues and causes swelling. Consequently, venous return is reduced and blood pressure declines; at the same time, heart rate accelerates and venoconstriction occurs in an attempt to counter the effects of venous pooling. If the upright position is still maintained, the subject eventually faints owing to insufficient cerebral blood supply. Tilting the person either horizontally or head down immediately restores circulation and consciousness is quickly regained. [16]

The average person has about 5 liters of blood or 10.57 pints (0.47 liters = 1 pint). [17] Some people may have slightly more or less blood depending on their body size, but not much, that is, the amount is not proportionally higher or lower in relation to actual body weight. It has been estimated that 60 to 70 percent of the body's blood is in the veins and the majority of that is below the diaphragm. If a singer maintains a stationary posture without any movement of the legs, as much as 2 pints of blood can pool in the lower extremities and not return to the heart. [18] Thus an insufficient amount of blood is available for the heart—sometimes referred to as an "uphill destination." This condition, as we mentioned, can lead to or cause dizziness or fainting (see Figure 60).

Similar situations leading to blood pooling have been noticed in the rigid positions of military personnel, especially when standing at attention for some time. We have observed honor guards at attention on Constitution Avenue in Washington, D.C., lined up on both sides of the street to greet visiting dignitaries or heads of state. After maintaining that position for approximately twenty or thirty minutes, some of the men collapsed. [19] The command "parade rest" was then given to ease the situation. [20]

[16] William D. McArdle, Frank I. Katch, and Victor L. Katch, *Exercise Physiology*, 2d ed. (Philadelphia: Lea & Febiger, 1986), p. 249.

[17] Ibid., pp. 271, 275. See also Abraham Noordergraaf, *Circulatory System Dynamics* (New York: Academic Press, 1978), p. 9.

[18] Arthur C. Guyton, *Textbook of Medical Physiology*, 7th ed. (Philadelphia: W. B. Saunders, 1986), p. 223.

[19] For further information on the physiological effects of this military posture, see Guyton, p. 223. See also Smith and Kampine, pp. 100-102.

[20] In recent years the military services have become more aware of this problem, and the U.S. Army advocates that personnel, while at attention, flex their knees, alternately tense the muscles in each leg, and wiggle their toes. This advice is not published, but has generally been passed on verbally; however, the Army Field Manual does state, "Keep the legs straight without locking the knees" (Field Manual No. 22-5, *Drill and Ceremonies*, Washington, D. C.: Department of the Army, 1984, p. 3-1). Air Force Regulation 50-14, "Drill and Ceremonies," states that while at attention the "legs are kept straight without stiffening or locking the knees" (*Air Force Regulations*, Department of the Air Force, 1975, p. 14).

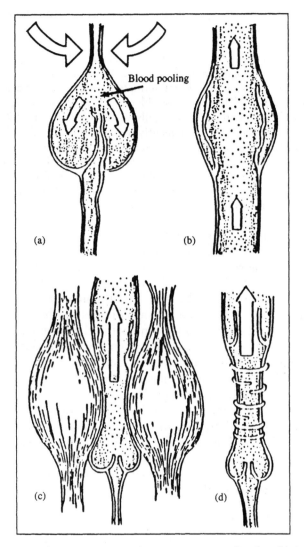

FIGURE 60 Valves in the veins (a) prevent returning flow but (b) do not hinder the normal flow very much. Blood can be pushed through veins (c) by nearby active muscle, or (d) by the action of the smooth muscle bands. (From H. Elias, and J.E.Pauly, *Human Microanatomy* and Philadelphia: F.A.Davis, 1966 and as adapted by W.D. McArdle, F.I. Katch, and V.L. Katch, *Exercise Physiology*, 2d ed. Philadelphia: Lea & Febiger, 1986, p. 249. Used by permission.)

According to Smith and Kampine, the "ancient practice of execution by crucifixion was largely based on the resultant circulatory stress from upright suspension," where no movement in the lower extremities of the body was allowed. [21] It is also interesting that test pilots wear pressurized suits along with special support stockings that aid in reducing the shifting of blood to the lower extremities of the body while in an upright position.[22] Conversely, in space, astronauts travel in a zero-gravity environment, so more blood flows to the head than would normally do so on earth. Symptoms of the common cold are the result—a runny or stuffy nose and a "full head" feeling.

The body does the best it can to prevent venous pooling. Even during quiet standing there is an unconscious, slight swaying action of the body as a result of the rhythmical cycles of reflex contraction and relaxation of the skeletal muscles of the lower extremities.[23] However, some people maintain so much rigidity in their bodies that even this natural response is suppressed and difficulties arise as a result.

To minimize the extent of venous pooling and to ensure the proper circulation of the blood, singers should stand with the knees slightly flexed, never rigid, stiff, or locked. For those people who have skied on either snow or water, the feeling will be natural because the bent knees in the postures for these sports serve as shock absorbers over the bumps. Singers should practice flexing their knees. Additionally, one foot should be placed several inches ahead of the other in order to maintain better balance when singing and to provide a foundation for the proper use of the breathing muscles.[24] The weight of the body should rest on the balls of the feet, the chest should be held relatively high, the abdomen drawn in, and spine kept straight. The head should be kept perpendicular to the shoulders and the music held in a position so the director can be seen without raising or lowering the head. In a seated position, singers should sit away from the backs of their chairs with some of their body weight distributed on the legs.[25] This will help singers maintain a firm foundation to support the breath, but also may remind them of the need for subtle and continual leg movements, such as tensing the muscles in the thighs and calves and wiggling the toes. Solo singers, of course, have ample opportunity for leg movements, either between selections or sometimes within a given piece during an extended rest or sectional changes in mood or tempo. All leg movements help to facilitate the "pumping" action of the leg muscles (see Figure 60b and c).

Choir singers generally remain stationary during a particular choral work, but between selections and during audience applause they can flex their knees and, perhaps even more important, shift their body weight alternately from one foot to the other, imitating a slow walking motion. This facilitates the muscle

[21] Smith and Kampine, p. 102.

[22] McArdle, Katch, and Katch, p. 250.

[23] Smith and Kampine, p. 100.

[24] For a poster illustrating correct singing posture, as well as instructive information that may be displayed on a rehearsal room bulletin board, see "The Choir Singer's Posture" by Robert L. Garretson, available from Collegiate Cap and Gown Co., 1000 N. Market St., Champaign, Ill. 61820.

[25] See "Achieving Correct Posture," pages 68–70.

contraction necessary to pump the blood back to the heart. (They can also alternately tense the muscles in each leg and wiggle their toes any time during singing.) These movements can be relatively slow and deliberate and usually are unnoticeable to the audience if done with care. Of course, such movements should be practiced during rehearsals and particularly during the final rehearsal prior to the performance.

During a concert, many choral directors like to use different standing arrangements depending on the stylistic nature of the music. For example, in a homophonic piece necessitating good choral blend, they may opt to use the scrambled arrangement. In a polyphonic piece, however, they would naturally prefer a conventional arrangement with, for example, the basses behind the sopranos and the tenors behind the altos. In still other pieces, such as Charles Ives's bitonal "Sixty-Seventh Psalm," where the women's parts are in C major and the men's parts in G minor, the director will want to separate these sections and have them stand together on the choir risers. Moving singers periodically throughout a concert for musical reasons can only have positive physical effects on singers, and along with the previous suggestions for physical movement should minimize venous pooling and keep a choir vigorous.

While the primary cause of dizziness and/or fainting is the pooling of blood in the lower extremities of the body, it will certainly contribute to a choir's overall preparedness if prior to concerts, as well as rehearsals, they utilize some stretching exercises to increase blood circulation and help them get "in tune" with their bodies. Stretching exercises, or prevocalizing warm-ups, are done with the group as a whole and may include neck stretches (lower head frontward and backward, and then from side to side, but avoid rotating the head); shoulder shrugs (raise shoulders toward the neck and then reach downward); arm circles (small ones, with arms extended sideways); upward arm stretches (reach toward the ceiling with first the left and then the right arm); and torso stretches (reach across the body with the right arm and then reach right with the left arm). These exercises, like the stretching exercises used by runners and other athletes prior to strenuous physical activity, will improve blood flow to the upper body muscles. As a final word: before moving from the warm-up room to the concert hall, remind the choir to utilize the body movements previously suggested during the concert and particularly those that they may do between selections.[26]

The singers' clear understanding of their bodies' circulatory system is essential if they are to protect themselves against any possible problems. Post an enlargement of the illustration in this chapter on the bulletin board so that all may see and study it. This will serve as a constant reminder to the singers of the importance of proper posture and the vital relationship between posture, bodily movement, and the circulatory system.

---

[26] For further information on singing posture and stretching exercises, see pages 68–70 and 71–73.

TOPICS FOR DISCUSSION

1. What is meant by the term "whole body health" and how does it relate to a singer's vocal health?
2. Under what circumstances do physicians advise persons, "Get lots of rest and drink lots of liquids"?
3. What information and advice would you as a choral director give to school cheerleaders who are members of your choir?
4. In what ways can choral directors demonstrate good vocal habits?
5. Under what circumstances should singers in your choir seek the advice and counsel of a laryngologist?
6. What lessons can be learned from the experience and advice of professional singers ?
7. Have you ever heard conflicting theories about why singers sometimes faint while standing on choral risers?
8. Describe the classic "tilt table" experiment.
9. If a singer maintains a stationary position without any movement of the legs, how much blood can pool in the lower extremities?
10. Explain the ancient practice of execution by crucifixion, how it affected the circulatory system, and how this understanding can lead to a better comprehension of the physical trauma that some singers experience from poor posture.
11. What difficulties may result from a singer's locked knee position?
12. Discuss some pre-performance exercises that would increase blood circulation and help singers to get more in tune with their bodies.

SELECTED READINGS

References on Maintaining Vocal Health

BOONE, DANIEL R. *The Voice and Voice Therapy* (3d ed.) Englewood Cliffs, N.J.: Prentice-Hall, 1983.

BRADLEY. MARK. "Prevention and Correction of Vocal Disorders in Singers." *The NATS Bulletin* 36, no. 5 (May/June 1980), 38–41, 49.

BRODNITZ, FREDERICK S. *Keep Your Voice Healthy* (2d ed.). Boston: College-Hill Press. Little, Brown, 1987.

COOPER, MORTON. "Vocal Suicide in Singers." *The NATS Bulletin* 26, no. 3 (February/March 1970), 7–10.

FEDER, ROBERT. "Vocal Health: A View from the Medical Profession." *Choral Journal* 30, no. 7 (February 1990), 23–25.

FLIPPIN, ROYCE. "Slow Down, You Breathe Too Fast." *American Health* 11, no. 5 (June 1992), 71–75.

FERGUSON, TOM. "Grandmother Knew Best." *The Mother Earth News*, no. 65 (September/October 1980), 140.

LAWRENCE, VAN. "Sermon on Hydration (The Evils of Dry)." *The NATS Journal* 42, no. 4 (March/April 1986), 22–23.

SANIGA, RICHARD D., MARGARET F. CARLIN, AND PATRICIA R. HAYS. "The Prediction of Vocal Abuse in Professional Voice Students." *The NATS Journal* 42, no. 4 (March/April 1986), 8–11.

SATALOFF, ROBERT T. "Bodily Injuries and Their Effects on the Voice." *The NATS Journal* 2, no. 1 (May/June 1987), 23–24.

———. "Professional Singers: The Science and Art of Clinical Care." *American Journal of Otolaryngology* 2, no. 1 (August 1981), 251–66.

———. "The Professional Voice: Part I. Anatomy, Function, and General Health." *Journal of Voice* 1, no. 1 (March 1987), 92–104.

THURMAN, LEON. "Voice Health and Choral Singing: When Voice Classifications Limit Singing Ability." *Choral Journal* 28 no. 10 (May 1988), 25–33.

References on Blood Circulation

FUNG, F. C. *Biodynamics Circulation*. New York: Springer-Verlag, 1984, p. 201.

GUYTON, ARTHUR. *Textbook of Medical Physiology* (7th ed.). Philadelphia: W. B. Saunders, 1986, p. 223.

LITTLE, ROBERT C., AND WILLIAM C. LITTLE. *Physiology of the Heart and Circulation* (4th ed.). Chicago: Yearbook Medical Publishers, 1989, p. 307.

MCARDLE, WILLIAM D., FRANK I. KATCH, AND VICTOR L. KATCH. *Exercise Physiology* (2d ed.). Philadelphia: Lea & Febiger, 1986, p. 249.

SMITH, JAMES L., AND JOHN R. KAMPINE. *Circulatory Physiology* (2d ed.). Baltimore/London: Williams and Wilkins, 1984, p. 102.

Children's Voices and the Boy's Changing Voice

Related to the matter of maintaining vocal health are the proper treatment and handling of children's voices and the boy's changing voice. The unique characteristics of these voices must be understood and dealt with properly to ensure their proper development and to avoid vocal difficulties.

CHILDREN'S VOICES

In working with children's voices it is important to understand their natural vocal characteristics, as well as how to vocalize them and develop the appropriate desired tonal characteristics and the necessary control. Additionally, knowledge of voice ranges is essential for the proper selection of music. The use of proper vocal models during rehearsals facilitates children's understanding and development. Also, an awareness of children's interests is vital in selecting appropriate vocalises and music and in achieving effective rehearsals.

Vocal Characteristics

The human voice has an inherent flexibility that enables it to imitate a variety of sounds. The vocal mechanism of a child, however, is smaller than that of an adult and lacks the maturity and development that result from continued training. The voices of fifth- and sixth-grade children are at a peak of development just prior to adolescence, and generally are clearer and more resonant than at any previous stage. Students at this age are sensitive, wish to do well, and take pride in their accomplishments. This is the time when a special continuing effort should be made to develop the children's head voice, which is light in quality, in contrast to the heavier chest voice, and which may be described as clear and flutelike, even ethereal. We are not implying that children's voices should always sound like angels, as the voice quality or color will necessarily change somewhat according to the poetic characteristics of the text of the music. This lighter voice quality, however, enables children to develop and utilize their upper range, which is less weighty, and produces less strain on the vocal mechanism. In working with children's choirs that include both boys and girls, you will note that there can be differences between their characteristic sounds. Frequently in boys' voices the pitch is pure and clearer, whereas the sound of girls' voices might be lighter, diffused, and somewhat airy.

Adult voices by comparison are inclined to sound somewhat dark and heavy, and children should never attempt to imitate this sound; it is unnatural and simply too much for young voices to try to do. Attempts to achieve any degree of adult voice quality can be injurious to young voices. In using their voices children need careful guidance. When singing in their upper range they sometimes may be inclined to use their playground voices, which are too heavy for use on higher pitches. Help children to use their light head voice on all higher pitches.

Sometimes parents become overzealous in promoting their children's vocal development, and may call their children's music teacher asking for the names of voice teachers. You should advise parents to delay private voice study until their children are in high school. Young children may try to match the quality of the adult woman's voice, which only creates problems in their vocal development. For young children, the best advice is to encourage their study of piano, or some other musical instrument, and to continue their choir participation—in school, church, or community.

Vocalises

As with choirs of all age groups, use various vocalises to improve tone quality, flexibility, and articulation. The essential beginning point, however, is the use of exercises to improve tone quality and placement. Therefore, for children's choirs in particular, we recommend downward vocalization on a $\overline{oo}$ vowel as a beginning point. Such vocalization should begin on about fourth line D above middle C and descend on a five-note pattern (see Exercise 21), and the voices should be allowed to float down to their lower register. Voices should never be pushed! Encourage children to carry the lighter quality of their voices smoothly downward as far as possible, without any break in the voice at all.

EXERCISE 21

1. Vocalize downward on the five-note patterns, beginning each pattern one half step lower.
2. Let the voices float down to their lower register. Don't push the voices.

It is often helpful to think of lining the child voice on the vowel o͞o, and a certain amount of vocalization on this vowel, preferably on descending patterns, can be helpful in developing in children's voices the type of voice quality they should be striving for. Use of the o͞o vowel on vocalises promotes a brighter quality than the other vowels, which sometimes may also be used, but sparingly, at least until the concept of the head voice is well established. Development of the head voice enables children to expand the upper range of their voices and thus be able to sing a wider variety of music. Listening to recordings of other experienced children's choirs can serve as a model for the desired tonal quality. It is particularly important for boys to learn to use their head voices, as they will have better control when their voices begin to change, and subsequently will feel better about themselves and their voices.

In striving for the desired tonal quality, it is usually best not to use the words *soft* or *loud*, but rather "sing more lightly," or sing with an "open, fuller sound." The message will get through. Never let singers push their voices. Tell your singers that anyone can sing loudly, but that it takes effort and concentration to sing softly.

Children generally need help in improving their articulation. The vocalization of various tonguetwisters is a good way to work on articulation. The McDonald's vocalise, which some years ago was used as a commercial, is still a good exercise for children (see Exercise 22). It is a real tonguetwister, and one way to use real experiences in a child's life. This exercise gives the tongue and facial muscles a good workout. Sing upward by half steps beginning on D to E♭, E, and F, or until the children become tired. An alternative exercise is to use the old tonguetwister "Peter Piper Picked a Peck of Pickled Peppers" and adapt the words to pitches (scalewise or chordwise) of your choice (see Exercise 23).

EXERCISE 22

THE MCDONALD'S VOCALISE

Two   all beef pat-ties, Spec-ial   sauce,   let-tuce, cheese, pic-kles,

on-ions on   a se-sa-me seed   bun.   *etc.*

Repeat vocalise beginning each one half step higher—E♭, E, F, and F♯.

EXERCISE 23

PETER PIPER

Pe-ter Pi-per picked a   peck of   pick-led pep-pers.

Repeat vocalise beginning each one half step higher—E♭, E, F, and F♯.

OR

Pe-ter Pi-per picked a   peck of   pick-led pep-pers.

Other exercises children enjoy that contribute to improved articulation are "Super Dooper Double Bubble Gum" and "Jack and Jill" (see Exercises 24 and 25). The singing of "Jack and Jill," which uses the chromatic scale, is also helpful as an ear-training device. To ensure accurate intonation, the exercise should be sung rather slowly at first, but after the singers have become secure in their pitches, the vocalise may be sung at faster tempos. It may also be sung as a two-part round with the second part beginning as the first part reaches point 2 (two beats later). For further variety, use other nursery rhymes, for example, "Mary had a little lamb, its fleece was white as snow" (ascending) and "Everywhere that Mary went the lamb was sure to go!" (descending).

EXERCISE 24

SUPER DOOPER DOUBLE BUBBLE GUM

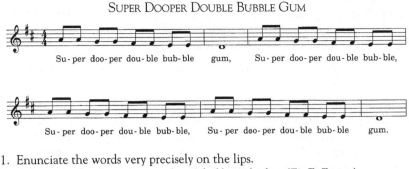

1. Enunciate the words very precisely on the lips.
2. Repeat vocalise beginning each one half step higher (E♭, E, F, etc.).

EXERCISE 25

JACK AND JILL

1. Enunciate the words very precisely on the lips.
2. Sing the exercise slowly at first to ensure reasonably accurate intonation, but after the singers have become secure in their pitches, the vocalise may be sung at faster tempos.
3. Repeat vocalise beginning each one half step higher (C♯, D, E♭, etc.).
4. For variety, sing the vocalise as a two-part round, with the second part beginning as the first part reaches point 2 (two beats later).
5. For further variety, use other nursery rhymes, such as "Mary Had a Little Lamb."

While the vocal exercises presented here are a good beginning point, considerable value may also be derived from the periodic use of the exercises presented in Chapter 2, particularly from exercises 6, 7, 9, and 14 (see pp. 83, 87).

Voice Ranges and Selecting Music

Participants in children's choirs in elementary schools are normally selected from students in the intermediate grades (4–6), and their ages usually range from nine to eleven.[1] Ages of children in church-affiliated choirs and

---

[1] The ages of children in middle school choirs (grades 6–8) may range from eleven to thirteen.

community groups will normally follow the same parameters; however, children somewhat older may also be allowed to participate. The old axiom that the range of children's music for this age group should lie within the treble staff is generally applicable for children with limited vocal experience and training. However, the range of children with reasonably trained voices may be considered to be [musical notation], and music selected for performance should generally lie within this range. Even more important than the occasional high or low note is the tessitura of the music, or the average range of a choral selection. Music with a high tessitura can be fatiguing to the singers, but it should not strain their voices if they are using proper vocal production. When teaching a new piece consider pitching it a step or two lower until the children are familiar with it. Then raise the pitch to its original level after it is reasonably well learned. Regardless of the age group of a choir, more vocal strain occurs when learning new music, and this is particularly true with children.[2]

In helping children to learn a troublesome part of the music, it is of little benefit for you to sing the part because of the mature sound unnatural to children. Instead, ask for one or two volunteers to sing a particular part to provide a good tonal model for the choir. If a choir member sings a part properly, then the singers' reaction may be "Well, if he or she can do it, I certainly can too!" Such a practice is not only advisable, but particularly necessary for music in a high range.

In children's choirs for this age group, some boys' voices may begin to change as early as the sixth grade. Be on the lookout for them! These voices will often drop an interval of a fourth during this change. Advise any singer you feel is bordering on a voice change to simply not sing any of the pitches that are uncomfortable for him or that seem to strain his voice. Then, as soon as possible, test the singer's voice individually to determine his vocal status. For suggestions in dealing with these singers, see the following section, "The Boy's Changing Voice."

Some Comments on Rehearsals

The success of children's choirs affiliated with churches or school choirs meeting at a designated time outside of the regular school schedule depends on all members being present and the rehearsal starting on time. Latecomers not only often miss announcements or instructions, but are a distraction when they enter the rehearsal room to find their seats.

Perhaps you have experienced choral rehearsals where all the singers were conversing and the director had to strive to get everyone's attention, and says, "All right, everyone, it's time to begin our rehearsal!" While all directors hope

---

[2] For further information on "The Child Voice and Singing," see Chapter 3 in Robert L. Garretson, *Music in Childhood Education*, 2d ed. (Englewood Cliffs, N.J.: Prentice-Hall, 1976), pp. 39–58.

that the rehearsal room is a place where everyone who enters it is ready to sing, this is certainly not always the case with many young singers. For her children's choir, one director has utilized a unique means of motivation. All the singers who enter the rehearsal room on time write their names on small pieces of paper and drop them in a container provided. At the end of the rehearsal, the director then draws one name from the container and awards this singer with a small candy bar. This motivation must be tremendous, as one young participant reportedly asked her mother to drive through a red light so she would be on time for the rehearsal and have a chance at the prize.[3]

Another idea that facilitates the prompt beginning of rehearsals is to give a tuning fork to one of the early arrivals. At the director's signal this individual sounds the tuning fork and then sings that pitch (A) on an **oo** vowel. The other singers know they must listen for and match that pitch.[4] The singing of this pitch is then followed by various other exercises, usually beginning with the downward vocalization on the **oo** vowel (see Exercise 21). Prior to any extensive vocalization, however, children can benefit considerably from various stretching exercises. For a detailed discussion of these exercises, see pages 71–73.

THE BOY'S CHANGING VOICE

Choral directors must thoroughly understand the boy's changing voice if they are to be at all effective in teaching at the the junior high school level. A view once generally held in Europe, and still believed by some people, is that singers undergoing voice change should refrain from singing until their voices are totally changed and settled. Most teachers in the United States, however, disagree with that concept and believe it is important for boys to continue singing during this time of their lives, but that particular caution should be taken by directors to handle these voices properly.

First of all, explain to all students, both girls and boys, what occurs physiologically when a boy's voice changes:

1. Voice change is a part of growing from a boy into a man; this is a gradual and natural change. The vocal cords in the adolescent male thicken and lengthen approximately one sixth of an inch, and cause the voice to drop an octave in pitch. Accompanying this are changes in the larynx, the structure of muscle and cartilage at the upper end of the trachea. Show anatomical illustrations of this area and discuss them with students to facilitate a more complete understanding (see Figures 46 and 47 in Chapter 2). Show film of the vocal cords in action to all the students in the class.[5]

[3] Credit for the "door prize idea" goes to Janelle Forney, Vocal Music Specialist, O'Dea Elementary School, Poudre R-1 Schools, Fort Collins, Colorado.

[4] The technique regarding the use of the tuning fork was observed at a workshop presented by Jean Ashworth Bartle, Director of the Toronto Children's Chorus.

[5] See, for example, the educational films *The Changing Voice* (45 minutes, 1959, produced by Florida State University) and *The Human Throat* (12 minutes, 1947, produced by Bray Studios,

2. Explain that adolescent males undergo changes in height and body weight, and in sexual characteristics such as the growth of facial and body hair, as well as the development of the Adam's apple, the projection in the front of the throat by the thyroid cartilage.

3. Students should understand that voice changes may begin as early as the fifth or sixth grade or be delayed until high school years. Most boys' voices change, however, when they are in the middle or junior high school. The change may take place in two or three months or it may take a year or so for the complete process. Although the voice may change in pitch in the length of time indicated, it may be several years before the voice is properly settled. Boys may worry about their changing voices when they are now unable to sing the higher notes. Encourage such boys to have patience. It should be understood that rapidly changing voices tend to become baritones or basses; slowly changing voices tend to become tenors.

Duncan McKensie states that, in his opinion, boys' voices begin to change earlier in southern California than in the East, due to the warm climate or perhaps the ethnic background of the singers, as well as in high altitude locations like Salt Lake City, Utah.[6] The author, having once taught at a junior high school in Reno, Nevada, and also in the East and Midwest parts of the United States, concurs with this belief.

It is most important to test boys' voices frequently during the period in which they are changing. Voice tests are advocated at least three times a year: after summer vacations, after Christmas break, and after Easter. Maintain a record that includes data on all voice tests: the boy's voice ranges on given dates, special vocal characteristics, and other pertinent information, such as the boy's age and observations on bodily growth. You should understand that experienced singers, by singing in their falsetto voice range, can sometimes hide their changing voices. So be especially vigilant in your observations of young boy singers. As you work with these voices, you will come to realize that understanding the boy's changing voice is a never-ending process.

Care of the Voice

Advise students on all voice parts never to force or strain their voices, and don't allow them to sing any louder than *mezzo forte* (*mf*). Also, remind students that loud yelling at athletic events can be most injurious to the human voice. Suggest that they restrain themselves whenever possible. The ranges of changing voices will be limited, so when singing any higher pitches have singers do so in a falsetto or very light head voice. Notes out of range—either high or

---

New York). Consult with your school's audiovisual department regarding sources, ordering procedures, and the availability of other similar and more recent films.

[6] Duncan McKensie, *Training the Boy's Changing Voice* (New Brunswick, N.J.: Rutgers University Press, 1956), p. 29.

low—are *not* to be sung. Class periods should begin with careful vocalization. The desirability of downward vocalizing on a five-tone scale pattern is advocated by many music educators.

If at any time a boy's voice breaks or cracks during singing, never allow other students to laugh or taunt the individual involved. Instead, comment positively: "— is becoming more of a man every day." In other words, make all boys proud of their gradual maturation. Never allow such incidents to disrupt the class, and return as soon as reasonably possible to the task at hand. Perhaps at another time remind students that all of the grown men they know today went through this period of the changing voice.

Students should understand the benefits of vocalizing, that its purpose is to improve the voice, and that it is not just an unrelated activity to go through before singing. Describe to young singers the extensive stretching exercises that professional football players go through before their games and compare the two activities. Have a discussion on the reasons that football players believe so strongly in warm-up exercises and taking care of their bodies. Students who have observed football players' warm-ups should be encouraged to describe them to their classmates. The end result of all this talk will hopefully be a more focused period of vocalization.

If any ascending vocalizes are ever used (in an arpeggio, for example), encourage all singers to use their falsetto or light head voices on upper pitches and never carry any heavy tone into the higher register. Use a wide variety of vocalises and alternate them periodically so none will become overused and lose their appeal. It is also essential that you devote time to a discussion and demonstration of proper singing posture and breathing techniques. A class period need not be entirely devoted to singing, but may be varied to include other activities, such as explaining aspects of music theory that may facilitate sight-singing, discussing various aspects of musical style, and listening to recordings of various choral groups.

As a reference point for changing voices, note that the unchanged boy's voice sounds light and clear and boys should be encouraged to sing with this flutelike quality for as long as they are able. Their vocal range is like the girls',

approximately .

Points of View on the Changing Voice

There are four music educators who have contributed substantially to our understanding of the boy's changing voice: Irvin Cooper, Duncan McKensie, Frederick Swanson, and John Cooksey. Their research and writings are listed in the references on the changing voice at the end of the chapter. Each of these men has made a significant contribution to the investigation and literature on the changing voice; however, they do not agree on all aspects of the nature and handling of these voices.

Irvin Cooper refers to the changing voices as *cambiata* (singular, an Italian term meaning changing) or *cambiate* (plural). He describes the collective range of these voices as approximately [musical notation], although in many instances individual voices will be substantially less. Cooper believes that voice changes occur very gradually and that the cambiata voice should not be confused with the boy alto, or alto-tenor. He also feels that after the summer vacation between the eighth and ninth grades, cambiate voices mostly change to baritone, with the following voice range [musical notation].[7] Between the ninth and tenth grades he feels that maturing tenors and basses begin to emerge and become identifiable as such.

Cooper advocates a group voice-testing procedure as follows:

1. Have all the boys sing "Old Folks at Home" ("Swanee River"), by Stephen Foster, in Bb major.
2. Move among the boys, identifying all those singing in the lower octave and tapping them on the shoulder—a signal for them to stop singing.
3. The remaining group consists of the unchanged soprano voices, and the cambiate (changing voices).
4. Have these boys sing the song again, but in the key of Gb major. Move among the group again and silence the identifiable sopranos. The boy sopranos are more readily identified when singing in this key. The remaining singers are cambiate voices.

After one of his well-known demonstrations in which cambiate are identified, Cooper used to state, "These boys are the heart and core of my choir. If you ask them to sing pitches not in their voice ranges they will have problems. If you have them sing within their proper range, they will sing with assurance and not have pitch problems."

A teacher who listens to a boy singing the E above middle C may mistakenly believe the student is singing the E below middle C, because of the unique sound of the boy's voice. Cooper referred to this as the "octave illusion." A teacher may even believe that the student is a baritone or a bass, when actually he is still in the process of voice change, and could eventually even become a tenor.

As for girls' voices in the middle school, Cooper felt that because there was little difference in the range and quality of their voices, there was little point in voice tryouts to determine soprano and alto voices. Instead he simply divided them arbitrarily, that is, "This group will sing soprano, and this group will sing alto," and alternated the parts on different songs.

One of the chief advocates today of the teachings of Irvin Cooper is Don L. Collins, who established the Cambiata Press, P.O. Box 1151, Conway, AR 72032. Cambiata Press publishes music specifically for the needs of changing voices. A copy of their catalog of publications is available upon request from

---

[7] Currently, boys' voices are changing much earlier than in previous years.

Malecki Music, Inc., 4500 Broadmoor St., P.O. Box 150, Grand Rapids, MI 49501 -0150, telephone 1-800-253-9692.

In 1979, the Cambiata Vocal Music Institute of America, Inc. was founded and incorporated as a nonprofit state-chartered institution. The primary purpose of the institute is to train music educators in the comprehensive philosophy and methodology of the cambiata concept by providing a sound basis for teaching vocal music to adolescents. For further information, contact Don L. Collins, the founder/director of the institute, at 1806 Bruce St., Conway, AR 72032, telephone 1-800-643-9967.

Duncan McKensie believes that the boy's unchanged voice moves from Soprano I to Soprano II to Alto and then to the Alto-Tenor range for a given length of time before true baritone and bass voices begin to emerge. McKensie's Alto-Tenor plan is based on the concept of the lowered voice that is still alto due to maturation but can sing in the tenor range. The quality, however, is neither a true tenor or bass. In singing four-part music for boys, it is the third part. The Alto-Tenor range is . Some voices, he feels, may be able to sing a few notes higher and some a few notes lower than the range indicated. McKensie likes to use the speaking voice as one indication of when boys should be considered and tested for a part change.

Following is a summary of McKensie's beliefs:

1. Downward vocalization is beneficial because it prevents the use of the chest voice. McKensie also advises singing with a soft tone.
2. A "rapid" or sudden lowering of the voice indicates that the voice is changing to bass, and a slow lowering indicates a likely change to tenor.[8]
3. If there is ever any doubt about the voice classification of a boy's voice, it is best to assign him to the lower one.
4. During voice changes, boys need to sing in the range where they feel most comfortable. McKensie feels the Alto-Tenor plan allows the greatest flexibility in achieving this goal.
5. The importance of unison singing is often overlooked, and is especially important for the development of vocal tone—in contrast to the use of only vocal exercises to achieve this objective.
6. The extensive use of formal vocal exercises has no place in a program for young adolescent voices; however, such devices as yawning to set the right physical conditions for achieving resonance, and "smelling a flower" to assist in developing proper breathing techniques are recommended.[9]

Frederick Swanson believes that voices often begin to change in the seventh grade and the voice changes rather rapidly, for example, over the summer

---

[8] Duncan McKensie, *Training the Boy's Changing Voice* (New Brunswick, N.J.: Rutgers University Press. 1956), p. 31.

[9] Ibid., pp. 54–55.

vacation or even within a few weeks. He also believes the term *cambiata* to be a misnomer. He indicates the range of the adolescent bass to be approximately

. Swanson indicates that many new basses retain their treble voices, but there is a blank spot between the two ranges. Through the use of a falsetto technique he advocates downward vocalization through the break area, so the two voices can be merged. In SACB arrangements (C means Cambiata), Swanson feels that the cambiata part will be too high for the real tenor voice and too low for the boy alto. Therefore, he advocates the following voice groups—boy alto, true tenor, and "new" bass. His suggested voice ranges are as follows:

Boy Alto   Tenor   Bass

John Cooksey considers the factors of range, tessitura, and vocal timbre to be the most important aspects of each stage of vocal development in the adolescent male.[10]

Cooksey identifies five stages of the changing voice (see Figure 61):

a. Stage 1 is the Boy Soprano, which is at its peak for one to two years. Grade 6 into part of grade 7. Age: 10 to 12.

b. Stage 2 is the Midvoice (or alto) that lasts from three to nine months. Grade 7 or early grade 8. Age 12 to 13.

c. Stage 3 and 3A is the Midvoice 2 that lasts from three to twelve months. This is the cambiata sound. Most boys in this stage are in grade 8. Age: 13 to 14. Cooksey believes this is a crucial period in a boy's vocal development, as alto parts are sometimes too high and tenor parts too low.

d. Stage 4 is the New Baritone voice that lasts from one to two years, and characterizes boys during the latter part of grade 8 or the beginning of grade 9. Age: late 14 or ages 16 to 17.

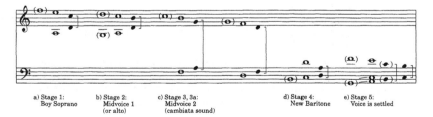

a) Stage 1:   b) Stage 2:   c) Stage 3, 3a: d) Stage 4:   e) Stage 5:
Boy Soprano   Midvoice 1   Midvoice 2   New Baritone   Voice is settled
                 (or alto)   (cambiata sound)

FIGURE 61   Ranges and tessituras for the changing male voice as indicated by John Cooksey. Notes in brackets indicate the tessitura of each voice.

[10] John Cooksey, "The Development of a Contemporary, Eclectic Theory for the Training and Cultivation of the Junior High School Male Changing Voice. Part 2: Scientific and Empirical Findings; Some Tentative Solutions," *The Choral Journal* 18, no. 3 (November 1977), 12.

e. Stage 5 is the time when the voice is reasonably settled even though some development will continue. Begins at age 17 or 18 and continues for some time. [11]

In classifying voices Cooksey prefers an individual assessment, however, and suggests the following procedure when dealing with large groups and when time is an important factor.

1. Ask the entire class (boys and girls) to sing *America* in the key of C major; then have the boys sing alone.
2. Walk around the room, identify boys singing in the lower octave, and ask them to stop singing. These are the baritones.
3. Have the remaining boys sing *America* in the key of F or G major, and identify those singing in the upper octave, which are boy sopranos or Midvoice I's. Assign these voices to a treble part—preferably alto. (Some of these voices may be assigned to tenor even though the part may be too low some of the time.)
4. Again, have the remaining voices sing *America* in F or G. These voices should be Midvoice 2's. Assign them to the tenor part.

Cooksey advocates a rather extensive system of vocalises to develop adequate vocal technique. [12]

Perusing the writings of Cooper, McKensie, Swanson, and Cooksey will help you better understand each point of view. Cooksey's work is explained in four articles published in *The Choral Journal*. The first of these articles, "The Development of a Contemporary Eclectic Theory for the Training and Cultivation of the Junior High School Male Changing Voice; Part 1: Existing Theories," reviews the positions of Irvin Cooper, Duncan McKensie, and Frederick Swanson, and the three other articles explain Cooksey's own point of view.

These four authorities disagree on some matters but agree on others. In studying their writings, combined with actual teaching experience in dealing with young voices, you will necessarily develop your own eclectic point of view—one that works best for you in your particular teaching situation.

After voices have finally settled, their classification should depend on the timbre of the voice and not just the range alone. As the eminent Harry Robert Wilson used to say, "Tenors are made, not born," the implication being that many tenors exist, but have never learned how to use their voices properly—particularly in the upper range. [13]

---

[11] Ibid, 12–14.

[12] See John Cooksey, "The Development of a Contemporary, Eclectic Theory for the Training and Cultivation of the Junior High School Male Changing Voice. Part 3: Developing an Integrated Approach to the Care and Training of the Junior High School Male Changing Voice," *The Choral Journal* 18, no. 4 (December 1977), 12–15.

[13] Harry Robert Wilson, *Artistic Choral Singing* (New York: G. Schirmer, 1959), p. 157.

Selecting Music

In selecting music, vocal range is the most important criterion. Cambiata Press provides quality choral literature arranged to fit the physical limitations of the changing voice. Consult the Appendix for a selected listing of recommended music for cambiate voices.[14] Other publishers that offer music for the changing voice do not usually label the cambiata part as such, but simply as parts 1, 2, and, 3.

Directors who are sensitive to girls' voices understand that true altos do not develop until later years. As previously indicated, Irvin Cooper, in working with large demonstration groups, liked to alternate the girls who were singing the treble parts to provide them equal experience. While some of the special Cambiata Press arrangements are arranged for SACB, a number of others are written for SSCB, with the idea in mind of limiting the lower pitches in the second part. Various other voice arrangements are available for SSC(B), SAB(B), SCB, SA, C/B, SSC, SAC, CCB, CBB, CCBB, SC, SS/CB, and SSACB. Cambiata Press releases a demonstration cassette tape annually that includes some older favorites and widely used arrangements as well as some new releases. These cassette tapes may be obtained from Malecki Music.

With junior high school choirs in which the voices seem reasonably settled, some easy four-part SATB music may be used for certain ninth-grade choirs. But pay particular attention to the tessitura of all voice parts, avoiding any selections that are too high. There are some directors who like to use SAB arrangements for these settled voices, presumably because of their "simplicity." While this music can be useful for some eighth- and ninth-grade choirs, its weakness is sometimes poor voice-leading in the middle and bottom parts. Be careful when selecting such music for choirs. Also, in these arrangements, the baritone part is usually a compromise, with the pitches ranging from the F below middle C to the D or E♭ immediately above middle C.

Cooksey suggests avoiding music that demands "great breadth, sustained intensity, and force in the sound," as in, for example, "How Lovely Is Thy Dwelling Place," by Johannes Brahms. Also avoid music that "contains rapidly shifting harmonies, fast moving rhythms, and angular pitch relationships."[15]

Finally, while singing in parts can be musically satisfying, don't overlook the advantages of using some unison music (with a limited range) or music with descants. The best overall range is B♭ below middle C to B♭ above. An even more comfortable singing tessitura is D to A (above middle C). If any of the male singers are required to sing beyond these limitations the intonation will be

---

[14] Cambiata Press has music available for a variety of voice combinations. For a list of all titles and voice arrangements, write or call Malecki Music, Inc., 4500 Broadmoor St., P.O. Box 150, Grand Rapids, MI 49501-0150, telephone 1-800-253-9692.

[15] John Cooksey, "The Development of a Contemporary Eclectic Theory for the Training and Cultivation of the Junior High School Male Changing Voice. Part 4: Selecting Music for the Junior High School School Male Changing Voice," *The Choral Journal* 18, no. 5 (January 1978), 6.

adversely affected, and many of the boys will be unable to sing in unison at all. The writer recently heard a mixed chorus from a small school in which the boys were actually singing a full half step below the girls for some unexplainable reason. Careful listening, of course, is essential and singing some music in unison where pitch discrepancies are more obvious may help boys to develop better listening habits.

Scheduling and Seating Arrangements

In middle schools (grades 6, 7, and 8), mixed choirs are often offered with students from all grade levels participating. In junior high schools separate choirs are sometimes maintained for both girls and boys. Other schools may offer only a mixed choir for eighth- and ninth-grade students. There are, of course, advantages to both arrangements. A preferable situation, however, is to schedule the boys' rehearsals on Mondays and Wednesdays, the girls' on Tuesdays and Thursdays, and combine the two groups on Fridays. On the days the students are not in choir they often participate in physical education classes. This scheduling arrangement allows the director time to work with the particular problems of the boy's changing voice. Some choral literature of special interest to boys may thus be rehearsed and performed. Additionally, time is available for the rehearsal of parts in preparation for the Friday rehearsals of combined voices. If the school enrollments allow, separate choirs for eighth- and ninth-grade students are preferable to only one junior high school choir.

For mixed ensembles it is desirable to place all the boys in the middle between the sopranos and altos. Additionally, seat the unchanged boys' voices next to the sopranos and the changing boys' voices adjacent to the altos. In such a seating arrangement boys with unchanged voices may sing the soprano or highest part, while the changing voices may sing the alto, cambiata, or tenor parts (see Figure 62). In any reference to voice sections avoid the terms *soprano* and *alto*, but rather refer to the *highest part* (soprano), the *middle part* (altos and changing boys' voices), and the *lowest part* (changed baritone voices). Some

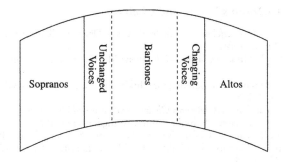

FIGURE 62 A suggested seating arrangement for young mixed choirs with boys' unchanged and changing voices.
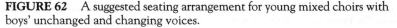

music does not identify the parts as soprano, alto, and baritone, but simply numbers them as parts 1, 2, and 3. This helps to avoid the stigma of boys singing girls' parts. Quite naturally at the early adolescent age, boys hate any reference that classifies them with the girls.

TOPICS FOR DISCUSSION

1. Describe the unique characteristics of both girls' voices and the unchanged boy's voice and contrast these sounds with adult voices. Why should any imitation by children of adult voices be avoided?
2. Describe some desirable procedures for vocalizing children's voices.
3. Discuss the limitations of children's voice ranges and the implications for the selection of music.
4. Describe some unique procedures for beginning the rehearsals of children's choirs.
5. What occurs physiologically when a boy's voice changes?
6. How early in life (age and grade level) may a boy's voice begin to change?
7. What good advice should be given to boys whose voices are beginning to change, and how should these voices be handled in the classroom?
8. Name the four individuals who have made the most unique and significant contributions to the understanding of the boy's changing voice.
9. What does the term *cambiata* mean? What is the plural of this word?
10. Describe the four steps of Irving Cooper's "group" voice testing procedure.
11. Name the six principles of Duncan McKensie's beliefs regarding the boy's changing voice.
12. Discuss the five identifiable stages that John Cooksey believes the boy's changing voice goes through.
13. Describe the four procedures John Cooksey advocates in testing the boy's changing voice.
14. What criteria should directors consider in selecting music for choirs with unsettled and changing voices?

SELECTED READINGS

References on Children's Voices and Choirs

BARTLE, JEAN ASHWORTH. *Lifeline for Children's Choir Directors.* Toronto, Canada: Gordon V. Thompson Music, 1988.

GARRETSON, ROBERT L. *Music in Childhood Education* (2d ed.). Englewood Cliffs, N.J.: Prentice-Hall, 1975.

HITE, TOM. "Some Ideas on Tone Building for Children's Choirs." *Journal of Church Music* 29, no. 8 (October 1987), 7–8.

LEE, JANET, A. *You Can Have a Children's Choir: Create a Joyful Noise with Children: A Step by-Step Guide for Church Leaders.* Nashville, Tenn.: Abingdon Press, 1988.

MCRAE, SHIRLEY W. *Directing the Children's Choir.* New York: Schirmer Books, 1991.

PHILLIPS, KENNETH H. "Training the Child Voice." *Music Educators Journal* 72, no. 4 (December 1985), 19–22, 57–58.

RAO, DOREEN. ed. *Choral Music for Children.* Reston, Va.: Music Educators National Conference, 1990.

———. *The Young Singing Voice.* New York: Boosey & Hawkes, 1987.

SWEARS, LINDA. *Teaching the Elementary School Chorus.* West Nyack, N.Y.: Parker Publishing Company, 1985.

TUFTS, NANCY POORE. ed. *The Children's Choir.* Philadelphia: Fortress Press, 1965.

References on the Boy's Changing Voice

ADCOCK, EVA. "The Changing Voice—The Middle/Junior High Challenge." *The Choral Journal* 28, no. 3 (October 1987), 9–11.

BUSCH, STEPHEN E. "Some Voice Classifications and Developments in Young Adolescent Choirs." *The Choral Journal* 14, no. 1 (September 1973), 21–24.

COFFMAN, WESLEY, S. "The Changing Voice—The Elementary Challenge." *The Choral Journal* 28, no. 3 (October 1987), 5–7.

COLLINS, DON L. *The Cambiata Concept: A Comprehensive Philosophy and Methodology of Teaching Music to Adolescents.* Conway, Ark.: Cambiata Press, 1981.

———. "The Changing Voice—A Future Challenge." *The Choral Journal* 28, no. 3 (October 1987), 19–20.

———. "The Changing Voice—The High School Challenge." *The Choral Journal* 28, no. 3 (October 1987), 13–17.

COOKSEY, JOHN M. "The Development of a Contemporary Eclectic Theory for the Cultivation of the Junior High School Male Changing Voice. Part 1: Existing Theories." *The Choral Journal* 28, no. 2, (October 1977), 5–14.

———. "The Development of a Contemporary Eclectic Theory for the Cultivation of the Junior High School Male Changing Voice. Part 2: Scientific and Empirical Findings; Some tentative Solutions." *The Choral Journal* 18, no. 3, (November, 1977), 5–16.

———. "The Development of a Contemporary Eclectic Theory for the Cultivation of the Junior High School Male Changing Voice. Part 3: Developing an Integrated Approach to the Care and Training of the Junior High School Male Changing Voice." *The Choral Journal* 18, no.4, (December 1977), 5–15.

———. "The Development of a Contemporary Eclectic Theory for the Cultivation of the Junior High School Male Changing Voice. Part 4: Selecting Music for the Junior High School Male Changing Voice." *The Choral Journal* 18, no. 5, (January 1978), 5–15.

COOPER, IRVIN. *Changing Voices in Junior High, "Letters to Pat."* New York: Carl Fischer, 1953.

———. "Study of Boy's Changing Voices in Great Britain." *Music Educators Journal* 51, no. 3 (November-December, 1964) 118–20.

———. AND KARL O. KUERSTEINER. *Teaching Junior High Music* (2d ed.). Boston: Allyn Bacon, 1970.

GROOM, MARY. *A Descriptive Analysis of Development in Adolescent Male Voices During the Summer Time Period.* Ph. D. dissertation, Florida State University, 1979.

GUSTAFSON, JOHN M. *A Study Relating to the Boy's Changing Voice: Its Incidence, Training, and Function in Choral Music.* Ph.D. dissertation, Florida State University, 1956.

HULS, H. S. *The Adolescent Voice: A Study.* New York: Vantage Press, 1957.

JOSEPH, WARREN. "A Summation of the Research Pertaining to Vocal Growth." *Journal of Researh in Music Education* 13 (Summer 1965), 93–100.

MCKENSIE, DUNCAN. "The Boy's Changing Voice." *Music Journal* 14, 9, (November 1956), 29, 38–39.

MCKENSIE, DUNCAN. "Training the Boy's Changing Voice." New Brunswick, N.J.: Rutgers University Press, 1956.

SWANSON, FREDERICK, J. "The Changing Voice: An Adventure, Not a Hazard." 16, *The Choral Journal* no. 7, (March 1976), 5–14.

———. "Changing Voices: Don't Leave Out the Boys," *Music Educators Journal* 10, no. 5 (January 1984), 45–50.

———. "Do We Short Change Our Boy Singers?" *Music Journal* 70, no. 7, (October 1959), 56–58, 84.

———. *The Male Voice Ages Eight to Eighteen.* Cedar Rapids. Iowa: Laurance Press, 1977.

———. *Music Teaching in the Junior High and Middle School.* New York: Appleton-Century-Crofts, 1973.

———. " The Proper Care and Feeding of Changing Voices," *Music Educators Journal* 48, no. 2 (November-December 1961), 63–66.

———. "The Vanishing Basso Profundo Fry Tones." *The Choral Journal* 17, no. 5 (January 1977), 5–10.

————. *Voice Mutation in the Adolescent Male: An Experiment in Guiding the Voice Development of Adolescent Boys in General Music Classes.* Unpublished Ph.D. dissertation, University of Wisconsin, 1959.

VIDEOTAPES

Barresi on Adolescent Voice, by Anthony Barresi. The University of Wisconsin at Madison, Department of Continuing Education in the Arts.

Gotta Sing . . . Gotta Dance! by John Jacobson, Step 4—Movement and Staging for the Young Choir. Hal Leonard Music Publishing Corporation, No. 08414640.

The Children's Choir with the Glen Ellyn Children's Chorus and immediate past conductor, Doreen Rao. American Choral Directors Association, Volume 1.

5

Style
and Interpretation

Your primary function as the conductor is to interpret the music. You must interpret it in such a way that the intentions of the composer are brought to life and projected to the audience. To do this properly, you need, among other qualities, a clear concept of the music's basic style. *Musical style* may be simply defined as the distinctive manner or mode in which musical thought is expressed. It includes those characteristics that make a particular musical work uniquely different from others.

An understanding of the main historical periods, as well as the different styles within each period, is a requisite to the proper interpretation of any composer's music. Basic styles of art expression change periodically as a result of various social, political, and economic forces. Although the characteristics of the music of any one period begin to develop in the previous period and carry over to the next, various points of demarcation may be determined. The main currents of musical expression since the year 1400 may be divided into five periods as follows: *the Renaissance period* (ca. 1400–1600), *the Baroque period* (1600–1750), *the Classic period* (1750–1820), *the Romantic period* (1800–1900), and the *Modern period* (1890 to the present).

Although the characteristics of the music of each period could be presented in a variety of ways, we have chosen the following five factors for discussion: meter and stress, tempo, dynamics, texture, and expressive aspects of the music. These factors have undergone change, were often distinctly different during the various periods, and can be controlled somewhat by the conductor in striving toward his or her interpretative goals.

THE RENAISSANCE PERIOD

Although we should not forget that cultural change is a slowly moving process and that ascribing particular dates to certain periods is an arbitrary matter, the approximate 200-year period that we call the *Renaissance* (ca. 1400–1600) does have certain salient characteristics. In some circles of European society, the religious orientation declined before rising secular interests. This shift of interest culminated in the development of modern scientific inquiry in the seventeenth century. Renaissance intellectuals began to emphasize their destiny here on earth, rather than considering life as only a prelude to the hereafter. They developed new confidence in their ability to solve their own problems and to determine their own fate. The wisdom of the Church usually was not denied, but in addition, the claims of other sources of truth were staked out.

Despite the considerable discussion that has taken place, there appears to be some uncertainty as to the exact beginning of the Renaissance period, but the year 1400 seems to be the most suitable date. Jeppesen concurs with this date and offers the following well-founded reasons:

> As far as can be discerned at present, there is a marked and very significant boundary line, especially in a musico-technical respect, at about the transition from the 14th to the 15th century. What happened at that time may be characterized as a change in the conception of consonance—the definite, practical recognition of the 3rd and 6th as not only having privileges in musical art equal to the 4th, 5th and 8th, but moreover as main consonants—tonal combinations decidedly preferred above all others, and regarded as fundamental factors in musical composition.[1]

Meter and Stress

Most of the music of the Renaissance period was unmetered, with stress occurring only through the emphasis of particular syllables in important words. The barline, with the resultant stress on the first beat of the measure, generally was not used. Although the barline did come into being during the latter part of the period, it was used only as a "measure" of elapsed time and as a means of keeping the singers together.[2] When metrical stress is used for music of this period, the inherent beauties and flow of the vocal lines are destroyed.

[1] Knud Jeppesen, *The Style of Palestrina and the Dissonance*, 2d ed. (Copenhagen: Ejnar Munksgaard, Publisher, and New York: Oxford University Press, 1946), p. 222. Used by permission.

[2] As a convenience to the singers, modern-day publishers employ several means to facilitate the reading of Renaissance music. Some employ the use of regular barlines; others utilize dotted barlines as a means of minimizing the natural stress following the barline. Still other publishers use

In Figure 63, an excerpt from Palestrina's *Missa Papae Marcelli* is shown, illustrating the use of the traditional barlines. The normal syllabic accents occurring on the words "*Ple*-ni sunt *coe*-li et *ter*-ra" are obscured, and the rhythmic counterpoint so necessary to the music does not occur with this manner of barring. Figure 63b, however, is barred according to the natural accent of the text, thus revealing the beauties of the rhythmic complexity of the music.

The conductor should be always alert to the tendency of singers to stress certain figures of rhythmic groupings in a manner that is inimical to the proper interpretation. For example, in the motet *Cantantibus Organis* by Marenzio (Pustet, No. B32), singers often have a tendency to stress, in a somewhat mechanical manner, the first and third of each group of four eighth notes (Figure 64). This practice should be avoided, because stress should occur only through the natural accent of particular syllables in important words. The sacred music of this period, in particular, should be performed in a smooth, flowing manner, and phrases should be thought of in terms of long ascending and descending lines.

Remind the singers to think always melodically and never chordally, except when tuning various intervals, and to avoid the regular recurring accents common to barred music. To help achieve the correct syllabic stress, ask the singers to read the text aloud with accents in the correct place and in accordance with the rise and fall of the various vocal lines. Use the *tactus*, or downward and upward movement of the hand and arm, to minimize any tendency toward metrical stress and to allow for the interplay of rhythmic polyphony.[3]

Tempo

The tempo of Renaissance music is determined largely by the syllabic setting of the text and the mood of the music. When one syllable is set to a melodic figure (*melisma*), the tempo should be restrained so that the inherent beauty of the vocal line may be revealed. On the other hand, when each syllable is set to a different note of a comparatively longer duration, the tempo may be pushed slightly forward.

The tempo should remain relatively steady throughout the entire composition, or at least throughout a particular section. Any change in tempo should result only through a contrasting change in the mood of the text and a resultant change in the musical texture. Any changes in tempo within a given

a short vertical line before certain words at regularly spaced intervals to serve as a guide to the singers.

[3] Each tactus has two beats in opposite directions—up-down or down-up (usually the latter is employed)—each one at a tempo ranging between M.M. = 60–80. This tempo was related to man's normal heartbeat (during quiet respiration) or his leisurely walking stride; thus the tempo of Renaissance music remained relatively steady. Both movements of the tactus were made with equal force whether it was conceived as down-up or up-down. For a further discussion of tactus, see Curt Sachs, *Rhythm and Tempo* (New York: W. W. Norton, 1953), pp 202–33.

FIGURE 63 Excerpt from *Missa Papae Marcelli*, by Palestrina: (*a*) illustrates the use of traditional barlines; (*b*) is barred according to the natural accent of the text. From *A History of Music and Musical Style*, by Homer Ulrich and Paul A. Pisk, © 1963 by Harcourt Brace Jovanovich, Inc.

FIGURE 63 (*cont.*)

section should be extremely gradual and subtle, lest the symmetry of the music be destroyed.

Rallentando, as we know it today, did not exist in the music of the Renaissance period. Composers of the period were, however, aware of this effect, and when it was felt desirable they made it a part of the music itself. That is, they

FIGURE 64   An excerpt from the series *Cantantibus Organis*. Madrigal by Luca Marenzio, in which mechanical stress should be avoided in the eight-note groupings in measures 2, 3, and 4, and the music performed in a smooth, flowing manner. Used by permission of Otto Heinrich Noetzel Verlag, Wilhelmshaven BRD.

achieved the effect by simply broadening or lengthening the musical notation. Therefore, avoid the deliberate use of rallentando, because this would only distort the musical interpretation.[4]

A somewhat greater freedom, however, exists in the performance of madrigals and related genre than in the masses and the motets of the Renais-

[4] Cf. Sachs, *Rhythm and Tempo*, pp. 218–19.

sance period. Madrigal composers were captivated by the expressive qualities of the words. The mood of the text, therefore, is an essential determining factor in the selection of the correct tempo (and the proper dynamics). Restraint and avoidance of extremes, however, should always be paramount in the conductor's mind.

Dynamics

The dynamics of the music of this period are related to and are dependent on any changes of mood in the text. Changes in dynamics would occur only as with changes in tempo—that is, with a contrasting mood between sections of the music. Within the overall framework of the music, however, dynamic levels should be moderate; extremes should seldom occur. Owing to the high degree of consonance, the pervading imitation, the lack of harmonic complexity, and the restraints inherent in the style, a climax seldom occurred and was not even sought by composers of the period.[5]

Through the use of the seamless technique, cadences were overlapped or dovetailed; that is, one phrase ended in two or more of the parts, while another began in the other parts. Through this technique many cadences were minimized, thus lessening the necessity for dynamic changes. It should be added, however, that dynamics, especially in the madrigal, frottola, and canto carnascialesco, may be realized simply through the natural tessitura of the voices, as well as in the intensity of the word symbolism.

Texture

The music of the period was primarily contrapuntal in texture; that is, the various vocal lines were conceived as horizontal in nature. Composers wrote using anywhere from three to six or more parts. When first examining music of the period, you might feel that some compositions or portions of others were conceived harmonically rather than contrapuntally. Upon careful examination, however, you will often discover that, for example, the third in a particular part may be omitted in an effort to achieve the best movement in the various vocal lines.[6]

Imitation as a contrapuntal device was used by composers from Dufay through the remainder of the period. The term *point of imitation* pertains to the introduction of a figure or motive in one part that is taken up successively in the other parts. These points of imitation should be emphasized slightly. The entrances need to be definite and precise, but vigorous accents are out of place and should be avoided. These entering parts should be brought out slightly, but

[5] Cf. Robert Stevenson, *Music before the Classic Era* (London: Macmillan & Co. Ltd., 1955), p. 42.
[6] See, for example, Jeppesen, *The Style of Palestrina*, p. 92.

should never overshadow the other contrapuntal lines. As other parts enter, they should recede into the background.

Expressive Aspects

The sacred music of the Renaissance period sounds remote and restrained, primarily because of the large degree of consonance. There was a wide use of unisons, thirds, fifths, sixths, octaves, and triad sounds. Dissonance of the unprepared variety was used sparingly and was considered something "vehement and violent." Therefore, the objective was to conceal or muffle it insofar as was possible.[7]

Renaissance music possesses very subtle points of harmonic arrival. As previously mentioned, with the seamless technique phrases were overlapped or dovetailed; that is, one phrase ended in two or more parts, while another began in the other parts. Through this technique many cadences were somewhat obscured and the tension of the cadence was minimized. Search out all the suspensions in Renaissance music, mark them in your score, and have the chorus lean on them ever so slightly during performance.

The masses and the motets of the Renaissance are impersonal in nature and should be performed with an atmosphere of quiet reflection and sincerity of feeling—in other words, as a prayer to God, and not as a concert. The tone quality, therefore, should be kept light and clear, with a minimum of vibrato. Heavy dramatic quality and excessive vibrato in the voices are inimical to the expressive character of the music; both should be eliminated.[8]

Renaissance music, when performed correctly, sounds remote and restrained. The resonance in the church or the hall in which it was originally performed contributed substantially to this effect. The impersonal quality of Renaissance sacred music is comparable to the detachment that may be observed in certain paintings of the period in which the Madonna is not caressing her child, but is maintaining a distance from him.[9]

---

[7] Ibid., p. 108.

[8] Singing in the early Church was limited to the voices of men and boys. During the early part of the Renaissance period, men singing in their falsetto voices often were used to reinforce the boys' voices. During the sixteenth century, falsettists eventually supplanted the boys and sang the treble, or upper two, voice parts. Today, these voices are called *countertenors*. An excellent example of their use and how these voices might have sounded during the Renaissance is demonstrated by the King's Singers (see the *Schwann Record Catalog* for a listing of their available recordings). Since choral conductors are concerned with authentic performance practices and since today's choirs use women (rather than falsettists) on the treble parts, the tone quality should be light and clear, with a minimum of vibrato—if any is used at all. Perhaps the best model of mixed voices performing Renaissance motets is the Roger Wagner Chorale in their album *Echoes from a 16th-Century Cathedral* (Angel S-36013).

For further information on the use of the falsetto voice during the Renaissance, see Robert L. Garretson, "The Falsettists," *The Choral Journal* 24, no. 1 (September 1983), 5–9.

[9] See, for example, the painting *The Niccolini-Cowper Madonna* by Raphael (1483–1520).

A somewhat greater freedom existed with the madrigals and related secular styles of the period. Composers were well aware of the expressive qualities of the text and often employed word painting in their music. That is, they used the music to portray, in a variety of ways, the character of certain words. For example, leaps in the melody were often used to depict joy, while the voices might ascend on such words as *heaven* and descend on words such as *earth*. To depict grief and sadness, a diminished or an augmented triad was often used, and dissonance was employed to represent such words as *sadness* and *pain*.

Study the score and identify the various word-painting devices employed by the composer, and for an effective performance, lead the singers to an understanding of those devices. The music must be sung with an emotional expressiveness that can result only through proper understanding of it. Secular music of the period, although light in texture, should never be sung in an insipid manner. The rhythmic interplay among the voices should be emphasized somewhat, and the text articulated in a crisp manner, especially in English secular music. While a firmness of approach is necessary to performance, the inherent emotion in the music should not be allowed to run rampant; rather, the music should be performed with a certain degree of restraint.[10]

THE BAROQUE PERIOD

The Baroque period began toward the end of the sixteenth century and is generally considered to have ended by 1750, the year of the death of Johann Sebastian Bach. The word *baroque* is said to have originated from *barrôco*, a Portuguese word meaning "a pearl of irregular form." In the nineteenth century, the term was used in a pejorative manner, implying that the exceptionally ornate style of the arts of this period was in poor taste and a debasement of the Renaissance style. Today, however, such a connotation of the word has largely disappeared and the Baroque is considered to be one of the greatest periods of dramatic expression.

The art forms of the Baroque period were characterized by expansiveness, grandeur, and impressiveness. Baroque architecture was expansive and monumental; paintings were dynamic, alive with color, and filled with the tension of opposing masses; and the interior decoration of churches was highly ornate and dramatic.

Through the Counter-Reformation, beginning about the middle of the sixteenth century, the papacy, utilizing all its resources, set out to regain the faith of the people previously lost to Protestantism. The Counter-Reformation sought converts by trying to reach the spiritual through the senses. A vigorous program, incorporating the impressive aspects of all the arts, was put into action. As a result, cultural forms were developed that were both grandiose and sublime.

[10] For a further discussion on the interpretation of madrigals, see Charles Kennedy Scott *Madrigal Singing* (London: Oxford University Press, 1931).

The period of the early Baroque began to take form during the pontificate of Sixtus V (1585–90), and the new Catholicism was reflected in all the arts.

> The early baroque was, at first, a period of Catholic churchly art, and it was again the Society of Jesus which gave this art its peculiar traits of character. From the sphere of quiet devotion, the faithful were lifted into the world of the triumphant Church whose cult was celebrated by richly decked clergy under the vaults of a mighty architecture, surrounded by statues and pictures, before scintillating altars ornamented with gold and silver, to the accompaniment of the impressive and resonant music of multiple choirs, orchestras, and organs. In elaborate processions with flags, candles, and torches, triumphal carriages, floats, and arches, with the marchers singing, accompanying soldiers' bands blaring forth with their trumpets, the bells tolling and cannon booming, priests and students, guilds and corporations with their emblems, princes and the populace all united to demonstrate their adherence to the regenerated triumphal Church.[11]

Whereas the Counter-Reformation prompted the creation of a vast amount of sacred art, Protestantism showed little interest in pictorial and decorative art, presumably because such churchly ornamentation would be contrary to the evangelical precepts of the church.[12] Protestant piety held that the proper reverence to God's word would be weakened if the congregation's attention was diverted by ornaments and decorations. In the main, therefore, the Protestant churches remained relatively simple, their architecture merely imitating that of pre-Reformation times. Although music also suffered as a result of this artistic hostility, it was the one art form that eventually became an integral part of the reformed faiths. After a while, music came to epitomize the highest degree of artistic expression in Protestantism.[13]

Meter and Stress

The barline and metered music came into being during the Baroque period; accentuations, therefore, generally occur at regularly spaced intervals. To evoke these accentuations in the performance of Baroque music, use a definite and precise beat. This approach is particularly appropriate for music such as Schütz's *Cantate Domino canticum novum* (Bourne, No. B201889). Avoid, however, a mechanical, machinelike stress following each barline. For example, in Carissimi's *Plorate filii Israel* (Bourne, No. B210369, E. C. Schirmer, No. 1172), a broad legato style with a minimum of stress is required. Analyze each selection under

---

[11] Paul Henry Lang, *Music in Western Civilization* (New York: W. W. Norton, 1941), p. 319. Copyright renewed 1968 by Paul Henry Lang.

[12] Extreme Calvinists sometimes went so far as to destroy stained glass windows and smash religious statues in their rejection of traditional symbolism.

[13] Lang, *Music in Western Civilization*, pp. 320–21.

consideration, and particularly each phrase, to determine those places requiring greater stress—sometimes those notes at the peak of the phrase.[14]

The frames of Baroque paintings usually did not encompass the entirety of a particular scene, but often cut through various objects, thus giving the illusion of boundless space.[15] Composers achieved a similar effect by often beginning their music on a beat following a rest, thus providing the feeling to the listener that the music was a continuation of something that had already been underway. This delayed entrance effected a tension and rhythmic drive leading to the nearest downbeat.[16]

The practice of lengthening the dotted note and shortening the complementary note is an important consideration in the proper interpretation of Baroque music. For example, the rhythm ¢ 𝄾 ♫♩. ♩ | should often be performed as ¢ 𝄾𝄾 ♫. 𝄾 ♩ | and ⁶⁄₈ ♩. ♩ ♩. ♩ | as ⁶⁄₈ ♩.. 𝄾 ♩.. 𝄾 | . Why is it that the composers did not indicate what they desired? Simply because it was easier to tell the performers how the music should be performed than to write out the notation. This treatment of the dotted note began during the early part of the seventeenth century and carried through to the beginning of the nineteenth century. The music of Monteverdi, Purcell, Bach, and Handel (as well as the later music of Haydn, Mozart, and Beethoven) all necessitate this treatment.[17] During the latter part of the eighteenth century, however, composers began to indicate more carefully their desired intentions in the music.

The purpose of this practice is the achievement of a crisp, clear manner of articulation, as opposed to a lazy and sluggish treatment. This manner of articulation also minimizes the tendency for performers to rush their parts. Of course, conductors should use discretion in applying this convention. One criterion for consideration is the general character of the music; that is, the lengthening of the dotted notes would be more appropriate to brilliant and majestic music and somewhat less appropriate to music of a lifting, graceful character.

A different treatment of dotted rhythms, however, should occur with trochaic rhythms in compound triple meter, which are sometimes written as dotted rhythms. For example, the rhythm notated as ³⁄₄ ♩. ♩ ♩. ♩ ♫♫³ | should be performed as ⁹⁄₈ ♩ ♪ ♩ ♪ ♫♫ | . To determine the proper handling of these

---

[14] It should be mentioned that in the Baroque period, two basic stylistic practices existed—the *stilo antico* and the *stilo moderno*. In the *stilo antico*, or old style, which was suitable for the Church, the music dominated the text. In the *stilo moderno*, or new style, the text dominated the music. These styles are sometimes referred to as *strict style* and *free style*. Some composers (Eberlin, for example) mixed these styles, rather than keeping them separate.

[15] See, for example, the painting *Landscape with the Chateau of Steen* (1636) by Peter Paul Rubens (1577–1640).

[16] Sachs, *Rhythm and Tempo*, p. 266.

[17] Thurston Dart, *The Interpretation of Music*, rev. ed. (London: Hutchinson Publishing Group Ltd., 1960), pp. 81–82.

rhythms, analyze the music; when the dominant rhythm is compound triple meter (often determined by the triplet groupings), than the passage should be performed as indicated in the second example in this paragraph.[18]

A somewhat more controversial problem is encountered in the handling of dotted eighth notes against triplets. An examples of this occurs in the Bach sacred cantata No. 4, *Christ lag in Todesbanden* ("Christ Lay in Death's Dark Prison"), *Versus VI.*[19] The dotted rhythm ♩♪ ♩♪ in the bass line of the orchestral accompaniment (continuo) occurs against the triplet figure ♩♩♩♩ in the parts for soprano and tenor. As a general rule, duplets should yield to triplets.[20] In this case the dotted eighth note should coincide with the first two triplets and the sixteenth note with the last triplet (Figure 65).[21]

Tempo

The tempo of baroque music should generally be moderate and deliberate, and extremes should be avoided. Even fast tempi should be performed with some restraint. During the Baroque period, Italian terms, such as *allegro* and *largo*, were used to indicate the character of the music, rather than as specific tempo markings. As a result some conductors, misunderstanding the meaning of these terms, are inclined to rush the music marked *allegro* and *vivace*, and to conduct too slowly music marked *adagio* and *largo*. Italian markings should be considered as an indication of mood rather than tempo. *Allegro* should be interpreted literally,

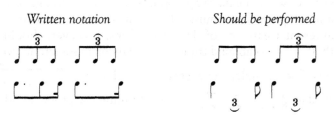

Written notation   *Should be performed*

FIGURE 65

[18] Ibid., p. 89.

[19] Another example of this problem occurs in Bach's *Jesu, Joy of Man's Desiring* (E.C. Schirmer, No. 317).

[20] For an example of the suggested interpretation, listen to the recording by the Robert Shaw Chorale, RCA Victor LSC-2273.

[21] For a further discussion of dotted rhythms, see Sachs, *Rhythm and Tempo*, pp. 303–6, and Dart, *The Interpretation of Music*, pp. 81–83, 88–89, 111, 125–26, and 171.

as merry, lively, brisk, rather than as fast; *largo* should be considered as simply broad, rather than as very slow.[22]

Handel often wrote the Italian marking *largo* at the end of many of his sacred choruses. The composer's intent in adding this marking at the end of a chorus implies simply that the quarter note for the *allegro* becomes exactly twice as long for the *largo*; for example, if the *allegro* has been conducted at ♩ = 120, then the *largo* will be conducted at ♩ = 60. He also, however, sometimes wrote notes of a larger or greater value as a means of achieving the desired intention of *largo*, that is, simply broad. For the conductor to further slow down the pulse of the music would make the ending too slow and thus distort the desired effect.[23]

In the early Baroque monody, a considerable flexibility existed in the tempo so that the emotions in the text and the music might be fully expressed. In the late 1630s, however, a reversal of this trend occurred and the tempi of music became more strict and restrained.[24] The relative freedom of emotional expression gave way to rhythmical shifts within a stricter tempo.

According to Machlis, one of the most notable characteristics of Baroque music is its steady pulsation or unflagging rhythm.[25]

> The Baroque, with its fondness for energetic movement, demanded a dynamic rhythm based on the regular recurrence of accent. The bass part became the carrier of the new rhythm. Its relentless beat is an arresting trait in many compositions of the Baroque. This steady pulsation, once under way, never slackens or deviates until the goal is reached. It imparts to Baroque music its unflagging drive, producing the same effect of turbulent yet controlled motion as animates Baroque painting, sculpture, and architecture.[26]

Although a steady pulsating drive is important to proper interpretation, this does not mean that the tempo should be completely unyielding. For instance, at cadences immediately prior to subsequent sections, a slight holding back of the tempo is often desirable. The exact treatment of each cadence, however, will vary according to the music itself.[27] In reference to the handling of cadences *Grove's* states:

[22] Richard T. Gore, "The Performance of Baroque Church Music," *Music Teachers National Association, Volume of Proceedings* 1950 (Pittsburgh: The Association, 1953), pp. 156–57.

[23] Ibid., p. 157.

[24] Sachs, *Rhythm and Tempo*, pp. 265–66.

[25] Exceptions to this general characteristic of Baroque music are the *recitative*, which is sung in a declamatory style with stress or accent occurring as a result of important words or particular syllables, and the *arioso*, which in style lies somewhere between the recitative and the aria and possesses some of the characteristics of each.

[26] Joseph Machlis, *The Enjoyment of Music*, 5th ed. (New York: W. W. Norton & Co., Inc., 1984), pp. 361–62.

[27] For a discussion of conflicting viewpoints in regard to tempo changes, see Sachs, *Rhythm and Tempo*, pp. 277–80.

Each needs its own natural flexibility, though this may vary according to circumstances from the merest easing scarcely consciously perceptible, at the one
extreme, to a majestic broadening at the other. It is for the performer to judge on
the merits of each case between sentimental excess and self-conscious rigidity. [28]

Accelerando and ritardando (or rallentando) are inappropriate and out of
place in baroque music, principally because these concepts of gradually increasing or gradually decreasing the tempo did not exist in this period. These concepts grew out of the Mannheim school in the latter part of the eighteenth
century. Another concept, often misunderstood, is the treatment of the fermata.
A fermata in baroque music simply indicates the end of a phrase and a point at
which the singers may take a breath. The concept of the fermata as an untimed
hold developed during the latter part of the eighteenth century, as did also the
modern concept of accelerando and ritardando.

Dynamics

The concept of crescendo and decrescendo did not widely exist during the
Baroque period, principally because the instruments of the period did not have
the necessary flexibility to achieve these ends. The organ, for example, did not
possess swell shutters, and the piano was not invented until the latter part of
the period. Therefore, contrast was sought by other means. [29] Contrast in
dynamics was achieved by adding or dropping out various instruments or voice
parts. This was referred to as *terraced dynamics*, meaning various levels or
plateaus of dynamics. Extremes in dynamics, therefore, should be avoided,
because the concept of terraced dynamics would render them undesirable. [30]
Usually the music itself will take care of the often slight dynamic changes in
terraced dynamics, and you should question editorial markings that seem to
place undue emphasis on these changes. Terraced dynamics are only part of the
change, however. The other is the density due to the increase or decrease of the
number of voices participating. Composers up through J. S. Bach generally did
not include dynamic markings, but in those instances where they did, it was to
make clear a change that might not have been recognized in the performance
practice of the time or where an absolute insistence of change seemed necessary
by the composer. Utilize a dynamic range only from *piano* to *forte*. Extending

[28] Eric Blom, ed., *Grove's Dictionary of Music and Musicians*, Volume 2 (New York: St. Martin's Press, Macmillan & Co., Ltd., 1954), p. 986. Used by permission of Macmillan, London and
Basingstoke.

[29] According to *Grove's Dictionary of Music and Musicians*, 5th ed., crescendo and
decrescendo were not entirely unknown to baroque composers, since written indications of it are
found in the mid-seventeenth-century music of the Italian composer Mazzochi (*Grove's*, Vol. 2, p.
988).

[30] Gore, "The Performance of Baroque Church Music," pp. 157–58.

the dynamics above or below these levels is inappropriate and should generally be avoided except on rare occasions.

Texture

The beginning of the Baroque period ushered in a change from a texture of independent but interrelated parts to a single melody or voice part supported by chords or chordal combinations. This change from modal polyphony to a homophonic style necessitated a change in the harmonic system—from the medieval church modes to a system of major and minor tonality. Whereas the polyphony of the Renaissance symbolized the submissiveness of the individual, the new style fulfilled the need for greater individual expression. Secular music gained vastly in importance, and the new style allowed for a greater emotional expression of the text. When polyphony returned, after a brief lapse, it did so within a different harmonic framework—the system of major-minor tonality.[31] Even when the new harmonic counterpoint came into vogue, some composers continued to write in the old style polyphony (*stile antico*), sometimes called the Palestrina style. Conductors, therefore, need to recognize and treat each style accordingly.

Because Baroque polyphony functions within a harmonic framework of tonality and generally well-defined chord progressions, cadences are important aspects of arrival, but may be different according to the overall texture of the music; that is, some may be lighter and others heavier (see previous section on tempo for a discussion on the treatment of cadences). Also, the complexity of the texture as well as the complexity of the chords, especially when some have been chromatically altered, may have an influence on the tempo of the music. In lighter textures the tempo may be pushed slightly forward; in denser textures the tempo may be held back somewhat. As to imitations, answering voices should be replicas of the announcing voice's treatment of the subject, including specific rhythmic patterns, trills, and so on.

Expressive Aspects

In contrast to the Renaissance composer, who expressed emotion with considerable restraint, Baroque composers gave freer vent to their emotions. Nevertheless, their music was still somewhat impersonal, with the emotion stemming not from an individual struggle, as in the Romantic period, but from the tumultuous and dramatic forces affecting all humankind.[32]

---

[31] While polyphony was rejected by most composers during the early Baroque period, it was never abandoned by the famous three S's: Johann Herman Schein (1586–1630), Samuel Scheidt (1587–1654), and Heinrich Schütz (1585–1672).

[32] George Howerton, *Technique and Style in Choral Singing* (New York: Carl Fischer, 1957), p. 133.

Within the new system of major-minor tonality, each chord assumed a definite relationship to the others. Harmonic tension and repose were well understood by composers of the period and were used as devices in composition. There were fewer but stronger cadences, and the drive to the keynote was apparent. There was a considerable increase in the intensity of the music and in the amount of dissonance that was used for the purpose of achieving emotional intensity. Whereas in the Renaissance period dissonance was permissible only when prepared—that is, when first heard with a consonant interval and introduced through a suspension—the use of unprepared dissonance became accepted and widely used as an expressive device.[33]

Tone painting, or the way in which the music portrayed the words, was increasingly given attention by composers of the period. Bach, for example, advised his students to "play the chorale according to the meaning of the words." It must be understood, however, that although the text gave birth to the musical idea, it was the music itself that ultimately reigned supreme.[34]

The Baroque period marked the first time in history that instrumental music assumed an equal position with vocal music. The spirit of the times prompted the development of new instruments and the improvements of the old. The new status of instrumental music has caused certain people to say that some music was conceived instrumentally rather than vocally. The performance of Baroque music, therefore, necessitates a most exacting rhythmic precision. Singers should be as exacting as instrumentalists. They should also maintain a steadiness and a purity of vocal line, devoid of excessive vibrato, since this may adversely affect the intonation and thus blur the polyphonic structure. These qualities are especially important in singing contrapuntal music.

The matter of the proper pitch level at which to perform Baroque music should be given due consideration. Between approximately 1600 and 1820, the standard accepted pitch level—although there were many deviations—was about a semitone lower than the present A-440. The implications of this fact are that, to perform Baroque music in as authentic a manner as possible, we ought to lower the pitch a half step to return it to its original key. Of course, practical considerations such as the difficulty of transposing the orchestral parts, or even the piano or organ accompaniment, often make this practice unfeasible. Another argument against this practice is the additional brilliance that is often achieved through performance in the higher key. On the other hand, when the tessitura of the various parts appears to be too high and thus negatively influences the tone quality, you may consider lowering the pitch. If you elect to do so, you then will have at least two justifications for your decision. By and large, however, you will minimize your problems if you perform the music in the key in which it is presently written.

---

[33] Claudio Monteverdi (1567-1643) is often credited with the first wide use of unprepared dissonance.

[34] Machlis, *The Enjoyment of Music*, 5th ed., pp. 360–61.

THE CLASSIC PERIOD

While Bach and Handel were carrying the Baroque style to its culmination in the first half of the eighteenth century, forces were already at work leading toward the formulation of a new style. The Classic era, generally considered to cover the period from 1750 to 1820, includes such diverse aesthetic trends as the Rococo (*Stile galant*), *empfindsamer Stil* (literally, "sensitive style"), Enlightenment, and *Sturm und Drang* (storm and stress). The Classic period thus lacked any unifying social and aesthetic philosophy such as shaped artistic expression in the Baroque period. While each of these aesthetic trends had its proponents, it was the master composers of the period—Haydn, Mozart, and Beethoven—who were able to synthesize the elements of each into their music.

The Rococo style (ca. 1720–70) repudiated the massive forms of the Baroque. The endless vistas gave way to intimate glimpses; the grandeur of Baroque decoration changed to delicate, often unnecessary, ornamentation; monumental sculpture decreased in size to figurines for the mantle; the center of life moved from the ballroom to the boudoir; and the grandiloquent language of the Baroque changed in manner and tone to witty, tête-à-tête conversations.[35] The expansiveness, grandeur, and impressiveness of Baroque music gave way to an expression of elegance in delicate proportions. The polyphony of the later Baroque was abandoned in favor of a homophonic style, with interest focused on the soprano line that often was adorned with a proliferation of ornamentation.

Whereas the music of Rococo was elegant and ornate and written to please the aristocracy, the *empfindsamer Stil* (or expressive style) was more the music of the middle class. This bourgeois style reflected the attitudes of honesty and goodness and often approached the borders of sentimentality. It is reflected, for example, in the title of a collection of songs by the German composer J. F. Reichardt, "Lullabies for Good German Mothers."[36]

The eighteenth-century Enlightenment, or Age of Reason, began as a reaction against supernatural religions, formalism, and authority. The underlying philosophical belief was that man should be "natural" in all these respects—that is, natural behavior as opposed to formality, and individual freedom as opposed to submission to authority.[37] Denis Diderot's *Encyclopédie*, or *Classified Dictionary of Sciences, Arts, and Trades*, was published serially beginning in 1751 and symbolizes rationalism and the spirit of scientific inquiry. Thomas Paine's *The Age of Reason* also reflects such rationalism. The Marquis de Condorcet's book, *The Progress of the Human Spirit* (1774), set forth ten stages through which man had progressed from primitive life to near perfection. This philosophy

[35] William Fleming and Abraham Veinus, *Understanding Music: Style, Structure, and History* (New York: Holt, Rinehart & Winston, 1958), pp. 309–10.

[36] Ibid., p. 312.

[37] Donald Jay Grout, *A History of Western Music*, 3rd ed. (New York: W. W. Norton, 1980), pp. 448–49.

expressed the belief that man, through the use of his rational and moral powers, could ultimately control his environment. Jean Rameau was an outstanding exponent of rationalism and sought to restore reason to musical thought. There is evidence of this philosophy in the optimism expressed in some of the music of Beethoven, who was the movement's most articulate spokesman. [38]

The *Sturm und Drang* (storm and stress) movement in Germany ran counter to the elegance of the Rococo, the optimism of the Enlightenment, and the restricted emotionalism of the *empfindsamer Stil*. [39] These aesthetic trends were rejected in favor of a search for emotional truth and a more flexible use of the imagination. This philosophy may be seen in the literary works of both Goethe and Schiller. The best known literary example is Goethe's *Faust*. Faust rejects the tenets of the Age of Reason, ceases to search for nature's secrets in books, and seeks the ultimate truth in experiences and emotion. It is felt by some authorities that Haydn, Mozart, and Beethoven were all influenced by this philosophy, as indicated by the pathos and the sometimes violent outbursts in some of their music. [40]

The center of cultural life in the Classic period was the palace. The ruling aristocracy surrounded itself with the arts, which it considered its privileged right. Beauty of expression and elegance of manner became formalized and permeated its existence. The artist of the period created for his patron, who was far above him in social rank. Composers were employed for what they could contribute to the aristocracy's "cultural" surroundings. In general, the patron was interested in the artist's creative output rather than in him as an individual. In other words, a certain degree of reserve existed between employer and employee. In this social setting, where the emphasis was on courtly manners, the artist avoided becoming too personal in his art, since this would have been considered poor taste. Objectivity and reserve, therefore, became necessary in the artist's creative expression.

Meter and Stress

The art of the Classic era, the Rococo style in particular, strove for elegance and more delicate proportions. These general characteristics were also reflected in the music of the period. Therefore, the pulsation of the music was more delicately marked than in the Baroque period. In order to convey this style clearly to your performers, use a lighter beat, yet with a definite or marked precision to delineate the crisp rhythmic patterns of the music. [41]

---

[38] Fleming and Veinus, *Understanding Music*, p. 313.

[39] Some authorities feel that the *empfindsamer Stil* and the *Sturm und Drang* are only different manifestations of an overall Classic-Romantic style.

[40] Fleming and Veinus, *Understanding Music*, p. 314.

[41] Howerton, *Technique and Style*, p. 142.

Tempo

Tempi in the Classic period were generally moderate, and extremes were avoided. Beginning with the Classic period composers indicated to a much greater extent what they desired in their scores. Markings indicating the desired tempo, correct phrasing, and tonal quality were often included. Tempo was often indicated through the use of Italian words (*allegro, adagio,* and so on), and signs indicating dynamic changes were written in.[42] In the waning years of the Classic period, composers, Beethoven in particular, were able to prescribe the desired tempo of their compositions through the use of metronome markings. (As we noted previously, the metronome was invented by Maelzel in 1816.)

Tempo rubato originated from the vocal art and eventually was utilized as a device in the interpretation of instrumental music. It was first discussed in a book on singing by Pier Francesco Tosi, published in 1723. The letters of Mozart reveal that he was well aware of the device and used it in his piano performances. In addition, Karl Philipp Emanuel Bach (1714–88) discussed tempo rubato in volume 2 of his *Versuch*.[43] It is reasonable to assume that other composers of the period were also aware of this interpretative device. It is suggested, however, in performing music of this period, that tempo rubato be used with discretion and restraint and that its more exaggerated use, as in the subsequent Romantic period, be avoided. In general, follow the principle of strict time. The exceptions where tempo rubato seems desirable will usually be dictated by the poetic aspects of the text.[44] The use of ritardando and accelerando became more frequent, especially during the latter part of the period. In accordance with the general characteristics of the music of the period, such alterations in tempi should be slight and performed with restraint.

Dynamics

Although dynamic contrast was an important part of the music of the period, composers did not seek the extremes that occurred during the later periods. One of the most significant developments growing out of the latter part of the eighteenth century was that of *crescendo-decrescendo*. This concept was in marked contrast to the terraced dynamics of the earlier Baroque period. While the concept of crescendo-decrescendo was not entirely unknown and had been utilized to some degree in Italy from the beginning of the century, it had not been widely used elsewhere. Through the efforts of Stamitz, the precision of the orchestra at Mannheim was developed to such a high degree that this carefully controlled crescendo became known as the *Mannheim crescendo*. In choral performances the crescendo-decrescendo should be performed with some restraint,

[42] Frederick Dorian, *The History of Music in Performance* (New York: W. W. Norton, 1942), p. 155.

[43] Ibid , pp 186–93.

[44] For a further discussion of tempo rubato, see Sachs, *Rhythm and Tempo*, pp. 306–10.

considering the general dynamic level of the passage. The crescendo should not begin from as low a dynamic level, or reach as high a level, as it would during the Romantic period. Generally, in crescendo and decrescendo, the dynamic level should change gradually just one degree higher or lower—for example, from p ⟪ mp, and rarely from p ⟪ f.

The *forte-piano* contrast was an unwritten law of dynamic execution; that is, repeated phrases or periods should be performed *piano*, as in an echo. Periods performed *piano* the first time should be performed *forte* on the repetition.[45] The harmony itself will provide you with further clues for the treatment of dynamics.

> Philipp Emanuel Bach points out that every tone foreign to the key can very well stand a *forte*, regardless of whether it occurs in dissonance or consonance. ... Quantz distinguishes clearly three classes of dissonances, to be played *mezzo forte*, *forte*, and *fortissimo*, respectively. He also explains that the theme of the composition calls for dynamic emphasis. Likewise, all other notes of importance (in a theme, in a contrapuntal passage, or in a harmonic structure) must be stressed by means of dynamics. The notes introducing the theme must be marked the dissonance must be made stronger than its resolution.[46]

It is also often necessary and desirable to adjust the dynamics to the acoustical conditions of the performance hall. You need to consider the character of the music, the number and the maturity of the performers, and the size and the acoustical conditions of the performance hall or auditorium. To maintain the classic proportions of the music, it should never become overbearing from the dynamic standpoint. An overly large musical organization, coupled with an auditorium with exceptionally live acoustical properties, can create a dynamic level that is much too high; to be effective, reduce the dynamic level in size and scope.

Texture

Composers sought for lightness and simplicity in their music. In place of the heavy Baroque texture, there was a combination of textures in which chordal patterns, running figures, unsupported melodies, and other devices were used alternately, depending on the expressive intentions of the composer. Contrapuntal devices were also sometimes used, particularly in the masses; however, polyphony was generally not sought by composers of the period. During the Baroque period, a polarity existed between the melody and the bass parts. The bass supported the melody, while the inner voices sometimes only completed the harmonies. During the Classic period, the inner voices assumed greater importance, and the previous supporting function of the bass part gave way to one of greater flexibility and interplay with the inner voices.[47]

---

[45] Dorian, *The History of Music in Performance*, p. 166.

[46] Ibid., p. 168.

[47] Homer Ulrich and Paul A. Pisk, *A History of Music and Musical Style* (New York: Harcourt Brace Jovanovich, 1963), pp. 322–23.

Expressive Aspects

In contrast to the late Baroque period, where the cadences were relatively infrequent and somewhat inconspicuous, and the phrases were spun-out, the composers of the Classic period used phrases of a regular two- or four-bar length that were shorter and more distinct. There were generally rather strong points of harmonic arrival, and the period structure was well defined. Although the harmonic vocabulary did not differ substantially from that of the late Baroque period, the harmonic progressions were certainly less weighty.[48] Melody reigned supreme; the other parts served to support and enhance it, and were often subordinate to it. Ornamentation developed to its fullest bloom. This embellishment of the melodic line, however, was only reflective of the spirit of the times, where elegance and grace were considered highly important, particularly to the patrons of the arts.

The music of the Classic period was generally abstract in nature and discreet in taste and was an integral part of a sophisticated mode of living. It was moderate in style, avoiding the extremes of the later Romantic period. Emotional content was less important, and unity of design became the composer's goal. Form served to eliminate the personal qualities and universalized the style. Symmetry, balance, clarity, and restraint summarized the composer's artistic creations.

THE ROMANTIC PERIOD

The French Revolution, beginning in 1789, resulted in the breakdown of the aristocratic way of life and led to the development of nineteenth-century liberalism. In the world of the arts, it was paralleled by the rise of the Romantic movement, in essence a revolt against formality and authority. Composers had for many centuries worked under the patronage of either the church or the princely courts; under that system, composers generally wrote music to please their patrons and were careful not to let their music become too personal in nature. With the breakdown of the patronage system, composers were free to express themselves individually. They were no longer inhibited or restricted by a patron's demands and were able to please their equals—the general public. With their greater freedom, composers sought out new and unique means of expression. This led to a greater display of emotion, heretofore largely restrained.

Although the composer, no longer bound to his patron, was able to express himself more freely, his financial insecurity often caused him to withdraw from the world about him. He sometimes became preoccupied with his own inner problems and pessimistic about the future. Nevertheless, these situations or conditions involving withdrawal, escape, mysticism, religion, as well as the need for self-expression, were often expressed in the composer's music, enriching the repertoire as a result.

[48] Grout, *A History of Western Music*, p. 417.

The term *Romanticism*, as it pertains to the nineteenth century, is inexact and somewhat misleading. The Romantic period contained many forces that seemingly run counter to its name. According to Machlis:

> The nineteenth century included many opposites: liberalism and reaction, idealism and the crassest materialism, bourgeois sentimentality and stark realism, mysticism and scientific inquiry, democratic revolution and royalist restoration, romantic optimism and no less romantic despair.[49]

Meter and Stress

Composers in the Romantic period, in their search for freedom from rules, often sought to break the strictness of the rhythm, yet remain within the time-honored rules. A widely used device to achieve this objective was the use of meter changes without changes in the meter signature.[50] An example of this device may be found in the Brahms *Requiem*. Such metric alteration results in displaced accents—that is, accents where they are not normally expected—in a relatively short space of time. Whereas Romantic composers achieved these unique rhythmic effects within the boundaries of the accepted rules, the modern-day composer would normally use alternately different meter signatures (see later section, "The Modern Period," in this chapter and discussion on meter and stress for examples). Other varied means of syncopation also became widely used during this period as an expressive device and as a means of evoking interest. Intricate rhythmic patterns and rhythmic surprise were characteristic of the music of the period. Composers sometimes used an irregular phrase structure of varying lengths. Brahms in particular was noted for his elongated or extended phrases; in some cases they were absorbed into contrapuntal textures so that it is difficult to determine where they actually do end.[51]

Tempo

The restraint typical of the Classic period was abandoned during the Romantic era. It was a period of extremes—fast tempi were often performed exceptionally fast and slow tempi exceptionally slow. Tempo was closely aligned with mood, and since the composer was often expressing varying moods within a composition, extreme, abrupt changes in tempo often occurred. Accelerando and ritardando were more frequently used than in the previous period. As an element of expressiveness, tempo rubato was developed to its ultimate.

During the Romantic period two diametrically opposed schools of interpretative thought existed. One, represented by Mendelssohn, was based on classical principles; the other was the highly romantic, sometimes called the

[49] Joseph Machlis, *The Enjoyment of Music*, regular rev. ed. (New York: W. W. Norton 1963), p. 85.

[50] Sachs, *Rhythm and Tempo*, p. 344.

[51] Ulrich and Pisk, *A History of Music*, p. 485.

"Neo-German," type of interpretation, which was initiated by Liszt and exemplified by Wagner. The Mendelssohn school sought to preserve the Classical tradition and to eliminate some of the practices that they felt were extreme. Mendelssohn was an exponent of regularity of rhythm and fluency of tempo. Wagner, on the other hand, favored broad, singing melody, and considerable liberty in tempi.[52] He felt that the correct tempo could be determined only through "a proper understanding of the melos."[53]

Although composers may be said to have had tendencies toward one or the other of these positions, and certainly were influenced in one way or another, it would be unwise, as well as impossible, to categorize them all in either group. The music of each composer must be considered individually. Only through a thorough analysis and study of the music can you determine a proper tempo. For example, music with a light texture may be performed in a faster tempo than music with a heavy, sonorous texture. The latter should be performed somewhat slower if it is to be effective. Relating to this point, the following statement by Robert Schumann is both interesting and revealing:

> You know how I dislike quarreling about tempo, and how for me only the inner measure of the movement is conclusive. Thus, an allegro of one who is cold by nature always sounds lazier than a slow tempo by one of sanguine temperament. With the orchestra, however, the proportions are decisive. Stronger and denser masses are capable of bringing out the detail as well as the whole with more emphasis and importance; whereas, with smaller and finer units, one must compensate for the lack of resonance by pushing forward in the tempo.[54]

Dynamics

In contrast to the restraint of the Classic period, composers of the Romantic period often used extremes in dynamics ranging from *fff* to *ppp*, but with a slight leaning toward the use of the lower dynamic levels. Some editions of the Verdi Requiem, even contain dynamic markings of *ppppp*.

Crescendo and decrescendo, or the gradual swelling and diminishing of tone, became a widely used expressive device by nineteenth-century composers. In certain compositions it was used to create the illusion of distance—that is, of a group or an object gradually coming closer and then receding into the distance.

Some composers employed a slight accelerando with a crescendo and a slight ritardando with a decrescendo. Rossini, in particular, was noted for combining "a gradual dynamic increase with a great rhythmic momentum."[55]

Composers in the nineteenth century indicated their intentions on their scores using a variety of tempo and dynamic markings. Some of these terms

---

[52] Dorian, *The History of Music in Performance*, pp. 230–31.

[53] Ibid, p 281.

[54] Ibid., p. 227. See Sachs, *Rhythm and Tempo*, p. 379.

[55] Ulrich and Pisk, *A History of Music*, p. 455.

encompassed both tempo and dynamics. For example, *morendo* (dying away) indicates that the music should be both slower and softer, and *andante maestoso* (moderately slow and majestic) implies a moderate tempo, yet with a full sonority.

In addition to crescendo and decrescendo, the use of more sudden climaxes also became a common practice. Grieg, for example, employs this device to a considerable extent in his *Psalms* (C. F. Peters). The use of dynamic accents, such as *sforzando* (*sfz*) and *sforzato* (*sf*), occurred with much greater frequency. See, for example, the Choral Finale to the *Ninth Symphony*, by Beethoven (H. W. Gray; G. Schirmer), *Elijah*, by Mendelssohn (G. Schirmer), the *Requiem Mass* and the *Stabat Mater*, by Dvořák (G. Schirmer), and the *29th Psalm*, by Elgar (Novello). In contrast to the moderately sized ensembles used in the various princely courts of the Classic era, the combined forces of large orchestras and choirs became the ideal medium for the expression of the dynamic extremes of the Romantic period.

Texture

New harmonic relationships were explored by composers of the Romantic period. Dissonance became more widely used, and an increasing use of melodic and harmonic chromaticism gave the composer a wider range of expressive devices.[56] There was a lessening of harmonic drive, with an increased tendency toward the use of deceptive resolutions and obscured cadences. That is, cadences were sometimes avoided, or resolved deceptively. In contrast to "wandering" chromaticism, composers sometimes used sudden harmonic and enharmonic changes, or shifts of tonal center.

Although a balance between harmony and counterpoint is said to have existed during the late Baroque period, the nineteenth-century Romanticist altered the balance in favor of harmony. The Romantic composer, however, often alternated the texture within a short time span. Counterpoint, when used, focused on the opposition of masses rather than on vocal lines. In contrast to the light and clear texture of the Classic period, the texture of music in the Romantic period was often somewhat dense and heavy.

Expressive Aspects

During the Romantic period some composers expressed their opposition to formality, convention, authority, and tradition; some others expressed a longing for the past—the "golden age"—and made efforts to recapture it in some way. Whereas the Classic composer was highly concerned with expression within a particular form, the Romanticist was not to be restricted by it. He was not to be bound by the previous forms and strove to develop a freer form through which he might better express himself.

[56] The effectiveness of dissonance is certainly related to tempo, since the listener's aural comprehension of a complex and dissonant passage may be blurred by a tempo that is too rapid.

Individual expression became the composer's principal goal. To express emotion freely, the composer drew on all the multitude of musical resources at his command. As a means of creating tension and expressing emotion, composers of this period experimented considerably in the field of harmony. Unusual harmonic effects, as well as unusual rhythmic effects, wide contrasts in dynamics, changing moods, and varying textures were all used as expressive devices.

While tone color has always existed as an integral aspect of music, it took on a new importance during the Romantic period. Through tone color, composers sought to express sensuous beauty and tonal enchantment. Musical terms such as *con amore* (with love), *con fuoco* (with fire), *con passione* (with passion), *dolce (sweetly)*, *gioioso* (joyous), and *mesto* (sad) were increasingly used by composers as an indication of their intention to the performers. These terms, in addition, indicate the frame of mind of the composers of the period. Music of this period, both vocal and instrumental, was influenced by the lyricism of the human voice. It is notable that many of the themes of instrumental music of the period have been adapted into popular songs. Their popularity is, in part, affected by their singability.[57]

The center of musical life in the nineteenth century was the concert hall, rather than the palace or the church. Because of the lack of restrictions in regard to size of performance organizations, composers during the latter part of the period increasingly wrote for larger groups and in a more colorful and grandiose style than was characteristic of the earlier part of the period.[58]

THE MODERN PERIOD

Toward the end of the nineteenth century the subjective expression of Romanticism had run its course. Some composers, however, continued to write in a modified Romantic style. Among the more notable of this group of late Romanticists were Sergei Taneyev (1856–1915), Edward Elgar (1857–1934), Gustav Mahler (1860–1911), Richard Strauss (1864–1949), Alexander Gretchaninov (1864–1956), Enrique Granados (1867–1916), Max Reger (1873–1916), and Sergei Rachmaninoff (1873–1943). Most composers, however, began to seek new means of expression. We now describe the main currents of musical expression in the Modern Period.

Impressionism

Impressionism developed as a reaction against the emotionalism and subjective aspects of Romanticism. It emerged during the last quarter of the nineteenth century and was exemplified in the music of Claude Debussy (1862–1918) and Maurice Ravel (1885–1937). Debussy was highly influenced

[57] Machlis, *The Enjoyment of Music*, regular rev. ed., pp. 86–88.
[58] Ibid., p. 88

by the Impressionist painters and the Symbolist poets, who avoided the exact and clear-cut representation of things, but rather sought to create a momentary impression of them. The painters often did not mix their paints, but juxtaposed daubs of pure color on the canvas, leaving the "mixing" to the eye of the viewer. Also seeking new paths, the Symbolist poets rejected emotionalism and turned to nebulous suggestion and dreamlike evocation of mood.[59]

Expressionism

Appearing about 1910 as a reaction against the "vagueness" of Impressionism, Expressionism is sometimes referred to as the German answer to French Impressionism. Expressionism also received its impetus from painting and poetry. Artists, perhaps influenced by Sigmund Freud's work in psychology, endeavored to capture on canvas the myriad thoughts from the unconscious. Distorted images, expressing the artist's inner self, took the place of the traditional concepts of beauty. Composers also rejected older aesthetic concepts and sought new means of expression.[60] Expressionistic music is characterized by its continuous intensity, high level of dissonance, angular melodic fragments, complex rhythms, and fluctuating tempi. Expressionist composers utilized all the devices at their command to express the conflicts, fears, and anxieties of humans' inner self. The outstanding exponents of Expressionism are Arnold Schoenberg (1874–1951), Alban Berg (1885–1935), Anton von Webern (1883–1945), and Ernst Krenek (b. 1900).

Neo-Classicism

In the phase of musical expression called Neo-Classicism, which appeared after World War I, composers sought to recapture the ideals of the eighteenth century, where the emphasis was on craftsmanship rather than on emotional expression. They sought to restore the proper balance between form and emotion and rejected the excesses of the Romantic period. The return to form was a primary consideration in composition, with emotional expression being a secondary factor. The Neo-Classicists decried the idea of program music and gave more stress to the intellectual aspects of music. Composers who have written in this style include Igor Stravinsky (1882–1971), Paul Hindemith (1885–1963), Darius Milhaud (1892–1974), Francis Poulenc (1899–1963), William Schuman (1910–1987), Benjamin Britten (1913–76), Irving Fine (1914–62), Vincent Persichetti (1915–87), and Lukas Foss (b. 1922).

---

[59] Joseph Machlis, *Introduction to Contemporary Music*, 2d ed. (New York: W. W. Norton, (1979), pp. 84–86
[60] Ibid., p. 335.

Some musicologists have applied the labels of Neo-Classicism and Neo-Romanticism to specific composers, most of whom have written in various styles. It is impossible to categorize the works of all composers in this manner. Students will need to analyze each work under consideration to determine the tag that most appropriately applies.

Neo-Romanticism

Twentieth-century composers have not all found the styles of Impressionism, Expressionism, or Neo-Classicism to their liking. Some, therefore, have utilized means of expression more closely aligned with the ideas of the Romanticists. This group has been referred to as the Neo-Romanticists. Music in the Neo-Romantic style is usually rich in sonorities, contains frequent climaxes, and is comparatively easy for the nonmusician to listen to. The Neo-Romantic composers utilize many of the tonal and rhythmic devices of the Neo-Classicist, but they convey them in a subjective manner—in such a way as to instill emotion and warmth in their music.

While, during the first part of the twentieth century, the majority of composers had rejected the ideals of the nineteenth century in favor of other modes of expression, the political and economic situation of the second quarter of the century led the way to a more emotional means of expression. World War II, in particular, created an atmosphere more receptive to romantic ideals and a need in some composers for a more personal means of expression, in which greater emphasis is placed on the poetic and dramatic aspects of music.[61] Some representative composers of this style are Ernst Toch (1887–1964), Carl Orff (1895–1982), Howard Hanson (1896–1981), William Walton (1902–83), Paul Creston (1906–85), Samuel Barber (1910–81), Gian Carlo Menotti (b. 1911), Norman Dello Joio (b. 1913), and William Bergsma (b. 1921).

In addition to the styles of musical expression just discussed, separate consideration must be given to those composers who utilize folk material in their music. This group has often been referred to as the Nationalists. Among the more prominent are Ernest Bloch (1880–1959), Zoltán Kodály (1882–1967), Ralph Vaughan Williams (1872–1958), Charles Ives (1874–1954), Randall Thompson (1899–1984), Aaron Copland (1900–90), Heitor Villa-Lobos (1887–1959), Carlos Chávez (1899–1978), and Alan Hovhaness (b. 1911).

Whereas nineteenth-century composers used folk material more for color effects and altered it when it did not fit their compositional scheme, the twentieth-century Nationalists incorporated more of the flavor of the original folk idiom in their music. Modal music and material with asymmetrical rhythms are often used to create fresh, new effects.[62]

[61] Ibid., p. 314.
[62] Ibid., p. 257

Meter and Stress

Impressionistic music possesses less tension and rhythmic drive than music of the Romantic period. Impressionist music, particularly that of Debussy, gives the impression of being "suspended in space." While Impressionistic music may give the feeling of vagueness, it is quite precise. Avoid any exaggeration of tempo fluctuations, and keep the beat clear and precise but flexible and responsive to all the subtle nuances in the music.

In contrast to Impressionism, Expressionistic music possesses considerable rhythmic incisiveness; that is, the rhythm is even more clear-cut. The rhythm of the music is generally aligned with the durational values of the text; however, as a means of achieving tension, the Expressionists often distorted the normal accentuations of words. This alteration usually necessitated the use of changing meter to accommodate the resultant rhythm.

A particular characteristic of Neo-Classic music is its rhythm. As a means of avoiding the monotony of the regular stress following the barline, composers employ various devices. One procedure is to alter the meter with each measure (sometimes referred to as *multimeter*).[63] The same effect, however, may be achieved by simply shifting the stresses or accents from point to point within the measure without changing the meter signature. In conducting rhythmic patterns with shifting accents, limit the scope of your patterns and utilize a precise rebound to each beat. On accented notes—whether on a downbeat or an upbeat—the stress should be reflected in the tension of the arms and shoulders, whereas limited, yet precise, movements should occur on the unaccented notes.

Still another rhythmic device is the division of traditional meters in non-symmetrical ways. For example, in 4/4 meter the eighth notes might be grouped as 3 + 3 + 2, or 3 + 2 + 3, rather than 4 + 4. (Another way of stating these rhythmic groupings is 1 2 3 1 2 3 1 2, or 1 2 3 1 2 1 2 3.) In 6/8 meter, a two-measure pattern might be alternately written as 3 + 3 + 2 + 2 + 2. In conducting rhythms in nonsymmetrical forms, you must alter your patterns to conform to the basic rhythm of the music.[64]

Although Neo-Romantic composers use many of the rhythmic devices of the Neo-Classicists, they do so in moderation. They place a greater emphasis on the poetic aspects of music and a means of personal expression that is more universally understood. When modern-day rhythmic devices contribute to this end they are used, and when they do not they are avoided.

---

[63] See, for example, various works by Jean Berger: "It Is Good to Be Merry" (Kjos), "The Good of Contentment" (Presser), "Lift Up Your Heads" (Summy-Birchard), and "Seek Ye the Lord" (Augsburg).

[64] For a discussion of this technique, see "Conducting Accent and Changing Meter" in Chapter 1.

Tempo

With Impressionistic music most tempi tend toward the moderate and the slow, with exceptionally fast tempi usually being avoided. A considerable degree of modern music following this period, however, exhibits a strong rhythmic drive. Movement and speed are an integral part of our modern-day life, and these characteristics are reflected in much of our music. The rhythm of Expressionistic music is generally somewhat irregular and rather complex. As a result of the normal accent of words being sometimes deliberately distorted, the tempo often fluctuates with the use of pauses, ritardandos, and accelerandos.

Tempo, of course, is related to both rhythm and mood, and, in determining the proper tempo, you should consider both of these factors carefully. Because clarity of line is essential to the performance of Neo-Classic music, a tempo that is too fast will impede the articulation, whereas a tempo that is too slow will sometimes lessen the intensity and the rhythmic drive. Mood is an important consideration in determining the tempi of Neo-Romantic music. With emotional expression being relatively important, the projection of textual meanings often necessitates a greater flexibility in tempi.

Dynamics

In contrast to music of the Romantic period, Impressionistic music possesses a relatively low level of dynamic intensity. *Fortissimo* occurs rather infrequently, with the medium and the lower dynamic levels, *mezzo forte*, *piano*, and *pianissimo*, used primarily. Crescendo and decrescendo, when employed, should be used with considerable care and restraint. In performing music from this period, take care to adapt the scope of your beat to the dynamic levels of the music. In conducting a *pianissimo* passage, for example, use very slight movements.

Following the Impressionistic period there has gradually developed an increasing use of dynamic extremes. Contrast is often achieved through a rapid change from an extremely low dynamic level to one of great intensity and volume. Modern-day composers are inclined toward using a multiplicity of dynamic effects in their music, including extreme contrast in dynamic levels, rapid crescendos and decrescendos, dynamic accents, and uniform levels of intensity.[65]

Texture

Composers of the Romantic period were highly interested in harmonic experimentation. This interest was intensified by composers of the Modern period. The Impressionists sought to escape the restrictions of the major-minor system of tonality. In the process, Debussy used a variety of devices, including the medieval modes, the whole-tone scale, and the pentatonic scale. Parallel fourths,

[65] Howerton, *Technique and Style*, pp. 179–80.

fifths, and octaves were often used above a pedal point, which resulted in unusual effects from the clash between the sustained and the moving harmonies.

Although previous harmonic systems focused on the relationship of chords and their progression from one to another, the Impressionists utilized individual chords for the sonorous and coloristic effects they created. Thus the tendency for chord resolution was certainly lessened. While triads were sometimes used, seventh, ninth, and eleventh chords were frequently employed either separately or in succession. Composers, furthermore, often utilized these chords on various scale degrees by shifting them up and down without alteration. This "gliding" use of chordal movement, utilizing blocklike chords in parallel motion, was an integral stylistic feature of Impressionism. Escaped chords—that is, those that are not resolved, but seem to "escape" to another key—were also an important characteristic of Impressionistic music. Impressionist composers often achieved a feeling of rest, or point of harmonic arrival, by simply using a less dissonant chord than those preceding it. Tonal color became equated with melody, harmony, and rhythm during this era.

Debussy often deliberately created a vagueness within his music, coupled with an indefiniteness of phrase structures. Ravel, on the other hand, utilized traditional forms and phrases to a much greater extent. The whole-tone scale was not used by Ravel because he desired a more definite triadic outline, clearer phrase structures, and more functional harmony.

Expressionism is generally considered to have begun with Schoenberg, and since twelve-tone music is associated with him, the two terms have become somewhat synonymous. It should be understood, however, that not all Expressionist music is twelve-tone music, because the Expressionistic movement began before this development. In Schoenberg's earlier works (his oratorio *Gurre-Lieder* [Universal], for example) he developed his use of chromaticism to its maximum potential. He then began to seek new means of expression.

Schoenberg's experimentation led to the development of the *twelve-tone method*, or *serial technique*, about 1923. With this method, all compositions are based on an arbitrary arrangement, or *set*, of the twelve chromatic tones. Each tone row or set is handled in such a manner that no particular tone becomes any more important than the others. After a tone has been introduced, it may not be used again until every other tone in the series has been used at least once. This is in marked contrast to the conventional major-minor tonal system. The row or set serves as a unifying factor in the music. After the basic set has been introduced, it may be repeated through a variety of means. It may be inverted—that is, turned upside down—it may be performed backward (retrograde), or inverted and performed backward (a retrograde of the inversion). The tone row is a type of variation technique in which great variety is achieved with only a minimum of material.[66] The guiding thought is that no idea should be repeated except in

---

[66] Machlis, *Introduction to Contemporary Music*, pp. 340–42.

a new form. The older style of repetition and sequence, balanced phrases and cadences, was rejected by the Expressionists.

In the nineteenth century, rhythm, harmony, and tone color were often considered as entities unto themselves, whereas Neo-Classicism considered each of these separate elements as subservient to the whole. The use of counterpoint by the Neo-Classic composers became increasingly important. To differentiate it, however, from the "harmonic" counterpoint of the Romantic era, this new polyphony is often referred to as "linear counterpoint." It is often marked by its transparency of texture and its dissonance and driving rhythm. While striking dissonance often occurs as a result of clashes between vocal lines, each line must maintain its forward drive or thrust.

In the music of the Neo-Romanticists, extreme harmonic complexity is usually avoided. Their music is generally characterized by its sensuous lyricism and its richness of harmony. It is often simply and directly stated, although some music possesses considerable rhythmic drive and intensity. Neo-Romantic music is primarily tonal in nature. Dissonance is used, but generally for comparatively brief periods to highlight the emotional and poetic aspects of the text. Although a considerable portion of Neo-Romantic music is harmonically conceived, some composers utilize contrapuntal devices as well. While their compositional techniques vary considerably, their one common characteristic is a more personal means of expression.

Expressive Aspects

The Impressionistic composer's aim was simply to suggest rather than boldly to state. Music in this style, therefore, should be approached in an objective manner and performed with considerable restraint. The excesses and extremes of the Romantic period should be avoided.

Expressionistic and Neo-Classical music should be approached with an even more objective point of view. Perhaps the most outstanding characteristic of Expressionistic music is its continuous dissonance (and lack of consonance that would allow for a lessening of the tension). Dissonance, along with such other devices as angular melodic fragments, irregular rhythm, and abrupt changes in tempi, is used as a means of expressing the conflicts of the inner self. The composer's concern is to use these varied devices to portray these inner feelings, rather than the expression of pure emotion in itself.

Neo-Classicists are concerned largely with craftsmanship and with the statement of their material in an impersonal, objective manner. Emotional expression is minimized. Although it will vary from composer to composer, it is always carefully controlled. Neo-Classicists endeavor to recapture the classic spirit by striving for symmetry and balance in their music, by utilizing more transparent textures, and by limiting the size of their musical forces.

Neo-Romanticists, however, seek a more universalized type of expression. Their goal is different from Neo-Classicists, since they desire a more personal means of communication. Although they use many musical devices similar to those of the Neo-Classical composers, since their purpose is different they use them in a different way. You should analyze the music and determine the *raison d'être* for each device if you are to employ it for its intended purpose.

In performing music of the Modern period, give particular attention to the tone quality and the manner of articulation. With Impressionistic music, the singers need to use a legato style of diction so as not to disturb the smooth flow of the carefully voiced chords often moving in parallel motion.[67]

The melody of Expressionistic music often moves in wide angular leaps, thus creating some serious intonation problems for the performers. Singers, obviously, need to listen carefully. And because any rigidity in the jaw will inhibit proper articulation, they need to maintain a rather relaxed jaw to facilitate a cleaner articulation of the various interval leaps.

In Neo-Classic music it is usually desirable to lessen the dramatic qualities of the voice so that the clarity of the structure may be brought out. Voices with excessive vibrato or tremolo are particularly detrimental to the interpretation of this style of music. In performing music in a Neo-Romantic style, the voice should be warm and expressive so as to convey best the subjective quality of the music.

MUSIC WITH ELECTRONIC TAPE/NONCONVENTIONAL NOTATION

The continued search for new means of musical expression brought forth, particularly during the 1970s, a variety of types of new choral music, including voices combined with electronic tape sounds, choric speech with singing, aleatoric (chance) music, and multimedia presentations. (We are presently in the midst of many new developments and therefore lack the perspective that we have of earlier music. It thus seems appropriate to include this material in a section separate from other twentieth-century music.)

Conventional notation for the vocal parts is usually employed in choral music with electronic tape. In some music, the time for specific cues is indicated in the score, and a stopwatch is necessary to coordinate the two separate sound sources. In other instances, a graphic illustration of the electronic sound is indicated in the score, thus assisting both the conductor and the singers to coordinate their efforts and making the use of a stopwatch unnecessary. Examples of both types are illustrated in Figures 66 and 67.

As composers continue to explore new means of music expression, they find that the conventional means of music notation do not allow them sufficient flexibility, nor do symbols always exist for the expression of their musical ideas. This has resulted in the creation of an entirely new means of notation. Specific notation now has been devised for spoken pitches, raising and lowering the pitch of the voice, shouts, screams, laughter, varying dynamic levels, tone clusters, stacca-

---

[67] For a discussion of legato diction, see "Styles of Diction" in Chapter 2.

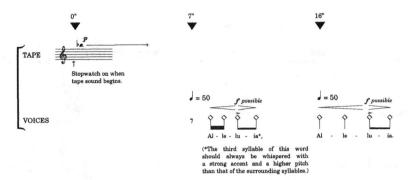

FIGURE 66 Excerpt from *Pentecost Sunday,* by Richard Felciano. Score indicates elapsed time in seconds for coordination of tape with choral parts. Copyright 1967, World Library Publications, Inc., 3815 N. Willow Rd., Schiller Park, IL 60176. All rights reserved. Used by permission.

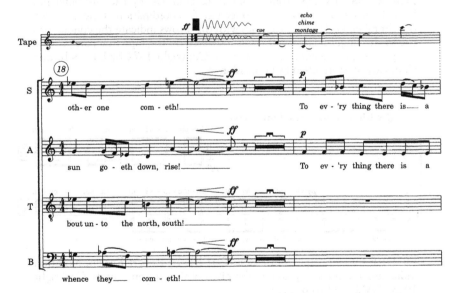

FIGURE 67 Excerpt from *A Time to Every Purpose,* by Gilbert Trythall. Graphic illustration of tape sounds for coordination of choral parts with tape. Copyright © 1972, Edward B. Marks Music Corporation. Used by permission.

to pronunciations, whispers, various lip sounds, tongue clicks, coughs, hissing sounds, giggles, hand claps, glissandos, vibrato, tempo, duration, accelerando, ritardando, and various other tonal effects.[68] Excerpts from a number of compositions representing this type of notation are illustrated in Figures 68 through 73.

---

[68] For a helpful and useful compilation of all these symbols, along with explanations, see Frank Pooler and Brent Pierce, *New Choral Notation* (New York: Walton 1971).

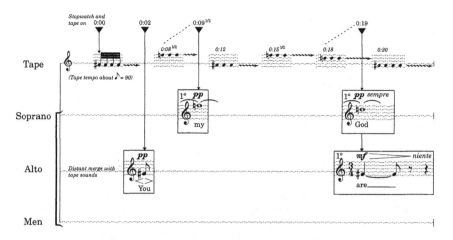

FIGURE 68   Excerpt from *Hymn of the Universe*, by Richard Felciano. Score indicates the elapsed time in seconds for coordination of the tape with the choral parts. The vertical lines with the arrows indicate the conductor's cue to the singers. The small notes indicated on the tape line part provide the pitches for the entering voice parts. Copyright 1974 by E.C. Schirmer Company, Boston. Used by permission.

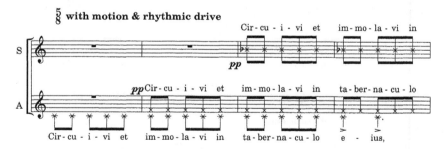

FIGURE 69   Excerpt from *Psalm* (Part III) by Robert Karlen. Notation indicates, as closely as possible, the pitch of the spoken sounds. Copyright 1968, A.M.S.I. Used by permission.

As part of the total musical diet, avant-garde music adds a new dimension to sound as an expressive art, and it can open singers' ears, so to speak, to new as well as older sounds. Young singers are generally receptive to music of this type, because it may be closer to their own popular musical culture. See Appendix for a selective list of choral music with electronic tape and with nonconventional notation. Most of this music will include explanatory information concerning the notational symbols and how to interpret them. Examination and study of these compositions by the conductor and performance of certain selected works will balance out the repertoire of the choir or chorus.

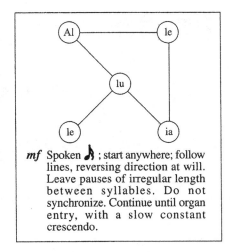

mf Spoken ♪ ; start anywhere; follow lines, reversing direction at will. Leave pauses of irregular length between syllables. Do not synchronize. Continue until organ entry, with a slow constant crescendo.

FIGURE 70 Excerpt from *Pentecost Sunday*, by Richard Felciano. Chart designed to elicit irregular, nonsynchronized speech sounds. Copyright 1967, World Library Publications, Inc., 3815 N. Willow Rd., Schiller Park, IL 60176. All rights reserved. Used by permission.

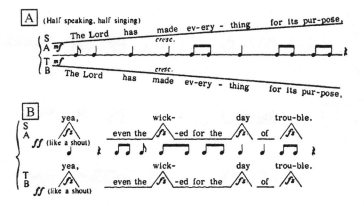

FIGURE 71 Excerpt from *All the Ways of a Man*, by Knut Nystedt. Rhythm and text given, but (A) pitch changes indicated by ascending and descending lines and (B) dynamic accents or "shouts" indicated by ⫽ꜛ⫽ . Copyright 1971, Augsburg Fortress Publishing House. Used by permission.

THE JAZZ/POP IDIOM

The twentieth century has seen many composers utilizing popular music and the rhythm of various dances as raw material for the more serious expression of their music. As the American composer Douglas Moore points out, we must acknowledge "popular forces, such as jazz, as typical American music products, which,

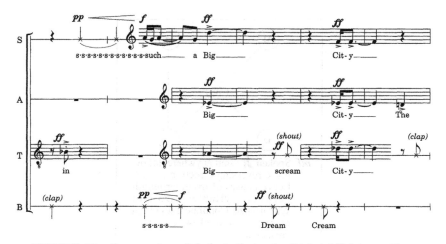

FIGURE 72 Excerpt from *Pshelley's Psalm*, by Richard Felciano. Note combination of designated pitches with other sounds, including hisses, shouts, and hand claps. Copyright 1974, E.C. Schirmer Company, Boston. Used by permission.

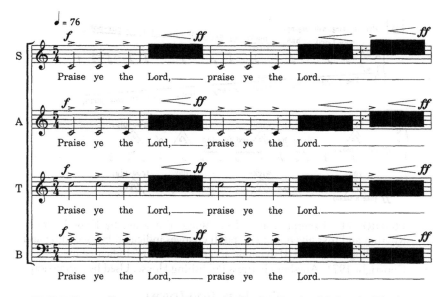

FIGURE 73 Excerpt from *Aleatory Psalm*, by Gordon H. Lamb. The box represents a tone cluster within the confines of the symbol (in this instance, a minor seventh in each part). Singers should try to avoid a pitch sung by another person. Copyright 1973, World Library Publications, Inc., 3815 N. Willow Rd., Schiller Park, IL 60176. All rights reserved. Used by permission.

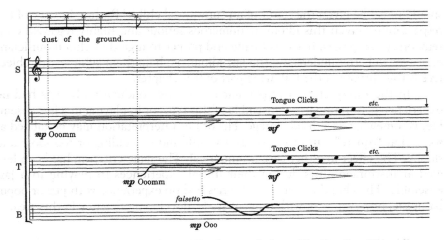

FIGURE 74 Excerpt from "*The Creation*", from *The Family of Man*, by Michael Hennagin; (*a*) approximate pitch level of vowel sound indicated by lines and (*b*) special effects, such as tongue clicks. Copyright 1971, Walton Music Corp. Used by permission.

despite their divided allegiance between commerce and art, are of much greater cultural value than the average American suspects."[69] The reason for the use of the elements of ragtime (the forerunner of jazz) and jazz is the composer's attempt to move away from the rhythmic sterility of post-Romanticism, and particularly its divisive even beats that were no longer in vogue.[70]

The use of ragtime occurred in "Golliwogs Cakewalk" from *Children's Corner*, by Claude Debussy (1908), in one of the dances in *L'Histoire du Soldat*, by Igor Stravinsky (1918), and in one of the dances in *Suite für Klavier*, by Paul Hindemith (1922). The jazz idiom appears in numerous twentieth-century works, including *Parade*, by Eric Satie (1917); *La Creation du Monde*, by Darius Milhaud (1923); the opera *Jonny spielt auf*, by Ernst Krenek (1926); *Rio Grande*, for chorus, orchestra, and solo pianoforte, by Constant Lambert (1928); *Suite* for jazz orchestra, by Dimitri Shostakovich (1934); and *Ebony Concerto* for clarinet and swing band, by Igor Stravinsky (1945).

Since World War II, many of the popular tunes from the 1920s and 1930s, now known as "golden oldies," have been rearranged for, and performed by, the many jazz/show choirs prevalent in high schools and colleges throughout the United States. Many of these works have also been performed by modern concert choirs as encores, or as part of a closing set of American music.

The use of the elements of jazz in contemporary music *does not* make it unrespectable, as some choral conductors presumably believe. Such music

[69] Frederick Dorian, *The History of Music in Performance* (New York: W. W. Norton & Company, 1942), p. 353.

[70] Curt Sachs, *Rhythm and Tempo: A Study in Music History* (New York: W. W. Norton & Company, 1953), p. 368.

should never be given the status of an "unwanted child." Rather, in view of the respectability given this idiom by numerous serious and highly regarded contemporary composers, it seems fitting and proper to urge that choral musicians endeavor to better understand the jazz idiom. To help them achieve this objective is the purpose of the following part of this chapter.

In the interpretation of popular music, the conductor who has had no experience performing in an ensemble of this type, or in playing in a jazz ensemble, is somewhat at a disadvantage. His or her interpretation may be tabbed as somewhat "square"—in other words, too stiff and unyielding or too loose and sloppy. The effect in either case is unmusical. The same criticism has been leveled at instrumentalists during their initial experiences in playing in a jazz ensemble. The choral conductor who has had no experience with jazz or popular music, however, can, with diligent study, develop proficiency in this area.

Rhythm

A basic aspect of interpretation pertains to the treatment of eighth notes. In most pop/rock tunes they are usually performed with equal duration and are generally notated that way; for example:

The underlying even eighth-note pattern in the percussion part of the combo accompaniment is an integral part of the style and helps to perpetuate the rhythmic drive. (Certain performers even say that they feel the music in 8, or at least a strong *and*, or second half of the beat.) Some publications provide directions in various ways. For example, in "Crazy Rhythm," by Meyer and Kahn, arr. Ellis Bretton (Warner Bros.), the initial directions are "Funky Rock (equal eighth notes)." In "Sausalito Strut," by Carl Strommen (Alfred Publishing Co.), the music is marked "Bright Rock ($\downarrow$ = 120)" and the drum part is notated

In "Just the Way You Are," by Billy Joel, arr. Ed Lojeski (Hal Leonard), under "Performance Notes" is the comment, "Rehearse slowly, counting each eighth note," and at measure 21 the percussion part includes the directions "Bossa Nova-rock feeling."[72] Eighth notes are also generally of equal length in music of a particularly slow tempo. Textual cues and notation within the total configuration of the music will usually enable the director to determine the proper desired effect. Directions and clues for performance in a pop/rock style may be found at various places in the music, and if none are there, then you

[71] From "Streets A fire!" by Mark Brymer (Hal Leonard Publishing Co.).

[72] For an interpretation of this song by the singer/composer, see the album *The Stranger*, Columbia 34987.

must make your own assessment of the musical style, listen to a current recording of the music, or both.

Singers should always strive to feel and respond to the pulse or forward drive of the music. Particularly after a rest, $\frac{4}{4}$ ♩ , the entrance of the group must be together, which is not likely to occur unless the singers feel the pulse of the third beat and respond precisely on the rebound, or second half of the beat (pop/rock style).

In performing offbeat rhythms, $\frac{4}{4}$ ♩ ♫♩ ♪♩♪ ♫♩ ♪♩♪, for example, such as occur in "Just the Way You Are," by Billy Joel, arr. Ed Lojeski (Hal Leonard) and "Baby Come Back to Me," by Nick Santamaria, arr. Jerry Nowak (Hal Leonard), singers should avoid simply trying to read individual notes and should try to develop a feel for the entire phrase. In pop/rock music, offbeat accents occur on the second half of the beat, while in vocal jazz they usually are held back and performed on the last third of the beat (see the following discussion on swing style). Directors should, therefore, determine the basic style and then assist their singers in its interpretation accordingly.

In music with a moderate tempo, there is a tendency for some singers to rush the figure ♪♩ ♪♩, particularly the eighth followed by the quarter note, thus creating a stiff or square effect. [73] Singers should be advised to stretch out or "lay back" on these two notes to create a more relaxed (and less corny) style.

In swing style, both equal eighth notes and dotted eighth and sixteenth notes are performed with a two-to-one, rather than a three-to-one, ratio. For example, the dotted-eighth-and-sixteenth-note pattern in the old standard "Louise," notated as $\frac{4}{4}$ ♫. ♫. ♫ ♫. ♫ | ♫. ♫ ♫. ♫ ♩ |, is not sung as indicated, but as $\frac{12}{8}$ ♩♪♩♪♩.♩♪ | ♩♪♩♪♩ |. .The three-to-one durational pattern would create a stiff or "square" effect, whereas the two-to-one relationship (as indicated in the example) makes the choir "swing." Another way of notating the two-to-one relationship is as follows: $\frac{4}{4}$ ♩ ♪♩ ♪♩♩ ♪♩ ♩ ♪♩ ♪♩ |.

However, in certain instances this notation can be somewhat difficult to read. An increasing number of arrangers are indicating on the score the style they desire. For example, in "I Hear Music," by Loesser and Lane, arr. Larry Lapin (Warner Bros.), the directions "Moderate Swing" (♫ = ♩ ♪) are indicated.

While all the eighth notes in this arrangement are written equally, the directions clearly indicate to the director that a two-to-one relationship is necessary in performance. If the music is not marked "swing style," then one may be

[73] See, for example, "Georgia on My Mind," by Hoagy Carmichael, arr. Gene Puerling (Studio P/R).

inclined to assume that equal eighth notes should be performed as written. However, there can be exceptions to this, and you must use your own musical judgment. In swing style, the dotted quarter note is similarly performed as: ♩.♪ = ♩⌣♩ ♪. Also in swing style, one may periodically encounter the rhythmic figure 4/4 ♩ ♩ ♩. ♩ ♩. ♩ |. As to the last two equal eighth notes, they have been performed in three ways: ♫ , ♩ ♪ and ♩ ♪. In such situations, try the pattern several ways; that is, experiment, think about what you feel is the most effective or sensitive way, and then do it!

In the first measure of the introduction to the arrangement of "I Hear Music," each chord (syllable) is notated on the second half of the first, second, and fourth beats, respectively; however, they are performed on the last one-third of each of the beats indicated. (Note the directions by the arranger—"Moderate Swing ♫ = ♩ ♪.") For the singers to respond to the rhythm accurately, they must feel the beginning of each beat and "bounce off," so to speak, so the accents are as precise as possible.

The question is often asked why arrangers don't notate the music the way they would like it to sound. Figure 75 shows the notated rhythm of an excerpt from "I Hear Music" followed by notation indicating the correct performance style. The latter two ways are obviously more difficult to read than the first. For this reason the traditional means of musical notation is generally used, with an indication of "swing style" given. Once you comprehend the basic swing style, you can usually read the notation quite easily.

In interpreting jazz rhythms, you will encounter innumerable patterns. For further study, see Clark Terry and Phil Rizzo, *The Interprerarion of the Jazz Lan-*

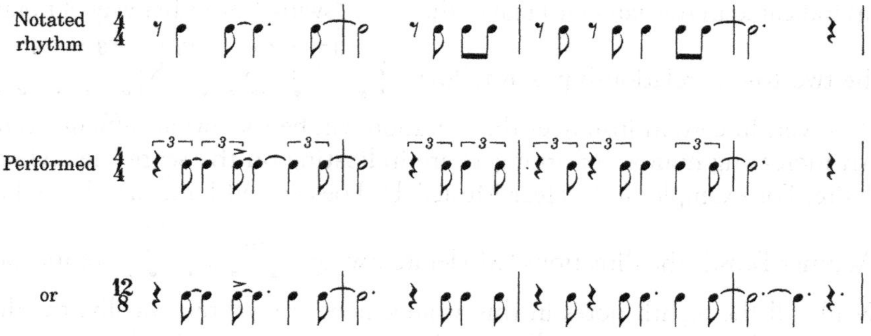

FIGURE 75   Rhythmic patterns from the introduction to "*I Hear Music*" as notated and as performed.[74]

[74] Notated rhythm from "I Hear Music," by Lane, arr. Larry Lapin. Warner Bros. No. CH 0926

guage, M.A.S. Publishing Co., Bedford, Ohio, 1977. In this publication, various rhythmic patterns are notated with a suggested appropriate jazz interpretation included on a line underneath.

Tempo

In the rendition of any vocal jazz or pop tune, the finding of the right groove is essential for the most precise articulation and overall impact of music. Directors will find the metronome markings helpful, but they should experiment a bit because, for example, the people who make up a group and the acoustics of the performance hall may have a subtle effect on the tempo that will seem right for that group. Once this is determined and marked on the conductor's score, many conductors like to refer to a pocket metronome to make certain of the tempo before it is given to the group. Performance conditions can have subtle effects on the groups, and they should be advised to hold rigidly to the given tempo—that is, don't rush and don't drag; keep on the beat!

On up-tempo tunes, there is often a tendency for the group to drag, or sing behind the beat. Conversely, on medium to slow tempos there is sometimes a tendency for a group to rush the tempo. As previously mentioned, an inward response to the pulse of the music is essential to maintaining a steady beat. On up-tempo tunes the singers should keep on top of the beat, so to speak, and have a feeling of leaning forward; that is, they should anticipate and respond to the "front" side of the beat. (However, they should avoid rushing up-tempo tunes to the extent that articulation becomes blurred.) On slow tempos, singers should be advised to lay back, relax, and respond to the back side of the beat.

Sometimes there is a tendency for singers to rush staccato notes that fall on the beat—for example, $\frac{4}{4}$ ♩ ♩ ♩ ♩ ♩ ♩ ♩♩♩♩ ♩. They should be advised to lay back and allow for the separation that should occur between the quarter notes.

Tone Quality

In vocal jazz, as well as in most pop tunes, singers should sing with a straight tone during all unison passages and in those with close or tight harmony; otherwise, the intonation and the blend will be adversely affected. Note, for example, the voicing in measure 2 of the excerpt from "When I Fall in Love" (Hal Leonard), shown in Figure 76. With the bass, tenor, and alto parts an interval of a major second apart, the clarity of the chord structure would most certainly be muddled were any vibrato to be used. Some vibrato, however, may be used occasionally for coloring purposes, but primarily on solo passages.

The same basic principles of correct tone production as related in Chapter 2 generally apply to pop singing (see section titled "Developing Choral Tone" in particular). As to diction, initial consonants should be clearly and precisely articulated, though the intensity of *middle* and *final* consonants should be minimized. The consonant *t*, in particular, needs to be softened. For example, on the

FIGURE 76 Excerpt from "When I Fall in Love," by Edward Heyman and Victor Young, arranged by Phil Azelton. © Copyright 1952, 1973 by Northern Music Corp., a division of MCA Entertainment, Inc., and Victor Young Publications. Used by permission.

final consonant in *doot*, minimize the *t* and keep the tongue in contact with the palate. Also, the function of the *t* in *doot* is to stop the sound.

As to the treatment of diphthongs, the second vowel will usually be omitted or at least softened. One of the most troublesome problems of choral singers, regardless of the music style, seems to be their dogged determination to anticipate the second vowel in diphthongs, and, of course, not all; do this at the same time, thus resulting in problems with choral blend. Pop singers, however, have numerous models to whom they listen regularly, so you can perhaps more readily make your point. In summary, tone and diction in pop style should not be forced, but should be somewhat relaxed and easygoing.

Vocal Jazz Articulations and Inflections

The following symbols are generally accepted as standard articulations and inflections for arrangements of vocal jazz ensemble music.

Accent markings

- = heavy accent held to fullest value. May occur on or off the beat.
- = heavy accent, usually on the beat and held less than full value.
- = heavy accent, but short as possible.

Tenuto and Staccato

- = note held to fullest value.
- = short and detached.

Shake

= a rather fast alternation between the written pitch and minimally a major second above. Some directors prefer a minor third or even a major third. Shakes need not be synchronized within the group.

Flip

= sound first note written, and just before its release raise the pitch and drop quickly to the next note.

Smear

= a slide into a note from below, reaching the pitch just before the next note. The length of the smear, then, depends on the length of the note.

Falloff

= a descending slide that may be either short or long, depending on the style and the tempo of the music. (The sigh is the essence of the falloff.)

Doit

= an ascending slide of one to five steps.

Plop

= a descending slide to the indicated note. Sing the main note at the last instant and "land" with force.

Indefinite Sound (Ghost Notes)

= an indefinite pitch for notes needing a soft but vital sound.

Glissando (Gliss)

= a slide from one pitch to another that may be up, down, short, or long.

or   Some arrangers simply mark the music as *slide* .

Downward Turn or Dip

= an inflection, generally occurring on the first beat of a measure, in which the singers bend a note downward, usually a half step, and resume the original pitch. [75]

In rehearsing music in the jazz/pop idiom, there are many subtleties of interpretation you should be aware of. The following activities, therefore, will enable you to develop greater sensitivity by (1) listening to and analyzing recordings of outstanding popular groups; (2) discussing various matters of inter-

[75] For further performance suggestions, see Kirby Shaw's *Vocal Jazz Style*, 2d ed. (Milwaukee: Hal Leonard, 1990).

pretation with your colleagues (most school systems have at least one person who has had experience with instrumental or vocal jazz ensembles); (3) attending concerts of other jazz/show choirs in the area; and (4) openly discussing interpretative matters with the students in the ensemble. Following are several performing groups whose recordings are suggested for listening and study: Manhattan Transfer, Singers Unlimited, The Hi Lo's, Rare Silk, Phil Mattson & the P.M. Singers, and the Swingle Singers.

SOME CONCLUDING THOUGHTS

Certainly characteristic of twentieth-century music is the wide diversity of musical styles. It is often difficult to place composers neatly in the previously mentioned categories, since some change their styles during their composing years. Other composers are eclectic, that is, they draw from the techniques and devices of various schools, depending on the musical thought to be expressed. To interpret properly the works of any particular modern-day composer, study and analyze the music as well as the writings of the composer. What composers say about their own music has obvious implications for proper interpretation. Whenever such writings do not exist or are unavailable, turn to the vast number of books on twentieth-century composers (as well as those of other periods). What others have written about the lives and the music of particular individuals will often provide the inquiring, analytical reader with fresh insights into the interpretation of music.

The study of style and interpretation is not a subject to be dealt with on a one-time basis—it should be studied throughout your musical career. The intent of this chapter has been to provide a summary of the most salient points for consideration. To be most meaningful, however, they must be studied in connection with actual music. With this background information, carefully study and analyze your scores. Only through reflective thought on the composer's intentions will the proper interpretation be achieved. Listen critically to the interpretations of various choral organizations—on recordings and in the concert hall. The listener will most likely find that the interpretation of a particular composition will vary somewhat from one conductor to another. "What is stylistically correct and what is incorrect about these performances?" and "What do I like and dislike about the performances?" These questions must be always present on the listener's mind if he or she is to make the proper evaluation essential to further musical growth. The young conductor must give these questions careful consideration if he or she is ultimately to achieve the correct interpretation.

Finally, the effective conductor must also be a scholar. You should devote considerable time to further reading in various sources of the main points discussed in this chapter. Develop a broad historical understanding of the various periods of artistic achievement. For these purposes, a selected list of publications recommended for further study is included at the end of this chapter. Particularly recommended is *Choral Music: History, Style, and Performance Practice*, by Robert L. Garretson, Englewood Cliffs, N.J.: Prentice Hall, 1993.

TOPICS FOR DISCUSSION

1. What are some problems you might encounter when trying to perform baroque music as it was originally intended?
2. Discuss the benefits and the drawbacks of the old system of princely patronage of composers. What ideas have been advanced for the support of composers in our present-day society?
3. What specific techniques might a choral conductor use in teaching an appropriate style for any given period or composer? Discuss each historical period and cite particular composers and works.
4. How should the conductor's beat vary in conducting music of various periods?
5. In striving toward an authentic performance, to what extent should you allow authenticity to give way to your personal idiosyncrasies?
6. Discuss the effect of geographical influences on the style and mode of expression of particular composers.
7. The Romantic era has been referred to as a "period of opposites." What is meant by this expression, and what are the implications for understanding the music of particular composers?
8. What is meant by the term *eclectic style?* Give some examples.

SELECTED READINGS

ALDRICH, PUTMAN C. "The 'Authentic' Performance of Baroque Music." In *Essays on Music in Honor of Archibald T. Davison*. Cambridge, Mass.: Harvard University Press, 1957.

APEL, WILLI. *The Notation of Polyphonic Music, 900–1600*. Cambridge, Mass.: Medieval Academy of America, 1942.

ARNOLD, DENIS. *The New Oxford Companion to Music* (2 vols.). Oxford, England: Oxford University Press, 1983.

ARTZ, FREDERICK. *From the Renaissance to Romanticism*. Chicago: University of Chicago Press, 1962.

BAKER, THEODORE. *Baker's Biographical Dictionary of Musicians* (7th ed., rev. Nicolas Slonimsky). New York: Schirmer Books, 1984.

BARRA, DONALD. *The Dynamic Performance: A Performer's Guide to Musical Expression and Interpretation*. Englewood Cliffs, N.J.: Prentice-Hall, 1983.

BLUME, FRIEDRICH. *Classic and Romantic Music*. New York: W.W. Norton & Co., 1970.

————. *Renaissance and Baroque Music*. New York: W.W. Norton & Co., Inc., 1967.

BORROFF, EDITH. *The Music of the Baroque*. Dubuque, Iowa: Wm. C. Brown, 1970.

BROWN, HOWARD. *Music in the Renaissance*. Englewood Cliffs, N.J.: Prentice-Hall, 1976.

BUKOFZER, MANFRED F. *Music in the Baroque Era: From Monteverdi to Bach*. New York: W.W. Norton & Co., Inc., 1947.

————. "On the Performance of Renaissance Music," *Music Teachers National Association, Volume of Proceedings*, 1941. Pittsburgh: The Association, 1942, pp. 225–35.

CALVOCORESSI, M.D. *A Survey of Russian Music*. Baltimore: Penguin, 1944.

CURTIS, MARVIN V. AND LEE V. CLOUD. "The African-American Spiritual: Traditions and Performance Practices" *The Choral Journal* 32 no. 4 (November 1991), 15–22.

DART, THURSTON. *The Interpretation of Music* (rev. ed.). London: Hutchinson Publishing Group, Ltd., 1960

DECKER, HAROLD A. AND JULIUS HERFORD. *Choral Conducting Symposium* (2nd. ed.), chaps. 3, 4. Englewood Cliffs, N.J.: Prentice Hall, 1988.

DOLMETSCH, ARNOLD. *The Interpretation of the Music of the XVIIth & XVIIIth Centuries*. London: Oxford University Press, 1946.

DONINGTON, ROBERT. *The Interpretation of Music*. London: Faber & Faber Ltd., 1963.

DORIAN, FREDERICK. *The History of Music in Performance*. New York: W.W. Norton & Co., Inc., 1942.

EINSTEIN, ALFRED. *The Italian Madrigal* (3 vols.). Princeton, N.J.: Princeton University Press,
———. *Music in the Romantic Era*. New York: W.W. Norton, 1947.
ETHERINGTON, CHARLES L. *Protestant Worship Music: Its History and Practice*. New York: Holt Rinehart & Winston, 1962.
FELLOWES, EDMUND H. *The English Madrigal Composers* (2d ed.) London: Oxford University Press, 1948.
FLEMING, WILLIAM, AND ABRAHAM VEINUS. *Understanding Music: Style, Structure, and History*, pp. 309–310. New York: Holt, Rinehart & Winston, 1958.
GARRETSON, ROBERT L. *Choral Music: History, Style and Performance Practice*. Englewood Cliffs, N.J.: Prentice Hall, 1993.
———. "The Falsettists." *The Choral Journal* 24 no. 1 (September 1983), 5–9.
GORE, RICHARD T. "The Performance of Baroque Church Music," *Music Teachers National Association, Volume of Proceedings*, 1950. Pittsburgh: The Association, 1953, pp. 155- 163.
GROUT, DONALD JAY. *A History of Western Music* (3rd ed.). New York; W.W. Norton & Co., Inc., 1980.
Grove's Dictionary of Music and Musicians (5th ed., 9 vols.). New York: St. Martin's Press, Macmillan & Co., Ltd., 1954.
HANSEN, PETER S. *An Introduction to Twentieth Century Music* (2nd ed.) Boston: Allyn & Bacon, 1967.
HARMAN, R. ALEC, AND ANTHONY MILNER. *Late Renaissance and Baroque Music*. London: Barrie & Rockliff, 1959
HEGER, THEODORE E. *Music of the Classic Period*. Dubuque, Iowa: Wm. C. Brown, 1969.
HOWERTON, GEORGE. *Technique and Style in Choral Singing*. New York: Carl Fischer, Inc., 1957.
JEPPESEN, KNUD. *The Style of Palestrina and the Dissonance*. Copenhagen: Ejnar Munksgaard, Publisher, 1946.
JORGENSEN, OWEN. *Tuning the Historical Temperaments by Ear*. Marquette: Northern Michigan University Press, 1977.
KENNEDY, MICHAEL. *The Oxford Dictionary of Music*. Oxford, England: Oxford University Press, 1985.
KJELSON, LEE, AND JAMES McCRAY. *The Conductor's Manual of Choral Music Literature*. Miami: CPP/Belwin, 1973.
LANG, PAUL HENRY. *Music in Western Civilization*. New York: W.W. Norton, 1941.
LEONARD, RICHARD. *A History of Russian Music*. New York: Macmillan, 1957.
LONGYEAR, REY M. *Nineteenth-Century Romanticism in Music* (3d ed.). Englewood Cliffs, N.J.: Prentice Hall, 1988.
MACCLINTOCK, CAROL, ed. *Readings in the History of Music in Performance*. Bloomington, Ind.: Indiana University Press, 1979.
MACHLIS, JOSEPH. *The Enjoyment of Music* (5th ed.). New York: W.W. Norton 1984.
———. *Introduction to Contemporary Music* (2nd ed.). New York: W.W. Norton 1979.
MANN, WILLIAM. *James Galway's Music in Time*. Englewood Cliffs, N.J.: Prentice-Hall, 1983.
MAY, JAMES D. *Avant-Garde Choral Music: An Annotated Selected Bibliography*. Metuchen, N.J.: Scarecrow, 1977.
MOE, DANIEL. "The Conductor and Twentieth Century Choral Music," in *Choral Conducting Symposium* (2nd ed.). Harold A. Decker and Julius Herford, eds. Englewood Cliffs, N.J.: Prentice Hall 1988.
MORLEY, THOMAS. *Plain and Easy Introduction to Practical Music*. London, 1597. Modern edition by R. Alec Harman, London, 1952.
New Grove Dictionary of Music and Musicians, The, ed. Stanley Sadie (20 vols.). London: Macmillan Publishers, Ltd., 1980.
PALISCA, CLAUDE V. *Baroque Music* (2nd ed.). Englewood Cliffs, N.J.: Prentice-Hall, 1981.
PATTISON, BRUCE. *Music and Poetry of the English Renaissance*. London: Methuen & Company Ltd., 1948.
PAULY, REINHARD G. *Music in the Classic Period* (2nd ed.). Englewood Cliffs, N.J.: Prentice-Hall, 1973.
POOLER, FRANK, AND BRENT PIERCE. *New Choral Notation*. New York: Walton, 1971.
QUANTZ, JOHANN JOACHIM. *Versuch einer Anweisung die Flöte traversiere zu spielen*. Berlin, 1752. Translation and study by E. R. Reilly. Unpublished Ph.D. dissertation, University of Michigan, 1958.

RANDALL, DON MICHAEL, ed. *The New Harvard Dictionary of Music*. Cambridge, Mass.: Harvard University Press, 1986.

REESE, GUSTAVE. *Music in the Renaissance*. New York: W.W. Norton, 1954.

ROBINSON, RAY, AND ALLEN WINOLD. *The Choral Experience: Literature, Materials, and Methods*, Part Four on Performance Practices. New York: Harper & Row, 1976.

ROSEN, CHARLES. *Classic Style*. New York: Viking, 1971.

ROTHSCHILD, FRITZ. *The Lost Tradition in Music: Rhythm and Tempo in J. S. Bach's Time*. New York: Oxford University Press, 1953.

—. *Musical Performance in the Times of Mozart and Beethoven: The Lost Tradition in Music*, Part 2 New York: Oxford University Press, 1961.

SACHS, CURT. *Rhythm and Tempo: A Study in Music History*. New York: W.W. Norton 1953.

SALZMAN, ERIC. *Twentieth-Century Music: An Introduction* (2d ed.). Englewood Cliffs, N.J.: Prentice-Hall, 1974.

SCOTT, CHARLES KENNEDY. *Madrigal Singing*. London: Oxford University Press, 1931.

SPARKS, EDGAR. *Cantus Firmus in Mass and Motet, 1420–1520*. Berkeley and Los Angeles: University of California Press, 1963.

STEVENSON, ROBERT. *Music before the Classic Era*. London: Macmillan & Co., Ltd., 1955.

STRUNK, OLIVER, ed. *Source Readings in Music History*. New York: W.W. Norton, 1950.

SWAN, HOWARD. *Conscience of a Profession* (ed. Charles Fowler). Chapel Hill, N.C.: Hinshaw, 1987.

TARTINI, GIUSEPPE. "Treatise on Ornamentation" (trans. and ed. Sol Babitz) *Journal of Research in Music Education* 4, no. 2 (Fall 1956), 75–102.

ULRICH, HOMER. *A Survey of Choral Music*. New York: Harcourt Brace Jovanovich, 1973.

—. AND PAUL A. PISK. *A History of Music and Musical Style*. New York: Harcourt Brace Jovanovich, 1963.

VIQUIST, MARY, and Neal Zaslaw. *Performance Practice: A Bibliography*. New York: W.W. Norton, 1971.

YOUNG, PERCY M. *The Choral Tradition*. New York: W.W. Norton, 1962.

VIDEOTAPES

A Renaissance of Monteverdi. Produced by Eugene Enrico and William Crane, 1981. Center for Music Television, University of Oklahoma, Norman, OK 73019.

Handel's Messiah: A Commemoration. Produced by Eugene Enrico and William Crane, 1984. Center for Music Television, University of Oklahoma, Norman, OK 73019.

Music of Antonio Vivaldi. Produced by Eugene Enrico and Dave Smeal, 1987. Center for Music Television, University of Oklahoma, Norman, OK 73019.

Music of Thomas Morley. Produced by Eugene Enrico and Dave Smeal, 1987. Center for Music Television, University of Oklahoma, Norman, OK 73019.

Wedding Cantata by Marc-Antoine Charpentier. Produced by Eugene Enrico and William Crane 1982. Center for Music Television, University of Oklahoma, Norman, OK 73019.

Rehearsal
Techniques

The success of the choral concert is determined in the rehearsal room. Effective musical results depend on a well-defined concept of your musical objectives and on your ability to transmit them to the members of the choral group. Although careful planning assists in the clarification of objectives, you must possess various techniques for implementing your ideas. Efforts in this direction will result in higher musical standards and increased satisfaction for both the performers and the audience.

PREREHEARSAL PLANNING

Choral directors are constantly asked to perform, and many, especially school music directors, feel that allocated rehearsal time is inadequate to develop their groups to the proper performance level. In view of this situation, rehearsals must necessarily be well planned to make the most effective use of your time. Careful prerehearsal planning is also likely to result in more meaningful learning experiences, which in turn provide the climate necessary for subsequent learning experiences. Following are some general suggestions concerning overall rehearsal planning.

1. Plan for a variety of musical types and styles.
2. Know the music well! Identify troublesome spots in the score and decide how you will handle them.

3. Study the text carefully, know its meanings, and identify any words with an unusual pronunciation.
4. Apply your knowledge of musical style.
5. What do you plan to say to the group? Write out some sample sentences.
6. Do you plan to demonstrate any ideas? If so, what and how?
7. Plan to take a positive attitude toward your singers.
8. Help your accompanist prepare for the rehearsal.
9. Determine beforehand and write the rehearsal order of selections on the chalkboard.
10. Consider matters of the group's progress that should be evaluated following each rehearsal.

Include a variety of music from all historical periods in the choral rehearsal. If choir members are to develop an understanding of, and appreciation for, various types of music, they should have some experience with choral music of the Renaissance, Baroque, Classic, Romantic, and Modern periods, as well as with folk music.[1] Furthermore, when you provide variety by alternating selections with contrasting styles, moods, and tempi, student interest is more readily maintained.

Never attempt to learn the music concurrently with your singers; study it carefully prior to each rehearsal. To become familiar with the music, read through the choral parts on the piano. Note specific difficulties or pitfalls such as intricate rhythmic patterns, difficult intervals in the various parts, unusual harmonic progressions, and particular diction problems. Mark your score with a colored pencil, indicating the anticipated difficulties.

Consider the teaching procedures you will use to clarify and solve rhythmic and tonal problems. Analyze and practice specific conducting techniques. It is advisable to sing through any portions of the vocal parts that are likely to cause the singers difficulty, so that they may be demonstrated adequately to the choir. Examine the text for words with an unusual pronunciation, and when in doubt, consult a dictionary. Any subtleties in the text should also be noted as a basis for achieving the proper interpretation.

In addition, you will want to draw on all your resources and musical background to achieve an effective musical interpretation. The practical application of knowledge gained in music theory and history classes will at this point be of inestimable value. Apply your knowledge of musical styles in various historical periods and, more specifically, your understanding of the unique styles of individual composers.

In determining the procedures for accomplishing your objectives, prepare and write out a set of sample sentences on how to state what you desire to say or do. Such a procedure will enable you to be more objective and precise about your procedures. Not too much should be said! Be succinct and consider the *impact* of what you plan to say or do! If you later find that your procedure is not really effective, then try another way. Your written plan will provide you with some basis for evaluating your actions.

[1] For a chronological listing of choral composers, see Appendix.

There are three basic ways or procedures for achieving your objectives: (1) verbally; (2) by demonstrating (singing to illustrate tone quality, pronunciation, enunciation, phrasing, and so on, and clapping or chanting to correct rhythmic difficulties); and (3) by using some psychological device or motivation such as "let the tone float—just as light as a feather." You must decide which of these three procedures will be most effective in solving the problem at hand.

Some directors, in their eagerness to facilitate the choir's learning, attempt to sing along with them, assisting various parts wherever necessary. This seldom helps much. You cannot blend with the choir, and you are at a decided disadvantage because when you are singing you are unable to hear the choir adequately and to identify specific tonal and rhythmic difficulties. It is helpful, however, to mouth the words periodically, particularly at points of entrance to help singers, for example, to initiate a new phrase. Maintaining close eye contact with the singers, both helps them feel more secure and encourages a more musical interpretation. Conducting the music by memory will enable you to maintain such eye contact and is sometimes admired by singers and the audience. However, for reference, or in case of a failed memory, always keep an open score on the stand. Better safe than sorry!

It is important that the director give reinforcement through words of approval or positive actions. If students are to improve, they need to know what they have achieved and what problems still remain to be solved. In short, they need careful guidance. Some teachers feel they shouldn't comment on progress until the rendition of a specific choral selection is almost perfect. This approach is not advisable—conductors should give *some* approval whenever possible. Teachers, however, should make an honest assessment. Actually, progress occurs in degrees, and directors may likewise respond with varying degrees of approval ranging from minimal approval to great satisfaction. The following succinct statements are provided as examples.

Minimal approval—"That's better! You have the idea!"
Moderate approval—"That's good! Much improved!"
Maximum approval—"I like it! That's great!"

Young conductors may sometimes have a concept in mind about how the music should sound and then conduct blithely away, seemingly oblivious to the reality of the situation. At times during a rehearsal you may wish to make corrections but are receiving so many stimuli that you are unable to find the words to express what you want. By identifying potential problems—and this skill improves through experience—and writing out appropriate statements or ways of seeking solutions, you will be better able to respond to the situation. By writing out succinct statements you will avoid the opposite pitfall of saying too much—to the extent that the impact is lost and valuable rehearsal time is lost.

Prior to the rehearsal, determine the order of the selections to be rehearsed and place them on the chalkboard. Singers, after they enter the rehearsal room, can then place their music in order, thus saving time and eliminating or at least minimizing any confusion prior to working on each selection.

Make certain that the accompanist is provided with any new music in ample time prior to the rehearsal, with instructions on tempo, dynamics, mood, and the like. The most carefully laid rehearsal plans can be of little avail if the accompanist is not adequately prepared.

After each rehearsal, it is desirable to take a few moments to evaluate the group's progress and to notate, either on the music or in a notebook, those points in the score that need further attention, and any approaches that might be effectively used in subsequent rehearsals.

THE SINGERS' RESPONSIBILITIES

To what extent do the singers in the choir share the director's objectives? Do they have a full understanding of what is expected of them? Do they realize that the conductor can achieve only so much without their complete understanding and support? While conductors can verbalize many of the choir's overall objectives to the singers, you must realize that the majority of persons are visually rather than aurally oriented. Therefore, prepare a list of objectives you consider most important. The list, prepared in the form of questions, should then be duplicated and distributed to the choir members, so that every singer can read and contemplate each question. Questions may deal, for example, with each singer's preparation for rehearsals, attention given to the director's instructions, attitudes about new music, encouragement of other singers in the choir, listening to one's own singing voice, understanding of the text of the music, efforts toward memorizing the music, visual attention to the director, efforts toward improving music reading skills, and expectations regarding the achievements of the choir.

All questions and statements serve to reinforce comments that the director has previously stated verbally. Singers are asked to evaluate themselves on each question and determine how they rate personally, and to periodically reassess their status. The list provides a basis for informal group discussions held preferably at the beginning of the year and periodically as occasions necessitate. For an example of a questionnaire that can be adapted for use with your choir, see the article "Responsibilities of the Choir Singer," by Robert L. Garretson in *The Choral Journal* 28, no. 9 (April 1988) pp. 34–36.

THE FIRST REHEARSAL

The success of a choral group depends to a great extent on the success of the initial rehearsal. In recruiting members, one of the best advertisements is a group of inspired singers. The word soon gets around that choral singing is an exciting adventure, and the question "Why don't you join too?" may be frequently asked.

Young singers entering the rehearsal room for the first time may possess mixed feelings about choral singing—they may eagerly anticipate an activity that they feel will be exciting and enjoyable, and yet be somewhat dubious of the outcome or the wisdom of their choice. It is your responsibility as the director to plan the rehearsal so that it will move smoothly toward its objective.

After the group has been seated, set the group at ease with a few words of welcome. Next, explain the general rehearsal procedures and tell the singers what they must do in order to retain their membership. Initial remarks, however, should be kept to a minimum, and the business of the actual rehearsal should be undertaken without unnecessary delay. Also keep in mind that overemphasis on technique in the beginning can have a deadly effect on a young choral group. These details are generally best introduced as the requirements of music dictate—and only a few at a time.

In selecting the music for the first rehearsal, consider the musical background of the group. Perhaps the singers have not been exposed to the standard choral literature and are generally unaware and unappreciative of its inherent beauties. In the beginning, it is helpful to concentrate on a variety of folk song arrangements of a rhythmical nature. In situations where the singers' backgrounds are extremely limited, intersperse a few easy rounds and canons with the rest of the repertoire. By providing the singers with music commensurate with their abilities and backgrounds, you can minimize individual feelings of frustration, and a more successful and enjoyable rehearsal will result. In the beginning, the singers should be provided with music they like, as long as it is within the limits of good musical taste. There will be ample time for raising musical standards and improving individual tastes.

The importance of having the first concert as soon as possible cannot be underestimated. Individuals constantly need a goal before them to guide their work if they are to make strides toward a consistently improved performance. This is especially important in the early stages of the development of a newly organized group. Soon the singers will anticipate the rehearsals for the sheer beauty of the music itself and the enjoyment and satisfaction that they receive. At this point you should implement your plans, on a gradual basis, for broadening the singers' musical interests and raising their tastes and musical standards.[2]

INTRODUCING MUSIC

In teaching new music, the best procedures are those that facilitate learning and achieve artistic singing in the shortest period of time. Some choral directors employ what is called the "note approach"; that is, after an attempt is made to read the music, each part is worked out separately with the aid of the piano, and finally all the parts are sung together. Such a procedure is extremely tedious, discipline is often difficult to maintain, and artistic singing is not readily achieved. One of the greatest objections to this procedure is that few of the emotional

[2] For further information on prerehearsal planning, see "Studying the Score," page 56.

qualities of the music survive this mechanical approach. The following suggestions are given in an attempt to remedy this dilemma.

If the singers have a fair amount of reading power, they should try to sing the entire number through from beginning to end (with or without the aid of the piano, depending on the development of their musicianship). In this way, not only will the reading ability of the group improve, but also an overall concept of the music will be attained.

When difficult compositions are being presented, the accompanist may play the music on the piano while each singer follows his or her part. If a good recording is available, it can be an invaluable aid in presenting new music. It is certainly not recommended that choral recordings be slavishly imitated by any group or conductor, but they can serve as an extremely useful guide and rehearsal aid. After the choir members have been introduced to the music and have an overall conception of it, then various sections may be rehearsed in detail.

Many choral conductors have found through years of experience that once the rhythmic problems have been overcome, the notes and the parts come faster. In studying sections of the music, it is very helpful to have the singers recite together the text of the composition in correct musical rhythm. Such an approach helps to solve problems of rhythm, diction, phrasing, and proper dynamics simultaneously.

This procedure does not preclude the necessity for occasionally devoting special attention to a particular voice part. At a specific point in the rehearsal, this may be the only means of achieving the desired musical results. Difficulties do sometimes arise, however, when directors devote too much time to this procedure. Discipline problems may be lessened considerably if you strive to maintain the group's interest at all times and if you stress the importance of using all the rehearsal time to the group's best advantage. In achieving this objective, you may use the following procedures alternately. First, while one part is being rehearsed, the other singers should be asked to study their part and listen to it in relation to the other parts. Second, all singers might be asked to sing a troublesome part in unison. This procedure also has value in developing an awareness of the relationships between parts. Third, request the choir members to *hum* their own parts softly while the troublesome part is being rehearsed.

Successful directors have found that effective rehearsals must be stimulating and move quickly. When the director maintains a fast pace and the singers are kept busy, much more is accomplished and confusion is reduced to a minimum.

SECTIONAL REHEARSALS

Many directors like to utilize sectional rehearsals periodically so that individual parts may be learned more readily. The desirability of such rehearsals, of course, depends on the choir and their ability to learn new music without a lot of attention being given to individual parts. If the latter situation is the case, then rehearsal time may be best used by dividing the choir, for example, for separate men's and women's sectional rehearsals. In addition to teaching singers their individual parts, sectional rehearsals let you focus on the development of a more homogeneous tonal quality for the various voice parts. This is not as readily attained in a full choir rehearsal with various voice timbres resounding throughout the rehearsal room. Voice qualities to strive for in a sectional rehearsal are a light, floating tone for sopranos; a fuller, somewhat heavier quality for altos; a high-forward resonance for tenor voices, with the utilization of a light head voice, or falsetto quality in the upper range; and a full-bodied resonant tone for baritones and basses.

IMPROVING MUSIC READING

In most areas of learning, conceptual understandings are likely to be most meaningful when learning is through a discovery process and not through simply being told the answer. Similarly, in music, sight-reading skills will improve most when singers have to struggle a bit to interpret the score. Once they hear the music through a recording or on the piano, they no longer need to rely on their musical memory in an attempt to recall the correct rhythm and pitches, for they already *have* the answer. To improve music-reading skills, singers need to be provided with challenges involving a wide variety of rhythmic and tonal experience.

If individuals are to improve, they must recognize and feel a need for improvement. Some persons are strongly motivated toward achieving success in all areas and have a strong desire for self-improvement. Such minds are highly receptive to improving music reading skills. However, not everyone possesses this degree of motivation, and you can assist persons who do not by helping them feel the satisfaction of achievement. Be positive in all your remarks and plan all music-reading experiences so that they are as challenging and interesting as possible. Any devices used should generally grow out of a problem in actually reading music. At least, they should relate to a specific problem of music reading. Abstract drills, unrelated in any way to actual music, can become most dull and serve little purpose.

If the sight-reading abilities of a choir are to be developed, attention must be given to their development during each rehearsal period. Sight-reading can be improved only by practice, based on musical understanding. Perhaps just past the midway point of each rehearsal, include at least one selection for sight-reading purposes. Procedures followed at music competition-festivals are suggested. The music should be carefully examined by the choir members while the director points out and discusses various pitfalls inherent in it. Upon first examination, singers should accustom themselves to looking first at the meter and key signatures and at the beginning chord, and then scanning their respective parts for intricate rhythmic patterns or figures, unfamiliar intervals (particularly wide ones), any chromatic alterations, and expression markings. Next, pitches should be given and the group should attempt to sing the music completely through from beginning to end without a break. General suggestions that the group should keep in mind are (1) keep the eyes moving ahead to grasp patterns or groups of notes; (2) respond to the pulse of the music in some way—perhaps by wiggling the toes inside the shoes;[3] (3) keep going and do not stop or fret about mistakes; (4) look for familiar patterns in the music both before and during the reading process. Following the initial reading, difficult aspects of the music should again be discussed, and, if time allows, the selection should be repeated in an effort to eliminate previous errors.[4]

In many instances, problems of rhythm and pitch arising from reading sessions should be dealt with simultaneously. In other cases, the learning process may be facilitated when each is dealt with separately. Suggestions for achieving rhythmic responsiveness and tonal awareness follow.

Rhythmic Responsiveness

A singer's perception of rhythmic patterns and the accuracy of his or her response constitute an important part of music-reading skills. The following approaches are suggested as a means of increasing a choir's responsiveness to rhythm.

1. Reciting the text of the music in correct musical rhythm, as discussed in the preceding section, is an excellent means of facilitating the learning of difficult rhythm patterns. To develop individual rhythmic responsiveness, however, ask the singers to peruse the rhythmic patterns silently by themselves before the group chants them together.
2. Clapping the troublesome rhythm patterns is a good way to elicit a bodily response to rhythm. Opportunity should be provided for everyone to respond in various ways—individually, in quartets, or in sections, rather than just in the entire group.
3. Accumulate a number of rhythmic problems confronted by the singers. To encourage more careful listening coupled with bodily response, chant a one-or-two-measure pattern, with the group responding immediately afterward. The response is more effective if the group taps the heel or the toe prior to the chanting, and maintains this steady response to the pulse throughout the activity. Rhythmic patterns may vary from the simple to the complex and encompass all musical styles. (For an illustration of this idea, see the discussion or rhythmic precision as it relates to attacks and releases, and Figure 77, later in the chapter.)
4. Isolate particular rhythm problems in the music and write them on the chalkboard. Analyze them and then respond in some way by chanting or clapping, or by some counting system.
5. Some students have difficulty reading music in meters other than 3/4 and 4/4 because, as a result of their limited experience, they usually expect each beat to be

---

[3] For other means of encouraging a response to the pulse of the music, see "Attacks and Releases" later in the chapter.

[4] To develop sight-reading skills, some directors like to use music selected from their choral libraries; others prefer to use a methods book designed for this purpose. A recommended book is *The Jenson Sight Singing Course*, by David Bauguess (New Berlin, Wis.: Jenson, 1984).

a quarter note. To correct this misconception, and to broaden their experience, it is helpful to write on the chalkboard a familiar tune in a meter other than the original. A tune originally in 4/4 meter might be written, for example, in 4/8, 4/2, or 12/8 meter. The familiar tune serves as a common element and through singing and comparing different ways of notating a tune, students gain insight into the relatedness of rhythms.

6. Write a phrase of a familiar song on the chalkboard and, after the group has sung it through once, alter the rhythm in some way. Use simple rhythmic alterations, but soon include the more difficult until a considerable number of rhythm patterns have been experienced. The familiar song provides a base from which to begin, so that attention may be focused on the rhythm and not on the tonal problems.

Tonal Awareness

The ability to perceive differences and relationships in pitch and to reproduce them accurately is essential to achieving any degree of skill in music reading. We suggest the following procedures as a means of developing tonal awareness.

1. A keen awareness of the tonal relationships between various intervals in pitch and the ability to reproduce them accurately is essential to the achievement of good intonation, as well as to achieve any degree of skill in sight-music reading. One suggested device is the singing in unison of various intervals without aid from the piano. Ask the group to sing "up a major third" and back to the initial pitch, then "up a perfect fifth" and back, then "down a perfect fourth" and back, and so on, until various intervals have been sung. Extended over a period of time, this device may encompass a wide gamut of interval experience, which will contribute substantially to the singers' musicianship. The introduction of this procedure presupposes, of course, some preliminary instruction in the theoretical aspects of intervals, and some initial practice in singing them with the aid of the piano and observing them on the chalkboard as they are sung. The practicality of this device, in terms of improving sight-reading skills, lies in the singers' ability to establish the connection between this aural experience and the visual recognition of the intervals. Therefore, to establish the connection more firmly, during the rehearsal of certain selections, ask the singers to identify specific intervals, recall their relationships, and then sing them with a reasonable degree of accuracy.

    A related procedure is to train the group to sing the pitch A = 440 without aid from the piano. In the initial stages periodical checking of the pitch with the piano will be necessary and will illustrate to the group their relative degree of success. After a while the singers will develop this skill and a degree of confidence will result from the accomplishment. Once the pitch has become firmly established in the singers' minds, a basic starting point is also provided for the singing of various intervals. Then, on another day, ask the choir to sing F or G. Use this procedure with all the pitches of a scale, until the group develops a more acute sense of pitch. Most pitches can be recalled and sung with accuracy after a reasonable amount of practice.

2. A procedure used to help cement tonal relationships is to relate the intervals to those found in the opening pitches of familiar songs. A list of suggested songs follows. If some of the singers don't know the songs, then teach them. Singers should learn the entire song so they can recall the intervals in their tonal context. Encourage them to add songs that they know, and particularly enjoy, to the list. You also should look for appropriate songs.

The practical aspect of this procedure is to transfer this tonal frame of reference to the choral rehearsal where singers are reading new and unfamiliar music. When the group has difficulty with particular intervals, the director will ask the singers to (a) identify the musical interval, (b) recall one or more songs in which the interval occurs and sing the pitches, and (c) apply the sound to the intervals and the choral music they are reading.

INTERVALS

Half Steps (Semitones)

Ascending—   "Stardust" (Hoagy Carmichael)
Descending—   Theme from "MASH," "Habanera" (from *Carmen*, Bizet), "Ciribiribin" (Italian)

Major Seconds (Whole Tones)

Ascending—   "America," "Happy Birthday," "Polly Wolly Doodle"
Descending—   "Mary Had a Little Lamb," "I Dream of Jeannie" (Stephen Foster), "Turkey in the Straw"

Minor Thirds

Ascending—   Lullaby (Brahms), "Impossible Dream," "Angels We Have Heard on High" (3rd and 4th pitches), "After the Ball"
Descending—   "This Old Man," "The Caisson Song," "Everytime I Feel the Spirit," "The Sidewalks of New York" (chorus), "When You and I Were Young, Maggie"

Major Thirds

Ascending—   "On Top of Old Smoky," "For He's a Jolly Good Fellow," "Kum Bah Ya," "When the Saints Go Marchin' In," "I Heard the Bells on Christmas Day," "Holy, Holy, Holy"
Descending—   "Swing Low, Sweet Chariot," "Blest Be the Tie That Binds," "My Old Kentucky Home"

Perfect Fourths

Ascending—   "The Farmer in the Dell," "Auld Lang Syne," "Here Comes the Bride," "Flow Gently Sweet Afton," "Taps," "Hark, the Herald Angels Sing," "Pop! Goes the Weasel"
Descending—   "I've Been Working on the Railroad," "Born Free," "March of the Three Kings" (Bizet)

Augmented Fourths

Ascending—   "Maria" (from *West Side Story*, Bernstein)

Perfect Fifths

Ascending—   "Twinkle, Twinkle, Little Star," "My Favorite Things" (from
               The Sound of Music, Rodgers and Hammerstein)
Descending—   "My Home's in Montana," "Feelings"

Minor Sixths

Ascending—   "Go Down, Moses" (spiritual)
Descending—   "Love Story"

Major Sixths

Ascending—   "My Bonnie," "My Wild Irish Rose," "It Came Upon the Mid-
               night Clear"
Descending—   "Nobody Knows the Trouble I've Seen"

Minor Sevenths

Ascending—   "Somewhere" (from *West Side Story*, Bernstein)

Major Sevenths

Ascending—   "Bali Hai" (from *South Pacific*) (1st and 3rd pitches)

Perfect Octaves

Ascending—   "Somewhere Over the Rainbow," "The Christmas Song" (Mel
               Tome), "Annie Laurie" (3rd and 4th pitches)

The preceding procedure must be considered as a training technique and used for
that purpose only, since it quite understandably can slow a rehearsal down
Through careful prerehearsal planning, however you can anticipate those portions
of the music where intervallic difficulties are most likely to occur and then utilize
the procedure quickly and only where most appropriate. On other occasions, you
can play on the piano the initial phrases of different songs and then ask the group
to identify the opening intervals

3. Ear-training devices are generally helpful in developing tonal awareness, but particularly so are those that increase a singer's sensitivity to half steps. The following
   exercise will contribute toward that objective.

a. Proceed upward by half steps, stopping periodically to tune chords.

b. Upon arrival at desired pitch level proceed downward: alto down two half steps; soprano down one half step; tenor and bass down one half step and alto up one half step upon change to new chord. Repeat sequence, indicating each tonal change by cueing choir sections.

c. Use various vowel and consonant sounds: *oo, thum* or *doom* (for a detached sound), *mee, may, mah, moh, moo,* and so on.

d. Sing at various tempi from moderate to fast.

e. Begin the exercise from varying pitch levels.

4. Singing the resolutions of dominant seventh chords develops a feeling for tonality and for modulation to new keys and, as a result, has a direct relationship to music-reading skills. A seventh chord creates tension and each pitch possesses a pull toward another. Initially, it is desirable for the choir to experience all the resolutions in the different inversions of the chord. Then, they may sing the key circle progression given in Figure 77. The use of notation, however, is not necessary. Each section is asked, upon signal, to move to the closest possible note that will create a feeling of rest The soprano, alto and tenor parts will move upward or downward either a half or a whole step, or they will remain on the same tone. The bass part moves downward a fifth and upward a fourth, except in third inversion chords (V_2) when the seventh is in the bass part. Begin on a major triad, then direct one of the upper voice parts doubling the root of the chord to move downward a whole step, thus creating the dominant seventh chord. Give the choir lots of time to feel the pull of their notes before resolving each seventh chord.

FIGURE 77   Resolving the dominant seventh.

5. An excellent device for developing tonal awareness is to teach the choir member to recognize the chord progressions they sing. A good starting place is to identify the cadences. Too many individuals sing the simple V-I cadence without knowing what it is. A few minutes of each rehearsal can be well spent in explaining to the group the function and purpose of the cadence, and the part each note plays in the chord. You may want to take the chord progression out of context and drill each chord until it is perfectly in tune—each time making sure that the singers are able to identify the progression.

   As the group improves in their identification of chord sounds, you will be able to extend the process to more complicated chord progressions and eventually even to modulation. Such a practice, if carried on over a long period of time, will most certainly show results not only in improved reading ability but also in better intonation and all-round musicianship.

6. When intonation difficulties occur within the group, the pitch variation is usually less than a half tone, since otehwise the group would be singing a wrong note and many, but not all individuals would recognize such a discrepancy. A helpful device is therefore to train the choir to sing *quarter tones*. First, select a note in the middle range and have the group sing downward a whole tone and back, then down two half steps and back, then down two *quarter tones* and back. Immediately check the pitch with the piano. In the beginning the choir will find this procedure difficult but after repeated daily attempts they will soon be able to sing quarter tones with comparative ease. After singers have developed an acute consciousness of pitch, you often will be able to signal various sections of the choir to make the slight adjustments sometimes necessary for maintaining accurate pitch, especially when singing music *a cappella*.

7. Encourage the choir to maintain the pitches in their minds when they are stopped for corrections or suggestions. Do not always provide the pitch on the piano, but ask them to remember it and sing upon direction. At first they may flounder and begin to sing in a variety of keys. Soon, however, they will retain and recall the correct pitches. The general alertness necessary to remember the pitches will often have a beneficial effect on the rehearsal.

8. As a further means of developing tonal awareness, and as a check to determine how well the singers know their notes and if they are hearing them in tune, the device of *silent singing* is suggested.

   First, give the pitch of a selection the group knows reasonably well. Then ask the choir to sing the music "silently" together at the tempo indicated by the conductor. At the appropriate time, prepare the group to sing aloud with the verbal command, "Sing!" spoken on the previous beat. Initially, the group may sing silently for only four to eight measures, but as they become more proficient the activity may be extended in length. The choir may also be directed to sing aloud at the beginning of a new phrase or, again as they develop proficiency, at any point within the phrase. The conductor will find silent singing to be an excellent means to stimulate concentration and alertness and to rejuvenate a sluggish choir.

Attacks and Releases

Precision of attacks and releases is essential to artistic choral singing and is dependent on several factors—namely, the general attentiveness of the group, the rhythmic response of the group, and the basic technique of the conductor.

A choral group with high morale, in which each individual possesses a feeling of belonging and exhibits a singleness of effort toward the group's objectives, is relatively easy to motivate toward a consistently improved performance. The attentiveness of the choral group depends to a very great extent on this group morale and on a high degree of motivation. Difficulties usually arise, not in the early stages of rehearsing a selection, but in the latter stages, just prior to the perfection of the number. Always look for ways to stimulate interest and capture the singers' imagination. Individuals who are highly motivated and desirous of improving their group's musical standards will not succumb to the pitfalls of slovenly body attitudes and the resultant lack of precision.

Rhythmic security in the music not only aids in the precision and the vitality of the performance but also reduces to some extent excessive muscular tension and improves the tone quality of the group. Rhythmic security can be increased by encouraging a stronger rhythmic response to the music.

Here is an approach to rhythmic responsiveness that usually creates enthusiasm on the part of the singers. After setting the tempo, instruct the choir members to tap their feet (not too loudly) in response to the basic pulse. Continue for several measures until the group is responding together precisely. While the group continues the tapping, sing a rhythmic or melodic pattern one or two measures long. In the following measure or measures, the group responds and imitates the pattern previously sung by the director (Figure 78). When figures extend to the last beat of a measure, it is best for the group to wait out a full measure and enter on the subsequent measure, often on cue. Patterns should be varied and may be sung on a single pitch or a melodic or "scat" pattern.

School-age youth especially enjoy responding to different rhythmic patterns. Try it—the possibilities are unlimited! In addition to evoking rhythmic response, this procedure is also beneficial as an ear-training device.[5]

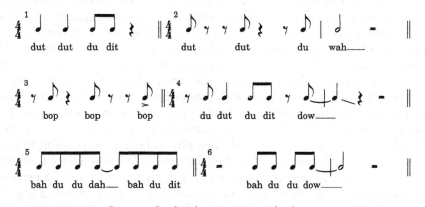

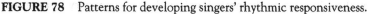

FIGURE 78   Patterns for developing singers' rhythmic responsiveness.

[5] This device is intended to be used in conjunction with music of a rhythmic, syncopated nature, such as the vigorous spiritual "Rock-a My Soul." It would provide an excellent means of evoking the necessary excitement and rhythmic awareness required for effective singing of this

Singers should develop a strong feeling for the pulsation of the music they are singing, especially if it is in a staccato or a marcato style. They are more likely to feel the pulsation if they make some large body movements while singing. Having the group either beat out the basic pulsation of the music on the knee or conduct the traditional conducting patterns can be exceedingly helpful.

The conductor should thoroughly prepare for all attacks and releases if they are to be clear to the performers. Many choral directors take too much for granted in this respect. Most singers soon learn to adjust to the indecisive movements of the conductor, yet as a group they are never quite sure of his intentions. The choral conductor's movements should be clear, precise, and rhythmical, and should reflect the mood of the music. Daily practice in front of a mirror can be very helpful. *See if you can follow yourself!*

BALANCE AND BLEND

To achieve correct balance, consider the voice quality of the individual singers, the range in which the voices are singing, the number of persons singing the various parts, and the harmonic aspects of the chords and the relative importance of the various vocal lines.

Voices of unusual and distinct tone quality often protrude from their sections, thus destroying the choral balance and blend. These voices must be subdued and blended with the group if artistic choral singing is to be achieved. You must be continually on the alert for such occurrences and strive to develop the singers' awareness of the problem. Often the difficulty results from poor voice production and improper breath control. In such instances, especially in the case of a wide tremolo, individual assistance is often necessary to correct the problem.

The problem of the tremolo, or excessively wide vibrato, usually occurs when a person tries to sing with an overly large, dramatic quality and does so without the proper breath support. To eliminate this condition, emphasize adequate breath support, a somewhat lighter tone quality, and practicing with a fairly straight tone. Through constant attention, the situation can be remedied.

When individuals are singing in the extreme high range of the voice, distortion is likely to occur. Voices with greater power and brilliance (resonance) in the upper registers must be subdued to the level of the entire group. If the proper balance and blend are to be maintained throughout the vocal range, choral groups should avoid using all their physical energy in an effort to sing as loud as possible. Distortion cannot help but result. The best advice is always to save some energy in reserve by singing only up to approximately 75 percent of the maximum vocal effort, and by concentrating on resonance and improved tone quality. Maximum dynamic levels will, of course, vary from group to group,

selection. Conversely, using the procedure immediately prior to a Bach chorale would by comparison make the chorale seem rather dull and would serve no purpose.

and the most effective dynamic ranges must necessarily be determined by the director for each specific group.

In music with divided parts, it may be necessary to redistribute some of the voices and assign them to the weaker parts in order to achieve the proper balance. It is suggested that a few selected voices in the chorus be designated as "roving" singers. This would mean, for example, that a few of the second sopranos need not be given definite voice assignments, but may sing either the soprano or the alto part as the musical situation demands.

Moving parts, especially when they occur in the lower voices, should be emphasized and brought out. When some of the parts are sustained, these moving parts often indicate a change of harmony and are of special interest to the listener. A much more musical effect often can be created by emphasizing the rhythmical movement of the vocal line, rather than by just singing the part a little louder. The problem of bringing out the melody usually occurs when it is in the lower parts. In such instances it might be well to mark the melody on all the music. Close attention to dynamics is most essential in securing balance between the melodic line and the supporting harmonic parts.

Other factors influencing choral blend, aside from those previously mentioned, pertain specifically to uniform vowel production and tonal and harmonic awareness. In singing, the tone is sustained on the various vowel sounds. Each vowel produced must be clear and distinct and uniform in production throughout the choir if any degree of blend is to be achieved. The choral director should stress the importance of *singing on the vowel*. As a basis for achieving good blend, present the following two concepts to the group and emphasize them continually.

1. Following the initial consonant, move to the vowel sound as quickly as possible—and *sing on the vowel*.
2. Listen carefully and try to blend your vowel sounds with the group.

Many directors have found it profitable to utilize all the primary vowel sounds in an exercise in which careful attention can be given to uniform production within the group. (See Exercise 26 for blending the vowels.)

EXERCISE 26

Mah may mee moh moo, mah may mee moh moo,

1. Vocalize within the middle range of the voice only.
2. Move smoothly from one vowel to another.
3. Listen carefully—strive for uniform production within the group.

Some singers appear to be completely unaware of the other voices in the group. Good blend, balance, and intonation will not be achieved unless all the singers are trained to listen to the entire ensemble as well as to themselves.[6] Singers should be advised never to sing so loudly that they can't hear the individuals and the parts next to them. Humming the music sometimes will allow the singers to hear the other parts better. This device can be used to improve the blend of all the parts, especially in legato singing. On easy and familiar choral selections, it is profitable for the singers occasionally to switch parts. This helps to develop an awareness of the other parts and subsequently may improve the blend of the group.

A procedure that has been found to give the most immediate (and sometimes startling) results is to place the entire choral group in quartets (SATB), or in the arrangement known as the *scrambled setup*.[7] Achieving results from these arrangements presupposes that the students know their parts. These seating arrangements separate the students who lean on each other and lessen the stridency in voices of students accustomed to sitting together. They generally result in a tone quality and a blend extremely satisfying to the group. In addition, they reveal the extent to which students have learned their parts.

A tape recorder can be put to very effective use in the choral rehearsal. Recordings of the group serve to reemphasize the suggestions made by the director. They are also valuable as a means of evaluating progress and determining future lines of endeavour.

PITCH AND INTONATION

Faulty pitch and intonation in choral groups are among the most troublesome problems confronting choral directors today. Some have learned to live with them, so to speak, and have accepted them as being common to untrained voices. The majority, however, continue to strive for perfection, and many have achieved a reasonable consistency of performance in their groups.

Accurate pitch and intonation are basically dependent on (1) correctly produced tones, properly supported by the breath, and (2) the degree of tonal awareness that each individual singer possesses. In addition to these two basic factors, both previously discussed, there are other, varied causes of poor intonation, which directors should be cognizant of if they are to deal effectively with the problem.

The Slurring Attack

Attacking the notes from below and sliding or slurring to the proper pitch is a particularly obnoxious fault common to singers. The problem can be somewhat alleviated if choir members are instructed to think of approaching the

---

[6] For a further discussion of the importance of singing without accompaniment, see "Rehearsing A Cappella" later in the chapter.

[7] For diagrams of both these seating arrangements, see Plans 6 and 7 in Chapter 8.

notes from above, rather than from below, the pitch. Another helpful device is to think of singing the consonants on the same pitch as the vowels.

Repeated Tones and Scale Passages

Intonation difficulties frequently occur on repeated tones. Since there is sometimes a tendency to sing each repeated tone a bit lower, it is helpful if the singers are instructed to think of each repeated tone as being a bit higher.

Intonation difficulties also often occur on ascending and descending scale passages. Many individuals are likely to sing the ascending scale steps too small and the descending scale steps too large. Both practices, of course, result in flatting. Ask choir members to think purposely of singing the ascending scale steps larger and of singing the descending scale steps smaller.

Diction

Lack of attention to careful enunciation of the words can create intonation difficulties. The best advice that can be given the singers in such instances is "Vitalize your words," or "Be more precise in your tongue, lip, and jaw movements, and work for clarity of diction."

Breath Control

The problem of breath control usually occurs on long, extended phrases. Advise singers to refrain from using all their available breath supply, since this results in an irregular flow of the breath, which in turn results in gradations in volume and slight variations in the pitch. The group should be instructed in the staggered method of breathing. On long, extended phrases, each individual should drop out when in need of breath, take a full breath, and unobtrusively reenter. Certain sections or groups probably should be told when to breathe in order that the best possible effect may be achieved.

Classification of Voices

Adolescent voices are unsettled and generally in a state of change. For this reason, and to protect the voices from unnecessary strain, retest each singer's voice frequently. Baritones singing tenor parts and altos singing soprano parts can lead to many difficulties.

Body Attitudes and Fatigue

Incorrect body attitudes, which generally reflect a lack of genuine interest, can have a decided effect on performance. Always be alert to this problem and encourage choir members to maintain correct posture while singing. Correct posture and alert body attitudes are essential to properly supported tones, and when singers fully realize this fact they are usually more eager to cooperate. One idea found profitable in action is to insist that the group maintain correct posture only when singing; between numbers they should relax. Good posture can become a habit. Strive for it!

The best time of day for the choral rehearsal is the middle to late morning. Individuals generally do not sing as well immediately following lunch or late in the afternoon, when body fatigue begins to occur. It is recognized that some school schedules prohibit using the most desirable hours for rehearsal and that many directors have little voice in determining the scheduling of classes. Try to discuss the problem with your school administrator. Administrators are eager to provide the best possible education for their students and if presented with a reasonable argument for making changes in the schedule, are usually most anxious to cooperate if they can.

When rehearsals become dull and uninteresting, body fatigue is bound to occur regardless of the time of day or the length of the rehearsal. Carefully plan and try to make all rehearsals exciting events for the choir members.

Tempo

The tempo of the music can have a decided effect on intonation. The tempo selected for a previous choral group—or the tempo originally chosen by the conductor—may not always be the best one. Become sensitive to the problem and determine through experimentation the tempo that is most suitable for your present group and, of course, for the most effective rendition of the music.

Seating Arrangements

In choral groups where a strict tryout is not mandatory for membership, there will usually exist a few voices that might be classified as "chronic flatters." If these individuals are allowed to sit together, their tone qualities are seemingly reinforced and can play havoc with the group's intonation. The problem, however, can be somewhat alleviated by judiciously placing each of those offenders between two or more stronger singers. In this way they are more likely to produce the tone qualities desired.

Acoustics

Many factors, including the size and the shape of the room and the finishing materials used, affect the acoustics of the rehearsal room or the auditorium stage. Again, the tempo at which the music is performed should be determined to some extent by the acoustical properties of the performance room. As a general rule, in rooms with little reverberation, avoid singing the music too slowly if accurate pitch is to be maintained, whereas in rooms that are exceedingly alive, avoid singing the music at too fast a tempo, lest the sounds emitted meet each other coming and going and produce a discordant and distasteful result.

Atmospheric Conditions

Atmospheric conditions also have their effect on intonation. On dark, dismal days most individuals do not respond physically in the same way that they do on bright, clear days. At such times, spirits are sometimes low and the group does not always display an abundance of vitality. It has been said that a person's vitality is to some extent dependent on the relative degree of humidity present in the atmosphere. During very humid days, body fatigue occurs sooner, the tone is generally not supported correctly, and intonation problems may result. What can be done to alleviate the situation? The director can only point out to the group the pitfalls that may occur and, through increased group effort, hope to avoid some of the difficulties. If this procedure does not produce the desired results, then all concerned would be wise to charge the difficulty to "just one of those days. "

Ventilation

Poor ventilation in the rehearsal room creates a stuffy, stale atmosphere that can have a decidedly detrimental effect on intonation. Recheck ventilation periodically during the rehearsal or assign the task to one or more interested singers.

Growing Stale

Most directors have experienced the problem of having choral selections grow stale. There is only one solution to this problem. Set the number aside and return to it at a later date. The problem can be avoided somewhat if the season's repertoire is planned early in the year. This provides ample time for singers to learn a new selection, which can then be set aside until rehearsals are renewed just prior to its presentation. This procedure can have a definite beneficial effect on raising standards of musical performance.

OTHER REHEARSAL CONSIDERATIONS

The effectiveness of a given rehearsal begins from the moment the choir members enter the rehearsal room. Encourage the singers to secure their music folders and immediately take their seats so that the rehearsal may begin promptly with a minimum of confusion. This process is facilitated if each singer's music is kept in an assigned folder and stored in a music cabinet near the entrance door.

Following are suggestions that will contribute to more effective and satisfying rehearsals.

Rehearsal Pace

Rehearsals should move quite rapidly—when they lag, discipline problems may arise. Confusion between selections can be lessened if the rehearsal order is carefully planned and written on the chalkboard prior to the rehearsal. Choir members should not be given the opportunity to waste time. In most cases, they will appreciate the director's efforts to make efficient use of rehearsal time.

Warm-up Exercises and Ear-Training Devices

Many conductors prefer to begin their rehearsals with a warm-up exercise or an ear-training device. To avoid monotony, it is desirable to alternate these exercises and devices and, above all, to keep them *short*. Get the music as soon as possible.

Establishing and Maintaining Rapport

It is advisable to begin rehearsals with *familiar* music of a reasonably vigorous nature that is straightforward, uncomplicated, and not too demanding vocally. Selections that are demanding vocally or that include various subtle nuances and shadings may be better dealt with later in the rehearsal when the singers are more adequately warmed up.

Study the technical aspects of the music before each rehearsal and know what you want to accomplish. Use the music as a reminder, glancing at it only when necessary. This leaves you free to concentrate on maintaining eye contact with the group. Whenever possible, inject a bit of humor into the rehearsals. A good laugh can lessen group tension and contribute substantially to the rehearsal's outcome. Through body attitudes, project your enthusiasm for the music to the group and spur the singers toward greater musical accomplishments.

Maintaining Correct Posture

If tones are to be adequately supported, correct posture must be maintained while singing. Unless the singers are continually encouraged, they are likely to fall into poor posture habits. Since the length of many choral selections will average about three minutes, choir members should be expected to maintain 100 percent effort for this minimum length of time. Between selections they should be instructed to stretch and relax. This same philosophy applies to those individuals who feel they must communicate with each other during the singing of a specific selection. The following rule should apply: *No talking during actual rehearsal! Time between selections will be allotted for questions and communication regarding musical problems of concern to the group.*

Avoiding Fatigue and Vocal Strain

There is a limit to what can be accomplished with a given selection during a single rehearsal. When the singers show signs of fatigue and boredom, set the music aside and return to it at the following rehearsal.

Provide a short break at the midway point in the rehearsal period. This time may be effectively utilized for special announcements, such as forthcoming concerts and musical events.

Rehearsing A Cappella

Too often singers become overly dependent on the piano for tonal and rhythmic support. As a result, they listen primarily to this instrument and not to the other vocal parts. Therefore, it is absoultely essential to rehearse some of the choral selections without accompaniment. Only in this way will the maximum degree of vocal independence, rhythmic security, and effective blend and balance be achieved.

Making Corrections

Errors in rhythm, pitch, and phrasing should be corrected immediately, before they become habitual. But do not be overcritical or belittle the singers, for this may discourage the group. Be positive—commenting about progress already made, as well as about the portions of the music that still require improvement.

When the conductor resorts to excessive talking, however, the singers' enthusiasm is lessened and valuable rehearsal time is lost. Therefore, be succinct in your comments and proceed with the rehearsal as quickly as possible.

Concentrate on rehearsing the troublesome parts of a choral selection. Much time can be wasted by simply repeating the sections that the singers already know. It is also advisable to periodically hold sectional rehearsals for a choir. This practice is essential if minor discrepancies in rhythm and pitch are to be corrected and if sectional tone quality and blend are to be improved.

Prior to the repetition of selections, avoid merely saying, "Let's sing it again." If singers are to improve, they must know what they are striving for. Therefore, tell them clearly what you want in every repetition.

Consideration should be given to possible starting points after the choir is stopped for corrections. A general procedure is to identify the point by referring to first the *page*, then the *score*, the *measure*, and finally the *beat* within the measure. After the choir is reasonably familiar with the music, a particular word or phrase may be identified as the starting point. After the singers have gained even further knowledge of the musical score, starting points may be identified as, for example, (1) after the double bar, (2) at the key change, (3) at the tenor entrance (thus forcing the other singers to identify this portion of the music to orient themselves).

Although demonstrating desired musical improvements and occasionally singing certain entrances is justifiable, avoid continually singing with the group. Instead, devote your attention to critical listening and assisting the group to a more effective interpretation of the music through your conducting technique.

Stimulating Concentration

It is important that singers give their undivided attention to the conductor and that they concentrate on achieving artistic singing. Following are suggestions that will contribute toward this objective.

Rehearsing from a standing position   Singers can become fatigued when rehearsing all the music from a sitting position. In addition, the maximum group effort cannot always be achieved unless the singers stand, assume the correct singing posture, and concentrate on artistic singing. Therefore, alternate selections should be sung from a standing position.

As a further means of developing more careful attention, time each selection with a stopwatch. While the resulting information is essential in planning the length of the final concert program, it has the added advantage of stimulating an extra group effort, particularly if the singers understand the purpose of the timing and the importance of being alert and responsive to the director's conducting movements.

"Erratic" conducting   When singers seemingly have their eyes glued to the music and are unresponsive to the subtleties of the conductor's movements, then it is helpful to purposely alter the tempo—faster and slower and employing the fermata at will. Singers enjoy this activity, and the challenge of following the conductor is an excellent means of developing attentiveness and responsiveness in a choir.

"Silent singing"   Mentally thinking together the pitch, rhythm, and tempo of a selection under a conductor's direction, before being asked to sing aloud at a designated point, is an excellent means of stimulating concentration and alertness. (For a more detailed discussion of this procedure, see end of section "Tonal Awareness," earlier in this chapter.)

Encouraging Individual Responsibility

Encourage the choir members to analyze their difficulties and to request assistance with particularly troublesome voice parts or sections of the music. Although you must use discretion and be the final judge of which problems should be undertaken first, you should encourage individual responsibility in regard to the various problems encountered in the music. Encouraging individual effort produces greater group solidarity, improved musicianship, and eventually a more effective interpretation of the music.

Ending the Rehearsal

Schedule a selection relatively familiar to the group during the final portion of the rehearsal—one that the singers particularly enjoy, so they will leave the rehearsal room with a feeling of genuine aesthetic accomplishment. Be prompt in ending the rehearsal, because most individuals have demanding time schedules. Nevertheless, the dismissal time must be considered the director's prerogative—the singers should not be mere clock watchers, but should wait to be dismissed.

INTERPRETATION

To achieve an artistic interpretation of choral music, a conductor must take into consideration a number of factors. The following are suggestions.

Style of the Music

Prior to the initial rehearsal of a choral selection, give ample thought to the style of the music. Essential points are the characteristics of music in various historical periods and the specific treatment of meter and stress, tempo, dynamics, texture, and expression. The unique characteristics of the music of each individual composer should also be understood.

Consideration should also be given to the stylistic features or characteristics of particular types of compositions, such as the chorale, the motet, the madrigal, the cantata, the oratorio, the mass, liturgical music, the folk song, the ballad or love song, and music in a popular idiom.

Another facet of style is the manner in which it is articulated—that is, legato, staccato, or marcato. The mood of the text as well as the musical markings will generally reveal these basic styles. Each musical selection requires a specific treatment in terms of diction, as well as in the projection of the mood or spirit of the song to the audience. The singers, therefore, must become aware of the differences in style if they are to interpret the music artistically.

Dynamic Range and Contrast

The dynamic range of a particular choral group depends on the age level, physical maturity, and vocal development of the singers in the group. The relatively immature voices of a junior high school chorus, for example, are obviously unable to achieve the same full *fortissimo* effects as an adult choral group. Avoid being overambitious and striving for effects that may prove harmful to younger students' voices. Contrast of dynamics is, of course, one of your objectives. Remember, however, that dynamics are relative. The dynamic extremes of one group need not necessarily equal those of another. Through experimentation, determine the maximum dynamic level that voices of your particular group may sing without distortion of sound and undue vocal strain-and then compensate at the other extreme of the dynamic range by reducing the level of the *pianissimo* effects. Although immature vocal groups will be unable to achieve the same *pianissimo* effects as an adult group, some adjustment toward the goal of achieving dynamic contrasts must necessarily occur at this end of the continuum. Only in this way will the voices be protected from undue vocal strain.

You must devote considerable attention to the achievement of effective dynamic contrasts. Adhere to crescendo and decrescendo markings. In the absence of such markings a slight crescendo on ascending vocal lines and a slight decrescendo on descending vocal lines will generally enhance the effectiveness of the interpretation. When in doubt about the general dynamic level, a thorough study of the text will reveal certain subtle implications—each suggesting, sometimes from phrase to phrase, a change in dynamic effects; to achieve effective interpretation, assist the singers in developing an awareness of the importance of dynamic contrasts. Through the use of teacher demonstrations, the tape recorder, choral recordings, and other means, the ineffective portions of a selection must be brought to the singers' attention, and the importance of dynamic contrasts should be continually stressed.

Tempo

Although choral conductors often differ in their opinions concerning the correct tempo of a selection, the majority agree they must determine the most effective tempo for their own groups. Factors determining the proper tempo are the basic style of the music, the mood of the text, the given musical markings, the physical maturity of the group, and the acoustical properties of the rehearsal room and the auditorium. Experiment to determine the most effective tempo for your particular group.

Nuances

Nuances may be defined as delicate changes in musical expression, either in tone, in color, in tempo, or in voulme. The various nuances and shadings necessary for the most effective performance of the music quite naturally develop as the singers gain increased understanding of the text. The singers should recite and study the words of the music individually and as a group. Only through this approach will certain subtle, hidden meanings—essential to the best interpretation of the music—be revealed.

One type of nuance, perhaps obvious only to the director, is the slight degree of tension and relaxation within each phrase essential to the most effective interpretation of choral music. The tension or emotional surge is usually characterized by a slight quickening of one phrase, whereas the relaxation aspect of the cycle is reflected through a slight slowing down of the tempo. The tension is not only balanced but also complemented by the relaxation. Improvement of a problem moves through three stages: an awareness of the problem, an evaluation or appraisal of present progress, and a renewed effort toward improvement. Therefore, to implement these effects in the music, demonstrate your desired objective by singing various vocal lines and by playing back tape-recorded portions of the music so that the group may evaluate their performance.

Projecting the Mood

Projection of the mood or spirit of a song is essential to an effective choral performance. Capturing the proper mood of a selection may occur only through diligent study of the text. Discuss the implications of the text with the singers, establish the proper mood for each selection, and make an effort to improve the projection with each subsequent rehearsal.

In achieving this goal, it is helpful to give special attention to the consonants. For example, in certain words, such as *thunder* and *glory*, the prevailing thought is quite dynamic. Therefore, the initial consonants should be stressed—almost exploded. Often the advice "Sing these as *Capital Consonants*" assists in creating in the singers' minds the desired mental picture. Conversely, other initial consonants, in such words as *dreams*, *softly*, and *lullaby*, demand the opposite treatment and must be handled more subtly and sung in a smooth, legato style.

Finishing the Musical Phrase

Perhaps one of the most obvious differences between a professional and an amateur choral group is the seeming inability of the latter to complete their musical phrases. Often, because of lack of proper breath control, choral groups anticipate the release of the phrase ending. You may eliminate this difficulty, to some extent, by employing what is called *staggered breathing*, thus enabling the singers to sustain the phrase until it is released by the conductor. It is also helpful if, during rehearsals, you employ a slightly modified type of interpretation by holding certain phrases a bit longer than others. In this way, choir members are trained to watch you more carefully, especially at the beginnings and ends of phrases.

One of the most troublesome faults in choral singing is that groups do not finish their words. Such singing is slovenly and detrimental to an effective projection of the mood or spirit of the music. Singers should be trained to include the final consonants on all words, and should be especially careful to include the final consonant on the release of the phrase by the conductor. For example, a problem often arises when one or more sections of the choir release the phrase at the end of the second beat, while another section begins a phrase on the third beat of the music. This is essentially a conducting problem, and the difficulty

FIGURE 79 Excerpt from "April Is in My Mistress' Face," by Thomas Morley.

can be avoided if the singers are instructed that the attack for one section will serve as the release for the other section (see Figure 79).

Eliminating Excessive Slurring

Exaggerated slurring or scooping is the scourge of effective choral singing. According to studies by the music psychologist Carl Seashore, some degree of "gliding attack" is characteristic of the human voice and is even desirable.[8] However, definite steps should be taken to avoid excessive slurring. Most objectionable slurring occurs because the jaw is tight and rigid and the mouth is kept too tightly closed. Slurring can be eliminated, to a considerable extent, by asking singers to drop their jaws prior to the initial attack or prior to wide pitch changes. When choir members learn to anticipate wide pitch or interval changes, and properly adjust the vocal mechanism, choral singing can be much more effective.

Singers' Facial Expressions and Audience Communication

Choral directors all understand the importance of their singers projecting to the listening audience an understandable and exciting interpretation of the poetic aspects of the text. Singers' faces that glow with enthusiasm and sparkle stand out in a choir and become focal points for an audience's attention. An often heard remark following a concert is, "Who is that singer on the left side in the front row? She really seemed to be enjoying her singing and I simply couldn't

[8] C.E. Seashore, *Psychology of Music* (New York: McGraw-Hill, 1938), p. 271.

take my eyes off her!" Admirable? Yes indeed, but why not have all choir singers appear this way to the listening audience? Many choral concerts are rendered less effective as a result of the stoic, expressionless faces of the singers. Through watching TV performers, choral directors have become more cognizant of the importance of facial expressions and body attitudes to the ultimate success of the concert program.

Directors realizing the importance of appropriate appearances endeavor to influence their singers with remarks like "smile," and "look pleasant." While this often helps, an alternative approach is to set up situations where the singers themselves have a strong concept of the poetic message of the text and thus are more likely to project it to an audience automatically. In short, the motivation comes from within each singer, rather than being externally imposed by the conductor. Examples of how directors may create such situations are as follows:

"Create in Me, O God" (from the Motet, Op. 29, No. 2), by Johannes Brahms G. Schirmer, No. 7504.

Create in Me, O God, a pure heart and grant anew, grant a right spirit within me.

This is a simple straightforward text of a sincere, repentant individual asking forgiveness for past transgressions and a chance to begin anew. This person is asking for a new opportunity to possess a positive attitude and the ability to help and work with fellow human beings—and only from this can true happiness result. A new fresh start in life! Isn't that worth praying for? Think about this important idea as we sing this beautiful music together.

"Toyland! Toyland!" (from *Babes in Toyland*), by Victor Herbert arr. Edward B. Jurey. Belwin Mills Publishing Corp., No. 60563.

Toyland, Toyland, Little girl and boy-land,
While you dwell within it, You are very happy then.
Childhood Joyland, Mystic merry Toyland!
Once you pass its borders You can ne'er return again.

When you were a young child do you remember the excitement about the gifts you expected during the holiday season and on special occasions? Think about this as we sing "Toyland, Toyland," and the happiness these thoughts brought to you!

"White Christmas," by Irving Berlin arr. Anita Kerr. Hal Leonard Publishing Co., No. 08565970.

Imagine it is a cold winter night and you are sitting beside an open fireplace. It is snowing outside, but you are warm and comfortable. Your little sister and brother are sitting beside you and you feel like hugging them both. If you are old enough, perhaps a boyfriend or girlfriend is also with you. You feel warm inside and the words of "White Christmas" come to mind. You would like to tell the entire world how good you feel!

The remarks just listed are only examples of what you might say to your choral groups. Of course, you should give thoughtful consideration to all choral works that are scheduled to be performed. Depending on the music, even more comments might be appropriate, or in other instances perhaps considerably fewer. Whatever is said should be considered essential to the preparation of the singers during rehearsals and immediately prior to concerts.

Memorizing the Music

If the mood of the music is to be projected effectively to the audience, music performed for programs and concerts must be thoroughly memorized. When music is memorized, the singers are able to watch the director more closely and concentrate on the interpretative aspects. The director is able to establish better rapport with the group and to transmit the desired musical interpretation through conducting technique, body attitudes, and facial expressions.

Some choral groups are able to memorize music more quickly than others. Memorization can be facilitated through increased musical understanding and through the principle of association. Students with a greater understanding of the musical score—that is, knowledge of form, harmonic structure, styles of music, and the like—will memorize their parts more quickly. Memorization of the text may be facilitated by identifying particular key words in the text and associating them with various facets of personal experience. When one connection fails, often singers can rely on others to assist in the recall process.[9] Memorization is dependent on a well-defined concept of the entire musical composition and on the relationship of the various parts to the whole. In short, a systematic, well-planned program of instruction, designed toward the goal of improving the musicianship and the understanding of the singers, will reap many benefits—only one of which is improved memorization.

MENTAL ATTITUDES

Each individual hears "two voices" (Self 1 and Self 2) while he or she is engaged in any physical activity, including singing. One is the trained self, the other the natural self. The trained self is the one that will become hypercritical, and we are often inclined to pay so much attention to this inner voice that it sometimes overrides the natural self. The hypercritical attitude inhibits freedom in performance.[10]

---

[9] An approach to the identification of key words is as follows. Write the complete text of the choral selection on the chalkboard, and ask the group to follow it when singing, rather than the text in the octavo publication. Prior to the next repetition, erase certain nonessential words, such as *and*, *or*, and *to*. Then, gradually, on each subsequent repetition erase other words, until only a small group of key words remains. Then suggest to the group that they give vent to their imaginations and associate these key words with as many related ideas as possible. Finally, erase all the words from the chalkboard and test the singers' recall ability.

[10] W. Timothy Gallwey, *The Inner Game of Tennis* (New York: Random House, 1974), pp. 14–15.

Before a performance, individuals should let go of their critical attitudes and try to enjoy themselves. Singers should be told to stop being critical, to let loose and release tension (see, for example, the exercises on p. 232) and any negative attitudes that would inhibit a performance, since it is usually too late immediately prior to a performance to make major changes anyway. We are in an age when students expect or try to be perfect; the public media, including radio, television, and recordings, have created this unrealistic expectation. We need to encourage singers to accept their performance at all stages of its development and to see it as an improving activity—one in which being expressive is as good as being perfect. This approach is particularly applicable to the solo singer, but it has validity for choruses as well.[11]

During the final chorus rehearsal and also immediately prior to the first concert, tell the choir, "We have worked diligently on technical matters in the music, and now they should take care of themselves. Let's not continue to dwell on these matters, but enter into the concert in a joyful spirit, enjoy ourselves, and transmit our feelings to the audience. It will be helpful if you watch me closely, and I will maintain close eye contact with you to help facilitate the communication of musical ideas.[12] Think about the message of the text, use your imaginations, and communicate with the audience. Now let's all make beautiful music together!"

Of course, developing the proper mental attitude of singers doesn't just begin at the final rehearsal, but should start when you first introduce the music. Teachers who always display positive attitudes and excite their students about the learning process contribute immensely to each individual's personal development. Many teachers, as a result of their love of teaching and helping students, automatically and often unknowingly, develop positive student mental attitudes. Thus it behooves all teachers to evaluate their own teaching procedures and to make changes when deemed necessary. (For an example of positive reinforcement relating to achievement in choral rehearsals, see p. 204)

Sports Psychology and Peak Performance

The use of imagery techniques has been used as a device to help athletes achieve peak performance. The alpine ski racer Jean-Claude Killy was known for his great achievement of winning gold medals in three Olympic events. Because of an injury, Killy was able to use only mental practice, yet the actual race turned out to be one of his best performances. The tennis player Chris Evert stated in a radio interview that she carefully rehearses her forthcoming matches.

[11] For helpful ideas on assisting the solo performer, see Barry Green, *The Inner Game of Music* (Garden City, N.Y.: Anchor Press/Doubleday, 1986). See also Green's videotape, *The Inner Game of Music,* produced by the Department of Continuing Education in the Arts, the University of Wisconsin at Madison.

[12] Maintaining eye contact with the singers is essential, not only for the interpretation of musical ideas, but also to help minimize tension in the singers. It helps them to loosen up.

"She focuses on anticipating her opponent's strategy and style and visualizes herself countering with her own attack."[13]

Jack Nicklaus, considered one of the world's best golfers, once described his use of mental imagery as follows: "I never hit a shot, not even in practice, without having a very sharp, in-focus picture of it in my head. It's like a color movie. First I 'see' the ball where I want it to finish, nice and white and sitting up high on bright green grass. Then the scene quickly changes and I 'see' the ball going there. Then there is sort of a fade-out, and the next scene shows me making the kind of swing that will turn the images into reality."[14]

The eminent sports psychologist Richard M. Swinn states that imagery rehearsal, such as VMBR—visual motor behavior rehearsal—can be helpful to persons in all walks of life including business executives, scientists, musicians, and government officials—to all those who desire to enhance themselves and improve their job skills.[15]

VMBR involves more than picture imagery. It includes deep body relaxation followed by the vivid imagery of a skill to be learned or performed. VMBR helps to program mind and body into a single unit to achieve peak performance. To use the procedure, first find a quiet, comfortable place in which to relax. With eyes closed, move from one muscle group to another by first slowly tensing and then relaxing them in the following order.[16]

1. Right hand into fist. Relax, then repeat. Do the left hand, repeat.
2. Flex right bicep. Relax, repeat, relax. Flex left bicep. Relax, repeat.
3. Frown to tense your forehead. Relax, repeat.
4. Clench your jaws. Relax, repeat.
5. Shrug your shoulders. Relax, repeat.
6. Take a deep breath. Hold it to tense your chest. Exhale, relax, repeat.
7. Tense abdominal muscles. Relax, repeat.
8. Point toes downward to tense your feet and legs. Relax, repeat. Finally, take three slow deep breaths. Exhaling should increase the sense of muscular relaxation.

Following this procedure, focus on the visualization, somewhat like turning on a videotape or a movie. First visualize a scene in which you performed well. The scene must be a real situation that actually happened. Visualize the scene

[13] Richard M. Suinn, "Psychological Techniques for Individual Performance Enhancement: Imagery," Handbook on Research in Sport Psychology, eds. Robert Singer, Milledge Murphy, and L. Keith Tennant (New York: Macmiuan, 1992).

[14] Jack Nicklaus, Golf My Way (New York: Simon & Schuster, 1974).

[15] Richard M. Suinn is a member of the Steering Committee for the Sports Psychology Advisory Panel of the U.S. Olympic Committee's Sports Medicine Council. He was also team psychologist for the 1976 and 1988 Winter Olympics, and psychologist for the Olympic athletes in the sports of track and field for the 1980 Summer games and Fencing for the 1988 Summer games. Dr. Suinn is currently Professor of Psychology, and Head of the Department of Psychology at Colorado State University.

[16] Richard M. Suinn, "Guide to Better Performance," Colorado State Magazine 1 no. 1 (Fall 1988), 39.

for a minute or so, then return to focusing on *muscle* relaxation. Next visualize the event again. Alternate the relaxation and visualization three to five times.

As skill is gained in the relaxation/visualization effort, you may shorten the procedure by eliminating the muscle tensing and only reviewing each muscle group, letting the relaxation predominate. You can later turn on the relaxation aspect by simply thinking the word *relax* and by using deep breathing. Finally, and most important, you should know specifically what physical actions are necessary for improvement. In the instance of music performance, you must ask/know how they as performers would like to feel when on stage, the image of themselves they would like to project, and the message of the music they would like to convey to the listening audience. (For a related discussion on this topic, see: "Singers' Facial Expressions and Audience Communication," pp. 228–30.)

VMBR has been used to reduce performance anxiety in musicians. In one case, the subject was asked to visualize being on stage, seeing the judges in the audience, and awaiting a signal to begin. The therapist then gave a verbal sign ("all right, start now"), after which the subject began to play mentally the piece selected for a forthcoming competition. She was asked to signal the therapist on finishing the piece, so that the procedure could then be repeated. Because time sequences in the visualization of an act do not correspond precisely with the passage of real time, a subject may "practice" several times within a one-hour session. After working with the therapist for five consecutive days, the subject qualified as a semifinalist in an open competition, and later as a semifinalist in a regional contest.[17]

The use of group therapy in sports centers on the elimination of interpersonal conflicts among players, the development of group cohesion and team spirit, and the improvement of coach/athlete rapport and communication.[18] In a parallel way, group meetings between choral directors and their choirs (outside of regular rehearsals) may also be used to improve rapport and communication. Often the best time is at the beginning of school in the fall when an overnight choir retreat may be held on a specified weekend. During this time a variety of topics that could improve the choir, may be discussed, interspersed between rehearsals. Topics might include the importance of rehearsals beginning on time, the necessity for certain specified special rehearsals (before choir tours or performances for chorus and orchestra), attentiveness during rehearsals, maintaining vocal health, relationships with other singers, and any special musical problems.[19]

[17] Richard M. Suinn, "Visuo-Motor Behavior Rehearsal for Adaptive Behavior," in *Counseling Methods*, eds. John D. Krumboltz and Carl E. Thoreson (New York: Holt, Rinehart and Winston, 1976), p. 364.

[18] Michael J. Mahoney and Richard M. Suinn, "History and Overview of Modern Sport Psychology," *The Clinical Psychologist* (Summer 1986), 65.

[19] The motivation derived from choir tours, either during vacation periods or European summer tours, is so strong, and such a close-knit feeling develops among singers and their director that such retreats, while always helpful, are not really necessary.

While there is absoultely no uncertainty about the application of such techniques to solo vocal performance, there has been minimal experimental study regarding large group participation. Nevertheless, the principles are sound, and a list of references for further study is given at the end of this chapter. We also encourage you to consult with a sports psychologist at a nearby college/university.

CONDUCTING CHORAL/ORCHESTRAL WORKS

To perform a work for chorus and orchestra you must not only carefully rehearse the chorus, but also be prepared to conduct the orchestra. You must have a working knowledge of orchestral instruments and stringed instrument bowings, know how to achieve proper balance and intonation, and organize efficient rehearsals. For an effective performance you must also consider acoustics and the use of a shell, seating arrangements and placement of the chorus, choral/orchestra balance, and concert protocol.

The Orchestral Instruments

It is presumed that you, the conductor, understand the nature of transposing instruments—that is, where particular pitches are written and where they actually sound—and that you are able to read the orchestral score to at least determine if the right notes are being played. Experience with orchestral instruments will help you understand their timbre or tonal characteristics so you will know better the composer's expectations regarding the orchestral scoring. (If you didn't know the characteristics of voices, it would be difficult to conduct a choir.)

To become acquainted with the range and tonal characteristics, the technical abilities, and the limitations of particular instruments, review a book on orchestration.[20] However, nothing will substitute for actually hearing the instruments and discussing them with instrumentalists. So talk with orchestral musicians about the nature of their specific instruments and the technical difficulties they might have. Be sure to ask about the physical capabilities and especially the limitations of each instrument.[21] Listen to recordings of numerous orchestral works, particularly choral/orchestral works. It is especially important, however, to listen to school orchestras in both rehearsals and concerts. Listen

[20] See, for example, Kent Kennan and Donald Grantham, *The Technique of Orchestration*, 3rd ed. (Englewood Cliffs, N.J.: Prentice-Hall, 1983). This text also includes suggested music for listening to specific instruments. (The Appendiex includes a listing of different instruments, and where particular pitches are written and where they actually sound.) See also Elizabeth A. H. Green, *The Dynamic Orchestra* (Englewood Cliffs, N.J.: Prentice Hall, 1987), pp. 19–59. (Professional musicians on all orchestral instruments have been interviewed and discuss both the strengths and limitations of their instruments.)

[21] For example, the C# on the flute and the G on the bassoon are inclined to be sharp, and the throat tones on the clarinet (from second line G to B♭) tend to be flat. Performers often use a combination of alternate fingerings and/or embouchure adjustments to minimize the problem.

carefully and make some judgments, however tentative, about articulation, phrasing, balance, intonation, and so on. Would you do anything differently if you were the conductor?

In working with school, college, and community orchestras, having an adequate number of players for each part is generally not a problem. However, church and community choirs who do not have these resources at their disposal generally have to employ musicians if they want to perform a choral/orchestral work. In this case, where finances are of some concern, thought may be given to the minimum number of players that can effectively perform the work with the chorus. If the orchestra is very small, never use two players on the first and second violin parts. Use either one or three players on a part, because of the tight or close frequencies. The third player neutralizes pitch problems and facilitates the blend. The violas and the cellos can get by with only two players on a part if using only normal ranges. Under most circumstances, however, the suggested minimum-sized string section would be three first violins, three second violins, two violas, two violoncellos, and one string bass.

To better understand why not to use two violins to a part (use either one or three as a minimum), examine the strings of a piano. Note that beginning with C# (second space, bass clef) and extending to the utmost upper limits of the instrument, each pitch has three strings. As an experiment, try damping (or holding down) one of the three strings, and then striking the key for that pitch. If one of the two remaining strings is only slightly out of tune you will hear a "whang" sound. However, when all three strings are allowed to vibrate this effect is minimized. Again, remember that a minimum of three violins to a part is a basic requirement, but that four violins is even better than three.

Bowings

String players need to utilize bowings that are the easiest to execute while achieving the desired musical effect. Different bowings achieve varying musical effects, and it is your responsibility as the conductor to determine the desired result (the bowings should conform to the vocal phrasing and breathing). The bowings printed on the music may not always be acceptable, and in such instances, the conductor should provide a bowed score for the string parts prior to the first rehearsal, so that each part may be properly marked. In school situations, this will be the conductor's responsibility. In professional orchestras, the responsibility may be delegated to the concertmaster and/or other string principals—subject, of course, to the approval of the conductor.[22]

You should understand the importance of using the upper part of the bow for delicate, soft, and understated passages and the lower part (where more weight is needed) for louder, heavier, and more dramatic passages. Also, know when to ask the instrumentalists to play on or off the strings. *Legato* means on,

---

[22] For detailed information on bowings, see Elizabeth A. H. Green, *The Dramatic Orchestra* (Englewood Cliffs, N.J.: Prentice-Hall, 1987), chap. 6.

spiccato means off, and *brush* is in between. Feel free to ask to hear the music played several different ways, and be guided by what you hear and what you want to hear. In determining a choice, understand that at a certain (faster) tempo, it is no longer possible to play staccato on the string. At a faster tempo staccato must be played spiccato. Spiccato means "bouncing bow" (off the strings), and was made possible by the modern bow invented by Francois-Xavier Tourte (1747–1835) and named after him. Prior to the Tourte bow, during the Baroque and early Classical periods, a somewhat unwieldy larger bow was used, that was incapable of controlling the spiccato. Articulation markings are often indicated as follows:

Legato means on

Spiccato means off

A brush stroke means raising and dropping the bow with each stroke (similar to the strokes of a paint brush) . To repeat, the faster the tempo, the more off the strings the articulation. Make sure the string basses (bass viols) are placed prominently and play strongly, since these low vibrations do not project as well, yet supply the fundamentals for all the upper harmonic partials. At the same time monitor them carefully in order to avoid a "grunting" quality by stopping the heavy strings firmly and using longer, lighter bowing.

The videotape *Guide to Orchestral Bowings through Musical Style*, developed by Priscilla Smith and Marvin Rubin, can be of immense help in understanding the various techniques of bowing and their application to the interpretation of music of various styles.[23]

In orchestral literature you may occasionally encounter an abbreviated form of notation, or shorthand, which is a way of expressing music without writing it all out. Four examples are given here:

a	b	c	d
4 ♪ = eighth notes (quavers)	8 ♪ = sixteenth notes (semiquavers)	16 ♪ = thirty-second notes (demisemiquavers or a tremolo)	= a trill or a tremolo

Examples *a* and *b* are actually measured notation, that is, when the tempo generally allows them to be articulated they are executed as eighth notes (quavers) and sixteenth notes (semiquavers), respectively. Example *c* could be called demisemiquavers or a tremolo depending on the tempo and/or the interpretation of the conductor (see Figure 80, excerpt from *L'Histoire du Soldat* by Igor Stravinsky). If the tempo is too fast to actually measure the number of notes, then it is a tremolo. The same principle also applies to example *d*, except that if

---

[23] See the videotape *Guide to Orchestral Bowings through Musical Styles*, by Pricilla Smith and Marvin Rubin. Produced by the University of Wisconsin at Madison, Department of Continuing Education.

FIGURE 80   Excerpt from *L'Histoire du Soldat*, by Igor Stravinsky.

the movement is between the two pitches of a major second, then it is a trill. If the interval is a major third or more, it is called a tremolo.

Balance and Intonation

In rehearsals, listen for a balance between instruments in one family and between sections of the orchestra. Again, note the markings in the score. What sounds right to you? Intonation, of course, is always a matter of concern. Following are some points to remember:

1. String players should use plenty of bow; if the sound is too loud, then reduce the pressure on the strings, not the amount of bow being used. As previously indicated, the bowing should conform to the vocal phrasing and breathing. Younger string players need to be encouraged to play with the whole bow.
2. Brass players can often diminish their volume without losing intensity by directing the bells of their instruments into the music stands; conversely, they can add brilliance by raising the bells of their instruments.
3. Check balance especially carefully with instrumental parts that double vocal parts (for example, the trombones in Beethoven's *Ninth Symphony*, Choral Finale, 3/2 section).
4. In performing choral/orchestral works, it is particularly important that singers not have vocal scores blocking their faces; if they do, the sound will become lost and not be properly projected. Singers should know their parts well enough that they

need the music for reference only and can keep their eyes and attention focused on the conductor.

5. Be aware of the orchestra's tendency to go sharper as instruments warm up, particularly with young orchestras. In some instances, the situation may necessitate retuning the orchestra between sections of a musical work. However, this problem may be minimized through adequate warm-up and tuning prior to the concert.

Seating Arrangements

Different orchestral seating arrangements each have certain advantages for the security of the players, tone quality, and balance, as well as the performance of music of different styles. Figure 81 illustrates the most widely used setup.

An optional arrangement would place the first violins to the conductor's left and the second violins to the right. The string basses in this setup are placed toward the back of the stage behind the first violins.

Placing all the violins together, however, as illustrated in Figure 82, allows for a rich sound, as all the F holes on the violins face the audience. This arrangement is, therefore, good for Romantic works. With the string basses on the right side and turned slightly toward the audience, these more slowly speaking instruments are more readily heard because they are closer to the audience than in the optional arrangement, where they are placed toward the back of the stage behind the violins. The same is also true, only to a much lesser extent, of the violincellos placed on the immediate right of the conductor.

It is likely that from time to time you will be working with various sizes of groups. For example, with a pit orchestra for opera performances, all the strings

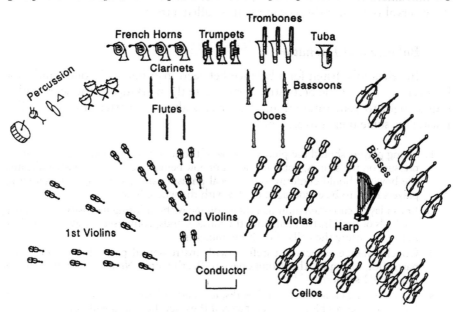

FIGURE 81   A commonly used orchestral seating arrangement.

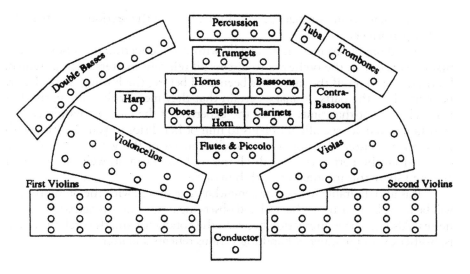

FIGURE 82   This seating arrangement creates or allows for an antiphonal effect in such words as the first movement of Beethoven's *Fifth Symphony*. It is also a desirable arrangement for Baroque and Classical Works.

are usually seated to the conductor's left, and the winds on the right. Whatever the seating arrangement, familiarize yourself thoroughly with it, and in individual score study, attempt to visualize the location of sections, and particularly entrances that need to be cued.

While this section focuses on the performance of choral/orchestral works, it is understood that some works may involve the performance of a chorus with symphonic band or wind ensemble. Seating arrangements for these two groups are presented in Chapter 7. (See pp. 265)

Preparing for Rehearsals

Identify possible troublesome parts in the orchestral score and mark your score accordingly. For example, if a particular troublesome spot occurs ten bars after letter F or eight bars before letter G, then circle this passage and mark on your score F+10, or G-8, so that you may instruct the orchestra where to begin again, for example, at ten bars after after letter F, or eight bars before letter G. This will save you the trouble during a rehearsal of counting the measures from the troublesome spot in the music to the orientation letter. Also, as previously mentioned, learn as much as you can about the characteristics of all the orchestral instruments, and familiarize yourself with the bowing of string instruments, the seating of players, different musical styles, the achieving of any special effects, and so on. The seating of players can be critical to achieving the best musical results. Endeavor to pair strong and weaker players together, or help the group by placing some stronger players in the back of the section to support the weaker performers.

It is desirable to meet individually with the Concertmaster prior to your first rehearsal with the orchestra to discuss all relevant matters, such as tempo, bowings and so on. If the music has been used before, the bowings may already be marked on the parts, so make certain that they meet with your approval or make changes at that time. Utilize the expertise of the Concertmaster as your Assistant and defer specific problems to him or her. Prior to your meeting with the Concertmaster, develop your overall concept of the work and what you expect from the performers—both chorus and orchestra, as well as soloists, if any, and share this information with him or her.

It is also desirable to become somewhat acquainted with the orchestra you will be using by visiting a rehearsal and observing its general strengths and weaknesses. Also note the interaction between the conductor and the orchestra, that is, his/her overall manner of handling various rehearsal matters.

Rehearsals

If you have selected a musical work to perform and have either made arrangements with the school orchestra or employed some musicians for rehearsals and performance(s), then it is desirable to rehearse the orchestra well in advance of the combined choral/orchestra rehearsal(s). Prior to the first rehearsal, familiarize yourself with the seating attangement of the orchestra or whatever instrumental ensemble will be performing.

Prior to beginning an actual rehearsal, make all comments on musical style and background brief and to the point. Remember that orchestral musicians do not respond to pep talks like some choirs. Before the first reading, however, it is usually desirable to point out possible troublesome passages, or those necessitating a specific desired treatment. However, be succinct in your comments and get to the music! Do not raise your arms until you are ready to begin, as this is a signal fot the players to raise their instruments. Any unnecessary delay after that point is tiresome and frustrating to orchestral musicians.

Before working details in rehearsals try to read through the entire work or movement so the orchestra can get a good feel for the entire work—that is, how it all fits together. Then go back and devote as much time as is necessary to those troublesome parts of the music. The subsequent detail work will be more effective and meaningful than if done out of context. During the read through, some errors will be corrected by the players themselves and often acknowledged through eye contact with the conductor, thus eliminating any reason to stop the rehearsal at those points for corrections Also, if you hear a wrong note, don't always assume that the player(s) made a mistake, but first check the score against their parts, particularly if the pitch is played by more than one player. If any stopping for corrections is deemed necessary, keep your comments brief. For problem passages, encourage the players to work on them on their own prior to the next rehearsal. A very useful device used by successful conductors is to make a list of anticipated problem passages and then rehearse/drill only these specific parts during the second rehearsal, after the players have obtained a basic overview of the entire piece from the first rehearsal. After this particular procedure, then play through the entire piece without any frequent stops.

Choral directors are sometimes inclined to be too fluid in their gestures when directing a chorus. An orchestra often expects more precision and definition in the conductor's movements or gestures. To help clarify your gestures, conduct with a baton rather than with the hands only. Some orchestral instruments, such as the string basses and the lower brasses and woodwinds, speak more slowly, and to coordinate the ensemble's efforts, direct your gestures toward those instruments, particularly during entrances, as well as at other times when they are prominent. The players can also help by slight anticipation.

The conductor should make his/her beat patterns as definite and clear as possible, avoiding any unnecessary flourishes or extra movements as are sometimes given to a choir, as they may only confuse the orchestra. In general be careful not to overuse the left hand in mimicking the right hand, but instead use it more for sculpting phrases, cues, dynamics, and attacks and releases. As to baton technique, orchestra players usually have their eyes on the music, and while it might seem they are not watching the conductor, they do see him or her through their peripheral vision.

As to the balance between the orchestra and the chorus, the orchestra may initially appear to be playing too loudly. Allow for a couple of readings before you try to give them any specific directions about playing more softly. By then the matter of balance, along with many other matters, may have taken care of themselves.

Some orchestral players often have lengthy rests, which they must count out. To avoid any possible error, however, it is important for the conductor to cue their entrances carefully and precisely. Players expect cues and have more respect for the conductor who assists them.

Orchestral musicians are usually trained to be especially observant of the conductor's beat when any musical passage is marked *accelerando* or *ritardando*. These changes, of course, should never be sudden or drastic, considering the large number of performers involved. And, it follows that conductors should remind the orchestral musicians of the importance of their necessary attention. In conducting a *ritardando*, gradually increase the size of the beat as the tempo is broadened. For an *accelerando*, the process is just the reverse. In conducting a fermata, the movement of the baton either ceases or continues to move very gradually until the preparatory movement to the next beat. In certain passages, you will find that letting your left hand and arm mirror the movements of your right will contribute to rhythmic stability. However, this device should not be overused. [24] Be aware of a chorus's tendency to sing behind the beat, as they're

[24] Cf. Don V Moses, et al. *Face to Face with an Orchestra* (Princeton, N.J.: Prestige, 1987), p. 29

sometimes listening to the orchestra's sound go out and come back rather than singing with the beat.

After each rehearsal, it is helpful to talk to the orchestra director about your conducting effectiveness with the orchestra. Are your conducting gestures understood by the orchestra? Ask for suggestions from the orchestra director! It is also helpful to record your orchestra rehearsals for later review. How do they square with your expectations of the chorus? Will they work together?

Memorize the choral score, so you need to make only minimal reference to it and can focus on the multiplicity of lines in the orchestral score. The chorus should become less and less dependent on the conductor for the subtle gestures often given during choral concerts. Begin to conduct the choral rehearsals from a full orchestral score well in advance of the combined choral/orchestral rehearsals. Thus, you can gradually give attention to the total ensemble, rather than using the full score only immediately prior to the orchestral rehearsals. In preparation for the choral/orchestral rehearsals, have the singers mark the measure numbers or letters at important selected points in their choral scores.

The appropriate and effective use of time is essential in the final choral/orchestral rehearsals. There can be nothing more frustrating to performers than to sit through any part of a lengthy rehearsal that does not directly involve them. Therefore, evaluate a group's progress continually, and plan to devote time to those players and singers who need special attention. For example, rehearse the soloists prior to the scheduled arrival of the chorus. Or, toward the end of a rehearsal, dismiss the singers and focus on the improvement of specific instrumental parts. In certain instances, part of the orchestra may be dismissed if attention needs to be given to a particular orchestral section. Each choral/orchestral work is different and will need its own specific and particular plan. In the final dress rehearsal, however, the entire work must be rehearsed in sequence, so that all individual performers comprehend their relationship to the total work.

The Concert Hall and the Performance

Many modern auditoriums have an acoustical ceiling and side panels that surround the stage. If the facility is not thus equipped, then all sound-absorbing materials, such as curtains, should be pulled or drawn aside and an acoustical sound shell placed behind the singers. An effective performance requires a surface from which sound can be reflected toward the audience and that will allow the singers and the orchestral musicians to hear themselves and each other better.

As previously mentioned, the balance between the chorus and the orchestra is highly important. During the combined choral/orchestral rehearsals, make an initial determination of the balance. Singers, of course, have physical limits to the sound they can produce; therefore, achieving an appropriate balance usually necessitates softening the orchestra to whatever degree is necessary. The best determination can be made during final rehearsals in the concert hall, and it is often helpful to have a colleague stand at the rear of the hall to provide feedback.

If the singers are placed behind the orchestra they will usually be on standing risers. (On long, extended works, seated risers would be preferable; however, elevated platforms and chairs take much more space.) In orchestral concerts, the wind players are often elevated on platforms to facilitate balance, as well as to improve visual sight lines. However, it is difficult for singers to project over the heads of orchestra members. Therefore, it is important that the wind players be seated on the floor rather than on risers. The only alternative to this arrangement is to place the singers on more highly elevated platforms. For example, standing choral risers may be placed on top of 4×8 foot partable staging, with two or more sections reversed to provide a straight, rather than a curved, stage arrangement. Portable 4×8 foot staging is available in elevations of 8, 16, 24, and 32 inches.[25]

When an auditorium has aprons in front of the proscenium arch, risers may be placed on each side of and in front of the orchestra to help achieve proper balance; however, the feasibility of this arrangement depends on the musical security of the group, as well as on the musical work being performed. A similar arrangement, except that all the singers are on the stage, is illustrated in Plan 3 on page 266. Another alternative is to place the chorus on the left side of the stage, as illustrated in Plan 2, page 265.

Singers should not have to stand any longer than is absoultely necessary; therefore, the orchestra should be seated, tuned, and ready to play before the chorus is asked to enter the stage. Following the concert, all performers should be recognized: first the soloists, then the chorus and the orchestra. After a limited amount of applause, the soloists and the conductor may leave the stage (or opt to remain on stage), only to return momentarily for continued recognition. Next, it is important for the conductor to acknowledge the person(s) who trained the orchestra or assisted with the chorus. At this point, after again recognizing the soloists and the chorus, the conductor should, with a hand motion, signal the orchestra to rise. Continue to accept the audience's applause as long as possible. After all, the performers deserve it! Performers should never leave the stage as long as the audience is still showing its appreciation through applause.

MUSICAL TERMS FOR THE ORCHESTRAL PLAYER/CONDUCTOR

Arco: With the bow
Attacca: Proceed directly to next movement
A2 or zu 2:   Double part (two players—on woodwind or brass parts)
Bouché: Stopped horn

---

[25] With the use of portable staging, choral risers may be positioned to accommodate from nine to as many as twelve rows of singers. For further information on these plans, contact the Wenger Corporation, 555 Park Drive, Owatonna, MN 55060.

Bratsche: Viola
Col legno: With the stick part of the bow
Concertmaster: Principal violinist of an orchestra; sets bowings, tunes the orchestra, and so on
Con sordino: With mute
Contra: Instrument sounding an octave below the written pitch
Corni: Horns
Crook: Tubing of a brass instrument
Détaché: Broad legato stroke (separate bows—⊓, ∨)
Divisi: Separated string parts; outside plays top, inside plays bottom or divided by stand
Doppio movimento: 2 × tempo, double the tempo
Down bow (⊓): A bowing stroke in which the bow is pulled down from the frog
Dur: Major
Fagott: Bassoon
Glissando: Sliding the fingers continuously in a smooth manner
Harmonic: Natural partial of a string
Leggiero: Light, delicate; generally implies a bouncing bow
Luftpause: "Air pause" (quick breath)
Marcato, Martelé: A sharp, accented stroke—literally, "well-marked"
Mit schwammschlagel: Strike with the soft (sponge) stick
Moll: Minor
Non divisi: Double stop (stopping two or more strings at once)
Pizzicato: Plucked
Portamento: Gliding from one note to another
Saltato, Saltando: Ricochet bowing ("throwing" the bow so it will bounce a series of rapid notes)
Scordatura: Unusual tuning of any string instrument for special effects
Senza sordino: Remove or without mute
Soli: "Solo" section
Spiccato: Controlled bouncing bow
Staccato: Short, detached stroke
Sul ponticello: To play at or near the bridge of a stringed instrument, resulting in an eerie tone
Sul tasto, Sur la touche: Bowing near or above the fingerboard
Talon: The heel or nut or frog of the bow
Tampon: Two-headed drumstick used to produce a roll on a bass drum
Timbale: Timpani
Tremolo: Reiteration of the same note, produced by rapidly moving the bow back and forth on the same pitch, or a sustained tremolo between two pitches wider than the interval of a second, such as from e to g
Tromba: Trumpet
Tromboni: Trombone
Unisoni: Marks the end of a divisi passage
Up-bow (∨): Bowing stroke in which the bow is pushed up from the tip
Vibrato: Rapid, regular oscillation of pitch above and below the tone

TOPICS FOR DISCUSSION

1. What are some of the personal characteristics of successful choral directors you have known?
2. In your experience as a participant in various choral groups, have you ever sensed or felt that the director was unprepared for the rehearsal? What were your feelings? What was the reaction of the group?
3. Discuss the effects on a chorus of a mechanistic approach to the teaching of new music.
4. Identify, if possible, the causes of poor pitch and intonation in some of the choral groups in which you have participated.

5. Recall the techniques utilized by the conductor for achieving effective interpretation in groups in which you have participated. Which techniques were most effective? Which were relatively ineffective?

6. Select a specific publication and try to analyze the difficulties that a particular group might encounter in rehearsals.

7. Why should accompanied selections be rehearsed, at least part of the time, without accompaniment?

8. Discuss the factors that prevent the attainment of effective balance and blend in a choral group. How would you remedy them?

9. Analyze the difficulties, if any, that hamper your memorization of music.

10. Should music be memorized for all performances? For what reasons would you have the chorus memorize the music? For what reasons would you have the chorus use the music at programs and concerts?

SELECTED READINGS

ALLEN, S. GAIL., AND HILARY APFELSTADT. "Leadership Styles and the Choral Conductor." *Choral Journal* 30, no. 8 (March 1990) pp. 25-31.

BAUGUESS, DAVID. *The Jenson Sight Singing Course (2 vols.).* New Berlin, Wis.: Jenson, 1984. There is both a student's edition and a teacher's edition.

BOYD, JACK. *Rehearsal Guide for the Choral Director.* Champaign, Ill.: Mark Foster Music Company, 1977.

—. *Teaching Choral Sight Reading.* West Nyack, N.Y.: Parker Publishing Company, Inc., 1975.

BRINSON, BARBARA A. *Choral Music: Methods and Materials.* New York: Schirmer Books, 1996.

CAIN, NOBLE. *Choral Music and Its Practice,* chaps. 9, 11, 12. New York: M. Witmark & Sons, 1942.

CHRISTY, VAN A. *Glee Culb and Chorus,* chaps. 4, 5. New York: G. Schirmer, 1940.

DAVISON, ARCHIBALD T. *Choral Conducting,* chaps. 4, 5. Cambridge, Mass.: Harvard University Press, 1945.

EHRET, WALTER. *The Choral Conductor's Handbook,* chaps. 1–7. New York: Edward B. Marks Music Corp., 1959.

FINN, WILLIAM. *The Art of the Choral Conductor,* chaps. 5–12. Boston: C.C. Birchard & Co., 1939.

GORDON, LEWIS. *Choral Director's Rehearsal and Performance Guide.* Englewood Cliffs, N.J.: Parker Publishing, 1989.

HEFFERNAN, CHARLES W. *Choral Music: Technique and Artistry.* Englewood Cliffs, N.J.: Prentice-Hall 1982.

HOGGARD, LARA G. *Improving Music Reading in the Choral Rehearsal.* Delaware Water Gap, Pa.: Shawnee Press, 1947.

JENNINGS, KENNETH. *Sing Legato.* San Diego, Calif.: Neil A. Kjos Music Co., 1982.

JONES, ARCUHIE N. ed., *Music Education in Action: Basic Principles and Practical Methods,* pp. 172–84, 186–99. Boston: Allyn & Bacon, 1960.

KRONE, MAX T. *The Chorus and Its Conductor,* chaps. 3, 6, 7. San Diego: Neil A. Kjos Music Co. 1945.

MURRAY, LYN. *Choral Technique Handbook.* Great Neck, N.Y.: Staff Music Publishing Co., 1956.

PFAUTSCH LLOYD. "The Choral Conductor and the Rehearsal," in *Choral Conducting Symposium* (2nd.ed.), ed. Harold Decker and Julius Herford. Englewood Cliffs, N.J.: Prentice-Hall, 1988.

STEPTOE, ANDREW. "Performance Anxiety: Recent Developments in Its Analysis and Management." *The Musical Times* 123, no. 1674 (August 1982) pp. 537–41.

SWAN, HOWARD. *Conscience of a Profession* (ed. Charles Fowler). Chapel Hill, N.C.: Hinshaw Music, 1987.

VAN BODEGRAVEN, PAUL, AND HARRY R. WILSON. *The School Music Conductor,* chaps. 2, 4, 5, 6. Chicago: Hall & McCreary Co., 1942.

WILSON, HARRY R. *Artistic Choral Singing*, chaps. 3, 4, 9, 11. New York: G. Schirmer, Inc., 1959.

REFERENCES ON MENTAL ATTITUDES

GALLWEY, W. TIMOTHY. *The Inner Game of Tennis*. New York: Random House, 1974.
GREEN, BARRY, AND W. TIMOTHY GALLWEY. *The Inner Game of Music*. Garden City, N.Y.: Anchor Press/Doubleday, 1986.
MALTZ, MAXWELL. *Psycho-Cybernetics*. New York: Pocket Books, 1969.
RISTAD, ELOISE. *A Soprano on Her Head*. Moab, Utah: Real People Press, 1982.

REFERENCES ON SPORTS PSYCHOLOGY

BENNETT, LUISE. "Achieving Peak Performance." *Colorado State Magazine* 1, no. 1 (Fall 1988), 38–39.
HACKFORT, DIETER, AND CHARLES D. SPIELBERGER. eds. *Anxiety in Sports: An International Perspective*. New York: Hemisphere Publishing Corp., 1989.
MAHONEY, MICHAEL J., AND RICHARD M. SUINN. "History and Overview of Modern Sport. Psychology." *The Clinical Psychologist* (Summer 1986), 64–68.
SCHOLLANDER, DON AND JOEL H. COHEN. *Inside Swimming*. Chicago: Henry Regnery Company, 1974.
SINGER, ROBERT, MILLEDGE MURPHY, AND L. KEITH TENNANT. *Handbook on Research in Sport Psychology*. New York: Macmillan, 1992.
SUINN, RICHARD M. *Anxiety Management Training: A Behavior Therapy*. New York: Plenum Press, 1990.
———. "Guide to Better Performance." *Colorado State Magazine* no. 1 (Fall 1988), 38–9.
———. "Imagery Rehearsal Applications to Performance Enhancement." *The Behavior Therapist* 8(1985), 155–59.
———. "Psychological Techniques for Individual Performance Enhancement: Imagery." In *Handbook on Research in Sport Psychology*, eds. Robert Singer, Milledge Murphy, and L Keith Tennant. New York: Macmillan, 1992.
———. *Seven Steps to Peak Performance*. Lewiston, N.Y.: Hans Huber Publishers, 1987.
———. "The 1984 Olympics and Sport Psychology," *Sport Psychology Today*, 7 (1985), 321-329.
———. "Visual Motor Behavior Rehearsal: The Basic Technique." *Scandinavian Journal of Behavior Therapy* 13 (1984), 131–42.
———. "Visuo-Motor Behavior Rehearsal for Adaptive Behavior." In *Counseling Methods*, John D. Krumboltz, and Carl E. Thoreson. New York: Holt, Rinehart and Winston, 1976.
TITLEY, ROBERT W. The Loneliness of a Long-Distance Kicker." *The Athletic Journal*, 57 no. 1 (September 1976), 74–80.

References on Conducting Choral/Orchestral Works

ARCHIBEQUE, CHARLENE, AND KERRY BARNETT. "Preparing Choirs for Orchestral Concerts and/or Singing with Other Conductors." *The Choral Journal*. 31 no. 7 (February 1991) 15–21.
BARNETT, KERRY. "A Choral Conductors Preparation for Choral/Orchestral Concerts," *The Choral Journal*. 31 no. 2 (September 1991) 29–40
DANLELS, DAVID. *Orchestra Music: A Handbook*. (2d ed.). Metuchen, N.J.: Scarecrow Press, 1982.
GREEN, ELIZABETH A. H. *The Dynamic Orchestra*. Englewood Cliffs, N.J.: Prentice Hall, 1987.
MOSES, DON V., ROBERT W. DEMAREE, AND ALLEN F. OHMES. *Face to Face with an Orchestra*. Princeton, N.J.: Prestige, 1987.
PRAUSNITZ, FREDERIK. *Score and Podium: A Complete Guide to Conducting*. New York: W.W. Norton, 1983
WESTRUP, JACK, with Neal Zaslow. "Orchestra." In *The New Grove Dictionary of Music and Musicians* (6th ed.), ed. Stanley Sadie. New York: Macmillan Publishers, Ltd., 1980, Volume 13, pp. 679–91.

Videotapes

The Art of the King's Singers (The King's Singers work with Karl Erickson's Choir at Gustavus Adolphus College). Hinshaw Music, Inc., No. 3056.

Guide to Orchestral Bowings through Musical Styles, by Priscilla Smith and Marvin Rubin. Produced by the University of Wisconsin at Madison, Department of Continuing Education in the Arts.

Excellence in Conducting. "The Natural Approach," by Eph Ehly. Volume 2. Expressivity. Hal Leonard Publishing Corporation, No. 08414150.

Howard Swan, An Interview by Gordon Paine. American Choral Directors Association, Volume 2.

The Inner Game of Music, by Barry Green. University of Wisconsin at Madison, Department of Continuing Education in the Arts.

Jester Hairston, A History of the Black Spiritual in America. American Choral Directors Association Volume 3.

Positive Motivation for the Choral Rehearsal, by Eph Ehly. Hal Leonard Publishing Corporation, No. 08416830.

Robert Shaw: Preparing a Masterpiece: A Choral Workshop on Brahms' A German Requiem. Videolab Cassettes, 506 Jersey Avenue, New Brunswick, New Jersey 08501.

Tuning the Choir, by Eph Ehly. Hal Leonard Publishing Corporation, No. 08417760.

Programs
and Concerts

Practically all choral conductors have at one time or another encountered difficulties in the preparation and presentation of choral programs. Problems of special concern include locating a variety of worthwhile choral materials, planning and staging programs of an artistic nature, and planning and implementing effective publicity. Individual conductors solve these problems as best they can and, in so doing, constantly obtain new ideas. Following are suggestions that may be helpful.

SELECTING THE MUSIC

The basic consideration in planning a choral program is selection of the music, since the success of the program depends to a great extent on the quality and the appropriateness of the music performed. Following are criteria that will serve as a guide in selecting good, usable choral materials.

1. Is the text worthwhile? Does it contain a message of sufficient value?
2. Is the music artistically conceived, and does it reflect the mood of the text?
3. Does the selection fit the needs and the interests of the particular age group for which it is being selected? Does the music have emotional appeal for the singers?
4. Does the music fit the physical limitations of the singers? Is the tessitura of the parts too high or too low? Are there extreme, awkward jumps in the voice parts that might prove difficult to execute?

5. Are the voice parts handled in such a manner as to make each part sufficiently interesting?
6. If the selection is an arrangement is it done in an authentic musical style? Is the authenticity of the music sacrificed for clever musical effects? (This criterion applies to arrangements of the masters as well as to folk song arrangements.)
7. Does the music justify the rehearsal time necessary to prepare it?
8. Are all the various types and styles of choral music being represented in your selections, so that the singers may have the broadest educational experience possible?

ETHNIC MUSIC AND MULTICULTURAL PERSPECTIVES

While folk songs and spirituals have long been part of the choral repertoire of choirs and choruses in the United States, there has been developing in recent years a steadily increasing interest in the performance of ethnic music from all cultures around the world. Ethnic, of course, refers to the designation of any group of peoples as distinguished by customs, characteristics, language, and common history.

Residents of the United States are no longer as isolated from the world as they were in prior years. With the advent of increased communication via satellite, the television viewer today has a closer view of worldwide events. Also, the study of ethnomusicology as a specialty in colleges and universities has become increasingly popular. For example, the college-level courses offered in "Semester-at-Sea" utilize qualified ethnomusicologists to teach music that is appropriate and relevant to the countries they visit during their various travel around the world.

In attempting to perform music of these styles, conductors should familiarize themselves with the performance traditions of the music selected, and also endeavor to understand not only the music but also the culture from which it comes. One will note that rhythmic figures are sometimes unusual, and that specific tone qualities are sometimes needed in performance. When, and if, they are called for, the editor will usually offer suggestions. When the text of the music is in a foreign language, a text in English is often given. When it is not included, then the editor often provides a guide for pronunciation. Also, a variety of percussion instruments are often used as accompaniment. This adds a unique flavor to the overall sound and can contribute to a stunning, exciting performance that is highly appealing to both singers and the listening audience.

While performing ethnic music, one should not endeavor to take on too much, but endeavor to maintain a balance between european art music and ethnic music—that is, don't let the tail wag the dog! Study and performance of ethnic music also can be helpful in breaking out of our elitist image, that is, the perceptions that some audience members may have about our choral programs.

To assist choral directors in their search and selection of choral music that is appropriate and to their liking, an extensive listing of octavo music is listed in the Appendix in the following categories:

Africa

Asia, the Pacific Rim, and Australia

British Isles (England, Ireland, Scotland)

Eastern Europe (Poland, Baltic States: Latvia, Lithuania, Estonia; Slavic Countries: Czech Republic, Hungary, Romania, Yugoslavia)

Israel

Latin America (Brazil, Venezuela, Argentina, Mexico)

North America (Canada and United States)
  Folksongs
  African-American Spirituals

Russia

Scandinavia (Norway, Sweden, Denmark, Finland)

Western Europe (France, Germany, Netherlands, Spain, Italy, Austria, Portugal)

In addition to the above-mentioned lists, refer also to the list of Folksongs and Spirituals in the Appendix, which includes earlier octavo music.

CONSIDERING THE AUDIENCE

Music has a variety of moods and must be appropriate to the occasion. Aside from individual musical tastes, the nature of the event quite often determines the receptivity of the group to various types of music. Performing at certain festive banquets, for example, can preclude the exclusive use of sacred music. If the occasion warrants the use of popular and novelty tunes, they should be used. This need not imply a lowering of musical standards, for to include in the program a variety of styles and types of music is often the most effective way of evoking enthusiastic audience reaction.

It is important to the success of the program that rapport be established as soon as possible between the audience and the performers. Prior to the beginning of the choral concert, the audience is usually unsettled, as evidenced by considerable shuffling around, coughing, and general confusion. To gain the complete attention of the audience, begin the program with music that is reasonably straightforward and vigorous. Placing quiet and subdued selections at the beginning of the program should be avoided, for here their effect is lost. Such numbers are more effective if placed later in the program, when the audience is more settled.

Consider the audience in planning the length of the program. Fatigue decreases not only the efficiency of the singers but also the receptivity of the audience. Choral programs generally should not exceed an hour and a quarter, including intermission. It is desirable to end the program with the audience wanting to hear more, since that will promote more enthusiastic support of the choral organization.

While the preceding criteria provide an important basis for the selection of choral music, outside forces often determine the choice of music. Selections are influenced by conductors' backgrounds and musical experiences, including groups in which they have performed as students and attitudes of directors they associate with. If, for example, groups you belonged to performed mostly sacred music, then unconsciously you may be inclined to favor and select a preponderance of this musical style. At the opposite extreme, if you were once an active member of a jazz or a show choir, you may tend to program more of this style of music. Neither extreme is desirable. A balance should be achieved between all types and styles of music, so that the singers under your tutelage acquire the broadest educational and musical experience possible. Make sure singers experience both sacred and secular music from the Renaissance, Baroque, Classic, Romantic, and Modern periods, folk and/or ethnic music from various countries, and at least some music in a popular idiom.

You may receive criticism about the study and performance of sacred music from people in the community who will cite the separation of church and state and the necessary omission of anything depicting religious ideals in the schools. Reassure these critics that you are *not* advocating religious dogma, but exposing young singers to the musical and artistic creations of some of the world's great composers. Art teachers, for example, have their students study the paintings of Leonardo da Vinci and Michelangelo. Prepare a syllabus in which you outline course objectives and study materials. Then the school principal will be better able to defend you when and if there are any complaints. Should a singer or group of singers in your choir complain about any aspect of the religious nature of the text or music being rehearsed or performed, seek a discussion of the matter in private where neither the individual feelings of the singer(s) nor the potentially controversial nature of the issue might be misunderstood publicly. And, it seems advisable to hold such discussions in the presence of another adult faculty member for the sake of both accuracy and verification of the conversation. For several years diverse religious and ethnic groups have suggested that a solely traditional seasonal concert such as a "Christmas" concert has failed to serve the increasing number of students with diverse religious and/or cultural beliefs in our public schools. The director might best consider the presentation of, say, a "Holiday" concert that offers both director and students the *opportunity* for more diverse literature and musical observances of different faiths and traditions.[1] In view of our profession's increasing recognition of wider-world cultures, ethnic and religious observances, the director might consider planning balanced programs of traditional (sacred and/or secular), ethnic, and multicultural literature. (Special programs, however, that are thematically, historically, or otherwise oriented would have their own design and balance.) This body of ethnic and multicultural literature, which increases annually in size, accessibility, and popularity, continues to gain wide acceptance because the needs of more students are served. Finally, a wider vision for music in the current world is both

---

[1] For those readers who wish to investigate further the topic of religious music in the public schools, see the list of references at the end of this chapter.

educationally prudent and sound, and ultimately essential to a healthy choral curriculum into the next century.

ACHIEVING UNITY AND VARIETY

For an effective choral program, it is important to maintain both unity and variety. Musical *variety* may be achieved by selecting numbers that contrast in style, mood, length, mode, and key. Variety in the program also may be obtained by

1. Featuring vocal or instrumental soloists, or both, either within or in addition to the choral selections.
2. Featuring either or both the male and the female voices in the choir in selected TTBB and SSA literature.
3. Presenting several of the school's music groups, both vocal and instrumental, in a combined program.

Unity, as well as variety, is often achieved in the choral program by selecting publications that fall into groups but which still possess a definite literary or stylistic relationship. A program of sacred music, folk songs, and contemporary music provides such variety of style, mood, and tempo yet still offers wide scope historically. A prevalent practice is to begin the program with a group of sacred selections, representing various historical periods, and to end the program with music of a lighter mood—either folk songs or contemporary music. Many directors also like to include the composers' dates on the printed program to indicate to the listening audience, and remind the singers of, the historical periods the music represents.[2] Program 1 illustrates these ideas.

The program sequence from serious to lighter moods and from early periods to contemporary compositions is, of course, heavily enmeshed in tradition and has many merits. However, some directors feel that the group of sacred songs is likely to be better received if it is placed later in the program. Furthermore, they believe that audience rapport may be more firmly established if the program begins with music of a lighter mood. Program 2 is presented as an alternative approach. The use of a choral prelude and a choral postlude may contribute further to the overall effectiveness of the program.

Since any given audience will usually contain people with varied musical tastes, you may wish to evoke maximum audience response and enthusiasm by including on the program a variety of musical styles and ensembles. In Program 3, for example, Part 1 includes sacred choral literature from various periods. In Part 2, while the singers are given a brief rest, the accompanist is featured in two piano selections. Including an extended choral work in Part 3 serves to highlight the first portion of the program, as well as providing a valuable musical experience for the participants. Following an intermission, it is often desirable to

---

[2] See the Appendix for a chronological listing of composers from the Renaissance to the present.

include music of a less serious nature. A group of folk songs from various countries, therefore, is appropriate at this point (Part 4). Further variety may be achieved by featuring one or more smaller vocal ensembles. Part 5 includes music particularly suitable for a men's octet; Part 6 includes music most appropriate for a small mixed ensemble of twelve to sixteen voices. At the culmination of the program, the entire chorus is featured in music of a light character. Selections from light opera and Broadway musicals are particularly appealing to most audiences and generally are enthusiastically received.

Using a Theme

Another means of achieving unity is to build the choral program around some theme. In choosing a theme, consider the various alternative subtopics around which the music may be grouped. Provided the text of the music under consideration is related to the central theme, a careful analysis of it will often reveal many possibilities for natural groupings. Christmas, Easter, and other important holidays or seasons provide a natural opportunity for this type of thematic treatment. For the imaginative choral director the possibilities are unlimited. Consider the following suggestions.

Christmas programs   A most effective Christmas choral program may be achieved by selecting numbers that fall into one of the following three categories: "The Advent," "The Nativity," and "The Rejoicing." By using this theme, you will find your problems somewhat minimized, since most of the choral publications of Christmas music may be placed into one of these three important periods of the Christmas season. Program 4 illustrates this idea.

Other categories that may be used in a similar manner for a Christmas program are "The Star of Bethlehem," "The Nativity of the Christ Child," and "Joy to the World."

"Christmas Around the World" is a flexible theme for a school assembly program. The program may be built around carols from all countries. The use of a narrator may further enhance the effectiveness of the program.

Whereas some directors prefer to use only sacred music at Christmas, others may wish to include some secular music, as well, on their programs. When this is done, the selections must be given careful consideration and judiciously placed on the program according to some particular plan. To help achieve this purpose, the theme "Music at Christmastide" is suggested. Appropriate categories for developing this theme are "Christmas Hymns and Carols," "Christmas Symbols and Greetings," and "Songs of Youth and Childhood." The program may be made even more effective through the use of an organ prelude, a brief choral prelude or fanfare prior to the processional, and the inclusion of selected masterworks for combined choirs immediately after the processional and just before the recessional. Further variety may be achieved by featuring different choral groups on all or part of each of the three major sections of the program.

Program 1

1

SACRED MUSIC

Jubilate Deo.. Orlandus Lassus
(1532–1594)

Day by Day We Magnify Thee .... George F. Handel
(1685–1759)

Contentment... W. A. Mozart
(1756–1791)

Nunc Dimittis .... Vassili S. Kalinnikov
(1866–1901)

The Last Words of David .... Randall Thompson
(1899–1984)

2

CONTEMPORARY MUSIC

It Is Good to Be Merry .... Jean Berger
(1909–   )

The Lobster Quadrille .... Irving Fine
(1914–1962)

Old Abram Brown .... Benjamin Britten
(1913–1976)

Sure on This Shining Night............................ Samuel Barber
(1910–1981)

Whether Men Do Laugh or Weep .... Ralph Vaughan Williams
(1872–1958)

3

FOLK SONGS

My Pretty Little Pink .... American Folk Song
arr. Joyce Barthelson

Dance to Your Daddie .... Scottish Nursery Song
arr. Edmund Rubbra

I Know My Love .... Irish Folk Song
arr. Parker-Shaw

May Day Carol .... English Folk Song
arr. Deems Taylor

Didn't My Lord Deliver Daniel? .... Spiritual
arr. Ralph Hunter

Program 2[3]

CHORAL PRELUDE

O Sing Your Songs . . . . Noble Cain

FOLK SONGS

Chiapanecas. . . . . Mexican Dance Tune
arr. Harry R. Wilson

Shenandoah* . . . . Early American Barge Song
arr. Tom Scott

Soon-Ah Will Be Done† . . . . Spiritual
arr. William L. Dawson

Charlottown . . . . American Folk Song
arr. Charles F. Bryan

SACRED MUSIC

O Filii et Filiae . . . . Volckmar Leisring

Ave Verum Corpus. . . . . W. A. Mozart

Salvation Is Created. . . . . Paul Tschesnokov

Glory to God in the Highest . . . . Randall Thompson

CONTEMPORARY MUSIC

Younger Generation. . . . . Aaron Copland

Old Abram Brown . . . . Benjamin Britten

Monotone . . . . Normand Lockwood

Stomp Your Foot (from The Tender Land) . . . . Aaron Copland

CHORAL POSTLUDE

Onward, Ye Peoples. . . . . Jean Sibelius

Program 5 illustrates this idea. If, as previously mentioned, there are diverse religious beliefs in one's community, the director may opt to present a "Holiday" concert instead. In this case, the headings or categories for presenting the music may be "Yuletide Carols," "Holiday Symbols and Greetings," and "Songs of Youth and Childhood."

Other categories or titles for grouping choral selections are "Music of the Masters," "Now We Go A-Caroling!" "The Many Moods of Christmas,"

[3] In this and subsequent programs, symbols indicate that selections are to be sung by (*) girls' glee club, (†) boys' glee club, and (‡) choir and audience. Undesignated selections are to be sung by the mixed chorus.

Program 3

1

Cantantibus Organis .... Luca Marenzio

Cantate Domino Canticum Novum .... Heinrich Schütz

Plorate Filii Israel .... Giacomo Carissimi

Ave Maria .... Sergei Rachmaninoff

Alleluia .... Alan Hovhaness

2

Reflets dans l'eau .... Claude Debussy

Alborada del gracioso .... Maurice Ravel

Mary Jones, Pianist

3

Polovetzian Dance and Chorus
(from Prince Igor) .... Alexander Borodin

INTERMISSION

4

Marching to Pretoria .... South African Veld Song
arr. Joseph Marais & Ruth Abbott

Ho-La-Hi. .... German Folk Song
arr. Roger Fiske

Ching-A-Ring Chaw .... Minstrel Song
arr. Aaron Copland & Irving Fine

When Love Is Kind .... English Folk Song
arr. Salli Terri

Ezekiel Saw the Wheel. .... Spiritual
arr. Harry Simeone

5

Josh'a Fit de Battle .... Spiritual
arr. Harvey Enders

Loch Lomond .... Scottish Folk Song
arr. Dede Duson

Men's Octet

6

A Wonderful Day Like Today . . . . Leslie Bricusse
& Antony Newley
arr. Norman Leyden

Am I Blue? . . . . Harry Akst
arr. Kirby Shaw

Just One of Those Things . . . . Cole Porter
arr. Roger Emerson

The Modernaires

7

Neighbors' Chorus
(from *La Jolie Parfumeuse*) . . . . Jacques Offenbach

Broadway Spectacular . . . . arr. Roger Emerson

"Christmas Favorites," "Yuletide Carols," "Loud Their Praises Sing!" and "Carols from Faraway Lands."

Easter program　An effective grouping of music for a sacred Easter program may be achieved by selecting music that falls into one of the following three categories: "The Holy Week," "The Crucifixion," and "The Resurrection."

General sacred programs　Groupings that may be used for general sacred choral music programs are "The Spirit of Glorification," "The Spirit of Trust," and "The Spirit of Peace."

Secular programs　Appropriate groupings for a secular program are "Songs of Work," "Songs of Love," and "Songs of Play," or "Songs of Nature," "Songs of Love," and "Songs of Travel." "I Hear America Singing" may be used as an appropriate title for a spring concert in which both sacred and secular music is included (Program 7).

Memorial Day program　An effective Memorial Day program may be achieved by grouping the music into the categories "The Ideals," "The Men and the Women," and "The Land." Program 8 illustrates the use of this theme.

PUBLICIZING THE CONCERT

Adequate publicity is essential to the overall success of concerts and programs. Singers perform best before an interested and enthusiastic audience; therefore, continually search for ways to increase the size and the quality of the audience

Program 4

CHORAL PRELUDE

Fanfare for Christmas Day . . . . Martin Shaw

THE ADVENT

While Shepherds Watch'd . . . . Old Yorkshire Carol
arr. Gustav Klemm

As Joseph Was A-Walking . . . . Don Malin

Lost in the Night . . . . Finnish Folk Melody
arr. F. M. Christiansen

The Three Kings . . . . Healey Willan

THE NATIVITY

Jesus, Jesus, Rest Your Head . . . . Appalachian Carol
arr. Niles-Warrell

Gentle Mary and Her Child . . . . Finnish Folk Melody
arr. Lundquist

Slumber Song of the Infant Jesus . . . . François Auguste Gevaert

Silent Night* . . . . Franz Gruber

THE REJOICING

Hodie Christus Natus Est . . . . Jan Pieters Sweelinck

Go Tell It on the Mountain . . . . Spiritual
arr. John W. Work

Glory to God in the Highest . . . . G. B. Pergolesi

CHORAL POSTLUDE

Joy to the World‡ . . . . George F. Handel

and to develop community support for the choral music program. Following are some suggested publicity techniques.

Newspaper Articles

Newspaper articles should be well written, giving all the vital information, such as date, time, place, soloists, and other special features of the program. This information, along with a copy of the program, should be forwarded to local newspapers well in advance of the program date. Most newspaper editors

Program 5
Music at Christmastide

ORGAN PRELUDE

Pastorale . . . . Arcangelo Corelli

Carol Rhapsody . . . . Richard Purvis

Organist: Mary Jones

CHORAL PRELUDE

Fanfare for Christmas Day . . . . Martin Shaw

PROCESSIONAL AND GLORIA

Adeste Fideles . . . . Old Latin Hymn

Gloria in Excelsis Deo . . . . Joseph Haydn

Combined Choirs

CHRISTMAS HYMNS AND CAROLS

Christmas Hymn . . . . 17th Century German

God Rest Ye Merry, Gentlemen . . . . Old English Carol

Still, Still, Still . . . . Austrian Carol

Carol of the Bells . . . . Ukrainian Carol

Concert Choir

CHRISTMAS SYMBOLS AND GREETINGS

Now Is the Caroling Season . . . . Dorothy Priesing

O Tannenbaum . . . . Traditional German

Silver Bells . . . . Jay Livingston

Mistletoe . . . . Fred Waring and Jerry Toti

Mixed Chorus

SONGS OF YOUTH AND CHILDHOOD

Sleigh Ride . . . . Leroy Anderson

Winter Wonderland . . . . Felix Bernard

Chestnuts Roasting on an Open Fire . . . . Torme and Wells

Toyland . . . . Victor Herbert

The Modernaires

CHORAL POSTLUDE AND RECESSIONAL

Hallelujah Chorus (from Messiah) . . . . George F. Handel

Combined Choirs

Joy to the World‡ . . . . George F. Handel

Audience and Combined Choirs

Program 6

1

O Magnum Mysterium .... Tomas Luis da Vittoria

Verbum Caro .... Gaspar von Weerbeke

Angelus ad Pastores............................. Hans Leo Hassler

Weihnachts Motette.............................. Luca Marenzio

2

Mi Yemalel (Who Can Retell?) .... Max Helfman

Saenu.. Yemenite Melody
arr. Charles Davidson

S'vivon (The Top) .... Folk Song
arr. Max Helfman

Light the Legend (A Song for Chanukah) .... Michael Isaacson

3

Break Forth, O Beauteous Heavenly Light...................... J. S. Bach

Joseph Tender, Joseph Mine .... Seth Calvisius

Lo, How a Rose E'er Blooming........................ Michael Praetorius

Hallelujah Chorus (from Messiah) .... George F. Handel

---

welcome such information and are usually willing to allot a limited amount of space in their publications as a public or community service. The younger set may best be reached by placing articles and announcements in the school newspaper. To provide a desirable learning experience for secondary school students, designate individuals in the choral organization to handle this latter aspect of public relations.

Radio Announcements

In communities displaying a high degree of interest in school, church, and community affairs, certain local radio stations have cooperated by broadcasting spot announcements of programs, sometimes during local news broadcasts, a few days before the event is to occur. Some local radio stations provide this assistance as a public service, without charge. In certain instances, stations have been known to interview choir members about aspects of a coming musical event or program.

Program 7

I HEAR AMERICA SINGING

CHORAL PRELUDE

A patriotic selection

OF HER FAITH

Sacred music of various faiths

OF HER PEOPLE

Secular or sacred music about particular societal organizations
or famous individuals

PRAISE TO THE LAND OF THE FREE

Appropriate patriotic music

CHORAL POSTLUDE

America the Beautiful‡

Complimentary Tickets

Perhaps one of the most effective means of publicity is the distribution of a specified number of complimentaty tickets to concerts for which there normally would be no admission charge. Tickets may be mailed to selected persons, or a certain number may be provided each choir member for distribution. Individuals do not, as a rule, destroy so quickly items to which they attach some value and having tickets is a constant reminder of the coming event.

To initially develop an audience, it is suggested that several announcements advertising a concert be placed on subsequent days in a local newpaper, well in advance of the concert. Indicate in the ad that complimentary tickets may be obtained by calling a designated phone number (at school) and have volunteer choir members "on duty" to take calls during specified hours during the day. Through this process an audience of strong and interested supporters of your choral program may be developed. Prior to subsequent concerts a letter announcing a forthcoming concert may be mailed to these persons, again offering complimentary tickets. Newspaper announcements prior to concerts may be continued until the audience has reached the maximum size for the auditorium

Program 8

LEST WE FORGET

CHORAL PRELUDE

The Star-Spangled Banner‡ .... John S. Smith

THE IDEALS

Born to Be Free .... Ralph E. Williams

What Makes a Good American? .... Singer-Gearhart

Give Me Your Tired, Your Poor .... Irving Berlin

THE MEN AND THE WOMEN

Anchors Aweigh .... Miles & Zimmermann

The Caissons Go Rolling Along .... E. L. Gruber

The Marine's Hymn .... L. Z. Phillips

The U.S. Air Force Song .... Robert Crawford

Reading: O Captain! My Captain! .... Walt Whitman

THE LAND

This Is My Country .... Al Jacobs

Homeland .... Noble Cain

God Bless America .... Irving Berlin

America the Beautiful. .... Samuel A. Ward

POSTLUDE

Taps‡ .... U.S. Army Bugle Call

or concert location. At this point directors will need to decide if they would like to present back to back concerts to meet the community's response.

Mailing of Programs

In many instances, a certain clientele may be lured by photocopies of the actual program. In contrast to the more formal appearance of a printed announcement, the actual program creates greater interest for the reader. Recognition of a familiar or a favorite choral selection sometimes provides the necessary extra motivation to leave the confines of a comfortable home on a cold winter night.

Posters

Attractive, eye-catching posters can also be an effective means of attracting attention and stimulating interest in choral programs. Posters may be printed by local printing shops for a nominal fee or in the school print shop. In most organizations there are a number of people with artistic ability who are willing to prepare some attractive posters. These same individuals will usually assume the task of distribution. Posters should be placed where traffic is heavy—in locations where they will be seen by the largest number of people—in schools, churches, stores, and various other locations in the community.

Word-of-Mouth

For many performances, a large segment of the audience will always consist of parents, relatives, and friends. This group is motivated to attend programs and concerts largely because of their individual interests in particular members of the performing organization. The personal touch is exceedingly important in all areas of human relations. Effective results may be achieved, therefore, if each participant in the organization is requested to extend a cordial, verbal invitation to at least twenty five people outside his or her immediate family. Singers may be provided with a printed reminder, perhaps in the form of an invitation, to make certain they remember to pass the word.

THE FINAL REHEARSAL

When programs are presented in a school or church auditorium, it is of paramount importance that the final rehearsal be held there so that the choir members may become accustomed to the acoustics and to the routine of the performance. (Indeed, the final rehearsal for any concert should always be held at the place where the concert is to be given.) The group should even practice marching on and off the risers so that this may be accomplished with a minimum of confusion.

Not everyone in an audience is capable of judging the musical accomplishments of a choral group, but most will surely be impressed one way or another by the singers general appearance. The importance of uniform dress is discussed in Chapter 8. In addition, emphasize the importance of body attitudes and facial expressions that reflect the mood of the music. Concentration on the emotional qualities of the music not only will result in an improved performance and greater audience appreciation, but also will serve to reduce excessive nervousness in the singers.

The choir should be advised always to keep their eyes on the conductor and not on the audience, never to turn their heads to look at the person next to them, never to call attention to any mistakes, and to maintain absolute silence between selections and when offstage. In short, the group should endeavor to be as professional as possible.

Turn part of the rehearsal over to a student conductor or a qualified assistant and listen from the back of the auditorium for choral balance, blend, precision, intonation, and general effect. Most persons generally wish to do their best, and last-minute suggestions are sometimes taken more seriously than advice given during previous rehearsals.

When the music has been memorized, the singers are able to pay closer attention to the conductor. Most individuals will have memorized the music by the time it is perfected and ready for performance. There may be occasions, however, when it is necessary to use the music. In such instances the singers should be reminded to hold their music so that they can easily see the director—they should keep their noses out of the music and watch him or her as closely as possible, especially at the beginnings and ends of phrases.

Final instructions concerning the dress for the performance and the meeting time and place prior to the concert should be reiterated at the last rehearsal. To avoid any misunderstanding, place these final instructions on both the bulletin board and the chalkboard. When the performance involves a number of different school, church, or community groups, photocopy the instructions and distribute a copy to each individual involved.

The placement of the piano in relationship to the chorus must be considered if it is to enhance the effectiveness of the music and if the correct balance and maximum security of the singers are to be achieved. Generally, the best location for a grand piano is immediately in front of the chorus, rather than at either side. If it is in this position, generally all singers can hear equally well. If only an upright piano is available, then the risers may be divided in the middle and the piano placed between the two sections in such a position that the director can be easily seen. This arrangement has the obvious disadvantage of dividing the singers, but it is outweighed by the increased tonal and rhythmic security they receive. [4]

When a band or an orchestral accompaniment is used, the chorus is usually placed on risers, or on the stage, immediately behind the band or orchestra (Plan 1). From the visual standpoint this arrangement is highly desirable. In addition, it usually enables all the performers to see the conductor more easily. The major problem that usually occurs with this arrangement lies in achieving a proper balance between the two groups. Unless an especially large choral group is performing, it is necessary to lessen considerably the volume of the instrumental group. This is sometimes best accomplished by assigning only one player to a part.

When a satisfactory balance still cannot be achieved, the problem can be lessened to some extent by placing the chorus on one side of the stage, as illus-

---

[4] This is only a suggested option for the placement of an upright piano. If it in any way creates an awkward situation, simply place the piano in front of, and perpendicular to the choir, but perhaps turned slightly toward you so you can be readily seen.

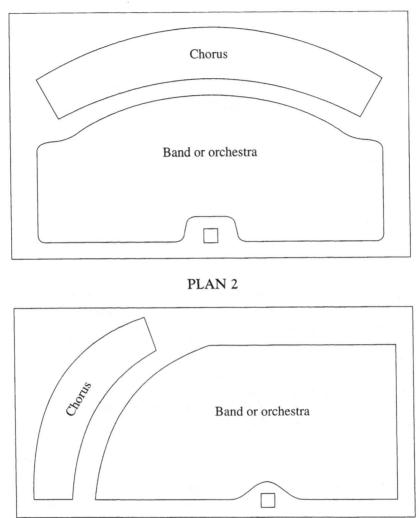

trated in Plan 2. This arrangement allows for a somewhat better projection of the voices.

Still another possibility is to divide the chorus and place them on both sides of the instrumental group and to the front of the stage (Plan 3). This arrangement allows for the highest degree of voice projection but has the obvious disadvantage of lessening, to some extent, the tonal and rhythmic security of the singers.

Musical productions presented on a stage with adequate facilities can be made much more effective by using appropriate lighting. Through the use of various colors, such as amber, red, blue, green, and pink, during the various choral

PLAN 3

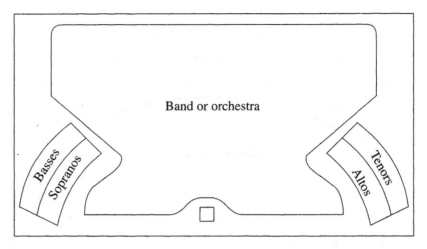

selections, the emotional effects of the music can be heightened considerably. Lighting color media (gels) for covering spot and stage lights may be obtained in a wide assortment of colors (approximately ninety-five). The imaginative director will be able to identify the predominant color mood or moods of each selection by careful analysis of the music. A cue sheet or a marked copy of the program should be prepared for the electrician, and all lighting effects should be carefully set during the final rehearsal.

Stress the importance of an adequate warm-up before the performance. Choir members should be in the rehearsal room at least forty-five minutes prior to the concert. It is important that the temperature of the rehearsal room be approximately that of the auditorium stage. Extreme differences in temperature can have a detrimental effect on the singers' voices.

A little time devoted to vocalization, reviewing general procedures, and renewing in the singers' minds the tempi and the general moods of the choral selections can prove a profitable aid in achieving an improved performance. It is especially important to review the order of the selections. It is helpful to start each number and sing at least the first phrase or so. This procedure helps the group accustom themselves to the routine of the program. Singers are often likely to be somewhat nervous and on edge immediately prior to the concert. Try to calm the group by talking and chatting informally with them in the warm-up room prior to entering the auditorium stage.[5]

Careful planning and attention to all the preceding details will contribute substantially to the overall effectiveness of the choral concert.

[5] For further ideas on this subject, see "Mental Attitudes," page 230.

THE MADRIGAL DINNER

The Madrigal Dinner, sometimes called a Christmas Madrigal Dinner, or an Elizabethan Madrigal Christmas Dinner, remains a very popular event in high schools, colleges, and universities. This event is generally scheduled on the first weekend of December. [6] The number of performances depends, of course, on the popularity of the event. These affairs provide an opportunity for the school's madrigal singers or chamber singers to perform before, during, and after the dinner being served to the attendees. Meals may be planned and served either by the school's dining services or through a local catering service. All time devoted by the director to menu planning and cost considerations will be well spent. In addition to the school's madrigal singers, a guest ensemble from another school may also be invited to participate. The event provides an opportunity to feature quartets, duets, soloists, recorder ensembles (or a Collegium Musicum if available), dancers, gymnasts, and jugglers. The event requires Renaissance costumes for all the participants. All music, dances, and other activities should be as authentic as possible.

The exact format of the printed program is difficult to illustrate in a book format, but one example of its most essential parts is duplicated here (see Figure 83). Printed programs should be on a good quality, cover weight, embossed off-white paper, using either a red or green ink for the printing. When laid out, the dimensions will be 11 inches wide by 17 inches deep, folded into thirds with the bottom third folded upward and the top third folded downward. On the interior of the program, the top panel (third) might include on the left the title of the event "Well-come to ye all, bothe more or less, to the Elizabethan Madrigal Christmas Dinner" followed by the place, date(s), and names of the group(s) presenting the affair. On the lower part of the top horizontal panel the Christmas feast or overall program could/might begin and continue downward through the middle horizontal panel (see Figure 84). On the left-hand side of the bottom panel the names of all the participants in the performing groups may be listed.

On the right-hand side, the top horizontal panel should offer the greetings (a paragraph) from the Lord of the Manor. Beginning on the bottom part of this panel and continuing on the middle panel will be printed "The Lord's Entertainments"—Part the First ... and Part the Second (see Figure 85). Note that the first part of the program occurs after the Seventh Fanfare by the Herald Trumpeters and Part the Second occurs after the Tenth Fanfare. Appearing on the right-hand side of the bottom panel are all acknowledgments.

On the reverse side of the complete 11 × 17-inch printed program, the top panel when folded downward may illustrate a group of Renaissance characters including the King and Queen, two children carrying the trains of the King's robe, other nobility, and the court jester. The inscription "Wel-come Ye to a

---

[6] An optional time to present a madrigal dinner is in February, with a Valentine's Day theme. The madrigal literature with love themes is very extensive.

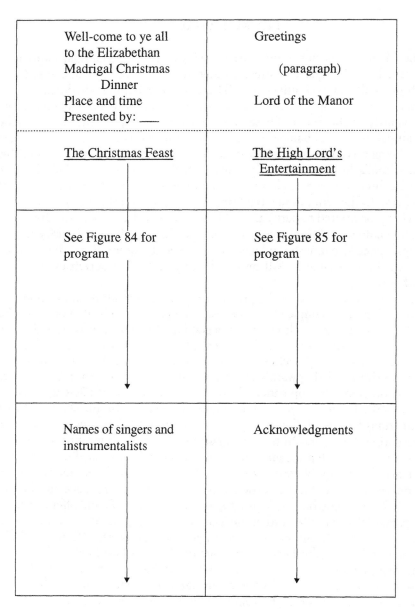

Well-come to ye all to the Elizabethan Madrigal Christmas Dinner Place and time Presented by: ___	Greetings (paragraph) Lord of the Manor
The Christmas Feast	The High Lord's Entertainment
See Figure 84 for program	See Figure 85 for program
Names of singers and instrumentalists	Acknowledgments

FIGURE 83   Layout of the interior of a Christmas Madrigal Dinner program. Overall dimensions are 11 × 17 inches. Folded panels are 5 ½ × 11 inches.

Madrigal Feast" might appear beneath the illustration (see Figure 86). On the middle and lower panels of the back side of this program may be listed the menu, the Rules of Etyquett, and the words of various Christmas carols.

The Christmas Feast

First Fanfare — Heralding the Outer Procession
Deck the Hall — Traditional Welsh — Set by Lee Egbert

Second Fanfare — Heralding the Welcoming of the Guests
Reading of the Booke ov Curtasye

Third Fanfare — Heralding the Seating of the Guests

Fourth Fanfare — Heralding the Processional
Mohrentanz — Tylman Susato, 1551

Fifth Fanfare — Heralding the Lighting of the Candles
Bring a Torch, Jeanette Isabella — Traditional French Carol

Sixth Fanfare — Heralding the Wassail Bowl Processional
Here We Come A-Wassailing — Traditional English Carol
Landlord, Fill the Flowing Bowl — Traditional English Carol

Seventh Fanfare — Heralding the High Lord's Entertainments, Part the First

Eighth Fanfare — Heralding the Boar's Head Processional
Boar's Head Carol — Traditional English Carol
Tallis' Canon — Thomas Tallis

Ninth Fanfare — Heralding the Serving of the Feast
Divers Dittyes of the Season

Tenth Fanfare — Heralding the High Lord's Entertainments, Part the Second

Eleventh Fanfare — Heralding the Serving of the Christmas Pudding
Flaming Pudding Carol — Traditional English Carol
Drum Salute
Eastern Townships
Fort Collins
March (MacCloud)/Strathspey (Duncan Johnstone)/Reel (Lexy McCaskill)
Amazing Grace
Exit March — *Scotland the Brave*
Fort Collins Pipe Band

Twelfth Fanfare — Heralding the Carol Medley
Carol Medley for the High Lord's Household and all the Noble Men and Noble Ladies in the Hall
A Merry Christmas — Arthur Warrell

Thirteenth Fanfare — Heralding the Recessional
Puer Nobis — Anonymous

FIGURE 84   The Christmas Feast. An example of the overall program of a Christmas Madrigal Dinner. Program courtesy of Lee Egbert, Director of Choral Activities, Colorado State University.

𝕿𝖍𝖊 𝕳𝖎𝖌𝖍 𝕷𝖔𝖗𝖉'𝖘 𝕰𝖓𝖙𝖊𝖗𝖙𝖆𝖎𝖓𝖒𝖊𝖓𝖙𝖘

𝕻𝖆𝖗𝖙 𝖙𝖍𝖊 𝕱𝖎𝖗𝖘𝖙 . . . .

I

Wassail Song .... Traditional English
        Court Singers of Colorado State
La Pastorelle .... François Couperin Le Grand
        Padre Parroco Roberto di Cavarra, Harpsichord

II

Greensleeves .... Traditional English
        Fräulein Johanna von Morgenthal, Mezzo-soprano
        Padre Parroco Roberto di Cavarra, Harpsichord

𝕻𝖆𝖗𝖙 𝖙𝖍𝖊 𝕾𝖊𝖈𝖔𝖓𝖉 . . . .

I

My Dancing Day .... set by Shaw-Parker
        Rocky Mountain Singers
There is no rose of such Virtue .... John Joubert
        Court Singers of Colorado State

II

Make We Joy Now in This Feast .... set by Judith Otten
        Lord John and Lady Barbara; Lady Virginia and Parson Michael
Carnival Songs of the Seasons .... LaNoue Davenporte
        Collegium Musicum

III

The Pavane: Pavan Lesquercarde (1571) .... Thinot Arbeau
The Galliard: La Volta .... William Byrd
        Court Dancers of Colorado State; Collegium Musicum

IV

My Bonnie Lass She Smileth .... Edward German
        Rocky Mountain Singers
Lirum, Lirum .... Thomas Morley
        Court Singers of Colorado State

V

Upon My Lap, My Sov'reign Sits .... Martin Peerson
        Court Singers of Colorado State; Paul Metz, Guitar
Ninna-Nanna A Gesú Bambino .... D. Lavinio Virgili
        Mary Jo Bonnema, Alto; Rocky Mountain Singers
Nativity Carol .... William Mathias
        Court Singers of Colorado State

VI

Masque: Oxfordshire St. Georges .... Anonymous

FIGURE 85 The High Lord's Entertainments. An example of the music portion of a Christmas Madrigal Dinner program. Program courtesy of Lee Egbert, Colorado State University.

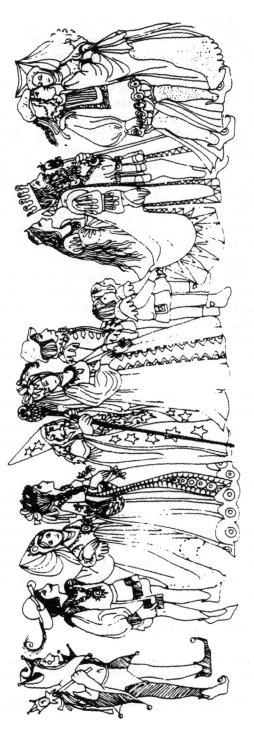

Well-come Ye to a Madrigal Feast

FIGURE 86 A Renaissance Scene for use of the foldover (reverse side) cover of an Elizabethan Madrigal Christmas Dinner program. Original size was 11 × 5 ⅝ inches. Illustration from *The Compleet Madrigal Dinner Booke* (C7832), by Paul Brandvik © 1978 Curtis Music Press, Neil A. Kjos Music Company, Dist. Used with Permission, 1992.

The program format described in the preceding pages is, of course, only one of various possibilities. For other ideas, see the references at the end of this chapter, attend madrigal dinners at other schools, and confer with other choral colleagues.

For more detailed information on planning Christmas Madrigal Dinners, see *The Compleet Madrigal Dinner Booke*, Paul Brandvik (San Diego, Calif.: Curtis Music Press, 1978). The book is indeed "compleet" with chapters on dates, performance place, division of duties, publicity, tickets, seating and programs, script, dramatic direction, makeup, lighting, staging, costumes, types and styles of music, ceremonial music for the royal court, the concert by the royal court, rehearsals and style, and repertoire lists and sources. This complete kit includes the book, a script for the speaking parts and general procedures, and twelve early English Christmas Carols. Another recommended book is *An Elizabethan Christmas Madrigal Dinner*, by John Haberlen (Champaign, Ill.: Mark Foster Music Company, 1978). This book includes a complete script, along with selected music for voices and instruments. For those directors who plan to include a recorder ensemble as part of the program, a suggested source book is *Renaissance Songs and Dances for Recorders*, Erich Katz (New York: Associated Music Publishers, 1967). A list of other suggested sources of information on madrigal dinners is listed at the end of this chapter.

After you have presented your first madrigal dinner, those in subsequent years should be somewhat easier to plan. However, other considerations will arise, such as

1. How can you change the program somewhat each year so the audience will want to return and see "what's new?"
2. What parts of the program should be retained from year to year, so the audience can anticipate certain events and then be able to tell their friends about "what's coming next"?

You may wish to encourage your audience to come in costume and then give a prize (perhaps two tickets for next year's dinner) to the best dressed person (or couple?). Prior to giving the prize, participants in this contest may be asked to parade before the head table or whoever is making the judgments. Actually, this best costume will probably already have been identified, but the parade allows the audience to see all of them, and besides, some people may even be flattered to show off their costumes, to which they probably have given considerable thought and time.

TOPICS FOR DISCUSSION

1. Maintain a file of programs of various types. Discuss the aspects of particular programs you like or dislike, in terms of musical value, unity and variety, and general format.
2. Discuss the importance of achieving audience rapport. By what means can this be achieved?

3. As a class project, prepare individual programs using a unique thematic idea. Discuss the strengths and the weaknesses of these programs in terms of the purposes for which they were designed.
4. Discuss the lighting effects that you feel would enhance the effectiveness of a particular choral program.
5. Discuss the effects of a good program of public relations upon concert attendance and school/community relationships.
6. Recall from your past experience as a singer situations in which the director's careful attention to details during the final rehearsal contributed substantially to the effectiveness of the choral concert.

SELECTED READINGS

ANDERSON, WILLIAM M. AND PATRICIA SHEHAN CAMPBELL, Editors, *Multicultural Perspectives in Music Education*, 2nd Edition. Reston, VA: Music Educators National Conference, 1996. (A companion audiotape, *Music Resources for Multicultural Perspectives*, is also available).
CAIN, NOBLE. *Choral Music and Its Practice*, chap. 13. New York: M. Witmark & Sons, 1942.
CHRISTY, VAN A. *Glee Club and Chorus*, chap. 8. New York: G. Schirmer, Inc., 1940.
DAVIS, ENNIS. *More Than a Pitchpipe*, chap. 8. Boston: C. C. Birchard & Co., 1941.
GARRETSON, ROBERT L. "Scheduling Choral Programs and Community Relations." *The Choral Journal* 20, no. 2 (October 1979), 17-19.
GRAHAM, FLOYD F. *Public Relations in Music Education*, chap. 7. New York: Exposition Press, 1954.
KRONE, MAX T. *The Chorus and Its Conductor*, chaps. 9, 10. San Diego: Neil A. Kjos Music Co., 1945.
WILSON, HARRY R. *A Guide for Choral Conductors*, chap. 4. Morristown, N.J.: Silver Burdett, 1950.

References on Religious Music in the Public Schools

ACDA, NATIONAL BOARD OF DIRECTORS. "Music with Sacred Text: Vital to Choral Music Education in the Choral Art." *Choral Journal* 23, no. 3 (November), 1982, 3.
AD HOC COMMITTEE ON RELIGIOUS MUSIC IN THE SCHOOLS, ALEX CAMPBELL CHM. "Religious Music in the Schools." *Music Educators Journal* 71, no. 3 (November, 1984), 28-30. (Updated version, with extensive bibliography, MENC, 1987.)
AQUIRO, JOHN. "Can We Still Sing Christmas Carols in Public Schools?" *Music Educators Journal* 63, no. 3 (November, 1976), 71-73.
BAGWELL, DONNA K. "Separation of Church and State: Vocal Music in the Public Schools." *Choral Journal* 22 no. 7 (March 1982), 11-13.
GILBERT, NINA. "Sacred Music in the Schools." *Choral Journal* 34, no. 5 (December, 1993), 4-5.
GRIER, REBECCA. "Sacred Music in the Schools: An Update." *Music Educators Journal* 66, no. 3 (November, 1979), 48-51.
MIMS, BOB. "Student Singer Wins Suit on Graduation Song." *The Denver Post*, June 7, 1995, 3B.
NEW YORK UNIVERSITY SCHOOL OF LAW. "Religious Holiday Observances in the Public Schools." 48, 1973, 1144.
NIERMAN, GLEN E. "Can Christmas Carols Still Be Included in Our Holiday Programs?" *The Nebraska Music Educator* 42, no. 2 (December, 1983), 8-9.
"Professor to Teach Free-Speech Class in Wake of High School Religion Flap." *The Denver Post*, July 22, 1995, 5B.
REYNOLDS, CHARLES. "Sacred Music: How to Avoid Cooking Your Holiday Goose." *Music Educators Journal* 71, no. 3 (November, 1984), 31-33.
SCAMMAN, JAMES. "Religious Music in the Public Schools." *Music Educators Journal* 53, no. 9 (May, 1967), 46-49.
SCHWADRON, ABRAHAM. "On Religion, Music, and Education." *Journal of Research in Music Education* 58, no. 2 (Summer, 1970), 157-66.
SCHWADRON, ABRAHAM A. "On Words and Music: Toward an Aesthetic Conciliation." *Journal of Aesthetic Education* 5 (July, 1971) 91-108.

SEKULOW, JAY ALAN. "Christmas Observances in Public Schools: A Legal Opinion." *Choral Journal*
    34, no. 5 (December, 1993), 54.

References for Madrigal Dinners

ARBEAU, THOINET. *Orchesography* (sixteenth-century dances). New York: Dover, 1966.
BRANDVIK, PAUL. *The Complete Madrigal Dinner Booke.* San Diego, Calif.: Curtis Music Press, 1984.
BRANDVIK, PAUL. *Madrigal Dinner Scripts.* Bemidji, Minn.: Knight-shtick Press, 1991.
COSMAN, MADELAINE P., *Medieval Holidays and Festivals: A Calendar of Celebrations.* New York:
    Charles Scribner's Sons, 1981.
DOLMETSCH, MABEL. *Dances of England and France: 1450-1600.* New York: Da Capo Press, 1975.
FISSINGER, EDWIN. *The Madrigal Concert: Choral Music for the Madrigal Dinner, Renaissance Feast, and
    Madrigal Concert.* Milwaukee: Jensen Publications, 1981.
HABERLEN, JOHN, AND STEPHEN ROSOLACK. *Elizabethan Madrigal Dinners.* Champaign, Ill.: Mark Fos-
    ter Music Co., 1978.
MCKELVY, JAMES ed., *A Christmas Madrigal Dinner at the Home of Charles Wesley.* Champaign, Ill.:
    Mark Foster Music Co., 1980. (rental production)
SCOTT, K. LEE ed., *Madrigals for Christmas.* New York: Carl Fischer, Inc., 1987. (includes choral
    music, accompanying instrument parts for trumpets, trombones, violin, viola, cello, and
    soprano-alto-tenor recorders)

VIDEOTAPES

The Inner Game of Music by Barry Green. University of Wisconsin at Madison, Department of Con-
    tinuing Education in the Arts.
The Art of the King's Singers. Hinshaw Music, Inc., No. 3056.

8

Planning and Management

A practical knowledge of planning and management procedures is as important to the choral director as the techniques of teaching: many times, the ultimate success of the music program depends on it. As a choral conductor, you are first an organizer, second a teacher, and finally a conductor. Without an understanding of organizational procedures you may be seriously impaired in your efforts to develop outstanding musical groups. Administrators often judge the effectiveness of the music director by his or her ability to plan and organize, rather than by musicianship. They can generally assume that the music teacher has had an adequate training in music; they cannot, however, always assume that the person is an effective organizer.

THE CHORAL CURRICULUM

The development of music education in America has been marked by different emphases during various periods or decades. During the 1930s, for example, there was much emphasis on the *a cappella* choir, and the choral literature of the time reflected this emphasis on unaccompanied singing. During the 1940s and the 1950s, the emphasis was on diction and methods and means of improving choral tone. Concurrently during the 1950s, certain educators expounded on the beauty and the spiritual value of choral music as a means of fulfilling a basic human need. During the 1960s, and perhaps related to the effect of "Sputnik" on

275

the American educational system, music began to be considered as an "academic discipline." In a way, many subjects in the school curriculum needed to prove their worth and be justified, particularly in view of the continually increasing costs of education. During this period, and also during the 1970s, choral music fulfilled a dual purpose of not only providing worthwhile aesthetic experiences, but also (perhaps to keep pace with the other subject-matter areas) developing a definite content of its own. An important aspect of these dual objectives focused on the adherence to authentic performance practices. This emphasis was extended and perhaps intensified beginning in the 1980s.

Fortunately, musicologists have provided the choral profession with considerable insight into the performance practices of music from various historical periods, while music theorists have developed college courses in musical styles (or analytical techniques) that develop the prospective teacher's capacities to analyze, and more thoroughly understand, the music of particular composers, as well as the more generalized characteritics of the music of different historical periods. Thus a sizable body of course content for choral conductors has developed, one that not only enhances the aesthetic experience, but also provides students with insights and understanding of the stylistic aspects of music of various historical periods. Students also gain a comprehension of the ongoing social economic, and political forces during the life of a particular composer and how these served as a famework for his creative output.

To develop student understanding of musical style and specific performance practices, do not resort to extensive lectures, which might prove deadly and defeat your purposes. Rather, try to relate, in a succinct manner, pertinent information as it applies to the performance of a particular musical selection. In this way, musical enjoyment can be increased, students will gain a greater understanding of their musical heritage, and the artistic level of musical performances may be increased substantially. With adequate college preparation you can achieve these goals without undue effort, providing you plan carefully for all your rehearsals.

Whereas dietitians and physicians speak of a balanced nutritional diet, musicians refer to a balanced musical diet—that is, the development of a choral curriculum that will provide students with some experience and comprehension of music of all types and styles, including music from the Renaissance, Baroque, Classical, Romantic, and Modern periods, folk music, and music of a popular, stylized nature. Often one particular choral group is unable to cover literature this broad in scope. Therefore, various groups are sometimes included in the choral curriculum, each with a slightly different focus, but all designed to meet the varied musical needs and interests of students.

In developing a balanced choral music program, you may ask, "How many and what types of choral groups should I have?" Certainly the answer to this question depends on the situation as it exists in a specific school. The size of the school and the existing need are both determining factors. The most successful school choral programs usually include a selected mixed choir or chorus with other junior groups used as feeders to the advanced group. This does not mean to suggest the exclusion of particular students from the advanced groups. Rather, it implies the necessity for choral experience commensurate with the level of each singer's musical development. The choral program should be based on meeting the needs of all students, and everyone with the desire should have the opportunity to participate in some choral group.

Students enter the junior high school with a variety of previous experience and backgrounds. Although most of them have benefited from the general music program in the elementary school, certain pupils may have been fortunate enough to participate in grade school choruses comprising selected fifth- and sixth-grade students. Figure 87 illustrates the type and the variety of

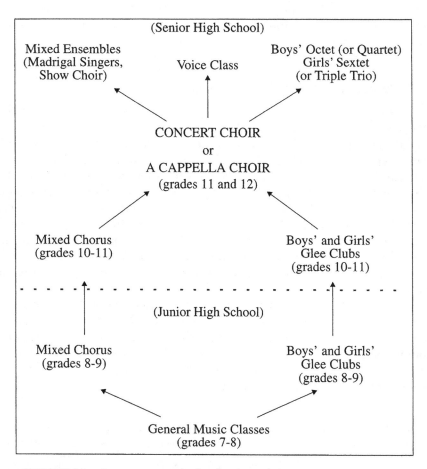

FIGURE 87   A junior-senior high school vocal music program.

choral groups that the secondary school may endeavor to maintain. It also illustrates two alternative approaches in the basic pattern of organization. Both programs are predicated on the philosophy of meeting the needs of all students—that is, providing an opportunity for all students who so desire to participate in choral singing.

The general music class is required by most junior high schools. In some instances this class is required only of seventh-grade pupils, while being optional or elective for eighth-grade students. In general music classes, students are provided the opportunity to explore special music areas of particular interest. Although some schools enroll seventh-grade students in selective choral groups, it is desirable to delay this particular experience until the eighth grade. At this point the music program usually becomes more selective, and students are encouraged to participate in some activity of special interest, whether it be choral or instrumental music, fine or industrial arts, home economics, or some other area. In the late spring, before the close of school, seventh grade students may be offered the opportunity of auditioning for the more selective eighth- and ninth-grade choral groups.

Junior High School Choral Groups

As indicated in Figure 87, the organization of special groups may follow one of several patterns. Some schools organize a boys' and girls' glee club for eighth- and ninth-grade students.[1] Where school enrollments are particularly large, separate boys' and girls' glee clubs are often maintained for *both* eighth- and ninth-grade students. This plan of organization is predicated on the belief that during early adolescence boys and girls enjoy participating in activities with their own gender. Another reason advanced is that the music composed or arranged for boys' and girls' glee clubs is more closely in line with their particular interests and musical tastes. Advocates of this position advance the argument that these types of musical experience differ considerably from the standard choral literature for mixed voices, and should be an integral part of the junior high school student's background.

Administrators and music educators in other schools feel that boys and girls should have experiences that bring them together under socially desirable conditions; thus they advocate the *mixed chorus* as the most ideal plan of organization. Still other schools, recognizing the value of both glee clubs and mixed groups, compromise between these two alternatives and thus capitalize on the strong points of both plans of organization.

---

[1] This plan is predicated on the belief that seventh-grade students entering junior high school have certain adjustments to make, and that a general music class designed to broaden their experience in music is a desirable curricular offering. Some schools, however, also offer a select choir for seventh-grade students. In middle schools, involving sixth, seventh, and eighth grades, choir participation is generally available to those students who are accepted after an audition.

Senior High School Choral Groups

In the senior high school, the "combined" plan may also be followed for the "junior" groups, but owing to scheduling difficulties students generally participate in either a mixed chorus or a boys' or a girls' glee club. (In certain schools, where the enrollment is exceptionally large, both types of organizations may be maintained.) It is desirable to schedule these groups for a minimum of three periods a week. In four-year high schools (grades 9–12), the membership in the mixed chorus (sometimes referred to as the junior choir) and the glee clubs generally comprises ninth- and tenth-grade students. In three-year high schools (grades 10–12), the membership in these organizations will consist primarily of tenth-grade students, plus a limited number of eleventh-grade students who were not accepted for membership in the advanced choir. Because of the greater variety and amount of literature available for mixed voices, and since in many cases it may be more practical to schedule one organization than two, the mixed chorus is felt to be the most flexible arrangement. In addition, since all "senior" or advanced choral groups depend on feeder organizations for their ultimate success, student experiences in singing music for mixed voices, prior to membership in the advanced choir, may contribute substantially to the degree of proficiency that the latter organization is able to achieve.

The "Concert Choir" and the "A Cappella Choir" are two names commonly given the selective choral group in the high school.[2] By maintaining a selective choral group, higher musical standards may be achieved and the participating singers will benefit from a higher quality of musical experiences. Because the school's musical groups provide a "bridge of understanding" between the school and the community, it is highly desirable to develop and maintain a choral group that achieves and maintains high musical standards. The membership will usually consist of eleventh- and twelfth-grade students (juniors and seniors). A selective choral group, to achieve the maximum degree of musical proficiency, should rehearse at least five days a week, Monday through Friday. The most effective rehearsal time is during the morning, since students often become overly fatigued during the afternoon hours.

Small Vocal Ensembles

For particularly talented and interested students, experience in various small ensembles should also be provided. Participation in either an octet or a quartet will provide an outlet for boys who desire male companionship and the

---

[2] Although the term *a cappella* choir is still used as a name for mixed choral groups in particular schools, it should be noted that the term is somewhat archaic and a holdover from several decades ago, when the trend was to perform music *a cappella* (without accompaniment) almost exclusively. Today, the practice is to choose the repertoire for its musical worth, and as a result, conductors generally achieve a reasonable balance between unaccompanied music and music with instrumental accompaniment—that is, with either piano, organ, string, wind, or percussion instruments, or an ensemble of instruments in various combinations.

opportunity to explore the literature composed and arranged especially for male voices. Participation in a sextet or a triple trio will provide a similar opportunity for the especially talented girls in the school.

The mixed ensemble, however, may provide a unique musical experience. Many schools organize a group of madrigal singers, with a membership usually of twelve to sixteen voices. These groups generally devote themselves to a thorough study of madrigal singing and related types of choral literature. Other schools may organize a show choir, ranging from sixteen to twenty-four voices, devoted to the study and performance of popular, stylized arrangements. Although the latter group is given various names, the title "The Modernaires" is descriptive of the choral music performed. Often the school enrollment and the degree of student interest necessitate the maintenance of both types of small mixed choral ensembles—that is, both a madrigal group and a "jazz" or "show" choir. If only enough students are available for one mixed ensemble, however, the group should study, rehearse, and perform a wider variety of choral literature, rather than devote itself to only one type or style of choral music.

Small vocal ensembles should rehearse at least twice weekly. In some cases the singers will find a free period during the day in which rehearsals can be scheduled. When this is not possible, rehearsals will have to be scheduled before or after school hours or during the noon period. The smaller ensembles, such as trios, quartets, sextets, and octets, may be encouraged to schedule, during the evening hours, an additional weekly rehearsal at one of the members' homes. Although the most desirable arrangement would have the director meet with the singers during every rehearsal, a busy schedule may not permit him or her to do so. Thus these evening rehearsals, if deemed necessary or desirable according to the local situation, may be conducted by one of the more talented student leaders. Such opportunity provides valuable experience for students who may eventually enter teacher training programs.

The Voice Class

The high school voice class is an adjunct of the choral program. It is usually taught by the choral director and may serve as a valuable training ground for student soloists in the advanced choir. Membership in the voice class should be selective and limited to those students who possess at least a reasonable degree of innate vocal and musical ability, and who display a keen interest in developing vocal proficiency. The particular value of the class approach to vocal training lies in the opportunity for singers to observe each other and discuss, as a group, common vocal difficulties. Although private vocal study is highly desirable, it may be financially prohibitive to many students; in addition, the opportunity for valuable group experience does not present itself. Therefore, by meeting the needs of a particularly interested and musically talented group, the high school voice class makes its unique contribution to the balanced vocal music curriculum.

RECRUITING SINGERS

The organization and development of new choral groups in various educational institutions, or the improvement of established programs, may in some instances pose a considerable problem to the inexperienced director. A successful choral group demands at least a specific minimum membership, without which it is difficult to achieve any measurable degree of success; naturally the long-range development of a program depends to some extent on this initial success. Following are suggestions that should prove profitable in the development of the choral music program.

Endeavor to show all individuals that singing can be an enjoyable and rewarding experience—not an uninteresting mechanical ritual! In schools this may be approached, in the beginning, through well-planned but informal songfests, preferably in groups that are not too large so that effective rapport and communication can be achieved.[3] In churches, informal sings may be promoted as an integral part of the program provided or sponsored for various age groups— that is, boy and girl scouts, youth groups, young married couples' groups, singles' groups, men's organizations, and women's societies.

At the outset of this program, use many familiar songs, sung in unison. Singing in unison, with good tone quality and clear diction, can be a satisfying musical experience. This activity, plus the singing of many rounds and canons, provides the background for and serves as a means of stimulating interest in the later group harmonization of favorite songs. Although the emphasis should always be on the recreational and not the technical aspects of the music, it is possible for the leader to stress the importance of good tone quality and clear diction as it relates to expressive singing. Remarks such as "When you open your mouths wide, you sound so much better," and "Enunciating your words makes this song more enjoyable to sing" contribute toward this end. Several highly successful choral programs were begun in this manner. From the musical seeds sown in these informal sings grew a strong desire on the part of many to explore further the vast wealth of choral literature.

With particular reference to school situations the following suggestions are offered. Inviting outstanding choral groups from neighboring schools and from the community at large to present assembly programs may serve to stimulate interest in singing and provide further impetus to the choral music program. One of the local barbershop quartets might prove of special interest to the male students. If individuals are to improve, they must know what they are striving for. Hearing other choral groups provides a means for students to evaluate their own attitudes and progress.

In certain schools, the biggest problem in recruiting students for choral groups is obtaining an adequate number of boys to sing four-part music for mixed

---

[3] For a variety of songs for recreational singing, see the listing at the end of this chapter.

voices (SATB). The reasons for this problem are many, including schedule con-flicts with other school activities and athletics. The solution usually comes down to ferreting out the remaining number of boys, making the choral program so attractive that an adequate number of singers are drawn from conflicting activi-ties, or both. The organization of a male quartet or octet that may be called on to sing in a school assembly or elsewhere in the community can have a most desirable effect on boys who consider choral singing to be a nonmasculine activ-ity. To combat this attitude, many successful directors have devoted special attention to establishing rapport with, and subsequently recruiting in the orga-nizations, the leaders of the school athletic teams. Once this group has been won over, the problem of recruiting additional boys is, for obvious reasons, lessened considerably.

Enlisting the cooperation of other teachers in the school to be on the look-out for students who display an interest in music, and who from all indications will be able to meet the established membership qualifications, has in many cases proven most profitable. Some students, to a greater or lesser extent, want to participate in choral groups, but either are unaware of their capabilities or lack courage enough to express their desires to the choral director.

It is advisable to heed the adage "Nothing succeeds like success." You should believe in the success of your choral groups. In other words, be optimistic; think in positive terms and avoid negative thoughts. A positive attitude is con-tagious and can have a decidedly beneficial effect on your singers.

TESTING AND CLASSIFYING VOICES

Among choral directors, it is accepted procedure to audition individuals before admitting them to membership in an organization. In some cases, the audition is used as a means of limiting membership and obtaining the best voices for the choir or chorus. Directors using the procedure primarily for this purpose justify it as a necessary means of providing the selected singers with the best possible musical experience. It is most desirable to develop and maintain highly selective choral groups, provided that the remaining individuals are not prevented from participating in some group as a result. Opportunity for participation in a wide variety of choral groups and ensembles should be provided, so that the musical and the social needs of *all* interested persons are met. Auditions also provide a means of determining the singer's vocal range and voice quality so that he or she may be assigned the most suitable voice part and thus make the best contri-bution to the group. Since most adolescent voices are quite unstable and are still in the process of change, retest voices periodically in order to avoid unnecessary strain from singing in an improper vocal range.

In classifying voices, you must take two criteria into consideration—*range* and *quality*. The following procedure is suggested as a means of determining these factors.

1. Determine the approximate middle range of the student's voice and start there.
2. Using Exercise 27, vocalize upward, noting the point at which excessive strain occurs or at which the quality of the voice changes to any noticeable degree.

EXERCISE 27

Ah,—————————————   Ah,—————————————   *etc.*

3. Using Exercise 28, vocalize from the middle range downward, noting the point at which the quality of the voice changes. The low range is as important as the higher limits of the voice. Little benefit can come to a voice that is forced downward in an attempt to sing too low a part.

EXERCISE 28

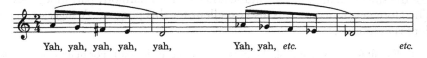

Yah, yah, yah, yah,   yah,   Yah, yah, *etc.*   *etc.*

The voice ranges in Figure 88 are only approximate classifications, and the ranges of many singers do not always fall easily into these categories. The vocal range of some individuals may be considerably smaller than, and some may conceivably cover the ranges of two or more of, the classifications presented. In any case, listen carefully to the quality of the voice and determine the range in which it sounds most natural—that is, where the person sings with the best voice quality and with the least amount of strain or effort. This is most readily accomplished by utilizing some easy song material. The well-known English folk song "Drink to Me Only with Thine Eyes" is excellent for this purpose, and may be found in many songbooks compiled for community singing.

As a further guide in determining the proper voice classification of singers, the following voice qualities are considered characteristic.

First Soprano—light, flutelike, lyric quality.
Second Soprano—similar in range to the first soprano, but has a fuller, more dramatic voice quality.

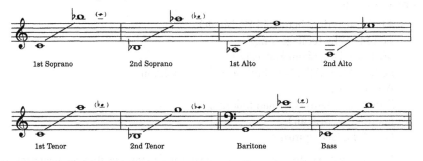

FIGURE 88   A general classification of voice ranges of untrained singers.

First Alto—similar in quality to the second soprano, but has a more developed lower range.

Second Alto—a heavier, deeper voice quality, especially in the lower range, which is more developed than the first alto voice.

First Tenor—light, lyric quality, especially in the upper range limits.

Second Tenor—similar in range to the first tenor, but has a fuller, more dramatic voice quality.

Baritone—often similar in quality to the second tenor, yet has a more fully developed middle and lower range. (Initial voice characteristics may be deceiving; it is in this category that many true tenor voices may be identified and developed. Periodical retesting is recommended.)

Bass—a heavier, darker, deeper quality, especially in the middle and lower ranges of the voice.

In addition to determining voice quality and range, many directors like to test the singer's ability to read music and to carry a harmony part independently. The aforementioned song is also excellent for this purpose. A suggested procedure is as follows:[4]

1. For all female voices, ask the person to sing the alto part. For male voices, request the individual to sing either the bass or the tenor part, depending on the singer's vocal range and previous musical experience.

2. Provide the starting note or a short introduction. Accompany the singer, playing all the voice parts *except* the one he or she is requested to sing. (Omitting this part enables you to determine more readily the extent to which a singer can carry a part without help from others in his section. This information is invaluable in assigning seating in an organization. "Followers" may be judiciously placed between "leaders," and from the reading standpoint the total effectiveness of the choral group will be enhanced.)

3. Because of some singers' lack of experience, it may occasionally be necessary to provide some assistance with their parts. This procedure is justifiable, since you really want to determine just how quickly the individuals catch on. In some instances, repeating the song a time or two (with less assistance each time) will help you determine the singer's musical memory and his ability to adjust to and profit from assistance provided during rehearsals.

Following is a suggested list of other songs that might be utilized for voice auditions. These selections may be located in most songbooks compiled for community singing.

All through the Night (old Welsh air)

Tell Me Why (college song)

My Homeland (from *Finlandia*)

Believe Me If All Those Endearing Young Charms

Annie Laurie

Fairest Lord Jesus (German folk song)

Juanita (Spanish air)

Jacob's Ladder (spiritual)

[4] It is assumed that the individual has been oriented to the song through singing the melody during the previous part of the audition.

Many choral conductors have found it advantageous to maintain a permanent record for each choir member. Readily available information, included on personnel cards, can be helpful in administering the total choral music program. Figure 89 shows a sample card, which may be altered or adapted to suit individual tastes.

SELECTING ACCOMPANISTS

Capable accompanists are essential to effective rehearsals and to the success of the choir. You should, of course, always be on the lookout for pianistic talents in the school. Some personal characteristics of a good accompanist are dependability, cooperativeness, and a desire to contribute to the school choral music program. Musical abilities include a piano technique sufficient to play the accompaniment to the choral music being performed, a reasonable ability to sight-read new and unfamiliar music, a sensitivity to the problems the choir is having, and, when the director stops the group for comments, knowing what pitches to provide the choir with for a fresh start. (This last ability may need to be developed through experience.)

When auditioning prospective accompanists, ask each student to first play two selections (or portions thereof) of contrasting musical styles—to enable the

---

PERSONAL DATA

Name: _____

Address: _____

_____ Phone: _____

Previous musical experience: _____

Part(s) previously sung: S1, S2, A1, A2, T1, T2, B1, B2

Height:_____ Weight: _____

. . . .

Range: | Voice timbre: S. A. T. B.
Comments: _____

Quality: 1 2 3 4 5   Part assigned: S1, S2, A1, A2
Intonation: 1 2 3 4 5   T1, T2, B1, B2
S. Reading: 1 2 3 4 5   Robe no. assigned: _____

FIGURE 89   A sample personal data card. The vocal range in which the individual sings with comparative ease may be indicated in red; the undeveloped part of the vocal range may be indicated in blue.

director to determine the overall level of technique and musicianship. In other words, what is he or she pianistically capable of? To determine the student's sight-reading abilities, have him or her play the accompaniment to one or more of the choral pieces that the choir is presently performing or that you are contemplating using. Other suggestions for sight-reading are Bach chorales and accompaniments to art songs.

When an ideal accompanist is found, you should feel fortunate; however, this will not always be the case. In high schools it is often desirable to have several accompanists, each of whom can be assigned to work on specific pieces and can substitute when one of the others is ill or absent. Also, more than one accompanist is necessary if sectional rehearsals are held periodically.

In schools with a relatively high socioeconomic level (where parents start their children studying piano at an early age), locating suitable accompanists may not be difficult. In less affluent schools, however, these conditions do not always exist, and you may be forced to employ some capable adult within the community to accompany the choir(s). Stay in touch with teachers and students in feeder schools to encourage piano study and to inform younger students of the musical opportunities that exist for them when they reach high school.

In working with accompanists, the following procedures are very important:

1. Give the accompanists their new music well in advance of the time they will be expected to play it and indicate or demonstrate appropriate tempi, dynamics, phrasing, and so on.
2. Meet with the accompanists prior to the first rehearsal of the new music, or the time they will be expected to play the accompaniments.
3. Identify any problems and apprise the students of their progress.
4. Be supportive and provide encouragement! Stimulate in each student the desire to improve his or her accompanying skills and to contribute to the choir.
5. Discuss with students the appropriate procedures for giving pitches (for example individual pitches played slowly from the lowest to the highest, proper dynamic levels, and so on).

Accompanists' names should always be listed on printed programs, and proper acknowledgment should be given them during each choral concert.

SEATING ARRANGEMENTS

Choral conductors generally have found, through experimentation, that certain seating arrangements are preferable to others. The type of arrangement selected usually depends on several factors, including the number of voices assigned to or available for each part, the comparative voice qualities of various members, and the relative musical experience of the singers. Plans 4 through 14 show several suggested seating arrangements for mixed voices, and the advantages of each are listed.

The advantages of the arrangement of Plan 4 are as follows:

PLAN 4

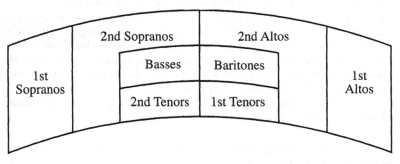

1. One of the problems confronting choral directors seems to be the development of tenor voices. When placed in the front of the choir, the tenors are more easily heard and may therefore sing in a more natural voice, thus improving the blend of the group.
2. At times the tenor part may need to be reinforced. If some of the second altos need to be used for this purpose, they will be close enough to effect a reasonably good blend.
3. The soprano and the bass sections are relatively close together. The proximity of these two sections, which are the outside two parts of the harmonic structure, can effect a stability to the chord and thus help to improve intonation.
4. The placement of a limited number of girls behind the boys can assist in the development of a better blend among the various sections. Choral blend is dependent to a great extent on the ability of the singers to hear the other parts adequately. This seating arrangement in which the female voices literally surround the male section increases the latter's awareness of the upper parts and provides increased tonal support, which is especially desirable for unstable adolescent male voices.

Plan 5 shows another suggested arrangement that may be used effectively when the membership of boys is adequate in both quantity and quality. The advantages of this arrangement are as follows:

1. With the taller students in each section standing toward the outside, a more uniform appearance is achieved—producing a total effect noticeably different from

PLAN 5

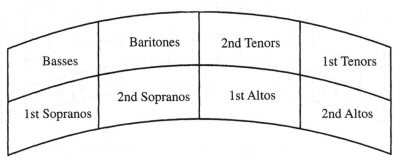

the first arrangement. The difference in height between the boys and girls is not accentuated, as it would be if they were placed in the same row.

2. Both choirs are reasonably close together and may function as separate units if necessary. (In terms of providing variety to a choral program, the inclusion of numbers arranged exclusively for male or female voices is highly desirable.)

3. In the event that the first tenor part needs to be reinforced with altos, the proximity of the second alto section would provide the maximum support and enable the singers to achieve a reasonably good blend.

4. The proximity of the soprano and the bass sections effects a certain stability to the harmonic structure and assists in improving intonation.

The preceding arrangements have one advantage in common; that is, the grouping together of the voices on the same part provides a degree of security for the singers, particularly those in young choirs. However, with the security of singing next to others on the same part also goes the danger of some singers becoming overly dependent on certain leaders within their section. If these leaders happen to be absent on a particular day, the effectiveness of the entire section is often hampered. It behooves you, therefore, to seek ways to strengthen the aural sense of all the singers in your groups. Your objective should be the development of individual security through vocal independence, not dependence. Seating arrangements may make their contribution to this end. After the choir members have had a certain minimal musical training, experiment with different seating arrangements, in which singers will be better able to hear themselves and to evaluate their efforts properly.

One arrangement, used for a number of years, is the placement of choir members by quartets; that is, SATB or any combination thereof, as shown in Plan 6.[5] The quartet seating arrangement usually results in the achievement of better balance and blend. Although the voice parts are arranged in rows from the front to rear of the choir, each singer is nevertheless able to hear himself or herself—and the other voice parts—better. Some conductors assign singers to quartets (or octets) on a continuing basis and utilize these groupings periodically for small ensemble practice. In school situations some conductors, at intervals of

PLAN 6

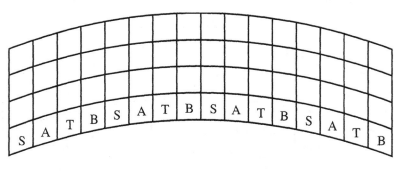

[5] Some directors use the arrangement TSAB, whereas others prefer BSAT.

about six weeks, will request each quartet to sing a portion of selected music for evaluative purposes.

Another arrangement involves placing each singer as far as possible from another singing the same part, thus enabling each to hear his or her own voice better and to evaluate his or her efforts toward improved tone quality, diction, balance and blend, and intonation. This arrangement, used by Robert Shaw, has been designated by Louis Diercks as the *scrambled setup*. Plan 7 is for a choir of nine first sopranos, seven second sopranos, eight first altos, seven second altos, five first tenors, seven second tenors, eight baritones, and seven basses.[6]

One of the most striking results of the use of this arrangement is improved balance and blend. The weaker singers are not in a position to affect the others in the section adversely, all singers can hear themselves better, and, with the sound of any particular part coming from all areas of the choir, there seems to be a better fusion of sound.[7]

Because the voices in the front row are nearest to and the first to reach the audience, Diercks suggests placing the more select singers in this position to serve as a "mask" to the choir.[8] Also, when a sufficient number of choir risers are available, it is desirable to space the singers slightly farther apart than usual. This also contributes to the objectives of this arrangement.

Some conductors prefer to use either the quartet arrangement or the scrambled setup exclusively, even when introducing new music. Others prefer to use a more conventional setup until they feel that the singers possess at least a minimal understanding of, and ability to sing, their parts. For the latter group, Plan 8 is suggested. While the singers are learning the music in their respective sections, the voice parts are at least divided or arranged so as to achieve a somewhat better blend, or fusion of sound, than in some of the traditional arrangements.

Directors of junior high school choirs often use SAB music arrangements because of a lack of well-developed tenor voices. Plan 9 is suggested for this

PLAN 7

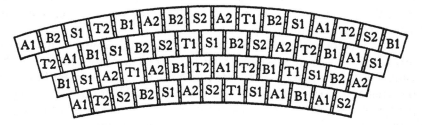

[6] Louis H. Diercks, "The Individual in the Choral Situation," *The NATS Bulletin* 17, no. 4 (May 15, 1961), 7. Used by permission.

[7] Both the quartet arrangement and the scrambled setup are desirable for use primarily with music of a homophonic texture. When performing polyphonic music, the choir should use a traditional formation, because the beauty of polyphony results from the interplay of the voice parts stemming from various sections of the choir.

[8] Diercks, "The Individual in the Choral Situation," p. 7.

PLAN 8

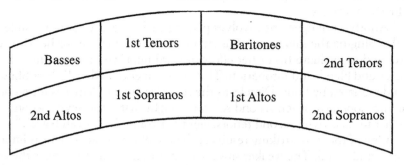

PLAN 9

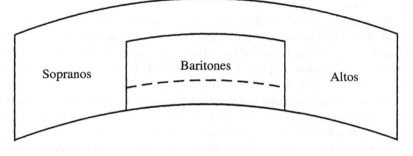

voice combination. Because of the insecurity of the male voices of this age group, place them toward the front of the choir where they will be nearly surrounded by the female voices. This will ensure their being heard more easily and will result in a better balance and blend. As the group progresses, and as the individual voices mature, it will become feasible to introduce some easy four-part (SATB) music. At this particular stage of development, the tenor voices are likely to be especially insecure, and perhaps fewer in number. Therefore, seating this group of voices in front of the baritones will also contribute to the balance and blend of the group.

For directors of treble voice choirs the seating arrangements shown in Plans 10, 11, and 12 are suggested. Plan 10 is for elementary school choirs comprising selected fifth- and sixth-grade students The plan allows for flexibility in rehearsing and programming a variety of music suitable for this age group. The repertoire will usually include a combination of two- and three-part music, some of which is learned in the general music class. When singing two-part music, the group placed in the center will sing their respective soprano or alto parts. When singing three-part music, they will sing the second soprano part. The group of students for this shifting, flexible role should be carefully selected through auditions held prior to the first rehearsal.

Plan 11 is suggested for girls' glee clubs in junior and senior high school and for women's choruses on the college or adult level. Although a sufficient

PLAN 10

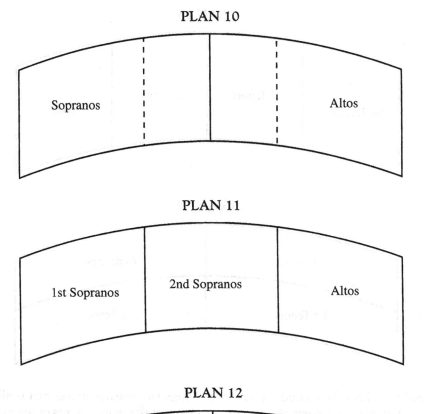

Sopranos

Altos

PLAN 11

1st Sopranos

2nd Sopranos

Altos

PLAN 12

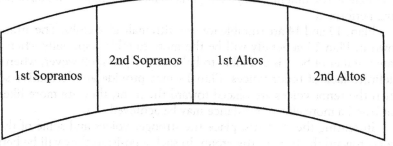

1st Sopranos

2nd Sopranos

1st Altos

2nd Altos

amount of three-part music is available for girls' glee clubs, the more proficient organizations may ultimately desire to include some SSAA music in their repertoires because of the more complete harmonic effects. In such instances, the alto parts will necessarily have to divide, as indicated in Plan 12.

Since both SSA and SSAA arrangements may be utilized in a given program, both Plan 11 and Plan 12 will be found practical because of the adjacency of the second soprano and the alto parts. To achieve an adequate balance, it may be necessary, for example, to assign a few second sopranos, designated as "roving singers," to the first alto part. Or, in other instances, a few altos may be

PLAN 13

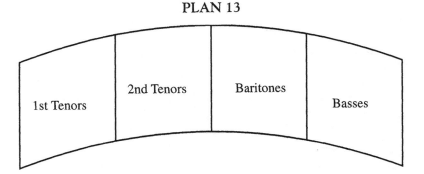

PLAN 14

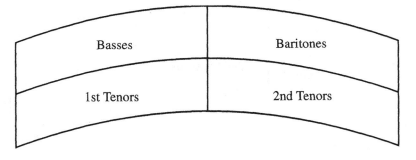

used to bolster the second soprano part. These two seating arrangements allow for a flexible assignment of adjacent parts to meet the requirements of the music being performed.

Plans 13 and 14 are suitable for use with male glee clubs. The arrangement shown in Plan 13 generally will be the more suitable, especially when an adequate number of boys is available to balance the parts. However, when there is a definite lack of tenor voices, Plan 14 may provide an alternative solution. When the tenor voices are placed toward the front, they are more likely to be heard, and a more effective balance may be achieved.

In seating the students, place the stronger voices and some of the better readers toward the back of the group. In such a position they will be better able to assist the rest of the singers. It is also advisable to scatter some of the better readers throughout the choir, in order to stabilize the group.

In an effort to achieve the best choral blend, place singers with strident voices between singers with a more natural vocal production. Individuals are inclined to simulate or assume the voice qualities of the persons nearest them. When several singers of a similar voice quality are seated together, this particular quality is sometimes strengthened and the resultant tone becomes stronger and out of proportion to the number of singers with that particular quality. The same principle may also adversely affect intonation. When several chronic flatters (caused by faulty voice production) are seated together, intonation problems are sometimes magnified. When these singers are distributed within the group, intonation problems are usually lessened considerably.

Another factor to take into consideration is each choir member's height. It is recommended that the taller individuals be placed toward the outside and the back of the group. Especially when the singers are on choral risers, this arrangement will enable them to see better the conducting movements of the director and will result in greater security of the entire group.

You will find it highly profitable to experiment with a variety of seating arrangements. Given plans may be more effective with certain groups than with others, and periodic changes in arrangements will sometimes contribute to the betterment of the choral organization.

STIMULATING INTEREST

Individuals are normally motivated in a variety of ways toward music participation. There are relatively few whose initial interest is entirely *intrinsic*—that is, whose desire to study music emerges primarily from a love of the music itself. Nevertheless, such interest not only is admirable, but also might well be considered one of the ultimate goals of music education. The skilled director who displays a great enthusiasm for music will normally make great strides in developing in individuals a love for music and the desire to explore and experience the vast wealth of music literature. It is not suggested, however, that you depend entirely on this intrinsic interest in the development of the choral music program. In a normal situation, we will find that everyone is interested in music to a greater or lesser extent. The problem usually occurs with the half-interested person who either is "exploring" the activity or is merely anxious to remain in the company of his friends. Experienced directors, however, take a realistic attitude and utilize many means to help accomplish their goal or purpose. Sometimes these techniques or methods are described as extrinsic means of motivation; that is, the director motivates such a person by taking advantage of interests that lie outside the music itself.

Following are suggestions that might be used in intrinsic situations, as a means of motivation to participate in music. If utilized, this will not only stimulate interest in music participation, but will also result in other values that contribute to the development of the choral music program.

Exchange Concerts

Exchange concerts with neighboring communities are valuable in that they provide the singers with a yardstick for the evaluation of the progress of their own music groups, as well as serving as an introduction to varied types of music literature. In addition, valuable and lasting friendships are sometimes made with individuals from other schools or communities.

Guest Conductors

Using guest conductors for rehearsals and concerts can be a valuable musical experience for chorus members. As a result of this experience, singers necessarily become more alert to the conducting movements of the director and develop an awareness of varying types of musical interpretation. Such an arrangement can usually be made on an exchange basis with directors from neighboring institutions. Whenever financial arrangements can be made, however, it would seem highly desirable to invite a nationally known choral conductor to work with the choir or chorus for a day or two. These rehearsals may culminate in a public concert. A practice that is quite prevalent, and certainly more economical, is for a number of neighboring schools or churches to join together and direct their efforts toward one large musical festival. Between schools, lines of communication usually are set up by the principals. Such choral festivals provide significant choral and social experiences for participating singers (both senior and junior high); they offer important opportunities to perform significant literature with leading conductors.

Attending Concerts

Group solidarity and a feeling of belonging—so important to the ultimate success of an organization—are often facilitated when members of a choral organization attend as a group various musical events presented in the community or in nearby towns or cities. In addition, a broader understanding and a greater appreciation of music are often developed by the group.

Choral Recordings

Recordings of professional, collegiate, church, and community choral groups are often used to introduce new musical selections to the group, and as a means of studying various types of interpretation. A variety of listening experiences is helpful in broadening the singers' musical horizons and in improving their musical tastes.

Tape Recordings as a Rehearsal Aid

The use of a tape recorder during rehearsals can be a most effective means of facilitating the singers' musical development. As an aid in improving the interpretation of a musical selection it is in many ways unsurpassable. Often the well-chosen words of the director, expressing a specific desired effect, are comparatively ineffective, whereas the playback of a tape recording usually has a profound effect on the listeners.

Production and Sale of Recordings

Provided the musical development of the organization warrants it, it may be profitable to produce and sell recordings of the group. Such a project not only serves to stimulate the singers' interest, but also focuses the community's interest on the choral music program—certainly a most desirable objective.

Group Photographs

The experienced director is well aware of the enthusiasm created when organization pictures are taken. They have for a long time been utilized as a means of developing *esprit de corps* in groups. People of all ages enjoy pictures, but school-age youth are especially interested in photographs that include themselves and their peers.

The Rehearsal-Room Bulletin Board

The bulletin board may be used advantageously—for posting general announcements, magazine or newspaper articles of general interest, organization photographs, and various other types of pictures and cartoons dealing with music topics. All of these are effective means for stimulating interest in music.

Radio and Television Broadcasts

The choral group that is fortunate enough to participate in radio or television broadcasts will usually be highly motivated to prepare for the programs.[9] As a result, most directors would agree that such opportunities are a profitable educational experience for the persons involved. Many local stations want to schedule programs of general public interest. Because the nature or the content of choral music programs is especially appropriate for programming during the Christmas and Lenten seasons, many community music groups may be heard at these times. Unfortunately, in some localities, opportunities such as these are not frequently available for all choral groups. In such instances, however, many directors endeavor to utilize these educational media in other ways—by announcing at rehearsals various noteworthy programs or posting notices of

[9] Choral conductors should know the necessary production hand signals used in television studios.

them on the bulletin board. In this way the choir members may benefit considerably from the programs themselves, as well as from discussions of them later.

Publication of Yearbooks or Newsletters

Many school music groups have found it extremely profitable, in terms of developing individual interest, to publish a yearly booklet in which photographs, comments on noteworthy performances, and various anecdotes about the organization's members are included. Other groups publish a newsletter periodically with equal success. In most groups there are people who have a keen interest in writing and who will benefit especially from this experience.

Awards

The presentation of letters, pins, or keys to outstanding students, or to students who have participated for a specified length of time, has long been an effective means of stimulating interest in school music groups. Some directors have found the establishment of a point system to be quite effective in implementing such a plan. That is, to receive an award a student must be credited with a specified number of points. For example, points may be given for attendance at regular and special rehearsals, participation in concerts and music festivals, or participation as a soloist or a member of an ensemble at competition festivals or at various functions in the community. It is usually advisable for a committee selected by the students to work with the director in setting up the system of awards.

Social Events

Dances, mixers, and parties provide a splendid opportunity for the development of esprit de corps and the feeling of belonging that can contribute so much to the eventual success of an organization. In addition to serving as a means of strengthening personal relationships within the group, they can be utilized as money-making activities.

Newspaper Publicity

Adequate newspaper coverage of concerts can be of considerable assistance in the development of the choral music program. Newspaper editors are eager to receive information concerning news events that they believe will be of special community interest. Many newspapers have a prescribed format to be followed in preparing news items. Learning and following these procedures will often facilitate communication and the release of the news item. Early submission of an item that has no particular release time enables a paper to use it whenever it will fit their makeup. The importance of maintaining friendly relationships with the local newspaper staff, and submitting articles that are carefully written, cannot be overemphasized.[10]

Music Festivals

Music festivals may contribute substantially to the development of the music program. Adjudicators' remarks may prove helpful to singers and director alike. Opportunity is also provided for hearing other school music groups and for making many lasting acquaintances with individuals from other communities. One major criticism often voiced against "contests"—not the only one, however—is that too much emphasis is placed on the competitive aspects, and that singers often become emotionally upset over the preparation, the performance, and the final ratings. In certain instances this criticism may be true; however, it should not be interpreted as a condemnation of contests. Prior to participation in such events, you must prepare your groups emotionally for an eventual outcome. Encourage concentrated effort during rehearsals and performances. Nevertheless, strive to develop in your singers a realistic life attitude. In our present-day society, too much emphasis is placed on winning first prize in various fields of endeavor, or being named the star of the show or the hero of the game. Individuals failing to reach their goals often assume a defeatist attitude. You can render a genuine service to your singers by helping them to develop a proper perspective.[11]

THE CHOIR/CHORUS RETREAT

The retreat is a day to a day-and-a-half meeting/rehearsal away from the normal confines of school at a different and neutral location, preferably near but just out of town. The objectives of such a retreat are to allow for an extended time for all singers in the group to meet together to discuss, define, and/or reaffirm their objectives, and to continue rehearsal of the new semester's music.[12]

Such retreats are best scheduled early in the year, beginning on a late Friday afternoon after school and concluding on Saturday afternoon after the group's initial objectives have been met. Ideal locations are boy/girl scout or church camps located nearby. The retreat location should obviously have both dining and recreational facilities, as well as a room of adequate size for rehearsals. It should also have a piano that is in reasonable tune and in good overall shape.

---

[10] See also the section on newspaper articles on page 258–260.

[11] For helpful ideas to utilize prior to music competition-festivals, see "Mental Attitudes" and "Sports Psychology and Peak Performance," pages 230–232.

[12] Many professional groups in business, education, and industry also periodically have retreats to likewise more clearly define objectives and make plans for the future.

The choir can often help identify locations not previously thought of. If a sufficient number of choir members have cars and are willing to drive and take passengers, they can provide transportation to the retreat site. When this is not feasible, then consider the use of school busses.

Following the group's arrival in the afternoon, people will first want to check into their assigned rooms and feel reasonably comfortable with the environment. Then, perhaps no later than 4:30 P.M., they can have their initial meeting. It is good to begin with a discussion of the group's overall objectives for the year and how each singer can maximize his or her contribution. Suggested initial discussion questions are as follows:

1. How good do we want our choir to be this school year, particularly at music festivals? The answer, of course, is rather obvious, nevertheless this is a good question with which to begin the discussion.
2. What do we want our audiences to think about our choir during and after concerts?
3. Each choir member should ask, "How can I maximize my contribution to the choir? Some group discussion on this topic should follow; the amount of time devoted to it will usually vary according to the maturity of the group. Certain topics can be revisited at other specified times during the year. Following the discussion of objectives, the group should begin/continue rehearsal of the music that has been provided them. Before the dinner hour singers should have a mental concept of the choir's sound and how they personally might contribute to the group's overall improvement.

Following the dinner hour, a reasonable break should be given the choir before returning to the rehearsal room. It is hoped that the discussion by the choir members of the group's objectives will result in a more highly focused group during all subsequent rehearsals. Obviously, before the group settles down for the night there will be a lot of personal excitement shown by all the students, and the group's officers should discuss a reasonable time for "lights out." The next day (Saturday) will alternate rehearsals with certain varied recreational activities of a not too strenuous nature. If desired, additional time may be alloted for a continued discussion on the group's objectives; however, don't go overboard on this activity! In determining the overall schedule for this day's activities, the director would do well to set up the schedule in collaboration with the choir's elected officers. The day's activities should certainly culminate no later than 4:00 P.M. to allow the singers to return home at a reasonable hour.

Before the choir leaves for home, one activity that can prove beneficial is to have each member review the article "Responsibilities of the Choir Singer— An Individual Assessment," by Robert L. Garretson. This article initially appeared in The Choral Journal 28 No. 9 (April, 1988), 23-36 and is reprinted on the following pages. The article includes fifteen questions that singers should ask and evaluate themselves on. Some directors may prefer to utilize this personal assessment during one of the first rehearsals of the choir very early in the school year. In that case, the time devoted at the retreat will only be a review or an update of the earlier assessment.

RESPONSIBILITIES OF THE CHOIR MEMBER— A SELF-ASSESSMENT[13]

To the Choral Director

To what extent do the singers in your choir share your objectives? Do they have a full understanding of what is expected of them? Do they realize that the conductor can achieve only so much without their complete understanding and support? While conductors can verbalize the choir's objectives with the singers, one must realize that the majority of persons are visually, rather than aurally oriented. Therein lies the purpose of this article: to provide a listing of fifteen major responsibilities of choir members that each person can read, contemplate, and thereby evaluate themselves. It may be modified or altered according to a director's own personal objectives. This article may be duplicated and distributed to each choir member. It provides a basis for informal group discussions held preferably at the beginning of the year and periodically as occasions necessitate.

To the Choir Member

1. Are you prepared to sing when you enter the rehearsal room? Are you mentally alert? Is your body in tune with itself? Stretching exercises of some kind are essential prior to physical exercise, and they also prepare the body for vocalization and singing. Much rehearsal time can be saved if singers will do some stretching exercises immediately prior to entering the rehearsal room. Ask your director for suggestions.

2. How much of your attention and energy do you give to the director and the choir during rehearsals? Sixty percent? Ninety percent? How about 110 percent to achieve a maximum contribution?

3. Do you listen carefully when your director gives instructions? Do you have a pencil available and make a note of what is said? It is important to reinforce the director's comments by making notes. See if you can remember what your director says without it being unnecessarily repeated. Challenge yourself!

4. Do you decide if you like or dislike new and unfamiliar music after only its first reading? Do you allow some time to adequately understand and appreciate it? Wouldn't you be disturbed if, after first being introduced to other persons, you learned that they made a negative judgment about your character or personality? Of course you would be concerned because they hardly know you! Likewise, one needs to allow some time to fully understand and appreciate new and unfamiliar music.

5. Do you encourage others? Whatever your attitude is about the music or the group, it will be sensed or felt by your fellow singers. So why not make it a positive attitude?

[13] Garretson, Robert L. Reprinted from *The Choral Journal* 27 No. 9 (April, 1988), 34-36. Used by permission.

6. Do you ever talk to your neighbors during rehearsals or when the director is giving instructions? Appreciate and support your neighbors, but *don't talk* to them during rehearsals!

7. Do you endeavor to listen to your own singing voice? Are you oversinging or forcing your voice? Does your voice blend and balance with the voices of the other singers?

8. Do you ever study your music outside of rehearsals? Do you play troublesome parts on the piano or work on parts with another singer? Do you devote at least fifteen minutes a day to your choral music?

9. Do you thoroughly understand the meaning of the text of the music? Do you ever read the words and note their inflections?

10. Do you maintain a list of common mistakes and their solutions in a notebook or on a separate sheet of notepaper?

11. Do you memorize your music quickly? If not, do you try each successive time to test yourself to determine how much you can sing without looking at the music?

12. Do you watch the director carefully or is your nose buried in the music? Does your director maintain eye contact with you?

13. Do your facial expressions reflect the mood of the music? Did you know that people in the audience look at each singer and their eyes settle on those persons who, they feel, are most attentive to the director and have appropriate facial expressions? Try singing before a mirror. If perchance you don't like what you see, then endeavor to change it!

14. Can you read music, or do you depend or lean upon the person next to you? Ask yourself, "What can I do about this matter?" Do you need a contest for motivation, or can you become self-motivated? Music reading involves responding to symbols of rhythm and pitch. Following are some steps you can take to help both yourself and the choir.

a. Rhythm   Identify rhythmic problems in your music and write these measures on a sheet of paper and give them to your director. They can then be written on a chalkboard, analyzed, and then clapped or sung on a neutral syllable. After enough rhythmic problems have been accumulated, a syllabus of rhythmic problems can be compiled and be of use to future singers in the choir. The responsibility for the identification of these problems should be shared with the director.

b. Pitch and intervals   An interval is the distance between two pitches. If this concept is not understood, ask your director to devote rehearsal time to an explanation of intervals. After you can identify the intervals visually, endeavor to relate them to the *beginning two pitches* in familiar songs. Then, with the other singers in the group, develop a list of songs with several examples for each interval. When you have difficulty with intervals, endeavor to recall one of these songs. Ask your director for assistance in this matter, but be prepared for his/her help! Music reading improves only with diligent practice!

15. Finally, what are your musical expectations for the choir? Just how good would you like the choir to be? Every individual is an important part of the choir and collectively everyone contributes to the overall strength or weakness of the group. All singers should endeavor to set daily and weekly goals for what they personally would like to accomplish. No one will achieve their fullest potential in any area unless they set goals. Without goals little is likely to be accomplished. "Nothing succeeds like success" is an axiom based upon the importance and necessity of group confidence. But to succeed in any area necessitates considerable individual effort. Everyone will have peaks and valleys in their life, but effort will help you to avoid many of the valleys.

After reading and evaluating yourself on each of the preceding fifteen questions, how do you rate personally? What is your composite score? Ask yourself again, are you hiding in any respect behind the collective efforts of others in the group, or are you giving your utmost? Think about the questions again and discuss them personally with your director and/or the other members of the group. Evaluation is not a one step procedure, but a continuous ongoing process. So, for this self-evaluation to be useful and helpful, re-read this article next week, next month, etc., and reassess your status and renew your on-going goals and objectives.

The Evaluation of Chorus Members

The evaluation of choir members should be a continuous process from the first rehearsal to the end of each formal grading period. Without specific established criteria, directors may easily succumb to the pitfall of giving all the students the same grade. This is certainly an undesirable practice, for if a group is to progress at a desired level, then the students must be evaluated on the basis of their accomplishments.

For a group to be properly evaluated, students must know the course objectives and the teacher's expectations. In this respect, it is suggested that teachers prepare a course syllabus that includes the following: objectives of the course; content of the course—that is, music to be rehearsed and performed (this information is helpful to parents as well); expectations as regards attendance; performance dates, time, and place, and an indication of the total number that will occur during the school year; the importance of attitude toward the achievement of the group's performance objectives; the care of choir robes or other attire; and specific criteria that will be used in the grading procedure and the percentage allocated to each. For example:

Written examinations	40%
Performance (singing exams)	40%
Attendance, effort, and attitude	20%
Total	100%

Examinations are, of course, time consuming, both in their preparation and in the grading, but it is felt that there should be some balance between the written and the performance types, since both contribute to improved musicianship. Various types of written tests may be given. One might simply cover the text of the music. A particular phrase could be given with directions for the student to write, in the space provided, the words of the succeeding phrase. This type of quiz may be given periodically and is helpful in that it stimulates singers to make a special effort to memorize the words of a piece. Some students learn words quite readily; some, however, can sing a piece for an entire semester or even longer and not memorize the text by simple repetition. These students, in particular, need the stimulation of quizzes to force them to make a special effort. In the memorization of poetry, students are advised to identify and memorize the key words in each phrase to help trigger their recall. [14]

Written exams or quizzes may also be given on such content as musical markings, texture, harmonic structure of a particular piece, rhythmic patterns, and melodic patterns (for example, "Circle the wrong pitch or note in the following phrase").

In evaluating performance capabilities, consider each singer's tone quality, ability to carry his or her own part, and blend and balance with other singers. To help set a procedure for determining this, divide the entire choir into quartets (SATB) and during the evaluation period identify the quartet and the specific beginning point in a selected piece. The length of time each quartet sings will depend on your having adequate time to focus on each individual singer in the quartet and make a judgment on tone, blend, balance, phrasing, and the ability to carry his or her part. It is advisable to rotate the selections used for various quartets, and when exams are given periodically, note in your gradebook both the grade and a code number for the selection so that a different tone may be used on the next exam. Some directors may prefer to set aside a particular time and have each quartet sing in the choral office; however, this is more difficult to arrange and certainly more time consuming. One advantage of the quartet assignment is that students may be encouraged to practice together during out-of-school hours in preparation for the next exam. When this occurs, many benefits may accrue to the singers as a result of this small ensemble experience where they all more readily hear their own parts, which will facilitate the development of improved tone quality, balance, blend, and general musicianship. [15]

---

[14] For further suggestions or procedures on memorization, see "Memorizing the Music" near the end of Chapter 6, page 230.

[15] As an alternative to assigning students in quartets, you may wish to play three parts on the piano, with the singer filling in the fourth part to make up the quartet.

THE MUSIC BUDGET

The cost of educating our children and running our schools continues to rise and the problem has become more and more acute. School administrators, therefore, must become more watchful of the amount of the budget allotted to each department. Departments not demonstrating a definite need for the funds allotted them are likely to suffer a decrease. Many music educators are especially concerned with the problem because, as their program develops and more students participate in it, additional funds are needed to purchase music and equipment necessary to provide the best musical education for the students. One bright spot: the more students enrolled, the lower the per capita cost.

Among administrators there seems to be a growing interest in a performance type of budget, in which the emphasis is on values received rather than on facts and figures. It might, therefore, prove most profitable for the music educator to discuss with the administration the benefits of music study in terms of its aesthetic, expressive, cultural, personal, social, avocational, and vocational values. Although most administrators are familiar with these benefits, it is nevertheless desirable for them to understand the music educator's particular point of view.

It is suggested that music educators demonstrate an interest in matters of budget. They should familiarize themselves with the proper procedures for requisitioning materials and keeping accounts and records. They should set up a system of filing and maintaining music materials, and should demonstrate knowledge of how to repair torn and overused music. If administrators feel that the music educator is spending money wisely, and if they feel that materials are well cared for, they are more inclined to grant a request for an increase in the music department budget.

After careful planning and estimating of future choral department needs, discuss the budget problem with your administrator, emphasizing the fact that the quality of instruction depends to a great extent on adequate teaching materials and equipment. A long-term approach to departmental needs is highly recommended. The budget for the approaching school year might be divided into three categories: "Desirable and Helpful," "Highly Desirable," and "Essential" for the operation of the program during the ensuing school year. Administrators are generally most appreciative of such a businesslike approach to the budget problem. (See Budget 1.)

Another approach to the budget problem is to list the items under two, rather than three categories. Under "Operating Expenses," list the items necessary for the efficient functioning of the department for the ensuing year. Under "Nonrecurring Expenses" (or "Capital Equipment Needs"), list the items that are important to the further development of the program. Since the funds for special purchases are not likely to be available in any one year for the acquisition of all special needs, the items in this category should be listed in the order of importance. This will be of considerable assistance to the administrator in making the final budget allotments. Any items that the school is unable to acquire in

---

BUDGET 1   CHORAL MUSIC DEPARTMENT

Proposed budget for the Academic Year ____

		Amount
A.	*Essential and Necessary Items* *	
	1. Octavo music (SATB, SSA, TTBB)................	$ ____
	2. Music folders	____
	3. Music storage boxes..............................	____
	4. Uniform maintenance and repairs..................	____
	5. Equipment maintenance	____
	6. Choral recording and tapes	____
	Total	$ ____
B.	*Highly Desirable Items* †	
	1. Additional storage cabinets.......................	$ ____
	2. Photographs (for publicity purposes)...............	____
	3. Additional rehearsal-room risers	____
	4. Additional chairs (for rehearsal room)	____
	5. Additional standing risers (for concerts).............	____
	6. New bulletin board	____
	Total	$ ____
C.	*Desirable and Helpful Items* ‡	
	1. Film and video rentals	$ ____
	2. New tape-recording equipment.....................	____
	3. Compact disk (stereophonic record player, optional)....	____
	4. Transportation expenses (festivals and contests)	____
	5. Additional piano (for student practice)	____
	6. Visiting conductor's fees	____
	Total	$ ____
Grand total...		$ ____

* Essential for operation of the department or activity during the ensuing scholl year.
† Highly desirable for the future growth of the program.
‡ Desirable and helpful in terms of providing the best educational experiences for the students.

a particular year may be included on the following year's budget request and perhaps ranked higher in their order of importance. Sample Budget 2 illustrates this idea.

Regardless of the form used, it is helpful to attach to the proposed budget a concise description of each item and the reasons for its need. This information will minimize questions of a general nature and thereby will facilitate the budget conference held between the choral director and the school administrator. Whenever conferences are held with administrators, a businesslike approach to the budget problem will be appreciated by the administrators and will be to your advantage. Study carefully your groups' needs and be prepared to explain the importance of each item. Be thoroughly familiar with the exact specifications of each requested item and be able to explain its desirability over other products of a similar nature but lower in cost.

CARE OF CHORAL MUSIC

Indexing and Storing

A practical method of indexing and storing choral music has many advantages. It protects the music from unnecessary wear and tear, selections are easily located, and a neat appearance is usually created in the rehearsal or storage room. In general, choral directors find one of the following two methods suitable for their particular situations. Some directors prefer to place each choral selection into a separate 9 × 12-inch manila filing envelope, and to file the music alphabetically by title in a metal filing cabinet. So that selections may be easily located, the title is placed in the upper left-hand corner of the envelope, along with other pertinent information such as the composer, the arranger, the voice arrangement, and the number of available copies. For easy reference, these data may also be kept on 3 × 5-inch cards and maintained in a metal file box.

Other music directors prefer to file their music in $7\frac{1}{2}$ × 11-inch reinforced cardboard boxes and to place them on conveniently situated shelves. (Boxes are available in 1-, 2-, and 3-inch widths.) Each box is labeled and numbered so that selections may be easily located. Again, all pertinent information, as previously described, may be placed on 3 × 5-inch cards, along with the number of the box in which the music is stored. All cards are

---

BUDGET 2   CHORAL MUSIC DEPARTMENT

Proposed Budget for the Academic Year ____

A. *Operating Expenses*   *Amount*
   1. Octavo music . . . . $ ____
   2. Music folders . . . .   ____
   3. Music storage boxes . . . .   ____
   4. Uniform maintenance . . . .   ____
   5. Equipment maintenance . . . .   ____
   6. Choral recordings and tapes . . . .   ____
   7. Photographs . . . .   ____
   8. Film and videotape rentals. . . . .   ____
   9. Transportation expenses . . . .   ____
        Total . . . . $ ____

B. *Nonrecurring Expenses*
   1. Additional chairs (for rehearsal room) . . . . $ ____
   2. Additional risers. . . . .   ____
   3. Additional piano . . . .   ____
   4. Additional storage cabinets . . . .   ____
   5. Choir robe replacements . . . .   ____
   6. New recording equipment . . . .   ____
   7. Compact disk, record player . . . .   ____
        Total . . . . $ ____

Grand total . . . . $ ____

filed alphabetically by title in a file box so that pertinent data or particular selections may be easily located. A separate index by composers is often helpful in quickly locating certain selections. Although file boxes are slightly more expensive than manila envelopes, the latter system will be less expensive to maintain. As the music library grows, it will be slightly less expensive to build additional shelves for storing music than to purchase additional filing cabinets.

Distribution

Choral directors distribute the music in various ways. Most find it a practical timesaver to insert the music in a folder of some type. Some use a plain 9 × 12-inch manila filing folder; others use a folder with cloth reinforced edges ($8\frac{1}{2}$ × 11-inch) with flaps that hold the music in place and prevent it from falling out. This type of folder, although a bit more expensive than manila folders, is well worth the investment; it is described in several music distributors' catalogs. Some directors utilize the services of student librarians to distribute the choral folders. Others file the music in a music cabinet near the door, so that students may pick up a folder as they enter the room (cabinets may be constructed or purchased ready-made for this purpose). Choir members are instructed to leave the music in the same place when they leave the room. This procedure saves a great deal of time and energy and is a practice far superior to collecting music left haphazardly about the rehearsal room.

Repair

After choral selections have been removed from the folders and before they are filed, they should be examined carefully and repaired with mending tape whenever necessary. When selections have been numbered, they should be replaced in order and filed in their appropriate locations. Disorderly piles of music not only are unsightly, but also can make a poor impression on school administrators.

Many of the duties just described can be assigned to responsible students. In this way, desirable training can be provided younger persons and you can be freed from many time-consuming chores, thus having more time to coordinate and develop the total choral music program.

SELECTING CHOIR APPAREL

Uniformity of dress has always been an important consideration for choirs and choruses because it contributes to developing the group into a unified and cohesive whole. It minimizes attention on individuals, which could be distracting during a performance, and focuses it on the total ensemble.

By attending an American Choral Directors Association convention or a state music competition-festival, you will observe the wide variety of apparel in use today. With each passing year, it seems even more options become available. Outfits chosen, however, will range from the very simple to the highly elaborate, depending on the age level of the singers, the sophistication of the group, and the financial resources of individuals or the group.

In schools where finances are of immediate concern, consider inexpensive options, including some items of clothing that singers may already have in their wardrobes. For example, some children's choirs have looked very appropriate in jeans and T-shirts, particularly for their age group. For high school groups, most boys usually have a sport coat, slacks, and matching shirts and ties. Girls usually have a white blouse (with long sleeves), and they can make a floor-length skirt or have one made. First, determine the color and the material most appropriate, and how much will be needed. Before purchasing, inquire about a discount on a quantity order of material. Then provide each girl with the necessary amount of material and a skirt pattern (several may be shared). Make certain, however, that a qualified person is doing the cutting and distribution of the material. Some girls have the ability to make the skirts themselves; others may require help from parents or from a local seamstress. When members leave the chorus upon graduation or for other reasons, they may sell their skirts to incoming members, and a choir apparel committee or the director may serve as a liaison for these arrangements. (This type of apparel is often worn for performances by college and adult women as well, but the men appear in formal wear.) For a splash of color with white blouses and dark skirts, consider adding a maroon cummerbund, or a scarf in dark red or some other tasteful color. A dark red scarf also seems to work nicely with an all-black dress.

In considering unique apparel for a choir, first look at the broad field. A wide variety of attire is available, including multicolored women's dresses and men's tuxedos in various shades such as black, white, silver grey, charcoal grey, light blue, navy blue, burgundy, brown, and cream, as well as tux shirts, bow ties, and cummerbunds in different colors. The uniqueness of available apparel will be appealing to all choirs. Initially, explore the wide range of possibilities and their costs. Send for catalogs and secure bid prices, and specific terms of payment, from manufacturers or distributors (see the Appendix for a listing of manufacturers/distributors of choir apparel and their addresses). Consult with local merchants to determine what they might be able to supply. Consider the quality of the material and the tailoring, as well as the cost per outfit. Better materials usually wear longer and often look much better.

It is desirable to create a special student committee (of not more than three persons) to study the various possibilities and narrow the options down to a few reasonable choices to present to the choir for discussion. Then, secure sample outfits from firms. Request specific sizes for a male and a female singer and have the outfits modeled before the choir. Let the group consider (1) flexibility of uses, (2) taste and style, (3) cost (to each individual, the school, or a combination), and (4) availability of the apparel in the future. In other words, will replacements be available for new members?

Allow ample time for discussion, and encourage everyone to be candid but courteous. The members must all realize that this is a costume and not an outfit designed specifically for themselves. Suggest that they all keep an open mind before making a choice. Then take a straw vote and think about the decision for a while. If individual members are to assume the cost, then be certain that they discuss the matter with their parents. In course descriptions, state that part of the course requirement is that members furnish a portion or all of their performing attire. That way, students know beforehand all the course expectations. The final selection may be voted on by the choir, or the decision may be made by the choir apparel selection committee in consultation with the choir director (in most cases a preferable option). Of course, involved in this decision-making process is the question of who is to pay for each outfit—the individual students, the school, or a combination of the two (that is, through school funds and monies acquired through fund-raising activities). If the school decides to purchase the outfits, then it is always helpful to purchase a few extra sizes to accommodate future members who wear unusual sizes and to allow for any increase in choir membership.

Fund-raising activities are frequently necessary to pay for uniforms. Various concerts may be designated and advertised for this purpose, with each choir member being responsible for selling a specified number of tickets. Another option, particularly appropriate in colleges and universities, is for the school to purchase the attire with monies from a school revolving account or to borrow the funds from a school foundation, or an alumni association, with the understanding that the monies will be repaid within a specified number of years. If each student pays a minimum yearly rental fee of 20 to 25 percent of the total cost, then the outfits could be paid for in four or five years. Continued rental charges, at a reduced rate, will also help to build a fund for the future replacement of outfits, as well as providing funds for a limited number of extra outfits for unusual sizes each year. Such a plan should initially be applied to the purchase of men's tuxedos and accessories, since these are much more expensive than women's outfits and since no option usually exists for less expensive attire, as it does for the women's outfits.

Once attire has been purchased, rules should be established as to the maintenance of outfits, dry cleaning, and so on. All statements of policy should be put in writing and distributed to the choir members to minimize any possible misunderstandings. For example, what should be done about a lost outfit that belongs to the school? How and when is it to be paid for? The policy should state the dates that school-owned outfits are to be returned and what will be done about an unreturned outfit. It is also suggested that all students sign a checkout card that specifies their responsibility and their agreement to specific conditions.

Choir Robes

While choir robes will necessarily be the choice of apparel for most church choirs, they are also a practical option for school choirs. Choir robes provide a comparatively cool garment, which may be donned with little effort and in a minimum amount of time. This advantage is especially important when program schedules allow only a limited amount of time for warming up and dressing. Following is information to help in choosing this type of attire.

Color To obtain individuality, many directors select robes and accessories in school colors. Two-tone color effects and pleasing color harmony may be achieved through the use of various accessories that can be worn with the choir robe. There are also robes now available that are constructed entirely of one material, but in a combination of two colors.

Many church choir directors purchase robes that blend with the interior decorations of the church. Some time ago, the Protestant church would not select choir robes in any color except black. However, today the trend is to use color in their choir apparel—color that is pleasing and will complement and blend with the interior of the church.

According to manufacturers, the most popular colors are shades of (1) blue, (2) gold, (3) green, (4) maroon and cardinal, and (5) black. White is sometimes used on special festive occasions such as Christmas and Easter, and also during the summer months. In addition to these colors, a wide range of delicate pastels is now available and is becoming increasingly popular. You may choose from such colors as pale yellow, powder blue, ivory, mint green, and aqua, to name a few.

Style Styles are available to fit many individual tastes. There are robes designed specifically for children's, intermediate, and adult choirs. After you determine your needs, consult various manufacturers' catalogs before making the final decision. Upon request, manufacturers will provide detailed pictures, swatches of material, sample robes, and other pertinent information. Also available are special robes for the director, the pianist, and the organist. They are altered by changing the sleeve construction to allow greater hand visibility and freedom.

Fabric In areas of the country where there is heavy industry, unless the material is specially treated, various chemical gases in the air will affect the robes, causing the color to fade. In such an area, you should take great care to determine if the fabric has been treated to prevent fading. Question the manufacturer before making a purchase. The quality of the frabric will determine the price of any given style. The better fabrics wear longer, retain their shape, are more comfortable, have better draping qualities, do not fade, and are less subject to wrinkling. A wash-and-wear fabric for robes is not necessarily practical. Some of the newer polyester materials are well suited for robes as they more effectively resist wrinkling; others are not. Check the quality carefully by examining samples.

Yoke   The foundation of any robe is the yoke, and the importance of its construction should not be overlooked. The yoke should be constructed of a substantial material so that it will hold its shape and prevent the body of the robe from drooping. It should be made of a strong yet lightweight material—lightweight for comfort, but possessing strength so that the body will retain its shape. The yoke shouldn't shrink, and should lie flat when dry cleaned.

Fluting   The fluting gathers the fullness of the robe over the shoulders and across the back, allowing the robe to hang in attractive folds. It is most desirable to purchase robes that have ample fullness so that large or small persons can wear them.

Closures   Various companies recommend different kinds of closures. Here are some of the advantages and disadvantages of each: (1) zipper—faster and looks neater; care must be taken that clothes are not snagged; (2) hook and eye—hooks may pull out, causing some gapping; (3) snap placket—snaps may pull out if they are merely tacked on; however, if care is taken they are quite satisfactory; and (4) Velcro—sometimes difficult to align properly and not as serviceable as a zipper, but far less destructive should a robe get caught in a door while being worn.

Robe sizes and assignments   Choir robes should be purchased in a range of sizes that will fit the average group. If funds are available, a few extra robes should be bought, because it may not be possible to purchase the same material in future years to replace damaged robes or to increase the quantity. The mill that manufactures the fabric may discontinue it, and in dyeing new fabrics, it may not be possible to match the shade exactly.

Computer programs are available to fit robes to members so that the length above the floor is uniform.

Care and repair   When robes are purchased, it is wise to sew in a numeral near the label; robes can then be assigned by number, and choir members can more easily locate their own robes. The director can maintain a list of all the choir members and the robe number that is assigned to each member.

All robes should be treated as one would treat fine clothes. To be protected against moths, they should be stored when not in actual use; they should be kept in a closet, away from light, since light will fade some robes as it will other fabrics. All robes should be dry cleaned at least once a year; with proper care, choir robes should last ten years or more. The proper maintenance and upkeep of robes is a wise way in which to protect your investment.

SUGGESTIONS FOR ADJUDICATORS OF CHORAL MUSIC FESTIVALS

The basic purpose of the festival is for music groups to perform and be evaluated, so they can learn from the experience. If the students learn little from the experience, then it is not worthwhile and did not fulfill the need for which it was intended.

When directors receive their evaluation sheets following their performance, the first thing they usually look at is the rating they received. The second thing they look at are the evaluations in the column of specific criteria, such as tone, intonation, diction, technique, balance, interpretation, musical effect, suitability of musical selections, and stage presence, to see if they match the overall rating. So, it is suggested that judges doublecheck the accuracy of this aspect of their final ratings.

Adjudicators are also advised to give heed to the "Three Cs," that is compliment, critique, and indicate a course of improvement They should first of all find something positive to say so they can honestly compliment the group. A compliment will always get a group's attention and takes away some of the threat of being adjudicated. In critiquing, comment only about what you hear and nothing else. Lastly, indicate a course of improvement or how a group and its director can chart a course for future improvement. Avoid generalities that will not lead to the improvement of specific aspects of the musical performance. Be specific and concise! After the festival, directors often provide feedback to the festival chairperson, and if many negative comments about specific adjudicators are received these persons will ultimately be excluded from future festivals.

TOPICS FOR DISCUSSION

1. Try to recall your personal reactions to hearing an outstanding choral group from a neighboring community. In what way did this experience serve as a means of motivating your own music study?
2. What musical experiences or events in high school made the greatest impression on you? Why do you feel these experiences made such a lasting impression?
3. Why are certain seating arrangements more effective with some choral groups than with others?
4. From a psychological viewpoint, why is it more desirable to schedule music classes every day, rather than, for example, only twice a week?
5. Outline an instructional program in choral music designed to meet the musical and social needs of a specific school or church. What choral groups and ensembles would you organize, and what membership requirements would you specify?
6. In what way is the budget problem related to the scheduling problem?
7. Discuss the types of attire available for various choral groups. Discuss the appropriateness of attire in relation to various types of musical programs and in relation to particular occasions.
8. Utilizing the criteria of purpose, price or cost, and durability, discuss the strengths and the weaknesses of essential musical equipment, such as pianos, risers, tape

recorders, compact disc players, directors' stands, music folders, music storage cabinets, choir robes (and storage cabinets), and other suitable attire.

9. What supplies and equipment do you consider basic to the effective operation of a balanced choral program?

SELECTED READINGS

BRINSON, BARBARA A. *Choral Music: Methods and Materials.* New York, Schirmer Books, 1996.

CAIN, NOBLE. *Choral Music and Its Practice*, chaps. 6, 7, 8. New York: M. Witmark & Sons, 1942.

CHRISTY, VAN A. *Glee Club and Chorus*, chaps. 2, 3. New York: G. Schirmer Inc., 1940.

DIERCKS, LOUIS H. "The Individual in the Choral Situation." *The NATS Bulletin* 17, no. 4 (May 15, 1961), 6–10.

DYKEMA, PETER W., AND KARL W. GEHRKENS. *The Teaching and Administration of High School Music*, chaps. 29, 30. Evanston, Ill.: Summy-Birchard Company, 1941.

GARRETSON, ROBERT, L. "Music Curricula." In *International Encyclopedia of Education*, vol. 6, pp. 3457–63. Oxford, England: Pergamon Press, Ltd., 1985.

————. "Scheduling Choral Programs and Community Relations." *The Choral Journal* 20, no. 2 (October 1979), 17–19.

GRAHAM, FLOYD F. *Public Relations in Music Education*, chap. 3. New York: Exposition Press, 1954.

KLOTMAN, ROBERT H. *Scheduling Music Classes.* Vienna, Va.: Music Educators National Conference, 1968.

KRONE, MAX T. *The Chorus and Its Conductor*, chaps. 1, 2. San Diego: Niel A. Kjos Music Co., 1945.

MENC Committee on Music Rooms and Equipment, Elwyn Carter, Chairman. *Music Buildings, Rooms, and Equipment* (rev. and enlarged ed.). Vienna, Va.: Music Educators National Conference, 1955.

SNYDER, KEITH D. *School Music Administration and Supervision* (2d ed.), chaps. 7, 8, 9. Boston: Allyn & Bacon, 1965.

SUNDERMAN, LLOYD F. *Choral Organization and Administration.* Rockville Center, N.Y.: Belwin Mills, Inc., 1954.

————. *Organization of the Church Choir*, chaps. 2, 6. Rockville Center, N.Y.: Belwin Mills, 1957.

VAN BODEGRAVEN, PAUL, AND HARRY R. WILSON. *The School Music Conductor*, chaps. 10, 12. Minneapolis: Schmitt, Hall & McCreary Co., 1942.

WILSON, HARRY R. *Artistic Choral Singing*, chap. 10. New York: G. Schirmer, 1959.

————, AND JACK L. LYALL. *Building a Church Choir*, chap 5. Minneapolis: Schmitt, Hall & McCreary Co., 1957.

VIDEOTAPES

Publicity/Public Relations for the Choral Program, by Fritz Mountford. Hal Leonard Publishing Corporation, No. 08416760.

SONGS FOR RECREATIONAL SINGING [16]

Introductory Songs

Hello! (*Sing Together*)
How D'ye Do (*357 Songs We Love to Sing*)
A Laugh Provoker (*357 Songs We Love to Sing*)

[16] In organizing a "community sing," it is suggested that at least one song be selected from each of the categories listed.

The More We Get Together (*The Biggest Little Song Book*)
Sweetly Sings the Donkey (*The Biggest Little Song Book*)
Viva l'Amour (*Singing Time*, No. 79)

Action Songs

Alouette (*The Golden Book of Favorite Songs*)
Daisy Bell (*Singing Time*)
Little Tom Tinker (*The Biggest Little Song Book*)
MacDonald's Farm (*357 Songs We Love to Sing*)
Oh! Susanna (*357 Songs We Love to Sing*)
She'll Be Comin' Round the Mountain (*The Biggest Little Song Book*)
Sweetly Sings the Donkey (*The Biggest Little Song Book*)

Rounds and Canons

Alleluia (*Rounds and Canons*, No. 24)
Alphabet, The (*Rounds and Canons*, No. 41)
Are You Sleeping? (*357 Songs We Love to Sing*)
The Bell Doth Toll, (*357 Songs We Love to Sing*)
De Bezem (The Broom) (*357 Songs We Love to Sing*)
Dona Nobis Pacem (*Singing Time*, No. 103)
Down in the Valley (*The Biggest Little Song Book*)
Early to Bed (*Silver Book*)
Fare Thee Well (*Sing Together*)
French Cathedrals (*Sing Together*)
Frog Round (*Sing Together*)
Ifca's Castle (*Carl Fischer Octavo*, No. CM 4708)
Little Tom Tinker (*The Biggest Little Song Book*)
Lovely Evening (*The Golden Book of Favorite Songs*)
Merrily, Merrily (*357 Songs We Love to Sing*)
The Merry Lark (*Sing Together*)
Morning Is Come (*Sing Together*)
Old Hungarian Round (*Sing Together*)
Reuben and Rachel (*357 Songs We Love to Sing*)
Rise Up, O Flame (Praetorius)(*Sing Together*)
Row, Row, Row Your Boat (*The Biggest Little Song Book*)
Scotland's Burning (*357 Songs We Love to Sing*)
Sing Together (*Sing Together*)
White Coral Bells (*Sing Together*)
Wise Old Owl (*Singing Time*)

Combined Songs

Are You Sleeping—Three Blind Mice (*357 Songs We Love to Sing*)
Old Folks at Home/Humoresque (*Singing Time*)
Solomon Levi—The Spanish Cavalier (*357 Songs We Love to Sing*)
Tipperary—Pack up Your Troubles (Chappell & Co., Inc.)
Yankee Doodle—Dixie (*357 Songs We Love to Sing*)

Songs for Harmonizing

All Through the Night (*357 Songs We Love to Sing*)
Annie Laurie (*Singing Time*, No. 68)
Battle Hymn of the Republic (*357 Songs We Love to Sing*)

Carry Me Back to Old Virginny (*Singing Time*, No. 27)
Clementine (*Singing Time*, No. 132)
Down by the Old Mill Stream (Forester Music Publishers)
Down in the Valley (*Singing Time*, No. 50)
Good-bye, My Lover, Good-bye (*357 Songs We Love to Sing*)
Home on the Range (*Singing Time*, No. 60)
In the Evening by the Moonlight (*Singing Time*, No. 62)
I've Been Workin' on the Railroad (*Singing Time*, No. 130)
Jacob's Ladder (*Singing Time*, No. 124)
Little Annie Rooney (*Singing Time*, No. 83)
My Bonnie (*357 Songs We Love to Sing*)
Old Folks at Home (*The Golden Book of Favorite Songs*)
On Top of Old Smoky (*Singing Time*, No. 6)
Standin' in the Need of Prayer (*Singing Time*, No. 120)
Tell Me Why (*Singing Time*, No. 74)

Closing Songs

All Through the Night (*357 Songs We Love to Sing*)
America (*The Golden Book of Favorite Songs*)
Auld Lang Syne (*357 Songs We Love to Sing*)
Fare Thee Well (*Sing Together*)
God Be with You (*357 Songs We Love to Sing*)
God Bless America (*Irving Berlin, Inc.*)
Good Night Canon (*Sing Together*)
Good Night, Ladies (*357 Songs We Love to Sing*)
Good Night to You All (*Rounds and Canons*, No. 60)
Jacob's Ladder (*Singing Time*, No. 124)
Now the Day Is Over (*The Biggest Little Song Book*)
Softly Now the Light of Day (*Silver Book of Songs, No. 170*)
So Long, It's Been Good to Know Ya! (*Folkway Music Publishers*)
Taps (*The Gray Book of Favorite Songs*)

Community Songbooks

Aloha Oe. Miami Beach: Hansen House, 1983.
Amazing Grace. Miami Beach: Hansen House, 1983.
The Biggest Little Song Book (comp. John Christopher). Miami: McAfee Music Pub., n.d.
Christmas Caroler's Book in Song and Story (arr. Torstein O. Kramme). Miami: Schmitt, Hall & McCreary, 1935.
Christmas in Song (arr. Theo Preuss). Miami: Rubank, Inc., 1947.
Fred Waring Song Book (comp. and ed. Hawley Ades). Delaware Water Gap, Pa.: Shawnee Press, 1962.
The Golden Book of Favorite Songs. Miami: Schmitt, Hall & McCreary, 1923.
Good Fellowship Songs. Delaware, Ohio: Cooperative Recreation Service.
The Gray Book of Favorite Songs. Miami: Schmitt, Hall & McCreary, 1941.
Joy to the World. Miami Beach: Hansen House, 1982.
Rounds and Canons (ed. Harry R. Wilson). Miami: Schmitt, Hall & McCreary, 1943.
Silver Book of Songs. Miami: Schmitt, Hall & McCreary, 1935.
Sing Around the Clock (arr. Howard Ross). Miami Beach: Hansen House, 1955.
Singing Time (arr. Ruth Heller and Walter Goodell). Miami: Schmitt, Hall & McCreary, 1952.
Sing Together (3rd ed.). New York: Girl Scouts of America, 1973.
Spirituals (arr. William Stickles). Miami Beach: Hansen House, 1946.
357 Songs We Love to Sing. Miami: Schmitt, Hall & McCreary, 1938.

Appendix:
Source
Information

CHORAL COMPOSERS

This chronological list does not presume to be complete, but it does include most of the major contributors to choral literature from approximately 1400 to the present. Although some composers may be known as well or perhaps even better for compositions other than choral music, all have made contributions significant enough to justify their inclusion here. This list was developed primarily from the choral compositions listed in the Appendix. For representative compositions of these composers, see lists under sections titled Choral Octavo Publications, Choral Collections, and Extended Choral Works.

PRE-RENAISSANCE (ca. 1200–1400)

Perotin (Perotinus Magnus)	b. France	ca. 1183–ca. 1238
Adam de la Halle	b. Arras, France	ca. 1240–1287
Guillaume de Machaut	b. France	ca. 1304–1377

RENAISSANCE PERIOD (ca. 1400–1600)

John Dunstable	b. Dunstable, England	ca. 1370–1453
Gilles Binchois	b. Mons, Belgium	ca. 1400–1460
Guillaume Dufay	b. Hainaut, Belgium	ca. 1400–1474
Johannes Okeghem	b. East Flanders, Belgium	ca. 1430–1495
Pierre de La Rue	b. Tournai, Belgium	ca. 1430–1518
Heinrich Isaac	b. Brabant, Belgium	ca. 1450–1517
Josquin Després	b. Hainaut, Belgium	ca. 1450–1521
Jacob Obrecht	b. Berg-op-Zoom, Netherlands	ca. 1452–1505
Loyset Compère	b. Flanders, Belgium	ca. 1455–1518
Juan del Encina	b. Salamanca, Spain	1468–1529
Antonio de Ribera	b. Salamanca Spain	1468–1529
Jean Mouton	b. Haut-Wignes, France	ca. 1470–1522
Antoine Brumel	b. Flanders	ca. 1475–1520
Martin Luther	b. Eislenben, Germany	1483–1546
Clément Janequin	b. Châtellerault, France	ca. 1485–1560
Ludwig Senfl	b. Zurich, Switzerland	ca. 1490–1543
Costanzo Festa	b. Rome, Italy	ca. 1490–1545
Nicolas Gombert	b. Flanders, Belgium	ca. 1490–1556
Thomas Créquillon	b. Ghent, Belgium	?–1557
Claudin de Sermisy	b. France	ca. 1490–1562
Passereau	Early 16th-century French composer	?–?
Adrian Willaert	b. Bruges, Belgium	ca. 1490–1562
Robert Carver	b. Scotland	ca. 1491–ca. 1546
Johann Walther	b. Kahler, Thuringia	1496–1570
Cristóbal Morales	b. Seville, Spain	ca. 1500–1553
Christopher Tye	b. England	ca. 1500–ca. 1572
Jacob Arcadelt	b. Liège, Belgium	ca. 1505–1560
Claude Goudimel	b. Besançon, France	ca. 1505–1572
Mattheus Le Maistre	b. near Liège, Belgium	ca. 1505–1577
Thomas Tallis	b. Leicestershire (?), England	ca. 1505–1585
Jacobus Clemens	b. Ypres, Belgium	ca. 1510–1556
Pierre Certon	b. Paris, France	ca. 1510–1572
Antonio Scandello	b. Brescia, Italy	1517–1580
Noé Faignient	b. Flanders, Belgium	?–1595
Hubert Waelvant	b. Tongerloo, Belgium	ca. 1517–1595
Pedro Guerrero	b. Seville, Spain	ca. 1518–??
Andrea Gabrieli	b. Venice, Italy	ca. 1520–1586
Philippe de Monte	b. Mons, Belgium	1521–1603
Fernando Franco	b. La Serena, Mexico	ca. 1525–1585
Giovanni Pierluigi da Palestrina	b. Palestrina, Italy	ca. 1525–1594
Francisco Guerrero	b. Seville, Spain	1528–1599
Claude Le Jeune	b. Valenciennes, France	1528–1600

Costanzo Porta	b. Cremona, Italy	1529–1601
Richard Farrant	b. England	ca. 1530–1581
Guillaume Costeley	b. Pont-Audemer, France	1531–1606
Orlando di Lasso	b. Mons, Belgium	1532–1594
Cornelius Freundt	b. Plauen, Germany	1535–1591
Giaches de Wert	b. Weert, Netherlands	ca. 1535–1596
Andries Pevernage	b. Courtrai, Belgium	1543–1591
William Byrd	b. Lincolnshire (?), England	ca. 1543–1623
Marco Antonio Ingegneri	b. Verona, Italy	1545–1592
Giovanni Maria Nanino	b. Tivoli, Italy	1545–1607
Giulio Caccini	b. Rome, Italy	ca. 1546–1618
François-Eustache Du Caurroy	b. Beauvais, France	1549–1609
Tomás Luis de Victoria	b. Avila, Spain	ca. 1549–1611
Francesco Suriano	b. Soriano, Italy	1549–ca. 1621
Jacobus Gallus (Jacob Handl)	b. Reifnitz, Austria (now Yugoslavia)	1550–1591
Orazio Vecchi	b. Modena, Italy	ca. 1550–1605
Giovanni Matteo Asola	b. Verona, Italy	1550–1609
Giovanni Macque	b. Valenciennes, France	ca. 1550–1614
Luca Marenzio	b. Coccaglio, Italy	1553–1599
Johannes Eccard	b. Mühlhausen, Germany	1553–1611
Giovanni Gabrieli	b. Venice, Italy	ca. 1555–1612
Bartholomeus Gesius	b. Müncheberg, Germany	ca. 1555–1613
Sethus Calvisius	b. Gorsleben, Germany	1556–1615
Giovanni Gastoldi	b. Caravaggio, Italy	ca. 1556–1622
Thomas Morley	b. England	1557–1602
Jacques Mauduit	b. Paris, France	1557–1627
Jacopo Corsi	b. Florence, Italy	ca. 1560–1604
Giovanni Croce	b. Chioggia, Italy	ca. 1560–1609
Don Carlo Gosualdo	b. Naples, Italy	ca. 1560–1613
Felice Anerio	b. Rome, Italy	ca. 1560–1614
Melchior Vulpius	b. Wasungen, Germany	ca. 1560–1615
Hieronymus Praetorius	b. Hamburg, Germany	1560–1629
Peter Philips	b. England	ca. 1561–1628
Jacobo Peri	b. Florence, Italy	ca. 1561–1633
Jan Pieterszoon Sweelinck	b. Deventer (or Amsterdam), Netherlands	1562–1621
John Dowland	b. Ireland, possibly in County Dublin	ca. 1562–1626
John Bull	b. Somersetshire, England	ca. 1562–1628
Francis Pilkington	b. England	ca. 1562–1638
Gregor Aichinger	b. Regensburg, Germany	1564–1628
Ludovico da Viadana	b. Viadana, Italy	1564–1645
Michael Cavendish	b. England	ca. 1565–1628
Thomas Campion	b. London, England	1567–1620
Giovanni Gastoldi ·	b. Caravaggio, Italy	15??–1622
Adriano Banchieri	b. Bologna, Italy	1568–1634
Paul Peurl	b. Austria	ca. 1570–1624
Thomas Bateson	b. Cheshire, England	1570–1630
Salamone Rossi	b. Mantua, Italy	1570–ca. 1630
Christian Erbach	b. Hesse, Germany	1570–1635
Thomas Tomkins	b. St. David's, England	ca. 1572–1656

John Wilbye	b. Diss, England	1574–1638
Thomas Weelkes	b. England	ca. 1575–1623
Steffano Bernardi	b. Verona, Italy	1576–1636
Francisco Correa	b. Seville, Spain	ca. 1576–??
Melchoir Franck	b. Zittau, Germany	ca. 1579–1639
Michael East	b. London, England	ca. 1580–ca. 1648
Thomas Ford	b. England	ca. 1580–1648
Orlando Gibbons	b. Oxford, England	1583–1625
Adrian Batten	b. London, England	ca. 1585–1637

BAROQUE PERIOD (ca. 1600–1750)

Giulio Caccini	b. Rome, Italy	ca. 1546–1618
Giovanni Gabrieli	b. Venice, Italy	ca. 1557–1612
Hans Leo Hassler	b. Nuremberg, Germany	1564–1612
Claudio Monteverdi	b. Cremona, Italy	1567–1643
Michael Praetorius	b. Kreuzberg, Germany	ca. 1571–1621
Richard Deering	b. Kent, England	ca. 1580–ca. 1630
Gregorio Allegri	b. Rome, Italy	1582–1652
Melchior Teschner	b. Fraustadt, Austria	1584–1635
Adrian Batten	b. England	1585–1637
Heinrich Schütz	b. Kostritz, Germany	1585–1672
Johann Hermann Schein	b. Grünhain, Germany	1586–1630
Salamone Rossi	b. Mantua, Italy	ca. 1587–ca. 1630
Samuel Scheidt	b. Halle, Germany	1587–1654
Thomas Ravenscroft	b. England	ca. 1590–ca. 1633
Thomas Vautor	b. England	1590–16??
Johann Crüger	b. Grossbreece, Germany	1598–1662
John Hilton	b. Oxford, England	1599–1657
Pier Francesco Cavalli	b. Crema, Italy	1602–1676
Orazio Benevoli	b. Rome, Italy	ca. 1605–1672
Giacomo Carissimi	b. Marino, Italy	ca. 1605–1674
Andreas Hammerschmidt	b. Brüx, Bohemia	1612–1675
Guillame Bouzignac	Early 17th-century composer	?–?
Franz Tunder	b. Burg auf Fehmarn, Germany	ca. 1614–1667
Christoph Bernard	b. Danzig, Germany	1627–1692
Matthew Locke	b. Exeter, England	ca. 1630–1677
George Jeffries	b. England	?–1685
Jean-Baptiste Lully	b. Florence, Italy	ca. 1632–1687
Marc-Antoine Charpentier	b. Paris, France	ca. 1634–1704
Dietrich Buxtehude	b. Helsingborg, Denmark	ca. 1637–1707
Johann Christoph Bach	b. Erfurt, Germany	ca. 1642–1703
Johann Wolfgang Franck	b. Unterschwaningen, Germany	1644–ca. 1710
Pelham Humfrey	b. England	1647–1674
Michael Wise	b. Salisbury, England	ca. 1648–1687
Johann Michael Bach	b. Arnstadt, Germany	ca. 1648–1694
John Blow	b. Newark-on-Trent, England	1649–1708
Johann Pachelbel	b. Nuremberg, Germany	1653–1707
George von Reutter	b. Vienna, Austria	1656–1738
Philipp Heinrich Erlebach	b. Esens, Germany	1657–1714

Giuseppe Pitoni [1]	b. Rieti, Italy	1657–1743
Henry Purcell	b. London England	1659–1695
Johann Kuhnau	b. Leipzig, Germany	1660–1722
Alessandro Scarlatti	b. Palermo, Italy	1660–1725
Gregor G. Gorczycki	b. Cracow, Poland	c. 1664–1734
Antonio Lotti	b. Venice, Italy	1667–1740
Francesco Gasparini	b. Camaiore (near Lucca)	1668–1727
François Couperin	b. Paris, France	ca. 1668–1733
Antonio Vivaldi	b. Venice, Italy	ca. 1669–1741
Antonio Caldara	b. Venice, Italy	1670–1736
D. Pompeo Canniciari	b. Rome, Italy	ca. 1670–1744
William Croft	b. Nether Ettington, England	ca. 1678–1727
Georg Philipp Telemann	b. Magdeburg, Germany	1681–1767
Jean-Philippe Rameau	b. Dijon, France	1683–1764
Bohuslav Cernohorsky	b. Nimburg, Czechoslovakia	1684–1742
Francesco Durante	b. Frattamaggiore, Italy	ca. 1684–1755
Johann Sebastian Bach	b. Eisenach, Germany	1685–1750
George Frideric Handel	b. Halle, Germany	1685–1759
Benedetto Marcello	b. Venice, Italy	ca. 1686–1739
Niccola Antonio Porpora	b. Naples, Italy	1686–1768
Johan Helmich Roman	b. Stockholm, Sweden	ca. 1694–1758
Maurice Green	b. London, England	1696–1755
Francesco Antonio Vallotti	b. Vercelli, Italy	1697–1780
Georg Gottfried Wagner	b. Mühlberg, Germany	ca. 1698–1756
Johann Adolf Hasse	b. Bergedorf, Germany	1699–1783
Johann Ernst Eberlin	b. Jettingen, Germany	1702–1762
Karl Heinrich Graun	b. Wahrenbrück, Germany	ca. 1704–1759
Frantisek Ignac Antonin Tuma	b. Kostelec nad Orlici, Bohemia	1704–1774
Giovanni B Martini	b. Bologna, Italy	1706–1784
Giovanni Battista Pergolesi	b. Jesi, Italy	1710–1736
Thomas Ame	b. London, England	1710–1718.

CLASSIC PERIOD (1750–1820)

Wilhelm Friedemann Bach	b. Weimar, Germany	1710–1784
Gottfried August Homilius	b. Rosenthal, Germany	1714–1785
Christoph Willibald Gluck	b. Erasbach, Germany	1714–1787
Karl Philipp Emanuel Bach	b. Weimar, Germany	ca. 1714–1788
George Christoph Wagenseil	b. Vienna, Austria	1715–1777
James Nares	b. Middlesex, England	1715–1783
Johann Heinrich Rolle	b. Quedlinburg, Germany	1716–1785
Johann Christoph Altnikol	b. Bevna, Silesia	1719–1759
Johann Ernst Bach	b. Eisenach, Germany	1722–1777
Christian Friedrich Gregor	b. Dirsdorf, Germany	1723–1801
Johann Adam Hiller	b. Wendisch-Ossaog, Germany	1728–1804
Johann C. Geisler	b. Germany	1729–1815

[1] Although Pitoni lived during the Baroque period, he was of the Roman school, which rejected the styles and forms of Baroque music and directed its efforts toward composing liturgical music in the style of Palestrina.

Johann C. F. Bach	b. Leipzig, Germany	1732–1795
Franz Joseph Haydn	b. Rohrau-on-the-Leitha, Austria	1732–1809
Carl Friedrich Christian Fasch	b. Zerbst, Germany	1736–1800
Johann George Albrechtsberger	b. Klosterneuburg, Austria	1736–1809
Michael Haydn	b. Rohrau, Austria	1737–1806
Carl Michael Bellman	b. Stockholm, Sweden	1740–1795
Quirino Gasparini	b. Bergamasco, Italy	?–1778
John Antes	b. Frederickstownship, Pennsylvania	1740–1811
Luigi Boccherini	b. Lucca, Italy	1743–1805
William Billings	b. Boston, Massachusetts	1746–1800
Johann Friedrich Peter	b. Heerendijk, Holland	1746–1813
Abbé Vogler	b. Würzburg, Germany	1749–1814
Andrew Law	b. Milford, Connecticut	1749–1821
Dimitri S. Bortniansky	b. Glukhov, Russia	1751–1825
Jacob French	b. Early American composer	1754–18??
Wolfgang Amadeus Mozart	b. Salzburg, Austria	1756–1791
Carl Friedrich Zelter	b. Berlin, Germany	1758–1832
Johann Rudolph Zumsteeg	b. Sachsenflur, Odenwald, Germany	1760–1802
Luigi Cherubini	b. Florence, Italy	1760–1842
Joseph Eybler	b. Schwechat (near Vienna), Austria	1764–1846
Thomas Attwood	b. London, England	1765–1838
John Wall Callcott	b. Kensington (London), England	1766–1821
Samuel Wesley	b. Bristol, England	1766–1837
Ludwig van Beethoven	b. Bonn, Germany	1770–1827
Johann Christian Heinrich Rinck	b. Elgersburg, Germany	1770–1846

ROMANTIC PERIOD (1800–1900)

Ignaz von Seyfried	b. Vienna, Austria	1776–1841
Johann Neopmuk Hummel	b. Pressburg, Czechoslovakia	1778–1837
Johann Kaspar Aiblinger	b. Wasserburg, Germany	1779–1867
Konradin Kreutzer	b. Messkirch, Germany	1780–1849
Anton Diabelli	b. Mattee (near Salzburg), Austria	1781–1858
Vincent Novello	b. London, England	1781–1861
Konrad Kocher	b. Ditzinger, Germany	1786–1872
Gioacchino Rossini	b. Pesaro, Italy	1792–1868
Lowell Mason	b. Medfield, Massachusetts	1792–1872
Franz Schubert	b. Lichtenthal, Austria	1797–1828
Alexis F. Lvov	b. Reval, Russia	1798–1870
John Goss	b. Fareham, Hants, England	1800–1880
Gustav Wilhelm Teschner	b. Magdeburg, Germany	1800–1883
Hector Berlioz	b. Côte-Saint-André, France	1803–1869
Mikhail Glinka	b. Novosspaskoye, Russia	1804–1857
Feliz Mendelssohn	b. Hamburg, Germany	1809–1847
Edward L. White	b. Boston, Massachusetts	1809–1851
Robert Schumann	b. Zwickau, Germany	1810–1856

Samuel Sebastian Wesley	b. London, England	1810–1876
Franz Liszt	b. Raiding, Hungary	1811–1886
Richard Wagner	b. Leipzig, Germany	1813–1883
Giuseppe Verdi	b. Le Roncole, Italy	1813–1901
Robert Franz	b. Halle, Germany	1815–1892
Charles François Gounod	b. Paris, France	1818–1893
Jacques Offenbach	b. Cologne, France	1819–1880
Franz Abt	b. Eilenburg, Germany	1819–1885
Louis Lewandowski	b. Wreschen (near Posen), Poland	1821–1904
César Franck	b. Liège, Belgium	1822–1890
Peter Cornelius	b. Mainz, Germany	1824–1874
Anton Bruckner	b. Ansfelden, Austria	1824–1896
Johann Strauss (Jr)	b. Vienna, Austria	1825–1899
Stephen Collins Foster	b. Pittsburgh, Pennsylvania	1826–1864
François Auguste Gevaert	b. Huysse, Belgium	1828–1908
Anton Grigorievitch Rubenstein	b. Vykhvatinetz, Russia	1829–1894
Jean-Baptiste Fauré	b. Mouline, France	1830–1914
Johann von Herbeck	b. Vienna, Austria	1831–1877
August Soderman	b. Stockholm, Sweden	1832–1876
Alexander Borodin	b. St. Petersburg, Russia	1833–1887
Johannes Brahms	b. Hamburg, Germany	1833–1897
César Antonovitch Cul	b. Vilna, Russia	1835–1918
Camille Saint-Saëns	b. Paris, France	1835–1921
John Farmer	b. Nottingham, England	1836–1901
Mily A. Balakirev	b. Nizhny-Novgorod, Russia	1837–1910
Alfred Robert Gaul	b. Norwich, England	1837–1913
Theodore Dubois	b. Rosnay, France	1837–1924
Georges Bizet	b. Paris, France	1838–1875
Modest P. Moussorgsky	b. Karevo, Russia	1839–1881
Peter Ilich Tchaikovsky	b. Kamsko-Votkinsk, Russia	1840–1893
John Stainer	b. London, England	1840–1901
Antonin Dvořák	b. Mühlhausen, Czechoslovakia	1841–1904
Arthur Sullivan	b. London, England	1842–1900
Edvard Grieg	b. Bergen, Norway	1843–1907
Herman Schroeder	b. Quedlinburg, Germany	1843–1909
Nikolay A. Rimsky-Korsakov	b. Tikhvin, Russia	1844–1908
Gabriel Urbain Fauré	b. Pamiers, France	1845–1924
Leoš Janacek	b. Hulvaldy, Moravia	1845–1928
Alexander Arkhangelsky	b. Penza, Russia	1846–1924
Gustav Schreck	b. Zeulenroda, Germany	1849–1918
Mikhail M. Ivanoff	b. Moscow, Russia	1849–1927
Vincent D'Indy	b. Paris, France	1851–1931
Hugo Jüngst	b. Dresden, Germany	1853–1923
Alexander A. Kopylov	b. St. Petersburg, Russia	1854–1911
Engelbert Humperdinck	b. Siegburg, Germany	1854–1921
Leos Janáček	b. Hukvaldy, Czechoslovakia	1854–1928
Stevan S. Mokranjac	b. Negotin, Yugoslavia	1855–1914
Sergei I. Taneyev	b. Vladimir, Russia	1856–1915
Alexander Kastalsky	b. Moscow, Russia	1856–1926
Edward Elgar	b. Broadheath, England	1857–1934

Henry Louis Reginald De Koven	b. Middletown, Connecticut	1859–1920
Mikhail M. Ippolitov-Ivanov	b. Gatchina, Russia	1859–1935
Hugo Wolf	b. Windischgraz, Austria	1860–1903
Gustav Mahler	b. Kalischt, Bohemia	1860–1911
Edward MacDowell	b. New York, New York	1861–1908
Horatio Parker	b. Auburndale, Massachusetts	1863–1919
Pietro Mascagni	b. Leghorn, Italy	1863–1945
Frederick F. Bullard	b. Boston, Massachusetts	1864–1904
Richard Strauss	b. Munich, Germany	1864–1949
Alexander T. Gretchaninov	b. Moscow, Russia	1864–1956
Sean Sibelius	b. Tavastehus, Finland	1865–1957
Vassili S. Kalinnikov	b. Voin, Russia	1866–1901
Enrique Granados	b. Lérida, Spain	1867–1916
Granville Bantock	b. London, England	1868–1946
Louis Vierne	b. Pointiers, France	1870–1937
Franz Lehar	b. Komorn, Hungary	1870–1948
Henry Hadley	b. Somerville, Massachusetts	1871–1937
F. Melius Christiansen	b. Eidsvold, Norway	1871–1955
Max Reger	b. Brand, Germany	1873–1916
Sergei V. Rachmaninoff	b. Oneg, Russia	1873–1943
Antonio Ribera	b. Barcelonia, Spain	1873–1976
Hugh S. Roberton	b. Glasgow, Scotland	1874–1952
Samuel Coleridge-Taylor	b. London, England	1875–1912
Nikolai D. Leontovich	b. Monastirsh, Russia	1877–1921
Paul G. Tschesnokov	b. Vladimir, Russia	1877–1921

MODERN PERIOD (1890 TO PRESENT)

Claude Debussy	b. St. Germain-en-Lave, France	1862–1918
Frederick Delius	b. Bradford, England	1862–1934
Erik Satie	b. Honfleur, France	1866–1925
Georg Alfred Schumann	b. Konigstein, Germany	1866–1952
Vladimir Ivanovitch Rebikov	b. Krasnoyarsk, Siberia	1866–1920
Henry Thacker Burleigh	b. Erie, Pennsylvania	1866–1949
Ralph Vaughan Williams	b. Down Ampney, England	1872–1958
Gustav Holst	b. Cheltenham, England	1874–1934
Arnold Schoenberg	b. Vienna, Austria	1874–1951
Paul Pierné	b. Metz, France	1874–1952
Charles Edward Ives	b. Danbury, Connecticut	1874–1954
Maurice Ravel	b. Ciboure, France	1875–1937
Martin Shaw	b. London, England	1875–1958
Pablo Casals	b. Vendrell, Catalonia	1876–1973
Ernest Bloch	b. Geneva, Switzerland	1880–1959
Healey Willan	b. Balham, England	1880–1968
Béla Bartók	b. Nagy Szent Miklos, Rumania	1881–1945
Robert Nathaniel Dett	b. Drummondville, Quebec, Canada	1882–1943
Zoltàn Kodály	b. Kecskemet, Hungary	1882–1967
Igor Stravinsky	b. Oranienbaum, Russia	1882–1971
Anton Webern	b. Vienna, Austria	1883–1945

Deems Taylor	b. New York, New York	1885–1966
Marcel Dupré	b. Rouen, France	1886–1971
Konstantin N. Shvedov	b. Moscow, Russia	1886–19??
Sigmund Romberg	b. Szeged, Hungary	1887–1951
Norris Lindsay Norden	b. Philadelphia, Pennsylvania	1887–1956
Heitor Villa-Lobos	b. Rio de Janeiro, Brazil	1887–1959
Ernst Toch	b. Vienna, Austria	1887–1964
Hall Johnson	b. Athens, Georgia	1887–1970
Božidar Sirola	b. Zakanj, Yugoslavia	1889–1956
Joseph W. Clokey	b. New Albany, Indiana	1890–1960
Heinrich Lemacher	b. Solingen, Germany	1891–1966
Arthur Honegger	b. Le Havre, France	1892–1955
Darius Milhaud	b. Aix-en-Provence, France	1892–1974
Felix Labunski	b. Ksawerynów, Poland	1892–1979
John Jacob Niles	b. Louisville, Kentucky	1892–1980
Bernard Rogers	b. New York, New York	1893–1968
Peter Warlock (Philip Heseltine)	b. London, England	1894–1930
Walter Piston	b. Rockland, Maine	1894–1976
Paul Hindemith	b. Hanau, Germany	1895–1963
Albert Hay Malotte	b. Philadelphia, Pennsylvania	1895–1964
Malcolm Sargent	b. London, England	1895–1967
Leo Sowerby	b. Grand Rapids, Michigan	1895–1968
William Grant Still	b. Woodville, Mississippi	1895–1978
Carl Orff	b. Munich, Germany	1895–1982
Gordon Jacob	b. London, England	1895–1984
Richard Kountz	b. Pittsburgh, Pennsylvania	1896–1950
Howard Hanson	b. Wahoo, Nebraska	1896–1981
Virgil Thomson	b. Kansas City, Missouri	1896–1989
Henry Cowell	b. Menlo Park, California	1897–1965
Alexander Tansman	b. Lodz, Poland	1897–1986
Roy Harris	b. Lincoln County, Oklahoma	1898–1979
William L. Dawson	b. Anniston, Alabama	1898–1990
Hugh Ross	b. Langport, England	1898–1990
Francis Poulenc	b. Paris, France	1899–1963
Carlos Chávez	b. Mexico City, Mexico	1899–1978
Alexander Tcherepnin	b. St. Petersburg, Russia	1899–1977
Randall Thompson	b. New York, New York	1899–1984
George Antheil	b. Trenton, New Jersey	1900–1959
Aaron Copland	b. Brooklyn, New York	1900–1990
Ernst Krenek	b. Vienna, Austria	1900–
Otto Luening	b. Milwaukee, Wisconsin	1900–
Gerald Finzi	b. London, England	1901–1956
Max Helfman	b. Radzin, Poland	1901–1963
Harry Robert Wilson	b. Salina, Kansas	1901–1968
Olaf C. Christiansen	b. Minneapolis, Minnesota	1901–1984
Jester Hairston	b. North Carolina	1901–
Edmund Rubbra	b. Northampton, England	1901–1986
William Walton	b. Oldham, England	1902–1983
Maurice Durufle	b. Louviers, France	1902–1986
Seno Takacs	b. Siegendorf, Austria	1902–
Luigi Dallapiccola	b. Pisino, Italy	1904–1975

Undine Smith Moore	b. Jarrett, Virginia	1905–1989
Paul Creston	b. New York, New York	1906–1985
Dmitri Shostakovitch	b. St. Petersburg, Russia	1906–1975
Normand Lockwood	b. New York, New York	1906–
Henk Badings	b. Bandoeng, Java	1907–1987
Miklos Rozsa	b. Budapest, Hungary	1907–
Hugo Distler	b. Nuremberg, Germany	1908–1942
Elliot Carter	b. New York, New York	1908–
Oliver Messiaen	b. Avignon, France	1908–
Halsey Stevens	b. Scott, New York	1908–1989
Jean Berger	b. Hamm, Germany	1909–
Samuel Barber	b. West Chester, Pennsylvania	1910–1981
Julius Chajes	b. Lwow, Poland	1910–1985
William Howard Schuman	b. New York, New York	1910–1992
Franz Reizenstein	b. Nuremberg, Germany	1911–1968
Alan Hovhaness	b. Somerville, Massachusetts	1911–
Gian Carlo Menotti	b. Cadegliano, Italy	1911–
Benjamin Britten	b. Lowestoft, England	1913–1976
Norman Dello Joio	b. New York, New York	1913–
Morton Gould	b. New York, New York	1913–
Jan Meyerowitz	b. Breslau, Germany	1913–
Gardner Read	b. Evanston, Illinois	1913–
Leland B. Sateren	b. Everett, Washington	1913–
Irving Fine	b. Boston, Massachusetts	1914–1962
Gail Kubik	b. South Coffeyville, Oklahoma	1914–1984
Cecil Effinger	b. Colorado Springs, Colorado	1914–1990
Knut Nystedt	b. Oslo, Norway	1915–
Vincent Persichetti	b. Philadelphia, Pennsylvania	1915–1987
Houston Bright	b. Midland, Texas	1916–1970
Alberto Ginastera	b. Buenos Aires, Argentina	1916–1983
Gordon Binkerd	b. Lynch, Nebraska	1916–
Scott Huston	b. Tacoma, Washington	1916–1991
Ulysses S. Kay	b. Tucson, Arizona	1917–
Norman Luboff	b. Chicago, Illinois	1917–1987
Leonard Bernstein	b. Lawrence, Massachusetts	1918–1990
Vaclav Nelhybel	b. Czechoslovakia	1919–
Dave Brubeck	b. Concord, California	1920–
Paul Feller	b. Philadelphia, Pennsylvania	1920–
Edwin Fissinger	b. Chicago, Illinois	1920–1990
William Bergsma	b. Oakland, California	1921–
Lloyd Pfautsch	b. Washington, Missouri	1921–
Ariel Ramirez	b. Santa Fé, Argentina	1921–
Lukas Foss	b. Berlin, Germany	1922–
George Walker	b. Washington, D.C.	1922–
Anton Heiller	b. Vienna, Austria	1923–1979
Peter Mennin	b. Erie, Pennsylvania	1923–1983
Daniel Pinkham	b. Lynn, Massachusetts	1923–
Ned Rorem	b. Richmond, Indiana	1923–
Kirke Mechem	b. Wichita, Kansas	1925–
Gunther Schuller	b. New York, New York	1925–

Friedrich Cerha	b. Vienna, Austria	1926–
Carlisle Floyd	b. Latta, South Carolina	1926–
Arnold Freed	b. New York, New York	1926–
Frank Pooler	b. LaCross, Wisconsin	1926–
Dominick Argento	b. York, Pennsylvania	1927–
Emmy Lou Diemer	b. Kansas City, Missouri	1927–
Donald Erb	b. Youngstown, Ohio	1927–
Samuel H. Adler	b. Mannheim, Germany	1928–
Aminadav Aloni	b. Tel Aviv, Israel	1928–
Lena J. McLin	b. Atlanta, Georgia	1928–
Karlheinz Stockhausen	b. Mödrath (near Cologne), Germany	1928–
Ron Nelson	b. Joliet, Illinois	1929–
Richard Felciano	b. Santa Rosa, California	1930–
Gilbert Trythall	b. Knoxville, Tennessee	1930–
Wendell P. Whalum	b. Memphis, Tennessee	1931–
John Biggs	b. Los Angeles, California	1932–
Krzysztof Penderecki	b. Debica, Poland	1933–
Nicolas Roussakis	b. Athens, Greece	1934–
Eugene Butler	b. Durant, Oklahoma	1935–
David Eddleman	b. Winston-Salem, North Carolina	1936–
Michael Hennigan	b. The Dalles, Oregon	1936–
Dede Dusan	b. El Campo, Texas	1938–
James E. McCray	b. Kankakee, Illinois	1938–
Brent Pierce	b. Ogden, Utah	1940–
John Rutter	b. London, England	1945–
Henry Mollicone	b. Providence, Rhode Island	1946–
Libby Larsen	b. Wilmington, Delaware	1950–
Z. Randall Stroope	b. Albuquerque, New Mexico	1953–
Steven Curtis Lance	b. Santa Ana, California	1954–

CHORAL OCTAVO PUBLICATIONS

The octavo publications listed here are particularly suitable for nonprofessional choral groups. SATB publications are suggested for use with high school, college and university, church, and community choirs and choruses. Also listed are SSA and TTBB publications that are appropriate for this age group/level.

For very young choirs, two-part (SA or TB) selections are listed. Music that takes into consideration the vocal capabilities and limitations of the boy's changing voice (cambiata) is included, with the following voice arrangements: SSCB, SACB, SSACB, SAC/B, and SSC(B). Music for young choirs that lack sufficiently developed tenor voices is included with arrangements for SAB. Following this listing of choral octavo music are suggested choral collections, including arrangements for mixed voices (SATB and SAB), for treble voices (SA, SSA, and SSAA), and for male voices (TB, TTB, and TTBB). Finally, a listing of extended major choral works is included, listed alphabetically by composer.

Because of the comparatively large number of publications included for use with mixed voices (SATB), all the music is listed under various categories so you may easily locate the selections you seek. These categories are "Christmas," "Easter and Lent," Ethnic/Multicultural Music, "Folk Songs and Spirituals," "Special Occasions," "General: Sacred and Secular," "Music with Electronic Tape/ Nonconventional Notation," and "Music for Jazz/Show Choirs." For the other voice classifications, publications are generally included under only three categories: "Sacred," "Secular," and "Folk Songs and Spirituals."

Most of the music listed has stood the test of time and is considered standard/classical literature. Music publishers, however, are continually marketing new compositions, editions, and arrangements. These newer works, which were published only in the past several years, are listed separately (before the standard/classical choral music listings), so you may more readily identify and acquire examination copies if you so desire.

Following the title, composer, and/or arranger, the publishers and the catalog number are given. This information is provided to facilitate the ordering of music. Since you will wish to know if the selection is to be performed *a cappella* or with accompaniment, this information is also provided. All publications have been graded according to difficulty, using the following terms: Easy, Moderately easy, Medium, Moderately difficult, and Difficult. Also indicated are those publications having incidental solos. Prices have not been included since they are subject to change. It is suggested that current prices be requested from local dealers immediately prior to placing an order; in this way, both billing and budgeting problems may be minimized. In selecting music, obtain for examination purposes single copies of particular octavo selections from the publisher or their local dealer, whichever is more convenient. The lists here provide a helpful starting point, but only through careful analysis of each selection in relation to the needs of a specific choral group will the most effective programming be achieved.

As the demand for particular choral publications increases, they can sometimes become temporarily out-of-stock. Therefore, ask music dealers to give you an approximate date of availability. In some other cases, music may become permanently out-of-print. If you have a single reference copy, write to the director of choral publications of the music publisher who holds the copyright and request permission to duplicate a specific number of copies. For this privilege, publishers usually charge a nominal fee per copy, and after the required amount has been submitted to a publisher, you may duplicate the specified number of copies, but *not* until written permission has been received.

An appeal from music publishers: "The unofficial copying of music has the effect of reducing the number of works available in print, and very often those works that are available become more expensive because of reduced print runs and subsequent higher costs. In order to protect our choral repertoire (our choral heritage), adherence to copyright law is essential."[2]

Publications for Mixed Voices (SATB)

Christmas (More Recently Published Sacred and Secular Music)

A Choral Fantasy (God Rest Ye Merry, Gentlemen)—Mark Riese. E. C. Schirmer No. 4059. Chamber orchestra or keyboard accompaniment. Medium.

Beautiful Star (17th-century carol)—arr. Libby Larsen. E. C. Schirmer No. 4202. Handbells accompaniment Easy.

The Bells Are Ringing on Christmas Day (Norwegian carol)—arr. Walter Ehret. Carl Fischer No. CM 8269. Accompanied. Easy.

Deux Chansons de Noel (French carols)—arr. Dede Duson. Neil A. Kjos No. ED 8672. Accompanied (finger cymbals). Moderately easy.

Good News Is in the Air—Hans Leo Hassler, arr. Hal H. Hopson. Hope Publishing No. AA 1686. Optional accompaniment. Moderately easy.

I Saw Three Ships—Mark Riese. E. C. Schirmer No. 4391. Chamber orchestra or keyboard accompaniment. Medium.

Maria Wanders through the Thorn (15th–16th-century German carol)—arr. Shirley W. McRae. Neil A. Kjos No. ED 8703. Accompanied (organ, finger cymbal, clarinet or oboe). Moderately easy.

O Hark the Bell's Glad Song (11th-century carol)—arr. Libby Larsen. E. C. Schirmer No. 4201. Accompanied. Moderately easy.

O Star That Makes the Stable Bright (from Nativity)—Norman Dello Joio. Associated No. 50488442. Accompanied. Medium.

O Tannenbaum (German folk song)—arr. Gregg Smith. G. Schirmer No. 50481500. A cappella. Medium.

Oh, Sleep Now, Holy Baby (Hispanic folk melody)—arr. Robb/Laster. Augsburg Fortress No. 11-2543. Accompanied. Easy.

On Christmas Night (traditional carol)—arr. R. Vaughan Williams. Galaxy No. 1.5130. Unison or unaccompanied mixed voices. Easy.

Orietur Stella—Jacob Handl, ed. Lee Egbert. Broude Brothers No. CR 54. Organ ad libitum. Medium.

Patapan (Burgundian carol)—arr. Greg Smith, G. Schirmer No. 50323220. Accompanied, with optional bells. Medium.

Puer Natus in Bethlehem—Samuel Scheidt, arr. Rod Walker, CPP/Belwin No. SV 8712. Optional accompaniment. Medium.

The Shepherds All Are Waking (16th-century carol)—Libby Larsen. E. C. Schirmer No. 4205. String orchestra and handbells accompaniment.

Silent Night—Franz Gruber, arr. David Conte. E. C. Schirmer No. 4562. Accompanied. Moderately easy.

This Is the Night—Leland B. Sateren. Neil A. Kjos No. C9012. A cappella. Moderately easy.

Three Christmas Motets—Jacob Handl, ed. Lee Egbert. Broude Brothers No. CR 57. A cappella. Medium

The Virgin Mary Had a Baby Boy (West Indian carol)—arr. Lohn Leavitt. Augsburg Fortress No. 11-2545. Percussion (claves and conga drum) accompaniment. Moderately easy.

Wassail Song—R. Vaughan Williams. Galaxy No. 1.5008. A cappella. Medium.

Christmas (Standard/Traditional Sacred and Secular Music)

A La Nanita Nana (Spanish carol tune)—arr. Walter Ehret. Shawnee Press No. A-674. Piano accompaniment. Moderately easy.

And the Trees Do Moan (Carol of the Mountain Whites)—arr. Gaul. Oliver Ditson No. 332. Optional accompaniment. Moderately easy.

[2] Music Publishers' Association of the United States, 1987.

Angelus ad pastores ait—Giovanni Gabrieli. C. F. Peters No. 5930. Two choirs—12 parts. Optional accompaniment. Difficult.

As Dew in Aprille (from *A Ceremony of Carols*)—Benjamin Britten, arr. Harrison. Boosey & Hawkes No. 1829. Accompanied. Medium.

Behold a Star from Jacob Shining—Felix Mendelssohn, arr. Davison. E. C. Schirmer No. 1683. Organ accompaniment. Medium.

Birds and the Christ Child, The (Czechoslovakian carol)—arr. Max Krone. Carl Fischer No. CM 4612. *A cappella*. Easy.

A Boy Was Born—Benjamin Britten. Oxford No. X92. *A cappella*. Medium.

Break Forth, O Beauteous Heavenly Light—J. S. Bach. Oliver Ditson No. 13744. Accompanied. Easy.

Carol of the Bells (Ukrainian carol; secular)—Nikolai D. Leontovich, arr. Peter Wilhousky. Carl Fischer No. CM 4604. *A cappella*. Easy.

Carol of the Birds (traditional French Christmas carol)—arr. Noble Cain. Schmitt, Hall & McCreary No. 1507. Optional accompaniment. Moderately easy.

Carol of the Italian Pipers (traditional carol)—arr. Zgodava. Shawnee Press No. A-967. Optional accompaniment. Moderately easy.

Carol of the Russian Children (White Russian carol)—arr. H. B. Gaul. G. Schirmer No. 6770. Optional accompaniment. Moderately easy.

A Child Said—James McCray. National Music Publishers No NMP-151. Piano and oboe. Optional solo. Moderately easy.

The Chocolate Burro (Mexican carol)—arr. Roy Ringwald. Shawnee Press No. A-1318. Piano accompaniment. Moderately easy.

A Christmas Carol (Hungarian traditional tune)—arr. Zoltán Kodály. Oxford No. 84.091. *A cappella*. Moderately easy.

Christmas Gift—Jester Hairston. Bourne No. S1033. Piano accompaniment. Moderately easy.

The Christmas Song—Mel Torme and Wells, arr. Walter Ehret. Edwin H. Morris No. E9822a. Piano accompaniment. Moderately easy.

Christmas Spirituals (Mary Had a Baby and Rise Up, Shepherd)—arr. Scandrett. Carus-Verlag. *A cappella*. Moderately easy.

Das neugeborne Kindelein (The Newborn Child)—J. S. Bach. National Music Publishers No. NMP-175. Piano or organ accompaniment. Medium.

Enter the Stable Gently (Spanish carol)—arr. Hal Hopson. Music 70 No. M70-249. *A cappella*. Moderately easy.

Fanfare for Christmas Day—Robert Shaw. G. Schirmer No. 8745. Optional organ accompaniment. Moderately easy.

Fum, Fum, Fum, (Catalonian carol)—arr. Alice Parker and Robert Shaw. G. Schirmer No. 10182. *A cappella*. Medium.

Gentle Mary and Her Child (Finnish folk melody)—arr. Lundquist. Elkan-Vogel No. 1152. *A cappella*. Easy.

Glory to God in the Highest—Giovanni Pergolesi. Wood No. 289. Organ accompaniment. Moderately difficult.

Gloucestershire Wassail (traditional old English yule song)—arr. Tom Scott. Shawnee Press No. A45. Accompanied. Bass or alto solo. Medium.

God Rest You Merry, Gentlemen (old English Christmas carol)—arr. Stevens. Pro Art No. 1420. Accompanied. Easy.

Good Christian Men, Rejoice (traditional German)—arr. Alice Parker and Robert Shaw. G. Schirmer No. 10183. *A cappella*. Moderately easy.

Go Tell It on the Mountain (Christmas spiritual)—arr. Work. Galaxy No. 1532. *A cappella*. Soprano and tenor solos. Medium.

Hawaiian Lullaby—Sargent. Oxford No. X85. *A cappella*. Medium.

He Is Born (II est né)—arr. Roger Wagner. Lawson-Gould No. 663. *A cappella*. Easy.

Here 'mid the Cattle (Alsatian carol)—arr. Eugene Butler. Carl Fischer No. CM 8065. Piano or organ accompaniment. Baritone solo. Moderately easy.

Here We Come A-Wassailing (traditional)—arr. Herbert Goodrich. National Music Publishers No. WHC–129. *A cappella*. Moderately easy.

Hodie Christus natus est—Jan Pieterszoon Sweelinck. Edw. B. Marks No. MC 4301. A *cappella*. Moderately difficult.

The Holly and the Ivy, (traditional English)—arr. Alice Parker and Robert Shaw. G. Schirmer No. 10187. A *cappella*. Moderately easy.

The Holy Child (Puerto Rican carol)—arr. Hruby. Pro Art No. 2687. Accompanied. Easy.

How unto Bethlehem (traditional Italian)—arr. Alice Parker and Robert Shaw. G. Schirmer No. 40194. A *cappella*. Moderately easy.

The Hunter—Johannes Brahms. E. C. Schirmer No. 1680. A *cappella*. Moderately easy.

I Heard an Angel—Ernst Krenek. Rongwen No. 3540. A *cappella*. Medium.

An Infant Sweet and Gentle (Polish carol)—arr. Walter Ehret. Presser No. 312-40765. Accompanied. Moderately easy.

In Fields Not Far from Bethlehem (Austrian carol)—arr. Walter Ehret. Elkan-Vogel No. 362-03117. Accompanied. Moderately easy.

I Saw Three Ships (traditional English)—arr. Alice Parker and Robert Shaw. G. Schirmer No. 10188. A *cappella*. Moderately easy.

It's the Most Wonderful Time of the Year—Pola and Wyle, arr. Hawley Ades. Shawnee Press No. A-1101. Piano accompaniment. Moderately easy.

I Wonder As I Wander (Appalachian carol)—arr. Niles and Horton. G. Schirmer No. 8708. Optional accompaniment. Soprano or tenor solo. Medium.

Jesus, Jesus, Rest Your Head (Appalachian carol)—arr. Niles and Warrell. G. Schirmer No. 8302. A *cappella*. Moderately easy.

Jesus' Christmas Lullaby (Bohemian folk song)—arr. Walter Ehret. Elkan-Vogel No. 1140. Accompanied. Moderately easy.

Joseph Dear, Oh Joseph Mild—Sethus Calvisius. Associated No. A-396. A *cappella*. Medium.

La Virgen Lava Panales—arr. De Cormier and Sauter. Lawson-Gould No. 52227. Piano accompaniment. Medium.

Let Heaven Rejoice and Sing (German carol)—arr. Walter Ehret. Sam Fox No. CC7. Accompanied. Easy.

Lo, How a Rose E'er Blooming—Hieronymus Praetorius. G. Schirmer No. 2484. A *cappella*. Easy.

Los Reyes Magos (The Three Kings)—Ariel Ramirez. Lawson-Gould No. 51748. Harpsichord, percussion, and guitar accompaniment. Moderately easy.

Lost in the Night (Finnish folk melody)—arr. F. M. Christiansen. Augsburg No. 119. A *cappella*. Soprano solo. Moderately difficult.

Love Came Down at Christmas—Lloyd Pfautsch. Lawson-Gould No. 52278. A *cappella*. Medium.

A Maiden Most Gentle (French tune)—arr. Carter. Oxford No. X266. Organ accompaniment. Easy.

Mary Had a Baby—William L. Dawson, Kjos No. T118. A *cappella*. Soprano solo. Medium.

Masters in This Hall (traditional French)—arr. Alice Parker and Robert Shaw. G. Schirmer No. 10192. A *cappella*. Medium.

O filii et filiae—Leisring, arr. Row. R. D. Row No. 283. A *cappella*. Medium.

Old Polish Christmas Carol—arr. Liszniewski. Huntzinger No. 4049. A *cappella*. Easy.

O magnum mysterium (O Wondrous Nativity)—Tomas Luis de Vittoria. G. Schirmer No. 7626. A *cappella*. Medium.

O Sanctissima (Sicilian folk melody)—arr. Alice Parker and Robert Shaw. G. Schirmer No. 10194. A *cappella*. Medium.

Our Day of Joy Is Here Again (Swedish folk melody)—arr. Lundquist. Elkan-Vogel No. 1151. A *cappella*. Easy.

Quem vidistis pastores? (Shepherds, Tell Us Your Story)—arr. Felis. Edw. B. Marks No. 4491. Optional accompaniment. Medium.

The Saviour Is Born (Austrian carol)—arr. Warner. Summy-Birchard No. 15787. Accompanied. Easy.

Shepherds All, and Shepherdesses (Allon, gay, gay)—Guillaume Costeley. Oxford No. OCS 1667. A *cappella*. Medium.

Shepherds' Chorus (from *Amahl and the Night Visitors*)—Gian Carlo Menotti. G. Schirmer No. 10801. Accompanied. Soprano and bass solos. Medium.

Silent Night—arr. Malcolm Sargent. Oxford No. OCS 876. A *cappella*. Moderately easy.

Sleep in Peace, O Heavenly Child—Michael Haydn. G. Schirmer No. 11043. Accompanied. Moderately easy.

The Slumber Song of the Infant Jesus—Francois Auguste Gevaert. E. C. Schirmer No. 1163. *A cappella.* Easy.

So Blest a Sight (English traditional)—arr. Alice Parker and Robert Shaw. G. Schirmer No. 10196. *A cappella.* Moderately easy.

Songs of Praise the Angels Sang (Swedish folk melody)—arr. Lundquist. Elkan-Vogel No. 1145. *A cappella.* Easy.

Still, Still, Still—Norman Luboff. Walton No. 3003. Accompanied. Easy.

Sweet Mary Tends Her New-Born Son (German carol)—arr. Walter Ehret. Elkan-Vogel No. 362-03116. Accompanied. Medium.

Sweet Was the Song (old English tune)—arr. Clausen. Mark Foster No. MF 550. *A cappella.* Moderately easy.

There Shall a Star from Jacob—Felix Mendelssohn. Carl Fischer No. CM 6228. Accompanied. Medium.

This Little Babe (from *A Ceremony of Carols*)—Benjamin Britten, arr. Harrison. Boosey & Hawkes No. 1830. Harp or piano accompaniment. Moderately easy.

Three Far-Eastern Carols—Malcolm Sargent. Oxford No. X73. *A cappella.* Moderately easy.

The Three Kings—Willan. Carl Fischer No. OCS 718. *A cappella.* Medium.

Three Old English Carols—arr. Gustav Holst. Schmidt No. APS. 15171. Accompanied. Moderately easy.

'Tis the Time of Yuletide Glee—Thomas Morley. Music 70 No. M.70-235. *A cappella.* Moderately easy.

Two Folk Carols (Star in the South and Zither Carol)—arr. Malcolm Sargent. Oxford No. X50. *A cappella.* Moderately easy.

We Wish You a Merry Christmas (English folk song; secular)—arr. the Krones. Kjos No. 4006. Accompanied. Easy.

What Child Is This? (old English)—arr. Alice Parker and Robert Shaw. G. Schirmer No. 10199. *A cappella.* Moderately difficult.

While by My Sheep (17th-century Christian hymn)—arr. Hugo Jungst. G. Schirmer No. 2532. *A cappella.* Easy.

Ye Watchers and Ye Holy Ones (17th-century German melody)—arr. Archibald T. Davison. E. C. Schirmer No. 1780. Accompanied Moderately easy.

Easter and Lent (Standard/Traditional Music)

Alleluia—Randall Thompson. E. C. Schirmer No. 1786. *A cappella.* Moderately difficult.

Alleluia, Alleulia—Dietrich Buxtehude. Presser No. 312-40668. Accompanied. Medium.

All Glory, Laud and Honor (Palm Sunday)—Gustav Wilhelm Teschner, arr. Noble Cain. Flammer No. 81127. Accompanied. Easy.

Ave verum corpus—William Byrd. Associated No. NYPMA 7. *A cappella.* Medium.

Cheer Up, Friends and Neighbors (old French Easter carol)—arr. Paget. Lawson-Gould No. 52334. *A cappella.* Easy.

Christ Is Arisen—Hans Leo Hassler. Edw. B. Marks No. 26. *A cappella.* Moderately easy.

Christ Is Arisen—Franz Schubert. E. C. Schirmer No. 2686. *A cappella.* Moderately easy.

Christ ist erstanden (Christ Is Arisen)—Franz Schubert. National Music Publishers No. CH-4. *A cappella.* Medium.

Crucifixus (from *Mass in B minor*)—J. S. Bach. E. C. Schirmer No. 1174. Accompanied. Medium.

Ecce, quomodo moritur—Jacobus Gallus (Jacob Handl). G. Schirmer No. 8424. *A cappella.* Moderately easy.

Four Chorales from the *Saint Matthew Passion*—J. S. Bach, ed. Walter Ehret. Lawson-Gould No. 686. *A cappella.* Moderately easy.

God So Loved the World—John Stainer. G. Schirmer No. 3798. *A cappella.* Easy.

Go to Dark Gethsemane—Noble. Gray No. CMR 501. *A cappella.* Medium.

He Never Said a Mumbalin' Word (spiritual)—arr. Harry R. Wilson. Paul Pioneer. *A cappella*. Moderately easy.

Hosanna (Palm Sunday)—F. M. Christiansen. Augsburg No. 57. *A cappella*. Difficult.

Lamb of God (Chorale 1540)—arr. F. M. Christiansen. Augsburg No. 133. *A cappella*. Easy.

Lamb of God—Hans Leo Hassler. Lawson-Gould No. 800. *A cappella*. Moderately easy.

Light Divine (scene and prayer from *Cavalleria Rusticana*)—Pietro Mascagni. G. Schirmer No. 5959. Accompanied. Moderately difficult.

Magdalena—Johannes Brahms. G. Schirmer No. 9953. *A cappella*. Medium.

My Savior Dear, What Woe of Soul—J. S. Bach, arr. Lundquist. Willis No. 5503. *A cappella*. Medium.

O Jesus, Crucified for Man—Franz Schubert. National Music Publishers No. CH-10. Accompanied. Medium.

O Lamb of God—Vassili S. Kalinnikov, arr. Walter Ehret. Pro Art No. 1513. *A cappella*. Moderately easy.

Osterlied (Easter Song)—Franz Schubert. National Music Publishers No. CH-9. Accompanied. Easy.

The Palms (Palm Sunday)—Gabriel Fauré, arr. Howorth. Belwin Mills No. 790. Accompanied. Medium.

Ride On! Ride On! (Palm Sunday)—Thompson. Gray No. CMR 1154. *A cappella*. Medium.

Sunrise Alleluia—Houston Bright. Shawnee Press No. A-852. Accompanied. Moderately easy.

Surely, He Bore Our Sorrows (Lent)—Tomas Luis de Victoria. E. C. Schirmer No. 2217. *A cappella*. Medium.

Surely He Hath Borne Our Griefs (from *Messiah*)—George Friderick Handel. G. Schirmer No. 6598. Accompanied. Medium.

Surrexit Pastor Bonus (The Shepherd Has Arisen)—Orlando di Lasso. G. Schirmer No. 7685. *A cappella*. Medium.

This Is the Day Which the Lord Hath Made—Dimitri S. Bortniansky. Bourne No. BL3041. *A cappella*. Medium.

Three Lenten Poems of Richard Crashaw—Daniel Pinkham. E. C. Schirmer No. 2693. Accompanied. Medium.

Tree of Sorrow—Carlos Chávez. Mercury No. MP-113. *A cappella*. Difficult.

Were You There? (spiritual)—arr. Henry T. Burleigh. Ricordi No. NY423. Optional accompaniment. Medium.

Ethnic/Multicultural Music

To assist choral directors in locating particular sought selections this listing of choral music is alphabetical— first by continent or region, and then by title. Various vocal arrangements are listed, however, unless otherwise indicated they are for mixed voices (SATB). Whether the work is to be performed *A cappella*, or with Piano and/or other instrumental accompaniment is also indicated, lastly followed by the level of difficulty ranging from Easy to Difficult. As indicated, all music is listed under the following categories:

Africa (Congo, Cameroon, Ghana, Kenya, Liberia, Nigeria, South Africa)

Asia and the Pacific Rim (China, India, Indonesia, Japan, Korea, Mongolia, New Zealand, Somoa)

British Isles (England, Ireland, Scotland)

Eastern Europe (Baltic States: Latvia, Poland, Sweden; Slavic countries: Bohemia, Hungary, Romania, Russia)

South America Latin America (Argentina, Bahamas, Brazil, Caribbean Islands, Cuba, Guatemala, Honduras, Jamaica, Mexico, Puerto Rico, Trinidad, Venezuela, West Indies)

Middle East (Arabia, Israel, Jordan, Lebanon)

North America (Canada and United States)

    Folksongs

    African-American Spirituals

Western Europe (Austria, France, Germany, Italy, Netherlands, Spain)

Africa. (Congo, Cameroon, Ghana, Kenya, Liberia, Nigeria, South Africa)

African Mass–Norman Luboff. Walton Music Corp. No. WM-110. For mixed chorus, solo voices, and tuned drums. Medium.

African Noel–Ronald Kauffmann. Elkan-Vogel No. 362-03288. SSATBB, with optional wood block and bongo drums. Medium.

Andeleli Oboduo (Congo)—arr. Aleksandar S. Vujic. Alliance Music Publications No. AMP 0059. *A cappella.* Medium.

Betelehemu (Nigerian Christmas song, via Olatunji and Wendell Whalum)—arr. Barrington Brooks Lawson-Gould No. 52744. *A cappella* with optional drums. Pronunciation guide for Yorba text included. Medium.

Betelehemu (Nigerian Christmas song, Via Olatunji)—arr. Wendell Whalum. Lawson-Gould No. 52647.TTBB with optional drums (ad lib). Pronunciation guide for Yoruba text included. Medium.

Cameroon—Dorothy Masuka, arr. Michael Scott. Warner Bros. No. SV9533. Two-part, with piano accompaniment. Easy.

Fill Us With Your Love (Ghana folk song)—arr. Carlton R. Young. Words by Tom Colvin. Agape No. AG 7256. Accompanied. Easy.

Freedom Is Coming (Songs of Protest and Praise from South Africa)—ed. Anders Nyberg. Walton Music Corporation No. WB-528. Fifteen songs that may be performed with the following voice arrangements: SATB, SAB, SSA, TTB, and SA. Moderately easy.

Hombe (Kenya (Luo) folk song)—arr. Laz Ekwueme. Lawson Gould No. 51807. *A cappella.* Alto solo. Pronunciation guide included. Moderately easy.

Iddem-Dem Mallida (based on an Itneg tribal chant)—arr. Elmo Q. Makil. Lawson Gould No. 62216. *A cappella.*

Jesu, Jesu (Ghanian folk song)—adapted by Tom Colvin, arr. William N. Simon. Carl Fischer No. CM8373. Accompanied. Moderately easy.

Kyrie (from *Missa Afro-Brasileira*)—Carlos Alberto Pinto Fonseca. Lawson Gould No. 52103. *A cappella.* Medium.

Mangwani Mpulele (Zulu folk song)—arr. Lana Walter. Warner Bros. No. SV9521. Two or three part with large drum, small drum, rattle, and optional piano. Easy.

O Sifuni Mungu—Marty McCall, David Maddux, Mmunga Mwenebulongo, and Asukuku 'Yunu Mukalay, arr. David Maddux. Word Music No. 3010467168. *A cappella.* Moderately easy.

Praise The Lord (traditional Cameroon melody)—arr. Ralph Johnson. Earthsongs. A processional song, with triangle, wood block, shakers, and conga drums. Medium.

Sing Hallelu (Liberian folk song)—arr. Donald Moore, Warner Bros. No. SV9554. Piano, with optional maracas, claves, and conga drum. Moderately easy. Also available for SAB, TTB, and SA.

Siyahamba (South African folk song)—arr. Donald Moore. Warner Bros. No. SV9530. Optional percussion instruments. Moderately easy. Also available for SAB and SA. Accompaniment cassette available.

South African Suite (South African folk songs)—arr. Henry Leck. Plymouth Music No. HL-200. A *cappella,* SSA or SSAA. Easy.

Three South African folk songs (Thula Sizwe, Icala, and Angilalanga)—arr. Caroline Lyon. Alliance Music No. AMP 0093. Shaker and high, medium, and low drums. Easy. Pronunciation/full performance cassette available.

Urukumbuzi Song—Aleksandar S. Vujić Alliance Music No. AMP 0058. Easy.

Wah Gee Tee Bee (Liberian dance song)—arr. Agnes Nebo. Lawson Gould No. 51509. Percussion instruments. Easy.

We Are Singing, for the Lord is Our Light (Zulu traditional song)—arr. Hal H. Hopson. Agape No. HH 3949. Accompanied. Easy.

Welcome (African Carol Igbo)—arr. Laz Ekwueme. Lawson-Gould No. 51824. A cappella. Pronunciation guide provided. Moderately easy.

Xire Ogun (War Game, ritual African text)—Carlos Albertos Pinto Fonseca. Lawson Gould No. 52136. A cappella. Medium.

Asia and the Pacific Rim (China, India, Indonesia, Japan, Korea, Mongolia, New Zealand, Philippines, Samoa)

Ahrirang (Korean folk song)—arr. Robert de Cormier. Lawson Gould No. 51540. Accompanied. Easy.

Arirang (Korean folk song)—arr. Shin-Hwa Park. Alliance Music No. AMP 0092. SSA. A cappella. Easy.

Autumn Night Song—Francis Baxter. Laurendale Associates No. CH-1064C. Accompanied. Pronunciation guide included. Easy.

Basant ("Spring,"-from Six Seasons)—Vanraj Bhatia. Earthsongs. A cappella. Moderately difficult.

Chi-Chi Pap-Pa (Japanese children's song)—arr. Salli Terri. Lawson Gould No. 51201. A cappella. Pronunciation guide included. Easy.

Crescent Moon Now Floating By (Chinese folk song from Qinghai Province)—arr. Cui Yuwen. Lawson Gould No. 52357. A cappella. Medium.

The Dawn of Spring—Francis Baxter. Laurendale Associates No. CH-1064A. Accompanied. Easy. Pronunciation guide included.

Dravidian Dithyramb—Victor Paronjoti. Earthsongs. A cappella. Medium. Also available for TTBB.

Faleula E! (a Samoan chant)—arr. Christopher Marshall. Vaia'ata Print. A cappella. Translation and performance notes included. Medium.

Four Chinese Children's songs—arr. Francis H. Baxter. Lawson Gould No. 52722. SA. Accompanied. Easy.

Four Haiku—Paul Parthun. Mark Foster No. MF 3017. Flute and harp (or piano) accompaniment. Medium.

Grishma ("Summer"-from Six Seasons)—Vanraj Bhatia. Earthsongs. A cappella. Medium.

Hemant ("Winter")—Vanraj Bhatia. Earthsongs. A cappella. Difficult. English translation included.

Hie Tsuki Bushi (Japanese folk song)—arr. Francis Baxter. Santa Barbara Pub. No. SBMP 59. Accompanied. Easy.

Iddem-Dem Mallida (Itneg tribal chant)—arr. Elmo Q. Makil. Lawson Could No. 52216. A cappella. Moderately easy.

Itsuki No Komori Uta (Japanese folk song)—arr. Francis H. Baxter. Lawson Gould No. 52733. Accompanied, with optional flute. Pronunciation guide included. Medium

Kashiri—Tae Kyun Ham (Korea). Earthsongs. Accompanied. Moderately difficult. Pronunciation suggestions included. Also avaiable for SSA and Piano.

Kiso Bushi (Japanese folk song)—arr. Francis Baxter. Santa Barbara No. SBMP 58. Piano accompaniment, with wood block. Moderately easy. Pronunciation guide included.

Kokiriko Bushi (Japanese folk song)—arr. Wendy B. Stuart. Music 70 No. M70-670. SSAA with percussion (woodblock and triangle). Easy.

Kompira Fune Fune (Japanese folk song)—arr. Francis H. Baxter. Lawson Gould No. 52725. Accompanied. Moderately easy.

Kuroda Bushi (Japanese folk song)—arr. Francis H. Baxter. Lawson Gould. Accompanied. Medium.

La'u Lupe (Samoan folk song)—arr. Christopher Marshall. Vaia'ata Print. A cappella. Moderately easy. Translation and performance notes included.

Minoi, Minoi (Samoan folk song)—arr. Christopher Marshall. Alliance Music Pub. No. AMP 0100. A cappella. Easy. Pronunciation guidelines included.

Moemoe Pepe (Samoan folk song)—arr. Christopher Marshall. Vaia'ata Print. A cappella, Easy. Translation and performance notes included.

Muge (Chinese folk song from Inner Mongolia)—arr. Qu Xixien. Lawson Gould No. 52315. *A cappella*. Medium.

Nodle Kangbyon (Traditional Korean folk song)—arr. Wallace Hornady. Earthsongs. Accompanied. Medium.

Okaoka La'u Honey (Samoan folk song)—arr. Christopher Marshall, Vaia'ata Print. *A cappella*. Moderately easy. Translation and performance notes included.

Otemoyan (Japanese folk song)—arr. Francis H. Baxter. Francis H. Baxter, California State University, Los Angeles. Accompanied. Moderately difficult.

Pengyou, Ting! (Traditional Chinese melody)—arr. Carolyn Jennings. Earthsongs. *A cappella*. Medium.

Pusi Nofo (Samoan folk song)—arr. Christopher Marshall. Vaia'ata Print. *A cappella*. Translation and performance notes included. Easy.

Sado Okesa (Japanese folk song)—arr. Francis H. Baxter. Francis H. Baxter, California State University, Los Angeles. Accompanied. Medium.

Sakura (Japanese folk song)—arr. Norman Luboff. Walton Music No. W3041. Accompanied, Easy.

Sakura Sakura (Japanese folk song)—arr. Jester Hairston. Bourne Co. No. 11276. Accompanied. Easy.

Sau La'u Teine Samoa (Samoan folk song)—arr. Christopher Marshall. Vaia'ata Print. *A cappella*. Translation and performance notes included. Easy.

Sharad ("Autumn")—Vanraj Bhatia, Earthsongs. *A cappella*. Difficult.

Shepherdess of Sadness (Mongolian folk song)—arr. Francis Baxter. Laurendale Associates No. CH-1068. Accompanied, with optional flute. Pronunciation guide included. Easy.

Shishir ("Harvest")—Vanraj Bhatia (India). Earthsongs. *A cappella*. Moderately difficult.

Snow on the River—Francis Baxter. Laurendale Associates No. CH-1064D. Accompanied. Pronunciation guide included. Easy.

Soran Bushi (Japanese folk song)—arr. Francis Baxter. Santa Barbara Pub. No. SBMP 60. Accompanied. Pronunciation guide included. Easy.

Sulram (Indonesian Lullaby)—arr. Robert De Cormier. Lawson Gould No. 51755. Flute and Piano Accompaniment. Easy.

Summer Day in the Garden (Shan Ting Xia Ri)—Francis Baxter. Laurendale Associates No. CH-1064B. Accompanied. Pronunciation guide included. Moderately easy.

Three New Zealand Songs—Christopher Marshall. Vaia'ata Print.
  Song At Summer's End
  Elegy In A City Railyard
  The Magpies
  A cappella. Medium.

Varsha (Monsoon)—Vanraj Bathia (India). Earthsongs. *A cappella*. Difficult.

Yosakoi (Japanese folk song)—arr. Francis H. Baxter. Francis H. Baxter, California State University, Los Angeles. Accompanied. Moderately easy.

British Isles (England, Ireland, Scotland)

A Ballynure Ballad (Irish folk song)—arr. Alice Parker. Lawson Gould No. 51457. *A cappella*. Medium.

A Wee Drappie O't (Scottish folk song)—arr. Laura Shur. Lawson Gould No. 52705 *A cappella*. Medium.

Annie Laurie (Scottish ballad)—arr. Gail Kubik. Southern Music Pub. No. 01-000262-135. *A cappella*. Medium.

Annie Laurie (Scotch tune)—arr. Alice Parker and Robert Shaw. Lawson Gould No. 647. *A cappella*. Moderately easy.

Cold Blows the Wind (English folk song)—arr. James McCray. Mark Foster No. MF 859. SA with piano and optional C instrument. Easy.

The Croppy Boy (Irish folk song)—arr. Alice Parker, Lawson Gould No. 51410. Harp or Piano accompaniment. Easy.

Dance Ti' Thy Daddy (Northumberland, British Isles, folk song)—arr. Robert De Cormier. Lawson Gould No. 51753. *A cappella.* Moderately easy.

Danny Boy (traditional Irish)—arr. Roger Wagner. Lawson Gould No. 52599. *A cappella.* Moderately easy.

The Girl I Left Behind Me (Irish tune)—arr. Alice Parker. Lawson Gould No. 51460. *A cappella.* Moderately easy.

I Know My Love (Irish folk song)—arr. Alice Parker and Robert Shaw. Lawson Gould No. 657. *A cappella.* Moderately easy.

I Know Where I'm Goin' (Irish folk song)—arr. Alice Parker. Lawson Gould No. 51444. *A cappella.* Moderately easy.

Ilkley Moor Baht 'At (Yorkshire folk song)—arr. Robert De Cormier. Lawson Gould No. 51403. Baritone Solo. Accompanied. Medium.

Irish Lullaby—arr. Steven Sametz Alliance Music No. AMP 0088. SSAA with soprano solo. Moderately easy.

Johnny, I Hardly Knew Ye (Irish folk song)—arr. Alice Parker. Lawson Gould No. 51452. *A cappella,* Moderately easy.

The Laird O'Cockpen (Scottish folk song)—arr. Laura Shur. Lawson Gould No. 52589. Accompanied. Moderately easy.

The Last Rose of Summer (Irish air)—arr. André Bellefeuille. Lawson Gould No. 52574. *A cappella,* Easy.

The Minstrel Boy (Irish tune)—arr. Alice Parker. Lawson Gould No. 51411. Harp or piano accompaniment. Easy.

She's Like the Swallow (traditional folk song)—arr. Eleanor Daley. Alliance Music Pub. No. AMP 0070. SSAA with solo. Accompanied, Moderately easy.

Silent, O Moyle, Be the Roar (Irish folk song)—arr. Alice Parker. Lawson Gould No. 51442. *A cappella.* Moderately easy.

The Tailor and the Mouse (English folk song)—arr. Edgar F. LaMance, Jr. Lawson Gould No. 52276. *A cappella.* Medium.

The Three Ravens (Old English song)—arr. Steven Porter. Lawson Gould No. 52573. SAB. *A cappella.* Easy.

Three Scots Songs (Ye banks and braes, The bonnie Earl o' Murray, and The Piper o' Dundee)—arr. Shena Fraser. Roberton Publications, No. 63210. *A cappella.* Medium.

'Tis Pretty to Be in Balinderry (Irish folk song)—arr. Alice Parker. Lawson Gould No. 51441. *A cappella.* Easy.

The Water Is Wide (English folk song)—arr. Arnold Freed. Coronot Press No. 392-41530. Accompanied. Easy.

Wear'n of the Green (Irish folk song)—arr. Alice Parker. Lawson Gould No. 51451. *A cappella.* Easy.

The Whistling Gypsy (Irish folk song)—arr. Robert de Cormier. Lawson Gould No. 51611. Baritone Solo. Accompanied. Moderately easy.

Who Killed Cock Robin? (English folk song)—arr. Robert De Cormier. Lawson Gould No. 51710. Incidental solos. *A cappella.* Moderately easy.

Eastern Europe (Baltic States: Latvia, Poland, Sweden; Slavic Countries: Bohemia, Hungary, Romania, Russia)

Ave Maria—Sergei Rachmaninoff. H. W. Gray No. 6-(5). *A cappella.* Medium.

Ave Regina Coelorum—Jan Dismas Zelenka. Carus-Verlag No. 40.465/01. Accompanied. Medium.

Birch Tree Variations (traditional Russian folk song)—arr. Steven Porter. Alliance No. AMP 0013. Accompanied. Easy.

Blaženni jaže izbral/ Wie glueklich, die du erwählt—Peter I. Tschaikovsky. Carus-Verlag, Stuttgart No. CV 40.177/60. *A cappella.* Moderately difficult.

Bogoróditse Dĕvo, ráduyšya (Virgin Mother of God, rejoice)—Sergei Rachmaninoff. Earthson's. *A cappella.* Russian pronunciation guide included. Medium.

Cherubim Song—Mikhail Glinka, ed., English text by Walter Ehret. Theodore Presser No. 312-41355. *A cappella.* Moderately easy.

Cherubim Song (No. 7)—Dimitri Bortniansky, arr. Peter I. Tchaikovsky. Oliver Ditson No. 332-14622. *A cappella.* Moderately easy.

Chindia (based on a Romanian folk-dance tune)—Alexandru Pascanu. Santa Barbara Music Pub. No. SBMP 44. Accompanied. Medium.

Credo quod Redemptor meus vivit—Jan Dismas Zelenka. Carus-Verlag No. 40.463/01. Accompanied. Medium.

Dance (from Balkan folklore)—Aleksandar S. Vujic. Alliance Music Pub. No. AMP 0057. *A cappella.* Moderately difficult.

Domaredansen (Swedish folk song)—arr. Bengt Hallberg, English text by Norman Luboff. Walton Music Corp. No. SK-102. Moderately difficult.

Dance with Me, Tuka (Belorussian folk tune)—arr. Robert G. Olson. Lawson Gould No. 51606. *A cappella.* Medium.

Érik A Som (Cherries Ripen: based on a Hungarian folk song)—Lajos Bárdos. Santa Barbara Music Pub. No. SBMP 47. *A cappella.* Easy.

Exultate Justi In Domino—Andreas Hakenberger. Mark Foster No. MF 173. SSATBB. *A cappella.* Moderately difficult.

The Fall of Night—Anton Nikolsky. Southern Music Publ. Co. No. 794-6. *A cappella.* Moderately easy.

Hopak Dance (Ukrainian dance song)—Modest Mussorgsky. Southern Music Pub. Co. No. 679-9. *A cappella.* Moderately easy.

Nochevála túchka zolotáya (The Golden Cloudlet)—Peter I. Tchaikovsky. Earthsongs. *A cappella.* Moderately easy.

Kas Tie Tadi (Latvian folk song)—arr. Steven Sametz. Alliance Music Pub. No. AMP 0087, *A cappella.* Medium.

Kde Sú Krávy Moje (Slovak folk tune)—H. A. Schimmerling. Associated Music Pub. No. HL.50232780. *A cappella.* Moderately easy.

Let Freedom Ring—Alexander Borodin. Southern Music Pub. Co. No. 786-6. Accompanied. Medium.

May There Always Be Sunshine (Russian)—arr. Robert De Cormier. Lawson Gould No. 52717. Accompanied. Medium.

The Miller's Tears (East European folk song)—arr. Maurice Goldman, Lawson-Gould No. 52329, Baritone solo. Accompanied. Medium.

Milosť mira ("A Mercy of Peace," from *The Liturgy of St. John Chrysostom*)—Peter I. Tchaikovsky. Earthsongs. *A cappella.* Moderately easy.

Neslēgtais Gredzens (The Unclosed Ring)—Juris Karlsons (Latvia). Earthsongs. SSSSATB. *A cappella.* Difficult.

Nu ar det Jul igen (Swedish dance carol)—arr. Ron Jeffers. Earthsongs, SSA. *A cappella.* Moderately easy.

Polish Carol (Lulajże Jezuniu)—arr. Anthony J. Palmer. Mark Foster No. MF 816. SA with piano. Easy. Pronunciation guide included.

Praise the Madrigal—Alexander Arkhangelsky. Southern Music Pub. Co. No. 827-4 *A cappella,* Medium.

The Road to Siberia—Dmitri Shostakovitch. Southern Music Pub. Co. No. 946-8. Accompanied. Medium.

Three Hungarian Folk Songs—Matyas Seiber. G. Schirmer No. 10715. *A cappella.* Moderately easy.

Three Hungarian Madrigals—Rezso Sugar. Shawnee Press No. A-1442. *A cappella.* Medium.

Three Latvian Carols, Set 1—Andrejs Jansons. Earthsongs. *A cappella.* Medium.

Three Latvian Carols, Set 2—Andrejs Jansons. Earthsongs. *A cappella.* Moderately easy.

Three Russian Folk Songs—arr. Joseph Roff. Carl Fischer No. CF7959. SA with piano and optional flute and hand drum. Easy.

Thy Holy Wings (Swedish folk tune)—arr. Daniel Kallman. Mark Foster No. YS 102P. Unison, with descant. Accompanied. Easy.

Treputé Martela (The Flax-Picking Song, Old Lithuanian folk song)—Vaclovas Augustinas. Alliance Music Pub. No. AMP 0043. SSAATTBB, with Percussion. Pronunciation guide included. Moderately difficult.

Two Latvian Carols—Andrejs Jansons. Earthsongs. SSA. *A cappella.* Pronunciation guide included.

Two Russian Folk Songs—John Biggs. Consort Press No. CP 31. *A cappella*. Medium.
The Young Cossack—Mikhail Glinka. Southern Music Pub. Co. No. 01-12184-122. Accompanied. English text. Moderately easy.

South America Latin America (Argentina, Bahamas, Brazil, Caribbean Islands, Cuba, Guatemala, Honduras, Jamaica, Mexico, Peru, Puerto Rico, Trinidad, Venezuela, West Indies).

A La Nanita Nana (Mexican folk song)—arr. David Eddleman. Carl Fischer No. CM8303. SA. Accompanied. Easy.
All My Trials (spiritual from the West Indies)—arr. Albert McNeil. Gentry Publications No. JG2026. *A cappella*, with solo. Easy.
All My Trials (West Indian spiritual)—arr. Robert DeCormier. Lawson Gould No. 52772. Accompanied. Easy.
All My Trials (Bahamian spiritual)—arr. David L. Brunner. Somerset Press No. SP 778. *A cappella*. Easy.
Alma Llanera (Soul of the Plains)—Pedro Gutierrez, arr. Angel Sauce. Earthsongs. *A cappella*. Medium.
Antigua (Guatemala)—Felipe de J. Ortega. Alliance Music Pub. No. AMT 0064. Piano or marimba accompaniment. Medium.
Ave Maria—Hector Villa-Lobos. Lawson Gould No. 52625. *A cappella*. Pronunciation guide included. Medium.
Ay, Ay, Ay (Creole Serenade)—arr. Leonard de Paur. Lawson Gould No. LG 654. *A cappella*. Medium.
Caballo Viejo (Costa Rica)—Simon Diaz, arr. Rolando Brenes Rojas. Alliance Music Pub. No. AMP 0065. *A cappella*. Moderately difficult.
Canciones De Cuna ("Cradle Songs")—Alberto Grau (Venezuela). Earthsongs. *A cappella*. Moderately easy.
Candu (Honduran folk song)—arr. Ruth De Cesare. Ludwig Music No. L-8101. SSA. Accompanied. Easy.
De Amor Heridos (traditional Mexican song)—arr. Ramon Noble. Alliance Music Pub. No. AMP 0025. *A cappella*. Easy.
De Tierra Lejana Venimos (Puerto Rican folk song)—arr. Donn Weiss. Music 70 No. M70-215. *A cappella*. Moderately easy.
Duerme Negrito (Cuban Lullaby)—arr. Robert DeCormier. Lawson Gould No. 52571. *A cappella*, with percussion. Moderately easy.
El Jarbe Tapatio (Traditional Mexican song)—arr. Ramón Noble. Alliance Music Pub. No. AMP 0024. SSA. *A cappella*. Moderately easy.
Eyes of Time (Ojos de tiempo)—Carlos Guastavino. Lawson Gould No. 52203. *A cappella*. Moderately easy.
Galo Garnizé (Mineiro folk song, Brazil)—arr. Carlos Alberto Pinto Fonseca. Lawson Gould No. 51979. *A cappella*. Medium.
Gloria (from *Misa Criolla*)—Ariel Ramirez, arr. Padre Jesus Gabriel Segade. Lawson Gould No. 51596. Piano or harpsichord and percussion accompaniment. Moderately difficult.
Good Evening, Mrs. Flanagan (Jamaican calypso)—Leonard de Paur. Lawson Gould No. 886. *A cappella*. Baritone and alto solos. Medium.
Jamaican Market Place—Larry Farrow. Gentry Publications No. JG2092. *A cappella*. Medium.
Kasar Mie La Gaji ("The Earth Is Tired")—Alberto Grau (Venezuela). Earthsongs. *A cappella*. Moderately difficult.
Ky Chororo—Anibal Sampayo, arr. Eduardo Gomez. Lawson Gould No. 52241. *A cappella*. Tenor or alto solo. Medium.
Kyrie (from *Misa Criolla*)—Ariel Ramirez. Lawson Gould No. 52653. Solos. Tenor drums (muffled). Moderately easy.
La Flor De La Miel ("The Flower of the honey")—Alberto Grau (Venezuela). Earthsongs. Solo. SSA divisi. *A cappella*. Medium.

Las Mañanitas (traditional Mexican song)—arr. Ramón Noble. Alliance Music Pub. No. AMP 0026. *A cappella.* Moderately easy.

Latin American Folk Songs—arr. Luis Sandi. Peer International Corp. *A cappella.* Medium.

La Virgen Lava Panales—arr. Robert DeCormier and Eddie Sauter. Lawson Gould No. 52227. Accompanied. Medium.

Marry a Woman Uglier Than You (Trinidad Calypso)—arr. Leonard de Paur. Lawson Gould No. 979. Tenor solo. *A cappella.* Medium.

Mata Del Anima Sola ("Tree of the Lonely Soul")—Antonio Estévez (Venezuela). Earthsongs. Tenor solo. *A cappella.* Moderately difficult.

Nights of Santa Fe (Noches de Santa Fe)—Carlos Guastavino. Lawson Gould No. 52239. *A cappella.* Medium.

On the Highways (Pampamapa)—Carlos Guastavino. Lawson Gould No. 52200. *A cappella.* Medium.

The Panana in a Zamba (El Parana en Una Zamba)—Ariel Ramirez. Lawson Gould No. 52243. Accompanied. Moderately easy.

Riqui, Riqui, Riqurrán (Venezuelan folk song)—arr. Gregg Smith. G. Schirmer No. 11299. *A cappella* or with string bass (or guitarone) Accompaniment. Moderately easy.

Romance de Roman Castillo (traditional Mexican ballad)—arr. Ramon Noble. Alliance No. AMP 0027. Accompanied. Easy.

Salmo 150 (Psalm 150)—Ernani Aguiar (Brazil). Earthsongs. *A cappella.* Medium.

The San Pedran (El Sampedrino)—Carlos Guastavino. Lawson Gould No. 52204. *A cappella.* Medium.

San Sereni (Puerto Rican Singing Game)—arr. Salli Terri. Lawson Gould No. 51234. *A cappella.* Moderately easy.

See De Stick She Go Bang (Caribbean Island folk melody)—arr. Walter Rodby. Lawson Gould No. 52645. Accompanied, with optional clapper. Easy.

Shut de Dō—Randy Stonehill, arr. Mark Hayes. Word Music No. 301 0262 167. Accompaniment: Claves, low drum, and temple blocks. Medium.

Song of the River (Peruvian folk song)—arr. Ruth DeCesare. Ludwig Music Pub. No. L-8102. SSA. Accompanied. Moderately easy.

Tangueando—Oscar Escalada. Lawson Gould No. 52729. *A cappella.* Pronunciation guide included. Moderately difficult.

Te Quiro ("I Adore You")—Alberto Favero (Argentina)—arr. Liliana Cangiano. Earthsongs. *A cappella.* Also available for SSA. Moderately easy.

Three Traditional Cuban Songs—Joaquin Nin-Culmell. Rongwen Music. 1) The Lost Child. Easy. 2) Come Here For Your Fruit-Pulp. Moderately easy. 3) Where Is the Ma Teodora? *A cappella.* Moderately difficult.

Tumbando Cana (Cuban folk song)—arr. Howard A. Roberts. Lawson Gould No. 51685. African drum accompaniment. Easy.

Tutu Maramba (Brazilian lullaby)—arr. James Erb. Lawson Gould No. 637. SSA. Accompanied. Easy.

With Wings He'll Touch Your Eyelids (Con Alas En Los Ojos)—Alberto Balzanelli. Lawson Gould No. 52202. *A cappella.* Medium.

Yo Paso Las Noches (Traditional Mexican song)—arr. Ramon Noble. Alliance No. AMP 0028. Accompanied. Easy.

Zamba For You—Ariel Ramirez, arr. Eduardo Gomez. Lawson Gould No. 52242. *A cappella.* Easy.

Middle East (Arabia, Israel, Jordan, Lebanon)

Adoration (traditional)—arr. A. W. Binder. Transcontinental Music Pub. No. 991614. For cantor, mixed choir, and organ. Moderately easy.

Avinu Malkeinu—Max Janowski. Transcontinental Music Pub. No. 991606 For cantor, mixed choir and organ. Medium.

Avinu Malkeynu (Our Father, Our King)—Max Janowski. Friends of Jewish Music. No. G-030. For solo, choir and piano or organ. Medium.

Ayn Charod (Palestinian folk song)—arr. A. W. Binder. Marks Music Corp. No. 2005. Alto solo. Accompanied. Moderately easy.

Boruch Atoh (You Shall Be Blessed)—Solomon Golub, arr. Joshua Jacobson. Transcontinental Music Pub. No. 991339. Accompanied. Pronunciation guide included. Easy.

Chanukah Song (Mi Y'Mallël, "Who Can Retell?")—Julius Chajes. Transcontinental Music Pub. No. 990211. Baritone solo. Accompanied. Moderately easy.

Dance for Hanukkah—David Eddleman. Coronet Press No. 392-41815. SA with keyboard accompaniment. Easy.

Dundai (Israeli folk song)—arr. Sonya Garfinkle. Mark Foster No. MF 329. Accompanied. Easy.

Halalujoh, halalu el b'kod'sho (Hallelujah, Praise Ye the Lord, Psalm CL)—Louis Lewandowski. G. Schirmer No 7454. Organ accompaniment. Medium.

Hallelujah (Psalm 150—Louis Lewandowski. Transcontinental Music Pub. No. 990792. Organ accompaniment. Medium.

Hanukkah Blessings (Dedication)—Ron Jeffers. Earthsongs. A cappella. Medium.

The Hanukkah Land—David Eddleman. Carl Fischer No. CM8354. SA with keyboard and tambourine. Easy.

Hanukkah Madrigal (Mi Y'mallel)—Herbert Fromm. Transcontinental Music Pub. No. 990239. A cappella. Moderately easy.

Hanukkah Song (Mi Y'Mallel, Who Can Retell)—arr. Julius Chajes. Transcontinental Music Pub. No. TCL 211. Piano or organ accompaniment. Moderately easy.

Hanukkah Song (Israeli folk song)—arr. Donald E. Sellew. Schmitt, Hall & McCreary Co. No. 1178. A cappella. Easy.

Harken To My Prayer—Julius Chajes. Transcontinental Music Pub. No. 99-0759. Optional organ accompaniment. Easy.

Hatikvah (Israeli National Anthem)—arr. Maurice Goldman. Ludwig Music No. L-1185. Accompanied. Pronunciation guide included. Medium.

Hava Nageela (Israeli folk song)—srr. Maurice Goldman. Lawson Gould No. 51270. Accompanied. Medium.

Hava Nagila (Israeli folk dance)—arr. Abraham Kaplin. Lawson Gould No. 51486. A cappella. Medium.

Hava Nagila (Israeli folk song)—arr. Robert L. Beckhard. Pro Art Pub. No. 2197. SAB. Accompanied. Dance directions included. Moderately easy.

Hava Neytzey B'Machol (Israeli folk song)—arr. Maurice Goldman. Lawson Gould No. 51615. Accompanied. Moderately difficult.

Hiney Mah Tov (Hebrew folk tune)—arr. Iris Levine. Mark Foster No. MF 3025. A cappella. Medium.

Horah: "Chanitah" (from Three Palestinian Dances)—arr. Ralph Hunter. Lawson Gould No. 569. A cappella. Moderately easy.

How Good It Is (Hebrew folk song)—arr. Maurice Goldman. Lawson Gould No. 51821. Accompanied. Easy.

In Nature's Ebb and Flow—Samuel Adler. Southern Music Pub. Co. No. 1080-22. Treble choir (SSAA) and piano. Medium.

The Lights We Have Kindled (Hanëros Halolu—Hanukkah Song)—Hugo Ch. Adler. Transcontinental Music Pub. No. TCL 779. Accompanied. Moderately easy.

Lullaby (Jordanian folk song) and Black Cat (Arabic folk song)—arr. Lois Land and Sally Monsour. AMC Publications No. AMC 1004. SA and SSA with Accompaniment. Easy.

Matai Yavo (Israeli folk tune)—arr. Maurice Goldman. Lawson Gould No 51269. Baritone or tenor solo. Accompanied. Moderately difficult.

Mi Yemalel (Who Can Retell?)—arr. Max Helfman. Transcontinental Music Pub. No. 991500. A cappella. Medium.

Mi Y'Maleil (Traditional)—arr. Steve Barnett. Transcontinental Music Pub. No. 991294. A cappella. Pronunciation guide included. Medium.

My Homeland (popular melody from Lebanon)—arr. Lois Land, SSA Accompanied. And My Home So Far Away (based on the Lebanese melody "Ya Laura Houbooki")—arr. Lois Land. SA Accompanied, AMC Publications No. AMC 1005. Easy.

Psalm 100 (Shout Joyfully to our God)—Louis Lewandowski, ed. Samuel Adler. Transcontinental Music Pub. No. 991391. Accompanied. Pronunciation guide included. Medium.

Rock of Ages (Maoz Tsur—Hannukah Song)—arr. Samuel Adler. Transcontinental Music Pub. No. 990134. Optional accompaniment, Easy.

Rounds of Israel (Shalom Chaverim, A Kum Bachur Atsel, Hiney Matov)—arr. Robert De Cormier. Lawson Gould No. 51542. Accompanied. Moderately easy.

Shemen Zach—Chaim Parchi, arr. Joshua Jacobson. Transcontinental Muusic Pub. No. 991340. Solo voice, piano, and optional guitar. Moderately easy.

Shiviti Adonai (memorial prayer)—Louis Lewandowski, ed. Samuel Adler. Transcontinental Music Pub. No. 991083. Organ accompaniment. Moderately easy.

Shirei Shabbat (sabbath songs)—Theodore Morrison, Earthsongs. Piano or organ accompaniment. Pronunciation guide included. Medium.

Shuru Habitu (Israeli folk song)—arr. Lois Land. Alliance Music Pub. No. AMC 1007. SA. Accompanied. Pronunciation guide included. Easy.

Song of Galilee (El Yivneh Hagalil)—arr. Julius Chajes. Transcontinental Music Pub. No. 99-0214. Accompanied. Medium.

S'Vivon (The Top—Folk Song)—arr. Max Helfman. Transcontinental Music Pub. No. 991501. *A cappella*. Easy. Pronunciation guide included.

S'Vivon (Traditional Jewish folk song)—arr. Valerie Shields. Earthsongs. SA. Piano accompaniment, with 2 violins. Easy. Pronunciation guide included.

Tafta Hindy (Arabic folk song)—arr. Lois Land. AMC Publications No. AMC 1006. Accompanied. Easy.

Three Songs From Israel: 1) Shir Haavoda (Song of Work), 2) Shir Shomrim (Watchman's Song), 3) Have Netze Bemachol (Come and Dance)—arr. Morris Browda. Shawnee Press No. A-956, Accompanied. Medium.

The Story of Hanukkah—David Eddleman. Carl Fischer No. CM8318. SA. Accompanied. Easy.

Sim Shalom (Prayer for Peace) Max Janowski. Friends of Max Janowski No. F-053. Solo. Accompanied. Easy.

Tchum Bi-Ri Tchum (Israeli folk tune)—arr, Maurice Goldman. Lawson Gould No. 51888. Accompanied. Moderately easy.

Tumbalalaika (Yiddish folk song)—arr. Robert De Cormier. Lawson Gould No. 51225. Accompanied. Moderately easy.

Ya Ba Bom (Jewish folk tune)—arr. Maurice Goldman Lawson Gould No. 51814. Piano accompaniment, with optional String Bass and Drums. Medium.

Yiboneh Hamikdosh (Classic folk tune)—arr. Max Janowski. Friends of Max Janowski No. C-60. Accompanied. Medium.

Yom Seh Le-Yisrael (traditional sabbath table hymn)—arr. Dudley Cohen. Boosey & Hawkes No. W-155. *A cappella*. Medium.

Zum Gali—Dance the Hora (Israeli folk tune)—arr. Maurice Goldman. Lawson Gould No. 52026. Accompanied. Moderately difficult.

North American Folk Songs (Canada and United States).

Adam in the Garden Pinnin' Leaves (American folk song sketch)—Gail Kubik. Lawson Gould No. 52148. Incidental solos. *A cappella*. Medium.

A La Claire Fontaine (French-Canadian folk song)—arr. Robert DeCormier, Lawson Gould No. 51544. *A cappella*. Easy.

An American Hymn ("America the Beautiful")—arr. Cecil Effinger. G. Schirmer No. 50314230. Organ or piano accompaniment. Moderately easy.

Beautiful River—Robert Lowry (1886)—arr. Robert DeCormier. Lawson Gould No. 52395. With brass, handbells and piano. Easy.

The Blue Tail Fly (American minstrel song)—arr. Salli Terri. Consort Press No. CP 38. Baritone or bass solo. Optional guitar and bass accompaniment. Moderately easy.

By'm Bye (Traditional American Lullaby)—arr. Alice Parker. Lawson Gould No. 51513. *A cappella.* Easy.

California Mission Music (composite mass and hymns)—ed. John Biggs. Consort Press No. CP-5. Accompaniment: Two flutes, two violins, cello or bassoon, string bass, and hand bells. Medium.

Carols of French Canada 1) Mon Petit Jésus, 2) D'ou Viens-tu Bergère? 3) Noël, Noël)—Louis Applebaum. Gordon V. Thompson No. VE. 1.1123. Accompanied. Also available for SSA. Moderately easy.

Charlottown (American folk song)—arr. William Martin. Lawson Gould No. 51155. Accompanied. Easy.

Chic-A-Boom (source: East Texas)—arr. Samuel Adler. Lawson Gould No. 950. *A cappella.* Easy.

Cindy (American folk song)—arr. Walter Ehret. Theodore Presser No. 312-41186. Accompanied. Easy.

Colinda (Cajun French folk song)—arr. Michael Scott. Warner Bros. Pub. No. SV8924. SA. Accompanied. Easy.

The Colorado Trail (American folk song)—arr. James Erb. Lawson Gould No. 52661. Soprano and tenor solos. *A cappella.* Easy.

The Courtin' Song (based on a Kentucky Mountain song)—Jean Ritchie, arr. David Dusing. Lawson Gould No. 52323. *A cappella.* Easy.

Dance, Boatman, Dance (American folk song)—arr. Robert DeCormier. Lawson Gould No. 52525. Baritone and bass solos. Accompanied Easy.

Deep Blue Sea (American folk song)—arr. Robert DeCormier. Lawson Gould No. 51754. Accompanied. Easy.

The Dyin' Californian—arr. Salli Terri. Lawson Gould No. 52116. Tenor solo. *A cappella.* Easy.

Elanoy (American Ballad)—arr. Mary Hoffman. Lawson Gould No. 52668. Accompanied. Easy.

El Padre Nuestro (The Lord's Prayer from "California Mission Music")—ed. John Biggs. Consort Press No. CP-5f. TTBB. *A cappella.* Easy.

En Roulant (French-Canadian folk song)—arr. Charles Pelletier. Mark Foster No. MF 1072. TB with baritone solo. *A cappella.* Moderately easy.

Ev'ry Night When the Sun Goes In (American folk song)—arr. Wendy Williams. Lawson Gould No. 52193. Accompanied. Easy.

Fish, Fish, Fish, Fish (from Sea Chanteys)—Sydney Hodkinson. Merion Music No. 342-40105. *A cappella.* Easy.

Follow the Drinking Gourd (source unknown)—arr. John Horman, Somerset Press No. SP782. SAB. Accompanied. Easy.

Frankie and Johnny—arr. Robert DeCormier. Lawson Gould No. 52040. Soprano, alto, tenor, and baritone solos. *A cappella.* Moderately easy.

Frog Went a-Courtin' (American folk song)—arr. David Dusing. Lawson Gould No. 52579. Accompanied. Medium.

Goin' to Boston (American folk song)—arr. Alice Parker. Lawson Gould No. 51738. *A cappella.* Medium.

Hallelujah, I'm A Bum—arr. Donald Cobb. Lawson Gould No. 52277. *A cappella.* Moderately easy.

He's Gone Away (American folk song)—arr. S.C. Terri, ed.Roger Wagner. Lawson Gould No. 633. Female and male solos. *A cappella.* Medium.

He's Gone Away (American folk song)—arr. Alice Parker and Robert Shaw. Lawson Gould No. 672. Soprano solo. *A cappella.* Medium.

Hicks Farewell (source: Virginia)—arr. Samuel Adler. Lawson Gould No. 951. *A cappella.* Moderately easy.

The Huron Carol (Jesous Ahatonhia)—arr. Howard Cable. Gordon V. Thompson No. VG-253. SA. Accompanied. Moderately easy.

The Huron Carol—arr. Robert B. Anderson. Gordon V. Thompson No. VE.I.1075. *A cappella.* Medium.

I Ride an Old Paint (traditional)—Gail Kubik. Lawson Gould No. 52149. *A cappella.* Medium.

Imprisoned Once at Nantes (French-Canadian folk song)—arr. Charles Pelletier. Mark Foster No. MF 962. SSA. *A cappella.* Optional triangle. Moderately easy.

I'se the B'y (folk song from Newfoundland)—arr. Robert de Cormier. Lawson Gould No. 52051. Accompanied. Easy.

I've Been Workin' on the Railroad (American folk song)—adapted by Robert DeCormier. Lawson Gould No. 52386. *A cappella.* Medium.

Jenny Jenkins (American play party song)—adapted by Robert DeCormier, Lawson Gould No. 51612. Accompanied. Medium.

Johnny Has Gone for a Soldier (American Revolutionary War folk song)—arr. Alice Parker and Robert Shaw. Lawson Gould No. 502. *A cappella.* Moderately easy.

In the Good Old Colony Days (early American song)—arr. Robert DeCormier, Lawson Gould No. 51281. *A cappella.* Moderately easy.

John Henry (American folk song)—arr. Laura Shur. Lawson Gould No. 52700. Accompanied. Medium.

John Henry (American folk song)—adapted by Robert DeCormier. Lawson Gould No. 52310. Soprano and baritone solos. *A cappella.* Medium.

Lolly Too-Dum (American folk song)—Gail Kubik. Lawson Gould No. 52151. Incidental solos. Accompanied. Medium.

Lowlands (Mississippi folk song)—arr. Clifford Taylor. Lawson Gould No. 51537. Tenor solo. *A cappella.* Medium.

Native American Spring Songs—Nancy Grundahl. Mark Foster No. MF 963. SSAA, with flute. Easy.

Oh, Fare You Well, My Own True Love (American folk song)—arr. Walter Ehret. Lawson Gould No. 52284. Accompanied. Easy.

The Old Fool (American folk song)—arr. David Dusing. Lawson Gould No. 52606. Accompanied. Moderately easy.

Papillon, Tu Es Volage (folk song from Quebec)—arr. Jonathan Thompson. Alliance Music Pub. No. AMP 0079. *A cappella.* Easy.

Play Party (American folk song)—adapted by Robert DeCormier. Lawson Gould No. 51274. Optional accompaniment. Easy.

Poor Wayfarin' Stranger (American folk song)—arr. Salli Terri. Lawson Gould No. 831. Two solo voices. *A cappella.* Medium.

Red River Valley (traditional)—arr. Robert Nelson. AMC Publications, No. AMC 1011. SA. Accompanied. Easy.

Revolutionary Tea Party (traditional)—arr. George Brandon. Lawson Gould No. 51811. Accompanied. Moderately easy.

Rodeo (based on Western tunes)—arr. Mary Hoffman. Lawson Gould No. 59669. Accompanied. Medium.

Salish Song (Canadian folk song from southern British Columbia)—arr. Derek Healey. Gordon V. Thompson No. VE.I.1017. Optional accompaniment. Medium.

Shenandoah (American Sea Chanty)—arr. Salli Terri. Lawson Gould No. 581. Male solo. *A cappella.* Medium.

Skip to My Lou (American dance tune)—arr. Paul Christiansen. Schmitt, Hall & McCreary. No. SCHCH 07617. Optional piano accompaniment. Moderately easy.

Soldier, Soldier Won't You Marry Me? (early American song)—arr. Robert DeCormier, Lawson Gould No. 51280. *A cappella.* Easy.

Somebody's Knockin' at Your Door (traditional)—arr. Ronald Melrose. Carl Fischer No. CM8302. *A cappella* with optional tambourine. Easy.

Song for Mother Earth (Native-American chants)—arr. Lana Walter. Warner Bros. Pub. No. SV9523. SA (opt. SSA) with piano, drum and rattle. Easy.

Songs of Early Canada—arr. Donald Patriquin, Earthsongs. SATB with piano and optional percussion. Easy.

Innoria (Huron Dance Song)

The Wreck of the Steamship Ethie (Newfoundland folksong)

Ah! si mon moine voulait danser (Folk song—Quebec)

The False Young Man (Ontario)

Morning Star (Saskatchewan folk song)

Savory, Sage, Rosemary and Thyme (British Columbia)

The Streets of Laredo (American Cowboy Song)—arr, Salli Terri, Lawson Gould No. 694. *A cappella.* Easy.

Streets of Larado (traditional American)—arr. Anthony J. Palmer. National Music Pubishers No. WHC-149. TTB with Piano. Easy.

The Sunny South—arr. Salli Terri. Lawson Gould No. 52269. Medium solo voice. *A cappella.* Easy.

Sweet Betsy from Pike—arr. Robert DeCormier. Lawson Gould No. 52133. Accompanied. Easy.

Three Mountain Ballads (He's Gone Away, Will He Remember? Barbara Allen)—arr. Ron Nelson, Elkan-Vogel No. 362-03379. Piano with optional string bass SSA. Medium.

Timber (traditional)—arr. Anthony J. Palmer, National Music Publishers No. WHC-172, TBB. Bass solo. Accompanied. Easy.

Two Shaker Songs (Simple Gifts and I Will Bow)—arr. Edwin Earle Ferguson. Lawson Gould No. 51352. Organ or piano accompaniment. Easy.

Two White Horses—Lee Hays, Bernie Krause, arr. Robert DeCormier. Lawson Gould No. 52327. Baritone solo. Accompanied. Easy.

The Unconstant Lover (American Midwest folk song)—arr. Salli Terri. Lawson Gould No. 52094. *A cappella.* Easy.

Wailie, Wailie (The Water Is Wide; American folk song)—arr. Robert DeCormier. Lawson Gould No. 51541. Tenor solo. *A cappella.* Moderately easy.

Wayfaring Stranger—arr. Robert DeCormier. Lawson Gould No. 51625. *A cappella.* Easy.

When I First Came to This Land—Oscar Brand, arr. Robert DeCormier. Lawson Gould No. 51935. Optional piano accompaniment. Moderately easy.

When I Was Single (American folk song)—arr. Arthur Hardwicke. Oliver Ditson No. 332-40132. SAB. Accompanied. Easy.

Willows by the Waterside (Pueblo Indians)—Robert Kreutz. Shawnee Press No. A-1323. *A cappella.* Medium.

Wondrous Love (traditional hymn)—arr. Alice Parker and Robert Shaw. Lawson Gould No. 907. *A cappella.* Easy.

Yankee Doodle (American folk song)—arr. Robert DeCormier. Lawson Gould No. 52215. Accompanied. Moderately easy.

Yellow Rose of Texas (Minstrel Song)—arr. Alice Parker and Robert Shaw. Lawson Gould No. 587. Accompanied. Moderately easy.

Young Hunting (North Carolina)—arr. Samuel Adler. Lawson Gould No. 949. *A cappella.* Moderately easy.

African-American Spitituals

Amazin' Grace (old hymn tune)—arr. Wendell Whalum. Lawson Gould No. 51750. Organ accompaniment. Moderately easy.

Amazing Grace (traditional hymn)—arr. Alice Parker and Robert Shaw. Lawson Gould No. 918. Tenor solo. *A cappella.* Medium.

Battle O' Jericho (spiritual)—arr. Roger Wagner. Lawson Gould No. 51570. *A cappella.* Medium.

Deep River (spiritual)—arr. Salli Terri. Consort Press No. CP 400. Soprano solo. Double SATB chorus. *A cappella.* Medium.

Dere's No Hidin' Place (spiritual)—arr. Alice Parker and Robert Shaw. Lawson Gould No. 51110. Tenor solo. *A cappella.* Medium.

Didn't My Lord Deliver Daniel? (spiritual)—arr. Ralph Hunter. Lawson Gould No. 957. Accompanied. Moderately easy.

Ezekiel Saw the Wheel (spiritual)—arr. Robert DeCormier. Lawson Gould No. 52581. Baritone and soprano (obligato) solos. *A cappella.* Moderately difficult.

Fare Ye Well—arr. Brazeal W. Dennard. Alliance Music Publications No. AMP 0030. Baritone solo. *A cappella.* Medium.

Fix Me, Jesus (traditional spiritual)—arr. Augustus O. Hill. Alliance Music Publications No. AMP 0042. Solo. Accompanied. Medium.

He's Got the Whole World in His Hands (spiritual)—arr. Robert DeCormier. Lawson Gould No. 51921. *A cappella.* Moderately easy.

I Got Shoes (spiritual)—arr. Alice Parker and Robert Shaw. Lawson Gould No. 51116. *A cappella*. Medium.

I'll Take Sugar in my Coffee-O—Jester Hairston, arr. Nathan Scott. Lawson Gould No. 52642. Optional Soprano solo. Accompanied. Medium.

I'm Goin' to Sing (spiritual)—arr. Alice Parker and Robert Shaw. Lawson Gould No. 51101. *A cappella*. Moderately easy.

I Want Jesus to Walk with Me (traditional spiritual)—arr. Eurydice V. Osterman. Alliance Music Pub. No. AMP 0107. Optional solo. *A cappella*. Easy.

Joshua Fit the Battle of Jericho (spiritual)—arr. David Paul Henry. Lawson Gould No. 52474. Accompanied. Moderately easy.

Let My People Go (spiritual)—arr. Howard A. Roberts. Lawson Gould No. 51556. *A cappella*, with optional percussion. Moderately easy.

Lit'le David, Play on Yo, Harp (spiritual)—arr. Roger Wagner. Lawson Gould No. 51192. *A cappella*. Moderately easy.

Little Wheel a Turn'n (religious folk song)—arr. Lloyd Pfautsch. Lawson Gould No. 547. Tenor Solo. *A cappella*. Moderately easy.

Lord, I Want to Be a Christian (traditional)—arr. Brazeal W. Dennard. Alliance Music Publications No. AMP 0029. *A cappella*. Medium.

My Lord, What a Moanin' (traditional)—arr. Adolphus Hailstork. Alliance Music Publications No. AMP 0073. *A cappella*. Moderately easy.

Nobody Knows (spiritual)—arr. Alice Parker and Robert Shaw. Lawson Gould No. 51108. Solo. *A cappella*. Easy.

Oh' What a Beautiful City (spiritual)—arr. Donald McCullough. Lawson Gould No. 52300. *A cappella*. Moderately easy.

Pick a Bale of Cotton (traditional work song)—arr. Robert DeCormier. Lawson Gould No. 51375. Accompanied. Moderately easy.

Plenty Good Room! Sit Down Servant—arr. Robert DeCormier. Lawson Gould No. 52544. Mezzo soprano or tenor and baritone solos. Accompanied. Medium.

Raise a Ruckus (folk song)—arr. Robert DeCormier. Lawson Gould No. 51277. Baritone or tenor solo. Piano accompaniment with guitar or Banjo. Medium.

Same Train (spiritual)—arr. Alice Parker and Robert Shaw. Lawson Gould No. 51113. Accompanied. Moderately easy.

Sometimes I Feel (spiritual)—arr. Alice Parker and Robert Shaw. Lawson Gould No.51112. Contralto solo. *A cappella*. Medium.

Sometimes I Feel Lika a Motherless Child (spiritual)—arr. Robert DeCormier. Lawson Gould No. 51479. Soprano and alto solos. Accompanied. Moderately easy.

Standin' in the Need of Prayer (spiritual)—arr. Howard Roberts. Lawson Gould No. 52539. *A cappella*. Medium.

Steal Away (spiritual)—arr. Alice Parker and Robert Shaw. Lawson Gould No. 51104. *A cappella*. Medium.

Swing Low, Sweet Chariot (spiritual)—arr. Alice Parker and Robert Shaw. Lawson Gould No. 984. *A cappella*. Medium.

That Lonesome Valley (spiritual)—arr. Alice Parker and Robert Shaw. Lawson Gould No. 51103. Baritone solo. *A cappella*. Medium.

Were You There? (spiritual)—arr. Robert DeCormier. Lawson Gould No. 51613. Solo voice. *A cappella*. Medium.

Western Europe (Austria, France, Germany, Italy, Netherlands, Spain)

Adoration of the Wise Men (15th-Century Freneh melody)—arr. Crawford R. Thoburn. Carl Fischer No. CM8379. Accompanied. Easy.

A La Nanita Nana (traditional Spanish carol)—arr. Roger Folstrom. Mark Foster No. MF 547. Piano, guitar, or harp accompaniment. Medium.

A La Nanita Nana (traditional Spanish carol)—arr. Noé Sánchez. AMC Publications No. AMC 1010. SSA. *A cappella*. Easy.

Alouette (French folk song)—arr. John Bertalot. Roberton Publications No. 312-41658. *A cappella*. Medium.

Alouette (French folk song)—arr. Robert DeCormier. Lawson Gould No. 51233, Accompanied. Medium.

Amor Vittorioso—Giovanni Gastoldi (c. 1550-1622)—ed. Jim Leininger. Alliance Music Pub. No. AMP 0095. *A cappella*. Easy.

Auprès de ma Blonde (French folk song)—arr. Alice Parker and Robert Shaw. Lawson Gould No. 644. *A cappella*. Text in French. Moderately easy.

Baile De Gaita (Spanish folk song)—arr. Roger Wagner and Frank Ahrold. Lawson Gould No. 636. *A cappella*. Medium.

Bella Bimba (Italian folk song)—arr. Robert DeCormier. Lawson Gould No. 51256. Accompanied. Moderately easy.

Bon Jour, Mon Coeur—Orlando di Lasso/John Biggs. Consort Press No. CP-2. Accompanied. Medium.

Cantaremos (traditional Spanish dance)—arr. Ramón Noble. Alliance Music Pub. No. AMP 0023. Text in Spanish. *A cappella*. Moderately easy.

¡Como esta sola mi vida! (Loneliness is all that I feel)—Juan Ponce. ed. Josquin Nin-Culmell. Broude Brothers No. SCT 19. *A cappella*. Easy.

¡Con Qué La Lavaré? (With what, how shall I cleanse?)—Juan Vasquez. ed. Josquin Nin-Culmell. Broude Brothers, No. SCT 7. *A cappella*. Moderately easy.

Cuatro Sonetos De Amor—Jacobo Ficher. Southern Music Pub. Co. No. 2146-13. 1) Miverso, como el alba, te saluda, 2) Para alumbrar tu corazòn en vela, 3) Amor, mi buen amor! 4) A traves de la noche. Text in Spanish. *A cappella*. Moderately difficult.

Da droben vom Berge (traditional Austrian carol)—arr. Ron Jeffers. Earthsongs. *A cappella*. Easy.

Das ist ein köstliches Ding (This is a precious thing)—Georg Schumann Earthsongs *A cappella*. English translation included. Medium.

Dejó La Venda—Francisco Guerrero (1528-1599), ed. Josquin Nin-Culmell. Broude Brothers No. SCT 13. SSAT. *A cappella*, or with optional instrumental doubling. Moderately easy.

De Los Álamos Vengo, Madre (From the Poplar Trees I Come)—Juan Vásquez (16th century). ed. Josquin Nin-Culmell. Broude Brothers No. SCT 9. *A cappella*. Moderately easy.

Donde Hay (a Spanish proverb)—Paul F. Page. Mark Foster No. MF 210. *A cappella*. Easy.

En El Portal A Belén (traditional Spanish carol) and Fum, Fum, Fum (traditional Catalonian carol)—arr. Noe Sanchez. AMC Publications No. AMC 1099. Spanish text. SSA. *A cappella*. Easy.

En La Fuente Del Rose (By the spring near roses red)—Juan Vasquez. ed. Josquin Nin-Culmell. Broude Brothers No. SCT 8. *A cappella*. Easy.

Esclarecida Juana (O dazzling, dazzling Juana)—Francisco Guerrero, ed. Josquin Nin-Culmell. Broude Brothers Ltd. No. SCT 15. SSAT. *A cappella*, or with instrumental doubling ad libitum. Moderately easy.

Four Spanish Christmas Carols (Alegria, alegria, alegria; El desembre congelat; Soy un pobre pastorcito; Vamos todos a Belen)—arr. Oscar and Noé Sanchez. AMC Publications No. AMC 1008. *A cappella*. Easy.

Freré Jacques (French folk song)—arr. Salli Terri. Lawson Gould No. 988. Optional celeste or piano accompaniment. Moderately easy.

Fum, Fum, Fum (traditional Catalonian carol)—arr. Josquin Nin-Culmell. Rongwen Music No. R.M. 2096. Tambourine accompaniment. Moderately easy.

Gran placer siento yo ya (Great delight do I sense now)—Pedro De Escobar. ed. Josquin Nin-Culmell. Broude Brothers. No. SCT 16. *A cappella*. Easy.

Jamais Je n'Aimerai Grand Homme (Your Haughty Heart—16th-century chanson)—ed. Linda Allen Anderson. Alliance Music Pub. No. AMP 0077. *A cappella*. Easy.

J'Entends le Moulin (I hear the millwheel—French chanson)—arr. Donald Patriquin. Earthsongs. Accompanied. Also available for SS and Piano. Medium.

Komm, heil'ger Geist (Come Holy Spirit)—Georg Schumann, Earthsongs. SSAATTBB. *A cappella*. English translation included. Moderately difficult.

Kyrie (from *Missa Brevis*)—Andrea Gabrieli (c. 1510-86)—ed. Rod Walker. Alliance Music Pub. No. AMP 0050. *A cappella.* Medium.

La Mi Sola Laureola (One and only Laureola)—Juan Ponce. ed. Josquin Nin-Culmell. Broude Brothers Ltd. No. SCT 18. *A cappella.* Easy.

La Virgen Lava Panales (Mary Was Washing the Linen)—Josquin Nin-Culmell. Rongwen Music No. R.M. 2062. *A cappella,* with tambourine. Easy.

Le Sommeil de l'Enfant Jésus (traditional French carol)—arr. Ron Jeffers. Earthsongs. SSA. *A cappella.* Easy.

Maria Walks Amid the Thorn (late 15th-century German carol)—arr Ron Jeffers. Earthsongs. *A cappella.* English translation included. Easy.

O Beautiful Young Maiden (French folk dance)—arr. Abraham Kaplan. Lawson Gould No. 51454. *A cappella* with optional drum accompaniment. Easy.

O Más Dura Que Mármol! (O resistant like marble!)—Pedro Guerrero. ed. Josquin Nin-Culmell. Broude Brothers No. SCT 12. *A cappella.* with optional instrumental doubling ad libitum. Moderately easy.

O Tannenbaum (traditional German)—arr. John Carter. Alliance Music Pub. No. AMP 0082. Accompanied. Easy.

Por Do Comenzare? (O how shall I begin?)—Pedro Guerrero (16th-century). ed. Josquin Nin-Culmell. Broude Brothers No. SCT 11. *A cappella* with optional instrumental doubling ad libitum. Moderately easy.

Por Unos Puertos Arriba—Antonio de Ribera (16th-century) and Quien Te Trajo, Caballero?—Juan Del Encina (1468-1529), ed. Josquin Nin-Culmell. Broude Brothers Ltd. No. SCT 3. *A cappella,* with optional instrumental doubling ad libitum. Moderately easy.

Prado Verde Y Florido (Meadow verdant and flowered)—Francisco Guerrero. ed. Josquin Nin-Culmell. Broude Brothers Ltd. No. SCT 14. SSAT. *A cappella* with optional instrumental doubling ad libitum.

Quedaos, adios (We leave, goodbye)—Pedro De Escobar. ed. Josquin Nin-Culmell. Broude Brothers Ltd. No. SCT 17. *A cappella.* Moderately easy.

Quelle est cette odeur agréable? (What is this lovely wondrous fragrance?—Noel Anciens)—arr. Donald Patriquin. Earthsongs. *A cappella.* Moderately easy.

Qu'es De Ti, Desconsolado? (What of thee, disconsolate one?)—Juan del Encina. STB. *A cappella* with instrumental doubling ad libitum, and Levanta, Pascual, Levanta (Arise, run, Pascual, run)—Juan del Encina. STB. Accompaniment of trumpet, Two trombones, and tambourine. ed. Josquín Nin-Culmell. Broude Brothers Ltd. No. SCT 5. Moderately easy.

Resonet in Laudibus (14th-century German carol)—arr. C. L. Alwes. Roger Dean Pub. Co. No. 10/1264R. Accompanied. Difficult.

See the Star (Spanish carol)—arr. Anthony J. Palmer. Highland Music Co. No. 8. Piano, claves and bongos. Moderately easy.

Si Ch'io Vorrei Morire—Claudio Monteverdi (1567-1643)—ed. Kenneth Fulton. Alliance Music Pub. No. AMP 0041. SATBB. *A cappella.* Medium.

The Snow-White Messenger (Netherland folk song)—arr. Lloyd Pfautsch. Lawson Gould No. 52641. Accompanied. Moderately easy.

Still, Still, Still (traditional Austrian carol)—arr. Ron Jeffers. Earthsongs SSA. *A cappella.* Easy. English translation included.

Three Spanish Carols: 1) A La Nanita Nana (traditional Spanish carol), 2) Gifts for the Child (traditional Spanish carol), 3) Come To Him, Dear Lady (traditional Spanish carol)—arr. Gene Grier and Lowell Everson. Warner Bros. Pub. No. SV9551. Piano with optional hand drum, castenets, and tambourine. Editions also available for SSA (SV 9552) and SAB (SV 9553). Moderately easy..

Tous Les Bourgeois De Chârtres (all villagers of Chartres)—arr. Donald Patriquin. Earthsongs. SSAATBB. *A cappella.* Medium.

Triste Espana, Sin Ventura! (Spain, Sad Spain, Misfortunate One), and A Tal Perdida Tan Triste (For a Lass so bleak, oh so sad)—Juan del Encina. Broude Brothers Ltd. No. SCT 1. *A cappella,* or with Instrumental doubling ad libitum. Easy.

Venez, mes enfants (Come my children)—Noel d'Alsace. arr. Donald Patriquin. Earthsongs SSAATBB. Moderately easy.

Vos Me Matastes (You have wounded me)—Juan Vásquez (16th century). Broude Brothers Ltd. No. SCT 10. SSATB A cappella. Moderately easy.

The White Dove (German folk song)—Johannes Brahms. ed. Charles F. Manney. CPP/Belwin No. 64096. A cappella. Medium.

Ya Viene La Vieja (traditional Spanish)—arr. Jim Leininger. Alliance Music Pub. No. AMP 0101.TBB with keyboard or guitar. Easy.

Folk Songs and Spirituals (More Recently Published Music)

Afton Water (Scottish song)—arr. Brent Pierce. Plymouth Music No. BP-113. A cappella. Moderately easy.

By and By (spiritual)—arr. Alice Parker. Jenson No. 43509063. A cappella. Medium.

Cockles & Mussels (Irish folk song)—arr. Roger Folstrom. Mark Foster No. MF 3031. A cappella. Easy.

Deep River (spiritual)—arr. Rene Clausen. Mark Foster No. MF 2064. A cappella. Soprano or tenor solo. Medium.

Don't You Let Nobody Turn You 'Roun' (spiritual)—arr. Phillip McIntyre, Mark Foster No. MF 294. A cappella. Moderately easy.

Don't You Let Nobody Turn You 'Round (spiritual)—arr. Lena J. McLin. Neil A. Kjos No. ED. GC 166. Accompanied. Moderately easy.

The Fountain (French folk song)—arr. Norman Luboff. Walton No. WW 1133. Flute, guitar, and bass or two-piano accompaniment. Easy.

Give Up the World (spiritual)—arr. Lena J. McLin. Neil A. Kjos No. ED GC 169. A cappella. Moderately easy.

Gonna Rise Up in the Kingdom (spiritual)—arr. Lena J. McLin. Neil A. Kjos. No. ED. GC 167. A cappella. Moderately easy.

High Barbary (sea chanty)—arr. Gregg Smith. G. Schirmer No. 50311420. A cappella. Tenor and baritone solos. Moderately difficult.

Incognito Young Man, The (Mexican folk song)—arr. Stan DeWitt. Aberdeen Music No. 1084. Accompanied. Medium.

Irish Shepherd's Psalm (traditional Irish)—arr. K. Lee Scott. Carl Fischer No. CM 8223. Organ or piano accompaniment. Easy.

I Want Two Wings (spiritual)—arr. Alice Parker. Jenson No. 43509062. A cappella. Medium.

Joshua Fit the Battle of Jerico (spiritual)—arr. Edwin Fissinger. Plymouth No. PCS-166. A cappella. Medium.

Just a Closer Walk with Thee (spiritual)—arr. James McLeod. Neil A. Kjos No. C8715. Dixieland band or piano accompaniment.

Kum Bah Ya (spiritual)—arr. Allen Koepke. CPP/Belwin No. 02524. A cappella. Moderately easy.

Little David Play on Your Harp (spiritual)—arr. John Leavitt. CPP/Belwin No. SV 9050. Optional accompaniment. Medium.

Londonderry Air (Irish folk tune)—arr. Phil Mattson. Neil A. Kjos No. C8923. Accompanied. Medium.

Lord, I Don't Feel No-ways Tired (spiritual)—arr. Phillip McIntyre. Mark Foster No. MF 2035. A cappella. Moderately easy.

Lord, I Want to Be a Christian (spiritual)—arr. Paul Christiansen. Augsburg Fortress No. 11-2449. A cappella. Moderately easy.

Oh Mary, Don't You Weep (spiritual)—arr. Donald Moore. CPP/Belwin No. SV 9059. Optional accompaniment. Medium.

Peace Like a River (spiritual)—arr. Philip E. Baker. Augsburg Fortress No. 11-2573. Accompanied. Easy.

Round Dance (Russian folk song)—arr. Patrick C. Williams. Plymouth Music No. PCS-180. Accompanied. Medium.

Shenandoah (American folk song)—arr. Gregg Smith. G. Schirmer No. 50310420. A cappella. Medium.

Sow Took the Measles, The (early 19th-century humorous Yankee farmer song)—arr. Walter Ehret. Tetra/Continuo No. TC 423. Accompanied. Easy.
Steal Away (spiritual)—arr. Paul Criswell. Carl Fischer No. CM 8265. Accompanied (piano or organ). Easy.
Swing Low, Sweet Chariot (spiritual)—arr. Philip M. Young. Beckenhorst Press No. BP 1355. Accompanied. Easy.
There Is a Balm in Gilead (spiritual)—arr. Carol Sams. Plymouth Music No. PCS-165 A *cappella*. Moderately easy.
Three German Folk song—arr. Bruce Chamberlain. Southern Music No. SC 138. A *cappella*. Medium.
Three Spirituals (1. You May Bury Me in the East, 2. Have You Got Good Religion, 3. Done Found My Lost Sheep)—arr. Phillip McIntyre. Augsburg Fortress No. 11-4519. Soprano or tenor and alto or bass solos. Medium.
Two Spirituals (1. Sometimes I Feel Like a Motherless Child, 2. Deep River)—arr. Robert Fountain. Neil A. Kjos No. C 8907. A *cappella*. Medium.
Walk in Jerusalem Just Like John (spiritual)—arr. Donald P. Moore. Mark Foster No. MF 288. Accompanied. Easy.
Water Is Wide, The (American folk song)—arr. Roger Folstrom. Mark Foster No. MF 3027. A *cappella*. Medium.
WereYouThere? (spiritual)—arr. Richard Felciano. E. C. Schirmer No. 4061. A *cappella*. Easy.

Folks Songs and Spirituals (Standard/Traditional Music)

Ain'-a That Good News? (spiritual)—arr. William T. Dawson. Kjos No. T103. A *cappella*. Moderately easy.
All Beauty within You (Italian love song)—arr. Riley. Music 70 No. M70-261. Accompanied. Moderately easy.
All My Trials, Lord (spiritual)—arr. Warren Swenson. Galaxy No. 1.2824.1. Accompanied. Moderately easy.
Ash Grove, The (Welsh air)—arr. Jacob. Oxford No. F9. A *cappella*. Easy.
Black Is the Color of My True Love's Hair (Appalachian folk song)—arr. Churchill. Shawnee Press. Accompanied. Moderately easy.
Carmela (traditional Mexican song)—arr. Schillio. Theodore Presser No. 312-40740. Accompanied. Easy.
Charlottown (southern folk song)—arr. Bryan. J. Fischer No. 8136. A *cappella*. Medium.
Chilly Waters (spiritual)—arr. Roberton. Curwen No. 61420. A *cappella*. Easy.
Ching-A-Ring Chaw (minstrel song)—arr. Aaron Copland and Irving Fine. Boosey & Hawkes No. 5024. Accompanied Medium.
Cicirinella (Italian folk song)—arr. Max T. Krone. Witmark No. 5-W2592. Accompanied. Easy.
Cindy (American folk song)—arr. Walter Ehret. Presser No. 312-41186. Accompanied. Easy.
Climbin' up the Mountain (spiritual)—arr. Smith. Kjos No. 1001. A *cappella*. Easy.
Czechoslovakian Dance Song—arr. Max T. Krone. Witmark No. 5-W2608. Optional accompaniment. Moderately easy.
Dance to Your Daddie (Scottish nursery song)—arr. Edmund Rubbra. Belwin Mills No. 322. A *cappella*. Moderately easy.
Dark-Eyed Sailor, The (English folk song)—arr. Ralph Vaughan Williams. Galaxy No. 128. A *cappella*. Medium.
Deer Chase, The (American folk song)—arr. Norman Luboff. Walton No. W3053. Accompanied. Moderately easy.
Didn't My Lord Deliver Daniel? (spiritual)—arr. Ralph Hunter. Lawson-Gould No. 957. Accompanied. Moderately easy.
Drei Volkslieder (Three folk songs)—arr. Felix Mendelssohn. European American No. EA 413. A *cappella*. Medium.
The Drunken Sailor (sea chantey)—arr. Schumann and Erickson. Boume No. C3004. A *cappella*. Medium.

Each Little Flower (Swedish folk melody)—arr. Lundquist. Elkan-Vogel No. 1150. *A cappella*. Easy.

Early One Morning (English folk song)—arr. Van Christy. Schmitt, Hall & McCreary No. 1115. A *cappella*. Moderately easy.

Elijah Rock (spiritual)—arr. Jester Hairston. Boume No. S 1017. Optional accompaniment. Medium.

Every Time I Feel de Spirit (spiritual)—arr. Murray. Boosey & Hawkes No. 1737. Accompanied. Moderately easy.

Ezekiel Saw the Wheel (spiritual)—arr. Harry Simeone. Shawnee Press No. 0130. Accompanied. Moderately difficult.

Farewell (Swedish folk song)—arr. Norman Luboff. Walton No. W3095. *A cappella*. Moderately easy.

The Farmer's Daughters (traditional English)—arr. Williams. G. Schirmer No. 8116. *A cappella*. Easy.

Fireflies (Russian)—arr. Henry Clough-Leighter. E. C. Schirmer No. 1178. *A cappella*. Easy.

Frankie and Johnny (traditional)—arr. Robert De Cormier. Lawson Gould No. 52040. *A cappella*. Soprano, alto, tenor, and baritone solos. Medium.

Gay Fiesta (Mexican folk song)—arr. Riegger. Flammer No. 81149. Accompanied. Moderately easy.

Gentle Annie—Stephen Foster, arr. Eliot. Beckenhorst Press No. BP 113. Accompanied. Easy.

Gently, Johnny, My Jingalo (English folk song)—arr. Alice Parker and Robert Shaw. Lawson-Gould No. 643. *A cappella*. Moderately easy.

The Girl with the Buckles on Her Shoes (Irish traditional)—arr. Nelson. G. Schirmer No. 10968. Accompanied. Moderately easy.

Good Night (German folk song)—arr. Manney. Wood No. 292. Accompanied. Moderately easy.

Goodnight Ladies (college song)—arr. Norman Luboff. Walton No. W3097. *A cappella*. Moderately easy.

The Great Angelic Host (Norwegian folk song)—arr. Edvard Grieg. Carl Fischer No. CM 530. A *cappella*. Medium.

Hawaiian Lullaby—arr. Malcolm Sargent. Oxford No. X85. *A cappella*. Medium.

Ho-La-Hi (German folk song)—arr. Fiske. Oxford No. F53. *A cappella*. Easy.

How Good It Is (Hebrew folk song)—arr. Maurice Goldman. Lawson-Gould No. 51821. Accompanied. Moderately easy.

Itca's Castle (Czechoslovakian folk song)—arr. Harley-Aschenbrenner. Carl Fischer No. CM 4708. *A cappella*. Easy.

I Know My Love (Irish folk song)—arr. Alice Parker and Robert Shaw. Lawson-Gould No. 657. Accompanied. Moderately easy.

I'm Goin' to Sing (spiritual)—arr. Alice Parker and Robert Shaw. Lawson-Gould No. 51101. A *cappella*. Moderately easy.

In Dat Great Gittin' Up Mornin' (African-American folk song)—arr. Jester Hairston. Bourne No. B206516-357. *A cappella*. Tenor solo. Moderately easy.

I Ride an Old Paint—arr. Houston Bright. Shawnee Press No. A-661. *A cappella*. Moderately easy.

Island Sheiling Song, An (folk song from the Hebrides)—arr. Arch. Boosey & Hawkes No. 5669. A *cappella*. Moderately easy.

I Sowed the Seeds of Love (Hampshire folk song)—arr. Gustav Holst. G. Schirmer No. 11149. A *cappella*. Medium.

I Won't Kiss Katy (Yugoslavian folk song)—arr. Smith and Aschenbrenner. Carl Fischer No. CM4596. *A cappella*. Moderately difficult.

Jacob's Ladder (spiritual)—arr. Harry R. Wilson. Ricordi No. NY1476. Optional accompaniment. Moderately easy.

Jesus on the Water Side (spiritual)—arr. Walter Aschenbrenner. Fitzsimons No. 1032. A *cappella*. Moderately difficult.

Jesus Walked This Lonesome Valley (spiritual)—arr. Harris. Music 70 No. M70-361. *A cappella*. Easy.

Just as the Tide Was Flowing (English folk song)—arr. Ralph Vaughan Williams. Galaxy No. 1.5020.1 *A cappella*. Medium.

The Keys of My Heart (North country traditional song)—arr. Warrell. G. Schirmer No. 8474. A *cappella*. Moderately easy.

The Lark on the Morn (folk song from *Sommersetshire*)—arr. Randall Thompson. E. C. Schirmer No. 1782. *A cappella.* Easy.

Linden Lea (old English folk song)—Ralph Vaughan Williams, arr. Salter. Boosey & Hawkes No. 1401. Accompanied. Moderately easy.

Little Duck in the Meadow (Russian folk song)—arr. Nikolsky. G. Schirmer No. 6669. *A cappella.* Moderately easy.

Marching to Pretoria (South African song)—arr. Marais and Abbott. G. Schirmer No. 10423. Four-hand piano accompaniment. Easy.

Mary Had a Baby (spiritual)—arr. William Dawson. Kjos No. T118. *A cappella.* Moderately easy.

Mayday Carol (English folk song)—arr. Deems Taylor. J. Fischer No. 4838. Accompanied. Moderately easy.

Miner's Lament (Tune: Lilly Dale)—arr. Robert De Cormier. Lawson-Gould No. 51975. *A cappella.* Moderately easy.

Moan to the Moon (Estonian folk song)—arr. Ralph Hunter. Lawson-Gould No. 954. Accompanied. Moderately easy.

Morning Now Beckons (Czechoslovakian folk song)—arr. Manney. Wood No. 355. Accompanied. Easy.

My Lord, What a Mornin' (spiritual)—arr. Henry T. Burleigh. Ricordi No. 412. *A cappella.* Medium.

My Pretty Little Pink (American folk song)—arr. Barthelson. Lawson-Gould No. 792. Accompanied. Moderately easy.

Nine Hundred Miles from Home (Appalachian Mountain folk song)—arr. Schillio. Associated No. A-712. Accompanied. Moderately easy.

Oh, Dear! What Can the Matter Be? (English folk song)—arr. Bantock. Joseph Williams, Ltd. No. 19. *A cappella.* Moderately easy.

Oh! Susanna—Stephen Foster, arr. Hayes. Shawnee Press No. A-1745. Accompanied. Moderately easy.

Oh, What a Beautiful City (spiritual)—arr. William Dawson. Kjos No. T100. *A cappella.*

The Old Woman and the Peddler (old English)—arr. Kinscella. G. Schirmer No. 7819. *A cappella.* Moderately easy.

Peasant and His Oxen (Yugoslavian folk song)—arr. Smith and Aschenbrenner. Carl Fischer No. 4595. *A cappella.* Medium.

Prince Charlie's Farewell (traditional English air)—arr. Robertson. G. Schirmer No. 8512. *A cappella.* Moderately easy.

A Red, Red Rose (Scottish folk tune)—arr. Alice Parker and Robert Shaw. Lawson-Gould No. 645. *A cappella.* Tenor solo. Medium.

Ride the Chariot (spiritual)—arr. Smith. Kjos No. 1015. Optional accompaniment. Medium.

Rock-a My Soul (spiritual)—arr. De Vaux. Bourne No. B-211128. Accompanied. Moderately easy.

Russian Picnic (based on Russian folk tunes)—arr. Harvey Enders. G. Schirmer No. 9544. Accompanied. Moderately easy.

Saenu (Yemenite melody)—arr. Davidson. Transcontinental No. 990744. Optional accompaniment. Moderately easy.

Sakura Sakura (Japanese folk song)—arr. Jester Hairston. Bourne No. J1. Optional accompaniment. Moderately easy.

See the Gipsies (Hungarian folk song)—arr. Zoltán Kodály. Oxford No. X61. *A cappella.* Medium.

Shenandoah (sea chantey)—arr. Moore. Mark Foster No. MF 3011. Optional accompaniment. Moderately easy.

She's Like the Swallow (Newfoundland folk song)—arr. Chapman. Oxford No. X64. *A cappella.* Moderately easy.

Silver Moon Is Shining, The (Italian folk song)—arr. Katherine K. Davis. E. C. Schirmer No. 1754. *A cappella.* Moderately easy.

Soon-Ah Will Be Done (spiritual)—William Dawson. Kjos No. T102. Optional accompaniment. Medium.

The Spring of the Year (English folk song)—arr. Ralph Vaughan Williams. Galaxy No. 129. *A cappella.* Moderately easy.

S'vivon (The Top)—arr. Helfman. Transcontinental No. 991501. *A cappella.* Moderately easy.

Tchum Bi-Ri Tchum (Israeli folk tune)—arr. Goldman. Lawson-Gould No. 51888. Accompanied. Moderately easy.

Tender Love (Cajun folk song)—arr. Norman Luboff. Walton No. 3070. Accompanied. Moderately easy.

There Is a Balm in Gilead (spiritual)—arr. William L. Dawson. Kjos No. T105. A cappella. Soprano solo. Medium.

There's a Lit'l' Wheel a-Turnin' in My Heart (spiritual)—arr. William L. Dawson. Kjos No. T121. A cappella. Medium.

Tomorrow Shall Be My Dancing Day (traditional English carol)—arr. Willcocks. Oxford No. 84.141. A cappella. Medium.

The Turtle Dove (English folk song)—arr. Ralph Vaughan Williams. G. Schirmer No. 8105. A cappella. Baritone solo. Moderately easy.

Twenty Eighteen (English folk song)—arr. Deems Taylor. J. Fischer No. 4846. Accompanied. Easy.

Two Macedonian Folk song—arr. Srebotnjak. G. Schirmer No. 11315. A cappella. Moderately easy.

Two Negro Spirituals (Deep River and Dig My Grave)—arr. Henry T. Burleigh. G. Schirmer No. 5815. A cappella. Medium.

Wade in the Water (spiritual)—arr. Kirk. Carl Fischer No. CM 8022. A cappella. Solo. Easy.

Waltzing Matilda (Australian song)—arr. Cowan-Wood. Oxford No. OCS 790. A cappella. Medium.

Waters Ripple and Flow (Czechoslovakian folk song)—arr. Deems Taylor. J. Fischer No. 5675. Accompanied. Soprano and baritone solos. Moderately difficult.

Weep, O Willow (mountain tune)—arr. Sven Lekberg. Summy-Birchard No. 5009. A cappella. Soprano solo. Medium.

The Well-Beloved (Armenian folk song)—arr. Deems Taylor. J. Fischer No. 4844. Accompanied. Soprano solo. Moderately easy.

When Love Is King (English folk song)—arr. Salli Terri. Lawson-Gould No. 843. A cappella. Moderately easy.

When the Saints Go Marching In (spiritual)—arr. Norman Luboff. Walton No. 3068. Accompanied. Moderately easy.

Ya Ba Bom (Jewish folk tune)—arr. Goldman. Lawson-Gould No. 51814. Piano accompaniment, with optional string bass and drums. Medium.

Yarmouth Fair (English folk song)—arr. Warlock-Gibbs. Oxford No. X37. A cappella. Moderately easy.

Zum Gali (Israeli folk tune)—arr. Maurice Goldman. Lawson-Gould No. 52026. Accompanied. Medium.

General: Sacred (More Recently Published Music)

Adoramus Te—Orlando di Lasso, ed. John B. Haberlen. Mark Foster No. MF. 921. A cappella. Easy.

Agnus Dei—Hans Leo Hassler, ed. Rod Walker. CPP/Belwin No. SV8918. A cappella. Easy.

Agnus Dei—Orlando di Lasso, arr. Robert S. Hines. Music 70 No. M70-589. A cappella. Easy.

Agnus Dei (from Missa Simile est Regnum coelerum)—Tomas Luis de Vittoria, ed. Walter Ehret. European American No. B. 232. A cappella. Medium.

All Earth, Sing Forth Your Joyful Praise (Laudate Nomen Domini) Christopher Tye, ed Hal H. Hopson. Ausburg Fortress No. 11-4676. Optional accompaniment. Easy.

Alleluia—Jacobus Gallus (Jacob Handl), ed. Daniel Pinkham. E. C. Schirmer No. 3007. For double chorus, A cappella. Moderately difficult.

Alleluia! Christus Surrexit—Felice Anerio, ed. Percy M. Young. Broude Brothers No. MGC 43. A cappella. Moderately difficult.

Almighty and Everlasting God—Orlando Gibbons, ed. James McKelvy. Mark Foster No. MF 2032. A cappella. Moderately easy.

Amazing Grace—W. Walker, arr. Richard Wienhorst. Mark Foster No. MF 2010. Two flutes or keyboard. Moderately easy.

And Peace Attend Thee—Daniel Pinkham. E.C. Schirmer No. 4036. Organ or piano accompaniment. Medium.

Ave Maria—Tomas Luis da Victoria, arr. Max T. Krone. M. Witmark No. 2712. A cappella. Medium.

Be Ye Sure That the Lord, He Is God (from *Utrecht Jubilate*)—George Frideric Handel, arr. Walter Ehret. Carl Fischer No. CM 8295. Accompanied. Medium.

Break Forth into Song—Allen Pote. Hope No. A 639. Keyboard and optional percussion. Moderately easy.

Break Out Shouting Joy (Psalm 100)—Paul Lisicky. World Library No. 7993. Cantor and piano. Moderately easy.

Call to Remembrance—James Nares, ed. Percy M. Young. Broude No. MGC 48. Organ accompaniment. Moderately difficult.

Cantate Domino—Giuseppe Ottavio Pitoni, ed. Patrick M. Liebergen. Carl Fischer No. CM 8274. *A cappella*. Moderately easy.

Cantate Domino—Z. Randall Stroope. Mark Foster No. MF 2016. *A cappella*, with tambourine. Moderately difficult.

Cantique de Jean Racine—Gabriel Fauré, ed. James Laughlin. Tetra/Continuo No. TC 882. Accompanied. Medium.

Christ Is the King—Melchior Vulpius, arr. Carolyn Jennings. Neil A. Kjos No. ED C8702. Organ and optional trumpet. Moderately easy.

Come Sunday (from *Black, Brown and Beige*)—Duke Ellington, arr. Alice Parker. G. Schirmer No. 50481495. Alto solo. Accompanied. Medium.

Confitebor Tibi—Johann Adolf Hasse, ed. Martin Banner. Carl Fischer. No. CM 8271. Accompanied. Medium.

De Profundis—Johann Georg Albrechtsberger, ed. Martin Banner. Carl Fischer No. CM 8316. Accompanied. Moderately difficult.

Dona Nobis Pacem—Franz Schubert, arr. Carl J. Nygard. Beckenhorst No. BP 1359. Accompanied. Easy.

Factus Est Dominus—Orlando di Lasso. Arista No. AE 306. *A cappella*. Medium.

Gaude Maria Virgo—Tomas Luis de Victoria, ed. James McKelvy. Mark Foster No. MF 153. *A cappella*. Medium.

Gloria (from the *Heiligmesse*)—Franz Joseph Haydn, ed. Bennett Williams. Plymouth No. FS-104. Accompanied. Easy.

Gloria in Excelsis (from *Gloria*)—Antonio Vivaldi, ed. Mason Martens. Walton No. W2043. Medium.

The Glory of This Day—Daniel Moe. Augsburg Fortress No. 11-0542. *A cappella*. Medium.

Glory to God (from *Judas Maccabaeus*)—George Frideric Handel, arr. Noel Goemanne. Neil A. Kjos No. ED. GC149. Organ accompaniment. Easy.

Grieve Not the Holy Spirit of God—John Stainer, ed. James McKelvy. Mark Foster No. MF 2029. Optional accompaniment. Medium.

Holy Wings (Swedish hymn)—arr. Bradley Ellingboe. Curtis No. C 9001. *A cappella*. Moderately easy.

How Beautiful Are the Feet (from *Messiah*)—George F. Handel, arr. Arthur Frackenpohl. Mark Foster No. MF 566. Accompanied. Easy.

If Ye Love Me, Keep My Commandments—Thomas Tallis, ed. Brian Busch. CPP/Belwin No. 02515. *A cappella*. Moderately easy.

In Thee, O Lord, Do I Put My Trust (In Te Domine Speravi)—Heinrich Schutz, arr. John Kingsburg. Plymouth No. SC 117. Accompanied. Medium.

In You Is Gladness (In Dir Ist Freude)—Giovanni Gastoldi, ed. Edward W. Klammer. G.I.A. No. G-3526. *A cappella*. Moderately easy.

In Virtute Tua—Grzegorz G. Gorczycki, ed. William Bausano. Mark Foster No. MF 2008. Organ and two violins. Moderately difficult.

Jesus, the Christ, Is Risen Today—George F. Handel, arr. Hal H. Hopson. Hope No. AA 1687. Accompanied. Moderately easy.

Jubilate (O Be Joyful)—Wolfgang Amadeus Mozart, ed. Patrick M. Liebergen. Carl Fischer No. CM 8324. Accompanied. Medium.

Jubilate Deo (Alleluia! Praise God)—Orlando di Lasso, ed. Elwood Coggin. Lawson-Gould No. 52438. *A cappella*. Moderately easy.

Justice, O God (Richte Mich, Gott)—Felix Mendelssohn, ed. Kenneth Jennings. Neil A. Kjos No. ED 8694. *A cappella*. Medium.

Kyrie (from *Mass in C Major*)—Ludwig van Beethoven, ed. K. Lee Scott. Carl Fischer No. CM 8213. Accompanied. Medium.

Kyrie—Jacob Handl, ed. Rod Walker, CPP/Belwin No. SV8738. *A cappella*. Moderately easy.

Kyrie, K. 341—Wolfgang Amadeus Mozart, ed. Jonathan Barnhart. E. C. Schirmer No. 4131. Accompanied. Medium.

Kyrie (from *Missa: O quam gloriosum*)—Tomas Luis de Victoria, ed. Robert S. Hines. Plymouth No. SC 52 *A cappella*. Medium.

Kyrie Eleison (Lord Have Mercy on Us)—Hans Leo Hassler, ed. Patrick M. Liebergen. Carl Fischer No. CM 8325. *A cappella*. Medium.

Laudate Dominum (O Praise the Lord, Our God)—Hans Leo Hassler, ed. Patrick M. Liebergen. Tetra/Continuo No. TC 1104. Optional accompaniment. Moderately difficult.

Laudate Dominum (Praise Ye the Lord with Song)—Giuseppe Ottavio Pitoni, ed. Patrick M. Liebergen. Carl Fischer No. CM 8255. *A cappella*. Moderately easy.

Lift Up Your Heads—Samuel Coleridge-Taylor, ed. William Tortolano. Broude Bros. No. CR 61. Organ accompaniment. Medium.

Lo, How a Rose E'er Blooming (Rhineland folk melody)—Johannes Brahms, arr. Arthur Frackenpohl. Mark Foster No. MF 563. Accompanied. Moderately easy.

Lord, Have Mercy Upon Us (Kyrie Eleison) from *Mass in C*—Ludwig van Beethoven, ed. John Kingsbury. Plymouth No. PCS-175. Accompanied. Medium.

Magnificat—George Christoph Wagenseil, ed. Martin Banner. Carl Fischer No. CM 8293. Accompanied. Medium.

Mi Zeh Y'maleil—Joshua R. Jacobson. Transcontinental No. 992016. Baritone solo. Tof (an Arab clay drum) and tambourine accompaniment. Medium.

My Peace I Leave with You—Ludwig van Beethoven, arr. Lon Beery. Beckenhorst No. BP 1329. Accompanied. Easy.

Natus Est Nobis—Jacob Handl. Arista No. AE 286. *A cappella*. Medium.

Now Thank We All Our God (from *A Psalm of Thanksgiving*)—Randall Thompson. E. C. Schirmer No. 4008. Accompanied (keyboard or orchestra). Moderately easy.

Nunc Dimittis—Josquin des Prez, ed. James Erb. Lawson-Gould No. 52251. *A cappella*. Medium.

O Bone Jesu (O Blessed Jesus)—Giovanni Pierluigi Da Palestrina, ed. Patrick M. Liebergen. Carl Fischer No. CM 8299. *A cappella*. Easy.

O Bread of Life from Heaven—Heinrich Isaac, ed. Hal H. Hopson. Carl Fischer No. CM 8206. Optional accompaniment. Moderately easy.

O Lamb of God—Gunther Schuller. Margun No. MM-26. *A cappella*, with optional organ or piano accompaniment. Difficult.

O Lord, We Beseech Thee—Thomas Attwood, ed. Percy M. Young. Broude Bros. No. MGC 44. Organ accompaniment. Medium.

O Magnum Mysterium—Jacob Handl, ed. Vahe Aslanian. Lawson-Gould No. 51893. Double chorus *A cappella*. Moderately difficult.

O Spirit of the Living God—Gunther Schuller. Margun No. MM-27. *A cappella*, with optional organ or piano accompaniment. Moderately difficult.

O Vos Omnes (O Ye People)—Pablo Casals. Tetra/Continuo No. TC 1103. *A cappella*. Moderately easy.

Psalm 148—Gustav Holst. Galaxy No. 1.5015. Organ and strings, or brass choir accompaniment. Moderately difficult.

Requiem—Giacomo Puccini. Ricordi No. 50481477. Organ accompaniment, with solo viola. Medium.

Requiem Aeternam—Giovanni B. Pergolesi, ed. James McCray. Music 70 No. M70-610. Accompanied. Medium.

Resonet in Laudibus (Let Praise Sound from Heav'n on High)—Orlando di Lasso, ed. Harold Schmidth C. F. Peters No. 6621. *A cappella*. Medium.

Salva Nos, Stella Maris (Save Us, Star of the Sea)—Cristobal de Morales, ed. Martin Banner. Lawson-Gould No. 51971. *A cappella*. Medium.

Sancta Maria, Succurre Miseris (Holy Mother, Succor the Wretched)—Tomas Luis de Victoria, ed. Martin Banner. Lawson-Gould No. 51980. *A cappella*. Medium.

Sanctum Domini Dei Nomen Est (Lord, God, We Praise Thy Holy Name)—Antonio Caldara. E. C. Schirmer No. 3076. Optional organ accompaniment. Moderately difficult.

Sanctus (Holy Is the Lord)—Franz Schubert, ed. Don Craig. Plymouth No. CD-109. Optional accompaniment. Easy.

Sanctus—Tomas Luis de Victoria, ed. Robert S. Hines. Music 70 No. M70-212. *A cappella.* Medium.

Sanctus and Benefictus—Gioacchino Rossini, arr. Robert N. Roth. Tetra No. TC 1108. Soprano and tenor solos. Optional accompaniment. Medium.

Send Forth, O God, Thy Light and Truth—Henry Mollicone, E. C. Schirmer No. 3083. *A cappella.* Medium.

Sent Forth by God's Blessing (Welsh folk song)—Omer Westendorf, arr. John Schiavone. World Library No. 8517. Organ accompaniment with trumpet. Easy.

Serve the Lord with Gladness—Antonio Caldara, ed. Benjamin Suchoff. Plymouth No. SC-120. Accompanied. Easy.

Sheep May Safely Graze (from *Was mir behagt*)—J. S. Bach, arr. Julia Morgan. Beckenhorst No. BP 1369. Accompanied (piano and two flutes). Moderately easy.

Sheep May Safely Graze—J. S. Bach, arr. James Winfield. Somerset No. MW 1244. Accompanied (organ and two flutes). Moderately easy.

Si Consistant Adversum Me (Lord, from Thee Comes Our Strength)—Antonio Caldara. E. C. Schirmer No. 3075. Optional organ accompaniment. Moderately difficult.

Sicut Locutus Est (Sing Joyful Songs to God)—Johann Sebastian Bach, ed. Gerald R. Mack and Martha Banzhaf. Optional accompaniment. Medium.

Simeon's Song—Alexander Gretchaninov, arr. Curtis Hansen. Curtis No. C9018. *A cappella.* Medium.

Sing Dem Herrn—Michael Praetorius, arr. Wallace DePue. CPP/Belwin No. SV8640. *A cappella.* Medium.

So Are They Blest Who Fear the Lord—George Friedrich Handel, arr. Robert S. Hines. Neil A. Kjos. No. ED 8699. Accompanied. Medium.

Sound the Trumpet (from *Miryams Siegesgesang*)—Franz Schubert, arr. Hal H. Hopson. Carl Fischer No. CM 8321. Piano accompaniment, with optional Bb trumpet. Medium.

Tenebrae Factae Sunt—Marc Antonio Ingegneri, ed. Harold A. Decker. National Music No. 140. *A cappella.* Moderately easy.

Tenebrae Factae Sunt—Carl Friedrich Zelter. E. C. Schirmer No. 4121. *A cappella.* Moderately easy.

Thine, O Lord—Craig Courtney. Beckenhorst No. BP 1276. Accompanied. Moderately easy.

Timor et Tremor (Trembling and Terror)—Orlando Di Lasso, ed. Maynard Klein. G. Schirmer No. 12129. *A cappella.* Medium.

Tu Es Petrus—Giovanni Pierluigi da Palestrina. Arista No. AE 378. *A cappella.* Medium.

Tu Es Petrus—Giovanni Pierluigi da Palestrina. National Music No. RCS-100-9. *A cappella.* Medium.

Twelve Canticles—Randall Thompson. E. C. Schirmer.
    1. Praise Ye the Lord. No. 4100.
    2. God Is a Spirit
    3. When Thou Liest Down. No. 4101.
    4. My Grace Is Sufficient. No. 4102.
    5. The Old and the Young.
    6. I Call to Remembrance. No. 4103
    7. Arise, Shine.
    8. The Past of the Just. No. 4104.
    9. Face Answereth to Face.
    10. Fear Thou Not. No. 4105
    11. Farewell.
    12. Amen. No. 4106
    All are of medium difficulty.

Veni Creator Spiritus—Johann Micheal Haydn, ed. Martin Banner. Carl Fischer No. CM 8317. Accompanied. Medium.

When the Stars Are Gone—Henry Mollicone. E. C. Schirmer No. 4510. Accompanied. Easy.

Whoso Dwelleth under the Defence of the Most High (from *The Company of Heaven*)—Benjamin Britten. Farber Music No. 50481206. A *cappella*. Difficult.

General: Sacred (Standard/Traditional Music)

Absalom—Thomas Tomkins. Chappell No. 6140. A *cappella*. Medium.

Adoramus Te—Jacopo Corsi, arr. Greyson. Bourne No. ES15. A *cappella*. Moderately easy.

Adoramus Te—Francesco Gasparini. Belwin Mills No. 2148. A *cappella*. Medium.

Adoramus Te—Orlandus Lassus. Music Press No. MP-76. A *cappella*. Medium.

Adoramus Te—W. A. Mozart. G. Schirmer No. 9932. Optional accompaniment. Moderately easy.

Adoramus Te, Christe—Giovanni Pierluigi da Palestrina. Carl Fischer No. CM 6578. A *cappella*. Easy.

Agnus Dei (Lamb of God)—Orlando di Lasso. Raymond A. Hoffman No. R-2002. A *cappella*. Moderately easy.

Agnus Dei—Hans Leo Hassler. Shawnee Press No. A-1482. A *cappella*. Easy.

Agnus Dei—Antonio Lotti. Edw. B. Marks No. 4365. A *cappella*. Moderately easy.

Agnus Dei—Thomas Morley, arr. Greyson. Bourne No. ES36. A *cappella*. Medium.

Agnus Dei—Giovanni Pergolesi. Mercury No. MC 147. Accompanied. Medium.

Agnus Dei (from *Deutsche Messe*)—Franz Schubert. Piedmont No. 4449. Accompanied. Medium.

Agnus Dei—Tomas Luis de Victoria. Lawson-Gould No. 925. A *cappella*. Medium.

All Breathing Life (from the motet *Sing Ye to the Lord*)—J. S. Bach. G. Schirmer No. 7470. Optional accompaniment. Difficult.

Alleluia (from the motet *Exsultate, Jubilate*)—W. A. Mozart, arr. Rosenberg. Carl Fischer No. CM 541. Accompanied. Medium. (Soprano solo, difficult.)

Alleluia—Randall Thompson. E. C. Schirmer No. 1786. A *cappella*. Moderately difficult.

Alleluia—J. S. Bach. C. F. Peters No. 6106a. Accompanied. Medium.

Alleulia, Alleulia—Dietrich Buxtehude. Presser No. 312-40668. Accompanied. Medium.

All Glory Be to God on High (melody of Gregorian origin)—arr. Don Malin. Summy-Birchard No. 345. Accompanied. Moderately easy.

All Hail the Power—Ralph Vaughan Williams. Oxford. Accompanied. Moderately difficult.

All the Earth Doth Worship Thee—G. F. Handel. Ricordi No. NY2030. Accompanied. Moderately easy.

All This Night—Gerald Finzi. Boosey & Hawkes No. 5127. A *cappella*. Medium.

Almighty and Everlasting God—Orlando Gibbons. Bourne No. ES35. A *cappella*. Moderately easy.

Almighty Father (Chorale from *Mass*)—Leonard Bernstein. G. Schirmer No. 11948. A *cappella*. Moderately easy.

Almighty God, Who Hast Me Brought—Thomas Ford. C. F. Peters No. 1558. A *cappella*. Moderately easy.

Amen—Alessandro Scarlatti, arr. Walter Ehret. European American No. EA 231. Organ or piano accompaniment. Moderately easy.

And Draw a Blessing Down (from *Theodora*)—G. F. Handel, arr. Don Malin. Edw. B. Marks No. 4535. Accompanied. Medium.

The Angelic Greeting—Johannes Brahms, ed. Mattfeld. E. C. Schirmer No. 2477. A *cappella*. Medium.

Ave Christe, Immolate—Josquin Desprez. Éditions Salabert No. MC 531. A *cappella*. Medium.

Ave Maria—J. S. Bach-Charles F. Gounod, arr. Tolmadge. Staff No. 243. Accompanied. Easy.

Ave Maria—Johannes Brahms. C. F. Peters No. 66136. Accompanied. Medium.

Ave Maria—Anton Bruckner. Edw. B. Marks No. 47. A *cappella*. Moderately easy.

Ave Maria—Cesar Franck, arr. Borucchia. McLaughlin & Reilly No. 1072. Organ accompaniment. Moderately easy.

Ave Maria—Jean Mouton. Music Press No. DCS 40. A *cappella*. Moderately easy.

Ave Maria—Sergei V. Rachmaninoff. Oliver Ditson No. 332-14564; Lawson-Gould No. 52344. A *cappella*. Medium.

Ave Maria—Peter 1. Tchaikovsky. Boston Music Co. No. 1064. A *cappella*. Moderately easy.

Ave Maria—Giuseppe Verdi. C. F. Peters No. 4256a. A *cappella*. Moderately difficult.

Ave Maria—Tomas Luis de Victoria. Music Press No. MP-79. *A cappella.* Moderately easy.

Ave Maria, gratia plena—Josquin Desprez. Associated No. 28. *A cappella.* Medium.

Ave Maria No. 20—Hector Villa-Lobos, new text by H. R. Wilson. Consolidated. *A cappella.* Medium.

Ave Maris Stella—Josquin Despréz. Associated No. 35. *A cappella.* Medium.

Ave Maris Stella—Hans Leo Hassler. Kjos No. 5012. *A cappella.* Moderately easy.

Ave Regina Coelorum—Orlandus Lassus. Associated No. A-406. *A cappella.* Medium.

Ave Regina Coelorum—Adrian Willaert. Ricordi No. NY1887. *A cappella.* Medium.

Ave verum corpus—William Byrd. Bourne No. ES44. *A cappella.* Moderately easy.

Ave verum corpus—W. A. Mozart. G. Schirmer No. 5471. Organ accompaniment. Moderately easy.

Awake the Harp (from *The Creation*)—Franz Joseph Haydn, ed. Neuen. Lawson Gould No. 51982. Accompanied. Medium.

Beautiful Savior (Silesian folk tune)—arr. F. M. Christiansen. Augsburg No. 51. *A cappella.* Medium.

Behold a Hallowed Day—Jacob Handl. Concordia No. 98-1690. *A cappella.* Medium.

Be Joyful, Be Joyful—Gottfried August Homilius. Sam Fox No. MM5. Accompanied. Moderately easy.

Benedixisti (Thou Hast Been Gracious, Lord)—Giovanni Gabrieli. G. Schirmer No. 7625. *A cappella.* Medium.

The Best of Rooms—Randall Thompson. E. C. Schirmer No. 2672. *A cappella.* Medium.

Blessed Are the Faithful—Heinrich Schütz, ed. Shaw and Speer. G. Schirmer No. 10114. *A cappella.* Moderately difficult.

Blessed Savior, Our Lord Jesus—Hans Leo Hassler. G. Schirmer No. 7563. *A cappella.* Medium.

Bless the Lord for Ever and Ever—W. A. Mozart, arr. Hilton. Mercury No. 352-00459. Accompanied. Moderately difficult.

Blest Be the Lord—Franz Joseph Haydn. McLaughlin & Reilly Co. No. 2217. Accompanied. Medium.

Brother James' Air (Marosa)—G. Jacob. Carl Fischer No. OCS763. *A cappella.* Easy.

Call to Mary—Johannes Brahms, ed. Mattfeld. E. C. Schirmer No. 2480. *A cappella.* Medium.

Call to Remembrance—Richard Farrant, arr. Greyson. Bourne No. ES 17. *A cappella.* Moderately easy.

Cantate Domino—Giuseppe Ottavio Pitoni. Bourne No. ES 5. *A cappella.* Moderately easy.

Cantate Domino—Heinrich Schütz. Arista No. AE 356; Bourne No. B201889. *A cappella.* Moderately difficult.

Cantique de Jean Racine—Gabriel Fauré. Broude Bros. No. 801. Accompanied. Moderately easy.

Cherubic Hymn (Greek liturgy)—arr. Aliferis. Witmark No. 5-W3063. *A cappella.* Moderately difficult.

Cherubim Song—Mikhail Glinka. Music 70 No. M70-423. *A cappella.* Moderately easy.

Cherubim Song—Alexander Gretchaninov, arr. Noble Cain. Hoffmann No. 46012A. *A cappella.* Medium.

Cherubim Song No. 3—Peter Ilich Tchaikovsky. G. Schirmer No. 2561. Piano or organ accompaniment. Moderately difficult.

Cherubim Song No. 7—Dimitri S. Bortniansky, arr. Tchaikovsky. G. Schirmer No. 2560. *A cappella.* Easy.

Christus factus est pro nobis—Anton Bruckner. C. F. Peters No. 6316. *A cappella.* Moderately difficult.

Clap Your Hands—David Eddleman. Cart Fischer No. CM 8039. Optional percussion. Moderately easy.

Come, Blessed Rest—J. S. Bach. Kjos No. 2004. *A cappella.* Medium.

Come, Then, O Holy Breath of God—Giovanni Pierluigi da Palestrina. Piedmont No. 4414. *A cappella.* Medium.

Come Let Us Start a Joyful Song—Hans Leo Hassler. Bourne No. ES 74. *A cappella.* Moderately easy.

Come Thou, O Savior—J. S. Bach. Summy-Birchard No. 5203. *A cappella.* Moderately easy.

Comfort All Ye My People—Gabriel Fauré, arr. Hopson. Carl Fischer No. CM 8017. Piano or organ accompaniment. Moderately easy.

Contentment—W. A. Mozart. Lawson-Gould No. 937. Accompanied. Soprano solo. Moderately easy.

Corporis mysterium (Sacrament of Priceless Worth)—Giovanni Pierluigi da Palestrina. Ricordi No. NY1852. A cappella. Moderately easy.

Create in Me, O God, a Pure Heart—Johannes Brahms, arr. Williamson. G. Schirmer No. 7504. A cappella. Moderately easy.

Crucifixus (from B. Minor Mass)—J. S. Bach. Hope Publishing Co. No. CY 3356; E. C. Schirmer No. 1174. Accompanied. Medium.

Crucifixus—W. A. Mozart. National Music Publishers No. WHC-141. Accompanied. Medium.

Dance Alleluia—Arnold Freed. Hansen Publications No. C566. Accompanied (piano, string bass, bongos, and wood block). Moderately easy.

David's Lamentation—William Billings. C. F. Peters No. 66336. Optional accompaniment. Moderately easy.

Day by Day We Magnify Thee—G. F. Handel. Lawson-Gould No. 797; Edw. B. Marks No. 4516. Accompanied. Medium.

De profundis (Out of the Deep)—Randall Thompson. Weintraub. A cappella. Moderately difficult.

Der Gott, unsers Herrn, Jesu Christi (To God, Our Lord and Saviour)—George Philipp Telemann. Lawson-Gould No. 52207. Accompanied. Medium.

Dies irae (from Requiem)—W. A. Mozart. G. Schirmer No. 10016. Accompanied. Medium.

Dies sanctificatus—Giovanni Pierluigi da Palestrina. National Music Publishers No. RCS-102. A cappella. Medium.

Dona nobis pacem—Ludwig van Beethoven. National Music Publishers No. WHS-143. A cappella. Medium.

Ehre sei Dir, Christe (Christ, Be Thine the Glory!)—Heinrich Schütz. G. Schirmer No. 10123. Optional accompaniment. Medium.

Et misericordia—Antonio Vivaldi, arr. Lee Kjelson. Belwin Mills No. 2236. Accompanied. Moderately easy.

Every Thing You Do—Dietrich Buxtehude. Sam Fox No. CM 19. Accompanied. Medium.

Exaltabo Te, Domine—Giovanni Pierluigi da Palestrina. G. Schirmer No. 7620. A cappella. Medium.

Exultate Deo (Sing and Praise Jehovah)—Giovanni Pierluigi da Palestrina. G. Schirmer No. 7672. A cappella. Medium.

Exultate Deo—Alessandro Scarlatti. G. Schirmer No. 11001. A cappella. Medium.

Exultate justi—Lodovico Viadana, ed. Maynard Klein. G.I.A. No. G-2140. A cappella. Medium.

Glaube, Hoffnung und Liebe (Faith, Hope and Love)—Franz Schubert. National Music Publishers No. NMP-185. Accompanied. Medium.

Gloria (from Mass No. 3 in G minor)—J. S. Bach. Gentry No. JG2021. Accompanied. Medium.

Gloria—Antonio Vivaldi. National Music Publishers No. NMP-132. Accompanied. Medium.

Gloria in excelsis (from Harmoniemesse)—Franz Joseph Haydn. Hal Leonard No. 08679600. Accompanied. Medium.

Gloria in excelsis—W. A. Mozart. G. Schirmer No. 3515. Accompanied. Medium.

Gloria—Only Begotten Son—Alexander Gretchaninov, arr. Tellep. Boosey & Hawkes No. 5097. A cappella. Medium.

Gloria Patri (Glory to God)—Giovanni Pierluigi da Palestrina, arr. Norman Greyson. Bourne No. ES46. A cappella. Easy.

Glory—Antonio Lotti. Edw. B. Marks No. 4366. A cappella. Moderately easy.

Glory and Honor Are Before Him—J. S. Bach. Kjos No. 5150. A cappella. Medium.

Glory and Worship—Henry Purcell. E. C. Schirmer No. 1108. Organ accompaniment. Moderately easy.

Glory Be to God—Sergei V. Rachmaninoff, arr. Tkach. Kjos No. 6528. A cappella. Medium.

Glory to God—J. S. Bach, ed. Harry R. Wilson. Ricordi No. NY1397. Optional accompaniment. Moderately difficult.

Glory to God—Dimitri S. Bortniansky. Witmark No. 5-W2743. A cappella. Moderately easy.

Glory to God—G. F. Handel. Lawson-Gould No. 796. Accompanied. Medium.

Glory to God in the Highest—Randall Thompson. E. C. Schirmer No. 2470. A cappella. Medium.

Graduale—Sancta Maria—W. A. Mozart. Broude Bros. No. 77. Accompanied. Medium.

Grant unto Me the Joy of Thy Salvation—Johannes Brahms. G. Schirmer No. 7506. *A cappella.* Moderately difficult.

Great and Glorious—Franz Joseph Haydn. Wood No. 316. Accompanied. Medium.

Haec dies—William Byrd. Oxford No. TCM 50. Optional accompaniment. Moderately difficult.

Hail, Thou Gladdening Light—Alexander Gretchaninov. Wood No. 594. *A cappella.* Moderately difficult.

Hail, Thou Holy One—Peter I. Tchaikovsky, arr. Noble Cain. Boosey & Hawkes No. 1979. *A cappella.* Medium.

Hallelujah (from *Mount of Olives*)—Ludwig van Beethoven. G. Schirmer No. 2215. Accompanied. Difficult.

Hallelujah—G. F. Handel. Music 70 No. M70-330. Accompanied. Medium.

Hallelujah, Amen (from *Judas Maccabaeus*)—G. F. Handel. G. Schirmer No. 9835. Optional accompaniment. Medium.

Hear, O Lord, Hear My Prayer—Orlando di Lasso, arr. Lundquist. Elkan—Vogel No. 1110. *A cappella.* Moderately easy.

Hear My Prayer—Alexander A. Kopylov. Boston Music Co. No. 1294. *A cappella.* Medium.

Hear Our Supplication—W. A. Mozart, arr. Hilton. Mercury. No. 352-00378. Accompanied. Medium.

Heavenly Light—Alexander A. Kopylov, arr. Peter J. Wilhousky. Carl Fischer No. CM 497. *A cappella.* Moderately easy.

The Heavens Are Declaring—Ludwig van Beethoven. G. Schirmer No. 3032. Accompanied. Easy.

The Heavens Are Telling (from *The Creation*)—Franz Joseph Haydn, arr. Phillips. Carl Fischer No. CM 127. Organ accompaniment. Moderately difficult.

Here Is Thy Footstool—Paul Creston. G. Schirmer No. 11146. *A cappella.* Medium.

He Shall Rule from Sea to Sea—Ned Rorem. Boosey & Hawkes No. 5651. Accompanied. Medium.

He Is Watching over Israel (from *Elijah*)—Felix Mendelssohn. G. Schirmer No. 2498. Accompanied. Moderately difficult.

He Who with Weeping Soweth—Heinrich Schütz. G. Schirmer No. 10115. Optional accompaniment. Moderately difficult.

Hide Not Thy Face, O My Savior (Finnish folk melody)—arr. Lundquist. Willis No. 8469. *A cappella.* Moderately easy.

Hodie nobis coelorum Rex—Houston Bright. Shawnee Press No. A-812. Accompanied. Medium.

Holy, Holy, Holy (Sanctus and Hosanna)—Franz Joseph Haydn. Mercury No. 352—00469. Accompanied. Moderately easy.

Holy, Holy, Holy (Sanctus)—Antonio Lotti. E. C. Schirmer No. 2216. *A cappella.* Medium.

Holy, Holy, Holy—Alessandro Scarlatti. Chappell No. 6141. *A cappella.* Medium.

Holy Is the Lord—Franz Schubert. Presser No. 312- 21416. Accompanied. Easy.

Honor and Glory—J. S. Bach. Plymouth No. SC10. Accompanied. Moderately easy.

Hosanna in excelsis Deo—Charles François Gounod. Gentry No. G-136. Accompanied. Medium.

Hospodi Pomilui—Alexis F. Lvov, ed. Peter J. Wilhousky. Carl Fischer No. CM 6580. *A cappella.* Medium.

How Lovely Is Thy Dwelling Place—Johannes Brahms. G. Schirmer No. 5124. Accompanied. Moderately difficult.

Humility before Thee—C. P. E. Bach, arr. Walter Ehret. Elkan-Vogel No. 1268. Piano or organ accompaniment. Medium.

The Hundredth Psalm—Felix Mendelsshon, ed. Hines. Concordia No. 98-2215. *A cappella.* Moderately Ncult.

Hymn to Saint Peter—Benjamin Britten. Boosey & Hawkes. Organ accompaniment. Soprano solo. Moderately difficult.

Hymn to the Trinity—Alexander A. Kopylov. Kjos No. 5337. *A cappella.* Easy.

If I Flew to the Point of Sunrise—Jean Berger. Kjos No. ED 5992. *A cappella.* Medium.

If Ye Love Me, Keep My Commandments—Thomas Tallis. E. C. Schirmer No. 2269. *A cappella.* Medium.

Incline Thine Ear, Oh Lord—Alexander Archangelsky. Witmark No. 5-W2689. *A cappella.* Medium.

In excelsis Deo (from *Mass in C*)—W. A. Mozart. Presser No. 312-41198. Accompanied. Medium.

In memoria aeterna (from *Beatus Vir*)—Antonio Vivaldi, ed. Doug McEwen. Hinshaw No. HMC-179. Accompanied. Medium.

In omnem terram—André Campra, arr. Conan Castle. Wood No. 44-964. Organ or piano accompaniment. Moderately difficult.

In Thee Is Joy—J. S. Bach. Somerset Press No. MW 1229. Accompanied. Moderately easy.

Iustorum animae—William Byrd. E. C. Schirmer No. 327. *A cappella.* Medium.

I Will Clothe Thy Priests with Salvation—Johann Fredrich Peter, arr. Kroeger. Boosey & Hawkes No. 6004. Accompanied. Medium.

Jesu, Joy of Man's Desiring—J. S. Bach. E. C. Schirmer No. 317. Organ accompaniment. Moderately easy.

Jesu dulcis memoria—Tomas Luis de Victoria. G. Schirmer No. 5573. *A cappella.* Easy.

Jesus, Now to Thee I Turn Me—Luigi Cherubini, arr. Lundquist. Elkan-Vogel No. 1159. *A cappella.* Easy.

Jubilate Deo—Orlandus Lassus. Mercury No. MP-80. *A cappella.* Moderately easy.

Jubilate Deo—W. A. Mozart. Pro Art No. 1007. *A cappella.* Moderately easy.

Justum deduxit Dominus (Lord, God Has Led the Righteous Man)—W. A. Mozart. Lawson-Gould No. 52137. Accompanied. Moderately difficult.

King of Glory—W. A. Mozart, ed Walter Ehret. Gentry No. G-345. Accompanied. Medium.

Kyrie—W. A. Mozart G. ed. Landon. G. Schirmer No. 12067. Accompanied. Medium.

Kyrie (from *Mass in G*)—Franz Schubert. Kjos No. ED 5989. Accompanied. Soprano solo. Medium.

Kyrie eleison—Francesco Durante. Pro Art No. 2279. *A cappella.* Moderately easy.

Kyrie eleison—Franz Joseph Haydn, arr. Walter Ehret. Heritage No. H 94. Accompanied. Moderately easy.

Lacrymosa—Luigi Cherubini, ed. De Pietto. Lawson Gould No. 51853. Accompanied. Medium.

Lacrymosa (from *Requiem*)—W. A. Mozart. G. Schirmer No. 10017. Accompanied. Medium.

Lasciatemi morire—Claudio Monteverdi. Ricordi No. NY841. *A cappella.* Moderately easy.

The Last Words of David—Randall Thompson. E. C. Schirmer No. 2294. Accompanied. Medium.

Laudate Dominum—Jan Pieterszoon Sweelinck. Concordia No. 97-5450. Optional accompaniment. Medium.

Laudate pueri—W. A. Mozart. Lawson-Gould No. 51166. Associated No. A-683. Accompanied. Medium.

Lend Thine Ear to My Prayer—Alexander Archangelsky, arr. Peter J. Wilhousky. Carl Fischer No. CM 613. *A cappella.* Moderately difficult.

Let All Mortal Flesh Keep Silence—Gustav Holst. Galaxy No. 3.2309.1. Accompanied. Medium. 3.2309.1. Accompanied. Medium.

Let Every Nation His Praises Sing—Cesar Franck. Sam Fox No. CM 20. *A cappella.* Medium.

Let My Prayer Come Up (Offertorium)—Henry Purcell. Gray No. 1527, Mercury No. 352-00440. Accompanied. Moderately easy.

Let Nothing Ever Grieve Thee—Johannes Brahms. C. F. Peters No. 6093. Accompanied. Moderately easy.

Let Their Celestial Concerts All Unite (from *Samson*)—G. F. Handel. E. C. Schirmer No. 312. Accompanied. Moderately difficult.

Let Thy Holy Presence—Paul G. Tchesnokov, arr. Noble Cain. Summy-Birchard No. 12. *A cappella.* Medium.

Libera me—Gabriel Fauré. Belwin Mills No. 2032. Accompanied. Medium.

Light the Legend (A Song for Chanukah)—Isaacson. Transcontinental No. 991024. Accompanied. Moderately easy.

Like As the Hart—Giovanni Pierluigi da Palestrina. G. Schirmer No. 3509. *A cappella.* Moderately easy.

Lo, I Am the Voice of One Crying in the Wilderness—Heinrich Schütz. G. Schirmer No. 10116. Optional accompaniment. Moderately difficult.

Locus iste a Deo factus est—Anton Bruckner. C. F. Peters No. 6314. *A cappella.* Easy.

Lord, Have Mercy upon Us—Ludwig van Beethoven. Chappell No. 6145. Accompanied. Moderately easy.

Lord, Hear Our Pryaer (from *Otello*)—Giuseppi Verdi, arr. Huguelet. Carl Fischer No. CM 616. Optional accompaniment. Medium.

Lord, How Lovely Is Your Dwelling Place—Alexander Gretchaninov, arr. Hal Hopson. Carl Fischer No. CM8214. *A cappella.* Medium.

Lord, Remember Not—Felix Mendelssohn. Walton No. 6010. Optional accompaniment. Medium.

Lord We Love the Place—Karl Heinrich Graun. Sam Fox No. MM 6. Accompanied. Medium.

The Lord Bless You and keep You—Peter Lutkin. Summy-Birchard No. 1089. *A cappella.* Easy.

Lord Christ, Son of God (Christe Dei Soboles)—Orlando di Lasso. G. Schirmer No. 9414 *A cappella.* Medium.

Lord God, in Power and Glory—Franz Joseph Haydn. Curwen No. 80782. Optional accompaniment. Moderately easy.

The Lord Is My Sheperd—Randall Thompson. E. C. Schirmer No. 2688. Accompanied. Moderately easy.

Lord of Love, to Thee I Flee—Peter Cornelius. Sam Fox No. MM 26. Accompanied. Medium.

The Lord Shall Be Unto Three (from *Requiem*)—Randall Thompson. E. C. Schirmer No. 2641. *A cappella.* Medium.

Lovely Appear (from *The Redemption*)—Charles Gounod. G. Schirmer No. 2013. Accompanied. Medium.

Magnificat—Giovanni Gabrieli. Curwen No. 10565. *A cappella.* Three choirs. Difficult.

Magnificat—My Soul Doth Magnify the Lord—Buxtehude. C. F. Peters No. 66288. Accompanied. Moderately difficult.

Magnificat and Nunc dimittis—Henry Purcell. C. F. Peters No. 66266. Optional accompaniment. Medium.

May We Ever Praise the Father—G. F. Handel. Lawson-Gould No. 52235. Optional accompaniment. Moderately easy.

A Mighty Fortress is Our God—Martin Luther. Witmark No. 5W2835. Optional accompaniment. Moderately easy.

Miserere mei—Antonio Lotti. Boosey & Hawkes No. 1938. *A cappella.* Easy.

Miserere mei—Giovanni Pergolesi. Walton No. 6011. Accompanied. Medium.

Mi Yemalel (Who Can Retell?)—Max Helfman. Transcontinental No. 991500. *A cappella.* Moderately easy.

My Heart Overflows—Harrer, ed. Frank. Sam Fox No. MM 1. Piano or organ accompaniment. Medium.

Ne irascaris—William Byrd. Alexander Broude No. 216-9. *A cappella.* Moderartely difficult.

Now God Be Praised in Heav'n Above—Melchoir Vulpius. E. C. Schirmer No. 1693. Optional accompaniment. Moderately easy.

O, Lord in Thee Have I Trusted—G. F. Handel., Kjos No. 5481 C. Accompanied. Medium.

O, Love Divine (from *Theodora*)—G. F. Handel, arr. Don Malin. Edw. B. Marks No. 4543. Accompanied. Moderately difficult.

O Be Joyful! (Freut Euch, Freut Euch)—W. A. Mozart. Sam Fox No. MM 9. Accompanied. Medium.

O Be Joyful in the Lord—John Rutter. Oxford No. A 346. Accompanied. Medium.

O Blessed Lord—Peter I. Tchaikovsky. Wallace Gillman No. 4001. Optional accompaniment. Moderately easy.

O bone Jesu—Giovanni Pierluigi da Palestrina. Oliver Ditson No. 332-03070. *A cappella.* Easy.

O Cast Me Not Away from Thy Countenance—Johannes Brahms. G. Schirmer No. 7505. *A cappella.* Moderately difficult.

O Clap Your Hands—Ralph Vaughan Williams. Galaxy No. 222. Organ accompaniment. Moderately difficult.

O Divine Redeemer—Charles Gounod, arr. Noble Cain. Schmitt, Hall & McCreary No. 1602. Accompanied. Moderately easy.

O Glorious One—Alexander Gretchaninov, arr. Noble Cain. Hoffman No. 46,339. *A cappella.* Moderately easy.

O God, I Thank Thee—Robert Schumann, arr. Lundquist. Willis No. 8466. *A cappella.* Easy.

O God Who Reigns in Heav'n Above—William Byrd, arr. Walter Ehret. Gentry No. JG-439. Optional accompaniment. Moderately easy.

Oh, Blest Are They—Peter I. Tchaikovsky, arr. Noble Cain. Remick No. 3024. *A cappella.* Moderately difficult.

O Hear Me When I Call on Thee—Franz Schubert. E. C. Schirmer No. 2684. Accompanied. Medium.

O Jesu, Salvator—Domenico Alberti, ed. Jack Boyd. Lawson-Gould No. 51843. Accompanied. Medium.

O Lord, Have Mercy on Us (Kyrie eleison)—Dietrich Buxtehude. Sam Fox No. CM 6. Optional accompaniment. Medium.

O Lord, Hear Thou My Prayer—Robert Schumann, arr. Maurice Goldman. Lawson-Gould No. 51968. Piano or organ accompaniment. Soprano solo. Medium..

O Lord Most Holy (Panis angelicus)—Cesar Franck. Summy-Birchard No. 396. Accompanied. Medium.

O magnum mysterium—Ned Rorem. Boosey & Hawkes No. 6006. *A cappella.* Medium.

O Mighty Hand (Dor Nifia)—Maurice Goldman. Transcontinental No. 991033. Organ or piano accompaniment. Moderately easy.

The Omnipotence—Franz Schubert. G. Schirmer No. 10146. Accompanied. Medium.

Once I Had Hoped from Thee—Philippe De Monte. Piedmont No. 4427. *A cappella.* Medium.

Onward, Ye Peoples!—Jean Sibelius, arr. Lefebvre. Galaxy No. 938- 10. Accompanied. Moderately easy.

O Rejoice, Ye Christians, Loudly—J. S. Bach, Carl Fischer No. CM 6600. *A cappella.* Moderately easy.

O Savior, Throw the Heavens Wide (*Motet*, Op. 74, No. 2)—Johannes Brahms. G. Schirmer No. 8545. *A cappella.* Moderately difficult.

O Sing unto the Lord—Hans Leo Hassler. G. Schirmer No. 10872. *A cappella.* Moderately easy.

O Sing unto the Lord—Henry Purcell. E. C. Schirmer No. 1103. Optional accompaniment. Moderately easy.

O Sing unto the Lord a New Song—Walter Piston. Associated No. A-640. Accompanied. Moderately difficult.

Os justi—Anton Bruckner. G. Schirmer No. 8121. *A cappella.* Medium.

Our Father—Alexander Gretchaninov, English text by Kimball. Presser No. 332-13000. *A cappella.* Moderately difficult.

Our Soul Doth Wait upon the Lord—John Antes, arr. Kroeger. Boosey & Hawkes No. 5941. Organ accompaniment. Medium.

O vos omnes—Francisco Correa. Lawson-Gould No. 52225. *A cappella.* Easy.

O vos omnes—Tomas Luis de Victoria. Ricordi No. NY1875. *A cappella.* Medium.

Pater Noster—Igor Stravinsky. Boosey & Hawkes No. 1833. *A cappella.* Medium.

Pater Noster (Our Father)—Peter I. Tchaikovsky. G. Schirmer No. 5475. *A cappella.* Moderately easy.

Plorate filii Israel (from *Jephtah*)—Giacomo Carissimi. Bourne No. ES 34; Kjos No. ED 29; E. C. Schirmer No. 1172. Accompanied. Medium.

Praise Be to Thee—Giovanni Pierluigi da Palestrina, arr. Lundquist. Willis No. 5678. *A cappella.* Easy.

Praise Him—J. S. Bach, arr. Steele. Raymond A. Hoffman No. H-2005. Accompanied. Moderately easy.

Praise Him, Praise Ye the Lord—Antonio Caldara, ed. Walter Ehret. Elkan-Vogel No. 362-03145. Piano or organ accompaniment. Soprano, alto, tenor, and bass solos. Moderately easy.

Praise the Lord in Song—Alessandro Constantini. Music 70 No. M70-341. *A cappella.* Moderately easy.

Praise Ye the Lord—James McCray. Music 70 No. M70-374. *A cappella.* Medium.

Prayer and Chorale—Felix Mendelssohn. Lawson-Gould No. 849. *A cappella.* Moderately easy.

Psallite—Hieronymus Praetorius, arr. Norman Greyson. Bourne No. ES 21. *A cappella.* Easy.

Psalm 43—Felix Mendelssohn. Hope Publishing Co. No. APM 006. *A cappella.* Medium.

Psalm 92—Franz Schubert. Alexander Broude No. AB 823. *A cappella.* Baritone solo. Moderately difficult.

Psalm CL (Praise Ye the Lord)—Cesar Franck. Oliver Ditson No. 332-14082. Organ accompaniment. Medium.

Psalm 150 (Hallelujah, Praise Ye the Lord)—Louis Lewandowski. Schmitt, Hall & McCreary No. 1640; Transcontinental No. 990792. Optional *A cappella.* Medium.
Psalm 61—Alan Hovhaness. C. F. Peters No. 6255. Organ accompaniment. Medium.
Quando corpus (from *Stabat Mater*)—Gioacchino Rossini, ed. Leonard van Camp. Music 70 No. 205. *A cappella.* Medium.
Rejoice in the Lord—David Amram. C. F. Peters No. 66517. *A cappella.* Medium.
Rejoice in the Lord Alway—Henry Purcell. Novello No. 1581. Accompanied. Moderately easy.
Religious Meditation—Hector Berlioz, ed. Prussing. Tetra No. AB 833. Organ accompaniment. Medium.
Requiescat—William Schuman. G. Schirmer No. 8926. Accompanied. Medium.
Salvation Is Created—Paul G. Tschesnokov, arr. Norden J. Fischer No. 4129. *A cappella.* Medium.
Salve Regina—Orlando di Lasso. Music Press No. MP-73. *A cappella.* Medium.
Sanctum Domini Dei nomen est—Antonio Caldara. E. C. Schirmer No. E.C.S. 3076. Optional accompaniment. Medium.
Sanctus (from *B Minor Mass*)—J. S. Bach. G. Schirmer No. 5654. Accompanied. Difficult.
Sanctus (from *C Major Mass*)—Ludwig van Beethoven. Walton No. 6014. Accompanied. Medium.
Sanctus (from *Requiem*)—Gabriel Fauré. Fitzsimons No. 2119. Accompanied. Easy.
Sanctus (from *16th Mass*)—Franz Joseph Haydn, arr. Hilton. Mercury No. MC 399. Accompanied. Medium.
Sanctus (from Mass VII)—Antonio Lotti. G. Schirmer No. 9407. *A cappella.* Moderately easy.
Sanctus—Gioacchino Rossini, ed. Ferguson. Lawson-Gould No. 51890. Accompanied. Moderately difficult.
Sanctus—Tomas Luis de Victoria. Music 70 No. M70-212. *A cappella.* Medium.
Sanctus and Hosanna—Giovanni Pergolesi. Music 70 No. M70-405. Accompanied. Medium.
Send Out Thy Light (Emitte Spiritum Tuum)—Franz Joseph Schuetky. Carl Fischer No. CM 548. *A cappella.* Moderately easy.
Serve the Lord with Gladness—G. F. Handel. Lawson-Gould No. 794. Accompanied. Medium.
Sicut Moses serpentem—Heinrich Schütz. Associated No. A-412. Accompanied. Difficult.
Sing a New Song—Michael Haydn. Flammer No. A-5970. Accompanied. Moderately easy.
Sing to the Lord (Gloria in excelsis Deo)—Franz Joseph Haydn. G. Schirmer No. 5414. Accompanied. Moderately easy.
Sing unto the Lord Most High—Giovanni Pergolesi. Boosey & Hawkes. *A cappella.* Easy.
Sing We All Now with One Accord—Hieronymus Praetorius. G. Schirmer No. 7543. Accompanied. Moderately easy.
Sing with Gladness—Jan Pieterszoon Sweelinck, ed. Sateren. AMSI No. 337. *A cappella.* Moderately difficult.
Sing Ye to the Lord (Jauchzet dem Herrn)—Johann Pachelbel. Music 70 No. M70-192. Accompanied. Moderately easy.
Sixty-seventh Psalm—Charles Ives. Associated No. A-274. *A cappella.* Moderately diffficult.
Song of Galilee (El Yivneh Hagalil)—transcribed by Julius Chajes. Transcontinental No. TCL 214. Accompanied. Medium.
Song of Repentance—J. S. Bach. Broude Bros. No. 65. *A cappella.* Medium.
Sound the Cymbal—Franz Schubert. Schmitt, Hall & McCreary No. 1745. Accompanied. Medium.
Stabat Mater—Franz Schubert. Belwin Mills No. 2164. Accompanied. Moderately easy.
Surgens Jesus—Orlando di Lasso. Arista No. AE 309. *A cappella.* Medium.
Tarry Here and Watch—Giuseppi Ottavio Pitoni, arr. Kingsbury. Tetra No. A.B. 757. *A cappella.* Medium.
Te Deum—William Schuman. G. Schirmer No. 9453. *A cappella.* Medium.
This Is the Record of John—Orlando Gibbons, ed. Alice Parker and Robert Shaw. Lawson-Gould No. 550. Organ accompaniment. Tenor solo. Medium.
Thou Art the King of Glory—G. F. Handel. Kjos No. 5481A. Accompanied. Moderately easy.
Thou Art Worthy of Praise—Franz Joseph Haydn. Sam Fox No. MM 13. *A cappella.* Moderately easy.
Thou Must Leave Thy Lowly Dwelling (from *Childhood of Christ*)—Hector Berlioz. Gray No. 1898. Accompanied. Medium.
To Him Who Never Faileth—Johann Christoph Altnikol, ed. Frank. Sam Fox No. MM 3. Accompanied. Moderately easy.

Tribulationes civitatum—Virgil Thomson. Weintraub. *A cappella*. Moderately difficult.

Tribus miraculis—Luca Marenzio. World Library. *A cappella*. Medium.

Turn Back, O Man—Gustav Holst. Galaxy No. 6. Accompanied. Medium.

Tu solus qui facit mirabilia—Josquin Després. Mercury No. 352-00045. *A cappella*. Medium.

The Twenty-Third Psalm—Harry Robert Wilson. Bourne No. 703. *A cappella*. Medium.

Unto Thee I Lift My Spirit—Hiller. Sam Fox MM No. 7. Accompanied. Moderately easy.

Veni Jesu—Luigi Cherubini, arr. Riegger. Flammer No. 84189. Accompanied. Medium.

Venite, exsultemus Domino (O Come Let Us Sing)—Jan Pieterszoon Sweelinck. Summy Birchard No. 5517. Optional accompaniment. Medium.

Veni Virgo Sacrata—Georg von Reutter, ed. Young. Broude Bros. No. MGC 21. Organ accompaniment. Medium.

Von Himmel hoch (From Highest Heav'n)—J. S. Bach. Lawson-Gould No. 903. *A cappella*. Medium.

Vouchsafe, O Lord—Alexander Gretchaninov. Galaxy No. 1356. Optional accompaniment. Medium.

We Adore Thee (Adoramus Te)—Antonio Lotti. Chappell No. 6149. *A cappella*. Moderately easy.

We Have No Other Help—Alexander Arkhangelsky, arr. Gnotov. Witmark No. 5-W3005. *A cappella*. Moderately easy.

We Pledge You Forever (from Cantata No. 208)—J. S. Bach, ed. Don Malin. Belwin Mills No. 2406. Accompanied. Moderately difficult.

We Praise and Bless Thee (from *Messe Solennelle*)—Charles Gounod, arr. Witford. Oliver Ditson No. 332-40049. Accompanied. Moderately easy.

We Praise Thee—Alexander Gretchaninov, arr. Noble Cain. Hoffman No. 46,335. *A cappella*. Easy.

We Will Rejoice in Thy Salvation—G. F. Handel, ed. Don Malin. Belwin Mills No. 2407. Accompanied. Moderately difficult.

While As a Stone, Yet Living—Luca Marenzio. Piedmont No. 4485. Optional accompaniment. Moderately easy.

Who Shall Separate Us?—Heinrich Schuetz. Chantry Music Press. Organ or piano accompaniment. Medium.

Who With Grieving Soweth—Johann Herman Schein. Mercury No. 19. *A cappella*. Moderately difficult.

With a Voice of Singing—Martin Shaw. G. Schirmer No. 8103. Accompanied. Moderately easy.

With Sorrow Shaken—K.P.E. Bach. Elkan-Vogel No. 362-03103. Piano or organ accompaniment. Alto solo. Moderately easy.

Ye Are Not of the Flesh (from the motet *Jesus meine Freude*)—J. S. Bach. Lawson-Gould No. 785. Accompanied. Difficult.

Your Voices Tune (from *Alexander's Feast*)—G. F. Handel, ed. Malin. Belwin Mills No. 2408. Accompanied. Medium.

General: Secular (More Recently Published Music)

A Capital Ship—arr. Norman Luboff. Walton No. WW 1081. Two-piano accompaniment. Medium.

Americana Medley—arr. Rhonda Sandberg. Aberdeen Music No. 1088. Accompanied. Moderately easy.

America the Beautiful—Samuel A. Ward, arr. John Ness Beck. Beckenhorst Press No. BP 1370. Accompanied. Moderately easy.

America the Beautiful—Samuel A. Ward, arr. Robert Berglund. Neil A. Kjos No. C8822. Accompanied (optional band or full orchestra). Moderately easy.

An American Tribute—arr. Robert Cundick. TRO No. S7067. Accompanied. Moderately easy.

A Warning—Wolfgang A. Mozart, arr. Ernest Gold. Lawson-Gould No. 52518. Accompanied.

The Dark-Eyed Sailor (English folk song)—arr. Ralph Vaughan Williams. Galaxy No. 1.5097. *A cappella*. Medium.

The Falcon—Johannes Brahms, ed. Terry Eder. Greystone Press No. GRP-1001. *A cappella*. Medium.

Homeward Bound—Carl Strommen. CPP/Belwin No. SV 9060. Accompanied. Moderately easy.

In the Forest—Felix Mendelssohn, ed. Frank Mueller. Music 70 Publishers No. M70-604. *A cappella.* Medium.

Island in Space—Kirke Mechem. G. Schirmer No. 50481434. *A cappella.* Moderately difficult.

Je Ne Fus Jamais Si Aisé—Clement Jannequin, arr. William D. Hall. National Music Publishers No. CMS-117. Brass, woodwind, or recorder accompaniment. Medium.

Joy of Living—Franz Schubert, ed. Cennen Gordon. Tetra/Continuo No. TC 258. Accompanied. Medium.

Just as the Tide Was Flowing (English folk song)—arr. Ralph Vaughan Williams. Galaxy No. 1.5020. *A cappella.* Medium.

Look, Mistress Mine—Francis Pilkington, ed. John Kingsbury. Music 70 No. M70-239. *A cappella.* Moderately easy.

Look upon Me, My Beloved—Giovanni Gastoldi, ed. Francis J. Guentner. CPP/Belwin No. SV8719. *A cappella.* Medium.

My Old Kentucky Home—Stephen Foster, arr. Donald P. Moore. Mark Foster No. MF 3028. *A cappella.* Moderately easy.

No Man Is an Island—Edwin Fissinger. Walton No. WW1141. *A cappella.* Moderately difficult.

O Mistress Mine—Ralph Vaughan Williams. Galaxy No. 1.5017 *A cappella.* Moderately easy.

Peaceful Vale—Felix Mendelssohn, ed. Frank Mueller. Music 70 No. M70-603. *A cappella.* Moderately easy.

Pluck the Fruit and Taste the Pleasure—Libby Larsen. E. C. Schirmer No. 4291. *A cappella.* Medium.

Sängerlust-Polka—Johann Strauss. Doblinger No. D.17636. Accompanied. Medium.

Songs of Love—James McCray. Mark Foster No. MF 3037. *A cappella.* Medium.

The Spring Time of the Year (English folk song)—arr. Ralph Vaughan Williams. Galaxy No. 1.5013 *A cappella.* Medium.

Three Chansons—Orlando di Lasso, ed. Francis J. Guentner. Broude Brothers No. CR 60. *A cappella.* Medium.

Three Italian Partsongs (Viva Sempre by Donato; Basciami, Vita Mia by Hassler; Chi La Gagliarda by Donato)—ed. Victoria Glaser. E. C. Schirmer No. 3042. *A cappella.* Medium.

Trout as You Like It (Variations on Schubert's Song)—Franz Schoggl. English version by Eugene Hartzell. Doblinger No. D.17.269. *A cappella.* Medium.

Twilight—Jean Berger. John Sheppard No. 2011. *A cappella.* Moderately easy.

Two Worlds—Randall Thompson. E. C. Schirmer No. 3041. Accompanied. Medium.

Walkin' on Air (from *Quotations*)—Morton Gould. G. Schirmer No. 12535. For double chorus and wind orchestra. Moderately difficult.

Welcome Sweet May—Orlando di Lasso. Carl Fischer No. CM7566. *A cappella.* Medium.

Wie Melodien Zieht Es Mir—Johannes Brahms, arr. Gregory Vancil. Southern Music No. SC 223. Moderately easy.

General: Secular (Standard/Traditional Music)

Adieu, Sweet Amarillis—John Wilbye, ed. Kaplan. Lawson-Gould No. 51865. *A cappella.* Medium.

Ah, Love, to You I'm Crying—Hans Leo Hassler, ed. Walter Ehret. Tetra No. A.B. 759. *A cappella.* Medium.

Anima mia perdona—Claudio Monteverdi, ed. Don Malin. Belwin Mills No. 2380. *A cappella.* Medium.

Anthony O Daly—Samuel Barber. G. Schirmer No. 8909. *A cappella.* Medium.

April Is in Her Mistress' Face—Thomas Morley. Ricordi No. 1398; E. C. Schirmer No. 1612. *A cappella.* Moderately easy.

As Long As Beauty Shall Remain—Johannes Brahms, arr. Christy. Schmitt, Hall & McCreary No. 1172. *A cappella.* Easy.

As Torrents in Summer—Edward Elgar, arr. Noble Cain. Flammer No. 81068. *A cappella.* Moderately easy.

Aug dem See (On the Lake)—Felix Mendelssohn. National Music Publishers No. NMP-184. *A cappella.* Medium.

Autumn Rain—Samuel H. Adler. Associated No. A-263. *A cappella*. Medium.

Ballad of Green Broom—Benjamin Britten. Boosey & Hawkes No. 1875. *A cappella*. Moderately difficult.

Beggar's Canon (from *The Brigands*)—Jacques Offenbach. Broude Bros. No. 117. Accompanied. Medium.

Blow, Blow, Thou Winter Wind—John Rutter. Oxford No. 52.024. Accompanied. Moderately easy.

Chanson on *Dessus le Marche d'Arras*—Orlando di Lasso. Associated No. NYPM 32. *A cappella*. Medium.

Choose Something like a Star—Randall Thompson. E. C. Schirmer No. 2487. Accompanied. Moderately easy.

Chorus of the Hebrew Captives (from *Nabucco*)—Giuseppi Verdi. Music 70 No. 224. Accompanied. Medium.

Chorus of the Office Clerks (from *Fortunio's Song*)—Jacques Offenbach. Broude Bros. No. 4066. Accompanied. Medium.

Come, Let Your Hearts Be Singing—Giovanni Gastoldi, arr. Greyson. Bourne No. ES 26. *A cappella*. Moderately easy.

Come and Sing (from *Die Fledermaus*)—Johann Strauss. Carl Fischer No. CM 4628. Accompanied. Moderately difficult.

The Coolin—Samuel Barber. G. Schirmer No. 8910. *A cappella*. Moderately difficult.

Dedication—Robert Franz, arr. Riegger. Flammer No. 81043. *A cappella*. Medium.

Der Gang zum Liebchen (Journey to My Love)—Johannes Brahms. National Music Publishers, No. WHC-132. Accompanied. Medium.

Dixie—Daniel Emmett, arr. Norman Luboff. Walton No. 3004. *A cappella*. Medium.

Early Spring—Felix Mendelssohn. Music 70 No. M70-259. *A cappella*. Medium.

Eloquence (Die Beredsamkeit)—Franz Joseph Haydn. Elkan-Vogel No. 1133. Accompanied. Medium.

Evening—Zoltán Kodály. Boosey & Hawkes No. 1110. *A cappella*. Difficult.

A Fable—Norman Dello Joio. Carl Fischer No. CM 6299. Accompanied. Moderately easy.

Face to Face (from *Ten Songs*)—Dimitri Shostakovitch. G. Schirmer No. 12121. *A cappella*. Moderately difficult.

Fair Is the Crystal—Orlando di Lasso. Piedmont No. 4384. *A cappella*. Medium.

Fall, Leaves, Fall—Houston Bright. Shawnee Press No. A-945. *A cappella*. Medium.

Farewell, The (Horch, der Wind klagt in den Zweigen)—Johannes Brahms. Sam Fox No. RC 2. Accompanied. Moderately easy.

Farmer's Wife Lost Her Cat—W. A. Mozart. Edw. B. Marks No. 1. *A cappella*. Moderately difficult.

Fa una canzone—Orazio Vecchi. Lawson-Gould No. 556. *A cappella*. Easy.

From Grief to Glory (Verse 2—Love in Grief)—F. Melius Christiansen. Augsburg No. 175. *A cappella*. Difficult.

Frühzeitiger Frühling (Early Spring)—Felix Mendelssohn. National Music Publishers No. NMP-167. *A cappella*. Medium.

Geographical Fugue (speaking chorus)—Ernst Toch. Belwin Mills No. 347. Difficult.

Glory (March from *Aida*)—Giuseppi Verdi. Willis No. 2892. Accompanied. Moderately difficult.

The Gondoliers (Finale)—Gilbert and Sullivan. E. C. Schirmer No. 356. Four-hand piano accompaniment. Medium.

Happiness (O Seligkeit)—Franz Schubert, ed. Freed. Sam Fox No. RC 4. Accompanied. Moderately easy.

Have Courage, Friends (from *Ten Songs*)—Dimitri Shostakovitch. G. Schirmer No. 12118. *A cappella*. Medium.

Herbstlied (Autumn Song)—Felix Mendelssohn. Lawson-Gould No. 52180. *A cappella*. Medium.

Hunting Song—Felix Mendelssohn. Sam Fox No. RC 9. *A cappella*. Medium.

If All My Heartfelt Thinking—Johannes Brahms. Associated No. A-407. *A cappella*. Medium.

If I Should Part from You—Claudio Monteverdi. Presser No. 312-40939. *A cappella*. Moderately easy.

I Myself When Young Did Eagerly Frequent—Emma Lou Diemer. Boosey & Hawkes No. 5778. *A cappella*. Medium.

In Silent Night—Johannes Brahms. G. Schirmer No. 5848. *A cappella.* Easy.

In Swift Light Vessels Gliding (Opus 2)—Anton Webern. Universal No. E6643A. *A cappella.* Moderately difficult.

In the Quiet Night—Peter Mennin. Carl Fischer No. CM 6417. *A cappella.* Medium.

In These Delightful, Pleasant Groves—Henry Purcell. Novello No. M. T. 1. *A cappella.* Medium.

In Winter—Paul Hindemith. Associated No. AS 19432V. *A cappella.* Medium.

It Is Good to Be Merry—Jean Berger. Kjos No. 5293. *A cappella.* Medium.

Je pleure (I Weep)—Claude Le Jeune. Éditions Salabert No. 23-6. *A cappella.* Moderately easy.

Je serais enchanté (I Should Be Overjoyed)—Charles Gounod. Alexander Broude No. 252-3. Accompanied. Moderately easy.

Jig for Voices—C. E. Rowley. Boosey & Hawkes No. 1699. Optional accompaniment. Medium.

Joyful Day—G. F. Handel. National Music Publishers No. NMP-143. Accompanied. Medium.

Lady, So Fair Thou Seemest—Glaches de Wert. Belwin Mills No. 60778. *A cappella.* Moderately easy.

Lark, The (Lerchengesang)—Felix Mendelssohn. Music 70 Publishers No. M70-252. *A cappella.* Moderately easy.

Las Agachadas—Aaron Copland. Boosey & Hawkes. *A cappella.* For solo group and eight-part chorus. Moderately difficult.

Lebenslust (Joy of Living)—Franz Schubert. Alexander Broude No. 258. Accompanied. Medium.

Life Is Happiness Indeed (from *Candide*)—Leonard Bernstein, arr. Page. G. Schirmer No. 12024. Accompanied. Medium.

A Lonely Boat Drifts Slowly—Robert Schumann. Broude Bros. No. 135. Soprano solo, flute, and horn. Medium.

Lost Youth (Verlorene Jugend)—Johannes Brahms. Presser No. 312-40946. *A cappella.* Medium.

Love Is a Blue Star—James McCray. National Music Publishers No. WHC-137. *A cappella.* Medium.

Love Song—Brahms, arr. Harry R. Wilson. Ricordi No. NY1475. Optional accompaniment. Moderately easy.

Lullaby (Wiegenlied)—W. A. Mozart. Associated No. A-84. Accompanied. Soprano solo. Moderately easy.

Madrigal—Don Carlo Gesualdo. Edw. B. Marks No. 52. *A cappella.* Medium.

Matona, Lovely Maiden—Orlando di Lasso. Carl Fischer No. CM 4637. *A cappella.* Moderately easy.

Modern Music—William Billings. C. F. Peters No. 66340. *A cappella.* Medium.

Monotone—Normand Lockwood. Kjos No. 8. *A cappella.* Medium.

Music the Comforter (Trösterin Musik)—Anton Bruckner. Sam Fox No. MM 12. Accompanied. Moderately easy.

My Love Dwelt in a Northern Land—Edward Elgar. G. Schirmer No. 2366. *A cappella.* Moderately easy.

The Nightingale—Felix Mendelssohn, ed. Mason. Walton No. 7010. Optional accompaniment. Moderately easy.

Nuptial Chorus (from *The Guardsman*)—Peter I. Tchaikovsky, ed. Malin. Belwin Mills No. 2405. Accompanied. Medium.

O, Dearest Love of Mine (Herzlieb zu Dir allein)—Hans Leo Hassler. Boston Music Co. No. 13703. *A cappella.* Medium.

O Be Joyful Ye Lands—Henry Purcell. Gentry No. JG-459. Accompanied. Easy.

O Care, Thou Wilt Despatch Me—Thomas Weelkes. Boston Music Co. No. 13705. *A cappella.* Moderately easy.

O Death, Pray Come—Claudio Monteverdi. Boston Music Co. No. 2890. *A cappella.* Medium.

Oh, When My Husband Comes Back Home—Orlando di Lasso. Pro Art No. 2365. *A cappella.* Moderately easy.

Oh Love Divine (from *Theodora*)—G. F. Handel. Carl Fischer No. ZCM108. Accompanied. Medium.

Old Abram Brown—Benjamin Britten. Boosey & Hawkes No. 1786. Accompanied. Easy.

Old Joe Has Gone Fishing (from *Peter Grimes*)—Benjamin Britten. Boosey & Hawkes No. 1784. Accompanied. Moderately difficult.

The Old Man (Der Greis)—Franz Joseph Haydn. Associated No. A-618. *A cappella.* Medium.

O Lovely Mai (O Sussex Mai)—Johannes Brahms. Belwin Mills No. 2174. *A cappella.* Moderately easy.

On the Way to My Sweetheart—Johannes Brahms, arr. Matesky. Gentry No. G-4007. Accompanied. Moderately easy.

O Swiftly Glides the Bonny Boat—Ludwig van Beethoven. National Music Publishers No. CMS-126. Violin, cello, and piano accompaniment. Moderately easy.

O voi che sospirate a migliore note—Luca Marenzio. Dartmouth Publications No. A-977. *A cappella.* Medium.

O Wondrous Harmony—Franz Joseph Haydn. Lawson-Gould No. 52065. Accompanied. Medium.

O World, I Now Must Leave Thee (Innsbruck, ich muss dich lassen)—Heinrich Isaac. Alexander Broude No. 251-3. *A cappella.* Medium.

A Party of Lovers at Tea—Dominick Argento. Boosey & Hawkes No. 5712. *A cappella.* Medium.

Pavane pour une infante défunte—Maurice Ravel. Broude Bros. No. 100. Accompanied. Moderately difficult.

Placido e il mar (from *Idomeneo*)—W. A. Mozart. Belwin Mills No. 2403. Accompanied. Medium.

Pleasure Awaits Us (from *La Finta Gardiniera*—W. A. Mozart. Belwin Mills No. 2403. Accompanied. Medium.

Prelude—William Schuman. G. Schirmer No. 8929. *A cappella.* Soprano solo. Moderately difficult.

The Primrose (Die Primel)—Felix Mendelssohn. Associated No. A-382. *A cappella.* Medium.

The Promise of Living (from *The Tender Land*)—Aaron Copland. Boosey & Hawkes No. 5020. Piano duet accompaniment. Moderately difficult.

Rest, Sweet Nymphs—Francis Pilkington. National Music Publishers No. CMS-121. String quartet or recorder consort accompaniment. Moderately easy.

Rise Up, Oh Flame—Hieronymus Praetorius, arr. Harley and Aschenbrenner. Carl Fischer No. CM 4712. *A cappella.* Moderately easy.

The Road Not Taken—Randall Thompson. E. C. Schirmer No. 2485. Accompanied. Moderately easy.

Roses of the South—Johann Strauss, arr. Gibb. Homeyer No. 437. Accompanied. Moderately easy.

See How Aurora Comes with Brow All Glowing—Luca Marenzio. Piedmont No. 4438. *A cappella.* Medium.

A Sigh Goes Stirring through the Wood—Johannes Brahms. Associated No. A-379. *A cappella.* Medium.

Since All Is Passing—Paul Hindemith. Schott No. AP 37. *A cappella.* Moderately easy.

Sing a Song of Sixpence—Houston Bright. Shawnee Press No. A-851. *A cappella.* Medium.

Sing of Spring—George Gershwin. Lawson-Gould No. 51964. Accompanied. Medium.

Six Balletti—Giovanni Gastoldi. C. F. Peters, Set I, No. 6877a. *A cappella.* Moderately easy. Set II, No. 6877b. *A cappella.* Medium.

Six Love Songs—Johannes Brahms. Summy-Birchard. Four-hand accompaniment. Moderately difficult.

The Skylark's Song—Felix Mendelssohn. Belwin Mills No. 2181. Optional accompaniment. Moderately easy.

Song of the Lark (Lerchengesang)—Felix Mendelssohn. Sam Fox No. RC 11. *A cappella.* Moderately easy.

Songs Filled My Heart—Antonin Dvořák. Presser No. 312-40813. Accompanied. Moderately easy.

So wahr die Sonne scheinet (As Surely As the Sun Shines)—Robert Schumann. National Music Publishers No. WHC-117. Accompanied. Medium.

Springtime—Paul Hindemith. Schott No. 19432, IV. *A cappella.* Moderately difficult.

Stomp Your Foot (from *The Tender Land*)—Aaron Copland. Boosey & Hawkes No. 5019. Piano duet accompaniment. Moderately difficult.

Strings in the Earth—Samuel Adler. Associated No. A-264. *A cappella.* Medium.

Sunrise—Sergei I. Taneyev. G. Schirmer No. 2623. *A cappella.* Difficult.

Sure on This Shining Night—Samuel Barber. G. Schirmer No. 10864. Accompanied. Moderately easy.

A Swan—Hindemith. Schott No. 19432, 11. *A cappella.* Medium.

Sweet Day—James McCray. J. Fischer No. 10132. *A cappella.* Moderately easy.

These Are My Heartfelt Tears (madrigal)—Giovanni Pierluigi da Palestrina. Lawson-Gould No. 51029. *A cappella.* Moderately easy.

This World (from *Candide*)—Leonard Bernstein, arr. Page. G. Schirmer No. 12027. Accompanied. Medium.

Thought Like Music, A—Johannes Brahms, arr. Suchoff. Plymouth No. A. S. 103. Accompanied. Moderately easy.

Three Nocturnes—Carlos Chávez. G. Schirmer No. 9522. *A cappella.* Moderately difficult.

To All, To Each—William Schuman. Presser No. 342-40013. *A cappella.* Medium.

To All Our Hearts Are Now Returning (from *Julius Caesar*)—G. F. Handel. Belwin Mills No. 2404. Accompanied. Medium.

To Music—Elliot Carter. Peer International. *A cappella.* Moderately difficult.

Tones Enchanted (Durch der Töne)—Franz Schubert. Kenbridge Music No. K-103. Accompanied. Medium.

Trysting Place, The (Der Gang zum Liebchen)—Johannes Brahms. E. C. Schirmer. No. 391. Accompanied. Medium.

Under the Willow Tree (from *Vanessa*)—Samuel Barber. G. Schirmer No. 10861. Accompanied. Soprano solo. Moderately difficult.

Up Sprang a Birch Tree Overnight—Antonin Dvořák. Mercury No. 312-40816. *A cappella.* Medium.

Valse (Speaking Chorus)—Ernst Toch. Belwin Mills No. 60564. Optional percussion. Medium.

Voix Célestes (humming chorus)—John Alcock. Chappell No. 2055. *A cappella.* Medium.

Walking on the Green Grass—Michael Hennagin. Boosey & Hawkes No. 5443. *A cappella.* Medium.

Warm Was the Sun (Scaldava il sol)—Luca Marenzio. Piedmont No. 4545. *A cappella.* Medium.

Warning—David Diamond. Elkan-Vogel No. 362-03143. Accompaniment. Moderately difficult.

We Are Brave Matadors (from *La Traviata*) Giuseppe Verdi. G. Schirmer No. 5435. Accompanied. Medium.

Welcome Sweet May (Wohl kommt der Mai)—Orlando di Lasso. Carl Fischer No. CM 7566. *A cappella.* Moderately easy.

When Evening Comes Chimes Fill the Forest—Antonin Dvořák. Mercury No. 312-40814. Accompanied. Medium.

When the Bright Sun—William Byrd. Belwin Mills No. A-202. *A cappella.* Moderately easy.

Whether Men Do Laugh or Weep—Ralph Vaughan Williams. Oxford No. X66. Accompanied. Medium.

A Woman Is a Worthy Thing—Carlos Chávez. G. Schirmer No. 9611. *A cappella.* Medium.

A Wonderful Life (Lebenslust)—Franz Schubert. Sam Fox No. MM 8. Accompanied. Medium.

Younger Generation—Aaron Copland, arr. Swift. Boosey & Hawkes No. 1723. Accompanied. Moderately easy.

Zamba for You—Ariel Ramirez. Lawson-Gould No. 52242. *A cappella.* Medium.

Zigeunerleben (Gypsy Life)—Robert Schumann. Walton No. 2706. Accompanied. Moderately easy.

Special Occasions (Commencement, Thanksgiving, Patriotic Holidays)

Battle Hymn of the Republic (patriotic)—William Steffe, arr. Roy Ringwald. Shawnee Press No. A 0028. Accompanied. Moderately easy.

Battle Hymn of the Republic (patriotic)—William Steffe, arr. Peter J. Wilhousky. Carl Fischer No. CM 4743. Accompanied. Medium.

Come, Let Us Sing to the Lord (Thanksgiving)—Konstantin Schvedov, arr. Noble Cain. Boosey & Hawkes No. 1800. *A cappella.* Difficult.

Give Me Your Tired, Your Poor (patriotic or commencement)—Irving Berlin, arr. Roy Ringwald. Shawnee Press No. A 0019. Accompanied. Medium.

Give Thanks (Thanksgiving)—William. Flammer No. 84191. Accompanied. Soprano solo. Easy.

In Solemn Silence (memorial anthem)—Mikhail M. Ippolitov-Ivanov, arr. Peter J. Wilhousky. Carl Fischer No. 635. *A cappella.* Medium.

Land of Hope and Glory (commencement)—Edward Elgar. Boosey & Hawkes No. 1161. Accompanied. Moderately easy.

Let All Creatures of God His Praises Sing (Thanksgiving)—Vassili J. Kalinnikov, arr. Noble Cain. Boosey & Hawkes No. 1801. *A cappella.* Medium.

Now Thank We All Our God (Thanksgiving)—Johann Crüger, arr. Gustav Holst. Kjos No. 5138. Accompanied. Moderately easy.

Now Thank We All Our God (Thanksgiving)—Randall Thompson. E. C. Schirmer No. 4008. Accompanied (keyboard or orchestra). Moderately easy.

Ownward, Ye Peoples! (commencement)—Jean Sibelius, arr. Lefebvre, Galaxy No. 938-10. Accompanied. Medium.

Prayer of Thanksgiving (Netherlands folk song; Thanksgiving)—arr. Kremser. G. Schirmer No. 4345. Accompanied. Easy.

Recessional (Memorial Day)—Henry DeKoven. Presser No. 322-35015. Accompanied. Moderately easy.

To Music (commencement)—Franz Schubert, arr. Harry Wilson. Schmitt, Hall & McCreary No. 1070. Accompanied. Moderately easy.

Publication for Mixed Voices (SAB)

Sacred and Secular (More Recently Published Music)

Benedictus—Orlando di Lasso, ed. Audrey Snyder. CPP/Belwin No. SV 8626. A cappella. Moderately easy.

Blow Thy Horn, Hunter—William Cornyshe, ed. Harold Owen. CPP/Belwin No. SV 8638. A cappella. Easy.

Climbin' Up the Mountain (spiritual)—arr. Walter Ehret. Carl Fischer No. CM 8270. Accompanied. Moderately easy.

Come and Adore (Basque Christmas carol)—arr. Curt Hansen. Neil A. Kjos No. C9013. Accompanied. Moderately easy.

Cum Sancto Spiritu—Antonio Lotti, ed. Patrick Eiebergen. CPP/Belwin No. SV 9112. A cappella. Easy.

The Day of Resurrection (16th-century hymn tune from Nurenberg)—arr. Walter Ehret. Tetra/Continuo No. TC 1109. Accompanied, with optional obbligato for two Bb trumpets). Moderately easy.

Domine Deus—Jacob Regnart, ed. Audrey Snyder. CPP/Belwin No. SV 8845. A cappella. Moderately easy.

Give Ear, O Lord—George F. Handel, arr. Hal H. Hopson. Mark Foster No. MF 2014. Accompanied. Moderately easy.

God's Glory Shines on All the Earth—Peter Ilyich Tchaikovsky, arr. Hal H. Hopson. Neil A. Kjos No. C8905. Organ accompaniment. Moderately easy.

Good News! (spiritual)—arr. Ruth Artman. Neil A. Kjos No. C8718. Accompanied. Moderately easy.

The Heav'ns Declare God's Mighty Power (from Samson)—George Frederick Handel, arr. Hal H. Hopson. Mark Foster No. MF 2059. Accompanied. Moderately easy.

In God Rejoice—Peter Ilyich Tchaikovsky, arr. Walter Ehret. Carl Fischer No. CM 8220. Accompanied. Moderately easy.

My Pigeon House (folk ballad)—arr. David L. Plank. Neil A. Kjos No. C8914. Accompanied. Easy.

O Word Incarnate—Orlando Gibbons, ed. Anthony Greening. World Library Pub. No. 8533. Accompanied. Moderately easy.

Rejoice in the Lord—Georg Philipp Telemann, arr. James McKelvy. Mark Foster No. MF 2031. Accompanied. Medium.

Rock-a My Soul (spiritual)—arr. C. Edward Thomas. Neil A. Kjos No. C 8816. Accompanied. Easy.

Rosebud in June (English folk song)—arr. Craig Davis. CPP/Belwin No. SV 8925. A cappella, with optional hand drum or tambourine and recorder or flute. Easy.

Sanctus (from Theresienmesse)—Joseph Haydn, arr. Robert S. Hines. Neil A. Kjos No. ED 8690. Accompanied. Medium.

Shir Hama-Alot—Salamone Rossi, ed. Joshua R. Jacobson. Broude Brothers No. CR 52. Optional accompaniment. Medium.

Simple Gifts (Shaker song)—arr. Martin R. Rice. Performers' Editions SAM 3. Accompanied. Moderately easy.

Sing with Joy—Lodovico da Viadana, arr. Barbara Owen. Boston Music No. 14095. Optional accompaniment. Moderately easy.

Strike It Up, Tabor—Thomas Weelkes, ed. Harold Owen. CPP/Belwin No. SV 8639. *A cappella.* Easy.

This Day We Sing Together—Jacques Arcadelt, ed. Patrick M. Liebergen. CPP/Belwin No. SV 9041. *A cappella.* Easy.

Sacred (Standard/Traditional Music)

Adoramus Te, Christe (We Adore Thee)—Jacopo Corsi, arr. Walter Ehret. Carl Fischer No. CM 8208. *A cappella.* Moderately easy.

Alleluja (from the motet *Exsultate, Jubilate*)—W. A. Mozart, arr. Riegger. Flammer No. 88522. Accompanied. Moderately difficult.

As Torrents in Summer—Edward Elgar, arr. Noble Cain. Flammer No. 88046. Optional *A cappella.* Easy.

Ave Maria—Charles Gounod, arr. Downing. G. Schirmer No. 9450. Accompanied. Moderately easy.

Blessing, Glory and Wisdom—J. S. Bach, arr. Walter Ehret. Elkan-Vogel No. 362-03118. Optional accompaniment. Medium.

Bless the Lord, O My Soul—Michael Ippolitov-Ivanov, arr. Richardson. Boston Music Co. No. 2801. *A cappella.* Moderately easy.

Canon of Praise—Johann Pachelbel, arr. Hal H. Hopson. Somerset Press No. MW 1226. Accompanied. Moderately easy.

The Cherubic Hymn (Opus 29)—Alexander Gretchaninov, arr. Howorth. Pro Art No. 1031. *A cappella.* Moderately easy.

Cherubim Song No. 7—Dimitri S. Bortniansky, arr. Tchaikovsky. G. Schirmer No. 9753. Accompanied. Moderately easy.

Christus resurgens (Christ Being Raised)—Lodovico Viadana. Leeds No. L-441. Organ accompaniment. Moderately easy.

Come Souls, Behold Today—J. S. Bach, arr. Nelson. Augsburg No. 1171. *A cappella.* Moderately easy.

Dona nobis pacem (old German canon)—arr. Harry R. Wilson. Schmitt, Hall & McCreary No. 5510. *A cappella.* Moderately easy.

For the Beauty of the Earth—Konrad Kocher, arr. Davis. Remick No. 4-R3231. Accompanied. Easy.

God So Loved the World—John Stainer, arr. Martin. Schmitt, Hall & McCreary No. 5509. *A cappella.* Easy.

The Heavens Are Declaring—Ludwig van Beethoven, arr. Kountz. Witmark No. 2565. Accompanied. Easy.

The Heavens Are Declaring—Ludwig van Beethoven, arr. Mueller. G. Schirmer No. 10670. Accompanied Easy.

The Heavens Are Telling—Franz Joseph Haydn, arr. Harry R. Wilson. Lorenz No. 7020. Accompanied. Moderately easy.

In God Rejoice—Peter I. Tchaikovsky. Carl Fischer No. CM 8220. Accompanied. Moderately easy.

Jesu, Joy of Man's Desiring (from Cantata No. 147)—J. S. Bach. G. Schirmer No. 10023; Remick No. R3279. Accompanied. Easy.

Jesu, Son of God (Ave verum corpus)—W. A. Mozart. Schmitt, Hall & McCreary 5502. Accompanied. Moderately easy.

Lead Me, O Lord—Samuel W. Wesley, arr. Gladys Pitcher. Willis No. 8493. Accompanied. Easy.

A Legend (from the cycle *Songs for Young People*)—Peter I. Tchaikovsky, arr. Deis. G. Schirmer No. 10035. Accompanied. Medium.

Let Our Gladness Know No End (old Bohemian Christmas carol)—arr. Ryg. Belwin Mills No. 1761. *A cappella.* Moderately easy.

Lift Thine Eyes (from *Elijah*)—Felix Mendelssohn, arr. Gladys Pitcher. Willis No. 8486. Optional accompaniment. Moderately easy.
The Moon Shines Bright (old English carol)—arr. Harry R. Wilson. Bourne No. T8. Accompanied. Moderately easy.
O Give Thanks unto the Lord—Franz Joseph Haydn, arr. Hines. Raymond A. Hoffman No. H-2030. Accompanied. Moderately easy.
O Little Jesus (16th-century German carol)—arr. Gordon. Belwin Mills. No. 1873. Accompanied. Easy.
O Lord, Our God—Schvedov, arr. Harry R. Wilson. Bourne No. T5. Optional accompaniment. Medium.
O Lord Most Holy—Cesar Franck, arr. Gladys Pitcher. Willis No. 8489. Accompanied. Easy.
Praise the Almighty, My Soul, Adore Him—Zipp. Concordia No. CH 1086. *A cappella*. Moderately easy.
Praise Ye the Father—Charles Gounod, arr. Gladys Pitcher. Willis No. 8482. Accompanied. Moderately easy.
A Prayer for Peace (Panis angelicus)—Cesar Franck, arr. Hoffman. Hoffman No. 46,107. Accompanied. Moderately easy.
Send Out Thy Light—Charles Gounod, arr. Mueller. G. Schirmer No. 8695. Accompanied. Medium.
Shepherd of Eager Youth—Roff. Elkan-Vogel No. 507. Accompanied. Moderately easy.
Sing to the Lord, Our God (Cantate Domino)—Giovanni Matteo Asola. Music 70 No. M70-350. *A cappella*. Medium.
Sing Ye Praises unto the Father—W. A. Mozart. Gentry No. G-151. Accompanied. Medium.
To Realms of Glory—Johann Herman Schein, arr. Nelson. Augsburg No. 1169. *A cappella*. Easy.
Turn Thy Face from My Sins—Thomas Attwood, arr. Gladys Pitcher. Willis No. 8487. Accompanied. Easy.

Secular (Standard/Traditional Music)

Bells of St. Mary's—Adams, arr. Stickles. Chappell No. 7006. Accompanied. Easy.
Bells of the Sea—Solman, arr. Harry R. Wilson. Sam Fox No. 542. Accompanied. Moderately easy.
Carol of the Bells (Ukrainian carol)—Leontovich, arr. Peter J. Wilhousky. Carl Fischer No. 4747. Optional *A cappella*. Easy.
Come Sirrah Jack Ho—Thomas Weelkes. National Music Publishers No. CMS-122. Clarinet trio accompaniment. Medium.
Danse Macabre—Charles Saint-Saëns, arr. Lorenz. Lorenz No. 7098. Accompanied. Moderately difficult.
Dedication—Robert Franz, arr. Harry R. Wilson. Paull Pioneer. Accompanied. Moderately easy.
Down South—Michael Myddleton, arr. High. Edw. B. Marks No. 403. Accompanied. Easy.
Follow Me, Sweet Love—Michael East. National Music Publishers No. CMS-120. Recorder consort accompaniment. Moderately easy.
Follow the Drinking Gourd (source unknown)—arr. Horman. Somerset Press No. SP782. Accompanied. Moderately easy.
Green Cathedral—C. Hahn, arr. G. Montrose. Presser No. 322-35447. Accompanied. Easy.
Homing—Del Riego, arr. Stickles. Chappell No. 7007. Accompanied. Easy.
Kentucky Babe—Giebel, arr. Stickles. Edwin H. Morris No. 8003. Accompanied. Easy.
Ol' Man River—Jerome Kern, arr. Stickles. Chappell No. CR77. Accompanied. Moderately easy.
Pines of Home—Luvaas. Carl Fischer No. 6452. Optional *A cappella*. Moderately easy.
Prayer from *Hansel and Gretel*—Englebert Humperdinck, arr. Riegger. Flammer No. 88019. Accompanied. Easy.
Shortnin' Bread—Wolfe, arr. Riegger. Flammer No. 88088. Accompanied. Moderately easy.
Sing, Sing a Song for Me—Orazio Vecchi, arr. Greyson. Bourne No. ES 53C. Optional accompaniment. Moderately easy.
Sing Songs of Jubilation—Johann Pachelbel, arr. Petker. Gentry No. JG-474. Accompanied. Medium.

Three Madrigals from the XVIIth Century. J. Fischer No. 9455.
    1. Your Shining Eyes—Thomas Bateson.
    2. As Late in My Accounting—Thomas Weelkes.
    3. Follow Me, Sweet Love—Michael East.
    A cappella. Medium.
Tickling Trio (Vadasi via di qua)—Giovanni B. Martini. Witmark No. 4-W2750. *A cappella.* Moderately easy.
To Music—Franz Schubert, arr. Harry R. Wilson. Schmitt, Hall & McCreary No. 5011. Accompanied. Moderately easy.
Turn Ye to Me—Wilson, arr. Churchill. Belwin Mills No. 1619. Accompanied. Moderately easy.

Folk Songs and Spirituals (Standard/Traditional Music)

Certainly, Lord (spiritual)—arr. Theron Kirk. Pro Art No. 1834. Accompanied. Moderately easy.
Cindy (American folk song)—arr. Barthelson. Belwin Mills No. 1984. Accompanied. Moderately easy.
Cindy (American folk song)—arr. Walter Ehret. Presser No. 312-41185. Accompanied. Moderately easy.
The Cowboy's Meditation (American folk song)—arr. Harry R. Wilson. Paul Pioneer. Accompanied. Moderately easy.
Ezekiel Saw de Wheel (spiritual)—arr. Noble Cain. Belwin Mills No. 1131. Accompanied. Medium.
From Lucerne to Weggis Fair (Swiss folk song)—arr. Harris. Pro Art No. 2369. Accompanied. Medium.
Gonna Ride Up in the Chariot (spiritual)—arr. Richardson. Presser No. 312-41187. Accompanied. Easy.
He Never Said a Mumbalin' Word (spiritual)—arr. Harry R. Wilson. Paul Pioneer. Optional accompaniment. Moderately easy.
I Ain't Gonna Grieve My Lord No More (spiritual)—arr. Walter Ehret. Belwin Mills No. 1661. Accompanied. Medium.
I Got Shoes (spiritual)—arr. Noble Cain. Flammer No. 88047. Accompanied. Easy.
Jennie Jenkins (American dialogue song)—arr. Churchill. Belwin Mills No. 1893. Accompanied. Easy.
John Anderson, My Jo (Scottish folk song)—arr. Gordon. Belwin Mills No. 1494. Accompanied. Moderately easy.
Little David, Play on Your Harp (spiritual)—arr. Noble Cain. Flammer No. 88054. Accompanied. Moderately easy.
Night Herding Song (country folk ballad)—arr. Barker, Belwin Mills No. 1828. Optional accompaniment. Moderately easy.
Rock-a My Soul (spiritual)—arr. Harry R. Wilson. Bourne No. T 11. Accompanied. Moderately easy.
Rocking Carol (Czech carol)—arr. Graham. Presser No. 312-40698. Optional accompaniment. Moderately easy.
Russian Picnic (based on Russian folk tunes)—arr. Harvey Enders. G. Schirmer No. 9632. Accompanied. Medium.
Simple Gifts (American Shaker tune)—arr. Theron Kirk. Pro Art No. 2662. Accompanied. Moderately easy.
The Turtle Dove (English folk song)—arr. Ahrold. Presser No. 312-40700. Accompanied. Moderately easy.
Vreneli (Swiss folk song)—arr. Walter Ehret. Presser No. 312-41189. Accompanied. Easy.
Water Boy (African-American work song)—arr. Gladys Pitcher. Boston Music Co. No. 2359. Accompanied. Baritone solo—melody in baritone. Easy.
Were You There? (spiritual)—arr. Harry R. Wilson. Bourne No. T 2. Accompanied. Medium.

Publications for Changing Voices (SSCB, SACB, SSACB, SAC/B, SSC(B), SATB) [3]

Sacred and Secular

Adolescence—Don Collins. Cambiata Press No. L97558. SSCB.

Adoramus Te, Christe—W. A. Mozart, arr. Collins. Cambiata Press No. D97812. SSCB.

Alleluia—J. S. Bach, arr. Roger Emerson. Jenson No. 40301000. SATB.

All Praise to Thee—Thomas Tallis, arr. Stone. CPP/Belwin No. 2223. SATB.

Aren't You Glad That It's Christmas?—Hoover. Cambiata Press No. A97811. SAC/B.

Au Clair de la Lune—Jean-Baptiste Lully, arr. Stone. CPP/Belwin No. 2156. SATB.

Ave Verum Corpus—William Byrd, arr. Don Collins. Cambiata Press No. D978121 SSCB.

Ave Verum—W. A. Mozart, arr. Lyle. Cambiata Press No. M17552. SACB.

Blessed Is the Man—Eugene Butler. Cambiata Press No. C97203. SSCB.

Blow the Wind Southerly—arr. Vance. CPP/Belwin No. 2168.

Cherubim Song—Dimitri S. Bortniansky, arr. Don Collins. Cambiata Press No. D978119. SSCB.

Christmas Secular Songs—arr. Don Collins. Cambiata Press. Collection of eleven arrangements. Variable voicing.

Climbin' Up the Mountain (spiritual)—arr. Walter Ehret. Studio PR. SACB.

Climbin' Up Those Golden Stairs—Wiley. Pro Art No. 2997. SSCR.

The Colorado Trail (American folk song)—arr. Lyle. Cambiata Press No. U17316. SSCB.

Da Pacem Dòmine—Cesar Franck, arr. Pardue. Cambiata Press No. M979126. SSACB.

Deck the Hall (old Welch air)—arr. Knight. CPP/Belwin No. 2988. SSCB.

En La Fuente De Rosel—Juan Vasquez. Lawson-Gould No. 51376. SATB.

Ezekiel Saw the Wheel (spiritual)—arr. Walter Ehret. Studio PR. SACB.

Fa Una Canzona—Orazio Vecchi. Lawson-Gould No. 556. SATB.

Feelin' Good—Myers, arr. Rodman. Celebration Press No. G3666. SATB.

Give Me Liberty or Give Me Death—Don Collins. Cambiata Press No. P47434. SSCB.

Gloria (from Gloria)—Antonio Vivaldi, arr. Don Collins. Cambiata Press No. M117207. SSCB.

Go and Tell John—arr. Wiley. CPP/Belwin No. 2976. SACB.

Gonna Build a Mountain—Bricusse/Newley/Carlyle. Plymouth No. SCC2002. SACB.

Hallelujah (Baptismal Shout)—arr. Don Collins. Cambiata Press No. S485192. SSCB.

Hallelujah, Amen—G. F. Handel, arr. Taylor. Cambiata Press No. M17312. SAC/B.

Hosanna—Gregor, arr. Lyle. Cambiata Press No. M979135, double chorus. SA and SSC(B).

I Come to This Hallowed Hour—Artman. Studio PR No. V7921-2. SATB.

I Got Shoes (spiritual)—arr. Melton. Cambiata Press No. S980156. SACB.

Infant Joy—Moore, arr. Blake. Beckenhorst No. BP1089. SATB.

Jesu, Priceless Treasure—Cruger-Bach, arr. Don Collins. Cambiata Press No. M982170. SSCB.

Laudate Dominum—Giuseppe Ottavio Pitoni, arr. Wiley. Pro Art No. 2893. SACB.

Lullay, Lullay Thou Little Tiny Child—arr. Tappan. Studio PR. SACB.

Masters in This House—Morris, arr. Vance. CPP/Belwin No. 2249. SATB.

May Day Carol—arr. Vance. CPP/Belwin No. 20022-7. SATB.

Night Song—Harley. Carl Fischer No. CM4710. SATB.

Nobody Knows the Trouble I've Seen (spiritual)—arr. Don Collins. Cambiata Press No. S97320. SSCB.

Now Let the Heavens Adore Thee—J. S. Bach, arr. Don Collins. Cambiata Press No. D978122. SSCB.

O Bone Jesu—Giovanni Pierluigi da Palestrina. Pro Art. SATB.

O Occhi Manza Mia—Orlando Di Lasso, arr. Walter Ehret. Walton No. 800463. SATB.

Oh Sinner Won't You Listen?—Spevacek. Jenson No. 47315010. SSAB.

Our Savior on Earth Now Is Born—arr. Walter Ehret. Studio PR. SSCB.

Plenty Good Room (spiritual)—arr. Melton. Cambiata Press No. S983279. SACB.

---

[3] Note that in this listing there are several voice arrangements for SATB. These are included only because of the limited range of the parts for tenor voice.

Praise God in His Holiness—arr. Theron Kirk. CPP/Belwin No. 2978. SACB.
Ride the Chariot (spiritual)—arr. Melton. Cambiata Press No. S117450.
Set Down Servant (spiritual)—arr. Walter Ehret. Tetra No. AB428. SATB.
Sing to His Name, for He Is Gracious—Eugene Butler. Cambiata Press No. C17429. SSC(B).
Sing to the Lord—Wilson, arr. Foster. Studio PR No. V7917. SATB.
Sing to the Lord Who Reigns Above—Hadley. CPP/Belwin No. 2975. SACB.
Sourwood Mountain—arr. Walter Ehret. Lawson-Gould No. 653. SATB.
Star Spangled Banner—Smith, arr. Don Collins. Cambiata Press No. D978123. SSCB.
Teacher, Help Me—Spencer. Cambiata Press No. ARS980154. SACB.
Tenebrae Factae Sunt—Ingegnere, arr. Don Collins. Cambiata Press No. D981155. SSCB.
Three Easter Songs—arr. Don Collins. Cambiata Press No. U485191. SSCB.
Three Sacred Christmas Songs—arr. Don Collins. Cambiata Press. Variable voicing.
Wade in the Water (spiritual)—arr. Lyle. Cambiata Press No. S117570. SACB.
We Sing with Grace in Our Hearts—Don Collins. Cambiata Press No. C117449. SSCB.

Publications for Two Parts (SA or TB)

Sacred and Secular (More Recently Published Music)

A Hora for Hanukkah—David Eddleman. Carl Fischer No. CM 8268. Accompanied. Easy.
A la Nanita Nana (Mexican folk song)—arr. David Eddleman. Carl Fischer No. CM8303. Accompanied. Easy.
Alleluia Amen—Wolfgang Amadeus Mozart, arr. Aden G. Lewis. Plymouth No. SC-521. Accompanied. Easy.
The Alphabet—Wolfgang Amadeus Mozart, arr. Walter Ehret. Tetra/Continuo No. TC 407. Accompanied. Easy.
Bourree for Bach—J. S. Bach, arr. Bennett Williams. Sam Fox No. FXCX 109. String bass (or cello), piano, and snare drum accompaniment. Easy.
The Bumblebee—Jean Berger. Neil A. Kjos No. ED 6206. Accompanied. Moderately easy.
Cindy (American folk song)—arr. Michael Scott. CPP/Belwin No. SV 8849. Guitar and piano accompaniment. Easy.
Come, O Jesus, Come—M. Cherubini, arr. Walter Ehret. Plymouth No. S.C. 501. Accompanied. Easy.
Five Songs by Charles E. Ives (unison)—compiled by Barbara Tagg. Peer International No. 02-093576-101. Accompanied. Moderately easy.
Gloria (from *Heiligmesse*)—Joseph Haydn. Plymouth No. PCS-566 Accompanied. Easy.
Hashivenu (Israeli folk song)—arr. Doreen Rao. Boosey & Hawkes No. B6430. Accompanied. Easy.
Heidenröslein (Unison)—Franz Schubert, ed. Henry H. Leck. Plymouth No. HL—500. Accompanied. Easy.
Keep in the Middle of the Road (spiritual)—arr. Curt Hansen. Neil A. Kjos No. C8925. Accompanied. Moderately easy.
Laudamus Te (from *Gloria*)—Antonio Vivaldi, ed. Mason Martens. Walton No. W 5014. Accompanied. Moderately easy.
Merrily Sing—Harriett Bolz. Boston Music No. 14182. Accompanied. Moderately easy.
Mr. Mozart—Frederick Silver. Genesis III No. SM 103. Accompanied. Moderately easy.
O Lord, Most Holy (Panis Angelicus)—Cesar Franck, arr. Hal H. Hopson. Hope Publishing No. AA 1685. Keyboard accompaniment, with optional handbells, C instrument, or F horn. Easy.
Panis Angelicus—Cesar Franck, arr. István Bogár. Mark Foster No. MF 817. Soprano solo, piano or organ accompaniment. Easy.
Poor Man Lazrus (spiritual)—arr. Wilhelm Krumnach. Neil A. Kjos No. C9015. Accompanied. Easy.
River in Judea—Jack Feldman, arr. John Leavitt. Shawnee Press No. EA-139. Accompanied. Easy.
Rock-A My Soul (spiritual)—arr. Warren Williamson. Tetra/Continuo No. TC 439. Accompanied. Easy.

Shenandoah (traditional folk song)—arr. Danny Green. Galleria Press No. GP-504. Accompanied. Easy.

Simple Gifts (Shaker tune)—arr. Hal H. Hopson. Agape No. HH 3940. Accompanied. Easy.

Sing a Song of Hanukkah—David Eddleman. Carl Fischer No. CM 8243. Accompanied. Easy.

Slumber Song—Johannes Brahms, ed. Nancy Grundahl. Neil A. Kjos No. C 9009. Four-hand piano accompaniment. Easy.

Solstice—Randall Thompson. E. C. Schirmer No. 4289. Accompanied. Easy.

Song of May (Ländliches Lied)—Robert Schumann, arr. Owen Goldsmith. Plymouth No. PCS-588. Accompanied. Easy.

The Sow Took the Measles (early 19th-century humorous Yankee farmer song)—arr. Walter Ehret. Tetra/Continuo No. TC 919. Accompanied. Easy.

Wayfarin' Stranger (spiritual)—arr. Donald Moore. Mark Foster No. MF 2033. Accompanied. Moderately easy.

Sacred and Secular (Standard/Traditional Music)

Achieved Is the Glorious Work—Franz Joseph Haydn, arr. Davies. Oxford No. E111. Accompanied. Medium.

Ah, Lovely Meadows (Czech folk song)—arr. Lee Kjelson. Belwin Mills No. 1901. Accompanied. Easy.

The Ash Grove (Welsh folk song)—arr. Stone. Belwin Mills No. 2199. Accompanied. Moderately easy.

As Lately We Watched (Austrian carol)—arr. Stocker. Kjos No. ED.6144. Piano and optional instrumental accompaniment. Moderately easy.

At the Gates of Heaven (Basque folk song)—arr. Lee Kjelson. Belwin Mills No. 1903. Accompanied. Moderately easy.

Bright Star (Polish carol)—arr. Walter Ehret. Edw. B. Marks No. 4407. Accompanied. Moderately easy.

Christ Is Born to You Today (German folk song)—arr. Walter Ehret. Edw. B. Marks No. 4408. Accompanied. Moderately easy.

Cielito Lindo (Mexican folk song)—arr. Tate. Oxford No. T72. Accompanied. Medium.

Cindy (American folk song)—arr. Barthelson. Belwin Mills No. 1746. Moderately easy.

Come, All Ye Lads and Lassies (old English melody)—arr. Howorth. Belwin Mills No. 1874. Medium.

Coventry Carol (English carol)—arr. Stone. Belwin Mills No. 2142. Accompanied. Moderately easy.

Cuckoo, the Nightingale, and the Donkey, The—Mahler. Oxford No. T75. Accompanied. Medium.

The Cuckoo Cries—Mahler, arr. Swift. Belwin Mills No. 1436. With solo voices. Medium.

De Gospel Train (spiritual), and There's Music in the Air (G. F. Root)—arr. Rhea. Bourne No. MD2. Easy.

Drill, Ye Tarriers, Drill (American ballad)—arr. Lee Kjelson. Belwin Mills No. 1904. Moderately easy.

Dyby Byla Kosa Nabróšená (If There Were a Sharpened Scythe)—Antonin Dvořák. National Music Publishers No. WHC-91. Accompanied. Easy.

Elephant and the Flea, The (nonsense song)—arr. J. Barthelson. Belwin Mills No. 01747. Moderately easy.

Go Tell It on the Mountain (Christmas spiritual)—arr. Barthelson. Belwin Mills No. 1833. Moderately easy.

He's Goin' Away (American folk song)—arr. Holworth. Belwin Mills No. 1848. Moderately easy.

He's Got the Whole World in His Hands (spiritual)—arr. Holworth. Belwin Mills No. 1777. Optional solo. Moderately easy.

Holding Wonder—Goldsmith. Flammer No. E-5242. Accompanied. Easy.

I Love Little Willie (southern mountain song)—arr. Barthelson. Belwin Mills No. 1748. Easy.

I'm Goin' to Leave Old Texas Now (cowboy song)—arr. Gladys Pitcher. Belwin Mills No. 1835. Easy.

Jesus Christ Our Saviour Is Born (Lithuanian carol)—arr. Gordon. Belwin Mills No. 1844. Moderately easy.

Kentucky Babe—Giebel, arr. Churchill. Belwin Mills No. 1836. Easy.

Little Cradle Rocks Tonight in Glory, The (spiritual)—arr. Walker. Concordia No. 98-2139. Xylophone and percussion accompaniment. Moderately easy.

My Heart Ever Faithful—J. S. Bach, arr. Bempton. Presser No. 312-40474. Accompanied. Moderately easy.

O Come, All Ye Children (German Christmas carol)—arr. Gordon. Belwin Mills No. 1720. Easy.

O Thou Good and Faithful Servant (Serve bone)—Charpentier, arr. James McCray. Mark Foster No. MF 805. Accompanied. Moderately easy.

Patapan (Burgundian carol)—arr. Jacques. Oxford No. T86. Accompanied. Easy.

Serve bone—Orlando di Lasso. Mark Foster No. MF 801. *A cappella.* Moderately easy.

Shenandoah (sea chantey)—arr. L. Stone. Belwin Mills No. 02141. Accompanied. Moderately easy.

Sing Hallelujah, Praise the Lord (Moravian melody)—arr. Mueller. G. Schirmer No. 10754. Moderately easy.

Sing Ye Praises unto the Father—W. A. Mozart, arr. Walter Ehret. Gentry No. JG-524. Accompanied. Medium.

So Far Away (Wie kann ich froh und lustig sein?)—Felix Mendelssohn. Gentry No. JG-527. Accompanied. Medium.

Standin' in the Need of Prayer (spiritual)—arr. Lee Kjelson. Belwin Mills No. 1902. With solo voice. Moderately easy.

Still, Still (German carol)—arr. Sumner. Scholin No. 2021. Easy.

Sweet Betsy from Pike (American folk song)—arr. Swift. Belwin Mills No. 1622. Moderately easy.

There's a Little Wheel a-Turnin' (spiritual)—arr. Vance. Belwin Mills No. 1898. Optional third voice and solo. Medium.

Today with Loud Rejoicing—W. A. Mozart, arr. Heinrich. Boston Music Co. No. 3117. Easy.

Velvet Shoes—Randall Thompson. E. C. Schirmer No. 2526. Accompanied. Easy.

Viennese Lullaby (Viennese popular song)—arr. Harry R. Wilson. Bourne No. B214056. Easy.

Publications for Treble Voices (SSA)

Sacred and Secular (More Recently Published Music)

An Den Vetter (To a Cousin)—Franz Joseph Haydn, arr. Gregory Vancil. Southern Music No. SC-244. Accompanied. Medium.

The Crawdad Song (traditional southern U.S. folk song)—arr. Aden G. Lewis. Plymouth Music PCS-216. Solo. Accompanied. Moderately easy.

Four Songs for Three Voices—Johannes Brahms, ed. Vernon Cotwals and Philip Keppler. Broude Brothers No. CR 47. *A cappella.* Medium.

Go Now, My Love—Claudin de Sermisy, arr. Jerry Weseley Harris. CPP/Belwin No. 02535. *A cappella.* Moderately easy.

Hymn to Freedom—Oscar Peterson, arr. Seppo Hovi. Walton No. WW 1135. Accompanied. Medium.

Praise Ye the Lord—George Philipp Telemann, arr. Wallace Depue. CPP/Belwin No.SV 8926. *A cappella.* Medium.

Shenandoah (American folk song)—arr. Mary Goetze. Boosey & Hawkes No. OCTB6257. *A cappella.* Easy.

South African Suite (South African folk and freedom songs). arr. Henry Leck. Plymouth Music No. HL-200. *A cappella.* Moderately easy.

Sweet Day—Ralph Vaughan Williams, arr. W. R. Pasfield. Galaxy No. 1.5012. *A cappella.* Moderately easy.

Sacred Standard/Traditional Music

Adoramus Te (We Adore Thee)—Giovanni Pierluigi da Palestrina, arr. Swift. Belwin Mills No. 1655. Accompanied. Moderately easy.

Alleluia—W. A. Mozart, arr. Riegger. Flammer No. 89024. Accompanied. Medium.

Angel Ever Bright—G. F. Handel, arr. Overby. Augsburg No. 1013. Optional accompaniment. Moderately easy.

Angels and the Shepherds—Zoltan Kodály. Universal No. 312-40593. A cappella. Medium.

Angelus ad pastores ait and Hodie Christus natus est (from Sacrae Cantiunculae)—Claudio Monteverdi. Mercury No. 352-000-24. A cappella. Medium.

Ave Maria—Jacob Arcadelt. Bourne No. ES 3. A cappella. Moderately easy.

Ave Maria—Zoltan Kodály. Universal No. 312-40592. A cappella. Moderately easy.

Ave verum—Josquin Després, arr. Greyson. Bourne No. ES 88A. A cappella. Moderately easy.

Away in a Manger (traditional carol)—arr. Terri. Lawson-Gould No. 666. A cappella. Moderately easy.

Bless Ye the Lord—Mikail M. Ippolitov-Ivanov, arr. Peter J. Wilhousky. Carl Fischer No. 639. A cappella. Moderately easy.

Blest Is the Man—Orlando di Lasso. Augsburg No. PS603. A cappella. Moderately easy.

Bring a Torch, Jeannette, Isabella (old French carol)—arr. Nunn. E. C. Schirmer No. 496. A cappella. Moderately easy.

The Call of the Shepherds (French Noël)—arr. Don Malin. B. F. Wood No. 826. A cappella. Moderately easy.

Cantate Domino—Giuseppi Ottavio Pitoni. Flammer No. 89181. A cappella. Moderately easy.

Carol of the Italian Pipers (traditional carol)—arr. Zgodava. Shawnee Press No. B-321. Accompanied. Moderately easy.

Cherubic Hymn—Musitcheskoo. Boosey & Hawkes No. 5026. Accompanied. Medium.

Christ Is Born (Ukrainian carol)—arr. Boberg. Carl Fischer No. 7455. A cappella. Moderately easy.

Christmas Hymn (17th century)—arr. Hugo Jüngst. G. Schirmer No. 9890. A cappella. Moderately easy.

Come, O Jesus, Come to Me—Luigi Cherubini, arr. Walter Ehret. Plymouth No. S.C. 201. Accompanied. Moderately easy.

Come to Me—Ludwig van Beethoven, arr. Aslanoff. G. Schirmer No. 8711. Accompanied. Easy.

Come, Ye Gay Shepherds—Guillaume Costeley, arr. Cramer. Edw. B. Marks No. 4482. Optional accompaniment. Moderately easy.

Come, Ye Lofty, Come, Ye Lowly (Breton carol)—arr. Don Malin. Summy-Birchard No. 1419. Accompanied. Moderately easy.

Coventry Carol (English carol)—arr. L. Stone. Belwin Mills No. 2070. Accompanied. Moderately easy.

Crucifixus—Andrea Gabrieli, ed. Walter Ehret. Edw. B. Marks No. 4332. A cappella. Medium.

Glory to God in the Highest!—Giovanni Pergolesi, arr. Riegger. Flammer No. 89041. Accompanied. Medium.

The God of Abraham Praise (traditional Hebrew melody)—arr. Malmin. Augsburg No. 1238. Accompanied. Easy.

God Rest You Merry, Gentlemen (English carol)—arr. Scholin. Belwin Mills No. 1625. Accompanied. Moderately easy.

Hear Our Supplication—W. A. Mozart, arr. Hilton. Mercury No. 352-00460. Accompanied. Moderately easy.

The Holy Infant's Lullaby—Norman Dello Joio. Edw. B. Marks No. 4392. Accompanied. Moderately easy.

How Far Is It to Bethlehem?—Chesterton. World Library No. AC-595-3. A cappella. Easy.

Hush My Babe—Rousseau-Stone. Belwin Mills No. 2067. Accompanied. Easy.

Incline Thine Ear, O Lord—Alexander Archangelsky, arr. Max Krone. Witmark No. 3220. A cappella. Medium.

Jesu, Joy of Man's Desiring—J. S. Bach, arr. Treharne. G. Schirmer No. 8388. Accompanied. Easy.

Lacrymosa—W. A. Mozart. Carl Fischer No. CM 6945. Accompanied. Medium.

A Legend—Peter I. Tchaikovsky. Carl Fischer No. CM 6325. Accompanied. Moderately easy.

Lift Thine Eyes (from Elijah)—Felix Mendelssohn. Willis No. 698. A cappella. Moderately easy.

Lo, a Voice to Heaven Sounding—Dimitri S. Bortniansky, arr. Katherine K. Davis. E. C. Schirmer No. 1079. A cappella. Moderately easy.

The Lord Is My Sheperd—Franz Schubert, arr. Watson. Remick No. 2-G1646. Accompanied. Moderately difficult.

O Little Jesus (16th-century German carol)—arr. Gordon. Belwin Mills No. 1874. Accompanied. Moderately easy.

Once in Royal David's City (Finnish folk melody)—arr. Lundquist. Elkan-Vogel No. 3079. *A cappella.* Easy.

Praise to the Lord (17th-century German tune)—arr. Whitehead. Gray No. 2095. Organ accompaniment. Moderately easy.

Praise Ye the Lord—J. S. Bach, arr. Trusler. Plymouth No. TR-103. Piano or organ accompaniment. Moderately easy.

Praise Ye the Lord of Hosts—Camille Saint-Saëns. Belwin Mills No. 698. Accompanied. Easy.

Prayer of Thanksgiving (old Dutch melody)—arr. Kremser. G. Schirmer No. 6812. Accompanied. Easy.

Puer natus est—Christóbal de Morales. Bourne No. ES 73. Optional accompaniment. Medium.

Rejoice, Holy Mary (French carol)—arr. Don Malin. Belwin Mills No. 693. Accompanied. Moderately easy.

Send Out Thy Light—Mily A. Balakirev. Boosey & Hawkes No. 1924. *A cappella.* Medium.

Shepherd's Carol—William Billings. Gray No. 3024. Accompanied. Moderately easy.

Slumber of the Infant Jesus—Francois Auguste Gevaert, arr. Katherine K. Davis. E. C. Schirmer No. 1088. *A cappella.* Medium.

This Little Babe (from *A Ceremony of Carols*)—Benjamin Britten. Boosey & Hawkes No. 5138. Accompanied. Moderately easy.

To Our Little Town (French carol)—arr. Don Malin. Belwin Mills No. 692. *A cappella.* Moderately easy.

To Us There Comes a Little Child (German melody)—arr. Don Malin. Belwin Mills No. 704. Accompanied. Moderately easy.

Two Czech Carols—arr. Peloguin. McLaughlin & Reilly No. 2047. *A cappella.* Moderately easy.

Vere languores nostros—Antonio Lotti. Bourne No. ES 22. *A cappella.* Moderately easy.

While Shepherds Watched (17th-century melody)—arr. Peter Tkach. Kjos No. 6044. Accompanied. Easy.

Whither Going, Shepherd? (Hungarian folk song)—arr. Deems Taylor. J. Fischer No. 5054. Accompanied. Moderately easy.

Wolcum Yole! (from *A Ceremony of Carols*)—Benjamin Britten. Boosey & Hawkes No. 1755B. Accompanied. Medium.

Ya Ba Bom (Jewish folk tune)—arr. Maurice Goldman. Lawson-Gould No. 51958. Piano and percussion accompaniment. Medium.

Secular Standard/Traditional Music

Adelaide—Ludwig van Beethoven. Boston Music Co. No. 3045. Accompanied. Moderately easy.

Adieu, Mignonne, When You Are Gone—Norman Dello Joio. Carl Fischer No. 6784. Accompanied. Moderately difficult.

Amarilli, Mia Bella—Giulio Caccini, arr. Deems Taylor. J. Fischer No. 4375. Accompanied. Medium.

An Offering—Baldwin, arr. Watson. Witmark No. 5W3362. *A cappella.* Moderately easy.

As Fair as Morn—John Wilbye. Edw. B. Marks No. 4331. *A cappella.* Moderately easy.

As from the Earth a Flower Grows—Claudio Monteverdi, arr. Zipper. Edw. B. Marks No. 45. *A cappella.* Moderately easy.

A Bird Flew—Joseph Clokey. J. Fischer No. 5506. Accompanied. Medium.

Bois épais—Jean-Baptiste Lully, arr. Deems Taylor. J. Fischer No. 4562. Accompanied. Moderately easy.

Calm as the Night—Boehm, arr. Noble Cain. Schmitt, Hall & McCreary No. 2016. Accompanied. Moderately easy.

Carol of the Bells (Christmas)—Leontovich, arr. Peter J. Wilhousky. Carl Fischer No. 5276. Optional accompaniment. Medium.

Come, Let Us Start a Joyful Song—Hans Leo Hassler. Bourne No. ES 31. Optional accompaniment. Moderately easy.

Come, Sirrah Jack Ho—Thomas Weelkes. E. C. Schirmer No. 840. *A cappella.* Medium.

Come, You Maidens—Peter I. Tchaikovsky. Boosey & Hawkes No. 5031. Accompanied. Moderately easy.

Danza, Danza—Francesco Durante, arr. Deems Taylor. J. Fischer No. 4378. Accompanied. Medium.

Dreams—Wagner, arr. Shelley. Presser No. 10687. Accompanied. Medium.

Enchanting Song—Béla Bartók. Boosey & Hawkes No. 1954. A cappella. Medium.

Go 'Way from My Window—John Jacob Niles, arr. Ross. G. Schirmer No. 9805. Accompanied. Soprano solo. Medium.

Hark! Hark! the Lark—Franz Schubert, arr. Bliss. Willis No. 2338. Accompanied. Easy.

He Came to Me—Robert Franz. Schmitt, Hall & McCreary No. 2127. Accompanied. Easy.

In Summer Fields—Johannes Brahms. Boston Music Co. No. 3044. Accompanied. Moderately easy.

In the Mill—Vladimir I. Rebikoff, arr. Sammond. J. Fischer No. 5689. A cappella. Medium.

In These Delightful Pleasant Groves—Henry Purcell. Bourne No. ES 28; Gray No. 519. A cappella. Moderately easy.

Invocation of Orpheus—Jacopo Peri. Witmark No. W 2728. Accompanied. Medium.

The Lass with the Delicate Air—Thomas Arne, arr. Chambers. Gray No. 515. Optional accompaniment. Moderately easy.

Let Us Sing—Jean-Philippe Rameau. Witmark No. 2-W 2988. Accompanied. Medium.

Linden Lea—Ralph Vaughan Williams, arr. Harrison. Boosey & Hawkes No. MFS 219. Accompanied. Moderately easy.

A Little White Hen (Ein Hennelin weiss)—Antonio Scandello, arr. Norman Greyson. Bourne No. ES 29P. Optional accompaniment. Medium.

Loafer—Béla Bartók. Boosey & Hawkes No. 1671. Accompanied. Moderately easy.

Love Song—Johannes Brahms, arr. Gibb. Boston Music Co. No. 3046. Accompanied. Moderately easy.

Marienwürmehen (My Lady Bird)—Robert Schumann, arr. Robinson.. G. Schirmer No. 10743. Accompanied. Medium.

Mocking of Youth—Béla Bartók. Boosey & Hawkes No. 1955. A cappella. Medium.

Mother, I Will Have a Husband—Thomas Vautor. Bourne No. ES 11. Optional accompaniment. Moderately easy.

Musetta's Waltz Song (from La Bohème)—Giacomo Puccini. Boosey & Hawkes No. 5120. Accompanied. Moderately easy.

My Mistress Frowns—John Hilton, arr. Stoufer. National Music Publishers No. CMS-123. A cappella. Recorder consort accompaniment.

The Nightingale—Thomas Weelkes, arr. Leslie. E. C. Schirmer No. 1008; Gray No. 671. A cappella. Medium.

O Lovely Spring—Johannes Brahms, arr. Grant. Belwin Mills No. 1839. Accompanied. Medium.

Over the Gods Love Holds His Sway—Jacob Arcadelt, ed. Don Malin. Belwin Mills No. 2413. A cappella. Moderately easy.

Pat-a-Pan (Burgundian carol; Christmas)—arr. Katherine K. Davis. E. C. Schirmer No. 1052. A cappella. Medium.

Prayer from Hansel and Gretel—Engelbert Humperdinck, arr. Riegger. Flammer No. 83087. Accompanied. Easy.

Pretense—Joseph Clokey. J. Fischer No. 7361. Accompanied. Moderately easy.

Robin Loves Me—De La Halle. Edition Musicus No. 014. Optional accompaniment. Easy.

Silent Strings—Granville Bantock, arr. O'Shea. Boosey & Hawkes No. 1467. Accompanied. Moderately easy.

The Silver Swan—Orlando Gibbons, arr. Norman Greyson. Bourne No. ES 12A. A cappella. Moderately easy.

Sing Songs of Jubilation—Johann Pachelbel, arr. Petker. Gentry No. JG-460. A cappella. Medium.

Slumber, Beloved One—Maurice Ravel, arr. Douty. Presser No. 21434. Accompanied. Moderately difficult.

Slumber Song—Alexander Gretchaninov. G. Schirmer No. 1510. Accompanied. Moderately easy.

The Smith—Johannes Brahms. Presser No. 312-40035. Accompanied. Easy.

Song from Ossian's Fingal—Johannes Brahms. E. C. Schirmer No. 495. Horn and harp accompaniment. Medium.

Song of Sorrow—Robert Schumann. Leeds Music No. L-423. Optional accompaniment. Moderately easy.

Songs My Mother Taught Me—Antonin Dvořák, arr. Cain. Flammer No. 83097. Accompanied. Moderately easy.

Spanish Serenata—Enrique Granados, arr. Harris. G. Schirmer No. 7814. Accompanied. Moderately difficult.

Sweet Day—Ralph Vaughan Williams, arr. Pasfield. Galaxy No. 695. Optional accompaniment. Moderately easy.

The Tambourine—Robert Schumann. Leeds Music No. L-428. Optional accompaniment. Medium.

To Schumann with Love (Three Songs from the *Dichterliebe*)—Robert Schumann, arr. Harris. National Music Publishers No. WHC 119. Accompanied. Medium.

Weep, O Mine Eyes—John Wilbye. E. C. Schirmer No. 841. *A cappella.* Moderately easy.

While the Birds Are Singing—Luigi Boccherini, arr. Ambrose. Schmidt No. 747. Accompanied. Moderately difficult.

Who Is Sylvia?—Franz Schubert. G. Schirmer No. 733. Accompanied. Moderately easy.

Within My Heart Breathes Music—Johannes Brahms, arr. Gibb. J. Fischer No. 9158. Accompanied. Moderately easy.

You Lovers That Have Loves Astray—John Hilton, arr. Stoufer. National Music Publishers No. CMS-119. Recorder consort accompaniment. Medium.

Younger Generation—Aaron Copland, arr. Swift. Boosey & Hawkes No. 1722. Accompanied. Medium.

Folk Songs and Spirituals—Standard/Traditional

Ay, Ay, Ay!—Freire, arr. Don Malin. Piedmont No. 4372. Accompanied. Moderately easy.

Charlottown—Bryan. J. Fischer No. 7993. *A cappella.* Medium.

Chiapanecas (Mexican dance song)—arr. Marlowe. Huntzinger No. 2039. Accompanied. Moderately easy.

Czechoslovakian Dance Song—arr. Row. R. D. Row No. 234. *A cappella.* Easy.

Dancing-Song (traditional Hungarian)—Zoltán Kodály. Oxford No. 54:942. *A cappella.* Medium.

The Dove on the Lily Tree (Swedish folk song)—arr. Vené. Carl Fischer No. CM 6280. Accompanied. Easy.

Down by the Sally Gardens (old Irish air)—arr. Donovan. Galaxy No. 555. Accompanied. Moderately easy.

Early One Morning (old English folk song)—arr. Tom Scott. Shawnee Press. Accompanied. Medium.

An Eriskay Love Lilt (folk song from the Hebrides)—arr. Arch. Boosey & Hawkes No. 5665. Accompanied. Moderately easy.

Farewell (Austrian folk song)—arr. Kanitz. Carl Fischer No. CM 6397. Accompanied. Easy.

Goin' to Boston (Kentucky folk song)—arr. Katherine K. Davis. Summy-Birchard No. 1573. Accompanied. Medium.

Good Night (German folk song)—arr. Don Malin. Wood No. 830. Accompanied. Moderately easy.

Gute Nacht (German folk song)—arr. G. Wallace Woodworth, E. C. Schirmer No. 819. Accompanied. Medium.

Hi, Ho, Sing Gaily (Swiss folk tune)—arr. Luvaas. Summy-Birchard No. 1505. Accompanied. Moderately easy.

Ifca's Castle (Czechoslovakian folk song)—arr. Harley and Aschenbrenner. Carl Fischer No. 5223. *A cappella.* Moderately easy.

I Got Shoes (spiritual)—arr. Noble Cain. Flammer No. 83206. Accompanied. Moderately easy.

I Live Not Where I Love (traditional English tune)—arr. Parry. Oxford No. W45. Accompanied.

The Keel Row (Tyneside air)—arr. Fletcher. Curwen No. 71227. Optional accompaniment. Medium.

The Lass from the Low Country (British folk song)—arr. LaMance. Lawson-Gould No. 52187. French horn accompaniment. Medium.

Linden Lea—Ralph Vaughan Williams. Boosey & Hawkes No. MFS 219. Accompanied. Moderately easy.

Little Bird (Mexican folk song)—arr. Grant. Belwin Mills No. 1723. Accompanied. Moderately easy.

Little David, Play on Your Harp (spiritual)—arr. Noble Cain. Flammer No. 83178. Accompanied. Easy.

The Little Sandman (German folk song)—arr. Harley & Aschenbrenner. Carl Fischer No. CM 5280. A cappella. Easy.

Lollytoodum (American folk song)—arr. Bell. Shawnee Press No. B 0096. Accompanied. Medium.

May Day Carol (English folk song)—arr. Deems Taylor. J. Fischer No. 4872. Accompanied. Moderately easy.

Meadows, Grow Ye Greene (Austrian folk song)—arr. Kanitz. Carl Fischer No. CM 6395. Accompanied. Easy.

Memories (Irish folk tune)—arr. Luvaas. Summy-Birchard No. 374. A cappella. Easy.

Meneate, buena moza (Spanish folk song)—arr. Don Malin. Piedmont No. 4374. Accompanied. Moderately easy.

My Desert Flower (North African folk song)—arr. Marshall. Belwin Mills No. 1821. Accompanied. Moderately easy.

O Can Ye Sew Cushions? (old Scottish cradle song)—arr. Mansfield. Belwin Mills No. 711. Accompanied. Moderately easy.

The Old Woman and the Pedlar (English air)—arr. Katherine K. Davis. E. C. Schirmer No. 1060. A cappella. Medium.

O Little Star in the Sky (Swedish folk tune)—arr. Katherine K. Davis. E. C. Schirmer No. 1065. Accompanied. Medium.

O Mary, Don't You Weep (spiritual)—arr. Siegmaster and Ehret. Bourne No. 25. Accompanied. Medium.

Rock-a My Soul (spiritual)—arr. De Vaux. Bourne No. 195. Accompanied. Medium.

Shy Love (Ukrainian folk song)—arr. Boberg. Kjos No. 6088. Accompanied. Easy.

Song of a Happy Heart (Ukrainian folk song)—arr. Boberg. Kjos No. 6091. Accompanied. Easy.

The Swallow's Wooing (Hungarian children's song)—arr. Zoltan Kodály. Oxford No. 542. A cappella. Medium.

Swing Low, Sweet Chariot (spiritual)—arr. Burleigh. Ricordi No. 116469. Accompanied. Moderately easy.

Three Hungarian Folk songs—Béla Bartók, arr. Suchoft. Boosey & Hawkes No. 5488. Accompanied. Medium.

Three Songs from Sweden—arr. Hallstrom. Shawnee Press No. B-215. Accompanied. Moderately easy.

Vreneli (Swiss folk song)—arr. Lester. Belwin Mills No. 1830. Accompanied. Moderately easy.

Waters, Ripple, and Flow (Czechoslovak folk song)—arr. Deems Taylor. J. Fischer. No. 5065. Accompanied. Moderately difficult.

We Wish You a Merry Christmas (English folk song)—arr. Max Krone. Kjos No. 1211. Optional accompaniment. Medium.

When Love Is Kind (traditional English or Austrian)—arr. Trinkaus. Carl Fischer No. 6139. Accompanied. Moderately easy.

Publications for Male Voices (TTBB)

Sacred and Secular (More Recently Published Music)

Down among the Dead Men (old English air)—arr. Ralph Vaughan Williams. Galaxy No. 1.5025. A cappella. Medium.

Drei Lieder für Mannerchor, Op. 13.—Hugo Wolf. A cappella.

    Nr. 1. Im Sommer. Doblinger No. 54015. Medium.

    Nr. 2. Geistegrus. Doblinger No. 54016. Medium.

    Nr. 3. Mailied. Doblinger No. 54017. Medium.

Gird Yourself with Lamentations—Frank Pooler. Walton No. WW1129. A cappella. Medium.

Gloria in Excelsis (from Gloria)—Antonio Vivaldi, ed. Mason Martens. Walton No. 9000. Medium.

Go Down Moses (spiritual)—arr. Norman Luboff. Walton No. W1018. A cappella. Medium.

O Come (Adeste Fideles)—arr. Dede Duson (TBB). Neil A. Kjos No. ED 5565. Brass accompaniment (two trumpets and two trombones) included. Moderately easy.

O Love, O Love (Sicilian folk song)—arr. Paul Hendrickson. Music 70 No. M70-609. Accompanied. Medium.

O, What Joy That I Have Jesus (Jesu, Joy of Man's Desiring)—J. S. Bach. Southern Music No. SC 325. For male voices in three choirs, with keyboard accompaniment and optional violin; oboe or flute; cello, bassoon, or bass; and trumpet. Medium.

O Vos Omnes (O Ye People)—Pablo Casals. Tetra/Continuo No. TC 242. *A cappella.* Medium.

Stars of the Summer Night—Isaac Woodbury, arr. Don Large. Plymouth No. DL-301. *A cappella.* Medium.

Still, Still, Still (Austrian carol)—arr. Norman Luboff. Walton No. W1009. Accompanied. Medium.

12th Street Rag—Euday L. Bowman, arr. Bobby L. McCullar. Plymouth No. PCS-309. *A cappella.* Medium.

When the Saints Go Marching In (traditional)—arr. Don Large. Plymouth No. VJSR-300. Accompanied. Medium.

Sacred (Standard/Traditional Music)

Adoramus Te—Giovanni Pierluigi Palestrina, arr. Norman Greyson. Bourne No. ES 16. *A cappella.* Easy.

Adoramus Te, Christe—Jacopo Corsi, arr. Noble Cain. Choral Art No. R180. *A cappella.* Moderately easy.

Alleulia—G. F. Handel, arr. Dawe. G. Schirmer No. 9412. Accompanied. Tenor solo. Moderately difficult.

All Glory Be to God on High (chorale melody of Gregorian origin)—arr. Don Malin. Summy-Birchard No. 1538. Accompanied. Moderately easy.

Ave Maria (Give Ear unto My Prayer)—Jacob Arcadelt, arr. Norman Greyson. Bourne No. ES 4. Optional accompaniment. Moderately difficult.

Ave, maris stella (Hail, O Star; Christmas)—Edvard Grieg, arr. Gladys Pitcher. Summy-Birchard No. 881. *A cappella.* Moderately difficult.

A Babe, So Tender (old Flemish carol)—arr. Manton. E. C. Schirmer No. 543. *A cappella.* Medium.

Beautiful Savior (Silesian folk tune)—arr. F. M. Christiansen and Wycisk. Augsburg No. 263. *A cappella.* Moderately easy.

Behold That Star (spiritual; Christmas)—arr. Cunkle. Shawnee Press No. 10. *A cappella.* Bass solo. Medium.

Cantate Domino—Hans Leo Hassler, arr. Beveridge. E. C. Schirmer No. 2194. *A cappella.* Medium.

Carol of the Russian Children (White Russian carol)—arr. Gaul. G. Schirmer No. 7363. Optional accompaniment. Medium.

Christ Is Born of Maiden Fair (ancient carol)—ed. H. Clough-Leighter. E. C. Schirmer No. 515. *A cappella.* Medium.

Christmas Hymn (17th century)—arr. Hugo Jüngst. G. Schirmer No. 1414. *A cappella.* Moderately easy.

Come, Sweet Death—J. S. Bach, arr. Reed. G. Schirmer No. 8956. *A cappella.* Moderately easy.

God Rest You Merry, Gentlemen (English carol)—arr. the Krones. Kjos No. 1117. Optional accompaniment. Moderately easy.

Hallelujah (from *Mount of Olives*)—Ludwig van Beethoven. G. Schirmer No. 10774. Accompanied. Moderately difficult.

Hallelujah, Amen—G. F. Handel, arr. Davison. E. C. Schirmer No. 38. Accompanied. Medium.

The Heart Worships—Gustav Holst, arr. Duey. Boston Music Co. No. 2952. Accompanied. Medium.

Heavenly Light—Alexander A. Kopylov, arr. Peter J. Wilhousky. Carl Fischer No. CM 611. *A cappella.* Moderately difficult.

I Wonder As I Wander (Appalachian carol)—arr. Niles and Horton. G. Schirmer No. 9292. *A cappella.* Medium.

Jacob's Ladder (spiritual)—arr. Harry R. Wilson. Ricordi No. NY1680. Optional accompaniment. Medium.

Joseph, Dear One, Joseph Mine (German carol)—arr. Barrow. E. C. Schirmer No. 2158. *A cappella.* Moderately easy.

A Joyous Christmas Song (Norwegian carol)—arr. Hokanson. Summy-Birchard No. 3142. *A cappella*. Moderately easy.

Let All Give Thanks to Thee—J. S. Bach, arr. Treharne. G. Schirmer No. 8342. *A cappella*. Moderately easy.

Let Nothing Ever Grieve Thee—Johannes Brahms. C. F. Peters No. 6009. Accompanied. Medium.

Let Thy Holy Presence—Paul G. Tschesnokov, arr. Walter Ehret. Boosey & Hawkes No. 5022. *A cappella*. Moderately easy.

Matthew, Mark, Luke, and John (West Country folk song)—arr. Gustav Holst. Curwen No. 50616. *A cappella*. Tenor solo. Moderately easy.

May Now Thy Spirit—Franz Joseph Schuetky, arr. Trehame. Willis No. 5641. *A cappella*. Medium.

May Thy Blessed Spirit—Paul G. Tschesnokov, arr. Cookson. Fitzsimons No. 4062. *A cappella*. Medium.

Nature's Praise of God—Ludwig van Beethoven. G. Schirmer No. 6566. Optional accompaniment. Moderately easy.

Noel, Noel—François Auguste Gevaert, arr. Norman Grayson. Kjos No. 5513. Accompanied. Easy.

Now Thank We All Our God—Johann Crüger, harmonized by Mendelssohn. Boston Music Co. No. 471. Organ accompaniment. Easy.

O bone Jesu—Giovanni Pierluigi da Palestrina. Bourne No. ES 45. *A cappella*. Easy.

O Light Divine—Alexander Arkhangelsky, arr. Bement. Oliver Ditson No. 15182. *A cappella*. Medium.

O Lovely, Holy Night (Christmas)—Kremser, arr. Biedermann. J. Fischer No. 3344. *A cappella*. Medium.

Praise the Name of the Lord—Ivanoff, arr. McKinney. J. Fischer No. 9166. *A cappella*. Medium.

Release Them, Lord (Absolve Domine)—Peter Cornelius. Music 70 No. M70—303. *A cappella*. Medium.

Requiem aeternam—Luigi Cherubini. Edition Musicus No. 1013. *A cappella*. Moderately easy.

Since Christ Our Lord Was Crucified—Heinrich Schütz, arr. Archibald T. Davison E. C. Schirmer No. 88. *A cappella*. Moderately difficult.

Sleep of the Child Jesus—François Auguste Gevaert, arr. Lefebvre. Franco Colombo No. NY773. *A cappella*. Easy.

The Stars—Franz Schubert, arr. Larson. Summy-Birchard No. 5021. *A cappella*. Tenor solo. Medium.

Tell Me, Shepherds, Dear (Polish carol)—arr. H.G.M. E. C. Schirmer No. 2105. *A cappella*. Medium.

Thanks Be to Thee—G. F. Handel, arr. Lefebvre. Galaxy No. 1222. Accompanied. Tenor solo. Easy.

Then Round About the Starry Throne (from *Samson*) G. F. Handel. E. C. Schirmer No. 907. Accompanied. Medium.

They Sang That Night in Bethlehem—Franz Schubert, arr. Deis. G. Schirmer No. 8292. *A cappella*. Medium.

Thou Must Leave Thy Lowly Dwelling—Hector Berlioz. Galaxy No. 2065. Accompanied. Medium.

Who Ne'er His Bread with Tears Did Eat—Franz Schubert. Lawson-Gould No. 876. Accompanied. Medium.

With a Voice of Singing—Martin Shaw. G. Schirmer No. 10454. Piano or organ accompaniment. Medium.

Ye Watchers and Ye Holy Ones (17th-century German melody)—arr. Archibald T. Davison. E. C. Schirmer No. 65. Piano or organ accompaniment. Medium.

Your Voices Raise—G. F. Handel, arr. Archibald T. Davison E. C. Schirmer No. 86. Accompanied. Difficult.

Secular (Standard/Traditional Music)

Aura Lee—Poulton, arr. Ralph Hunter, Alice Parker, and Robert Shaw. Lawson-Gould No. 527. *A cappella*. Moderately easy.

Battle Hymn of the Republic—William Steffe, arr. Roy Ringwald. Shawnee Press No. A 0028. Four-hand piano accompaniment. Baritone solo. Medium.

Brothers, Sing On!—Edvard Grieg, arr. McKinney. J. Fischer No. 6927. *A cappella*. Medium.

By the Sea—Franz Schubert, arr. Bantock. Belwin Mills No. 1145. *A cappella*. Moderately easy.

The Crown of Roses—Peter I. Tchaikovsky, arr. Bell. Belwin Mills Music No. 1085. *A cappella.* Medium.

Death Came Knocking—Carlisle Floyd. Boosey & Hawkes No. 5368. Accompanied. Moderately difficult.

Dreams—Richard Wagner, arr. Scherer. Gray No. 436. Accompanied. Medium.

The Gambler's Lament—John Jacob Niles. G. Schirmer No. 10305. Accompanied. Medium.

Good Fellows Be Merry—J. S. Bach, arr. Duey. Boston Music Co. No. 2944. Accompanied. Difficult.

Holiday Song—William Schuman. G. Schirmer No. 9866. Accompanied. Moderately easy.

Hunting Song (Jaglied)—Felix Mendelssohn, arr. Mueller. G. Schirmer No. 12074. *A cappella.* Medium.

In the Doorways I Will Linger—Franz Schubert, arr. Rider. Lawson-Gould No. 875. Accompanied. Medium.

Laura Lee—Stephen Foster, arr. Alice Parker and Robert Shaw. Lawson-Gould No. 874. *A cappella.* Moderately easy.

Liebe—Franz Schubert. Mark Foster No. MF 1059. *A cappella.* Medium.

The Night (Die Nacht)—Franz Schubert. Lawson-Gould No. 786. *A cappella.* Medium.

Nocturne—Felix Mendelssohn, arr. Treharne. Boston Music Co. No. 2987. Accompanied. Moderately difficult.

Passing By—Henry Purcell, arr. Alice Parker and Robert Shaw. Lawson-Gould No. 967. *A cappella.* Moderately easy.

Pilgrims' Chorus (from *Tannhäuser*) Richard Wagner, arr. Dawson. Kjos No. 5490. *A cappella.* Medium.

Pilgrim's Song—Peter I. Tchaikovsky, arr. Treharne. G. Schirmer No. 8802. Accompanied. Moderately difficult.

The Rain Has Kissed the Rose—Robert Schumann. G. Schirmer No. 412. *A cappella.* Moderately easy.

A Red, Red Rose—Robert Schumann, arr. Lloyd Pfautsch. Lawson-Gould No. 781. *A cappella.* Medium.

Rest (Du bist die Ruh)—Franz Schubert, arr. Bantock. Belwin Mills No. 1146. *A cappella.* Medium.

Rhapsodie—Johannes Brahms. Boston Music Co. No. 229. Accompanied. Alto solo. Moderately difficult.

Serenade—Franz Joseph Haydn, arr. Schultz. G. Schirmer No. 1087. *A cappella.* Easy.

Sophomoric Philosophy—Antonin Dvořák. Remick No. 9G 1108. *A cappella.* Moderately easy.

A Stopwatch and an Ordinance Map—Samuel Barber. G. Schirmer No. 8799. Kettledrum accompaniment. Moderately difficult.

Stouthearted Men—Sigmund Romberg, arr. Scotson. Harms, Inc. No. 9-H1184. Accompanied. Moderately easy.

The Swan—Camille Saint-Saëns, arr. Boyce. G. Schirmer No. 10527. Humming chorus with violin solo and piano accompaniment. Medium.

Sweet Love Doth Now Invite—John Dowland. Bourne No. ES7. Optional accompaniment. Moderately easy.

To All You Ladies Now on Land—John Wall Callcott. E. C. Schirmer No. 533. *A cappella.* Moderately easy.

Winter Song—Frederick F. Bullard. Oliver Ditson No. 10160. Accompanied. Moderately easy.

Woods So Dense—Jean-Baptiste Lully, arr. Sodero. G. Schirmer No. 8568. *A cappella.* Moderately easy.

Folk Songs and Spirituals (Standard/Traditional Music)

Ain'-a That Good News (spiritual)—arr. William Dawson. Kjos No. T104. *A cappella.* Medium.

All through the Night (old Welsh song)—arr. Roy Ringwald. Shawnee Press No. C-21. Optional accompaniment. Medium.

A-Roving (sea chantey)—arr. Roger Wagner. Lawson-Gould No. 791. *A cappella.* Baritone solo. Medium.

Aura Lee—Poulton, arr. Alice Parker and Robert Shaw. Lawson-Gould No. 527. *A cappella*. Moderately easy.

Believe Me, If All Those Endearing Young Charms (old Irish air)—arr. Ralph Hunter, Alice Parker, and Robert Shaw. Lawson-Gould No. 528. *A cappella*. Medium.

Blow the Man Down (English sea chantey)—arr. Alice Parker and Robert Shaw. Lawson-Gould No. 51055. *A cappella*. Bass solo. Moderately difficult.

The Boar's Head Carol (English secular carol)—arr. Alice Parker and Robert Shaw. G. Schirmer No. 10179. *A cappella*. Easy.

Carol of the Bells (Ukrainian carol; Christmas)—Nikolai D. Leontovich, arr. Peter J. Wilhousky. Carl Fischer No. CM 2270. *A cappella*. Moderately easy.

Climbin' Up the Mountain (spiritual)—arr. Smith. Kjos No. 1101. *A cappella*. Medium.

De Animals a'Comin' (African-American spiritual)—arr. Bartholomew. G. Schirmer No. 8046. *A cappella*. Medium.

Down among the Dead Men (old English air)—arr. Ralph Vaughan Williams. Belwin Mills No. 1142. *A cappella*. Medium.

Down in the Valley (Kentucky folk tune)—arr. Mead. Galaxy No. 1716. Accompanied. Moderately easy.

Drink to Me Only with Thine Eyes (old English air)—arr. Ralph Hunter, Alice Parker, and Robert Shaw. Lawson-Gould No. 530. *A cappella*. Moderately difficult.

Go Tell It on the Mountain (spiritual)—arr. Huntley. Fitzsimons No. 4067. *A cappella*. Medium.

We Wish You a Merry Christmas (English folk song; secular)—arr. the Krones. Kjos No. 1114. Optional accompaniment. Moderately easy.

What Shall We Do with a Drunken Sailor? (traditional sea chantey)—arr. Bartholomew. G. Schirmer No. 7422. Accompanied. Easy.

Publications for Combined Chorus and Band and/or Orchestra

All Glory, Laud and Honor—Gustav Wilhelm Teschner, arr. Cain. Flammer. SATB—for chorus and band; chorus and orchestra.

Ave Maria—J. S. Bach and Charles Gounod, arr. Tolmadge. Staff. SATB—for chorus and band.

Battle Hymn of the Republic—William Steffe, arr. Roy Ringwald. Shawnee Press. SATB; TTBB—for chorus and band; chorus and orchestra.

Battle Hymn of the Republic—William Steffe, arr. Wilhousky. Carl Fischer. SSATTBB—for chorus and band; chorus and orchestra.

Beautiful Dreamer—Stephen Foster, arr. Frangkiser. Boosey & Hawkes. SATB; TTBB—for chorus and band.

Break Forth, O Beauteous Heavenly Light—J. S. Bach. G. Schirmer. SATB—for chorus and orchestra (orchestra parts available from publisher on rental only).

Chorale from *Organ Symphony No. 3*—Camille Saint-Saëns. Staff. SATB—for chorus and band.

Chorale: King of Glory—J. S. Bach. Staff. SATB—for chorus and band; chorus and orchestra; chorus, band, and orchestra.

Chorale: St. Antoni—Franz Joseph Haydn and Johannes Brahms, arr. Tolmadge. Staff. SATB—for chorus and band.

Chorale: St. Martin—arr. Gardner. Staff. SATB—for chorus and band.

Choral Procession (Finale to Cantata *The Song of Man*)—Kountz, arr. Campbell and Watson. Witmark. SATB—for chorus and band.

Christmas Day—Gustav Holst. Gray. SATB—for chorus and orchestra (orchestral parts available from publisher on rental only).

Fantasie on Christmas Carols—Ralph Vaughan Williams. Galaxy. SATB, with bar, solo—for chorus and orchestra (orchestra parts available from publishers on rental only).

Festival Finale—Joseph Maddy. Kjos. SATB—for chorus and band; chorus and orchestra; chorus, band, and orchestra.

Festival Song of Praise—Felix Mendelssohn, arr. Wilson and Harris. Bourne. SATB—for chorus and orchestra.

Gloria in excelsis (from *Twelfth Mass*)—W. A. Mozart. Presser. SATB—for chorus and orchestra.

Glory—Nikolai A. Rimsky-Korsakov. Witmark. SSAATTBB—for chorus and orchestra.

Glory and Triumph—Hector Berlioz. Mercury. SATB—for chorus and band; chorus and orchestra.

Glory to God in the Highest—Giovanni Pergolesi, arr. Bruce Houseknecht. Kjos. SATB—for chorus and band.

God of Our Fathers—arr. Gearhart. Shawnee Press. SATB—for chorus, with three trumpets, percussion, four-hand piano and organ accompaniment.

Hail, Glorious Day—Edward Elgar, arr. Schaefer. Boosey & Hawkes. SATB—for chorus and band.

Hallelujah Chorus (from *Messiah*)—G. F. Handel. Carl Fischer. SATB—for chorus and orchestra; chorus and band.

The Heavens Are Telling—Franz Joseph Haydn. Carl Fischer. SATB—for chorus and orchestra.

Holy, Holy, Holy—arr. Eric Ledizén. Bourne. SATB—for chorus and band.

How Lovely Is Thy Dwelling (from *Requiem*)—Johannes Brahms. G. Schirmer. SATB—for chorus and orchestra (orchestral parts available from publisher on rental only).

Hymn of Freedom—Johannes Brahms, arr. Tolmadge. Staff. SATB—for chorus and band.

Hymn of Praise—W. A. Mozart, arr. Tolmadge. Staff. SATB—for Chorus and band.

Hymn to America—McKay. Schmitt, Hall & McCreary. SATB—for chorus and band.

Land of Hope and Glory—Edward Elgar. Boosey & Hawkes. SATB; SSA—for chorus and band; chorus and orchestra.

Largo from *New World Symphony* (choral parts: "Behold Our God")—Antonin Dvořák. Belwin Mills. SATB—for chorus and band.

Let All Mortal Flesh Keep Silence—Gustav Holst. Galaxy. SATB—for chorus and orchestra.

Magnificat—Ralph Vaughan Williams. Oxford. SSA, with contralto solo—for chorus and orchestra (orchestral parts available from publisher on rental only).

Mannin Veen (Dear Isle of Man)—Wood. Boosey & Hawkes. SATB; SAB; SSA—for chorus and orchestra-chorus and band.

A Mighty Fortress Is Our God—Martin Luther. Staff. SATB—for chorus and band; chorus and orchestra; chorus, band, and orchestra.

The Nation's Creed—Williams. Schmitt, Hall & McCreary. SATB—for chorus and band.

Now Thank We All Our God—Randall Thompson. E. C. Schirmer. SATB—for chorus and orchestra.

O Clap Your Hands—Ralph Vaughan Williams. Galaxy. SATB—for chorus, brass choir and percussion.

The Omnipotence—Franz Schubert. G. Schirmer. SSAATTBB; TTBB; SSA—for chorus and orchestra (orchestral parts available from publisher on rental only).

One World—O'Hara, arr. Wilson and Leidzen. Bourne. SATB; TTBB; SSA—for chorus and band; chorus and orchestra.

Onward, Christian Soldiers—arr. Harry Simeone. Shawnee Press. SATB; TTBB—for chorus and band; chorus and orchestra.

Onward, Ye Peoples—Jean Sibelius, arr. Lefebvre. Galaxy. SATB; SSA; TTBB—for chorus and band; chorus and orchestra.

Pomp and Circumstance—Edward Elgar. Staff. SATB—for chorus and band; chorus and orchestra; chorus, band, and orchestra.

Rhapsody in Blue (choral finale)—George Gershwin, arr. Wamick. Harms Inc. SSATTBB—for chorus and band; chorus and orchestra.

Song of Destiny—Johannes Brahms. Staff. SATB—for chorus and band.

To Music—Franz Schubert, arr. Harry R. Wilson. Schmitt, Hall & McCreary. SATB; SAB; SSA—for chorus and orchestra.

Trumpet Voluntary—Henry Purcell. Staff. SATB; SAB, SSA; SA—for chorus and band; chorus and orchestra; chorus, band, and orchestra.

Turn Back, O Man—Gustav Holst. Galaxy. SATB—for chorus and orchestra (orchestral parts available from publisher on rental only).

Voice of Freedom—Anton G. Rubinstein, arr. Lucien Caillet. Boosey & Hawkes. SATB; TTBB—for chorus and band; chorus and orchestra.

With a Voice of Singing—Martin Shaw. (S. Schirmer. SATB—for chorus and orchestral (orchestral accompaniment available from publisher on rental only).

Choral Music with Electronic Tape/Nonconventional Notation

Aleatory Psalm—Gordon H. Lamb. World Library Publications No. CA 4003-8. SATB.
Alleluia, Acclamation and Carol—Daniel Pinkham. E. C. Schirmer Nos. 2954 and 2955. SATB, timpani, percussion, and electronic tape.
All the Ways of a Man—Knut Nystedt. Augsburg No. 11—9004. SATB.
Amens—Daniel Pinkham. E. C. Schirmer No. 3016. SATB and electronic tape.
The Call of Isaiah—Daniel Pinkham. E. C. Schirmer No. 2911. SATB with organ and electronic tape.
Collect—Leslie Bassett. World Library Publications No. CA2000-8. SATB, electronic tape.
Creation, The (from The Family of Man)—Michael Hennagin. Walton No. W2186. SATB.
Dialogue—Robert Karlén. A.M.S.I. No. AMS 175. SATB, tape recorder.
The Emperor of Ice Cream—Roger Reynolds. C. F. Peters. Eight singers, piano, percussion; bass; multimedia.
Etude and Pattern—Brock McElheran. Oxford. SSAATBB unaccompanied.
Etude and Scherzo—Brock McElheran. Oxford. SSAATBB unaccompanied.
Evergreen—Daniel Pinkham. E. C. Schirmer No. 2962. Unison chorus, electronic tape, and optional instruments (Autoharp, bells, harp, guitar, piano, and organ).
God Love You Now—Donald Erb. Merion No. 342-40099. SATB, speaker, assorted instruments, reverberation device.
Hymn of the Universe—Richard Felciano. E. C. Schirmer No. 2944. SAB and electronic sounds.
In the Beginning of Creation—Daniel Pinkham. E. C. Schirmer No. 2902. Mixed chorus, electronic tape.
In the Presence—Gilbert Trythall. Edw. B. Marks No. 4495. SATB, electronic tape.
I Saw an Angel—Daniel Pinkham. E. C. Schirmer No. 2973. SATB and electronic tape.
Kyrie—Donald Erb. Merion No. 342-40026. SATB, piano, percussion, electronic tape.
Out of Sight—Richard Felciano. E. C. Schirmer No. 2909. SATB, organ, and electronic tape.
Pentecost Sunday—Richard Felciano. World Library Publications No. EMP—1532-1. Unison male chorus, organ, electronic tape.
Praise to God—Knut Nystedt. Associated No. A-597. Mixed voices, a cappella.
Praise Ye the Lord—Gardner Read. Lawson-Gould No. 51871.
Psalm 27 (Part 3)—Robert Karlen. A.M.S.I. No. 160. SATB.
Pshelley's Psalm—Richard Felciano. E. C. Schirmer No. 2930. SATB.
Sic transit—Richard Felciano. E. C. Schirmer No. 2903. SAB chorus, organ, electronic tape, light sources.
Signs—Richard Felciano. E. C. Schirmer No. 2927. SATB, electronic tape and one, two, or three film strip projectors.
Susani—Richard Felciano. E. C. Schirmer No. 3002. Mixed voices, organ, percussion, and electronic tape.
Three-in-One-in-Three—Richard Felciano. E. C. Schirmer No. 2910. Chorus, organ, tape.
A Time to Every Purpose—Gilbert Trythall. Edw. B. Marks No. 4586. SATB, electronic tape.
Two Moves and the Slow Scat—Dennis Kam. Belwin Mills No. 2282. SATB.
Two Public Pieces—Richard Felciano. E. C. Schirmer No. 2937. Unison voices and electronic sounds.
Words of St. Peter—Richard Felciano. World Library Publications No. CA-2093-8. Mixed voices, organ, and electronic tape.

Music for Jazz/Show Choirs (Broadway Musicals/Popular/Vocal Jazz)

More Recently Published Arrangements

A Gershwin Portrait—George and Ira Gershwin, arr. Mac Huff. Warner Bros. No. 08721797. A medley of thirty arrangements organized into six categories: 1. Opening; II. Gershwin at the Opera; III. A Gershwin Swing Set; IV. Fascinating Rhythm; V. Gershwin in Love; VI. Sing a Gershwin Show Stopper. Piano, with optional instrumental accompaniment including trumpets I & II, tenor sax/flute/clarinet, trombone, synthesizer, guitar, bass, and drums. Medium.

All the Things You Are (from *Very Warm for May*)—Jerome Kern, arr. Kirby Shaw. Hal Leonard No. 08720244. *A cappella*. Solo. Medium.

Am I Blue?—Harry Akst, arr. Kirby Shaw. Warner Bros. No. 441-01044. *A cappella*. Easy.

And All That Jazz (from *Chicago*)—John Kander, arr. Kirby Shaw. Hal Leonard No. 08655471. Accompanied. Medium.

The Christmas Song (Chestnuts Roasting on an Open Fire)—Mel Torme and Robert Wells, arr. Gene Puerling. Edwin H. Morris No. 07359063. Piano, bass, and drums. Medium.

Embraceable You—George Gershwin, arr. Steve Zegree. Warner Bros. No. 43509052. *A cappella*. Moderately easy.

Etude in Jazz—Heinz Kratochwil. Doblinger No. D.16.315. *A cappella*. Medium.

Fascinating Rhythm (from "A Gershwin Portrait")—George Gershwin, arr. Mac Huff. Piano with optional instrumental accompaniment. Moderately easy.

For All We Know—J. Fred Coots, arr. Brent Pierce. Plymouth Music No. VJS-103. *A cappella*. Moderately easy.

Friendship—Cole Porter, arr. Norman Leyden. Plymouth Music No. CP 101. Accompanied. Moderately easy.

Georgia on My Mind—Hoagy Carmichael, arr. Kirky Shaw. Hal Leonard No. 08657630. Piano, with optional guitar, bass, and drums. Moderately easy.

Gershwin in Love (from "A Gershwin Portrait")—George Gershwin, arr. Mac Huff. Warner Bros. No. 08721785. Piano, with optional instrumental accompaniment. Medium.

Get Happy—Harold Arlen and Ted Koehler, arr. Kirby Shaw. Warner Bros. No. 441-07014. Accompanied. Medium.

Here's That Rainy Day—Jimmy Van Heusen, arr. Roger Emerson. Jenson No. 403-08214. *A cappella*. Medium.

How High the Moon—Morgan Lewis, arr. Stephen Zegree. Hal Leonard No. 07357659. Piano, with optional guitar, bass, and drums. Medium.

If I Loved You (from *Carousel*)—Richard Rogers, arr. Kirby Shaw. Hal Leonard No. 08665939. *A cappella*. Moderately easy.

I'll Be Seeing You—Irving Kahal and Sammy Fain, arr. Phil Mattson. Hal Leonard No. 08603316. *A cappella*. Moderately easy.

It Might as Well Be Spring (from *State Fair*)—Richard Rogers, arr. Kirby Shaw. Hal Leonard No. 08657871. *A cappella*. Moderately easy.

Johnny One Note—Richard Rogers, arr. Gene Puerling. Hal Leonard No. 08624171. Piano and rhythm section, with optional jazz ensemble. Medium.

Love Walked In—George Gershwin, arr. Steve Zegree. Hal Leonard No. 08704361. *A cappella*. Moderately easy.

Misty—Erroll Garner, arr. Ed. Lojeski. Hal Leonard No. 08720755. Piano, with optional instrumental accompaniment (guitar, bass, drums, and synthesizer). Moderately easy.

More Than You Know—Vincent Youmans, arr. Steve Zegree. Hal Leonard No. 08704491. *A cappella*. Moderately easy.

My Funny Valentine (from *Babes in Arms*)—Richard Rogers, arr. Roger Emerson. Jenson No. 40326051. *A cappella*. Moderately easy.

Phantom of the Opera (medley)—Andrew Lloyd Webber, arr. Ed. Lojeski. Hal Leonard No. 08252941. Accompanied. Medium.

Phantom of the Opera (title song)—Andrew Lloyd Webber, arr. Ed. Lojeski. Hal Leonard No. 08252881. Accompanied. Medium.

Take Me Out to the Ball Game—Albert von Filzer, arr. Donald Moore. Mark Foster No. MF 3033. Accompanied. Easy.

Broadway Musicals/Popular/Vocal Jazz (Standard/Classical Arrangements)

A Holly Jolly Christmas—Johnny Marks, arr. Harry Simeone. Shawnee Press No. A-768. Accompanied. Moderately easy.

Alexander's Ragtime Band—Irving Berlin, arr. Harry Simeone. Shawnee Press No. 0638. Piano accompaniment. Moderately easy.

Am I Blue?—Akst, arr. Kirby Shaw. Warner Bros. No. 441-01044. *A cappella*. Moderately easy.

An Old Fashioned Love Song—Paul Williams, arr. Stan Beard. Shawnee Press No. A-1336. Four-hand piano accompaniment. Medium.

Another Op'nin', Another Show (from *Kiss Me Kate*)—Cole Porter, arr. Cable. Hal Leonard No. 00346038. Piano accompaniment. Moderately easy.

A Wonderful Day Like Today—Bricusse and Newley, arr. Leyden. Musical Comedy Productions No. S7029. Piano accompaniment. Moderately easy.

Baby Come Back to Me—Santamaria, arr. Nowak. Hal Leonard No. 07357521. Piano with optional rhythm section. Medium.

Beautiful City (from *Godspell*)—Stephen Schwartz, arr. Ed. Lojeski. Hal Leonard No. 08200630. Piano with optional percussion, guitar, and string bass. Moderately easy.

Bill Bailey, Won't You Please Come Home—Cannon, arr. Kirby Shaw. Jenson No. 441-02014. Piano and optional rhythm section. Moderately easy.

Black and Blue (from *Ain't Misbehavin'*)—Waller, arr. Elliott. Chappell No. 3893. Piano accompaniment. Medium.

Blow, Gabriel, Blow—Cole Porter, arr. Roy Ringwald. Shawnee Press No. A-1638. Accompanied. Medium.

Blues Down to My Shoes—Kirby Shaw. Hal Leonard No. 07852435. Piano, bass, and drums. Moderately easy.

Blue Skies—Irving Berlin, arr. Roger Emerson. Jenson No. 403-02094. Piano and optional rhythm section. Medium.

Broadway Spectacular (What I Did for Love, Tomorrow, Put On a Happy Face, Hello Dolly, Mame)—arr. Roger Emerson. Jenson No. 403-02044. Piano and optional rhythm section. Moderately easy.

Bye Bye Blues—Hamm, Bennett, Lown, and Gray, arr. Harry Simeone. Shawnee Press No. A-0523. Piano accompaniment. Medium.

Celebration—Bell, arr. Chinn. Jenson No. 457-03014. Piano and optional rhythm section. Moderately easy.

C'est si bon (It's So Good)—Betti, arr. Weir. Hal Leonard No. 08623371. Piano, bass, and percussion, with optional jazz ensemble. Difficult.

Choral Highlights from *Annie*—Charles Strouse, arr. Roger Emerson. Jenson No. 403-01084. Piano, guitar, bass, and drums. Moderately easy.

The Christmas Song (Chestnuts Roasting on an Open Fire)—Mel Torme and Robert Wells, arr. Walter Ehret. Edwin H. Morris No. E9822a. Accompanied. Solo. Moderately easy.

Corner of the Sky (from *Pippin*)—Stephen Schwartz, arr. Cacavas. Belwin Mills No. OCT 02288. Piano accompaniment. Moderately easy.

Crazy Rhythm—Meyer and Kahn, arr. Bretton. Warner Bros. No. H2210. Piano, guitar, and bass. Moderately easy.

Cute—Hefti, arr. Averre. Warner Bros. No. 487-41008. Piano, bass, and drums. Moderately easy.

Day by Day (from *Godspell*)—Stephen Schwartz, arr. Norman Leyden. CPP/Belwin No. 0014DC1X. Piano, drums, and electric and bass guitars. Medium.

Don't Take Away the Music—Tawney, arr. Ed. Lojeski. Hal Leonard No. 08212800. Piano, guitar, percussion, and electric bass. Medium.

Ease on Down the Road (from *The Wiz*)—Smalls, arr. Beard. Shawnee Press No. A-1374. Piano accompaniment. Moderately easy.

The Entertainer—Scott Joplin, arr. Ed. Lojeski. Hal Leonard No. 08214000. Piano, guitar, string bass, and percussion. Moderately easy.

Everybody Loves My Baby—Palmer and Williams, arr. Kirby Shaw. Hal Leonard No. 0865781. Piano and optional instrumental accompaniment. Medium.

Everybody Rejoice (from *The Wiz*)—Vandross, arr. Hawley Ades. Shawnee Press No. A-1402. Piano accompaniment. Moderately easy.

The Gene Puerling Sound (Am I Blue, April in Paris, Autumn in New York, Dancing in the Dark, Indian Summer)—arr. Gene Puerling. Shawnee Press No. A-1291. Optional piano accompaniment. Medium.

Georgia on My Mind—Hoagy Carmichael, arr. Gene Puerling. Studio P/R No. VGP 8001. Piano, bass, and drums. Moderately difficult.

Georgia on My Mind—Hoagy Carmichael, arr. Carl Strommen. Studio P/R No. SV 8337. Piano and guitar accompaniment. Medium.

Getting to Know You (from *The King and I*)—Richard Rogers, arr. Gene Puerling. Hal Leonard No. 07359124. Piano with optional rhythm section. Medium.

Go for the Good Times—Mark Brymer. Jenson No. 445-07054. Piano and optional rhythm section. Medium.

Got to Get You into My Life—John Lennon and Paul McCartney, arr. Carl Strommen. Alfred No. 6823. Piano with optional guitar, bass, and drums. Stage band accompaniment also available. Medium.

Here Comes That Rainy Day Feeling Again—Tony Macauley, Roger Cook, and Roger Greenaway, arr. Ed. Lojeski. Hal Leonard No. 08223500. Piano, guitar, electric bass, and percussion. Moderately easy.

Home (from *The Wiz*)—Smalls, arr. Hayward. Shawnee Press No. A-1394. Piano accompaniment. Moderately easy.

How Lucky Can You Get—Kander and Ebb, arr. Jennings. Warner Bros. No. 408-08014. Piano accompaniment. Moderately easy.

I Can't Stop Loving You—Don Gibson, arr. Kirby Shaw. Hal Leonard No. 07853871. *A cappella.* Medium.

I Hear Music—Frank Loesser and Burton, arr. Larry Lapin. Warner Bros. No. CH 0926. Piano with optional guitar, bass, and drums. Moderately difficult.

The Impossible Dream (from *Man of La Mancha*)—Leigh, arr. Roy Ringwald. Shawnee Press No. A-0885. Piano accompaniment. Medium.

In the Mood—Garland, arr. Sterling. Shawnee Press No. A-1533. Piano with optional guitar, string bass, and drums. Moderately easy.

It Don't Mean a Thing (If It Ain't Got That Swing)—Duke Ellington, arr. Paris Rutherford. CPP/Belwin No. 64402. Accompanied. Medium.

I've Got the World on a String—Harold Arlen, arr. Paris Rutherford. CPP/Belwin No. 74404. Piano, guitar, percussion, and bass. Medium.

I've Got the Music in Me—Boshell, arr. Billingsley. Jensen No. 432-09024. Piano and optional rhythm section. Medium.

I've Got You under My Skin—Cole Porter, arr. Phil Mattson. Hal Leonard No. 08603340. Piano, bass, and drums. Medium.

Jailhouse Rock—Leiber and Stoller, arr. Kirby Shaw. Hal Leonard No. 08657893. Piano with optional instrumental accompaniment. Moderately easy.

Jubilation—Anka and Harris, arr. Kirby Shaw. Hal Leonard No. 07981226. Piano, electric bass, drums, trumpet, alto saxophone, and trombone. Medium.

Just One of Those Things—Cole Porter, arr. Roger Emerson. Warner Bros. No. 403-10104. Piano accompaniment. Easy.

Just the Way You Are—Billy Joel, arr. Ed. Lojeski. Hal Leonard No. 08234875. Piano, guitar, percussion, and electric bass. Medium.

The King and I Medley—Richard Rogers, arr. Anita Kerr. Hal Leonard No. 08565671. Piano and optional instrumental accompaniment. Moderately easy.

Let's Call the Whole Thing Off—George Gershwin, arr. Anita Kerr. Hal Leonard No. 08565696. Piano, guitar, bass, and drums. Moderately easy.

Let the Sunshine In—Kirby Shaw. Jenson No. 441-12014. Piano and optional rhythm section. Medium.

Little Girl—Madeline Hyde and Francis Henry, arr. Anita Kerr. MCA Music No. UC 755. Piano, bass guitar, and percussion. Moderately easy.

Louise—Richard A. Whiting, arr. Harry Simeone. Shawnee Press No. A 611. Accompanied. Moderately easy.

Love Is the Answer—Hannisian. Shawnee Press No. A-1382. Piano accompaniment. Moderately easy.

Magic to Do (from *Pippin*)—Stephen Schwartz, arr. Fisher. Belwin Mills No. OCT 02302. Piano with optional bass, guitar, and drums. Moderately easy.

Mama Told Me (Not to Come)—Newmann, arr. Kirby Shaw. Hal Leonard No. 08658250. Piano, trumpet, alto saxophone, electric guitar, electric bass, and drums. Medium.

Maybe God Is Trying to Tell You Somethin'—Crouch, Jones, Maxwell, and Del Sesto, arr Kirby Shaw. Warner Bros. No. 441—13034. Piano, bass, guitar, and drums.

Me and My Shadow—Jolson and Dreyer, arr. Hawley Ades. Shawnee Press No. A-0512. Piano accompaniment. Medium.

Mercy, Mercy, Mercy—Zawinul, arr. Sechler. Shawnee Press No. A-1153. Piano with optional guitar, drums, and bass. Moderately easy.

Michelle—John Lennon and Paul McCartney, arr. Gene Puerling. Shawnee Press No. A-1344. A cappella. Soprano and tenor solos. Difficult.

Mood Indigo—Duke Ellington, arr. Harry Simeone. Shawnee Press No. A-0800. Piano and optional guitar, string bass, and drums. Medium.

Mood Indigo—Duke Ellington, arr. Paris Rutherford. CPP/Belwin No. 64395. Piano, guitar, percussion, and bass. Moderately easy.

Moonglow—Will Hudson, Eddie DeLange, and Irving Mills, arr. Teena Chinn. CPP/Belwin No. SVJ8601. Accompanied. Moderately easy.

My Funny Valentine—Richard Rogers arr. Kirby Shaw. Hal Leonard No. 08658800. A cappella. Medium.

My Romance—Richard Rogers, arr. Kirby Shaw. Jenson No. 441-13014. A cappella. Moderately difficult.

Mystery—Temperton, arr. Steve Zegree. Hal Leonard No. 07357770. Piano and optional instrumental accompaniment. Moderately difficult.

New York Afternoon—Cole, arr. Phil Mattson. Jenson No. 463-14024. Piano, bass, guitar, and drums. Moderately difficult.

New York City Rhythm—Manilow and Panzer, arr. Hyde. Big 3 No. 4027. Piano with optional guitar, percussion, and bass. Medium.

One (from A Chorus Line)—Marvin Hamlisch, arr. Anita Kerr. Edwin H. Morris No. 08565753. Piano, guitar, bass, and percussion. Moderately easy.

One Hand, One Heart (from West Side Story)—Leonard Bernstein, arr. William Stickles. G. Schirmer No. 10606. Accompanied. Easy.

Paddlin' Madelin' Home—Woods, arr. Grusin. Shapiro, Bernstein & Co. No. sb 7006. Piano accompaniment. Moderately easy.

People—Styne, arr. Gene Puerling. Hal Leonard No. 07359307. A cappella. Baritone solo. Moderately difficult.

Pippin (choral medley)—Stephen Schwartz, arr. Casey. Belwin Mills No. SB 00939. Piano with optional bass, guitar, and drums. Medium.

Powerhouse—Roger Emerson. Jenson No. 403-16074. Piano accompaniment. Medium.

Reach for the Stars—G. Fry. Belwin Mills No. OCT 02427. Piano with optional guitar, bass, and drums. Medium.

Rock-A-Bye Your Baby with a Dixie Melody—Jean Schwartz, arr. Paris Rutherford. CPP/Belwin No. 64405. Piano, with optional guitar, bass, and drums. Medium.

Rudolph, the Red-Nosed Reindeer—Johnny Marks, arr. A. Hawley Barry. Shawnee Press No. A-333. Accompanied. Medium.

Save the Bones for Henry Jones—Barker, Lee, and Jones, arr. Kirby Shaw. Hal Leonard No. 07248725. Piano, electric bass, and drums. Moderately easy.

The Shadow of Your Smile (from The Sandpiper)—Johnny Mandel, arr. Gene Puerling. CPP/Belwin No. SVCP501. Piano or vocal solo. Piano, bass, and drums. Medium.

The Shadow of Your Smile—Johnny Mandel, arr. Carl Strommen. Shawnee Press No. A-1764. Piano with optional guitar, bass, and drums. Medium.

Side-by-Side—Woods, arr. Coates. Shawnee Press No. A-1389. Piano accompaniment. Moderately easy.

Silent Night—Franz Gruber, arr. Gene Puerling. Shawnee Press No. A-1315. A cappella. Optional soprano and tenor solos. Moderately difficult.

Sleigh Ride—Leroy Anderson, arr. Hawley Ades. Shawnee Press No. A-669. Piano and sleigh bells. Moderately easy.

Smile—Chaplin, arr. Steve Zegree. Hal Leonard No. 08603699. A cappella. Medium.

Smiles (A choral montage of songs, 1900-1920)—arr. H. Ades. Shawnee Press No. A-1322. Piano accompaniment. Moderately easy.

Snow, Snow, Beautiful Snow—Sherm Feller, arr. Harry Simeone. Shawnee Press No. A-664. Accompanied. Medium.

Solitude—Duke Ellington, arr. Paris Rutherford. CPP/Belwin No. 64401. Piano, and optional guitar, bass, and drums. Medium.

The Sound of the Singers Unlimited (We've Only Just Begun, Try to Remember, On a Clear Day, Emily, My Ship, Where Is Love)—arr. Gene Puerling. Shawnee Press No. A-1412. Instrumental accompaniment available. Medium.

Stardust—Hoagy Carmichael, arr. Chuck Cassey. CPP/Belwin No. 64414. A cappella. Medium.

Stardust—Hoagy Carmichael, arr. Roy Ringwald. Shawnee Press No. A-0689. Piano accompaniment. Medium.

Streets A-fire!—Mark Brymer. Hal Leonard No. 08639211. Piano with optional instrumental accompaniment. Moderately difficult.

Summer Nights (from *Grease*)—Casey and Jacobs, arr. Ed Lojeski. Hal Leonard No. 08264480. Piano with electric guitar, percussion, and electric bass. Moderately easy.

Summertime—George Gershwin, arr. Kirby Shaw. Hal Leonard No. 08664217. Piano, electric bass, and drums. Medium.

Sweet Georgia Brown—Bernie, Pinkard, and Casey, arr. Kirby Shaw. Warner Bros. No. 441-19064. Piano accompaniment. Moderately difficult.

Their Hearts Are Full of Spring—Troup, arr. Kirby Shaw. Hal Leonard No. 08664515. A cappella. Medium.

Theme from New York, New York (from *New York, New York*)—John Kander, arr. Irving Frank Metis. United Artists No. 2992. Piano, with optional guitar, percussion, and electric or string bass. Medium.

There's No Business Like Show Business—Irving Berlin, arr. Hawley Ades. Shawnee Press No. A-0637. Piano accompaniment. Medium.

They're Playing Our Song (choral medley)—Marvin Hamlisch, arr. Ed. Lojeski. Hal Leonard No. 08240600. Piano, electric guitar, electric bass, and percussion. Medium.

This Is It!—Mack David and Jerry Livingston, arr. Larry Lapin. Warner Bros. No. CH0873. Accompanied. Medium.

Twentiana (a choral montage of songs of the 1920s)—arr. Hawley Ades. Shawnee Press No. A-1261. Piano with optional string bass and drums. Moderately easy to medium.

The Varsity Drag—DeSylva, Brown, and Henderson, arr. Kirby Shaw. Hal Leonard No. 08665421. Piano with optional dixieland combo. Medium.

We—Mancini, arr. Frederickson. Kendor Music No. 4277A. Piano accompaniment. Medium.

We Wish You the Merriest—Les Brown, arr. Jack Halloran. Shawnee Press No. A-841. Accompanied. Medium.

When I Fall in Love—Edward Young, arr. Phil Azelton. Hal Leonard No. 07259001. A cappella. Medium.

When Sunny Gets Blue—Fischer, arr. Roger Emerson. Jenson No. 403-23304. A cappella. Solo (male or female). Moderately difficult.

When the Saints Go Marchin' In—arr. Kirby Shaw. Hal Leonard No. 08665921. Piano with optional bass, drums, and dixieland combo. Medium.

Winter Wonderland—Felix Bernard, arr. Leo Arnaud. Shawnee Press No. A-102. Accompanied. Medium.

Woodchoppers' Ball—Merman and Bishop, arr. H. Brooks. Hal Leonard No. 07259075. Piano, bass, and drums. Medium.

Yesterday—John Lennon and Paul McCartney. Shawnee Press No. A-1338. A cappella. Medium.

You Made Me Love You—James V. Monaco, arr. Gene Puerling. Edwin E. Morris No. 07359465. Piano, bass, and drums. Medium.

You're Never Fully Dressed without a Smile (from *Annie*)—Charles Strouse, arr. Frank Metis. CPP/Belwin No. T6540YC1. Piano, with optional guitar, percussion, and bass. Moderately easy.

CHORAL COLLECTIONS

Whether or not to use choral collections has been a subject of some concern to conductors. Your criterion in arriving at a decision should simply be: Is it possible to use the majority of the selections in the collection? If so, the use of a collection may be a saving to the budget. When it is not feasible to use most of the selections, then it is a better practice to utilize separate octavo publications. Following are particular collections we have found useful and that you will want to examine to see if they meet the particular needs of your groups.

Collections for Mixed Voices (SATB, SAB) [4]

The A Cappela Singer—edited by H. Clough-Leighter. E. C. Schirmer 1682. A collection of 30 secular selections, primarily madrigals, from the choral literature of the sixteenth and early seventeenth centuries. An excellent basic book for madrigal groups.

Cantiones Sacrae et Profanae—by Henk Badings. Volume 7. Ten selections for mixed voices with English, Latin, and Dutch texts. Harmonia, Hilversum (available from Foreign Music Distributors).

Carols for Choirs—edited and arranged by Reginald Jacques and David Willcocks. Oxford University Press. A collection of 50 Christmas carols, arranged mostly for mixed voices.

Choral Perspective—compiled by Don Malin. Marks Music Corp. A cross-section of choral music from the Renaissance to the twentieth century, with compositions representing 18 composers.

The Concord Anthem Book—compiled and edited by Archibald T. Davison and Henry Wilder Foote. E. C. Schirmer No. 13 (clothbound). Contains 40 anthems selected from the choral literature of the sixteenth through the nineteenth centuries. Music varies in difficulty from easy to moderately difficult.

Early American Sacred Choral Library, Vol. 1—compiled and edited by Barbara Owen, The Boston Music Company. A collection of ten works representing music by William Billings, Benjamin Carr, Edward Hamilton, Thomas Hastings, Samuel Holyoke, Lowell Mason, and William Selby.

A First Motet Book—compiled and edited by Paul Thomas. Concordia Publishing House. Contains 17 motets in a variety of styles from the Renaissance to the twentieth century.

Five Centuries of Choral Music—compiled by a committee of teachers in the Los Angeles City High Schools. William C. Hartshorn, Supervisor in charge. G. Schirmer, Inc. A collection of 30 compositions representing various types and styles from the Renaissance to the present.

Five English Folk Songs—arranged for unaccompanied mixed voices by Ralph Vaughan Williams. Galaxy Music Corporation. Each selection is also published separately.

The Golden Age of the Madrigal—edited by Alfred Einstein. G. Schirmer, Inc. Twelve Italian madrigals for five-part chorus of mixed voices.

Madrigals and Motets of Four Centuries. Associated Music Publishers. A choral songbook of 18 European classics.

Madrigals for Christmas. Six Elizabethan hymns and part songs for four-part chorus of mixed voices *a cappella* or accompanied, with optional readings. Collected and edited by K. Lee Scott. Carl Fischer.

Mosaic of Jewish Folksong. Ladino, Yemenite, and Israeli folk song, arranged for mixed choir (SATB) *a cappella* by Sid Robinovitch. Transcontinental Music Publications.

Nativity Madrigals—by Daniel Pinkham. For mixed voices and organ, piano, or harp.

Rediscovered Madrigals—edited by Don Malin. Marks Music Corp. A collection of sixteentht-century Italian madrigals and French chansons representing seven composers.

[4] All collections are for SATB unless otherwise indicated.

Reflections of Canada, Volume 3—30 four-part arrangements of Canadian folk song by Jean Anderson, Kenneth Bray, and Nancy Telfer. Edited by John Barron. The Frederick Harris Music Co., Ltd.

Renaissance Choral Music—edited by Don Malin. Edward B. Marks Music Corp. A collection of 14 secular choral works from the sixteenth century. Music is by French, English, German, and Italian composers, with notes on the background of each.

Renaissance to Baroque—edited by Lehman Engel. Harold Flammer. A collection, in seven volumes, of choral music from the Renaissance and Baroque periods. Volume 1, French-Netherland Music; Volume 2, Italian Music; Volume 3, English Music; Volume 4, German Music; Volume 5, Spanish Music; Volume 6, English Music; Volume 7, French Music.

The Second Concord Anthem Book—compiled and edited by Archibald T. Davison and Henry Wilder Foote. E. C. Schirmer No. 1200 (clothbound). Contains 40 additional anthems selected from the choral literature of the sixteenth through the nineteenth centuries. Music varies in difficulty from easy to moderately difficult.

Songs for Sight-Singing (Junior High School, SATB)—compiled by Mary Henry and Marilyn Jones. Consulting editor, Ruth Witlock. Southern Music Company.

Songs for Sight-Singing (High School, SATB)—compiled by Mary Henry and Marilyn Jones. Consulting editor, Ruth Whitlock. Southern Music Company.

3 to Make Music—Hawley Ades, and edited by Lara Hoggard. Shawnee Press. "Three-part songs for girls and boys." A collection of 32 songs—folk song, spirituals, patriotic, faith and brotherhood, Christmas and general secular. Difficulty: easy to medium.

Twelve Traditional Carols (from Herefordshire)—collected, edited, and arranged by E. M. Leather and Ralph Vaughan Williams. For unison voices and keyboard or unaccompanied mixed chorus. Galaxy Music Corporation.

Collections for Treble Voices (SA, SSA, SSAA)

Christmas Carols for Treble Choirs—arranged and edited by Florence M. Martin. Schmitt, Hall & McCreary, Auditorium Series No. 56 (SA and SSA). A collection of 15 Christmas carols. Difficulty: easy to medium.

Glenn Glee Club Book for Girls—edited by Mabelle Glenn and Virginia French. Oliver Ditson. A collection of 42 songs for use in junior and senior high schools.

Presser Choral Collection; Sacred and Secular Literature—Past and Present—general editors, Geraldine Healy and William C. Hartshorn. Theodore Presser Company. A collection of 40 compositions for treble voices. representing various types and styles of choral music, compiled by a committee of choral music teachers in the Los Angeles City Public Schools.

Reflections of Canada, Volume 1—45 two-part arrangements of Canadian folk songs by Kenneth Bray, Nancy Telfer, and Gerhard Wuensch. Edited by John Barron. The Frederick Harris Music Co., Ltd.

Reflections of Canada, Volume 2—36 three-part arrangements of Canadian folk songs by Kenneth Bray, Nancy Telfer, and Gerhard Wuensch. Edited by John Barron. The Frederick Harris Music Co., Ltd.

Collections for Male Voices (TB, TTB, TTBB)

Gentleman Songsters—Livingston Gearhart, edited by Lara Hoggard. Shawnee Press. A collection of 42 songs for boys' glee clubs in two, three, and four parts (TB, TTB, and TTBB). Sea chanties, songs of the American Revolution, ballads, folk song, classics, songs for Christmas and other special occasions, college songs and novelties, songs of faith and brotherhood, spirituals, and patriotic songs. Difficulty: easy to medium.

EXTENDED CHORAL WORKS

All choral conductors should familiarize themselves with the extended choral works of various composers, for if you are not familiar with major choral works, which in certain instances represent the crowning achievement of a composer, you have only an incomplete picture or concept of choral literature. Although the advanced high school choir could perform some of these works in their entirety, even an advanced choir could not perform certain others because of their overall difficulty. Conductors of college, university, and adult community choruses should examine all these works for possible use by their groups.

AHLE, JOHANN RUDOLF
   Be Not Afraid   Concordia

ANTHEIL, GEORGE
   Cabeza de Vaca   Templeton Pub. Co.

BACH, JOHANN CHRISTOPH
   The Childhood of Christ   J. Fischer

BACH, JOHANN SEBASTIAN

Beautify Thyself, My Spirit (Cantata No. 180)	G. Schirmer
Be Not Afraid (Motet IV)	C. F. Peters
Christ Lay in Death's Dark Prison (Cantata No. 4)	Breitkopf & Härtel; G. Schirmer
Christmas Oratorio	G. Schirmer
Coffee Cantata, The (3-part chorus)	G. Schirmer
Come, Jesus, Come (Motet V)	H. W. Gray; C. F. Peters
Come, My Spirit, Come Exalt (Cantata No.189)	Breitkopf & Härtel
Come, Thou Lovely Hour (Cantata No. 161)	E. C. Schirmer
Deck Thyself, My Soul, with Gladness (Cantata No.180)	E. C. Schirmer
For As the Rain and Snow from Heaven Fall (Cantata No. 18)	G. Schirmer
For the Righteous, Wedding Cantata (No. 195)	Breitkopf & Härtel
For Us a Child Is Born (Cantata No. 142)	Galaxy; Mark Foster
From Depths of Woe (Cantata No. 38)	E. C. Schirmer
Gerechten muss das Licht, Dem (Cantata No. 195)	Breitkopf & Härtel
Gloria in excelsis Deo (Cantata No.191)	G. Schirmer
God, the Lord Is Sun and Shield (Cantata No. 79)	G. Schirmer
God Is My King (Cantata No. 71)	Breitkopf & Härtel
God's Time Is The Best (Cantata No. 106)	G. Schirmer
Great David's Lord and Greater Son (Cantata No. 23)	E. C. Schirmer
Heaven Declare the Glory of God, The (Cantata No. 76)	Breitkopf & Härtel
The Heavens Laugh, the Earth Exults (Cantata No. 31)	G. Schirmer
How Brightly Shines Yon Morning Star (Cantata No.1)	E.C. Schirmer
If Thou Wilt Suffer God to Guide Thee (Cantata No. 93)	G. Schirmer
In God I Place My Faith and Trust (Cantata No. 188)	G. Schirmer
I Suffered with Great Heaviness (Cantata No. 21)	G. Schirmer
It Is Enough (Cantata No. 82)	Breitkopf & Härtel
Jesus, My Great Pleasure (Motet 111)	C. F. Peters
Jesus, Thou My Constant Gladness (Cantata No. 147)	H. W. Gray
Jesus, Thou My Wearied Spirit (Cantata No. 78)	G. Schirmer
Kantate	Breitkopf & Härtel
King of Heaven, Come in Triumph (Cantata No. 182)	E.C. Schirmer
Kyrie in D Minor	G. Schirmer
Let Songs of Rejoicing Be Raised (Cantata No. 149)	H. W. Gray
Lord, Enter Not into Wrath (Cantata No. 105)	E.C. Schirmer
Magnificat	Breitkopf & Härtel; C. F. Peters; G. Schirmer
Mass in B Minor	G. Schirmer

Messe No. 4 in G Major	C. F. Peters
Missa Brevis in G	H. W. Gray
My Soul Doth Magnify the Lord (Cantata No. 10)	G. Schirmer
My Soul Exalts the Lord (Cantata No. 10)	E. C. Schirmer
The New-Born Babe (Cantata No. 122)	G. Schirmer
Now Thank We Our God (Cantata No. 192)	G. Schirmer
Nun ist das Heil und die Kraft (Cantata No. 50)	Breitkopf & Härtel
O Christ, My All in Living (Cantata No. 95)	Novello
Ode of Mourning (Cantata No. 198)	G. Schirmer
O God, How Grievous (Cantata No. 3)	E. C. Schirmer
O Jesus Christ, My Life and Light (Cantata No. 118)	G. Schirmer
O Light Everlasting (Cantata No. 34)	E. C. Schirmer
O Lord, Relent, I Pray (Cantata No. 135)	E. C. Schirmer
O Lord, This Grieving Spirit (Cantata No. 135)	G. Schirmer
O Praise the Lord for All His Mercies (Cantata No. 28)	H. W. Gray
Out of Darkness Call I Lord to Thee (Cantata No. 131)	Breitkopf & Härtel
The Passion According to St.John	Breitkopf & Härtel; G. Schirmer
The Passion According to St. Mark	Chantry Music Press
The Passion According to St. Matthew	Breitkopf & Härtel; G. Schirmer
The Peasant Cantata	Paterson's Pub. Ltd.
Praise Him, the Lord, the Almighty King (Cantata No. 137)	Breitkopf & Härtel
Praise Our God in All His Splendor (Cantata No. 11)	G. Schirmer
Praise the Lord, All Ye Nations (Motet VI)	C. F. Peters
Sheep May Safely Graze (Cantata No. 208)	G. Schirmer
Sing Ye to the Lord (Motet I)	C. F. Peters
Sleepers, Wake! (Cantata No. 140)	H. W. Gray
The Spirit Also Helpeth Us (Motet II)	H. W. Gray; C. F. Peters
Stronghold Sure, A (Cantata No. 80)	G. Schirmer
There Uprose a Great Strife (Cantata No. 19)	G. Schirmer
Thou Guide of Israel (Cantata No. 104)	H. W. Gray
Thou Very God and David's Son (Cantata No. 23)	G. Schirmer
To Us a Child Is Given (Cantata No. 142)	G. Schirmer
Weeping, Crying, Sorrow, Sighing (Cantata No. 12)	G. Schirmer
We Must through Great Tribulations (Cantata No. 146)	G. Schirmer
When Will God Recall My Spirit? (Cantata No. 8)	E. C. Schirmer
BACH, KARL PHILIPP EMANUEL	
Holy Is God	Concordia
Magnificat	G. Schirmer
BADINGS, HENK	
Missa Antiphonica	Harmonia (Foreign Music Distributors)
BARBER, SAMUEL	
Prayers of Kirkegaard	G. Schirmer
BARTÓK, BELA	
Cantata Profana	Boosey & Hawkes
Shepherd's Christmas Songs	Boosey & Hawkes
BEETHOVEN, LUDWIG VAN	
Cantata on the Death of Emperor Joseph II	G. Schirmer
Choral Fantasia	Edwin F. Kalmus
Choral Finale to the Ninth Symphony	H. W. Gray; G. Schirmer
Christ on the Mount of Olives	Edwin F. Kalmus

Mass in C Major	Edwin F. Kalmus
Mass in D	Novello
Missa Solemnis, Op. 123	G. Schirmer
BERGER, JEAN	
Brazilian Psalm	G. Schirmer
The Fiery Furnace	Schirmer
Psalm 57	Presser
Vision of Peace	Broude Bros.
BERLIOZ, HECTOR	
Childhood of Christ	G. Schirmer
Childhood of Christ (abridged version)	H. W. Gray
Choral Suite from Benvenuto Cellini	Oxford
Grand Death Mass, Op. 5	Breitkopf & Härtel
Requiem	G. Schirmer
Te Deum	G. Schirmer
BERNSTEIN, LEONARD	
Chichester Psalms	G. Schirmer
Choruses from The Lark	G. Schirmer
Kaddish	G. Schirmer
BLITZSTEIN, MARC	
The Airbone (cantata)	Chappell
BLOCH, ERNEST	
Sacred Service	Broude Bros.
BOITO ARRIGO	
Prologue in Heaven (from Mefistofele)	G. Schirmer
BORODIN, ALEX	
Polovetzian Dance and Chorus (from Prince Igor)	G. Schirmer
BRAHMS, JOHANNES	
Love-Song Waltzes (Liebeslieder Walzer)	Associated
Marienlieder	Breitkopf & Härtel; C. F. Peters; E. C. Schirmer
Motet from Psalm LI, Op. 29, No. 2	G. Schirmer
Nänie	G. Schirmer; E. C. Schirmer
Neue Liebeslieder	Lawson-Gould
Requiem, Op. 45	Edwin F. Kalmus; G. Schirmer
Schicksalslied (Song of Destiny)	H. W. Gray E. C. Schirmer Belwin Mills
Triumphal Hymn, Op. 55	G. Schirmer; Kalmus
BRITTEN, BENJAMIN	
A.M.D.G. (Ad majorem Dei glorium)	Faber Music
Ballad of Heroes	Boosey & Hawkes
Cantata Misericordium	Boosey & Hawkes
Ceremony of Carols, A (SATB; SSA)	Boosey & Hawkes
The Company of Heaven	Faber Music
Festival Te Deum	Boosey & Hawkes
Hymn to St. Cecilia	Boosey & Hawkes
Rejoice in the Lamb	Boosey & Hawkes
Saint Nicolas	Boosey & Hawkes
Spring Symphony	Boosey & Hawkes

Voices for Today	G. Schirmer
War Requiem	Boosey & Hawkes
Wedding Anthem, A (Amo, ergo sum)	Boosey & Hawkes
BRUCKNER, ANTON	
Mass in E minor	Broude Bros.
Mass No. 1 in D minor	C. F. Peters
Mass No. 3 in F minor	C. F. Peters
Psalm 150	Musikwissenschaftlicher Verlag
Te Deum laudamus	G. Schirmer; C. F. Peters
BUXTHEHUDE, DIETRICH	
Aperite mihi portas justitiae (Open to Me Gates of Justice)	C. F. Peters
Good Christian Men, with Joy Draw Near	Concordia
Jesu, Joy and Treasure	C. F. Peters
Laudia Sion Salvatorem	Chantry Music Press
Missa Brevis	Mercury
Open to Me Gates of Justice	C. F. Peters
Rejoice, Earth and Heaven	C. F. Peters
Sing to God the Lord	Concordia
What Is the World to Me?	Concordia
BYRD, WILLIAM	
Magnificat and Nunc dimittis	Oxford
Mass for 5 Voices	Galaxy: Stainer & Bell
Mass for 4 Voices	Galaxy: Stainer & Bell
Mass for 3 Voices	Galaxy
CALDARA, ANTONIO	
Credo	E. C. Schirmer
CARISSIMI, GIACOMO	
Jephte	Ricordi
CERHA, FRIEDRICH	
Rubaijat des Omar Khajjam	Doblinger
COLLINS, DON L.	
Huckleberry Finn	Cambiata Press
CHARPENTIER, MARC-ANTOINE	
Midnight Mass for Christmas	Elkan-Vogel
Venite ad me	G. Schirmer
CHERUBINI, LUIGI	
Requiem in D Minor	C. F. Peters
Requiem Mass in C Minor	G. Schirmer
COLERIDGE-TAYLOR, SAMUEL	
Hiawatha's Wedding Feast	G. Schirmer
COMES, JUAN BAUTISTA	
Beatus vir	G. Schirmer
Lamentación	G. Schirmer
Magnificat	G. Schirmer
COPLAND, AARON	
Canticle of Freedom	Boosey & Hawkes
In the Beginning	Boosey & Hawkes
CRESTON PAUL	
The Celestial Vision	Shawnee Press
Isaiah's Prophecy	Franco Colombo
Missa Solemnis, Op. 44	Belwin Mills

DEBUSSY, CLAUDE
 The Blessed Damoiselle   G. Schirmer
 L'Enfant Prodigue   Elkan-Vogel
 Ode à la France   Elkan-Vogel
DELIUS, FREDERICK
 A Mass of Life   Universal
 Appalachia   Boosey & Hawkes
 Sea Drift   Boosey & Hawkes
 Songs of Farewell   Boosey & Hawkes
DELLO JOIO, NORMAN
 The Mystic Trumpeter   G. Schirmer
 A Psalm of David   Carl Fischer
 Psalm of Peace   Edw. B. Marks
 Song of Affirmation   Carl Fischer
 Song of the Open Road   Carl Fischer
 To St. Cecilia   Carl Fischer
 Years of the Modern   Edw. B. Marks
DIAMOND, DAVID
 This Sacred Ground   Southern Music
DORATI, ANTAL
 Missa Brevis   Belwin Mills
DUBOIS, THEODORE
 The Seven Last Words of Christ   G. Schirmer
DURUFLÉ, MAURICE
 Requiem   Durand
DVOŘÁK ANTON
 Stabat Mater, Op. 58   G. Schirmer
EFFINGER, CECIL
 The Invisible Fire   H. W. Gray
 The St. Luke Christmas Story   G. Schirmer
 Set of Three   Elkan-Vogel
EINEM, GOTTFRIED VON
 Missa Claravallensis, Op. 83   Doblinger
ELGAR, EDNVARD
 Dream of Gerontius   Novello
 48th Psalm   Novello
 29th Psalm   Novello
ETLER, ALVIN
 Ode to Pathos   Associated
FAURÉ, GABRIEL
 Requiem   H. T. Fitzsimons
FETLER, PAUL
 Now This Is the Story (SSA)   Carl Fischer
 Te Deum   Augsburg
FOSS, LUKAS
 A Parable of Death   Carl Fischer
 The Prairie   G. Schirmer
 Psalms   Carl Fischer
FRANCK, CÉSAR
 The Beatitudes (oratorio)   G. Schirmer
 Communion Service in A Major, Op. 12   E. C. Schirmer
GABRIELI, GIOVANNI
 Jubilate Deo   Bourne; G. Schirmer

Timor et tremor	Annie Banks
GALUPPI, BALDASSARE	
Kyrie	Lawson-Gould
GESUALDO, CARLO	
Illumina nos	Boosey & Hawkes
Tres sacrae cantiones	Boosey & Hawkes
GINASTERA, ALBERTO	
The Lamentations of Jeremiah	Mercury
GOUDIMEL, CLAUDE	
Messe audi filia	Editions Salabert
GOUNOD, CHARLES	
Gallia	G. Schirmer
Mass in C	G. Schirmer
Messe Solennelle (St. Cecilia)	G. Schirmer
Missa Choralis	E. C. Schirmer
Missa Paschalis	E. C. Schirmer
GRIEG, EDVARD	
Choral Suite	Hinrichsen & Peters
Psalms for Mixed Chorus, Op. 74	C. F. Peters
Vier Psalmen, Op. 74	Harmonia
HAMMERSCHMIDT, ANDREAS	
Holy Is the Lord	Concordia
How Then Shall We Find Bread?	Concordia
Now Death Is Devoured	Concordia
HANDEL, GEORGE FRIDERIC	
Acis and Galatea	Novello
Alceste	Novello
An Autumn Day	Oxford
Belshazzar	Associated
Canticle of Praise	G. Schirmer
Dettingen Te Deum	H. W. Gray
Foundling Hospital Anthem	C. F. Peters
Funeral Anthem for Queen Caroline	G. Schirmer
Israel in Egypt	G. Schirmer
I Will Magnify You	G. Schirmer
Joshua	Novello
Judas Maccabaeus	G. Schirmer
The King Shall Rejoice	Novello
Laudate pueri Dominum (Psalm 112)	C. F. Peters
Messiah	G. Schirmer
O Sing unto the Lord (Psalm 96)	G. Schirmer
Samson	G. Schirmer
Saul	H. W. Gray
Sixth Chandos Anthem	G. Schirmer
Solomon	Breitkopf & Härtel; H. W. Gray
Te Deum laudamus	Verlag Merseburger
The Utrecht Jubilate	Breitkopf & Härtel
The Utrecht Te Deum	G. Schirmer
HANSON, HOWARD	
Beat! Beat! Drums!	J. Fischer
The Cherubic Hymn	Carl Fischer
Song of Democracy	Carl Fischer

Song of Human Rights	Carl Fischer
Songs from Drum Taps	J. Fischer
HARRIS, ROY	
Mass in C (for Male Voices and Organ)	Carl Fischer
HASSLER, HANS LEO	
Mass No. 5	Concordia
Missa Super "Dixit Maria"	Arista
HAYDN, JOSEPH	
The Creation	G. Schirmer
Der Sturm (La Tempesta)	Belwin Mills
Mare Clausum	Doblinger
Mass in Time of War	G. Schirmer
Missa Brevis in F	Doblinger
Missa Sancti Nicolai	Arista
Missa Solemnis	C. F. Peters
The Seasons	G. Schirmer
The Seven Last Words of Christ	G. Schirmer
Sixteenth Mass	H. W. Gray
Stabat Mater	G. Schirmer
Third Mass (The Imperial or Lord Nelson)	G. Schirmer
HAYDN, MICHAEL	
Laudate populi	Breitkopf & Härtel
Timete Dominum (O Fear the Lord)	G. Schirmer
HINDEMITH, PAUL	
Apparebit repentina dies	Schott
Four Songs	Schott
Messe	Schott
114th Psalm	Novello
St. Paul (oratorio)	G. Schirmer
When Lilacs Last in the Door-Yard Bloom'd	Schott
HOLST GUSTAV	
The Coming of Christ	G. Schirmer
The Hymn of Jesus	Galaxy Music Corp.
HONEGGER, ARTHUR	
Cantate de Noël	Éditions Salabert
La Danse des morts	Éditions Salabert
King David	E. C. Schirmer
Nicholas de Flue	E. C. Schirmer
HOVHANESS, ALAN	
Glory to God	C. F. Peters
In the Beginning Was the Word	C. F. Peters
Look toward the Sea	C. F. Peters
Make a Joyful Noise	C. F. Peters
30th Ode of Solomon	C. F. Peters
JANEQUIN, CLEMENT	
Messe La Bataille	Editions Salabert
KODALY, ZOLTÁN	
Missa Brevis	Boosey & Hawkes
Psalmus Hungaricus	Universal
Te Deum	Universal
KUBIK, GAIL	
Litany and Prayer (TTBB)	Southern Music
A Record of Our Time	MCA Music

KYR, ROBERT
  Magnificat   E. C. Schirmer
LARSEN, LIBBY
  The Settling Years   E. C. Schirmer
  Three Summer Scenes   E. C. Schirmer
LASSO, ORLANDI DI
  Missa Puisque j'ay perdu   J. Fischer
LISZT, FRANZ
  Hymn to the Virgin Mary   Lawson-Gould
  The XIIIth Psalm   G. Schirmer
LOCKWOOD NORMAND
  A Ballad of the North and South   Associated
  Carol Fantasy   Associated
  The Holy Birth   Choral Services
LOTTI, ANTONIO
  Mass VII in the Doric Mode   E. C. Schirmer
LULLY, JEAN BAPTISTE
  Te Deum   Schott
MCDONALD, CARL
  Pioneers, O Pioneers   Elkan-Vogel
  Songs of Conquest   Elkan-Vogel
MATHEWS, PETER
  Missa Brevis   Southern Music Co.
MACHAUT, GUILLAUME
  Messe Notre-Dame   Éditions Salabert
MCKAY, GEORGE F.
  Choral Rhapsody   J. Fischer
MAHLER, GUSTAV
  VIII Symphonie   Universal
  Waldmärchen (Forest Legend)   Belwin Mills
MARTIRANO, SALVATORE
  O O O O That Shakespearian Rag   Schott
MENDELSSOHN, FELIX
  As the Hart Pants (42nd Psalm)   G. Schirmer
  Christus   G. Schirmer
  Come Let Us Sing (95th Psalm)   G. Schirmer
  Elijah (oratorio)   G. Schirmer
  The First Walpurgis Night Op. 60   G. Schirmer
  Hear My Prayer   Mark Foster; G. Schirmer
  Hymn of Praise   G. Schirmer
  Kyrie   Oxford
  Magnificat   Augsburg
  Psalm 115
  "Nicht unserm Namen, Herr"   Harmonia
MENNIN PETER
  The Christmas Story   Carl Fischer
  The Cycle (Symphony No. 4)   Carl Fischer
MENOTTI, GIANCARLO
  The Death of the Bishop of Brindisi   G. Schirmer
MILHAUD, DARIUS
  Cantate pour louer le Seigneur   Universal
  Cantique du Rhône   Elkan-Vogel
  Le Château du Feu   Associated

Miracles of Faith — G. Schirmer
Naissance de Vénus — Heugel
Pan et Syrinx — Éditions Salabert
Three Psalms of David — Associated

MOLLICONE, HENRY
A Christmas Celebration — E. C. Schirmer

MONTEVERDI, CLAUDIO
Laetatus sum — Mark Foster
Lagrime d'Amante al Sepolcro dill'Amata — Lawson-Gould
Magnificat Primo — Lawson-Gould

MOZART, WOLFGANG A.
Davidde penitente (K. 459) — Broude Bros.
Glory, Praise and Power — H. W. Gray
Grand Mass in C Minor — G. Schirmer
Litania in E Flat (K. 243) — Edwin F. Kalmus
Mass in C (K. 317, "Coronation") — Breitkopf & Härtel; G. Schirmer

Misericordias offertorium de tempore — G. Schirmer
Missa Brevis in C (K. 220) — Associated
Missa Brevis in D (K 194) — Edw. B. Marks
Missa Brevis in F Major (K. 192) — G. Schirmer
Regina coeli — Lawson-Gould; E. C. Schirmer

Requiem Mass — H. W. Gray; C. F. Peters; G. Schirmer

Vesperae Solennes de Dominica (K. 321) — E. C. Schirmer

ORFF, CARL
Carmina Burana — Schott
Catulli Carmina — Schott
Trionfo di Afrodite — Schott

PACHELBEL, JOHANN
Deus in adjutorium — Edw. B. Marks
Der Herr ist König — Concordia
Jauchzet dem Herrn (Shout Forth to the Lord) — Concordia
Magnificat in C — Summy-Birchard

PALESTRINA, GIOVANNI
Assumpta est Maria — Breitkopf & Härtel
Leichte Chore — Breitkopf & Härtel
Missa Aeterna Christi Munera — Arista
Missa Brevis — Breitkopf & Härtel; G. Schirmer

Missa Iste Confessor — Breitkopf & Härtel; Edw. B. Marks

Missa Papae Marcelli — S. Fischer; G. Schirmer
Missa Tu es Petrus — Breitkopf & Härtel
Pater Noster — Breitkopf & Härtel
Stabat Mater — Belwin Mills; G. Schirmer

PENDERECKI, KRZYSZTOF
Canticum Canticorum Salomonis (Song of Songs) — Schott
Kosmogonia — Schott
Passion According to St. Luke — Belwin Mills
Utrenia
The Entombment of Christ — Schott

The Resurrection of Christ	
PERGOLESI GIOVANNI	
The Magnificat	Walton Music
PERSICHETTI, VINCENT	
Celebrations	Elkan-Vogel
Mass	Elkan-Vogel
Stabat Mater	Elkan-Vogel
PIÉRNE, GABRIEL	
The Children at Bethlehem	G. Schirmer
PINKHAM, DANIEL	
Ascension Cantata	E. C. Schirmer
Canticle of Praise	E. C. Schirmer
Christmas Cantata	E. C. Schirmer
Daniel in the Lions' Den	E. C. Schirmer
Easter Cantata	C. F. Peters
An Emily Dickinson Mosaic (SSAA)	C. F. Peters
Fanfares	E. C. Schirmer
Four Elegies	E. C. Schirmer
Jonah	E. C. Schirmer
Jubilate Deo	E. C. Schirmer
Mass of the Word of God	E. C. Schirmer
Requiem	C. F. Peters
Saint Mark Passion	C. F. Peters
Wedding Cantata	C. F. Peters
POULENC, FRANCIS	
Gloria	Éditions Salabert
Messe en sol majeur	Éditions Salabert
Stabat Mater	Éditions Salabert
PRAETORIUS, MICHAEL	
Canticum trium puerorum	Sam Fox
PROKOFIEFF, SERGE	
Alexander Nevsky	Leeds Music
PUCCINI, GIACOMO	
Gloria (from Messa di Gloria)	Lawson-Gould
Messa di Gloria	Belwin Mills
PURCELL, HENRY	
Te Deum laudamus and Jubilate Deo	G. Schirmer
RACHMANINOFF, SERGEI	
The Bells, Op. 35	Kalmus; Boosey & Hawkes (rental)
The Liturgy of St. John Chrysostom	Galaxy Music Corp.
Springtide	G. Schirmer
RAMIREZ, ARIEL	
Misa Criolla	G. Schirmer
Navidad Nuestra (The Nativity)	G. Schirmer
REIZENSTEIN, FRANZ	
Voices of Night	H. W. Gray
RESPIGHI, OTTORINO	
Laud to the Nativity	Franco Colombo
RIMSKY-KORSAKOV, NIKOLAI	
Polonaise with Chorus	Boosey & Hawkes

RINCK, JOHANN CHRISTIAN HEINRICH
Todten-feyer   Harmonia (Foreign Music
                                                   Distributors)

ROGERS, BERNARD
A Letter from Pete   Southern Music
The Prophet Isaiah   Southern Music
ROREM, NED
From an Unknown Past   Southern Music
Two Psalms and a Proverb   E. C. Schirmer
ROSSINI, GIOACCHINO
Messa Di Gloria   G. Schirmer
Stabat Mater   Edition Kunzelmann
ROZSA MIKLOS
To Everything There Is a Season   Broude Bros; Breitkopf &
                                                   Härtel

SAINT-SAËNS, CAMILLE
Christmas Oratorio   G. Schirmer
SCARLATTI, ALESSANDRO
Salve Regina   Walton
Te Deum laudamus   Presser
SCHOENBERG, ARNOLD
De profundis (Psalm 130)   MCA Music
Gurre-Lieder   Universal
Kol Nidre   Boelke-Bomart
Ode to Napoleon (for speaker and string orchestra)   G. Schirmer
Peace on Earth   Schott
A Survivor of Warsaw   Boelke-Bomart
SCHUBERT, FRANZ
Gesang der Geister über den Wassern (for male voices)   Carl Fischer
Mass in A-flat   Breitkopf & Härtel;
                                                   Novello
Mass in F   G. Schirmer
Mass in G   H. W. Gray; G. Schirmer
Mass No. 3 in B-flat   Arista
Miriam's Song of Triumph   G. Schirmer
Rosamunde   G. Schirmer
SCHUMAN, WILLIAM
A Free Song   G. Schirmer
This Is Our Time   Boosey & Hawkes
SCHÜTZ HEINRICH
The Annunciation According to St. Luke   J. Fischer; G. Schirmer
The Christmas Story   G. Schirmer
Deutsches Magnificat   Bärenreiter-Ausgabe
84th Psalm   G. Schirmer
A German Requiem   G. Schirmer
Magnificat   Breitkopf & Härtel
Mein Sohn, warum hast du uns das getan?   Oxford
Nativity   Bärenreiter
The Passion According to St. John   Oxford
The St. Luke Passion   Oxford
The St. Matthew Passion   Augsburg; Breitkopf &
                                                   Härtel; Oxford

The Seven Last Words	Oxford; G. Schirmer; E. C. Schirmer
Symphonia Sacra No. 4	Oxford
SENFL, LUDWIG	
Ave Maria, gratia plena	Associated
Ich stund an einem Morgen	Lawson-Gould
SHOSTAKOVICH, DIMITRI	
Song of the Forests (cantata)	Leeds
SOWERBY, LEO	
The Ark of the Covenant	H. W. Gray
The Canticle of the Sun	H. W. Gray
Christ Reborn	H. W. Gray
Forsaken of Man	H. W. Gray
Great Is the Lord	H. W. Gray
The Throne of God	H. W. Gray
SPOHR, LOUIS	
Mass, Op. 54	Arista
STAINER JOHN	
The Crucifixion	G. Schirmer
The Daughter of Jairus (cantata)	G. Schirmer
STEVENS, HALSEY	
Magnificat	Mark Foster
STRAVINSKY, IGOR	
Cantata	Boosey & Hawkes
Canticum Sacrum	Boosey & Hawkes
The Flood	Boosey & Hawkes
Mass	Boosey & Hawkes
Les Noces	Boosey & Hawkes
Oedipus Rex	Boosey & Hawkes
Perséphone (ballet with chorus)	Boosey & Hawkes
Symphony of Psalms	Boosey & Hawkes
Threni	Boosey & Hawkes
SURINACH, CARLOS	
Cantata of St. John	Associated
SWEELINCK, JAN PIETERSZOON	
Psalm 150	E. C. Schirmer
TALLIS, THOMAS	
Lamentations (Parts I and II)	Oxford
TELEMANN, GEORGE PHILIPP	
Jesu, Joyous Treasure	Augsburg
THOMPSON, RANDALL	
Americana	E. C. Schirmer
A Concord Cantata	E. C. Schirmer
A Feast of Praise	E. C. Schirmer
Mass of the Holy Spirit	E. C. Schirmer
Nativity According to St. Luke	E. C. Schirmer
Ode to the Virginian Voyage	E. C. Schirmer
Passion According to St. Luke	E. C. Schirmer
The Peaceable Kingdom	E. C. Schirmer
The Place of the Best	E. C. Schirmer
A Psalm of Thanksgiving	E. C. Schirmer
Requiem	E. C. Schirmer

Testament of Freedom	E. C. Schirmer
THOMSON, VIRGIL	
Mass (unison)	E. C. Schirmer
Missa pro defunctis	H. W. Gray
TULL, FISCHER	
Missa Brevis	Southern Music Co.
VAUGHAN WILLIAMS, RALPH	
Dona nobis pacem	Oxford
Epithalamion	Oxford
Fanatasies on Christmas Carols	Galaxy
The First Nowell	Oxford
Five Mystical Songs	Galaxy
Five Tudor Portraits	Oxford
Four Songs of the Four Seasons	Oxford
Hodie	Oxford
Mass in G Minor	G. Schirmer
Pilgrim's Journey	Oxford
Sancta civitas	Oxford; G. Schirmer
A Sea Symphony	Galaxy, Oxford; Stainer & Bell
Serenade to Music	Oxford
A Song of Thanksgiving	Oxford
Thanksgiving for Victory	Oxford
This Day	Oxford
Toward the Unknown Region	Galaxy
A Vision of Aeroplanes (Motet)	Oxford
VERDI, GIUSEPPE	
Four Sacred Pieces	Franco Colombo
Requiem	G. Schirmer
Te Deum	G. F. Peters
VICTORIA, TOMAS LUIS DE	
O magnum mysterium	Associated; J. Fischer & Bros.
Missa "O Quam Gloriosum"	Arista
VIERNE, LOUIS	
Solemn Mass	Mark Foster
VIVALDI, ANTONIO	
Chamber Mass	Lawson-Gould
Gloria	Ricordi
WALTON, WILLIAM	
Belshazzar's Feast	Oxford
Coronation Te Deum	Oxford
Gloria	Oxford
In Honor of the City of London	Oxford
WEBER, CARLO MARIA VON	
Mass No. 1 in G	Lawson-Gould
WEBERN, ANTON	
Das Augenlicht, Op. 26	Universal
Kantate, Op. 29	Universal

Music Publishers/Distributors[5]

Aberdeen Music, Inc. (order from Plymouth Music Co.)
Addington Press (order from Hinshaw Music, Inc.)
Agape (order from Hope Publishing Co.)
Alexandria House, 468 McNally Dr., Nashville, TN 37211
Alfred Publishing Co., P.O. Box 10003, 16380 Roscoe Blvd., Van Nuys, CA 91410-0003
Alliance Music Publications, 4819 Feagan, Houston, Texas 77007
Altam Music Corporation, 9301 Wilshire Blvd., Beverly Hills, CA 90210
Antara Music Group, 468 McNally Dr., Nashville, TN 37211
Art Masters Studios, Inc., 2710 Nicollet Ave., Minneapolis, MN 55408-1630
Associated Music Publishers, Inc., 24 E. 22nd St., New York, NY 10010 (order from Hal Leonard
      Publishing Corp.)
Augsburg Fortress Publishing House, 426 S. Fifth St., Box 1209, Minneapolis, MN 55440
Bärenreiter Music Publishers (order from Foreign Music Distributors)
Beckenhorst Press, P.O. Box 14273, Columbus, OH 43214
Belmont Music Publishers, P.O. Box 231, Pacific Palisades, CA 90272.
Belwin-Mills Music (see CPP/Belwin Music)
Irving Berlin Music Corp., 29 W. 46th Street, New York, NY 10019
Big 3 Music Corp. (order from CPP/Belwin Music)
Birch Tree Group, Ltd., 180 Alexander St., Princeton, NJ 08540
Fred Bock Music Company, P.O. Box 570567, Tarzana, CA 91357
Boelke-Bomart, Inc., and Mobart Music Publications (order from Jerona Music Corp.)
Boosey & Hawkes, Inc.. 24 E. 21st St., New York, NY 10010-7200
Boston Music Company, The, 172 Tremont St., Boston, MA 02111
Bote & Bock Musikverlag (order from Hal Leonard Publishing Corp.)
Bourne Company, 5 W. 37th St., New York, NY 10018
Breitkopf & Härtel (order from Hal Leonard Publishing Corp.)
Broadman Press, 127 Ninth Ave. N., Nashville, TN 37234
Broude Brothers, Ltd., 141 White Oaks Rd., Williamstown, MA 01267
Cambiata Press, P.O. Box 1151, Conway, AR 72032
Carlin America, Inc., 126 East 38th Street, New York, NY 10016
Carus-Verlag, Stuttgart (order from Mark Foster Music Co.)
CPP/Belwin Music, (order from Warner Brothers Publications, Inc.)
Chantry Music Press, 32 N. Center St., Springfield, OH 45502
Chappell Music Co. (order from Hal Leonard Publishing Corp.)
Charter Publications (order from J.W. Pepper & Son, Inc.)
Cherry Lane Music Co., Inc., 10 Midland Ave., Port Chester, NY (order from Alfred Publishing
      Co.)
John Church Company (order from Theodore Presser Co.)
Franco Columbo Publications (order from CPP/Belwin Music)
Concordia Publishing House, 3558 S. Jefferson Ave., St. Louis, MO 63118
Consolidated Music Publishers. Inc. (order from Music Sales Corp.)
Consort Press, P.O. Box 50413, Santa Barbara, CA 93150
Coronet Press (order from Theodore Presser Co.)
Creative World Music Publications (order from Warner Brothers Publications, Inc.)
Curtis Music Press (order from Neil A. Kjos Music Co.)
J. Curwen & Sons (order from Hal Leonard Publishing Corp.)
Dartmouth Collegium Musicum (order from Shawnee Press, Inc.)

---

[5] As in any business, publishers may change addresses or make new arrangements for the sales and dlstribution of their music. Generally, music dealers are aware of these changes however, choral directors desiring reasonably up-to-date information may request a copy of the latest *Music Publishers Sales Agency list*, available from the Music Publishers' Association of the United States, 711 Third Avenue, New York, NY 10017

Roger Dean Publishing Company (order from The Lorenz Corporation)
Oliver Ditson (order from Theodore Presser Co.)
Earthsongs, 220 NW 29th Street, Corvalis, OR 97330
Edition Musica, Budapest, Hungary (order from Boosey & Hawkes, Inc.)
Edition Musicus, P.O. Box 1341, Stamford, CT 06904
Éditions Salabert (order from Hal Leonard Publishing Corp.)
Edizione Suvini Zerboni, Milan, Italy (order from Boosey & Hawkes, Inc.)
Elkan-Vogel, Inc. (order from Theodore Presser Co.)
European American Music Distributors Corp., 2480 Industrial Rd., Paoli, PA 19301
The Evangel Press (order from Art Masters Studios, Inc.)
Carl Fischer, Inc., 62 Cooper Sq., New York, NY 10003
J. Fischer & Bros. (order from CPP/Belwin Music)
H.T. Fitzsimons Co., P.O. Box 570567, Tarzana, CA 91357 (order from Antara Music Group)
Harold Flammer, Inc. (order from Shawnee Press, Inc.)
Foreign Music Distributors, 13 Elkay Drive, Chester, NY 10918
Mark Foster Music Company, Box 4012, Champaign, IL 61820
Sam Fox Music Sales Corp. (order from Plymouth Music Co., Inc.)
Frank Music Corp (order from Hal Leonard Publishing Corp.)
Friends of Jewish Music, 10 Strauss Lane, Olympia Fields, IL 60461.
Galaxy Music Corporation (order from E.C. Schirmer Music Co.)
Galleon Music, Inc. (order from Altram Music Corp.)
Galleria Press (order from Plymouth Music Co.)
Genesis III Music Corp. (order from Plymouth Music Co.)
Gentry Publications, P.O. Box 570567, Tarzana, CA 91357 (order from Intrada Music Group, P O.
    Box 1240, Anderson, IN 46012)
G.I.A. Publications, 7404 S. Mason Ave., Chicago, IL 60638
Glory-Sound (order from Shawnee Press, Inc.)
H. W. Gray Company, Inc. (order from CPP/Belwin Music)
Greystone Press (order from Plymouth Music Co.)
Hansen House, 1804 West Ave., Miami Beach, FL 33139
Hänssler Music, USA, 3773 West 95th Street, Leawood, Kansas 66206
Harmonia (order from Foreign Music Distributors)
T.B. Harms Co. (order from Warner Brothers Publications)
The Frederick Harris Music Co., Ltd., 340 Nagel Dr., Buffalo, NY 14225-4731
Heritage Music Press (order from The Lorenz Corporation)
Heugel and Cie (order from Theodore Presser Co.)
Highland Music Company, 1311 North Highland Avenue, Hollywood, CA 90028
Hinrichsen Edition (order from C. F. Peters Corp.)
Hinshaw Music, Inc., P.O. Box 470, Chapel Hill, NC 27514-0470
The Raymond A. Hoffman Co. (order from Antara Music Group)
Charles W. Homeyer & Co. (order from Carl Fischer, Inc.)
Hope Publishing Co., 380 S. Main Place, Carol Stream, IL 60188
Intrada Music Group, P.O. Box 1240, Anderson, IN 46012
Ione Press (order from E. C. Schirmer Music Co.)
Jenson Publications, Inc., 7777 W. Bluemound Rd., Milwaukee, W 53213
Jerona Music Corp., P.O. Box 5010, Hackensack, NJ 07606-4210
Joclem Music Publishing (order from Boosey & Hawkes, Inc.)
Edwin F. Kalmus & Company, Inc., P.O. Box 5011, Boca Raton, FL 33433-8011
Kenbridge Music (order from Jerona Music Corp.)
Kendor Music, Inc., P.O. Box 278, Delevan, NY 14042
E. C. Kerby, Ltd. (order from Hal Leonard Publishing Co.)
Neil A. Kjos Music Co., 4382 Jutland Dr.; P.O. Box 178270, San Diego, CA 92117-0894
Laurel Press (order from The Lorenz Corp.)
Laurendale Associates, 15035 Wyandotte Street, Van Nuys, CA 91405-1746
Lawson-Gould Music Publishers, Inc., 250 W. 57th St., Suite 932, New York, NY 10107

Hal Leonard Publishing Corp., 7777 W. Bluemound Rd., Milwaukee, WI 53213

The Lorenz Corporation, 501 E. Third, St., Dayton, OH 45401

Ludwig Music Publishing Co., 557 East 140th Street, Cleveland, OH 44110-1999

Malecki Music, Inc., 4500 Broadmoor, P O. Box 150, Grand Rapids, MI 49501-0150

Manna Music, Inc., 25510 Stanford Ave., Valencia, CA 91355

Margun/Gunmar Music, Inc., 167 Dudley Rd., Newton Centre, MA 02159 (order from Jerona Music Corp.)

Edward B. Marks Music Company (order from Hal Leonard Publishing Co.)

MCA Music Publishing, 1755 Broadway, 8th Floor, New York, NY 10019 (order from Hal Leonard Publishing Co.)

McLaughlin & Reilly Company (order from Warner Brothers Publications)

Mercury Music Corp. (order from Theodore Presser Co.)

Merion Music Corp. (order from Theodore Presser Co.)

Edwin H. Morris & Co., Inc. (order from Hal Leonard Publishing Corp.)

Music Press (order from Theodore Presser Co.)

Music Sales Corp., 225 Park Ave. South, New York, NY 10003

Music 70 Publishers 170 N.E. 33rd St., Ft. Lauderdale, FL 33334

National Music Publishers, 1326 Santa Ana, P.O. Box 8279, Anaheim, CA 92802

Novello Publications (order from Theodore Presser Co.)

Orpheus Music Co. (order from Plymouth Music Co., Inc.)

Oxford University Press, 200 Madison Ave., New York, NY 10016

Paterson's Publications, Ltd., London (order from Carl Fischer, Inc.)

Paull Pioneer Publications (order from Shawnee Press, Inc.)

Peer Southern Music, 810 Seventh Avenue, New York, NY 10019 (order from Theodore Presser Co.)

J. W. Pepper & Son, Inc., 2480 Industrial Blvd., Paoli PA 19301

Performers' Editions (order from Broude Brothers, Ltd.)

C. F. Peters Corp., 373 Park Ave. South, New York, NY 10016

Plymouth Music Co., Inc., 170 NE 33rd St., P.O. Box 24330, Ft. Lauderdale, FL 33334

Theodore Presser Co., Presser Place, Bryn Mawr, PA 19010

Pro-Art Publications (order from CPP/Belwin Music)

Providence Press (order from Hope Publishing Co.)

G. Ricordi & Co. (order from Hal Leonard Publishing Corp.)

Robbins Music (order from CPP/Belwin Music)

Roberton Publications (order from Theodore Presser).

Rongwen Music (Order from Broude Brothers, Ltd.)

R. D. Row Music Co. (order from Carl Fischer, Inc.)

Sacred Music Press (order from The Lorenz Corp.)

Santa Barbara Music Publishing, P.O. Box 41003, Santa Barbara, CA 93104.

E. C. Schirmer Music Co., 138 Ipswich St., Boston, MA 02215

G. Schirmer, Inc., 257 Park Avenue South, 20th Floor, New York, NY 10010 (order from Hal Leonard Publishing Corp.)

Arthur P. Schmidt Co. (order from Warner Brothers Publications)

Schmitt, Hall & McCreary (order from CPP/Belwin Music)

Schott & Company (order from European American Music Distributors Corp.)

The Shapiro, Bernstein Organization (order from Plymouth Music Co., Inc.)

Shawnee Press, Inc., Waring Drive, Delaware Water Gap, PA 18327-1099

John Sheppard Music Press, P.O. Box 6784, Denver, CO 80206

Somerset Press (order from Hope Publishing Co.)

Southern Music Co., 1100 Broadway, P.O. Box 329. San Antonio, TX 78292-0300

Spratt Music Publishers (order from Plymouth Music Co., Inc.)

Staff Music Publishing Co., Inc. (order from Plymouth Music Co., Inc.)

Stainer & Bell, Ltd. (order from E. C. Schirmer Music Co.)

Studio 4 (order from Alfred Publishing Co.)

Studio P/R, Inc. (order from Warner Brothers Publications)

Summa Productions (order from Art Masters Studio, Inc.)
Summy-Birchard Co. (order from Warner Brothers Publications, Inc.)
Tabernacle Publishing Co. (order from Hope Publishing Co.)
Templeton Publications (order from Shawnee Press, Inc.)
Tetra/Continuo Music Group (order from Plymouth Music Co., Inc.)
Gordon V. Thompson Music, 29 Birch Ave., Toronto, Ontario, Canada M4V IE2 (order from Hal
    Leonard Publishing Corp.)
Transcontinental Music Publications, 838 Fifth Ave., New York, NY 10021-7046
Triune Music, Inc. (order from The Lorenz Corp.)
TRO (The Richmond Organization), 11 W. 19th St., New York, NY 10011
Tuskegee Music Press (order from Neil A. Kjos Music Co.)
Twin Elm Publishing, 1626 Twenty-Seventh Avenue Court, Greeley, CO 80631.
UNC Jazz Press, College of Performing and Visual Arts, School of Music, Jazz Studies Division, Uni-
    versity of Northern Colorado, Greeley, CO 80639
Universal Edition (order from European American Music Distributors Corp.)
Vaia'ata Print, c/o Music Department, University of Otago, P.O. Box 56, Dunedin, New Zealand
Walton Music Corp. (order from Plymouth Music Co., Inc.)
Warner Bros. Publications, 15800 N.W. 48th Ave., Miami, FL 30014
Joseph Weinberger, Ltd., London (order from Boosey & Hawkes, Inc.)
Williamson Music Co., 598 Madison Ave., New York, NY 10019
Willis Music Co., 7380 Industrial Rd., Florence, KY 41042
Word Music, Inc., 5221 No. O'Conner Blvd., Suite 1000, Irving, TX 75039
World Library Publications, 3815 N. Willow Rd., P.O. Box 2701, Schiller Park, IL 60176
The Zondervan Music Group, 365 Great Circle Rd., Nashville, TN 37228

NATIONAL RETAIL MUSIC DEALERS/DISTRIBUTORS

Local music dealers in most communities are generally very helpful to choral directors. They can provide single copies of choral octavo music that you can peruse to determine its adaptability for use with your groups. They also expedite school music orders in every way possible. Additionally, they often carry in stock a reasonable variety of solo song literature and other materials and equipment.

Unfortunately, not all communities in our country can boast of such services. This leaves some directors in a difficult situation. Under these circumstances, we advise you to work through a music retailer that supplies music to schools across the country. A list of these firms and their addresses is listed as follows, along with their toll free 800 phone numbers (if available) through which they may be contacted.

A & D Music Distributors, 3305-B Taylor Road, Chesapeake, VA 23321
    (804) 686-8313; 1-800-729-2093
Brodt Music Co., P.O. Box 9345, Charlotte, NC 28299-9345
    (704) 332-2177; 1-800-532-6235 (State); 1-800-438-4129 (National)
Byron Hoyt Sheet Music, 2525 16th Street, 3rd floor, San Francisco, CA 94103
    (415) 431-8055; 1-800-858-8055 (CA); 1-800-858-8500 (National)
Carl Fischer of Chicago, 312 South Wabash, Chicago, IL 60604
    (312) 427-6652; 1-800-572-3272 (State); 1-800-621-4496 (National); FAX: 312-427-9545
Eckroth Music Co., 1221 West Divide Avenue, Bismarek, ND 58501
    1-800-437-1762
Eckroth Music Co., 1132 28th Avenue South, Moorhead, MN 56560
    1-800-525-9232

Fees' Sharp & Nichols, 1017 N.W. 6th, Oklahoma City, OK 73106
    (405) 235-5165; 1-800-522-3500 (State); 1-800-433-7823 (National)
Flesher-Hinton Music Co., 3936 Tennyson Street, Denver, CO 80212
    (303) 433-8891; 1-800-225-8742
Flesher-Hinton Music Co., 1878 S. Havana, Aurora, CO 80012
    (303) 337-2610; 1-800-225-8742
Head's House of Music, 5507 N. Florida Avenue, Tampa, FL 33604
    (813) 234-9181; 1-800-326-1199; 1-800-783-8030
J. W. Pepper & Son, Inc., P.O. Box 850, Valley Forge, PA 19482
    1-800-345-6296; FAX: 1-215-993-0563
Karnes Music Co., 2399 Devon Avenue, Elk Grove Village, IL 60007
    (708) 766-9320; 1-800-323-1001; FAX: 708-766-0388
Kidder Music Service, Inc., 7623 North Crestline Drive, Peoria, IL 61615
    (309) 692-4040; 1-800-322-2800 (State); 1-800-541-0533 (National)
Malecki Music, Inc., 4500 Broadmoor, S.E., P.O. Box 150, Grand Rapids, MI 49501-0150
    (616) 698-7000; 1-800-253-9692; FAX: 616-698-0228
Malecki Music, Inc., 3404 South Eleventh Street, P.O. Box 411, Council Bluffs, IA 51502-0411
    (712) 366-2591; 1-800-831-4197; FAX: 712-366 4109
Mannerino's Sheet Music, Inc., 7605 Hamilton Avenue, Cincinnati, OH 45231
    (513) 522-8975; 1-800-543-1721 (KY); 1-800-466-8863 (OH, National)
Mathis Music, Inc., 3800 South Tuttle Avenue, Sarasota, FL 34239
    1-800-749-2202; (813) 924-2202
Menchey Music Service, Inc. 80 Wetzel Drive, Hanover, PA 17331
    1-800-972-2917 (State); 1-800-872 2920; FAX: 717-637-1978
Music Mart Inc., P.O. Box 4280, 210 Yale Blvd. S.E., Albuquerque, NM 87106
    (505) 265-7721; 1-800-545-6204; FAX: 505-268-4074 (24 hr.)
Music Plus, 425 Main Street, Danbury, CT 06810
    (203) 744-4344
Musik Innovations, 9600 Perry Highway, Pittsburgh, PA 15237
    (412) 366-3631; 1-800-677-8863
Pender's Music Company, 314 South Elm, Denton, TX 76201
    1-800-772-5918; FAX: 1-817 382-0869
Pepper of Atlanta, P.O. Box 43186, Atlanta, GA 30336
    1-800-345-6296; FAX: 1-404-691-6504
Pepper of Dallas, P.O. Box 534052, Grand Prairie, TX 75053
    1-800-345-6296; FAX: 1 214-606-0679
Pepper of Detroit, P.O. Box 3520, Troy, MI 48007
    1-800-345-6296; FAX: I-313-588-1000
Pepper at Paige's, 5250 East 65th Street, Indianapolis, IN 46220
    1-800-345-6296; FAX: 1-317-517-5918
Pepper of Minneapolis, P.O. Box 44820, Eden Prairie, MN 55344
    1-800-345-6296; FAX: 1-612-944-5418
Pepper of Los Angeles, P.O. Box 550, Gardena, CA 90247
    1-800-345-6296; FAX: 1-213-538-3115
Pepper at Duncan, P.O. Box 24753, Winston-Salem, NC 27114
    1-800-345-6296; FAX: 1-919-659-8083
Perkins Music House, 279 Water Street, Gardiner, ME 04345
    (207) 582-8066; 1-800-752-7664 (State)
Pied Piper Music, 1200 3rd Avenue, Huntington, WV 25701
    (304) 529-3355
Poppler's Music, Inc., 123 DeMers Avenue, Grand Forks, ND 58201
    1-800-437 1755
Praise Unlimited, Columbia Heights Mall, 4035 Central Avenue N.L., Columbia Heights, MN 55421
    (612) 788-7775; 1-800-443-0612
RBC Music Co., Inc., P.O. Box 29128, San Antonio, TX 78229
    (512) 736-6902; 1-800-548-0917; FAX: 512-736-2919

Rockley Music Company, 8555 West Colfax Avenue, Lakewood, CO 80215
(303) 233-4444; 1-800-233-4444
Sampson Ayers House of Music, 621 North Argonne Road, P.O. Box 143088, Spokane, WA 99214-3088
(509) 928-2008;1-800-541-2001; FAX: 509-922-1066
Schmitt Music Centers, 88 South Tenth Street, Minneapolis, MN 55403
(612) 339-4811; 1-800-767-3434
Southern Music Company, 1100 Broadway, San Antonio, TX 78215
(512) 226-8167; 1-800-284-5443; FAX: (512) 223-4537
Stanton's Sheet Music, Inc., 330 South Fourth Street, Columbus, OH 43215
(614) 224-5256; 1-800-426-8742
Tempo Music Service, 480 East Rosecrans Avenue, P. O. Box 47040; Gardena, CA 90247-0904
(213) 516-1572; 1-800-383-1572; FAX: 213-516-7625
University Music House, 4578 North High Street, Columbus, OH 43224
(614) 262-0024
University Music Service, P. O. Box 354, Hershey, PA 17033
1-800-858-3000.
Volkwein Bros., Inc., 138 Industry Drive, Pittsburgh, PA 15275-1054
(412) 788-5900; 1-800-553-8742; FAX: 412-788-6055
Ward-Brodt Music Co., 2200 West Beltline Highway, Madison, WI 53713
(608) 271-1460; 1-800-369-6255
Wingert-Jones Music, Inc., 2026 Broadway, P.O. Box 419878, Kansas City, MO 64141
(816) 221-6688 (Kansas City); 1-800-258-9566; FAX: (816) 221-5398
Young's Music Store, Inc., 283 Fifth Street, Whitehall, PA 18052
(215) 437-5881; 1-800-628-6204

MANUFACTURERS OF MUSIC EQUIPMENT

In general, you will find that local dealers can meet your particular music equipment needs, especially as they pertain to audiovisual equipment, pianos, and storage cabinets. In the event that certain equipment is not available through local firms, contact the manufacturer directly for general information, including exact specifications and prices, as well as the name and address of the nearest dealer or company representative. Upon request, most companies will send catalogs as well as other pertinent information. The names of various companies and their addresses follow.

Audiovisual Equipment [6]

Microphones

AKG Acoustics, Inc., 77 Selleck St., Stamford, CT 06902
Electro-Voice, Inc., 600 Cecil St., Buchanan, MI 49107
Gotham Audio Corp., 1790 Broadway, New York, NY 10019-1412
Peavey Electronics Corp., P.O. Box 2898, Meridian, MS 39301
Shure Brothers, Inc., 222 Hartrey Ave., Evanston, IL 60204-3696
Telex Communications, Inc., 9600 Aldrich Ave., S., Minneapolis, MN 55420

[6] For descriptions and prices of audiovisual equipment see *The Equipment Directory of Audio-Visual, Computer, and Video Products*, published by NAVA, the International Communications Industries Association, 3150 Spring St., Fairfax, VA 22031, and available in many school audiovisual departments.

Motion Picture Projectors (16 mm)

Atlantic Audio-Visual Corp., 630 Ninth Ave., New York, NY 10036
Eastman Kodak Co., 343 State St., Rochester, NY 14650
Eiki International, Inc., 27882 Camino Capistrano, Laguna Niguel, CA 92677
Elmo Mfg. Corp., 70 New Hyde Park Rd., New Hyde Park, NY 11040
Hokushin Rangertone, 115 Roosevelt Ave., Belleville, NJ 07109
International Audio-Visual, P.O. Box 1096, Coquitlam, British Columbia, Canada V3J6Z4
International Cinema Equipment Co., 6750 NE Fourth Court, Miami, FL 33138
Kalart Victor Corp., Hultenius St., Plainville, CT 06062
Lafayette Instrument Co., P.O. Box 5729, Lafayette, IN 47903
Radmar, Inc., 1263B Rand Rd., Des Plaines, IL 60016
Telex Communications, Inc., 9600 Aldrich Ave. S., Minneapolis, MN 55420
Visual Instrumentation Corp., 903 N. Victory Blvd., Burbank, CA 91502

Record Players

Audiotronics Corp., P.O. Box 3997, 7428 Bellaire Ave., North Hollywood, CA 91609
Audio-Visual Devices, 99 Washington St., East Orange, NJ 07017
AVAS Corporation, 196 Holt St., Hackensack, NJ 07602
Califone International, Inc., 21300 Superior St., Los Angeles, CA 91311-4312
Dealers Audio-Visual Supply Corp., 1 Madison St., P.O. Box 105, East Rutherford, NJ 07072
Hamilton Electronics Corp., 2003 W. Fulton St., Chicago, IL 60612
Radio-Matic of America, P.O. Box 250, Maplewood, NJ 07040

Tape Recorders

Gotham Audio Corp., 1790 Broadway, New York, NY 10019-1412
Otari Corp., 2 Davis Drive, Belmont, CA 94002
Studer Revox America, Inc., 1426 Elm Hill Pike, Nashville, TN 37210
Tandberg of America, Inc., Labriola Court, Armonk, NY 10504
TEAC Corp. of America, P.O. Box 750, 7733 Telegraph Rd., Montebello, CA 90640
Telex Communications, Inc., 9600 Aldrich Ave. S, Minneapolis, MN 55420

Video Equipment

JVC Industries, 41 Slater Dr., Elmwood Park, NJ 07407
Olympus Corporation, 32A Kinderkamack Rd., Oradell, NJ 07639
Panasonic Industrial Co., Video Systems Division, Matsushita Electric Corp. of America, One Panasonic Way, Secaucus, NJ 07094
Sharp Electronics Corp., 10 Sharp Plaza, P.O. Box 588, Paramus, NJ 07652
Sony Corp. of America, Sony Dr., Park Ridge, NJ 07656

Acoustical Equipment

Acoustic Systems, P.O. Box 3610, Austin, TX 78764-9827
Sico Incorporated, 7525 Cahill Road, P.O. Box 1169, Minneapolis, MN 55440
Stage Engineering International Ltd., 325 Karen La., Colorado Springs, CO 80907
Wenger Corp., 555 Park Dr., Owatonna, MN 55060

Choir Apparel

Academic Choir Apparel, 9747 Independence Avenue, Chatworth, CA 91311-9622
Ascot Formal Wear, 7807 South Main, Houston, TX 77030

Bettina Uniform Co., 715 E. Armour Rd., 3rd Flr., North Kansas City, MO 64116
Collegiate Cap & Gown Co., 1000 N. Market St., Champaign, IL 61820
Colorifics, P.O. Box 329, Worthington, OH 43085
Formal Fashions, Inc., 1500 W. Drake, Tempe, AZ 85283
Ireland Needlecraft, 4216 San Fernando Rd., Glendale, CA 91204
Lyric Choir Robe Co., P.O. Box 16954, Jacksonville, FL 32245-9972
Masters Professional Performers Service, 315 Federal Plaza, W., Youngstown, OH 44503
E. R. Moore Co., 1810 W. Grace St., Chicago, IL 60613-9970
Murphy Cap & Gown Co., 4200 31st St. North, St. Petersburg, FL 33714-9987
Oak Hall Choir Robe Company, 840 Union St., Salem, VA 24153
Regency Cap & Gown Co., 7534 Atlantic Blvd., P.O. Box 8988, Jacksonville, FL 32239-9971
Shenandoah Robe Co., P.O. Box 6039, Roanoke, VA 24017-9959
Southeastern Apparel, Inc., 142 Woodburn Dr., Dothan, AL 36301-9984
Thomas Creative Apparel, Inc., One Harmony Place, New London, OH 44851-9932
Tuxedo Wholesale, 15636 N. 78th St., Scottsdale, AZ 85260
Uniformals, 940 West 19th St., Hialeah, FL 33010
Willsie Cap and Gown Co., 1220 South 13th St., Omaha, NE 68108

Choir Risers

Humes & Berg Mfg. Co., Inc., 4801 Railroad Ave., East Chicago, IN 46312
Mitchell Mfg. Co., 2740 S. 34th St., Milwaukee, WI 53215
Peery Products Co., P.O. Box 22434, Portland, OR 97269-2434
StageRight Corp., P.O. Box 208, Clare, MI 48617
Wenger Corp., 555 Park Dr., Owatonna, MN 55060

Music Stands

King Musical Instruments Corp., 33999 Curtis Blvd., Eastlake, OH 44094
Selmer Company, The, P.O. Box 310, Elkhart, IN 46515
Wenger Corp., 555 Park Dr., Owatonna, MN 55060

Pianos

Baldwin Piano & Organ Co., 422 Wards Corner Rd., Loveland, OH 45140-8390
Everett Piano Co., 6600 Orangethorpe Ave., Buena Park, CA 90622
Steinway & Sons, Steinway Pl., Long Island City, NY 11105
Story & Clark Piano Co., 825 E. 26th St., La Grange Park, IL 60525
Walter Piano Co., 700 W. Beardsly Ave., Elkhart, IN 46514
Wurlitzer Co., 403 East Gurler Rd., DeKalb, IL 60115
Yamaha International Corp., 6600 Orangethorpe Ave., Buena Park, CA 90622
Young Chang America, Inc., 13336 Alondra Blvd., Cerritos, CA 90701

Safety Candles (Battery Operated)

Gamble Music Co., 312 South Wabash Ave., Chicago, IL 60604
Strayline Products Co., 336 Putnam Ave., P.O. Box 4124, Hamden, CT 06514

Storage Cabinets

All-Steel, Inc., P.O. Box 871, Aurora, IL 60507
Gamble Music Co., 312 South Wabash Ave., Chicago, IL 60604
Humes and Berg Mfg. Co., Inc., 4801 Railroad Ave., East Chicago, IN 46312
Lyon Metal Products, Inc., Box 671, Aurora, IL 60507
Norren Mfg. Inc., 778 N. Georgia Ave., Azusa, CA 91702
Wenger Corp., 555 Park Dr., Owatonna, MN 55060

CHOIR TRAVEL/TOUR SERVICES

ACFEA Tour Consultants
120 Second Avenue. S.
Edmunds, WA 98020
1-800-886-3355

Ambassador Travel Services
148 E. Michigan Avenue
Kalamazoo, MI 49007
1-800-247-7035

C-S Travel Service, Inc.
10031 S. Roberts Road
Palos Hills, Ill. 60465
1-800-428-7883

European Incoming Services
565 Moody Street
Waltham, MA 02154
1-800-443-1644

Intropa
4950 Bissonnets, Suite 201
Bellaire, TX 77401
    or
1066 Saratoga Avenue, Suite 100
San Jose, CA 95129
1-800-Intropa

Keynote Arts Associates
1637 E. Robinson St.
Orlando, FL 32803
1-800-522-2213

Musica Mundi, Inc.
111 Main Street, Suite 2
Los Altos, CA 94022
1-800-947-1991

Witte Travel
3250 28th Street, S.E.
Grand Rapids, MI 49512
1-800-253-0210

Index